D0438173

THIS HOUR HAS SEVEN DECADES

THIS HOUR HAS SEVEN DECADES

PATRICK WATSON

RETIRÉ DE LA COLLECTION UNIVERSELLE
Bibliothèque et Archives nationales du Québec

McArthur & Company
Toronto

Published in 2004 by
McArthur & Company
322 King Street West, Suite 402
Toronto, Ontario M5V 1J2
www.mcarthur-co.com

Copyright © 2004 Patrick Watson

The use of any part of this publication reproduced, transmitted in any form or by any means, electronic, mechanical, photocopying, recording, or otherwise stored in a retrieval system, without the expressed written consent of the publisher, is an infringement of the copyright law.

Library and Archives Canada Cataloguing in Publication

Watson, Patrick, 1929-
This hour has seven decades / Patrick Watson.

ISBN 1-55278-440-1

1. Watson, Patrick, 1929-. 2. Canadian Broadcasting Corporation—Officials and employees—Biography. 3. Television journalists—Canada—Biography. 4. Broadcasters—Canada—Biography. 5. Authors, Canadian (English)—20th century—Biography. I. Title.

PN1990.72.W38A3 2004 384.55'092 C2004-904244-0

Composition, Design & f/x: *Mad Dog Design*
Printed in Canada by: *Friesens*

The publisher would like to acknowledge the financial support of the Government of Canada through the Book Publishing Industry Development Program, The Canada Council for the Arts, and the Ontario Arts Council for our publishing activities. We also acknowledge the Government of Ontario through the Ontario Media Development Corporation Ontario Book Initiative.

10 9 8 7 6 5 4 3 2 1

For Lucy and Stan

CHAPTER 1

WHAT IT LOOKED LIKE TO ME

THE SALUTATION OF THE DAWN

Listen to the Salutation of the Dawn.
Look to this day,
For it is life, and very life of very life.
In its brief course
Lie all the verities and realities of your existence:
The bliss of growth, the glory of action,
The splendour of beauty.
For yesterday is but a dream,
And tomorrow is only a vision.
But today well-lived
Makes every yesterday a dream of happiness
And every tomorrow a vision of hope.
Look well therefore to this day.
Such is the Salutation of the Dawn.

WHEN I FIRST HEARD that recited by a hundred and twenty or so boys and young men, I was in my father's arms, six months old, blinking in the early sunlight that splashed off the lake beside us. I would hear the same poem many times during that summer of 1930, and almost every summer morning for the next nine years, and so it became engraved in my memory and affected the shape and the rhythms of the rest of my life.

My father, Stanley Watson, had just turned thirty-six. I was his third son and fourth child, but the first of his second marriage. He was leading the morning ceremonies at the boys' summer camp Layolomi. He had been camp director now for four years, in partnership with Earle Anderson, a fellow teacher who had built the camp on the shoreline of *his* father's spreading farm near the little Ontario town of Sundridge, almost three hundred kilometres north of Toronto. We said miles then, 185 miles from Toronto.

They called Stanley "The Chief," and two or three times each summer he would don a splendid if culturally inappropriate war bonnet and a loincloth, and conduct a council ring, with ceremonial fire-lighting and the smoking of a ceremonial pipe to the four winds, and other probably imagined Indian rituals and games, perhaps based on some work by Ernest Thompson Seton. Stan's other two sons, Cliff, age eight, and John, age seven, were already campers "down the line," living in cabins with a couple of teenage supervisors known as counsellors. I would go down the line too, when I became old enough, six or seven. My brother Cliff, already an adored and provocative mentor, would be my first counsellor.

That camp, with its granite outcrops and enveloping forest of pine and birch, was built on a mythology of self-reliance within the beauty and power of nature. It informed the confidence and sense of connection to the earth that seems to have been shared by the whole family. Cliff would send me, his little brother, solo in a canoe at the age of six, saying to the father's objections that he, Cliff (then fourteen), knew that Pat could do it, so what was the problem? When I was nine, he tried to persuade Dad to let me enter the two-mile annual swim across Lake Bernard. Cliff lost that one – probably just as well – but the confidence he expressed in me from the beginning was persuasive. Much of that encouragement took place among the granite and pine and sand and water of Layolomi, and the constant invitation to adventure and experiment the place offered; ever since, the Precambrian landscape has been invested with power, nourishment, and a sense of the rightness of the world.

I have the impression that I always tried to understand things too quickly. Once during a group hike when I was seven years old and hiding in the woods from "the enemy," a mosquito landed on my arm. I was trying to be brave and not slap it or move in any way because the enemy was hunting me, stealing through the brush close by, some of them out on the road. I could see them through the trees, and the slightest movement would give me away. And so although the mosquito's proboscis stung and itched the moment it sank into my skinny little arm, I held perfectly still – probably thinking that this was a heroic part of the game. And then I began to wonder: if I continued to stay absolutely still and if the mosquito finished its meal in a leisurely way, might it just suck back out all the stuff that was causing the sting and the itch? This was a brand-new idea. In a fascination approaching trance, although my chest was heaving with the excitement of it, I watched the crouching insect's abdomen swell darkly with my blood. I tried to breathe through my nose and mouth simultaneously to reduce the sound of my gasping.

The idea about waiting for the venom to be sucked out would prove correct but badly timed. I was so cocky with pride over this quick understanding of how it might clean out its own venom if allowed to drink as deeply as it wanted, that when it slowly withdrew and sat there heavily and I saw that while the insect's abdomen was redly engorged, *my arm didn't sting; there was no swelling!* I could not refrain from a little crow of triumph. "See!" And so of course the enemy heard, and I was discovered, and that round of the game was over.

Back at camp the counsellor said, "Why do you like hiding so much? You're always running ahead and hiding, aren't you?" He said it affectionately. I think I knew why, but I did not know what to say about it. I could not come right out and say that it made me feel powerful to hide and to see without being seen; I doubt that the word occurred to me: "powerful." But I think that is what I felt about the hiding part. Hiding and observing.

Cliff taught me to sail at Layolomi and sent me solo in an Aykroyd dinghy. The Aykroyd was a stable, manoeuvrable fourteen-foot clinker-built catboat, gaff-headed. To raise the sail, with a gaff that was pretty heavy for a skinny little kid, you hauled the peak halyard until the gaff was at a 45-degree angle to the mast, then the peak and throat halyards together till the throat was taut, then the peak to taut. Then you tied both off on oak belaying pins, which function like cleats. I always loved and still do the loop and throw and draw motions of cleating or belaying. In the 1990s the dock of our cottage on Go Home Lake became an extension of that memory, festooned with a superfluous garland of hand-carved cleats along its edges.

Back then the little camper that I was could wander unsupervised in the tall redolent forests. The roar and the eerie whistle of the passing trains two miles away at night spoke of yearning and distant places. It was as much the poetry and the rituals and the investment of nature with spiritual power that the camp conveyed, as it was the activities and the comradeship. There was that powerful sense of a community, and there was a strong intellectual and creative component, as well as the spiritual and ritual and sensory.

There was no plumbing, of course. We washed in the lake and shat in outdoor toilets, one- or two-holers, which had garbage cans in them that were regularly collected for emptying by strange little silent men who came out of nowhere. The outhouse was known as the KYBO, which was said to stand for Keep Your Bowels Open. The dining hall tables had flowers in ketchup bottles, and on the posts and beams was a collection of West Coast tribal masks, a beauty that embedded itself permanently in my sensibility.

Upstairs in the lodge (the recreation hall) was a craft shop where we did metal and leather work and carved wooden animals or copied Northwest Coast masks. The lodge had a stage with rudimentary flies and some wing space and there were theatre nights three or four times each summer. My first theatrical role was as a baby crying offstage. But when my cue came, I dried. Bill Curry, the director, who was holding me on his lap in the wings and frantically cueing me, gave up in disgust and did a pretty good imitation of an infant howl himself, in time to cue the next onstage line.

Once or twice a season there would be a "feast," mostly roast potatoes and popcorn and watermelon, and staying up long after dark. And certainly a singsong; singing was very big, and the whole camp population turned out. We sang "The Road to Mandalay" (although few if any of us had the remotest idea what part of the world we were singing about), "The Song of the Woad," and another song celebrating the camp but using the tune of the University of Toronto's "Hail Toronto Mother Ever Dear." From time to time my father would lead off with an original Gilbert and Sullivan parody, including a memorable one whose chorus was "Now I am the Captain of Layolomi."

On Sunday mornings there was a kind of chapel service, where an old harmonium would be carried outdoors if the weather was good and everyone sat on logs or on the ground and we sang a hymn or two and had a talk from some visiting wise person. One hymn was memorable, "God Who Touchest Earth With Beauty." Mary Edgar, whom we all knew because she ran the girls' camp, Glen Bernard, on the opposite shore, had written it. My sister, Mary, was sent across the lake to Glen Bernard the summer she was fifteen, because, she said recently, "I had been, ah, interfering with the boys at Layolomi."

Miss Edgar's hymn was set to a lovely air by another distinguished Layolomi figure, Magistrate Jones, and I can still sing it, and be moved by it. It had almost nothing to do with Christianity but a great deal to do with nature and clarity and renewal. Magistrate Jones played that harmonium on Sunday and had a cottage just north of the camp, with a tree house in a tall pine where lucky boys were sometimes invited to spend the night. I received some of my early misinformation about sex up in that tree house, as of course it was difficult to actually sleep, however comfortable the bunks, when you were swaying in the branches thirty feet above the ground. So you talked all night and made up a good deal of boastful stuff.

By contrast with the tree house speculations, there was some wonderful valid information in the Sunday morning talks. A few of them may have been on religious subjects, but the ones that stuck were about life and science and goings-on in the world. I remember one from about 1937 or '38, by a visitor who told us about a great wreck that lay on the ocean bottom somewhere off Newfoundland, where it had struck an iceberg and gone down a quarter of a century earlier. It was called *Titanic*, he said. And now that Auguste Picard had dived to several thousand feet in his bathyscaphe and bathysphere, it was going to be possible to go down to *Titanic* and seal up the wounds in the hull, and then bring down huge air hoses from the surface and pump the ship full of air so that it would float to the surface. There would be a movie years later based on that notion, but we heard it first in one of those Sunday morning talks at Layolomi. We also heard talks about exploration and astronomy and other sciences.

I remember vividly the aha! feeling that came when a Sunday morning talker expounded a theory of the biomechanics of taste. He said that the taste of everything was caused by combinations of a very small number of basic tastes: salt, sweet, sour, and so on. He said that the molecules of sugar and salt, and the other substances that had these tastes, had a certain physical shape and that built in to the surface of the tongue were something like microscopic little pits that corresponded to those shapes, and if a molecule fitted just right into the salt pit, you tasted salt, into the sugar pit, you tasted sweet, and it was the combinations of these that produced the taste of everything from hamburgers to oatmeal porridge and even your own skin when you licked your arm on a summer day. What a beautiful feeling it was to *understand*, suddenly, something that a moment before had seemed as mysterious as a sunset.

Those Sunday morning talks had been another aspect of the camp's attempt to open up the natural world to the boys, not just as an experience but as a set of meanings with a narrative behind them. That was Stanley Watson, still being a teacher right through the summer holidays, far away from the city school where he was principal the rest of the year.

Stanley Alvin Watson was born in June 1896 at 163 Colborne Street West in the prosperous town of Orillia. The house still stands. As I write, Stanley's sister-in-law, my aunt Gertrude, still lives in it. Stanley liked to tell about how he as a six-year-old was brought out on the porch of that house to watch the fireworks on New Years Eve, as the century changed, and how his mother said, "Remember this, Stanley; you'll never see another."

Orillia is now a small city wrapped around the southwest end of Couchiching, a nine- by two-mile shallow turquoise limestone-bottomed lake, part of the Trent Canal system connecting Lake Ontario near Kingston to the southern tip of Georgian Bay. Small craft (once military and commercial, now recreational) use it to avoid the long, storm-wracked shallows of Lake Erie and the once dangerously fortified town of Detroit and the St. Clair River. Stan's boyhood was very much influenced by the canoe and the freedom and self-reliance that go with it.

The family legend was that on a canoe trip in the early summer of 1914 Stan and his younger brother, Gordon, known as "Skid," stopped at a railway shack where the river passed beneath the tracks, and were told by the telegraph operator there that war had broken out. The two young men paddled non-stop back to Orillia to join up. The official record shows that he enlisted in 1916 and trained at the big Ontario base called Camp Borden, whence he would soon enough be sent for further training at Aldershot in England and then off to the mud and horror of Flanders and France.

Somehow he survived those days of massacre, when crowds of boys would pour over the top from their rat-infested trenches and run straight into the chattering fire of German machine guns, ten thousand dead in the space of half an hour, while the generals sat in their comfortable Chateau HQ billets ten safe miles behind the front and spoke proudly over tea of their gallant lads, and of glory, and of how the next assault would be the one that broke the Hun.

Stan was concussed by an exploding shell during a night patrol to lay Bangalore torpedoes under the enemy barbed wire. He came to, thinking he was dead because of the hot, sticky mess of stuff all over his tunic, the smell of blood in it. When the next star shell burst above him and his cowering group of survivors, he saw that the mess was the brains of his young corporal, lying shattered beside him in the mud of the shell hole they were trying to shelter in.

In another battle, mustard gas or perhaps chlorine caught him before he could get his gas mask on, and he was hospitalized briefly while a blistered lung repaired itself. But soon he was back at the front, fighting through and incredibly surviving the bloodbath at Ypres, and then that stunning morning at Vimy Ridge when the Canadians had their chance at an enemy stronghold that had defied the British and the French for two years. The Canadian strategy there was to develop small night raids to bring back one or two prisoners for interrogation. Conn Smythe was a fellow soldier and a daring member of those night raids. Ten years later Smythe would start planning a hockey arena to be called Maple Leaf Gardens. Out of the intelligence Smythe and the other raiders brought back grew a plan for bombardment and the final assault that was to begin at first light and secure the till-then impregnable ridge by early afternoon.

They did just that, and once more Stan Watson came through alive and got promoted to lieutenant and mentioned in dispatches.

When he recounted all this at the dinner table, we listened wide-eyed and concluded that this was something you did when you grew up, you went off to war for King and Country, and although many would die all around you, you would not. You would come back afterward to tell about it, and if it had to happen again, why, then you would go off again. And indeed when World War II came along twenty-one years after the end of the First, Stanley Watson, now forty-eight years old, signed up again. He was commissioned Major and served until his health let him down less than two years later, by then promoted to Lieutenant Colonel.

But back to Ypres, and Vimy, and then Mons, and the end of it all, and the slim twenty-five-year-old came home covered in glory and full of tales. He had learned to smoke and to speak French. He had the DSO and the DCM and Bar, which military historians say was better than the Victoria Cross because the Victoria Cross was political. He came home to marry his sweetheart, Obie Mullett, who had waited straight and true all those four years. My sister, Mary, was born on November 23, 1919. Cliff came two years later. The two children flourished in a world glowing with the certainty that peace was now forever. You can see the untroubled eagerness in their eyes, in their photos, those two kids: princelings in a world where love would always survive calamity as Obie and Stan's had, where anything you set out to do you could do.

Except that when the next child was born, John, in 1922 – there was no penicillin, of course – the young mother was stricken with peritonitis (they called it "childbirth fever"), and within days Stan was a widower. Suddenly death was more real and present than it had been even in Flanders, and it was poor John's fault: he never quite came out from beneath that shadow, was never forgiven by his father for the death of the beloved Obie.

The family stock was small-town and rural Ontario going back into the middle of the nineteenth century. My younger brother, Roger, and my sister, Mary, have been scouting gravestones and village archives out around Harriston and Mount Forest trying to locate the first Alexander Watson we know of, my great-grandfather. His father probably came out from Glasgow, maybe in the 1830s. His son Alex, my father's father, was a cabinetmaker who had to make his own tools during his apprenticeship. Adelaide Wright, who had some Irish blood, Co. Cork we were told, was Alex's third wife and my father's mother. Women died young in those days. There was an older son from an earlier marriage, Uncle Fred, who vanished into Alberta somewhere – I think I saw him once – and a cousin Keith, likewise seen once and then forgotten. Something loose around the fringes of the family in that way. But there seems to have been a Methodist-Presbyterian master narrative behind it all that had to do with picking yourself up and getting on with it and not whining. Obie's father,

Sydney Mullett, was an English-born Methodist, a successful merchant, having founded and run the Orillia Hardware and then retired comfortably to the sprawling Croydon Cottage, on Couchiching Point. He was fearfully strict. But I spent many very entertaining summer weeks with his plump, deaf, jolly, and generous widow Charlotte, my "Granny" Mullett. She was a Latimer, Irish Presbyterian. She taught me how to play poker and once astounded me by telling an off-colour joke.[1]

I say Methodist-Presbyterian, although I don't recall anyone actually going to church. I never did. But there was a tactile air of probity and sobriety, a bit exclusive and even bigoted when you go back a couple of generations. I do not understand how it was that my father escaped that part of it. In my boyhood when Toronto was anti-Semitic and black people lived in story books perhaps (but certainly not in Toronto), Stanley Watson would not allow a word of racial discrimination.

As a prominent school principal and later Education Department official, he would invite home visiting teachers from strange lands and bring us kids out to meet them and to be impressed with the very special qualities they had brought from Japan or Palestine. When I was about eight, my sister, Mary, somehow got the idea that my friend Lawrence Harsar, a Jewish kid who lived around the corner, resembled the German dictator. She began to call him "Hitler," affectionately. I recall the Dad sitting her down quietly one morning and gently explaining to her why she must not do that ever again. We already knew a little about what was happening to the Jews in Germany, even before the war had begun, and he managed to communicate to the kids something about the magnitude of that evil, something that stuck.

But I have to back up a bit, because I have got John and Cliff and

1. A little girl has been admiring her fairly new baby brother, and asks her mother what that thing is between the little boy's legs. The mother says, "It's his whistle." The girl replies, "It can't be a whistle, for it don't blow." Granny Mullett was about eighty when she told me this, and I about thirteen. I did not know where to look.

Mary on the scene here, and we know about the tragic end of the Stan and Obie love affair, but I haven't told you yet the next love story, which is where Lucy comes in.

Camille Paglia in her provocative *Sexual Personae* wrote: "Every man harbors an inner female territory, ruled by his mother, from whom he can never entirely break free." I don't think I ever wanted to.

Lucy Bate was of United Empire Loyalist stock that my brother Roger has traced back to a woman named Jane Savage, who was born in England in 1596. Lucy grew up in southwestern Ontario, near Port Burwell on the shore of Lake Erie. Her father, Harry Bate, had a small general farm and was something of a horse breeder and trader, solid but never really prosperous, who worked the farm well into his seventies. He had a sense of humour and a radiant, easy-going affectionate way with the grandchildren. Probably Presbyterian too, though once again nobody ever seems to have mentioned the word "church." Lucy was born in Moose Jaw, Saskatchewan, where Harry was a trainman on the CPR at the time, and Moose Jaw was a Division Point.

When she showed signs of a mysterious nutritional disease that had already carried off her older brother Harley at the age of two and a half, her mother, Clare, and Harry brought Lucy back to Ontario, where Clare's mother's family, the Earls, were in dairy. The little girl would get properly stuffed with cream and butter and eggs and fresh vegetables. She survived, but at the age of six or seven was stricken with polio, which left her with one forearm and hand that did not grow and did not function very well. Somehow she learned to play the piano, helped by a remarkable teacher who showed her how to find the one note in the left hand that you absolutely needed – she had the strength and control for one note with her shrunken left hand. The piano was a requirement then if you wanted to teach school.

When I knew her as a mother and housewife, she managed around the kitchen balancing dishes and lids on the back of that tiny twisted left hand and getting on with it without whining. When my siblings asked me to speak at her funeral in 1981 and I talked about the arm and the hand, three women who had known her for decades came up to me afterward and said, "What arm? What hand? What are you talking about?"

Well, it was perfectly clear that a girl with a withered arm wasn't going to be much of a catch for a young man – she knew that. So after a few years teaching in one-room country schools and a year teaching in her native city of Moose Jaw to see what *that* was like (she hated it), she decided to press on with a career and applied for a job with the Toronto school board. The principal was a handsome young widower who struck quite a figure when he came out in his beribboned lieutenant's uniform on Friday afternoons to take the school cadet corps on parade. Many of the young women teachers in the school quite clearly had their caps set for this principal. Lucy, knowing that she would never be part of that game, found it entertaining to watch. She said years later that she really thought, well, she shouldn't say it, of course, but she really thought a lot of the girls were making fools of themselves, it was so obvious.

This all came out at my dinner table one evening about five years after my father's death (in 1962; he was only sixty-nine and was having a very gratifying retirement as a curriculum expert, sought after right and left as a consultant by hopeful textbook publishers). So Lucy was sitting there at the dinner table at 18 Glengrove West, my kids all wide-eyed as the old Grandmother told what was very quickly shaping up as a love story.

She said that she began to notice how the principal was dropping into her Grade Two classroom at recess perhaps oftener than he needed, to ask if she was getting along all right, could he help with anything, did she have the supplies she needed? One morning he said there was an interesting play opening that night at Hart House Theatre at the university, would she like to see it with him? So they did that. And then he said he hadn't been playing his violin much lately and would really like to get back at it and why didn't they play some duets together? So from time to time they would leave school early and rent a little piano studio at the Royal Conservatory for a couple of hours, and then go to a concert or a play afterward, or even a movie. And they would talk about books and ideas, and about his three kids who were parked with their grandparents in Orillia, where he went every Friday afternoon, climbing on the train at a station near the school for the two-hour trip.

It may have been on one of those trips away from her that he wrote a sonnet, classical form, entitled "Treasure." I discovered it only recently, in a little notebook filled with his meticulous handwriting.

Around me lie all things heart can desire . . . .
White birches changing in the moonlight by the lake
An ever-changing sky – sunlight and cloud,
And cooling winds & songs of birds that start
With dawn – Yet constantly complaint I make
That to be near you I am not allowed.
For where my treasure is, there is my heart.
S.A.W.

She said that Obie's still-mourning parents, the Mullets, were not pleased to learn that Stan was seeing somebody new, and they let it be known that Lucy would not be welcome in Orillia: their weekends were spent apart.

But there came a Thursday night after a concert when he walked her home to her rooming house on High Park Avenue a couple of blocks from the school and on the porch he asked her to marry him. "And I said yes, and I was so happy I cried myself to sleep," she told us.

My son Chris was fourteen. Greg eleven, my daughter Boo ten. They were open-mouthed.

She said that the next day, Friday, he came into her classroom at the morning recess and gave her a book, a blue cloth-bound copy of *Deirdre* by James Stephens. He said that of course he had a sacrosanct view of library books, you never marked them, but that he had found a passage in the Stephens book that spoke more eloquently than he could about how he felt. So he had made a fine line in the margin with an HH pencil – nobody would mind. And he said, Lucy, I am so sorry that I can't be with you on the weekend, the Mullets and the kids, you know, or something like that, and she said, Of course, Stan, she knew. And he said that he wanted her to read the book over the weekend while he was away because it would convey something important.

So on Saturday night she got into it, and about halfway through she found a fine pencil line in the margin, HH, very faint, marking a passage about the transforming power of love.

"And I started crying again," my seventy-year-old mother was saying, "because I was so happy." Lucy then said that a few weeks ago she had got to thinking about that book, wondering what it would be like to read it again. She had gone to the Yorkville branch of the Toronto Public Libraries, her nearest, but they didn't have a copy and had suggested she try the Central Circulating at St. George and College, where the university bookstore now is. The catalogue showed one copy on reserve. She filled out the card. You can see this coming. The librarian came out from the stacks and handed her a blue, cloth-bound book.

"The hair came up on the back of my neck," she said. "I just knew. I opened the book about halfway through. You know how you can sometimes find a page, just like that? And there was a fine pencil line in the margin, beside this passage about the transforming power of love. And I just stood there with the tears running down my face. And the woman behind the desk said, 'Is there something wrong, Mrs. Watson?' And I said, 'No, my dear. There is nothing wrong in the entire universe.'"

My son Chris said, "Gran! Gran! It's a movie!"

I am usually doubtful of authors who put quotation marks around words in a book of memoirs. How the hell can Frank McCourt remember all that dialogue! Of course he can't; he's making it up, he's inventing memories.

Well, I'm not. Those words are etched. So is Chris's face saying, "Gran! It's a movie!"

And that's how Stan and Lucy got me.

In approaching the challenge of writing what seems to me a long and richly textured life, after chancing two or three chapters of events chosen more or less at random, just because they presented themselves as I began to reflect on things, I decided that this would be the life that I remember, not necessarily what other people remember. I am encouraged in this by Gabriel García Márquez, whom I admire almost without reservation, and who has said something like this about his own recent autobiography, *Living to Tell the Tale.* The issue came to a head over James Bond, 007.

Sometime in the early 1960s, when I was producing *Inqui'ry*, a weekly national affairs television series in Ottawa, Munroe Scott proposed that we go to Jamaica together to film an interview with Ian Fleming. Scott's New York agent was also Fleming's agent and had undertaken to set things up with the author of the James Bond stories. Scott said all he wanted was to conduct the interview, that I should direct, and it would be a great caper.

There was no reasonable argument for using the *Inqui'ry* budget to do a literary interview, and I had no idea where the thing would be broadcast, but in those days a producer could make choices and take chances and figure out later how to justify them; so I said, Let's go.

At the last minute, there was some kind of national crisis that kept me in Ottawa, so I assigned a young producer named Cameron Graham to direct in my stead. Cam Graham was later responsible for bringing me back from a sort of exile in New York, he by then the senior current affairs producer in the Ottawa area. But in 1962 or '63, when this happened, he was just getting started.

Here is where the difference between what I remember and what others remember became an issue as I began to write this book.

Graham and Scott came back from Jamaica crowing about how well it had gone – Just wait till the film comes back from the lab, you'll be delighted.

And, Graham said, there had been a bonus. When Munroe Scott asked Fleming if the name James Bond had been his cover name when he was briefly an intelligence agent in MI-5, Fleming said that although the story was widespread, it was not true. James Bond, he said, was the name of Jamaica's best ornithologist, and as a rabid bird watcher he, Fleming, had decided to honour the man by using his name in the thrillers. Scott, of course, then asked if Fleming had met the real James Bond, and the author replied that, no, to his regret, he never had.

At that point, Cam reported, the waiter who had helped them set up the tables and lights on the hotel patio where they were filming whispered to Cam that the old gentleman having tea at a nearby table was "the man who write de books about de birds."

"So," said Cam with a big grin, "after we wrapped I introduced them."

I stared at him, shocked. "*After you wrapped?*" I said. "You had a camera there when Ian Fleming met James Bond and *you didn't film it?*"

Now: in *my* memory I chased him, screaming imprecations, down the hall. In Cameron Graham's memory it did not happen that way. He maintains that he did indeed film the Fleming-Bond meeting.

But Munroe Scott's memory, alas, has us both wrong. Scott said that the interview was filmed not at a hotel, but at Fleming's house. There was no waiter. There had been some talk of James Bond the ornithologist, but no meeting to film. Or not film.

We are, all three, convinced of what we recall.

And so, while I have done extensive research in my own journals, and in CBC and other archives (especially regarding chronology), the life I have written here is the life that *I* remember.

Chapter 2

THE THIRTIES

MY MOTHER SAID one day, "Do you realize that I am spending a dollar a day on milk! Ten quarts of milk a day!" That was probably in 1938 or 1939. If there were rumours of war, they hadn't quite made it through to me yet. At eight or nine years old, I was living something like an idyllic childhood, as yet untroubled by hormones, bliss it was to be alive, the world was full of promise, the streets were too, the universe was beckoning.

In my early years I was often ill. During my kindergarten year, a bout of pneumonia kept me out of school more than I liked, because I enjoyed school a lot, especially the girls. Those first few months, suddenly being in the midst of girls, lots of girls, was a transformation of the social landscape. One night at the dinner table I told the family how I had persuaded a girl from the kindergarten class to come behind the fence of the schoolyard with me so I could kiss her. Cliff said, "You're brave!" and I mistakenly thought he meant brave because I had kissed Mitzi Schmidt, not brave because I had recounted it at the table.

I invited the girl next door, Maggie Dale, to come and play in my little pup tent in the backyard. Maggie was four, I think. We agreed that we were curious about each other, she showed me hers and I showed her mine, and then we went on playing at whatever we were playing at. But I did not forget about this very interesting discovery and, feeling uneasy about what I had done, confessed it to my mother at bedtime that night. "Did you touch her?" she asked. I lied and said no. She put her hand kindly on my head and said, "Well, you may not believe what I am going to say now, but I know I'm right. You are going to remember this for the rest of your life."

Lucy taught me to read like this: she would read to me at bedtime. *Winnie-the-pooh* stories were favourites. She would say something like "Would you like another one?" Well, of course I would. She would start another and then say, "Oh, my goodness, look at the time! I really have to get the dishes started. Look here, Pat. This is 'T,' remember, and this is 'H' and this is 'E.' Now, it's funny, but when you put them together, they say 'The.' Now, here is P-O-O-H. Whenever you see that, that's 'Pooh.' Now, you read it as well as you can, and tomorrow night we'll have some more."

Within a short time I was begging for more instruction. I remember sitting in the yellow sunlight on the kitchen floor as she spread letter cards on the linoleum by the old icebox (yes, an icebox – our first electric refrigerator would not appear until after World War II). She taught me to piece together the sounds. By the time I was in kindergarten, I was reading fluently, and though I missed the society of kindergarten when those frequent illnesses kept me at home, I didn't really miss much else, except the girls. Drawing and watercolours and pasting together coloured papers were a normal part of the bedtime activities for the sick little boy; Lucy had, after all, been a Grade Two teacher. She reminded me years later that after I had accomplished the latest task with scissors and paste and coloured paper, or big darning needles and coloured thread and construction paper, I would start banging things and chanting,

I want
Something to DO!
Something different
And something new!

I kept this up until she gave up and dug into her resources and came up with a game or a puzzle or some art materials that would keep me quiet for another half an hour.

In any case, with all that home teaching, Grade One, when I arrived there the next year, was only a brief passage. Grade One in 1936 was all about reading, and when it was discovered that I read rapidly and well, and loved it, I was moved immediately into Grade Two. Then I skipped Grade Three as well. So as I arrived in Grade Four, I was two years younger than most of the others, and small for my age at that.

Perhaps it began about then, a tendency to be watchful about people older than I, suspecting they had power and were mildly menacing. That tendency twisted into an assumption that powerful people whom I meet must be older than I. When I was chairman of the board of the Canadian Broadcasting Corporation, I was looking around the boardroom table one day at the powerful and influential people over whose deliberations I was presiding. And I realized with a start that they were all younger than I. That amounted to cognitive dissonance. They were powerful, therefore they *must* be older.

Just a few months before that, I had noted in my diary:

> *And I will be sixty in less than 3 months, and if I don't find a way to get some fitness back, I'm going to start feeling old. And this is surprising. It has to do not with the stupidity I expected to come finally, but with moving slowly and finding pain in more places and at more junctures in the day and night. Moving like a slow, old man. But I still sense the boy in there. THEY are all still older than I am. I am still puzzled by the mysteries that puzzled me at ten, still afraid of the darknesses I feared then, still thrilled by the sunrises and the curve of a wing as I was then. So I have not lost the boy, but he moves very circumspectly, slowly, more prudently; and he can't carry much.*

My older siblings did not count in this particular field of irony; them I simply admired. Well, I was often in conflict with my brother

John, the closest to my age, a boy who nursed a lot of anger for very good reasons.

A new brother arrived in 1936. I was pleased when the roundness of my mother's belly was explained. I advised the parents that the new baby should be named Mark, after my then favourite author, Mark Twain. I was disappointed when my instructions were ignored and the baby was named Roger Knox instead. Knox was for Frank Knox, professor of economics at Queen's, one of Stan's soldier-comrades, a very close friend, and a great intellectual sparring partner. Roger would choose engineering when he got to university, and as of this writing is just back in Canada after five years running a geophysical mapping operation in Ghana.

School was almost always easy and invigorating. I fainted when I got my smallpox shots and at all the other immunization procedures that broke the skin and filled the school with the smell of rubbing alcohol. I was no good at hockey or any game involving a ball, but completely at home in the water. Arriving at high school, twelve years old and small, and finding a swimming pool and honours accorded to those who could swim fast, I finally found my sport and set an unofficial record (nine seconds) for a one-length sprint of the pool. But I always preferred swimming *under* water, and still do.

At home there was a catalogue of taboo words and topics. One of them – *fart* – was broken by a dog.

The first dog I knew personally was called Fanjo. I was two or three at the most when he was brought home from the pound in the second or third year of the Great Depression. I calculate this because I was still so young that "Fanjo" was my best approximation of the word "spaniel," which Fanjo was reputed to be in part. He looked more like a cross between a fox terrier and a beagle: lean, randy, and humorous, shorthaired and black with a ginger patch on his chest. A slight flop to the ears betrayed some kind of hound origins.

At the time I knew nothing of this multiplicity of genes, what would a few years later be called a Heinz Hound (after the pickle manufacturer who boasted "57 Varieties"). I just accepted the statement that he was a spaniel, so he defined spaniel. With the arrogance of definition that remained and remains part of my character, I would scold those who wickedly tried to lead me into error by applying the name to certain other dogs, dogs longhaired, nervous or deferential, pretty or haughty, but clearly, despite the fierce assertions of their owners, not *real* spaniels like my Fanjo.

Infinitely patient with and attached to me, Fanjo would roll on the living room floor with me and lick my nose, and, until discovered and scolded for it, I, discerning that this gesture was part of his language and that I could acquire part of his language even if he could not acquire much of mine, would lick his nose in return.

There was some access to liberty in the ferocity of Fanjo's farts. In the thirties, in the world I lived in, farting had not become the easy laugh it now is on television. It certainly was not a matter of family conversation.

But Fanjo's mighty rhetorical perfume could not be ignored. On a trip with my mother to visit her father at his farm near Port Burwell on the shore of Lake Erie, we took Fanjo with us in the 1935 Oldsmobile (which had at last replaced the derelict Hupmobile). It was just cold enough to keep the windows closed all the time. Car heaters were then recirculating devices; they brought in no fresh air from outside. Fanjo began to create. It was almost overwhelming. I darted Mum a glance. She looked back sternly but couldn't contain a giggle. She was a farm girl, after all.

Soon my mother and I were collapsed in laughter together over the dog's alchemical colonic genius. I can't remember what metaphor she came up with for the phenomenon, though I have to suppose it was not cruel but clever in an affectionate way, like most of the laughter that was part of my bond with her. The words that she said are forgotten, but the laughter they released ended the Laingian mute annihilation of *that* subject at least: Fanjo had made it possible to stop pretending that farts had not happened.

Not much later my father shot Fanjo dead with his World War I service revolver. It was at Layolomi. Fanjo had bitten a local child;

there was a rabies scare; the magistrate ordered the dog destroyed; Dad, characteristically, would not have someone else do it. Nobody remembered to tell me.

It was the close of summer, the last day of camp, the end of August. The car was packed. I had gone off into the woods calling, "Fanjo! Fanjo! Time to go." My mother found me wandering through the cedars. She came and took my hand (I was eight). She said, "He doesn't hear you," and told me why. Strangely, I felt no anger for my father, yet that was the first of the terrible young encounters with death and grief, in which I was to learn there lay strange beauty.

The close of summer is freighted. Eleven years after losing Fanjo, the end of August brought the dramatic death, in his Supermarine Seafire, of my brother Cliff, my only ever real hero, who had taught me to swim and to sail and told me I was brave. He died on August 23, 1949. Eleven-year cycles. Eleven years after Cliff's death, the end of August brought my catastrophic fall from the top of my proud new handmade geodesic dome, the fall that brought crashing down a whole chapter of my life – while another and perhaps better one began. Fanjo's death was the first of those August catastrophes. But my! Couldn't he fart, that spaniel.

School, for the most part, was an adventure. The only time I can recall being baffled by anything I had to learn was about the same time as Fanjo's death, maybe a couple of years later: multiplying fractions. I got so frustrated at my little desk under the seven windows, the sewing room where I slept in the tall house on Bracondale Hill Road, that my father found me hunched over the little desk, whimpering.

He sat down beside me: "Let's take a look at this, Old Man."

And in about five minutes of patient pointing and asking the right questions, he caused the veil to fall from my eyes. It was easy, after all – how had I ever been stumped by such ridiculously easy stuff? Not only easy, but, well, kind of fun. "Neat!" I probably said. We didn't say "cool" yet, or "groovy," but we did say "You bet" quite a lot, and "Naturally!" and "Sure!" If anyone ever said anything profane or obscene it was an event. "Holy cow" and "Holy Nelly" were common exclamations, and I remember how surprised I was – but it made total sense – when someone explained to me that "Golly" was a way of sidestepping "God," and "Gee" the same for "Jesus." "Crap" was also current, though never used in front of your parents, who would probably say that something was "stuff and nonsense" or "not worth a hill of beans."

But "neat" was the going word of approval, and I probably said it after that arithmetic lesson, and my father probably looked slightly disapproving – he admired precision in language. I regret that I did not tell him that night what a wonderful teacher he was, and that I now understood that when older kids, kids my older brothers' and sister's age, who had been pupils in his classes would take the time to tell me what a wonderful teacher he was, they were not just trying to be nice.

If the mark of fine teaching is the stimulus of curiosity, he certainly had that ability too. And while we were seldom really close, my father and I, we took a number of long walks at night during those years before the war, usually east toward the reservoir park, or down through Wychwood Park and back along Davenport Road to where Bracondale climbs its winding way up the hill to our house at number 22. On those walks I learned to gaze at the stars and wonder about them, and to catch the excitement of the idea that perhaps other forms of life were out there, which we could never meet because they were thousands of light-years away. And learned what a light-year was, and why we could never travel faster than light. I remember clearly that he managed to put into my young mind the idea that all material existence might be patterns of whirling energy, nothing really solid at all, a pretty new idea then, it seemed, for when I tried it out on my friends at school I met with ridicule or, at best, an uncomprehending tolerance. We talked about that plan to raise the *Titanic* by sealing up the rip in the hull and then filling the ship with air pumped down from the surface. That one went over quite well at school.

Sometimes my father would recite. He had a knack for doggerel.

He would convert something in the day's events into a couple of rhyming lines. Or he would do something out of A.A. Milne's *When We Were Very Young*, or *Now We Are Six*. At the dinner table whenever the butter dish ran dry, he'd do "The King's Breakfast," with comic voices for all the parts, including the Alderney cow. By the time I was seven or eight I had it by heart from hearing it so often. I still get asked for it at dinner parties.

Every one of us around that table seemed to enjoy goofy verses. When I asked my sister, Mary, about that recently, she was able to furnish a couple of lines that were missing from my recall of the following, which we all recited: there was a kind of athletic challenge in getting it right:

Once a big molicepan
Met a bittle lum
Sitting on the sturb cone
Chewing gubber rum
Said the big molicepan
Goncha wimme some?
Tinny on your nintype
Said the bittle lum.

"Ninny on your tintype" was a jocular insult from the late nineteenth century; a tintype was an early form of snapshot.

Dad smoked Turret cigarettes. My mother would take one, after dinner, and smoke it before she got up to see that the maid had left everything properly in the kitchen, the dishes done, the leftovers in the icebox. Summoned with a small tinkling bell, the maid would often serve the meal, during the short time, probably from 1936 to 1942, when even a humble school principal could afford a servant in the house. She would stay for about a year, at $5 a week plus room and board, until she could find something better.

Those Turret cigarettes were one cent each, and the Dad sometimes sent me down to the little corner store – we would say "convenience" store today – with a nickel to buy him a five-cent pack. When

I was about thirteen, I started buying them for myself, and a group of us used to gather in the two adjoining vacant lots on Frank Crescent – David Hamilton's father, Chester, was holding on to those lots until prosperity returned – where we were allowed to dig trenches and make fires with the plentiful deadfall from the huge old white oaks that spread over the east side of the property. We would make our fires and sit around them after dark telling ghost stories, smoking our cigarettes as long as no adult came by, and roasting potatoes in the coals, to be eaten with a bit of butter and salt swiped from the dinner table. John and Cliff and some of their contemporaries set out to build a dugout, like the ones Dad had lived in off a trench during the war. Those older boys dug a pit about ten feet in diameter and six or seven feet deep before they reached heavy clay and water that did not drain away. They had planned to roof it over and make a tunnel entrance, but it never got finished. It stayed there, the sides caving in bit by bit, and the shape getting softer and more grassed and natural, until the lots were sold soon after the war.

Those lots were known as The Field. We played a game there called Peggy. You dug two small pits, about a foot deep and a foot square, about twenty-five feet apart. Each batter stood by the pit with a cut-off broomstick, just as a cricket batter stands by the wicket. The bowler at the other end took another piece of cut broomstick about three and a half inches long, held between index finger and thumb and hurled overhand so that it spun like a propeller as it flew, trying to get it into the pit before the batter could hit it. If the bowler succeeded, the batter was out. If the batter hit it, he ran to the other pit and back to his own, trying to chalk up as many runs as he could before the peggy was retrieved and hurled into a pit. You had to have your stick in the pit before the peggy got there, or you were out. I have never seen this game played anywhere else.

There were some great smells. Smells and memory belong together. There was the smell of books. My father came into my room one day and handed me a new selection from the Book of the Month Club. "I think you might like this," he said. He was usually right, so

I opened the blue linen covers and savoured the smell, as I always loved to do with a new book, and plunged right in. I was ten years old. It was *The Sword in the Stone* by T.H. White, the first volume of what became the trilogy *The Once and Future King.*

I was rapt, enchanted, swept away. I read it through in a whoosh. Then I started at the beginning and read it through again. Before long I could quote parts of it. I bet I have read it twenty times. I still pick it up with delight. It is about a boy ill-thought of by his powerful half-brother and serious elders, but beloved of animals and – oh wonderful! – also of the great magician Merlin, who recognizes in him both a sacred royal legacy and a great spirit to be cultivated. It is a fable about loyalty and steadfastness, about the love of the texture of things and the beauty instinct in nature, and about the wonder of creation.

The book held some obvious enchantments for a ten-year-old in a family of five siblings, a boy given to fantasies about being special. There was also a rich eccentric humour and a poetry in the language that I responded to with curiosity and delight, piecing together from context the meaning of austringer and complines, coneys and mews. And thinking how fine it was that Merlin and his coterie of magical animals would say things elegant and mysterious like "I feel eternal longings in me" or ". . . might his quietus make, with a bare bodkin."

I would be amazed to find, as I made my way delightedly into Shakespeare for the first time, how very often Shakespeare (and many other great English poets) quotes lines they must have found in my favourite book, *The Sword in the Stone.* It was a form of plagiarism that bespoke the magician Merlin, who lived backwards in time, remembered everything that was going to happen but had a hard time recalling what he had eaten for breakfast.

"The bell invites me," said the mad goshawk, Colonel Cully, as he murderously approached the boy called The Wart (who will become King Arthur). "Hear it not . . . for it is a knell that summons thee to heaven or to hell." It was wonderful, years later, to discover Macbeth speaking the same words, Shakespeare obviously having admired T.H. White as much as I did.

Lately I have been turning my hand to fables for adults, disguised as children's novels. *Ahmek, A Beaver Odyssey* was published in April of 1999 and shortlisted by the Canadian Library Association for best children's book of the year, and as I write has been acquired by the animation producers, Nelvana, for a television series, and has been reissued in paperback. A second, *Wittgenstein and the Goshawk*, my favourite of all the books I've written, should be out by the time this book is. And I find that the model to which I turn with affection more than any other source of influence is *The Sword in the Stone.* I still have that same old, much-thumbed and loved and worn, blue hardbound copy, the one my father handed me more than sixty years ago. Part of the linen on the spine is missing. It still smells good.

And another great smell: Toronto streets were redolent with horse in the 1930s. Horse-drawn wagons delivered those ten-cent glass bottles of milk (some of them with pinched necks at the point where the cream floated on top of the milk, with a special hooked spoon for stopping the flow of the milk at that pinch so you could pour off the thick yellow cream). For a while we had a friendly milkman who would take me aboard on Saturday mornings. I'd be out there at 7:30 waiting for him, and he would let me take the reins through the hinged front window of the wagon and cluck to the horse and say, "Giddap" and "Whoa," even though the horse knew the route by heart and needed no commands. The spreading stains of horse piss were part of the coloration of the landscape, and in the humid summers the rising waves of heat off the asphalt carried the scent up and even into your house through the screened windows. I liked that smell.

Horse-drawn wagons brought what you ordered from the Eaton's catalogue or the Simpson's catalogue, delivered ice for the iceboxes, brought cords of firewood and sacks of coal, and carried off the garbage.

The junk man was bearded, hatted, slouched, and known as "The Sheeny." He cried out, "Rags! Bones! Bottles!" in a raucous wail as he drove along your street and was much criticized for the starved appearance of his horse, his neglect being explained by the fact that he was a Jew. Some modern English-Canadian writers like to scold Quebec for its anti-Semitism in the 1930s and '40's. Well, the disease was vicious and endemic in the Toronto I grew up in. It is not clear to me how my father, from a small Ontario Presbyterian community, escaped it and would not tolerate the slightest hint of it or any other expression of the then normal racial discrimination from his children.

Serious-looking moustached policemen in tall English-bobby style helmets patrolled the streets and cruised by your house two or three times a week, one hand behind their backs, pedalling with dignity, the seats of their police bicycles furnished with big coiled springs set on edge, like wheels under the seat, unlike any other bikes. They would daintily negotiate their path past any clusters of manure that had not yet been swept and would occasionally nod graciously to the little kid who watched wide-eyed from the curb.

Several times a week men in overalls went along the streets with push brooms sweeping the manure into the gutters, and then later into tall canisters on wheels. It was uncommon for gutters to be empty of horse balls. In the winter, frozen, they could serve as a substitute snowball and were occasionally so used in group fights, though throwing a horse ball at someone was seen as pretty serious stuff.

At camp Layolomi riding was a major part of the program, so I was at ease with horses and riding comfortably by the time I was six. I had learned to groom, saddle, and bridle the two small western ponies that I liked better than the big horses. The smell of a stable bespoke summer and good times, as well as my amiable Grandfather Harry Bate's farm. I liked horses; the smell of them still brings waves of comfort.

One of the biggest faults I find with films set in urban North America in the 1930s is that they seldom have horses in them. There are lots of enchanting vintage cars – a popular cinematic convention for conjuring up the period – but that real texture of steaming, manured streets and the comforting clop clop of shod hooves, often the first sound of the city to be heard upon awakening in that little sewing room with the seven windows, is absent from even the richest of such films, such as *The Sting*. I recently directed the sixty-seventh *Heritage Minute*. This is a series of one-minute theatrical films on significant moments and persons in Canadian history, "micro-movies" whose creative development I have directed since their inception in 1988. This one is set in Laurier House, in Prime Minister Mackenzie King's dining room, in 1926. The one exterior sound effect that penetrates those walls in the finished film is the faint sound of horses' hooves on the dark street outside. You may have to listen for them (I tend to favour subtlety in sound effects), but they are there.

There were of course lots of cars. The first family one I remember was a tan-coloured Hupmobile, probably once very grand, with a wire-spoked spare wheel in each of two wells sunk into the front mudguards and a big, leather trunk, strapped separately and mounted on the back.

The most familiar car on the streets was the Model A Ford, with its distinctive *pocketa-pocketa-pocketa*[1] exhaust noise. I remember becoming particularly aware of that sound one winter morning when Bracondale Hill was deep in snow. The streets were not ploughed then. I learned to ski on Bracondale Hill Road. An empty field ran from Davenport Road up to Hillcrest, two or three acres with a good steep slope where we skied and tobogganed and sledded. You had to be careful not to zip out into the middle of Davenport Road's traffic, but even if you did, it wasn't ploughed either, so the cars and the little two-way streetcar – the Toonerville Trolley, after a comic strip – would be going pretty slowly. This would have been about 1936, and the only cars regularly able to make it up the deeply drifted hill in front of our house were the Model As, *pocketa-pocketa-pocketa.* All cars dripped oil on the street, and that was another good smell. So was the hot asphalt, "tar" we called it, from the slowly bubbling square kettles of the street-repair rigs, also horse-drawn. The tar not only smelled good but could be chewed like gum, if you wanted to show off.

This was still Depression time and pleasures were simple. At the

1. Pocketa-pocketa: James Thurber fans will recognize that I am quoting here from his story "The Secret Life of Walter Mitty," which I first read when it appeared in *The New Yorker* in 1939, my father having suggested that I would like it.

schoolyard at the corner of Tyrrel and Winona we made an Elephant Wallow, by treading the mud until it became a mud hole. A purely existential game: the wallow had no purpose except to have been made, a basin of mud where none had existed before. We threw pennies up against the wall and played Buck Buck How Many Fingers Up. In the schoolyard we chanted,

Help, murder, police!
The teacher fell in the grease.
I laughed so hard I fell in the lard
Help, murder, police!

The Depression left a permanent mark. I still save string. You threw nothing out. Even though the wadding in the top of a bottle of vitamin pills is now only a disagreeable synthetic, I still feel wrong about throwing it away; it *looks* like the piece of genuine "cotton batting" that was an important part of the first-aid supplies. It feels as though it should not be thrown away. What now sounds like no money at all went a long way then. "Here's a dollar, Pat. Go to the store and get me five pounds of sugar and a pound of butter and a loaf of bread and be sure to count the change." A hamburger, even into the first year or so of the war, was ten cents. So was a milkshake, fifteen cents if you wanted ice cream in it.

My father had bought that tall ten-room solid brick house on Bracondale Hill Road for $10,000 in 1934. It had a partly finished basement with a little stage in it for the ladies to watch from as the men played billiards (The Billiard Room, or just "the Bill," we called it, though we never had a billiards table). You could buy a car for under a thousand. Sad men in tattered suits came to the door with big suitcases full of stuff to sell, pins and needles and thread and tubes of glue, and one time one of them had a lapel button showing he had served in the same battalion overseas as my father. He was brought in and served a big meal at the table, and he and my father sat and talked about comrades they both remembered until late at night. My father gave him money and looked sad when he went away, sad for the wretched life this ex-soldier was living while he, my dad, was prospering as a school principal, earning more than $2,000 a year. There was talk of another war coming, but the older boys all said, No, that could not be, the world war was the war to end wars, and besides it was less than twenty years ago, you couldn't have another war that soon.

One summer there was a polio scare. We were warned not to go to the Canadian National Exhibition. When September came, with the polio still rampant, I and hundreds of other kids were packed off to friends or relatives in small towns well out of Toronto, and so I spent a month in a strange school among strange kids, in Aylmer, Ontario, living with my mother's old school friend Marion Connor. My mother said that I was probably immune because of her having survived polio as a child (it was still called infantile paralysis). But she wasn't taking any chances. Aylmer smelled different. It smelled of old ladies and antique lace.

As I said earlier, smells are so evocative. The smell of your knees when you got back into short pants in the spring, and crouched over that little fire in the field while you poked spuds into the coals. Sometimes I would go over there alone and make a fire and roast my spuds. Nobody seemed to object to that. Then there was the smell of the oil in your roller skate wheels, especially one amazing pair of roller skates whose wheels were made of hard white rubber that rolled silently, unlike the scraping rattle of the ordinary skates, and those white rubber wheels had a pale white smell to them, as well.

Coal smoke was another comforting smell, bad as it was for our health and the environment. On a cold winter morning the scene from our upstairs windows on the crest of the hill that forms the ancient lake shore and looks out over the city, would be a branchless forest of coal smoke trunks, rising brightly in the early light. A railroad, a spur line, served the industrial complex just south of Davenport Road, and you could see and hear the puffing of the locomotives, though the trains themselves were out of sight. Every house had its plume, which, when the Dad or the elder brother went down to stoke the furnace in the morning, would thicken and darken for a while as the new coal caught and flamed before settling down into a rich red glow in the heart of the big cast-iron furnaces.

Living rooms had grates and in the grates you used cannel coal in big, mirror-surfaced chunks that burned with a soft blue flame and sometimes revealed a fossilized leaf and produced a lesson in paleontology if you had a teacher for a father. The first house I ever owned, on Rothsay Avenue in the Queensway in 1954, had a coal-fired hot-air furnace in the basement. Before going off to work you stoked it up so that it would burn quietly until you came home at night, and if you went away for a weekend you got a neighbour to come in and stoke it for you. (We tried car sharing from time to time in those days. From that Queensway house I rode in with a neighbour one bitterly cold December morning perhaps as late as 1955, and stopped, spellbound, as I walked across the Spadina Avenue Bridge up from Lakeshore Road. The railway marshalling yards below me to the east, where SkyDome is today, were a panorama of coal-fired locomotive columns of smoke, backlit in the rising sun and so compelling in their beauty that I was late for work.)

But back to the Hupmobile, twenty years earlier: when school came to an end in June the Hupmobile would be packed for the trip to camp, Dad smoking most of the time as he drove. I loved the smell of a cigarette being lit in a car. In 1935, Dad traded the Hupmobile in on a new Oldsmobile after the Hupmobile went all to pieces on one dramatic drive to Sundridge that summer. Mary, Cliff, and John had begun to object to the crowding on that long trip, once I was big enough to take up a place for myself. The Hupmobile had a big steel trunk strapped to the back. Even when Mary was sent by train to give us a little more room inside the car, bags and boxes were still crammed in the passenger space, while that trunk was so packed it had to have one set of leather straps holding it shut and another set holding it onto the rack just above the back bumper. Tied to those straps on the back of the trunk was a brand-new hammock. It had lovely gold cords and a kind of brocaded ornamentation, and we all loved it.

We had two flat tires even before we got to Orillia (where we always stopped to visit Grandpa and Granny Watson and Uncle Skid, my mother tapping her fingers impatiently to get moving again). Once past Orillia the pavement stopped and Highway 11 was a two-lane gravel road. Sometime after Gravenhurst a surprising number of drivers coming the other direction waved and pointed at us. My father waved back and remarked on how friendly everyone was, must be the lovely weather, and said, Tut tut, or Stuff and nonsense, when my mother said she thought they were trying to tell us something. Finally one man in an open car yelled loudly enough to be heard. It sounded like "Fire!" Cliff and John in the back looked out and saw the hammock on fire. The hammock was on the trunk and the trunk was right above the gas tank filler pipe. Dad pulled off the road by a highways department sand pile, had his pocket knife open before he hit the ground, cut the cords on the hammock, heaved it onto the sand pile, and had all of us scoop up sand with our hands to douse the flames. Every year after that when we passed that sand pile we would reconstruct the scene.

Roadside signs were thicker and thicker every year. There would be signs in front of small shops in villages, or at corners, advertising Shell Gasoline, or Esso, or Supertest. Dad liked Shell, with its big yellow scallop-shell sign. The gas pumps were hand-operated. A tapered round steel column had a long pump handle fixed near its base, the handle to be rocked back and forth beside the usually red cast-iron column that supported a glass cylinder about a foot in diameter, graduated with one-gallon marks at about three-inch spaces up the side of the glass, to the top, which was the ten-gallon mark. You pumped until you had as much in the glass cylinder as you thought you needed, and then it flowed down by gravity through the filler hose. There was only one grade of gas. Some hand-painted signs would announce

Others said GOOD EATS. I could never understand why we couldn't stop and try out those eats.

It was always an exasperating day, the drive to camp, but that one took the prize. Not long after the fire, when Dad rolled down his side window, the glass broke and fell out. Then the radiator boiled over and he scalded himself. By the time we had made it down the single-track, two-rut grass-centred little road that ran down the east shore of Lake Bernard to the camp, he was saying, "That's it. That's enough." And a few days later, in Sundridge, he had traded the Hupmobile in for a brand-new navy blue Oldsmobile with solid wheels – no spokes! – and a curved and elegant shape, nothing square, and a *built-in-trunk!* I still think of the Hupmobile with affection, though. My first memory of having an erection is in that car, and probably it was on that last trip, before everything began to go wrong. The erection was in the right front seat, I remember that clearly, waking up to it and having to pee; I would have been five.

If we were still skeptical about a coming war, before long the news from Europe left little doubt. The older teenage boys would often be seen walking thoughtfully on the beach in the evening, two or three at a time with their heads together, and I remember clearly being told how this one or that had decided that, if war did in fact come, he was going to join up. So many of them did, in fact, that the camp never opened again, having lost virtually its entire staff that autumn of 1939.

We lost John too. He had always seemed restless, a bit of an outsider, even in the family. He had chosen the High School of Commerce instead of the academically oriented Oakwood that Mary had already graduated from (she was in nursing now, at the Wellesley Hospital), and where Cliff was going into his final year, Grade Thirteen or, as it was called then, Fifth Form. Although many of his friends had gone straight off to the recruiting stations the day war broke out, Cliff wanted to join the navy, and the Canadian Navy was not recruiting then. Dad told him he would have a better chance of a commission if he finished high school, so he decided to do that. Not

John. He just disappeared, left a note: "I'm going to go to sea," and despite my father's enlisting help from the police and everyone else he could turn to, there was no further sign until a postcard came from South America. He was working on a tanker, loving it, don't worry he was all right, he would come home on his first leave. John was sixteen.

Cliff hung in and did well in that Fifth Form. The year before he had become junior Canadian diving champion and had been offered a lifeguard's job at the popular Crang's outdoor swimming pool, on the north side of St. Clair avenue just east of Oakwood, where a giant supermarket now stands, and worked there for his last summer as a civilian, the summer of 1940.

When the war broke out, I was in Grade Six at McMurrich Public School, and the lean and pince-nezed Miss Parkinson got the whole class knitting socks for soldiers and sailors, and read us the news every morning. I began to skate, holding hands with girls whenever possible, on the two big rinks at Hillcrest Park where the park staff brought out fire hoses at night and flooded what had been all summer the multiple tennis courts. Grade Seven (Miss Kelso) was where we got seriously interested in science, and Mr. Varcoe, the vice principal who always had a leather strap visibly protruding from his hip pocket, came to our class twice a week and did experiments with us. Once he lit a candle under a big square candy jar full of water in which he had dropped a few grains of potassium permanganate, whose purple traces would show us the phenomenon of convection when the water began to heat up. However, the corner of the jar broke after a few minutes above the flame, and Mr. Varcoe's trousers were soaked with the outflow. We laughed involuntarily, but shushed quickly, in terror, until this martinet who was famous for giving a kid the slugs[2] at the slightest provocation looked up and broke into laughter himself.

Two fat women who lived together near Christie and St. Clair shared us for Grade Eight: Miss Pethick for grammar and composition, math and science, and her pal, Miss Winterborn, for literature,

2. The Slugs: A punishment that entailed slapping a child's outstretched hand with a heavy leather strap.

music, history, and geography. They were superb teachers. We would make jokes about their vast arms and bosoms, or about how Miss Pethick's skirt rode up past her bloomers when she sat at her desk and you could see all that even from the back of the room. Miss Pethick was very stern, but my goodness, you paid attention, and she made the intricacies of grammar seem like a game, which she got us all playing eagerly. Once in Miss Winterborn's class I played a joke on her with a trick from the Arcade Magic and Novelty Shop, a tipped ink bottle with a japanned metal pool coming out of it, apparently a pool of spilled black ink. Earlier, she had lent me her own precious copy of *Moby Dick*, and I had gained some confidence in her goodwill when I had involuntarily laughed out loud over the passage at the beginning when the stuffy owners are signing up Queequeg. I realized that I had committed a real offence, laughing out loud in class, when she strode over to my desk with the strap in her hand, never mind sending for Mr. Varcoe, demanding to know what I was laughing at, and I pointed at the passage, still convulsing, and said that I couldn't help it, and she started to laugh. So now I had apparently spilled this big blob of ink on her precious book. I pretended not to notice, the book open on one corner of the desk, I apparently deeply engaged in writing some serious notes in a workbook as she prowled the room looking over the pupils' shoulders. There was a hiss of indrawn breath, and then an awful, an awe-full, whispered, "*What is this!*"

I revealed the joke. How I had the nerve to do it, I can't recall. But she almost collapsed with laughter after a moment, and I became something of a class hero.

On Sunday afternoons when family friends came to an afternoon tea, there were freshly baked tea biscuits, and sandwiches called Pinwheels, which you made by slicing a loaf very thin from end to end, spreading something like cream cheese with bits of chopped pimento or red and green pepper on the long thin slice, then rolling it up and cutting across the roll to produce tiny round slices with a colourful spiral of filling. These were served from a wickerware stand called a curate. A favourite entertainment at those afternoon teas was a kind of group quiz or *Jeopardy*, called Guggenheimer. Five or six people could play at once. Each of you had a sheet of paper that you ruled off, in pencil, into twenty-five spaces, five across and five down, each space big enough to write a word or two in. Across the top you put categories, and each player had the right to name one: Countries, Cities, Authors, Airplanes, Cars, Rivers, Chemicals, Buildings, Comic Strip Characters, Movies, Flowers, Vegetables, Animals . . . virtually anything, although I think the other players could challenge your choice if you got too clever or arcane. Down the side were letters of the alphabet, again each player having the right to name one. There was a time limit, and on the word Go you tried to fill in each square with the name of, say, a mammal, or a candy or a celestial object, that began with the letter on the corresponding left-hand column. Adults and kids played together, and there was much raucous challenging of the answers. A bit like the spirit around a lively Scrabble board.

There were always lots of reference works around, for the challengers and the challenged: a twenty-volume *Encyclopaedia Britannica* (thirteenth edition, 1926 – I still have it), and stacks of current magazines and newspapers. The *Globe and Mail*[3] and the *Toronto Star* were delivered every morning and afternoon respectively by Ernie McCullough, whose tinsmith father had made him a streamlined silver-painted sidecar for his bicycle, so that he could carry literally hundreds of papers, which he threw to the verandah with almost unfailing accuracy, thirty feet or more from the street, as he nonchalantly rode his three-wheeler along, whistling as he went. I tried to grab the papers first, to get at the comics: Popeye, Bringing Up Father, Gasoline Alley (with a hero called Skeezix), Little Orphan Annie, Buck Rogers (a rocket ship hero, with a girlfriend called Wilma and an eccentric on-board scientist named Dr. Huer, about which we snickered quite a lot when we got old enough to hear the pun in it). For a few years some of the major daily strips were re-issued in book form: "Big Little Books." These were hard-bound books containing

3. Which had been *The Mail and Empire* in living memory, before merging with the *Toronto Globe.*

two or three hundred pages of comics, each page only one frame and the overall dimensions of the book just the size of that single frame and its border, not quite three inches – perhaps eight centimetres square – but they were over an inch thick and gave your collected Buck Rogers or Mandrake the Magician a nice substantial feel.

We also got *National Geographic, Maclean's, Saturday Night, The Atlantic Monthly, The New Yorker*, and, for the brief time that I delivered it door to door from a big bag slung over my shoulder, earning a few cents a copy and prizes (including once a hatchet!) if you sold more than a certain number, *The Saturday Evening Post*, with covers by Norman Rockwell, whom some of my father's friends dismissed as not being a "real artist," a judgment I found incomprehensible and still do.

Movies were a frequent category in that Guggenheimer game. We all went to the movies. The Oakwood Theatre, on Oakwood Avenue just north of St. Clair, and the Christie on St. Clair just east of Christie Street were the favourites. You got a Saturday afternoon double feature for ten cents, and sometimes you sat with a girl and maybe even held hands. When Walt Disney's *Snow White* was released it was not just another movie, it was a revolution: nothing like this had been seen before. People went back three, four, five times. We sang "Whistle While You Work" on the way to school, and wondered aloud if there would ever be another movie like it. Other animation houses, mostly offering primitive short cartoons in black and white – Popeye, Betty Boop, Felix the Cat – were still enjoyed but were seen as belonging to a primitive world not comparable to the multi-dimensional wonders of this amazing breakthrough.

We loved horror movies, and bravely pretended we weren't really scared. They were not usually very bloody. One that we went back to several times, *Cat People* from 1943, had a crucial scene near the end in which the heroine is trapped by the marauding supernatural woman-turned-panther, in a dark basement swimming pool, a scene that was still gripping when I screened it sixty years later, in which you never see the invader, but only the victim's terrified face, and the shadows along the walls of the deserted pool as the heroine tries in vain to see the diabolical creature she believes to be stalking her. It was brilliant.

Girls always wore skirts to school. I don't remember seeing a girl in slacks before the war. Boys wore breeks, tied below the knee with laces running through the same kind of lace-holes you had on your shoes, and the bottom edge of the breeks were trimmed with leather. Some had leather patches at the knees. If you were lucky, your parents might buy you a pair of Hi-Cuts, which were strong leather boots that came halfway up the calf and were laced all the way, a laborious process but worth it for the status. If you were in the Cubs or the Scouts, as I was until girls became more interesting, you learned to launder your own shirts, and to iron both shirts and trousers with the crease just so, and always ironing the inside of the leg, with a damp cloth between the iron and the wool of the trousers. We did have electric irons, but not refrigerators until after the war. The big wooden icebox had a fifty-pound block in the upper compartment, which might drain into a tube running through the floor to a drain in the basement. The first electric fridge came home around 1947 or '48. The electric service was still 25 cycle then, and light bulbs had a slight, barely detectable flicker.

I fell in love with Evelyn Bell (there were a lot of boys after her; she wore lipstick). One night at the skating rink when we slipped away behind the lawn bowling huts for a little necking, I managed to get my hand under her sweater and actually on to her bare skin. At the back. But when I told her I loved her, she laughed at me. Oh well. High school was coming. There would be more opportunities. The war was exciting, we were certainly going to win. Dad joined up again, briefly, and was promoted to Lieutenant Colonel. To his deep regret, he was boarded out medically with a lung infection contracted after a training session in which he had to ride a motorcycle for hours in a freezing rainstorm. In his convalescence he was given a fairly undemanding assignment as a rural school inspector in the Bradford, Ontario, area. There he inspected schools in the famous market gardening area, the Holland Marsh. Japanese kids were in some of those classes, the children of British Columbians who had been forcibly deported to Ontario to reduce their menace as aliens, and were in fact in forced labour on those farms. I remember him telling us that when he came into one of those classes and the teacher told the kids to stand and sing "God Save the King," and the Japanese kids did, he had to turn away he felt so ashamed.

In December 1941 Japan had bombed Pearl Harbor, and the Americans had finally come into the war. John and Cliff were overseas and Mary was finishing her nursing training at the Wellesley Hospital and was engaged to be married. It was halfway through the Grade Eight year. I turned twelve and could get out of the Cubs and into the Scouts. In June Dad drove us to Fredericton, where he had a contract to teach summer school. He rented me a bike for the summer, and I explored the forested surroundings almost every day, met some older girls who told sex jokes but kept their distance, went to a Scout camp for ten days, drove around the Gaspé coast on the way back, discovered that my dad spoke what seemed fluent French (learned in the trenches and billets in World War I, I suppose) with a great accent (the whole family were actors and mimics, except Roger), and decided that speaking French would be really fun, I would want to do that myself. That would happen soon. I was about to enter high school.

Chapter 3

HIGH SCHOOL

THE HIGH SCHOOL YEARS were divided between Toronto and Ottawa: two years at Oakwood Collegiate, where Mary and Cliff had both graduated, then two years at Glebe Collegiate in Ottawa, when my father was made principal of the Ottawa Normal School, then back to Oakwood for Grade Thirteen.

That first year at Oakwood got off to a distressing start for me. My older siblings had not warned me that it wouldn't do to turn up in short pants, looking my age, which was twelve. I was also small for my age, so I took a lot of teasing at first and handled it badly. But before long my mother had fixed me up with long pants (with cuffs, of course), white socks, which were *de rigueur*, smartly polished shoes, shirt, tie and jacket, so I looked pretty much like all my schoolmates except that I was smaller.

My voice had changed, going within weeks from a light girlish alto to a robust bass not much different from what it is today. I joined the choir, singing bass under the direction of a gentle romantic named Earl Davison. Before long I had my first enchanted encounters with Palestrina and the choral music of J.S. Bach, and then Wagner (forbidden in my father's house, as a favourite of Hitler's), a charming group of English folk songs, and some very sophisticated close-harmony four- and five-part arrangements of pop classics, including "Moonlight Becomes You," arranged by the popular radio choral director Fred Waring (who was also famous for inventing the blender, then always known as the Waring Blender).

I was already performing magic. I had first seen the diminutive Maltese magician John Giordmaine at a birthday party for my next-door neighbour Maggie Dale (she with whom I had furtively played doctor a few years earlier). Watching him produce flamboyant silk scarves and bunches of flowers out of nowhere, and making a bowl of water change colours just by waving his hand over it, and of course pulling a rabbit out of a hat, I knew that I wanted to do that. Giordmaine had a magic counter in Eaton's Toyland, and when I found him there I asked him to get me started. Bit by bit he taught me the rudiments and gave me a lot of encouragement.

I remember with delight the evening when I announced at the dinner table that I had something to show the parents after dinner and, having practised it diligently in my bedroom until it was flawless, performed for them the classic Multiplying Billiard Balls Johnny Giordmaine had sold me (for seventy-five cents, I think), and had the intoxicating experience of seeing that they were, unmistakably, baffled, surprised, and delighted.

I began to haunt the library, where a child who asked was allowed into the adult section and you could read and make notes and drawings from *Modern Magic* by "Professor Hoffman," but you could not take the book out of the library. Soon I was making some of my own equipment and offering to "do" birthday parties for schoolmates. Cliff wrote from England, where he was training as a British Navy fighter pilot, to say that he was now too big for his suit of tails, and they could be sold. I badgered my mother to cut them down for me and sew in the special pockets that Professor Hoffman assured his readers every serious magician required. (What Cliff – a teenage boy in Depression Toronto – was doing with a suit of tails is not now clear to me, although even then the formal coming-out dances for debutantes were part of the high school social scene).

Dad's friend the publisher Wilfred Wees, for whom I would later work as an editor at W.J. Gage and Company, gave me a silk opera hat that opened with a satisfying snap and looked pretty magical all on its own. I still remember the satisfaction of producing an endless series of eggs out of that hat (thanks to Professor Hoffman) while wearing my tails with the secret pockets at Bobby Green's birthday party in his house on Ossington Avenue.

I mostly loved the schoolwork. The first encounter with Euclid, where you could prove things with irresistible logic, was intoxicating. Latin, which I had dreaded, proved easy and charming; the teacher, Miss Jessie Reade, was an enthusiast who radiated the assumption that we would all love the language and find it easy; so we all did. She taught us limericks and jokes in Latin and seasoned her teaching with laughter. Sadly, partway through that first year she left to do some kind of mysterious war work, and we were dismayed to lose her. A long time after, on the seventy-fifth anniversary of Oakwood Collegiate, Mary and I went to the celebrations together. The first person we saw as we walked in was Miss Reade, who was one of a group of greeters. She walked forward when we came in and said, "Well, Mary Watson! And Pat!" I had been in her class for only a few months, forty years earlier. Perhaps she'd seen my television work. But she did not address me as Patrick, so I like to think she remembered. She had taught Mary for at least a year, but that was fifty years before.

The French teacher was Bill Evanson, a good-looking man of about thirty-five who also coached basketball and helped out with the cadet corps. Like Miss Reade, he was an enthusiast, and he managed to make us feel that learning French was an adventure. He also showed us that we already knew far more than we imagined. I remember his opening class.

"How many of you speak French?" No one put up a hand. "Oh come on!" said Mr. Evanson. "I bet you do, at least a bit. Anybody know any French words?"

Someone put up a hand and said, "Oui!"

"Good," Evanson said, and wrote it on the blackboard.

"Anyone else?" Someone knew "le" and "la" and someone else knew "non." On the board.

"Anybody tell me what this means in English?" Evanson asked, and wrote "parlement."

"Parliament?" someone said.

"Good for you. What about this?" And he wrote "professeur."

"Professor?" someone said, a little tentatively. Then came "bonjour" (well of course!), "au revoir" (no problem); then "longue," "langage," "province," "rivière." The excitement grew as people in the class nailed each new word, and Evanson made sure that it wasn't just the brightest kids who got a chance. (Everybody knew "bonjour," and he picked one of the least likely kids to give that answer.)

"Good for you! What about this?" "Un" went on the board and was identified, and then "deux" and "cinq" . . . we had seen them on the one-, two-, and five-dollar bills. Then we made out the rest of the numbers by inference.

"Right. Here's a tough one. Anybody know this one?" and he wrote "s'il vous plaît." And of course someone recognized it. By the end of the class, the blackboard was full of French words all of which had been recognized by these Grade Nine students, few of whom had thought they knew any French when the class began. The sense of accomplishment! We had all been praised for our knowledge, and by a teacher. And when we came back into Evanson's class the next day, the eagerness was palpable.

Perhaps we were blessed by a singularly gifted group of teachers in that school. Not all were young – several had taught my sister ten years earlier, and she had spoken of some with admiration and even affection. What went on in the classroom was an adventure, and I recall very few instances of the deliberate humiliation of students or the unfair handing out of detentions or other punishments. I do recall that the business teacher (we had a business class every two weeks and learned how to write cheques and do simple bookkeeping) put a sample of my handwriting on the main-floor bulletin board as her choice for the worst handwriting in the class. She was a grim-faced, sour-smelling person, but she had a sense of humour.

I managed to stand first or second when we had exams, sharing the honours with a girl I'll call Ellen Young, who stood first when I stood second and vice versa, a small round girl with dark eyes and black curly hair, with whom I of course fell in love. I joined the drama group, tried my hand at football but was hopeless, joined the swimming team and was very good at the sprint and went into every swimming meet I could manage. There was a cadet corps. We took rifle training on a rifle range set up in the basement; I joined the Precision Squad and proudly wore my uniform to school on Fridays.

"Cool" had not yet entered the vocabulary, except as a descriptive for certain kinds of jazz. "Neat" was still functional, and it may have been about then that "swift" became current. If someone farted someone else was almost sure to ask indignantly, "Who cut the cheese?" One wag earned the class's respect for both wit and nerve when he was given a French class assignment to write on the board his French version of several common English phrases and sentences, and included "*Qui a coupé le fromage?*"

Charley Fick and I became inseparable friends, although I was a bit intimidated by his skill with a football as he quarterbacked the junior team. But I went off by train to his cottage in Haliburton that first summer, learned to run his father's ancient ten horsepower outboard motor, and sat up late talking about girls and religion and the universe. And once, after an intensely embarrassing series of avoidances and false starts, we got around to the subject of masturbation and all the dreadful things they said it would do to you.

Music became important. Lucy had assumed that, being her child, I would be able to play the piano, and had started me with a teacher when I was six or seven. I hated the teacher, who rapped my knuckles with a ruler when I made mistakes; so for a while I thought that I hated the piano. In fact I had enjoyed all the music that was part of the elementary school curriculum: learning to read first the sol-fa charts and later the standard notation, singing at first in unison and then in parts. My brother John brought home a ukulele and learned to sing lonesome cowboy songs in a soft, mournful tenor. He taught me enough of the chording that when he went off to sea, I took over the ukulele and soon began to learn the comic songs of the Lancashire comedian George Formby.

High school brought a new focus on music with that rich choral experience of the great classics along with sophisticated arrangements of contemporary pop standards. At the same time as we gingerly explored sexual relationships through dancing with girls, the Friday afternoon "tea dances" in the auditorium led to an obligation to know about the bands, the singers, and the songs. Weekend parties at a fellow student's home would always include dancing, and sometimes homemade music if anyone played the piano well enough. Popular teachers were invited to those parties, and came, and danced with the students and played games.

Some time in the thirties, Lucy had brought home an ancient hand-wound Victrola with a few ancient, scratched 78s, mostly comic songs. One was terribly racist, a southern voice singing, "Some folks say that a Nigger won't steal" (Way Down Yonder in the Co-orn Field). Oddly, I don't remember anyone, even my scrupulously anti-racist father, even commenting on it.

I appropriated that Victrola to the third-floor bedroom I had taken over from Cliff and John, and began to buy popular dance records by Tommy Dorsey and Glenn Miller. Then somebody introduced me to the music of Duke Ellington. That was a revelation. The Dorsey and Miller swing records were still great fun, but you had to actually *listen* to Ellington's jazz; it kept insisting in your head afterwards, so that I found myself going to the piano, trying to pick out at least the basic melodic line for "Take the A Train," "East Saint Louis Toddle-OO," "The Mooch." Ellington led to Fats Waller and Lionel Hampton, music that opened my ears to the blues, and before long to boogie-woogie, which was a very coarse piano subset of the blues. I would whip over to a record shop on St. Clair just west of Oakwood when I had some spare cash, to see if there was anything new from Albert Ammons or Meade "Lux" Lewis. This stuff was a serious regression from the sophisticated jazz of Duke Ellington, but the great thing about boogie-woogie was that it was easy for an untutored kid to break down and reproduce by ear, on the piano keyboard: a simple walking octave bass line:

or repeated fifths, in dotted eighths and sixteenths, with a flattened third/third flip after every two-fifths, thus

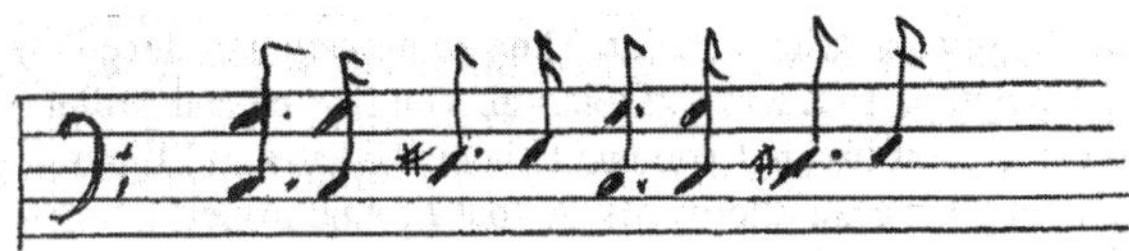

It would sound even dirtier, even more down-in-the streets if you dropped the dotted eighths and sixteenths and played straight eighths. The right hand was almost equally repetitious and easy, and before long I was relentlessly banging out this mean and rowdy 1-4-5 stuff, much to the despair of my usually tolerant parents.

In the late winter or early spring of 1943, a soldier friend of my father's, Dennis Healey,[1] invited me to meet him at the tank-training grounds at Camp Borden near Barrie, Ontario. That meeting turned into a day of wildly irresponsible rushing around in tracked vehicles, me furnished with a Tank Corps officer's beret and a fleece-lined combat coat. It was a day that so seduced me with the adventure of it all that I momentarily discarded my notion of being a fighter pilot like Cliff, and imagined instead tearing across the North African desert in a tank like Humphrey Bogart in *Sahara*, or indeed like Captain Dennis Healey himself, my host of the day.

Healey briefly usurped Cliff's role as my personal hero. He arranged for me to fire a simulated machine gun in the indoor gunnery range, from a rocking platform simulating a Bren gun carrier, an open box of a vehicle on tracks, like a tank, at miniature targets on a miniature desert. Then he taught me to actually drive a real Bren gun

1. No relation to the British Labour Party luminary.

carrier,[2] a kind of small tank without a top. I nearly turned us over on a slope, but Healey seemed to find it all hugely entertaining. He had taken an avuncular fancy to me, never having had children of his own. He invited me to come back the following week when he would arrange for me to drive a tank. A real tank with real guns on it. Jesus! I was only thirteen. But I was with Captain Healey and, though small, was wearing an officer's beret and ordinary soldiers were saluting me. "Return the salute," Healey had said, quite improperly, showing me how to do it.

He was one of that breed of adventurous guys who seem to feel invulnerable. Irish, perfectly fluent in French, and an actor by temperament, he had been in British intelligence and had parachuted into occupied France as a spy, staying there for nearly a year.

Now Healey wanted a different kind of action and had transferred to a Canadian armoured unit. He and Dad had met in a military hospital when they had both been invalided in 1942. At the close of that dizzyingly exciting day at Camp Borden (where my father had first trained as a young recruit), Healey had taken me to the officers' mess for dinner. I played chess with the Colonel, and lost. Healey (we all called him Dinty) drove me to the train in a Jeep. I went home and regaled the folks. I was too excited to notice their real reaction; after all, I had been playing Soldier, and Soldier was one of the most important roles that my father had played in life; so of course he would be as thrilled as I. If I looked at his face as I told my probably highly coloured stories of the day, I did not see what was forming there.

All during the following week I boasted and embroidered my exploits to my school chums. I was a hopeless scholar, daydreaming about the approaching weekend and able to focus on nothing else. A tank! Real guns! I was going to ride my bike over to the St. Clair Avenue CPR station at seven o'clock Saturday morning. Dinty would meet me at Barrie. We would have our adventurous day and another evening in the mess, and I would stay overnight in Officers' Quarters.

2. Also called the Universal Carrier.

In retrospect it all seems very improper; I have no idea how Healey was getting away with it, but that was the plan.

Friday night came. I was doing my last bits of homework in haste and distraction. There was a tap at my bedroom door, and Dad came in, looking very stern. "Pat," he said softly, "I know you are going to be very disappointed, but your weekend at Camp Borden is off. I've just been talking to Dinty."

I was shocked. What had happened, I asked. Was Dinty sick or something? No, Dad told me. "It was my decision. It's too dangerous. I told him that I'm not letting you go."

Tears of rage welled up. I couldn't speak. I sat there at my little desk shaking my head, uncomprehending. How could he betray me so, and at soldiering!

Dad came and put his arm around my shoulder. I can hear his soft voice still. He said, "Pat, I have one son who nearly lost his life in a plane crash a year ago. Now he's flying coastal patrol around the shores of Britain. He's in combat – do you realize what that means? I have another son I haven't heard from for thirteen months, who was shipwrecked and nearly died off the coast of Iceland two years ago. And he is on a merchant ship presumably somewhere off the coast of Africa, and may be alive or maybe not. We don't know. I am not going to take any risks with a third son."

It was the first time I had seen him vulnerable. It was, I think, the most loving moment that ever passed between us.

Perhaps it is appropriate to step out of the high school story here just long enough to reflect on the stories of my two extraordinary half-brothers, Cliff and John.

Chapter 4

CLIFF AND JOHN

WAR, RUMOURS OF WAR, and stories of war played a substantial role in my growing up. Often at the dinner table Dad would hold us all spellbound after the dessert, over cheese and crackers, with stories of his time in the trenches. The stories were sometimes quite bloody and appalling, but I don't think we knew then that they were appalling.

Perhaps Cliff knew. Cliff used to walk in his sleep. Dad had a big illustrated history of the Great War which I used to pore over, but even in face of the worst photos of the mud-filled trenches and the corpse-strewn battlefields, I seemed immune to the horror of it. The Great War was a mythic, remote, almost literary war from which my father had returned unscathed, a decorated hero. It was a war about which he told us stories with a certain relish, and I now think with a sense of wonder at his own invulnerability, and a rejoicing in that invulnerability. So I believed that this was what a dad did, he survived when others were falling all about him, and that was what I would do should circumstances so arise.

One day my father said the Great War book was missing, had any of us taken it? Mary remembered seeing Cliff sleepwalking a few nights earlier. She had come home late from a date and everyone else was asleep, and she had seen Cliff go into the study, where my dad's floor-to-ceiling bookshelves lined two walls, and come out again with a big book and head downstairs. Of course you never interfered with a sleepwalker; we all knew that. And then Dad remembered that when he had stoked the coal furnace the next morning he had been puzzled to see a thick pile of paper ash lying on top of the embers.

When I was thirty and for the first time read some serious history of that war, I realized how unusual it was that my father had survived it. It was only then that the meaning of those photos in the big book of the Great War began to sink in. But Cliff, who had a collection of Great War artefacts, a gas mask, a pineapple hand grenade, a British steel helmet, a bayonet, and some rounds of rifle ammunition, had evidently harboured some wise and distressing feelings about the war and about that book.

Like most boys of that era we played various kinds of war games. Paper games, like Battleship (we called it Sink the Swiss Navy). And fierce backyard battles, with snowballs, or wooden swords and garbage can lids for shields. I had been lent a pair of fencing foils and masks by a Cub master named Fred Tighe who was trying to seduce me sexually, and yet was kind and unaggressive, so that I knew I could hold him at bay, remain friends, and exploit him as in the case of the foils. Anyway fencing was taught at Layolomi and John was good at it, and we fenced in the cellar and imagined ourselves in knightly mediaeval wars, and invested war with glory in that way.

Once when I was about six or seven, I was in a snowball fight in the backyard at 22 Bracondale Hill Road, a member of the army ranged against the troops Cliff was leading. I led a charge into the hail of ice-coated and ferocious snowballs, was bloodied on the cheek but kept on coming. Our side stormed the others' snow fort and knocked it down. And Cliff said in unfeigned admiration, "Geez you're brave, Patchet." Well, I felt invulnerable, like my father.

Cliff and John, both of them meticulous craftsmen, made model airplanes, working in absorbed concentration by the light of an old gooseneck lamp, which I still own, producing exquisitely detailed Spads, SE 5s, Nieuports, and other Great War fighters. The two of them took me to see *Hell's Angels*, an unremittingly romantic film about the war in the air, featuring the very airplanes they were modelling. We eagerly speculated about What It Would Be Like.

And indeed, there was a fair amount of speculation about the possibility of a coming second war, but it seemed to us kids that another war would never happen. This was not because war as such was such a horrible thing, but because the Great War loomed so huge, so unique, that it was conceptually not possible that another could come in the lifetime of those who had fought in it.

In the summer of 1938 Dr. Hardy Hill, a history teacher at Oakwood Collegiate, took a small group of his students on a tour of Britain. Cliff was among them. Hill, a gunboat captain in the Royal Navy in the 1914–1918 war, arranged for the boys to spend ten days at sea on the battleship H.M.S. *Revenge.* Cliff was enchanted. He resolved that once out of school he would join the Royal Navy. He wrote a hilarious account of that sea voyage in the school yearbook, *The Oakwood Oracle of 1939.*[1] By the time that magazine was published the war clouds were almost overhead. At Layolomi that summer many of the young men of seventeen, eighteen, twenty – counsellors and instructors – walked the beach with their heads together contemplating a future in uniform.

It was not until 1989 that John told me Cliff had run away to join the navy in the fall of 1939 and that the police had found him in Halifax and brought him back. I had never heard that before. Mary's version is that he had got only as far as Montreal and ran out of money, and Dad arranged a train ticket to bring him back. In any case, in the summer of 1940 he worked as a lifeguard at the Crang pool on St. Clair Avenue, and organized a series of weekly aquatic comedy and fancy diving shows. The climax of those Wednesday evenings shows came when a blowsy comic blonde with huge boobs

1. And, in the same issue, drew a powerful pen and ink picture of a devastated tree in a Great War Battlefield, and wrote a moving short story about a nurse (Mary, his sister?) encountering a blinded soldier in a field hospital in Flanders, and realizing that the hideously wounded boy is her brother. That same summer of 1938 Mary, Granny Mullett, and Obie's sister Doris, only two years older than Mary, visited Italy and Germany together. Mary's stories of the trip, like Cliff's of his battleship adventure, contained no hint of the coming catastrophe.

and a lot of makeup came sauntering out of the dressing rooms, climbed jauntily to the first level of the diving tower, was egged on to the next level by the crowd, then to the ten-metre top, where she panicked and, amid gales of laughter, executed what began as a wildly gyrating fall and then transformed at the last moment into a perfect entry, from which Cliff surfaced in his trunks holding the girl's bathing suit and the falsies aloft in one hand and the blond wig in the other.

Someone bet him serious money he wouldn't have the nerve to disguise himself as a girl and enter the Toronto Police Games Beauty Contest. The side bets persuaded him; if he won, the money would secure his trip to Britain to join the British Navy, without his having to ask Dad for help. Mary taught him how to walk and helped make a realistic papier mâché bosom modelled on her own. He got through several rounds of elimination before being exposed and collected several hundred dollars on the bets. Now he had his boat fare. Off to war! Glorious excitement. I could not understand at the time why my father looked grim.

It was during that summer Cliff and I sailed together for the last time. He was eighteen, I was ten. That was the last time I saw him in civilian clothes. We had been having a great time together with Granny Mullett at Croydon Cottage, her summer place on Lake Couchiching. I slept in the sunroom on the lakefront side of the sprawling frame building, under its long west wall, which was all windows. Cliff had a small bedroom nearby. One evening he told me that Jim Harvey, a pal from Layolomi days, was going to pick him up before sunrise to go sailing, and that later in the morning he would drop Jim off in Orillia, borrow the little sloop for the rest of the day, and come back and get me.

I was awakened by a gentle knocking on the window over my head. It was about five o'clock. Jim Harvey whispered, "Wake Cliff up." I did, and he promised again that he'd be back for me around lunchtime. I was out on the long narrow dock for a swim when he turned up. Characteristically, Cliff let me do most of the sailing, and we must have done the whole length of Couchiching and back, cruising in as close to the little islands as we could, and heeling over giddily till the water nearly came over the side. We got quite sunburned. By the time we returned the boat to Jim Harvey at the government dock in Orillia, the sun was beginning to go down, and we were starved and shivering. Cliff ran to a phone box and put in a nickel to call Doris. She turned up in the big Buick and brought us back to the cottage. We hung out in the kitchen while Cliff made big back-bacon sandwiches and told me that there was nothing better after a day's sailing. I could not and cannot imagine that there could be anything better than that supper or the day itself, the companionship of an eighteen-year-old boy about to go off to war, and his adoring ten-year-old kid brother.

Doris had taken a photo of the two of us on the ramp of the boathouse that day just before we set off for our sail, the two of us grinning at the camera. But I did not see that picture until more than thirty years later.

At the end of August that summer of 1940 there was the great gag of the Police Games beauty contest, and then booking passage, and the excited goodbyes when he got on the train for Halifax to take ship for Britain. He told us later that when he got to the British naval recruiting office and showed them his school certificate, all that science and math caught their attention, and the next thing he knew another officer in another office was showing him a picture of a Fairy Swordfish[2] and asking if he wouldn't like to fly one of these magnificent machines? And so he joined the Navy's Fleet Air Arm. It was fairly early on in his training that an overseas call came to my father in the middle of the night. There had been a dreadful accident. Cliff was hospitalized with extensive injuries and might not survive. For days we stayed near the telephone, waiting for news.

He had finished his basic flying training, in the old de Havilland

2. A cloth-covered biplane torpedo bomber known as the String Bag. Vulnerable, even to small-arms fire, and due to be retired from service, it was nonetheless a major player in the sinking of a number of top-of-the line German warships in World War II, including the Battleship *Bismark.*

Tiger Moth cloth-covered biplanes, and had moved on to an advanced trainer, the Miles Magister, a low-winged single-engine trainer whose flying characteristics were a little closer to those of the fighters he would be assigned to in combat.

His instructor had taken him for a lesson on spins and recovery. The instructor had been teaching in the Tiger Moth for years but was new to the Magister. The Tiger Moth was an inherently stable very slow biplane. If you stalled it and kicked it into a spin and then took your hands off, it would recover from that spin in less than a single full turn. The Magister, like most smooth-skinned low-winged monoplanes, does a fairly vicious spin. The instructor demonstrated the spin entry at a low altitude that would have been safe for a Moth, was probably astonished by the rapidity with which the little monoplane began to rotate in a steep nose-down attitude, and somehow threw them inverted in his attempt at recovery. Cliff later said the last thing he remembered was flying upside down through the main street of the town of Luton, a little boy gaping at them from the steps of a church before they hit.

Somehow my father heard that a Canadian neurosurgeon named Plewes was stationed in the region; he tracked him down and asked him to see Cliff. Dr. Plewes called back to say that Cliff was in very bad shape, eleven vertebrae broken, as well as both arms and both legs, and a minor skull fracture. The first diagnoses had suggested that he would never walk again, and in any case would certainly never fly again.

But he, Plewes, was not so sure; he was going to propose further surgery after the initial shock and blood loss had been dealt with. It turned out that the instructor's irresponsibilities that day had included checking the flight out with only his name on the book, so that when the rescue workers dug his dead body out of the wreckage of the house that the Magister had crashed into, they had no idea there was another person involved. The nineteen-year-old student pilot lay there all night, covered with rubble, paralyzed and unable to call out, until they found him when the cleanup work began the next morning.

Dr. Plewes seems to have effectively taken charge of the case. The follow-up surgery went well. Within a couple of weeks, the boy who might never walk again was up and about and taking rehabilitation. Eight months later he had completed his training and was flying Hawker Hurricanes on coastal patrol. He was briefly home on leave in 1943. The only bothersome trace of that incredible set of fractures, he said, was a slight paralysis of the upper lip that wouldn't allow him to clean off a spoon without inverting it. My mother and I posed for a photograph with him in the backyard at Bracondale.

Not long afterward he was selected as one the Brits in a British Commonwealth Air Training project that brought two pilots from every country in the Commonwealth to Norfolk, Virginia, for an intensive course that had them fly every kind of aircraft then in active service in Commonwealth forces, including Lancaster bombers.

He served throughout the war, including the infamous Murmansk Run, and then the Italian campaign flying out of Malta, transferred to the Canadian Fleet Air Arm at the end of the war, was promoted to Lieutenant Commander, was head of training at the Shearwater base in Nova Scotia, and was head of the aerobatics team.

In the summer of 1948 he brought that team to the CNE's air show. I stood at the Downsview airport fence when the five Seafires came in to land after a performance, his lead aircraft swinging in closest to the fence, and felt dizzy with pride as he climbed out onto the wing, took off his helmet and goggles, turned to wave to the applauding crowd, spotted me, and called over, "Hello, Patchet!"

The next summer, 1949, he brought the team back to the CNE again. I was working at the Taylor Statten camp, Camp Ahmek in Algonquin Park. The afternoon before we were to leave for Toronto, Taylor Statten beckoned to me as I was racing back to my tent to finish packing, and told me that there had been an accident at the Ex, and Cliff was dead.

They had been rehearsing a formation roll, in which three planes do a complete roll around each other. The lead plane, slightly ahead but dangerously close to the other two, does a straightforward slow roll revolving on its axis of flight while the other two stay just off his wingtips, as if they were extensions of the leader's wings, rolling around him. Chuck Elton, the pilot on his left, lost control about two-thirds of the way through the manoeuvre, and slid in toward Cliff's plane, his propeller slicing right through the cockpit. Cliff was killed in less than a second. Fifty years later I met the third pilot, Joe McBrian, and only then heard a dispassionate and precise description of what he had seen. Elton's plane crashed in flames. The two twenty-seven-year old pilots were buried with military honours.

Cliff had married Joan Fawcett, the British nurse who had helped him through the recovery from the Luton crash, in 1941. They had a daughter, Wendy, who was three when Cliff died, and Joan was pregnant with a second daughter, Sally.

When I was about forty-five, Mary found the photograph that Doris had taken that last great summer day of sailing on Couchiching, and mailed me an eight-by-ten print. I had never seen it before. By then, he had been dead for over a quarter of a century. That night, deep in a dream, I saw the outside of Croydon Cottage, its long west wall of windows all boarded up, the building cold and deserted. And there was a knocking sound, knuckles knocking on wood. It was Cliff, I knew it, knocking to be let back into life.

John Oborne Stanley Watson, my second step-brother, had a tough life. He was one of the bravest men I ever met, but, unhappily, for much of our time together we did not get along very well. I was past fifty before I was able to put together a number of pieces of our story that helped me make sense of what had seemed an opaque set of contradictions, and only then did we get close enough to have the exchanges that brothers need.

John was strikingly handsome, even as an adolescent, a gifted mimic and raconteur. Although he had done badly at school, he was a bright, alert guy, and when he finally found his vocation at sea he taught himself the spherical trigonometry and other complexities of navigation and maritime command so that by the time he was twenty-five or twenty-six he had successfully written his master's papers, the equivalent of a B.Sc. in a British university, qualifying him to be a Merchant Marine Captain, almost entirely self-taught at sea.

Then came a severe reversal of fortune. During the war he had married a lovely Liverpool girl named Joan Heath. They had two children by now, Carol and Michael. Carol had severe spinal difficulties as an infant, and Joan pressed John to come ashore, give her a hand with the family, and act like a proper father. Giving up the sea before he got his own command, leaving the one way of life in which he had ever been happy, was the second great disaster in his life. The first had been the death of his mother as a result of his birth,[3] a loss that seems to have twisted my father's otherwise magisterially fair view of life to the point where he blamed John for that death and did not seem to consciously recognize that he was doing so. Dad constantly found fault with the poor kid and punished him frequently and physically.

I secretly witnessed an episode. I was four years old, and playing in a forbidden place, the coal bin in the cellar. When the door at the top of the stairs opened and I heard my father's angry voice, I hid and froze. Dad was dragging John down the stairs. He took off his belt and laid into the eleven-year-old with unrelenting ferocity. I crouched in my hiding place, terrified, until I heard someone calling me for dinner and went trembling upstairs expecting further horrors. It is the single episode that explains why I never got anywhere near as close to my father as I otherwise would, given the powerful shared interests and attitudes that we had: despite his always treating me kindly, if firmly, I must have been deeply afraid of him for the rest of his life. Lucy must have been profoundly distressed by his treatment of John; she told Mary shortly before her death that she had warned my father that if he ever laid a hand on me she would leave him.

Going through my sister's photograph album some time in my early fifties, I found a picture of the four of us, Mary, Cliff, John, and me, taken at Camp Layolomi when I was three. Cliff and Mary are radiant adolescents, eleven and thirteen years old, kids who clearly feel

3. April 29, 1922.

that they have the world under control and that only good things are going to happen to them. I look like a sunny, slightly fuddled, and baby-faced kid. But John looks as though tragedy had hit. He is cowering, looking at the camera as if it might hurt. There are black circles under his eyes. That photograph immediately conjured up the scene in the coal cellar. Now I knew why he had run away to sea at the first opportunity.

In his last years, we were able to talk through some of this together, and partly with his help, partly because of an unexpected encounter in Iceland with people who had known him as a young sailor, I was able to sort out some of the fiction from the fact, and to realize the magnitude of the courage the man was possessed of, that had allowed him to live at all, to find any sunshine outside the shadow of his grieving father's anger.

At about the same time as Cliff's near-fatal crash in the Miles Magister, letters from John stopped coming. He had at first been sailing out of Halifax to South and Central American oil ports in Imperial Oil tankers. But early in the war he found a berth on the *Persier*, a Belgian freighter plying the Halifax-Liverpool run. On his second eastbound crossing, the ship foundered in a storm off the south coast of Iceland. A group of Icelandic fishermen came out in fishing boats to help get the survivors ashore through the frigid surf, and John spent several weeks recuperating in the home of a family in the small southern village of Vik. When he told about it later, he had the group of them walking across the foot of a glacier to get to Vik from the site of the sinking, eight or ten survivors setting out in their still wet woollen gear, and several of them dying of exposure and exhaustion before they got to the village.

Then there was the story of how he and a shipmate returned the gallantry and kindness of some of those Icelanders when, walking on the cliff above Vik, they saw a fishing boat founder in the surf, ran down to the beach, waded out in the near-freezing water, saved three fishermen who would otherwise have drowned, brought them ashore, and revived one with artificial respiration. There was a clipping about it from, I think, a Liverpool paper. And there was a framed citation signed by the president of Iceland. It was on rich linen-based paper. At the top was a photograph of a bleak, storm-struck rocky shore, and beneath were the words "In memory of your heroic deed at this place."

He was seventeen at the time. Because of the German fighters off the west coast of Ireland, the government of Iceland had prohibited fishermen from sailing to England to sell their catch, but there were rumours of boats setting off secretly, taking their chances with those German planes because of the price they could get for fish in war-starved Britain. After a few months, John was able to get a berth on one of those contraband voyages, made it safely to Liverpool, met Joan Heath, and was married before he was twenty.

I remember further great tales of mysterious voyages around Africa, coming down with blackwater fever (*Haemoglobinuria)* and being hospitalized in Liberia. And then later about being first mate on a supply ship going in on the Normandy beaches on D-Day-plus-one and being sunk by a mine and spending half a day hanging onto a big marker buoy before he was rescued. Some of these stories became more dramatic with repetition and the passage of time. We said, Hey: sailors tell stories. But over the years, as I heard him telling of situations about which I had some reliable knowledge, I began to have some difficulty judging which parts to believe. One of those great stories, however, was resonantly verified forty-five years after it happened.

In the summer of 1986, starting work on our international co-production documentary series *The Struggle for Democracy*, my wife and I flew from Chicago to Reykjavik to film a sequence about the nine-hundred-year-old Icelandic parliament and its unbroken tradition of democracy going back to the days of the Althinge. The Althinge, an outdoor meeting place in a rift where the continental plates divide, functioned very much like the Athenian assembly of citizens in that world's first democracy.

I told John we were going and asked if he would like me to look up some of the people he had stayed with in Vik, and with whom he had kept up a correspondence for twenty years or so. He looked a bit embarrassed. I thought, Oh-oh! My suspicions may have been right. But I pressed him anyway, and after a few days he dug out some letters from an old file box and gave me the name and last known address of Erlendur Einarsson, the young man with whose parents he had lived in the village of Vik forty-six years earlier.

I called Einarsson a couple of days after we arrived in Reykjavik, and here are some journal notes from the next few days.

> *12 June 1986. I've spoken to Erlendur Einarsson and his wife, the guy who was John's contemporary, and he said he remembers John well, maybe his father, Einar is too weak to be visited, but we'll try. Mrs. E. called back, "please come for a plain family dinner on Sunday. it will be ten or eleven at table, including little children if you don't mind. We are very excited. We have heard so much about the men from the* Persier. *It is a very important part of our family story."*

> *15 June. Dinner at Erlendur Einarsson, the son of Einar Erlendson, the man who looked after John and his friends from the Persier in 1941, along with children and grandchildren . . . . We got a slightly more critical view of Democracy here, but even the somewhat rebellious (no, not rebellious, just dissenting or critical) young people were proud and patriotic.*

What follows is a letter I sent my bro John.

Reykjavik 16 Jun
Dear John:

I've just come from a visit with Einar and Borgerthi, at 89 and 91 still bright and clear of memory, and kind of amazed and thrilled to have this contact with you. I think you ought to investigate excursion fares out of New York; if you came for a visit you would be treated like some kind of returning Prince.

We went to Erlendur's house for dinner last night,

> Caroline and I, and met their children and Grandchildren, at least those who were there. . . . He is quite well off, has a grand collection of Icelandic art, some of which is quite spectacular. His wife Margit Helgassdottir is extremely beautiful, and very warm and affectionate. They both made it clear that if John Watson – who is well-remembered almost at the legendary level – should ever turn up here he would be welcomed in the warmest way.
>
> Einar and Borgerthi live in a comfortable nursing home, well looked-after. Both a bit frail, and Borgerthi's eyesight is very bad. But they talked and chuckled over the old times, and Einar remembered walking you home from the beach after your brave swim, you so exhausted and trembling with cold you could hardly walk and he holding on to your arm all the way back to the house. And Borgerthi said she put you in a hot bath and gave you a big cup of coffee.
>
> She said, "I cried and cried when he left; he was the finest boy I ever knew."
>
> Einar is still tall and straight. He insisted on walking us to the elevator when we left (Margit, Erlendur's wife, and I), shook hands long and warmly. "Bless, bless," he said. "Very good. Very good." . . .
>
> Well, it has been quite an encounter. A kind of confirmation of events so far away and long ago for me that they have a legendary quality to them. These people all think you are really sumpn. And I didn't tell them any different.

I would conclude that John himself, having told so many tales all his life, had begun to wonder if his own Icelandic Saga had in fact been as he told it, or had he made up some parts of that too, despite the photograph and the citation from the president.

Or was it simply that he feared that nobody there would remember him at all, and if they did, what would they say? That would explain his reticence, I thought, about digging out Erlendur's address.

When I got back to Canada, I went to see him, to tell him that he must go and visit those people. "I can't afford it, really," he said diffidently. I told him that I would give him a ticket, he could pay me back some day if he wanted, but he must go. I think he was a bit doubtful even as he got on the plane. But when he came back two weeks later, he was taller, straighter, brighter-eyed than I had ever seen him. He seemed to have grown a few inches. They had all remembered him. They had taken him to see the president too, *and* the prime minister (much more important) and had celebrated him nonstop.

Back in the 1950s, when Joan persuaded him to come ashore, be a father to their two kids Michael and Carol, stop this worldwide voyaging life that he loved so much, he went into sales. He had the gift of the gab; he was a good story teller; he had charm. He sold for Johnson & Johnson, then a fire-pump manufacturer, an advertising firm, and Procter and Gamble. He made a pretty good living, but he hated it; I knew that, even though he never said so. He did well enough that he was able to retire before he was sixty, built a cottage on Go Home Lake, set up a workshop there, and worked outdoors from snow to snow, building and repairing furniture with the same meticulous hands that I had once watched make model airplanes on the third floor at 22 Bracondale. We began to connect more, in those years at the lake. I would fly up from Ottawa and he would pick me up at the Muskoka airport; we would cruise over the lake and the islands in Georgian Bay, and he would talk about flying with Cliff once, in England during the war. And we finally got to the subject of our father, and that beating in the cellar, and the photograph of the four of us. I am glad that I was finally able to let him know that I knew.

He had started to smoke a pipe when he was sixteen, at sea, and it was his constant companion until the doctors told him, in his early seventies, that those sores under his tongue were cancer. He instantly gave up the lifelong tobacco habit and began to visit schools and talk to kids, himself as the prime example, about the dangers of smoking.

The early treatment was not working, and he was told he would have to go under the knife. The surgery left him horribly swollen for several months, and his speech permanently damaged. I never heard him complain. He told hilarious stories about the hospital, the nurses, the doctors, himself often the butt of the jokes. He was back in hospital for more surgery in the spring of 1996. My wife and I had planned a trip to Ireland, but I was reluctant to go until I knew he was safely home and recovering. I went to see him in the hospital several times, finding him often in a deep sleep, occasionally rousing for a hoarsely whispered hello, and trying to fire off a joke or two. One day he looked a bit better, still unable to sit up but his eyes fairly clear. I told him I was going to cancel the Irish trip until he was up and about. No way, he protested, mustering a twisted smile, and something like "You can't disappoint Caroline. I'm getting better. I know, you're hanging in because you're afraid I'm gonna pull a fast one and croak while you're out of town. Well, I'm not. So you go, and take me out to lunch when you get back."

Was he sure? I asked him. Sure, he was sure.

Five days later Mary called me at Roy Faibish's house in Strangford Lough to say that he was gone. A very complicated guy, my brother John. But one thing about him was not complicated at all: that immense reservoir of courage.

Chapter 5

HIGH SCHOOL PART II

IN THE EARLY 1940s when I was starting high school, there was as yet no television. But radio had played a significant role in our family life from as early as I can remember. Dad had a big parlour model Rogers Majestic with fluted black Bakelite knobs and one tiny illuminated brass-rimmed window behind which the dial rotated to show the selected frequency. Every evening at six it was CFRB and the Evening News with a red-faced, alcoholic, loud, and hearty newscaster named Jim Hunter. "Good Thursday evening, everyone!" he would thunder, once in a while getting the day wrong. I remember vividly a sense of the shrinking globe when my father woke us up about five o'clock one morning to sit around the Rogers Majestic and hear, live from Westminster Abbey, the funeral ceremony for King George V. Later, after the abdication of Edward VIII, we got up early again for the broadcast of the coronation of his younger brother, George VI.

Saturday afternoons it was the opera, from a station in Buffalo. Saturday night Edgar Bergen and Charley McCarthy, Jack Benny, Fred Allen. Maybe Fred Allen was Sunday night. Sunday afternoon was symphony time. And Sunday night was also *Lux Radio Theater*, one-hour radio renditions of current Hollywood movies, sometimes with the same stars.

Radio drama was a highly polished and popular form. There were gothic entertainments such as *The Shadow* and *Inner Sanctum* (brilliantly frightening ghost stories), and the classic *The Lone Ranger*. Almost nothing was Canadian, but I do recall asking Dad what the announcer meant who said, "*Ici Radio-Canada*: This is the Canadian Broadcasting Corporation" and his introducing me to the idea that this use of two languages represented something special about our country.

In 1941 the NBC station we received from Buffalo was broadcasting a jazz show on Saturday mornings, *The Chamber Music Society of Lower Basin Street*. It was presented live from New Orleans (almost everything, including the plays, went out live) by an eccentric young comic named Zero Mostel.

Buffalo radio was also the source of a lot of our American drama. Once we heard an exciting play about the development of something that was going to give the Americans, only recently engaged in the war, an invincible edge over the Axis powers. It was called the atom bomb, and the drama somehow managed to convey to me as an adolescent the idea that an element, uranium, could be modified into something called U-235 to make this prodigious weapon. How so much information about what was still a classified project ever found its way into a popular radio play I have no idea, but I do remember that I heard it with one or two young friends, that we fantasized war scenarios about it for days – wondering if it were fact or fiction – and that when the reality was unveiled with Hiroshima and Nagasaki, we felt that we had been in on a secret well ahead of anyone who had not heard that broadcast.

And presently the CBC and the afternoon live kids' radio serial were to inject me with a virus for which there is apparently no antidote: performing. At the beginning of my second year in high school, sometime in the second September, a radio producer and writer from Vancouver, Uncle Billy Hassel, came to Toronto. The Vancouver CBC radio station had contracted him to write, produce, and star in *The Kootenay Kid*, a children's daytime dramatized serial, live of course. *The Kootenay Kid* had played successfully for a year on the Vancouver station, and Hassel had decided to try his luck with it in the east.

There was little CBC network activity then. It seems odd now, when the contracting of independent producers to make programs with CBC facilities is thought of as a relatively recent innovation, that the Corporation would have gone outside for a radio drama producer. Hassel's initiative may well have been unique. But in any case he arrived at Oakwood Collegiate looking for young actors to play the adolescent characters in *The Kootenay Kid.* He auditioned members of the school drama group, and I was cast as Jake, the villain; a classmate, Robin Allen, as the female lead; and my friend and classmate, Bobby Green, as the eponymous hero, The Kid.

The school allowed us to leave class early to get to rehearsals at three o'clock, provided we kept up with our homework. And so every school-day afternoon we jumped on our bicycles and headed down to CBL, the CBC's Toronto station. It was in the old Canada Carbon Company building just west of the streetcar barns on Davenport Road at Bathurst. We ran through the fifteen-minute script a couple of times, learned how to manipulate the occasional sound effect the actors had to handle, and went to air live at 4:30.

I don't think we found it especially glamorous or heady, although it was a great deal of fun, spiced with the adrenaline rush of knowing you had no margin for error. Hassel was an amiable and helpful director who guided his young performers with kindness and humour. There was one sound-effects operator. He spun the occasional disk, and rippled his hand in a bowl of water for a gurgling stream, or massaged a wad of cellophane for a crackling fire. He had a supply of door and window frames for opening and shutting sounds, recordings for the neighing of horses and the singing of birds, and thunder and heavy rain. For walking on snow we made the crunch of our own footsteps with small cotton bags of cornstarch held in each hand, and the hoof beats of our horses (there were lots of horses) were produced by clapping coconut half-shells on our chests, tump-a-TUMP, tump-a-TUMP.

The plot was ongoing, with some attempt at cliffhanger endings for each fifteen-minute episode, but what they were about was not memorable; I can't recall an episode. All that remains are images of riding through rocky passes, camping by mountain streams, the occasional fistfight between me and The Kid, and the four of us around that little table, with the old RCA microphones hanging in front of us, clutching our scripts and grinning at each other.

Like some other afternoon children's serials – *Buck Rogers, Don Armstrong the All American Boy,* for example – we had a club you could write in to for your membership card, the Square Shooters' Club, with a code for secret messages. Sometime in the late winter or early spring Hassel rented Massey Hall for an appearance of the entire cast, all four of us, where we performed a special, one-time Saturday morning broadcast and filled at least the orchestra with members of the Square Shooters' Club. We were each paid $5 a week, we young actors. One dollar per program. Partway through that season the radio actors formed a new union, ACRA, the Association of Canadian Radio Artists. Overnight our salary went up to $15 a week. Munificent! I bought a brand-new bike, which, it being wartime, had no chrome on it, the handlebars being finished in flat black. But it was new and was exactly the bike I wanted.

Some CBC Radio programs were sponsored then. *The Kootenay Kid* was sponsored by a bread company whose factory was near Davenport and Spadina. At the end of the season Hassel sold both the sponsors and the CBC on a second season. He would have to spend the summer writing new scripts, and he hired me to help him with research. He also got me a job in the sponsor's bakery, taking bread out of the hot ovens and stacking the loaves on racks to be wheeled to the wrapping machines. It was a hot July when I started, and I was miserable. I kept looking for opportunities to get away from those ovens. One day the wrapping machines got fouled in melted wax from the wrapping, and on my own initiative, and knowing nothing about the machines, I undertook to try to clear the jam. Successfully. The foreman who came by to scold me for leaving my post ended up praising me for helping to keep the line going. I had visions of promotion to a cooler job somewhere, something to do with machines and maintenance. But it didn't materialize. When I hear the term "sweat shop" I think of that bakery. I think it was called Standard Bread. About two weeks into the job I was invited to go to work as a junior counsellor (age fourteen!) at my uncle Skid's YMCA summer camp on Lake Couchiching. At the same time, my father announced that he was moving us to Ottawa in August so there would be no more radio work for me. I gratefully quit the bakery, tearfully said goodbye to Billy Hassell, and headed for camp.

In recollection, the distress at leaving Toronto and friends (and Ellen Young) seems greater than any sense of loss regarding the interruption of my broadcasting career. I think it likely that the old refrain of *I want something to do, something different and something new!* was playing again in the back of my spirit. I had done radio. I could do it again, and thought I probably would, but I didn't feel compelled. And, lovesick and stricken as I made myself out to be, the prospect of finding those new somethings in a new town and a new school, and making my mark upon that new environment, had a whiff of adventure to it. So after a bit of conventional mourning, I arose like the narrator of *Lycidas* and twitched my

> . . . mantle blue
> Tomorrow to fresh woods, and pastures new.

There was some advantage, arriving in the new town, to having a girlfriend in the old one, a girlfriend to whom one would be faithful. While I went to the tea dances and the Friday night dances, and enjoyed the company of girls as much as ever, I felt a kind of freedom in knowing that I was not going to become involved; I could not; I was taken. A date was just a date. Some terminated with an amiable peck on the cheek, and the odd flirtation hinted at something more adventurous than that, but it was all lighthearted and playful. I wrote faithfully and soulfully to Ellen, and she to me, but there was no grief in it.

The sexual pressure of adolescence was powerful and led to frequent furtive trips to the bathroom or other private places. But the idea that one might actually have a sexual experience was, in those days, fantasy. I had graduated from tracing copies of the nudes in my father's *Thousand and One Nights*, to original drawings made from an artist's book of nude photographs that Cliff had left behind when he went off to war. The pubic areas had all been airbrushed to a kind of marble purity, but the breasts were enchanting, and I filled a ten-by-twelve-inch medium-tooth pencil sketchbook with my carefully rendered drawings of these fantasy women. On one page I made a life-size drawing of my own erection, feeling a good deal of pride in both the drawing and the subject. If police were to confiscate that drawing now I could be charged under the child pornography laws in our Criminal Code, which specify that the "sexual depiction of the sexual organs of a person under the age of eighteen" is an offence under the law. "Sexual depiction," as I learned forty years later when testifying as a media expert in the case of a Toronto artist charged under this definition, means depicted not for purely artistic purposes, but for the purpose of sexual arousal. My drawing, while I maintain that it was artistic enough, was certainly that of a person fourteen or fifteen years old, and certainly made for purposes of sexual arousal. There weren't many other opportunities.

Once at a football game at the old Ottawa Stadium a flashy sixteen-year-old redhead whom I knew about but had never met was sitting behind me. She tapped me on the shoulder and handed me a little card on which was printed "Everybody Likes a Nice Piece of Ass." I just laughed and dismissed it as a joke, and then later (too much later, alas) began to wonder if it had been a missed opportunity.

Optimism was in the air. In June of 1944 the Allied forces had landed in Normandy, among them Canadians who fought a distinguished campaign in the taking of those beaches. Step by step, Nazi-held Europe was falling apart. You could feel it in the streets, the assumption of imminent victory. If there was a setback, we all knew it was temporary. Cliff was in the Italian campaign, flying out of Malta, and his letters were exuberant.

My school in Ottawa, Glebe Collegiate, made Oakwood seem

anchored in the nineteenth century. Oakwood had been rewarding, but despite the eagerness of inquiry and the constant sense of possibilities, it was conventionally authoritarian; its principal administrative figures were awesome and distant. They wore rather formal clothes and were addressed with conventional deference. Classroom teachers had a sense of humour and even of adventure, but the school, as embodied in the principal and his dreaded vice principal (discipline, authority) was very much an institution.

Glebe was more like a community. I was astounded when I went to audition for the choir, The Lyre's Club. The pun was deliberate, mischievous, and the creation of the teacher who led the choir, Mr. McGregor. The other kids were addressing Mr. McGregor as Bob. After Oakwood this was astounding. We were assembled on the auditorium stage for the auditions. One of the kids looked out over the darkened hall and said quietly, "Hey! There's Chubby." McGregor said equally quietly, "He likes singing." In the gloom at the back of the hall I made out the figure of the school principal, W.D.T. Atkinson. A considerable scholar, my father had told me. Principal of Ottawa's biggest high school and they called him Chubby? Well, not to his face, I supposed. Not much later, an extremely distinguished gentleman in an elegant three-piece grey suit and gold pince-nez and chain walked quietly across the stage toward the storage room in the wings. One of the girls said, "Hi, Pop!" "Hello, Margery," he said pleasantly. Other kids said, "Hi, Pop!" Bob McGregor said, "How are you, Pop?" I was open-mouthed.

And not entirely approving. What if my father, war hero and now the distinguished principal of the Ottawa Normal School, had come in and they had said, "Hi, Stan!"? How would I feel about that?

Well, it turned out that Pop was the school janitor, who affected the pince-nez and the fine clothes, but apart from that was as approachable as all janitors, that being the tradition at the time. Students did not call the principal "Chubby" to his face. Or Dinny Ralph, or Nelly or Horse. But every teacher had a nickname, and sometimes in class they mischievously referred to each other by those nicknames. There was a subtle line of demarcation about who could actually utter the nicknames and under what circumstances. When you went for an interview with the principal, he would find an occasion to refer to himself as Chubby and to my extraordinarily eccentric Grade Eleven home room teacher, Clarence Thoms, as "Beaky."

I am indebted to Beaky Thoms. He would come into the room in the morning, take off his impeccable grey suit coat, and exchange it for a shiny black bookkeeper's jacket that hung on a hook behind the door and was covered with chalk dust. He too had a gold pince-nez on a gold chain around his neck, and before he opened the class he donned a green eyeshade like the ones traditionally worn by croupiers. He liked making dry, ironic comments both on the material we were reading and upon students' answers and observations: not cruelly, but deftly witty. But I allowed this to be more of an invitation to openness than it actually was, and once when he finished a harangue he looked up and saw me smiling broadly. "Why are you grinning like that, Watson!" he said. I replied, honestly if recklessly, "Because you are very amusing, sir."

"Amusing!" he roared, and pointed a bony finger at me, frowning fiercely.

"*Amusing*! You get down to the vice principal's office this minute!" he fumed, and chased me out of the classroom. He followed me to the top of the stairs, shaking his fist and continuing to sputter as I skipped down to the first floor as fast as I safely could. Mr. Bruce closed the door behind me and kindly asked, Was Mr. Thoms having one of his, ah, outbursts? Did I know it would be all forgotten soon? Did I think perhaps I should wait here in the VP's office for five minutes and then go back up looking chastened? Did I recognize that Mr. Thoms was really a very fine teacher?

If I did not recognize that right away, I soon came to. Beaky Thoms would often finish the last class on Friday afternoons by reading to us. We were doing *Hamlet* that year. Beaky would park on a stool against the front row of desks and just read quietly to us for the whole thirty-five-minute period. His voice was soft and undramatic, but there was a rhythmic resonance to it that was in love with the poetry. The class would be hushed, even the jocks and the flashy girls.

There was a sense of fun and of democracy about Glebe Collegiate, and of respect for the imagination. The auditorium held a new Casavant pipe organ, recently installed. Students were encouraged to play it if their keyboard skills were adequate. My friend Ward McAdam glowed with pride the first time he played the morning hymn in assembly. At the Christmas concert, W.D.T. Atkinson did a comic song dressed in lederhosen and referred to himself as Chubby, and was long and affectionately applauded when he worked into his original limericks the nicknames of many of the senior teachers.

Bob McGregor announced that he was going to form a classical string ensemble and needed somebody to play the double bass – there were two in the instrument room at the side of the auditorium stage, standing majestically in their racks, glowing warmly, noble, enticing. I diffidently explained that while I played the piano a bit by ear and could read well enough for choral work, I had never touched a stringed instrument but would love to try the bass. McGregor said, Sure, give it a try. I had a spare that afternoon. Somebody showed me how to tune and some rudiments of fingering, and that very afternoon, when the string ensemble sat down for its first session at the end of the school day, I lugged the gleaming instrument onto the stage, and within moments was playing a simple Haydn suite for strings. The bass part was sufficiently straightforward that I actually played some right notes, and simply backed off when I got lost.

The important thing was that I had fallen in love. A few days later a tall, wryly smiling Grade Twelve guy with bad acne and a head of curly red hair introduced himself to me in the hallway. Orville Johnson said he'd heard I was playing bass and would I like to join him in a jazz quartet – he already had a drummer and a guitar. In addition, the music teacher at the High School of Commerce, which was in the west end of the Glebe Collegiate building, organized a dance band and invited me to play bass in it.

And so within days, from a standing start, I had more extracurricular activity than I'd ever dreamed of at Oakwood. Orville Johnson was a gifted technician and loved to improvise. He and McGregor and the Commerce music teacher were tolerant of my beginner's fumbling with the bass. I didn't enjoy the dance band as much as the classical string ensemble: the reading was too hard. The jazz quartet was by far the best. I soon found that not thinking much about the names of the notes, but trusting the ear and the fingers, was the best strategy. At that first exciting practice session, Orville tossed it to me for a solo, and I just sailed into it, not too terrible, and soon we were getting gigs (unpaid) at dances and parties. Roy Cottee, Norm Polowin, and I worked up a song and dance act with a couple of comic numbers, of which I recall only one about a "Hot Dog Stand on the Road To Mexico City." We were invited to perform at other high schools as well as at the Friday afternoon tea dances at Glebe.

One awful day I put the bass up in its rack in the music room and forgot to secure it with the metal bar that locked across the top of the fingerboard. As I turned away, the huge, lovely, eloquent piece of wooden sculpture crashed to the floor, the front panel shattered, the fingerboard wrenched from its moorings by the strings, and I went into shock. In retrospect, it seems characteristic of the community spirit of that school that there was no blame, no punishment, lots of sympathy for my/our loss, and reassurance that it could be fixed, not to worry. There was a second instrument, which nobody had taken, so I continued to play, and in a few weeks the repaired bass came back, almost as good as new. The sound was a little less crisp now, but I had an emotional investment in that first bass. Number two went back in its rack and stayed there. With the metal bar in place.

A couple of years before writing this book, after a lot of Friday and Saturday evenings at the Woodside Restaurant in the Hockley Valley, where chef/owner Matthew Bach Jamieson brings in live jazz on the weekends, I found myself absently humming not the melodies but the bass lines, in the shower, dropping off to sleep, waking up, doing mindless chores. I asked one of the Woodside Regulars, Lenny Boyd, who used to play bass in the Winnipeg Symphony, if he could find me an instrument I could afford. Within a week he did so. And fifty-five years after saying farewell to my last high school bass, I brought home another, and was delighted to find I remembered quite a bit, and, as I write, am playing almost every day, occasionally blessed by a visit from musical friends such as Al Goodman or Laila Biali or Matthew Jamieson with his transverse flute, or a party at Kim McArthur's with her seventy-two-year-old mum, Jane, playing down and dirty blues, or at Barry Callaghan's with John Sheard, who can play anything. If I'm alone there are CDs to play along with, and sometimes I just sing, or hum, or play to whatever voices I am hearing in my imagination, be they horns, strings, percussion, or human.

Glebe held assembly every morning. About twice a month our string ensemble would play for the school. There were often visiting speakers. It might be a returning war hero, a former student now wrapped in glory. Once an old man (he was, well, at least fifty) who whistled the birdsongs in the Disney animated films gave us a wonderful talk about birds and pursed his lips and did cardinals and song sparrows and robins and bluebirds.

Not being obsessed with the girls around me, whom, because of Ellen Young, I had declared off limits except for casual dates and dances, I fell in with a group of eccentric boys who were passionate about model airplanes and other mechanical devices. For $3 I bought my first gasoline-powered model airplane engine, a Rogers, not a very good one, looked down upon by those who had Ohlsson 35s and Ohlsson 60s, which I could not afford. I spent hours in the basement in our rented house at the corner of Holland and Ruskin, trying to get the damn thing to run. I got my hands on a few ounces of ether. The decrepit Rogers would run on ether but not on gasoline. I got a bit intoxicated with the fumes, and the parents asked difficult questions, so the ether was dropped.

Here is a cultural observation. It is not, I believe, some antiquarian nostalgia. All my male friends at that time were on intimate terms with the internal combustion engine. It was like John Steinbeck's remark in *Cannery Row*, about two generations of American men knowing more about the carburetor than about the clitoris. I can't vouch for what my teenage friends knew about the clitoris (I had never heard of it), but I did know pistons and compression ratios, crankshafts, camshafts and valves and the difference between two-stroke and four-stroke. I could take an engine apart and put it back together again in working order. In my early twenties I would put my old Morris Minor up on blocks and drop the pan and replace the worn-out big-ends and get it running again, no problem. Now here comes the cultural observation: the teenage boys I know now – in fact, anyone I know who is forty or under – can't begin to tell me how a car engine works. The younger ones *do* know about RAM and gigabytes, and why defragging is a waste of time, and how to reformat, and what spyware is. But they do not know what a big-end is. I have no idea where they are with the clitoris, but suspect that they are a lot more advanced than we were.

Evenings we gathered at my house or another boy's house and spent hours carving hand-launched gliders out of balsa wood, newly available again after a brief wartime shortage. We outdid ourselves in competing to produce striking designs. Pure flying wings, deeply swept back, and with no fuselage or tail assembly, those were the great challenge. Then we'd go out under the streetlights and try them out, launching them by hand or occasionally with a rubber catapult.

Saturdays we went a few blocks south to the Dominion Experimental Farm, one of whose large meadows was at the corner of Carling and Holland, edged with stately elms, where we devised clever ways of launching our little gliders: elaborate long-throw catapults, slings and launching tracks with pulleys and weights. Ken Narraway, Bill Drysdale, Pudge Armstrong, and a pimply-faced boy named Ralph and I. No girls.

I found a recipe for rocket fuel, and we wound sheets of foolscap around broomsticks, using lots of paste to create a cylindrical rocket barrel, and then stuffed that barrel with our mixture, potassium chlorate and sulphur – was there a bit of sugar for the carbon? We would hang one of those paper barrels under the balsa wood fuselage of a new glider, or build wings onto the paper cylinder itself, and try to get a rocket plane flying. We generally got our hands a bit burned and never did figure out how to get a flight of any duration without incinerating the glider itself.

Then somebody suggested that fitting the tube with wheels would make a fine rocket-powered race car. Ralph and I made the first experiment. We wound an extra-long tube, packed in as much chemical fuel as it would hold, and twisted the end shut with a bit of candlewick sticking out for a fuse. Ralph stood on the sidewalk right by my front lawn, and I went a couple of hundred feet down the hill and set the little car between the streetcar tracks and lit the fuse. It started off very gratifyingly, but we had not really thought through the design problems related to directional stability (we used to talk like that then). Before long the little racer began to wander off course, toward the right-hand rail just where Ralph was excitedly watching. It slammed into the groove and lost its back wheels. It began to wriggle and spin like a wounded dragon spitting fire. Ralph, thinking to save the unused fuel, ran to it and stepped on the burning end to extinguish the flame.

Now, this particular mixture is quite explosive. We knew that, I think. Some kids had used it to make bombs with a cunning detonator made of a heavy nail and a match head and hurled them off rooftops with results that were crepitant at their least, thunderous at their best.

As Ralph's foot came bravely down on the flame-spewing end of our rocket car, there was an enormous bang. Ralph was thrown up and back. He landed in a heap on the lawn in front of my house. Doors opened up and down the street. People came out, looking alarmed. Ralph was stunned. Neighbours gathered around his inert form. Reproachful eyes scanned me up and down. I tried to explain but I had a hard time speaking. I was afraid that poor Ralph had had it. But then he sat up, holding his ears and shaking his head. He looked down at his scorched boot and said, "Wasn't that tremendous!"

Well, yes. But it was the end of rocket science for us. Not, however, of model airplanes. I designed a rubber-powered flying model with a streamlined, long, tapering, round fuselage, a single wheel tucked into the belly, double inverted tail fins to keep it upright on that single wheel after it landed so that the long, tapering gull wings would not hit the ground, and a folding propeller of my own design and construction. It flew very well and I'm sorry that I do not still have it, having given all my models away, in my university days, to an institution for handicapped children.

Those balsa-wood gliders continued to be the social glue for that group of boys in the west end. I had found in a book a design for a kite, a "French War Kite," a triangular box with narrow triangular fins on two sides, like short wings running along the length of the box. Bill Drysdale and Ken Narraway and I built one six feet long with a six-foot wingspread. Bill found a two-thousand-foot roll of light, strong cord somewhere. The kite went up like a dream and hung there painted on the sky. Ken said he thought it would make a great launching platform for those little balsa-wood gliders that we turned out in such profusion. He proposed putting a tiny ring in the nose of each glider, and a thread through the rings, looped around the release of a little two-ounce pneumatic timer he had (for stopping the gasoline engine in a gas-powered model). We could send up a dozen little gliders at a time. It took about thirty seconds for the kite to get to altitude at about five hundred feet. Then, after the two minutes it took for the timer's plunger to retract the restraining pin from its little screw-eye, we would see a shower of our gliders wheeling off in the northwest wind.

It worked, and we went back to the farm again with new loads of gliders, the designs progressively more fantastic. We seldom saw them again; they would often climb in the turbulent wind after their release, and mostly disappear off to the southeast, only the odd one – and usually an inferior performer – accidentally steering into the wind and coming back toward us. We taped little strips of paper with our names and addresses and phone numbers to the fuselages. "Maybe we'll get a call from Cornwall!" "Maybe we'll get a letter from New York!" We never did.

Ken Narraway had made a meticulously painted scale model of a Spitfire, carved out of solid pine. It was not intended to fly, but it looked aerodynamically correct, and one day he got a crazy idea. He decided to weight it so that it was the scale weight of the real thing, and balance it perfectly, the CG right at the one-third point in the wing chord, and drop it from the kite. No other way to get it up to flying speed. But it should fly. He drilled holes in the engine area and loaded it with BBs, checked the balance, and drilled another tiny hole in the spinner to make it ready to hang from the timer on the kite.

It was a glorious day. Just the Spitfire on the pneumatic timer release, no lesser craft. A west wind of about fifteen miles an hour was blowing. Bill handled the cord. Ken attached the Spitfire to the timer and held the big kite up in the wind, and then gave it a light toss – it always just seemed to lift smoothly out of your hand – and up it went.

Ken and Ralph and I watched from beside the stately elms along the north side of the farm.

The two minutes of the timer seemed very long. Suddenly a tiny dark speck detached from the kite. It dropped straight down like a stone, no, like an arrow. Faster and faster; it began to tremble.

"Look at it shudder!" Ken yelled. "Look!"

It was indeed shuddering, a scene from some movie about a fatal dive beyond the red line on the airspeed indicator, the unconscious pilot thrown clear of the disintegrating fighter. But then suddenly the little Spitfire was pulling out of its dive. It banked and headed straight toward us. It sped vividly past us about ten feet off the ground. The scale speed must have been four hundred miles an hour. It flew straight into the trunk of one of those great elms, and shattered.

I was thrilled but shocked. It had been so beautiful, so, well, real, as it flashed by us, a real, four-hundred-mile-an-hour Spitfire. But what a tragic ending. I turned to Ken. He was transfigured, illuminated.

"Wasn't that tremendous!" he said.

Someone said one day, You know, the kite was so stable and had such powerful lift, if we made, well, a really big one, way bigger than just six feet, say fifteen feet . . . we could put a little seat in it and send up a kid.

I asked Roger if he'd like to fly in a kite. He was about eight. He said, Sure, that sounded like a lot of fun. We started to build, and it is undoubtedly a very good thing, as far as the survival of my younger brother, that the big kite proved too much for us and we never finished it.

Those Carling Avenue elm trees are all gone now, lost to Dutch Elm Disease. What good is an experimental farm if it can't save the elms? But they gave us one more dizzy, wonderful, irresponsible adventure that autumn of 1944.

Someone made a dummy, life-size, real clothes, stuffed with grass or straw, an onion bag for its head. And someone else got the idea of hanging it from a branch of one of those elms – there was one you could climb – hang it on a long rope, looking like a suicide or a lynching, its head lolled sideways, at night, just at the height where the streetcars whose track ran not on Carling Avenue but parallel to it, on the farm, by the trees, just where the big headlight on the top of the cab, the light they turned on only for that run through the elms, would catch the slowly twisting feet.

The streetcars came every ten or twelve minutes. It was late October so it got dark early, and we might have time to hit two of them before the cops came. We kept an end of the rope on the ground so we could drop the corpse instantly.

The dummy was hard to see up there in the dark, but you could make out the lolling head. It twisted slowly. Along came a trolley, the big headlight on the roof streaming out before it. It got to within about fifty feet of the thing hanging there before the light caught the feet and legs; it looked very real when the light hit. We crouched in the long grass. There was a moment when nothing happened, then a screech as the motorman saw the sinister shape and hit the brakes.

Oh it was glorious! By the time the streetcar stopped, it was a hundred feet beyond the hanged man; it had been going at full speed. The motorman and a few brave passengers climbed out, spooked, came back along the tracks, peering up into the darkness. Then a man's voice said, My God! He's right! There it is! And the motorman said, Come on, there's a phone box by the next stop! And they clambered on board, and off they went, the trolley bell clanging.

We guessed that with a couple of minutes to get to the phone box, and a few more for the cops to come, we could risk waiting for another streetcar. So we did, but as soon as it was screeching past the hanging dummy with sparks flying from the braked wheels, Pudge Armstrong, I think it was Pudge on the rope, dropped the thing and we picked it up and folded it in half under somebody's arm, raced down Parkdale Avenue by the west end of the Civic Hospital, and found safety under some dark bushes, and gloried in our mischief and got our breath back.

The Parkdale bus came by, southbound from Carling. Its dim lights swept the road. There was nobody on the streets. Perhaps it was late now, I don't recall how late, but there were no passersby and not many passengers on the bus. Let's do the bus, someone suggested. No trees to hang the dummy from, but we could just lay it on the road, the bus lights were dim, maybe he'd run over it before he could stop and then we could pull it into the bushes where we were hiding.

Well, it worked for the first one, but the second one, twenty minutes later, must have been warned: the driver stopped before he hit the body on the road and was out of that bus as we started running between the houses, the furious driver yelling, Come back, you little buggers, and we laughing and tripping and running, knowing the backyards better than he did, and being young and slim and he fat and probably emphysematous, we got away, and ditched the dummy, and went home thinking that we had made a historic night.

Years later, in the sixties or seventies I think, in a taxi going out to Crawley films, not far from the scene of the crime, I was reminded of that night and told the elderly cab driver the story, and he laughed and said, "No shit! Was that you? It was all over the taxi stands that night. I remember that."

So we had made a historic night, after all.

In the summer of 1945, the war safely over, we moved to number 16, Maple Lane, in Rockcliffe, a long way from Glebe. In the fall Dad would drive me to school every morning on his way to the Normal School. The summer itself was something of a turning point. On a visit to Toronto on the way to my summer camp job on Lake Couchiching, I saw Ellen Young and made some clumsy sexual advances. I think that was the beginning of the end of *that* relationship. But I had found myself thinking about sex quite a lot more, all of a sudden, and the coming summer was to add pressure to that particular part of my mid-adolescence.

When the war ended many of us, still romantic about heroism, were a bit sorry that we had missed the adventure and the glory. I had not yet turned sixteen and I certainly did not look old enough to fake my age and try to follow Cliff's example and become a fighter pilot in the British Navy.

I did, however, successfully lie about my age in another arena. The summer I was fifteen I succeeded in persuading an eighteen-year-old girl that I too was eighteen. I'll call her Lorna. A lie about my age that would not have fooled a recruiting officer for seven seconds engendered in her a whole night of suspension of disbelief, willing or not. I was working that summer as a counsellor at my uncle Skid's YMCA camp, Summerland, at Breezy Point on the west shore of Lake Couchiching, and we boys had all been invited to a social evening at a nearby girls' camp. Lorna was a counsellor there, and we had sat together at the table when the snacks were brought out at the end of the evening.

Chemistry had its way with Lorna and me. We made a secret rendezvous. I discharged my bedding-down duties back at the YMCA camp and then, when all was silent, slipped out of the tent and loped along the shore to the girls' camp. She had got her charges settled down too. At about eleven o'clock when I arrived at the big boathouse, she was waiting in the shadows. We embraced hugely and kissed fiercely, but chastely so to speak: today's cinematic readiness of open mouths and exploring tongues was something alien in those days – foreigners did it, we knew; but it was not yet part of the local mores. However, we kissed at length, fiercely and hotly. We slipped quietly into the big boathouse. Emptied of its canoes and rowboats in summer, it was used as an indoor recreation space and had half a dozen sofas.

We stretched out on one of these, and began kissing again, hard kisses. After about half an hour of this rampant lip abrasion Lorna said, "Now that we are together like this, I want you to ask me to marry you."

"Of course," I said. I had played that game before. It had never meant anything thing in the past except that you would then get to do all the kissing and hugging you wanted to do.

"Kneel down and take my hand and ask me to marry you, then."

I did that. She accepted.

"So then you love me, and me alone, and forever?"

"I do," I said gravely. "You alone, and you alone forever."

"Then," she said, portentously, "I want you to know that my heart is yours. And my soul is yours. And . . . " there was a meaningful pause. "And," she concluded regally, "of course now that we are engaged, my body is yours." And she brought me back up on the sofa, and placed my hand decisively inside her blouse.

For a year or so I had been carrying a single, treasured, contraband condom in my wallet. Just In Case. The Just In Case had never before materialized. Back at Breezy Point, before setting out on my lover's lope down to the girls' camp, I had brought out my latex treasure to examine it. After two years in a sweaty adolescent's hip pocket wallet, the condom was in tatters. I bitterly threw it in the bushes as I trotted along the shore.

And so, nervousness compounded by knowing that the ultimate achievement had eluded me once again, I up to now had been nonetheless very energetically kissing and pressing myself against Lorna's generous body, wondering where this was going to end. But, oh well, it was our first date. My only real expectation, until the moment of the proposal and the introduction of my hand into her blouse, was that we would do some intense necking. That meant kissing roughly and long, but with closed mouths, of course.

I had gone so far as to think it not impossible (because of the frankness and eagerness of her invitation earlier that evening) that we might get to do some "petting," which meant hands on breasts and (wow, really? Could it be? On crotches?). Outside the clothes, of course. And I even thought that maybe tonight for the first time we might graduate to "heavy petting," which meant hands groping bare skin, *inside* the clothes. This was something that I had never done. I had never touched a bare breast, never had my hand in that so-much-imagined forbidden space between the legs.

Anyway, I supposed that the night's agenda might include – at its extreme limit – as much of one of the above as we could stand, and then a retreat to our separate quarters, a hand-produced release for me. . . . (And for her? The question, in those days, did not present itself.) In fantasy I had allowed myself to imagine that this time the gates might open to the Promised Land, but of course now the condom was gone, so forget about that. But never mind.

For the first time in my life I was having the delirious pleasure of real, naked female erogenous zones at my eager fingertips. Full, hard breasts with big fibrous nipples and a tantalizing pebblegrain of firm white skin, unexpectedly rough, which made it all the more arousing. Also unexpected: the virginal opening was tiny, very narrow, snug around my exploring finger and not very moist. How could my huge (and recently graphically celebrated) erection ever make its entry there, condom or no condom?

Lorna was frank and uninhibited, far less inhibited, in any case, than her naive young partner. She was open and sweet and generous. I was soon in pain from the pressure.

Intercourse was not thinkable. And it would not have occurred to me to ask her to, well, ah, to, ah . . . or to allow myself to, ah . . . It was one of those things that dared not speak its name, even more unspeakable than the missing condom.

In my confusion and anxiety I was rough and graceless. After a while Lorna said gently, "Slowly, gently. Like this." And she began to croon, wordlessly, the melody of *The Road to The Isles*, in a soft, dreamlike, interior way. "Just listen to the music and move like that," she said, "and you will get me ready."

Ready!!! Jesus, then what was *I* to do once *she* was ready? I could not, my whole fabric of mute taboo would not let me, speak directly about the missing condom. I mumbled, "See, I . . . I am not . . . I can't . . . I'm not ready. I can't be. I . . . " I was helplessly tongue tied.

She was holding me gently, stroking with the soft rhythms of her crooning voice. She said, "You seem ready enough to me. Come on. Let's try."

She pulled me on top of her. She spread her legs; I was astounded how widely they opened. She pulled aside the leg of her shorts. But we were both afraid, and the crooning had not really worked. She pulled me toward her, and I pressed, but I felt a wall of resistance. I had read about *The Hymen* in one of my sister's medical books, when she was in training at the Wellesley Hospital nursing school. I had formed the view that this intriguing membrane was filmy, supple, yielding. But here I had encountered something like a vulcanized chastity device. I think that in a way I was grateful and relieved, because I was so afraid of the pregnancy I had come to think unavoidable.

"Well, look," Lorna said after some of this shoving and grimacing and general awkwardness. "I know. Let's take all our clothes off . . . " (we were doing all this groping still half-clad, and even the clumsy attempt at penetration had been done around corners and hems, so to speak.) " . . . let's take all our clothes off, and go for a swim together, in the moonlight. I have always wanted to do that."

It was, in the calm moonlight, a magical way to end the night. In the water I somehow found my tongue. I have always felt strong and secure in the water. I told Lorna that I had had a contraceptive and that it had been torn. I swore that within the next few days I would by hook or by crook find another, several others, and we would gloriously consummate our love as often as we wished. Which love I was then called upon to swear once again. Lorna said that there was no need for a contraceptive; since we were to be married, she would be thrilled to become pregnant, but she accepted my declaration that it would be better, really it would, to wait till we both had jobs and some money.

We clung to each other and pressed our bodies together in the cool water. It was like a delicious dream. Finally I limped northward along the shore, bent over with the pain.

I slept through breakfast. At noon my uncle Skid called me into his tent. He told me that Lorna had wakened the director of the girls' camp before dawn and told an amazing story. He said that nobody in the camp management quite believed it, but that Lorna had cruised around the camp recounting it to all her friends. She had then become hysterical and had been taken into the hospital in Orillia, sedated, and was being sent back to her parents in Toronto.

Skid then recounted the story she had told, including the promise of marriage and eternal fidelity and the swim. I think part of what I read in his face when I dared raise my eyes and look at him was affectionate admiration. He said he expected I would remember this for the rest of my life, but that it was probably best that I not try to see Lorna in the city. And as far as I know he gave a sanitized version of the episode to my parents, for my dad made only a veiled reference, at the end of the summer, saying that Skid had allowed as how I had "an eye for a well-turned ankle."

It was difficult for me to accept what I had been told about Lorna, that she was seriously unstable, and that I should not have taken seriously her declarations. I knew somehow that she was *different*, but even when on reflection I allowed that "they" were right about her, I still felt grateful. There was a generosity about Lorna, I thought. I wanted to see her again, not because I thought we would resume where we had left off, but because the chapter was not really over.

It happened by accident, about two years later. I was going through Eaton's department store one afternoon, and there she was, behind a counter, a sales clerk in dry goods. I stood by while she finished a transaction and then caught her eye. It was all quite calm. We smiled at each other shyly.

"Hi."

"Hi."

"Are you okay?" I asked.

"Yeah, I've had a kind of bad time. I was, well, in the hospital for a while. I was . . . kind of . . . crazy, I guess. I'm okay now."

"They told me I shouldn't try to see you again."

"Yeah. Well, they're probably right. I'm glad you did. But they're probably right."

But I had been right too, at least about her generosity. And now it was closed. And I never saw Lorna again.

The Ottawa part of my school years had only a few months more to go, but they were very full months. In the late winter or early spring of 1946 my father was invited to become director of curriculum for the province of Ontario, and my parents and younger brother Roger moved back to Toronto, thoughtfully arranging for me to be billeted with friends so that I could finish my year at Glebe. I became art editor of the school magazine, the *Lux Glebana*, and drew several not very good cartoons for it (imitating Cliff, who always had had cartoons, good ones, in the *Oakwood Oracle*).

I fell in love with the editor of the *Lux Glebana*, a dark-eyed beauty a year and a half older than I, cool, brainy, a stunning figure and a great dresser. She was sought after by all the handsome jocks in Grade Thirteen, and it was clear there was no room there for me. But we got along famously putting the magazine together. She commissioned a story from me (which also was an imitation of one of Cliff's) and said she loved it. We went to a movie together, something related to the magazine. I got up my nerve and asked her to a dance. Amazingly, she accepted. I walked her home. She invited me in. Late, late that night, I found the courage to lean forward to kiss her. She threw her arms around me and kissed me back, warmly. I was speechless.

Something about the way it all happened, perhaps something she said, something careful, affectionate but not out of control, whatever it was, let me know that this was not, however, a beginning. By the end of term I came to understand that while the affection was real enough, it was more collegial than amorous. The kiss had been conventional. But I kept her photo with me, posting it on the wall at the camps I worked at the next summer, and feeling that an enduring privilege had flowed from that one kiss.

I fell in with a group of motorcycle enthusiasts a bit older than I. Paul O'Reilly had a 1934 500cc BSA, which he taught me to drive, and Pierre Dion had a 250cc Calthorpe, a low-slung British bike with a hand shift, painted a dark ivory, which he allowed nobody to ride. I spent a lot of time with Paul, on the back of that BSA, or long afternoons playing canasta with him and his two fat aunts in the vast, dark, perfumed, crucifix-strewn house just a couple of blocks from the school. One afternoon Paul allowed me to take the BSA off by myself on the River Road along the west side of the airport. We had gone to the flying club to watch the trainers take off and land, and when a young priest – a friend of the O'Reilly family – offered to take Paul up for a spin, he was so delighted that he spontaneously and unexpectedly waved me onto the bike, with no cautions, just a generous "Go ahead."

I decided to really let it run, sitting away back and leaning over the tank like a racing driver. The bike was not perfectly aligned, and when a speed-wobble developed, and I had no idea what was happening, I naturally tried to brake, the worst possible thing to do. I remember seeing the speedometer just touching 70 mph at the moment I and the machine parted company. I had learned in gym classes how to tuck and roll to protect head and limbs in a fall, and did that, and escaped with some torn clothes and a few scrapes on my knees and elbows. There was a fair amount of traffic on the road, and I have to suppose it was pure luck that I was not run over. Cars stopped and people helped me up and offered to take me to a hospital or a doctor, but all I could think of was the BSA. One of those alarmed drivers helped me wrestle it up out of the ditch, with nothing worse than a bent footrest. It started up first kick, and I rode it embarrassedly back to the flying club, where Paul was, amazingly, not angry but solicitous.

Dr. Harry Mount and his wife, Maude,[1] were pretty alarmed when I came home for dinner that evening with my nice sports jacket in tatters and had to tell them what had happened. They had already told my parents that they felt I was tearing around too much and neglecting my schoolwork, and now there would be another rocket, I supposed. However, the Easter term marks came out just about then, and I stood first or second in our class, with 80s and 90s in almost everything, and apparently the Mounts took it easy on me in their next Toronto report (people wrote letters in those days; a long distance phone call was a major event). In any case the motorcycle incident did not set off the row I had feared, although it certainly increased my respect for those machines.

I spent July at Uncle Skid's Y camp again, strong memories of Lorna, of course. And then worked as a counsellor at an Ontario Department of Education camp on the Oxtongue River, just west of Algonquin Park, where I became infatuated with and sexually optimistic about the camp nurse, who behaved in a way that was probably very unprofessional. However, in the end she hooked up with an older staff member.

On a day off I hitchhiked into Algonquin Park to visit Charley Fick, who was a counsellor in training (CIT) at the Taylor Statten Camps. Charley got me thinking about joining him there

1. Their son Balfour was just a "little kid" at the time. When I next saw him, forty-three years later, he was the nationally famous pioneer in palliative care for the dying, at Montreal's Royal Victoria Hospital. Maude Mount, born Maude Henry, had been a high school friend of my mother's at Alma College in Tillsonburg, Ontario, before World War I.

the following summer. And then it was back to Toronto, and Oakwood Collegiate for Grade Thirteen, the university entrance year.

At that time I was somewhat under the influence of my father's closest friend, Ken Jackson, head of engineering physics at the University of Toronto. Ken was a lovely guy with a warm sense of humour and seemingly inexhaustible generosity. He was also a fine teacher and a pioneer in stereoscopic photography. He had used stereoscopy as a method of range-finding in the trenches in World War I, where he and my father had met. Ken was a Scot with a touch of the Highlands in his voice and an idiosyncratic laugh that sounded like "Hut hut hut!" The character Pinch in my novel *Alter Ego*[2] is modelled on Ken Jackson, and I am named after him, my full name being Kenneth Patrick Watson.

In 1942 while my father was recuperating in a military hospital on the outskirts of Ottawa, Ken took over some fatherly duties, driving me from Toronto to Ottawa and back a couple of times, and once taking me to see some classified research at the National Research Council, where he was working as a dollar-a-year man. The NRC had built the prototype of an airplane that had no fuselage, only a huge wing within which the crew and weapons would be housed. It was called the Hill Pterodactyl. Ken said that I was to understand that this was secret stuff, nobody was to know about it, but he knew he could trust me.

The Pterodactyl was dropped after its flight trials – towed behind a DC 3 somewhere in Manitoba, and always in secret – but at the time I thought that the great gleaming plywood form, looming high over our heads in a huge hangar-like space at the NRC's building on the Montreal Road, was the most beautiful object I had ever seen. And I was strongly affected by Ken's declaration of confidence in my discretion; I was twelve years old at the time.

Hearing that man talk about the delights of making and understanding machinery, and having been taken by him on an enchanting

2. Lester and Orpen, Toronto, 1978, and in paperback with Penguin Canada and Fawcett (U.S.) in 1979.

tour of the Eng. Phys. building with its massive experimental machines when I was about thirteen, I had early on decided that engineering was for me too, probably not Eng. Phys., but maybe, *just maybe*, aeronautical engineering, to take that model-building experience to its logical conclusion and live out some of the fantasies that flying movies had engendered very early on, movies like *Captains of the Clouds*. I had managed to knock off one of the Grade Thirteen math courses, trigonometry, in that last year at Glebe – I found trig easy and rewarding – and that seemed to confirm that I was on the right track with this engineering thing.

So back at Oakwood in the fall of 1946 I loaded up the Grade Thirteen schedule with all the maths and sciences I could cram in, dropping history and Latin. History was no loss, being almost universally badly taught in those days, a matter of copying off the board and memorizing dates of battles and legislation and the names of kings and politicians, almost never conveying a sense of significance or narrative. But Latin: dropping that was a mistake. I loved Latin, consistently did very well in it. There was a group of us at Glebe who spoke it to each other and even made up the odd joke. But in my final year I dropped it, and I'm still sorry.

I worked professionally in radio again for a while when I was sixteen and seventeen, in that final year of high school. I was still spellbound by jazz, and Oakwood had a bass for me to play, which, once again, I was allowed to take home on weekends and even to the camp I worked at the summer after I graduated: Camp Ahmek in Algonquin Park. Ahmek always engaged a good pianist for the summer and that year it was Mario Bernardi, who would become conductor of the National Arts Centre and then the CBC orchestras. He and I played a fair amount of jazz together that wonderful summer of 1947.

The teenage culture had become big stuff in the early post-war period, and a very successful weekly tabloid, *Canadian High News* (for which I was briefly a stringer), started *High Variety*, a radio spin-off on CFRB. They engaged me as its jazz columnist. Jazz and swing were the acme of our musical experience then. In 1944 Duke Ellington came to the Oakwood Auditorium and played an hour of solo piano, with Betty Roché belting out a couple of his signature songs. Almost the whole student body crowded into the hall (standing; they took out all the seats as they did for our regular tea dances). We felt that a god had descended to shed his solar grace upon us.[3] I did not know enough about jazz to qualify as a columnist but I was already good at faking it.

At his house on Turner Avenue just around the corner from our Bracondale house, Mickey Colomby had the basement recreation room all to himself. Already, at the age of eighteen, he had been playing drums professionally in dance bands at summer resorts, but during the summer past a trumpeter had got him interested in brass and had given him a beat-up old cornet, which he took to with astounding facility and a line of improvisation that was fun to listen to and always recognizably related to the standard melody on which he was jazzing. Mickey proposed that we form a quartet. He had a solid grasp of chord structure and was one of my important music teachers, spending hours in that basement rec room taking me through the standards we loved, including "I'm in the Mood for Love," "Getting Sentimental Over You," and "The St. Louis Blues," and showing me how to anticipate the chord changes, and how to translate what I had learned into sequences for the string bass. The pianist, Lloyd Rotstein, was a union member and played with us under the name of Shoeless Joe Jackson. I forget who played the drums, but he got a lot of coaching from Mickey. A sultry, dark-haired girl who wore provocatively pointed bras, anticipating Madonna by a few decades, belted out torch songs when we played, sometimes the whole gig, for the Friday afternoon dances. Once when we were rehearsing in the auditorium, Principal W.H. Hannah (whom I remember in a swallowtail coat and

3. The proprietor of the Casino Theatre on Queen Street just west of Bay was the father of a fellow student, Marv Benny. This boy boasted that he could get the Duke to come to the school when he was playing the Casino, and promised, indeed, the whole Ellington band! Coming to Toronto from Detroit that day, the band had its instruments stolen from the bus, but Ellington had agreed to come and kept his word. The proceeds went to the war effort. Police recovered the instruments later that evening.

striped trousers, but that is likely an extrapolation from his manner) slipped into the hall and listened to us for a few numbers from the shadows under the balcony at the back, smiling and nodding in rhythm. His staying back there like that we took for a courtesy, and kept on playing. After a while he came down to the pit (we were on the stage), with a little half smile, and said, as we broke to acknowledge his coming among us, that he thought us really very good, but that there was one song we'd just rehearsed that he didn't want us to play: it was too suggestive for the younger students.

The offending piece was Cole Porter's "I've Got You Under My Skin."

My English Lit teacher that year was a kindly, cheerful old chap named Herbert Chrysler. Because of my odd mix of French, English, physics, chemistry, analytic geometry, and so on, I was not always with the same students in every class, and in Mr. Chrysler's English Lit. I found myself sitting beside one of Oakwood's distinguished jocks, a tall, handsome blond sixteen-year-old named John Kennedy. We did *Macbeth* that year. Kennedy and I were intrigued by The Scottish Play.[4] We used to sit in the cafeteria talking about it over our sandwiches. We developed a private conversational style, finding ways to use quotes from Shakespeare instead of colloquial English wherever we could. "The Devil damn thee black, thou cream-faced loon!" "He was a gentleman on whom I built/ An absolute trust." "Unsex me here." "If it were done when 'tis done, then t'were well/It were done quickly."

"The bell invites me" was an obvious one in a high school, and "Thou canst not say I did it; never shake thy gory locks at me" was a high-utility item.

I was impressed by the fact that the school's most elegant athlete was a Shakespeare enthusiast. Kennedy and I formed a friendship that has lasted almost sixty years. Under John's influence I came to realize that I loved Shakespeare, poetry, and literature even more than I loved

4. A persistent tradition in the theatre is that it is dangerously unlucky to speak the title; it is referred to by theatre people as *The Scottish Play.*

the mathematical and scientific components of engineering, and that my aeronautical engineering fantasy had been just that. I decided that university would be, at the very least, humanities (Social and Philosophical Studies, they were called then, "Soc. & Phil."), and maybe even that daunting haunt of the intellectual elites known as English Lang. & Lit.

Well, they wouldn't let me into Eng. Lang. & Lit. because I did not have Grade Thirteen Latin. I had the option of making up the Latin at summer school, or taking my first year in Soc. & Phil., with a Latin extra. I chose the second option so that I could go off to Camp Ahmek with Charley Fick and John Kennedy and the Oakwood bass fiddle. Kennedy and I by now were speaking Shakespeare almost all the time, inventing what sounded like Shakespearean dialogue if we couldn't find an appropriate line from *Macbeth*.

Chas Fick and I worked up a number of comic songs with bass and ukulele, and some cool renditions of "All of Me," Bobby Troup's hip version of "The Three Bears," and a couple of other songs in the style of the Page Cavanaugh trio, almost whispering the jazzed-up lyrics. We were even invited over to the girl's camp, Wapomeo, to do that Page Cavanaugh stuff, which I still remember and occasionally sing to myself while playing the bass. It was a legendary golden summer, a kind of farewell to youth. I won several sailing races. John Kennedy and I were assigned to a four-day girls' trip, to carry canoes, put up tents, and build the fires; almost nothing of what we fantasized happened, of course, but those four days took on a legendary quality all the same.

Fred Rainsberry was in charge of the C.I.T. program. Fred would ask us to examine the social and aesthetic considerations of our work: not only the great problems of telling the truth or dealing with our sexual frustrations or with spoiled and truculent children, but of such apparently meaningless and elementary things as the way in which we set a table, or the social and linguistic dynamics of obscenity and slang. Exposed to his challenging mind evening after evening, I began to understand what philosophical inquiry was about, and to regret that I had not been in his English Lit. classes at Oakwood. A deep and important friendship had been forged. Eight years later Fred's intervention would bring about a radical change in my life.

That Shakespeare talk with John Kennedy was one of the great playful delights of my life. If he had to acknowledge a major disappointment, Kennedy might say, "I am one, my liege, whom the vile blows and buffets of the world have so incensed that I am reckless what I do to spite the world." Brilliant. The whole summer was brilliant.

It was air and playing, lovely and watery, and fire green as grass.

And then it was September, and we were off to college.

Chapter 6

U OF T

OUR FIRST YEAR AT U.C., University College, seemed to be such a breeze that John Kennedy and I spent hours in the Junior Common Room with a card game called Casino, which we played almost every day.

Professor Marcus Long's introductory survey course in philosophy was a favourite. Long seldom lectured in a conventional way, and even in a class of forty or more he worked more like a seminar leader than a lecturer, throwing out provocative questions and treating the replies courteously. That was not the case with all the profs. I had heard about this spectacular prof from Victoria College, a guy in his thirties named Northrop Frye, and when he offered an evening colloquium in the Senior Common Room in Croft Chapter House a bunch of us came out to see what all the fuss was about. I tried to show off with a question, after Frye's initial presentation, which was about the nature of humour. The question was not only showy but stupid. Frye identified it as such with dismissive contempt. I was so upset that I was nearly sixty before I could read his books, and then had to upbraid myself for having missed all that brilliance for so long.

My Latin teacher was a warm-hearted young man who helped me catch up on what I had missed in Grade Thirteen, and soon I was even reading a little bit of Cicero for pleasure.

Anthropology was a relatively young department, and our introductory course was taught by its founding chair, and the star of the U of T anthropologists at the time, T.F. McIlwraith. We met him in a lecture room in the basement of the Royal Ontario Museum and were soon scouting the museum's halls with our sketchbooks, drawing primitive tools and other artifacts. McIlwraith was a charming lecturer. One of his themes was the vast amount of work entailed in the life of primitive humans. "Ladies and gentlemen, think of the labour involved!" McIlwraith would say dramatically, as he showed us a stone axe or a *coup-de-poing* and asked us to reflect on how difficult it must have been to make. Years later I would be fascinated to read in *Scientific American* the account by a couple of modern anthropologists about their surreptitiously following a group of tribesmen in a remote and primitive part of Papua New Guinea, who were said to go secretly to a riverbank where flints were plentiful, and ceremonially make a flint axe or two from time to time. Those anthropologists confessed that, like McIlwraith, they were thinking of the labour involved, and eager to watch it happening, hoping that the day's spying might be rewarded by at least one completed axe head. In fact what they saw was the half-dozen artisans wading into the river just long enough to pick up a few raw flints each, then coming up on the bank, going wham wham wham with one flint against another for the ten minutes or so it took to turn them all into keen-edged tools or weapons, then pausing for a smoke, some laughter and tale-telling, then back into the stream, and so on for a couple of hours during which about a hundred sharpened flints were produced. But McIlwraith's lectures were spellbinding; I briefly considered following my friend Ron Cohen into anthropology instead of English.

The University College Literary and Athletic Society, whose preserve the JCR[1] was, arranged for a series of talks on radio broadcasting. Lister Sinclair came and spoke on writing drama for radio. He was learned, funny, and practical at the same time. Here was a man whose voice I had heard on the radio for years, now, in the flesh, limping with a cane, his clothes in dreadful disarray (he was only twenty-

1. The Junior Common Room.

six) – but captivating and once again the source of thoughts about changing fields. Drama suddenly seemed necessary. I could write plays, I *knew* it.

My father gave me his old Underwood portable typewriter, and in the university bookstore I bought a second-hand typing course for fifty cents and learned to touch type. *Asdfg hjkl. Asdfg hjkl,* over and over again. It took about a month to get to the point where I could throw away the typing course and just work on speed. That month I neglected a lot of other work in order to master touch typing: it was one of the best investments of time I have ever made.

In saying that the first undergraduate year was easy I don't mean to suggest that we didn't take it seriously. There was a fine sense of privilege, of being on the edge of discovery and part of an enterprise of consequence. Kennedy and I were surprised that it seemed to take so little labour to produce the consistently good marks we were getting, and in retrospect I find it strange that we did so well: the following year was a nearly overwhelming disaster. In the spring of 1948 Chas Fick, Kennedy, and I went off to Fergus to help open up a new Department of Education campsite. There we met an engagingly comical Phys. Ed. student named Al Goodman. In July we all went northeast to Bark Lake, in Haliburton County, to build tent platforms and open up another camp, where we spent most of the summer teaching high school students how to be camp counsellors. We had plenty of free time and used to head off on marathon canoe escapades, visiting girls at cottages on the neighbouring lakes and rejoicing in our ability to run non-stop across the half-mile portage with a canoe on one's shoulders, a Coleman lamp hissing on the forward thwart with the glass globe removed in case of breakage. The companionship with Kennedy, Fick, and Goodman ripened. We composed and sang comic lyrics and told endless jokes. When the cook was fired for drinking I took over for a week, and specialized in a recipe of my mother's for Spanish Rice, until after presenting the rice dish for perhaps the third time I overheard John Kennedy's stage whisper, "That crap again!"

The camp nurse was flirtatious and loved having her back

rubbed. That was about as close as any of us got, I think, though it seemed as though one or the other of us was in her cabin most evenings of the week.

The camp's two-week sessions were not fully subscribed that first year, and for the last of the four sessions, in August, we looked after twenty-five boys from the Bowmanville reformatory. One of them was a personable and enthusiastic fifteen-year-old thief who boasted cheerfully of the more than twenty cars he had stolen, and of his plans to return to his chosen career as soon as he was released. "They'll never catch me again," he would say. His name was Ronald Turpin. On December 11, 1962, he was the last Canadian to be hanged for murder.[2]

The canoe was a significant part of my life. The nourishment it gave my self-confidence must have been powerful when my brother Cliff sent me out solo when I was six. There was a sleek cedar-strip canoe at Croydon Cottage, which could be sailed with a small leg-of-mutton sail and a pair of leeboards lashed to the centre thwart – polished oak panels that projected nearly three feet down into the water to prevent side slip, like the centreboard in any conventional small sailboat, or the keel on a yacht, and I have sailed it from one end of Lake Couchiching to the other many times, exulting in those white-capped days when the risk of capsizing was a constant. I had trained for those running portages at Bark Lake in the intervening years with dozens of canoe trips, sometimes going out for ten days at a time. I learned to cook elaborate meals over an open fire, especially with the help of the folding aluminum reflector oven. My mother had taught me to bake bread and biscuits when I was about ten. On canoe trips I loved showing off to my canoe-trip charges or partners by getting up early and whipping up a batch of fresh biscuits for breakfast, or a fruit pie. My greatest success was a lemon chiffon pie, for which I packed half a dozen eggs in a box of oatmeal so they wouldn't break – or if they did the oatmeal would form a tough glue around the cracks – and made the pie on the third or fourth day out on a seven-day trip in Algonquin

2. "Back to back," they said, with a professional hit man from Detroit, named Arthur Lucas.

Park during the Tamakwa days, rolling out the crust on a canoe bottom with a piece of perfectly round driftwood. I have slept in a canoe, anchoring it offshore on a hot night, and tried to get as close as one can to the joke about making love standing up in one (still a joke).

The silence of a tiny lake that can be accessed only by a long portage is a lovely thing. The choreography of that shell, as you find more and more ways to make it sideslip, or turn on a point with nearly invisible moves of the paddle, can become an addiction. The sound when waking from sleep under a canoe on a rainy night, with a loon calling in the distance, is unforgettable.

The autumn of 1948: optimistically back at University College for what I supposed would be another easy year, I dived into the extracurricular world a good deal more than into the library. I was strongly attracted to the Hart House Theatre, the first theatre I had ever seen in my life. When I was about three, my father had been obliged to carry me out of it, screaming in terror from a play about pirates. But whatever memory that carried was more of intrigue than fear, and soon I was auditioning for parts in both musicals and plays. I had been devouring books on makeup and had a great time building myself an outrageous, scene-stealing prosthetic nose for my Bardolph, in *Henry IV Part One*. I watched in awe the luminous performances of Kate Reid and Charmion King (whose *Antigone* was my introduction to ancient Greek drama). Years later, playing opposite those extraordinary actors on television,[3] the sense of privilege I experienced came in large part from the memory of their work at Hart House in their twenties.

Al Goodman and I worked up a male quartet with two medical students, Manie Rotenberg and David Silverstein.[4] At first it was largely barbershop standards: "I Want a Girl (Just Like the Girl That Married Dear Old Dad)," "The Moon Is Fair Tonight Along the

3. In my television series *Witness to Yesterday*, Reid played Queen Victoria, in 1973, and King played Mary Pickford in a script I wrote for her in 1998.

4. I was bass, Manie baritone, Al lead, and Dave tenor.

Wabash," "Down by the Old Mill Stream." But two interesting things happened. We discovered that we all had a fairly good knack of improvising our harmonies, and that led us into trying out anything that was fairly familiar and whose chord structure was not too challenging. Mickey Colomby's instruction had set, firmly (I still play the chord sequence he showed me for "Sweet Lorraine"). So I got the quartet to try some of those pop classics we had played in the quartet in Oakwood. The university, alas, did not have a bass to offer, and I could not afford one of my own, but I don't think I missed it much; there was so much else going on. The second thing that happened with the quartet was that David Silverstein wrote some arrangements for us, and while I think we enjoyed the improvising more than the learned pieces, we worked up two or three fairly sophisticated numbers to be mixed in to the performances we occasionally did at frats, singing for beers and for conviviality. Often we would just stroll along Bloor Street looking for a storefront with an indented entrance passing between converging glass display walls, such entrances providing plenty of resonance ("residence," Al called it, who was always making jokes with Yiddisher reference). I also sang bass in a more formal male quintet conducted by my old Glebe Collegiate friend Ward McAdam, who wrote intricate close harmony arrangements of some swing standards and got us gigs, dressed in tails, entertaining at big formal dances in the Hart House Great Hall.

The U.C. (University College) Follies was an attractive opportunity to try out some musical and comedy ideas. Bill Freedman (later a successful theatrical producer) and I wrote and performed some sketches together, and I did a couple of comic song numbers with an accomplished pianist and composer, Susie Davidson, who would later marry the scientist John Polanyi. Al Goodman arranged for me to get involved in the Phys. Ed. department's show *Health's a Poppin.* I bought some of those Fred Waring choral arrangements that Earl Davison had introduced to us at Oakwood ("Moonlight Becomes You" was one) and put together a thirty-voice choral group. Following the lead of the Glebe Collegiate music teacher Bob McGregor, I conducted from a front seat in the theatre, out of sight to most of the audience, a flashlight between my knees so that the singers could see my face and white-gloved hands. I appointed a basso with a pitch pipe in the back row to get the note just before the curtain went up on our act, the singers all humming sotto voce their start notes, so that as the curtain went up they could burst into song on my downbeat, with no fussing around or authoritarian showing-off from the conductor.

I had my first experience as a film actor. The University Film Society was not only a theatre in which I got to see the old classics for the first time, and took a great leap forward in my film education, it also took a few tentative steps toward original production. One of those steps entailed funding a partly dramatized account of the then seedy part of Toronto just south of the Art Gallery, and I was cast in a no-dialogue walk-on as a pimp, in zoot pants and broad-brimmed fedora. The director was Graeme Ferguson, who would go on to a distinguished career at the National Film Board (where we would later meet over somewhat more interesting projects) and who, with Roman Kroitor and some old pals from his hometown of Galt, Ontario, went on to devise and develop the revolutionary production and projection technology known as Imax.[5]

Chummy showed up that second year, Charmian Reading, another old friend from Glebe Collegiate, whom I had briefly dated there. We started to see each other and got sexually overheated, which was very frustrating for us both and, I think, the reason why we stopped "going out." None of my friends was having sex, though we were all getting dangerously close and painfully supercharged. If you had sex there was too big a risk of getting pregnant. Condoms were generally said to be untrustworthy. If the woman got pregnant, you got married. This may sound odd now, in the post-pill era, but the pill was still about a decade away. A good many love affairs went sour over

5. A considerable number of people contributed to Imax. Director Colin Low and cameraman Georges Dufaux had a lot of experience at large-format projection. A Danish inventor named Jan Jacobson designed the camera, and the initial project was financed by the Osaka World's Fair in Japan (1970). Bill Shaw and Robert Kerr from Galt, with whom Ferguson had published a community newspaper in his high school days, were key players on the business side.

the inevitable anger and frustration and fear that attended upon that damned forced restraint.

Another motorcycle joined the group, Ludovico Fecia Di Cossato – Louis – the son of the Italian ambassador in Ottawa. I think Louis was an exception to the above concerns. He also had what seemed an inexhaustible supply of money and very generously lent me his exquisite Triumph Tiger, a 500cc twin of recent vintage, for which I had a great deal of respect and upon which I stayed safe and had some great rides. John Kennedy borrowed it one afternoon and engaged the wrong gear while whizzing past the house at 22 Bracondale, ending up bruised and scraped, farther down the street, with the bike fairly seriously bent, the cost of unbending it eroding a good deal of our recreational scope for the rest of the year. Another U.C. friend (and still a good friend), Ben Marcus, had an ancient Velocette 500, which he too was generous with, and Charley Fick and I used it that summer to drive to our summer jobs near Fergus – I think we had by then bought it from Ben, it being close to its last legs. Or wheels.

In any case there was, as it turned out, far too much of that kind of thing and far too little time in the library or at the desk. I began to get severe comments scribbled on my essays, and when the marks came down after the end of term exams, mine were almost bad enough to lose me the whole year.

The summer of 1949 I went back to Camp Ahmek as a counsellor in the Senior section. I was too sexually distracted to do a very good job. Tay Statten, the founder's son and a psychiatrist by trade, was patient and wise, and helped pull me back into some simulacrum of responsible activity. A handsome athletic girl named Beverly Holmes, almost three years older than I, was a counsellor in the Inky section ("Inky" for Incubator). She was lean and smart, and held a Master Canoeist's certificate. All the canoe trip heroes and equestrian show-offs were dating her furiously. I decided that I would take her away from them, and succeeded, and we became an item. A chaste item, more or less, although a couple of days off with a canoe that got us several miles away from camp led to some fairly steamy times, steamy and frustrating enough to have sundered the relationship had it not been for my determination to show that I could land the most desirable girl in camp and thumb my nose at all the big shots.

It was the last day of that summer that the news came of Cliff's death. Back at U.C., racked with grief, I saw nobody, pulled out of all that extracurricular shit – as it seemed, in a bitter confused state, that trivial shit – and hit the books very hard. Bitter. I had no dates. I spent a lot of time at home. I lost weight and began to drink beer. In those days if you went out for a beer (you had to declare and often document that you were twenty-one or older) you went to a beverage room in a hotel. There were no bars. The beverage rooms, or beer parlours, were segregated, one section for men, one for "Ladies and Escorts." Both were murky with smoke. When you went to a liquor store for a bottle of wine or spirits, the LCBO made you fill out a form with your name and address, and a signed declaration that you were of age. There was no display in the shop, only a notice board listing the few available brands. A clerk took your form and vanished into the back to fetch your order. This was still the case as recently as twenty-five years ago.

One day I bumped into Bev Holmes. She was kind and comforting, and invited me to go across the street for coffee. We began to see each other. Her understanding of and undemanding response to my grief were such that I felt a rush of gratitude and asked her to marry me. She agreed. I came back into the sun then, and once more got deeply involved in music and theatre, but at the same time I found a new and very engaged interest in the academic work.

Many of the faculty in the department of English then deliberately and systematically humiliated and intimidated students by letting us know that if we hadn't read everything *they* had read, we could not consider ourselves serious scholars. If you came up with an original idea, you would be told that, well, of course, that was Trilling's notion, wasn't it, you'd have known that if you'd read Blackwell. Or if you'd read Trilling you'd know that your idea was discredited years ago. It was worse than condescending; it was a cruel, self-aggrandizing kind of crap that induced a dreadful anxiety among many of us. Even the department head, A.S.P. Woodhouse, was apt to talk like this sometimes. We forgave Woodhouse because he actually seemed to have read everything that was worth reading.

But there were also some humane and at least one or two spectacular teachers. A wild-eyed young Englishman named Douglas Grant joined the faculty at U.C. in time for my third year and electrified me with his course on Pope, Swift, and Johnson. That year was eighteenth century right across the board – the French lit was eighteenth century, and so was the philosophy, a beautifully integrated approach to the study of a period in the life of a culture: The West. What had been routine, something you do, getting through school, became important and meaningful. I believe I gave Beverly some of the credit for that, too, and allowed that gratitude to mask a growing awareness that we were not well-matched emotionally. In any case, in those days if you became engaged there was enormous pressure on you to go through with it. Tacit pressure, not directly spoken; but you did not Go Back On Your Word.

My marks in third year put me back up near the top. Beverly went back to Ahmek for the summer of 1950, and I went with Al Goodman to work at Camp Tamakwa on South Tea Lake, where I was sailing director. I became more closely acquainted than ever with Jewish culture and traditions. I sometimes even played the piano for Oneg Shabatt and learned to sing Hebrew folk songs. Manie Rotenberg was there too, that summer, and we got a quartet going, although we missed Dave Silverstein, who had gone off to New York to study orthopaedic surgery.[6]

My brother John had given me a spectacularly sharp sheath knife that he had made at sea, using the tempered blade from a power hacksaw and a piece of bone from a roast of pork. It was a beautiful piece of work and a great knife for the splicing and other rope work that I love. The Aykroyd dinghy was still the small sailboat of choice, and the rope was still three-strand natural manila. On calm days I would

6. As had his older brother Ezra, who in 1993 would do my hip replacement just before he retired.

take the sailing class on the dock and get eight or ten kids all working away at splices and sheeps' heads and other ornamental rope work. One day I left John's knife stuck in the dock near where we were working, forgot about it, and walked into it with my bare feet, slicing open my right big toe, right to the bone. Harry Shanoff, the young camp doctor, gave me a precautionary anti-tetanus shot (it was horse serum in those days), a very small dose, he said, to make sure there was no allergic reaction, and then he would give me a bigger one later. Within minutes I was floored with massive edema in my trachea and esophagus, young Dr. Shanoff bending over me hour after hour, pumping in adrenaline to try to keep the edema from closing down my windpipe altogether.

"That was very close," he said, when my breathing started to ease off and the swollen sensation in my throat abated. He warned me that I must never, *never* allow myself to be given an anti-tetanus shot again. Exactly ten years later, this would prove to be a matter of life and death.

That final undergraduate year was both tough and exhilarating. I finally began to feel at home in the academic environment, and to think that I might want to teach. A.S.P. Woodhouse assigned me an essay on John Milton's ideas about marriage and divorce. I wrote it as an imaginary dialogue between Milton and a young twentieth-century student recently arrived in heaven. Milton's dialogue and spelling were, of course, all seventeenth-century, and a great deal of the fun in the piece was the conjunction of the kid's twentieth-century language and attitudes with those of the great poet.

Woodhouse had assigned the marking of that set of essays to a graduate student, who didn't get it, marked the archaic spellings as errors, and gave me a C. I was sufficiently confident, even before the august presence of the Great Man, to go to Woodhouse and politely complain that I had been marked by a semi-literate. Woodhouse read the piece, gave me an A, and said I should consider doing an M.A.; he would find me a fellowship somewhere.

Beverly was now in teachers' college and agreed that we could get married in June and that she would support us by teaching for the year or two it would take me to do the M.A. Camp Tamakwa gave us a honeymoon cabin half a mile from the camp, a honeymoon that we somehow survived despite our already dramatic differences. Beverly was in charge of the girls' section of the camp, and I was teaching sailing again, and we did manage to get in a couple of very satisfying canoe trips before heading back to her first year at a tiny rural school in what is now downtown Mississauga, and I into what should have been an exhilarating set of seminars and research assignments in graduate school.

But the emotional load of that first year of marriage, with the financial uncertainty and the stress of graduate school, landed me in the Toronto General Hospital, mid-term, with "acute gastroenteritis of no known cause." We were able to talk to each other about the difficulties and resolved to try to make the marriage work. It would be years before I realized that this stoicism was hurtful to us both.

After the year of course work, Woodhouse found me a teaching fellowship at Queen's University in Kingston, for the year it would take me to finish my dissertation, directed by Professor Kenneth McLean. The thesis was entitled *The Mediaeval Mind of Henry Adams*, and my exploration of that era in late nineteenth- and early twentieth-century American literature and society was very satisfying. So was the teaching at Queen's, under the guidance of the amiable department head, Henry Alexander. I helped eke out Beverly's modest salary with some supply teaching in Kingston high schools, which I enjoyed more than I did teaching the Queen's engineering and medical students who sat restlessly in front of me for their mandatory minors in English. By the turn of the year Beverly was pregnant. The days of academic dreaming were over. I was going to have to seriously look for a job.

Chapter 7

CLOSE-UP

THE FIRST TELEVISION PROGRAMS I saw were at classmate Bud Weed's house in Wychwood Park, mostly children's programs from WBEN-TV, Channel 4, Buffalo, there being no television in Canada in 1946 or '47 when the Weeds got their first receiver. The pictures were hard to look at, distorted and very black: the contrast had somehow got cranked up to the maximum and nobody knew that this could be adjusted.

In the little bungalow at 51 Rothsay Avenue in the Queensway in the early fifties, the radio was often on in the evenings, and CBC was doing some powerful drama, including a series of remarkable productions of Shakespeare. But a friendly couple across the street invited us over for beer and spaghetti one night, and there we saw our first television dramas, mostly crime shows. We made fun of the primitive live shows and the frequent goofs when the wrong camera was cut and we saw stagehands standing around. I was earning about $2,500 a year then, and it would never have occurred to us to spend a few hundred dollars on a television receiver. We did not take it seriously

Just because I needed work badly, I had tried for a job in television after my year at Queen's University. A friend there had put me in touch with some CBC people – the scholarly, avuncular Neil Morrison, who was head of the department called Talks and Public Affairs and had an opening in radio, and Stuart Griffiths, who was head of the fledgling television service. I went in for interviews when we arrived back in Toronto in the spring of 1953, camping in with the in-laws to await the birth of our first child.

The interview with Stuart Griffiths was a shock. It was clear from the start that we had little to say to each other, and that he found me intellectually pretentious and out of touch with the populist, entertainment-oriented service that he was developing. Griffiths was a bluff, straight-talking guy. When the interview was over, he said unapologetically that it was clear to him I would never have a career in television, and that if the radio people were offering me a job I'd better take it.

The meeting with Neil Morrison went very well. I was struck by his dedication to the idea of public service and by the tremendous intellectual buzz of the place. He offered me a starting salary of $1,900. A year. Pretty tight, even then. Beverly had been making about that as a public school teacher, and supporting us, but now I was going to have to support her *and* a child, and we would have to find something more than the single room in a boarding house that had been adequate for us in Kingston.

My father was not happy about the prospect of my going into broadcasting and had spoken with his old pal Wilfred Wees, the head of W.J. Gage's publishing division. Gage also had a large and profitable printing operation in the big old brick factory building at 80 Spadina Avenue. Dr. Wees offered me a junior editor's job at $2,100 a year, and it was the extra $200 that forced the decision to turn down CBC Radio. Dad also offered us the third-floor apartment at 22 Bracondale, but Beverly's parents said they would help us buy a house if we could find something modest with a mortgage that my salary could carry. We still had the 1951 four-door Morris Minor ("The Birdcage," Beverly called it because it was so drafty in the winter), and I supposed I could commute from the Queensway when we found a house there for $11,000.

I enjoyed the work at Gage's. I was given some very challenging projects, including the development of a set of anthologies for Grades

Ten and Eleven, called *Creative Living*, which I still feel proud of. My editor-in-chief was Katherine McCool, the wife of another Department of Education colleague of my father's, Brian McCool. Katherine was bright, imperious, funny, and a very good teacher. She had a remarkable proofreader's eye and would catch an error in a tiny eight-point footnote on one of thirty-two pages on a whole four-foot-square press sheet spread out on her desk.

Frank Strowbridge, the jolly red-nosed sales manager, took me to lunch from time to time, introduced me to rye whisky (Wiser's Deluxe), and brought me to some of his sales and promotion events, which, among other things, were well catered and barred.

There were frequent trips to Chicago to deal with Scott, Foresman, the publishers of the Dick and Jane readers for which Gage had the Canadian rights. The colleagues in sales and editing were convivial. The printing operation, with its great roaring flatbed presses printing sheets with sixty-four pages on them, thirty-two to a side, and folding and cutting them with mesmerizing precision, the smell of ink and hot lead, and the magical operation of the bookbinding machines, added a satisfying textural, physical, olfactory, and mechanical element. For those first couple of years, although the marriage was stormy, and commuting with the cranky and surprisingly expensive Morris Minor was stressful, I felt that I was doing something worthwhile with a solid future.

During those evenings across the street at the neighbours', as we sniggered at the faltering efforts of the early television programs I felt no regrets about having been told I would never have a career in that medium. Print was exciting. Wilf Wees let it be known that he was grooming me to be his successor, and wanted me to have a Ph.D., as he did, and that the company would help me do that. I started summer courses at the University of Michigan, in English and Education, and planned a dissertation that was to be in the form of a textbook proposing a radical new approach to the teaching of introductory reading and writing. I had fallen in with a group of descriptive linguistics buffs in Ann Arbor, disciples of the pioneer Charles Fries. The idea that spoken English had a consistent structural logic that had nothing to do with the Latin-based grammar still being taught to bewildered kids all over the English-speaking world was for me one of those great gleaming light bulbs that go on in the heads of comic book characters. I suddenly saw what apparently nobody else had seen, that you could take that idea and design a whole elementary school reading-and-writing curriculum around it. My teachers at Michigan were supportive and, indeed, admiring. Wilf Wees was ecstatic. I knew that I was on to something genuinely original and a hell of a lot more fun than researching some obscure author or the history of the development of some educational theory, the numbing kind of esoterica that many doctoral candidates waste years upon.

With a couple of other print buffs at Gage's I bought an ancient hand-operated platen press, some type cases, and two or three point sizes of a font called Electra, and began to set up elegant little pages of verse in the basement of the house at 217 Douglas Avenue that we had just moved to. A second child was on the way.

But at the same time I began to feel that my career was being mapped out for me and was not of my making. It was the company's agenda. It was a good agenda, but it wasn't mine. Still, I was on the way to that Ph.D., it was promised that my salary would soon reach a comfort level, there were the perks of travel and big hotel meals at Frank Strowbridge's frequent events. So I stuffed my uneasiness into a back compartment, got on with it, and told myself that I was happy.

One day in the autumn of 1955 I got a call at my desk at W.J. Gage and Company, where I was editing and in some cases actually developing textbooks. The caller was Fred Rainsberry, who had been an English teacher at Oakwood and head of the Counsellor-In-Training program at Camp Ahmek when Chas Fick and John Kennedy and I were there as CITs the summer after we graduated from Oakwood, 1947. I had lost touch with Fred and was not aware that he had been named head of children's television when CBC TV started up in the spring of 1952.

I was, alas, a bit condescending about it. I said I was surprised that a man of his intellectual reach (Ph.D. in philosophy, among other accomplishments) would get involved in something as trivial as television. To Fred's credit he responded tolerantly. "You really don't have any idea of what we're doing over here, do you?" I remember him saying with a chuckle. He said that he was going to launch a regular Sunday afternoon magazine program (I had no idea what a magazine program might be), and that they were auditioning for hosts. He said he had admired the work he'd seen me do on the platform at Oakwood, emceeing various events, and similar stuff at Camp Ahmek, and that I would probably do well on camera. I should come over and spend some time with his people, he said, and I should also get a television set and watch some of their programs and some of the excellent stuff that was being broadcast from the United States, especially on Sundays. He mentioned Edward R. Murrow and Alistair Cooke.

I had by then begun to want a television set: now I had an excuse. And I did go to meet some of the children's television people, a lean, red-headed "Program Organizer" named Bruce Attridge, who also boasted a Ph.D and was a compulsive aesthete ("He can't brush his teeth without having an artistic experience," someone said), and Peggy Nairn, a confident, breezy producer/director in her late twenties, and Joan Hughes,[1] a big, hearty, and infectiously optimistic woman. Rainsberry had put together a very stimulating group. I agreed to come in for the *Junior Magazine* audition – sometime in November. I also started watching Alistair Cooke's elegant Sunday cultural magazine, *Omnibus*, and before long I realized that television could be superb.

Omnibus was the Ford Foundation's brief attempt to televise the best of the contemporary arts and letters, with an occasional whiff of science and philosophy. The programs produced by Robert Saudek were first broadcast on CBS, then moved to ABC and finally to NBC,

1. Joan later married the legendary and charming Nikolai Soloviov, a production designer who had worked with the great Eisenstein in Moscow. In a year or two I had the privilege of having him design a series for me.

beginning in 1952, and continuing until 1961. That was the venue in which Americans saw Orson Welles' acclaimed return to America to star in Peter Brook's *King Lear*, Rex Harrison and Lilli Palmer's *Henry VIII*, William Saroyan narrating an adaptation of one of his short stories, William Faulkner giving a guided tour of Oxford, Mississippi, James Agee's drama series on the life of Abraham Lincoln, S.J. Perelman's celebration of burlesque with Bert Lahr, Peter Ustinov's American début as Samuel Johnson, Jacques Cousteau's first underwater adventure film, and Les Paul and Mary Ford demonstrating the marvels of the then revolutionary techniques of multi-track recording. Just to name a few. It was this single enterprise that really spawned public television, again with a good deal of help from the Ford Foundation.[2] CBC TV briefly ventured into this kind of programming, and may yet do so again.

In any case, my feelings about television soon changed. Fred Rainsberry was a wise teacher and an enthusiast. A small group gathered once a month at his apartment or at Attridge's just to talk about ideas generally, but always speculating about how to make television richer, more challenging, how to bring ideas and the arts to wider audiences.

Meanwhile the first edition of *Junior Magazine* was recorded in mid-December, and I had my debut as a television host when it was broadcast on New Year's Eve, 1955. Starting in the New Year, the series went live on Sunday afternoons. Robert Goulet was a guest artist in that first program. There were science interviews and short films from the National Film Board, five or six items in each broadcast. My early nervousness soon evaporated. Attridge and Rainsberry were attentive and helpful. We would screen the programs on kinescope recordings after I got off work at Gage's later in the week, the producers generously correcting my early tics and mannerisms, and before long I felt at home. I began to hang around the cutting

2. See Chapter 8. *The Fifty-First State* was not only funded by the Ford Foundation, but to some extent devised by the foundation's director, Fred W. Friendly, who had been Edward R. Murrow's producer at CBS.

rooms helping where I could but really just there to soak it all in. The producers began to involve me in program planning. And then one Sunday afternoon when the broadcast was over, Rainsberry and Attridge invited me to the cafeteria in the basement of the old Radio Building at 354 Jarvis Street, for a chat. Over cups of tea they told me that the department would have a producer's position opening up in the spring. They said that the CBC was offering a training session, six weeks during which course members would get a crash course in directing, lighting, cameras and lenses, control room management, and program development, and they wanted me to take that course and accept a contract as a producer.

I protested that I was in the middle of my Ph.D. at Michigan, and that the coming year, starting in September, I would begin my mandatory year in residence there to try to complete the course work before getting down to developing my thesis. Fred Rainsberry asked me, Did I really *want* that Ph.D? I of course expostulated: here were the two of them sitting there across the table, both with their doctorates, how could they think I wouldn't want one? And Fred said with a characteristically challenging twinkle that he would just ask me not to dismiss his offer out of hand, to go home and think very carefully about whether I really wanted the Ph.D, and to call him in a few days. By the way, he added, Andrew Allan and Esse W. Ljungh – the production geniuses behind CBC's radio drama department, the guys who had invented the *CBC Stage* series that had held me, and often my mother and father as well, spellbound around the old Rogers radio, and later the brilliant Shakespeare series – Ljungh and Allan were also taking the course, as was my old high school friend John Kennedy, who had come over to TV from his reporter's job at the *Toronto Telegram*, and had been knocking around on a variety of journalistic assignments and would move into the Children's Department along with me, after the training course.

I might be sitting in with two of my intellectual heroes and a dear old pal? *That* was something to think about.

I believe it was that very night that I woke from a dream, and sat up in bed, and said to myself that it was not I who wanted that Ph.D.; *it was my father* who wanted it. He had always regretted not having the opportunity to take a graduate degree and was a little envious of Wilf Wees, whom everyone called "Doctor Wees." I was doing it for my father. I had not known that before. It was suddenly very clear. Yes, the thesis was a grand idea, needed to be done, maybe I could write an article about it, try to encourage somebody else to take on the work (I never did), but Fred's was an offer I could not refuse. I called him on Monday morning and began the painful work of letting my employers and colleagues at the publishing company know about my decision, and facing up to my father's dismay.

When I walked into the television building on Jarvis Street in mid-April to negotiate my first year's contract as a television producer, I was coming home. It was the CBC almost more than any other single force that had shaped my feeling for this country, largely through radio drama. This, I felt, was where I was meant to be. But the next few minutes began on a slightly unnerving note. John Barnes, the general manager of television, somewhat sheepishly had to tell me that there had been a mistake: there was no position available in Children's television after all. Their staffing budget had been used up. The CBC had, he acknowledged, undertaken an obligation to me, and he was prepared to give me a one-year contract (at $4,000) in the Public Affairs department, and then, at the end of that year, I might be able to move over to Children's. I was sent across the parking lot to meet Frank Peers, who had taken over from Neil Morrison as head of Talks and Public Affairs, and Eugene Hallman, who was Frank Peers's supervising producer for television. Hallman said that once the training course was over, I would be assigned to help other producers with existing programs until I knew the ropes, and then he would see about giving me an assignment of my own. I would share an office on the second floor of the Radio Building with two other producers who had been there from the beginning, Ted Pope and Gordon Babineau. Just up the hall was E. Ross McLean, the dean of the Public Affairs producers, with a reputation for being very difficult, very inventive, and very intolerant of anything less than excellence.

I moved in at the beginning of June and enrolled in the training course. We were about a dozen, mostly men. In addition to John Kennedy and my radio heroes, Andrew Allan and Esse W. Ljungh, there was the dazzlingly handsome young Englishman Eric Till, who was already a studio director[3] in the drama department and soon became one of the CBC's top drama producer/directors; among his feature film credits are *Hot Millions*, in which he directed Peter Ustinov and Maggie Smith. Another of my intellectual heroes, dramatist and radio essayist Lister Sinclair, was in the group. The classical actor Barry Morse became a friend during the course.[4] Syd Wayne, the younger brother of Johnny Wayne of Wayne and Shuster, was another member. Each of us would have to produce and direct our own program before the summer was over, and in the meantime we were given lectures and demonstrations by technical producers, lighting directors, audio technicians, program developers, writers, and experienced producer/directors.

Producers were their own directors then. None of us was on staff; we were all on contract, with no health plan, no pension, no benefits of any kind. It was said that the reason for not putting us on staff was that the work was so demanding that producers would burn themselves out in ten years. We were paid more than staffers, and it was whispered that the real hotshot producers, the Franz Kramers and Norman Campbells were making real money, some even suggested as much as $10,000 a year! I remember thinking, Boy, you'd never need to make any more than that – if it's true.

During the training course we hung lights, pushed cameras, operated the mike booms and the switcher, and got to know the tech-

3. Studio director was the CBC term for the man on the floor, linked to the director by headset, who is in some other TV worlds known as the floor manager or the stage manager.

4. Barry played both Shakespeare and G.B. Shaw in my historical interview series *Witness to Yesterday*, in the 1970s, appeared in about sixty movies, and become internationally known as Lt. Philip Gerard in the 1963 television series *The Fugitive*. His wife Sydney Sturgess gave a chillingly credible performance with me in *Witness To Yesterday* as Mary Todd Lincoln, the president's widow.

nicians. We were soon directing simple setups – interviews mostly – and learning the lingo and the protocols, the roles and responsibilities of the different specialized technicians in the control room. By the end of the summer when we made our sample programs,[5] we knew many of the technical people with whom we would soon be working and felt at ease in what had been a few weeks earlier the baffling complexity of a television control room.

Even before the course was over, I was assigned to direct the *National News* from time to time, under the supervision of the senior news producer, John Lant. Lant was the caricature of a British Army colonel, with a flamboyant red moustache, flashing eyes, all imperatives and enthusiasm. And a very good teacher. The News department did not have directors of its own: Public Affairs producers handled the task in rotation, and I was told that I might as well start as soon as I felt I could and get the hang of it. We had a fifteen-minute newscast at 6 p.m. and another at 11 p.m. It was a first-rate baptism of fire. There was no room for mistakes. We did a run-through half an hour before air, then fifteen minutes for notes, then to air on the hour. Lant stood behind the control room desk and delivered advice and orders in a half-bark, half-whisper if the new director got into trouble, and in any case the script assistants were old hands and the technical people would usually whisper corrections if they saw you about to do something inept. It was primarily a matter of one camera on the news announcer (Rex Loring, Larry Henderson, Earl Cameron), one for graphics, and rolling in film clips from telecine, on rare occasions a live reporter or guest in the studio. There was a delicious air of tension and accomplishment all the same, a kind of athletic buzz, like the starter's pistol and the unrelenting track stretching out ahead of you for the next fifteen minutes, everything to the second, all of this going out to thousands of people as you did it, no second chances, having to think very fast if the film broke or the announcer picked up the

5. Mine was a short illustrative drama followed by a discussion: it was called *So You Want to Buy a House.* Andrew Allan, who did not enjoy television, did a very creditable *Our Town* and Eric Till a superb ballet called *El Amor Brujo.*

wrong page or the map on the graphics camera was wrong. I am grateful for that battleground. I came out of it thinking that I could handle just about any challenge the studio control room had in store for me. I even offered to relieve my colleagues when they grumbled about being assigned to the news, just to rack up more hours. Lant and I became friends. Soon, when news specials were being planned, he sent for me, and when the first-ever network national election broadcast was undertaken (Diefenbaker's first win in 1957), Lant assigned me to direct it. I was now twenty-seven.

My friendship with Fred Rainsberry grew, despite my having not ended up in his department. Fred was a devout and thoughtful Christian and invited me to go with him to the high Anglican service at the Church of Saint Philip the Apostle. The rector, Father David Clarke, was an inspired teacher who came down into the congregation to preach and invited unconfirmed children to the communion rail to be blessed. Beverly and I became fascinated and started attending evening seminars Father Clarke was giving on the meaning of faith. It was a strange and warming experience to find ourselves in a genuinely worshipful congregation of people for whom the Church was not an instrument for keeping the lower orders in their place, but rather a community of seekers after the central truth of the Christian message.

I became so caught up in the spirit of it that I was baptized, took my first communion with a rush of powerful emotion, and stayed closely involved with the Church until after I moved to Ottawa a few years later and discovered how anomalous St. Philip's was. Father Clarke was most unusual. Too many churches were, as I had long felt, political in their intent, not interested in investigation, imagination, the elusive struggle with the mystery of being that was so present and energizing at St. Philip's. I have no regrets about that time; it illuminated my own intuitions and understanding of the depth and power of those mysteries. I felt, and feel, richer for having lived for a while in that congregation, and much clearer about the range of connections between deep imaginative probing, which animates believing communities and individuals, at one end and rank superstition and conformity at the other.

At work there was also a warm collegiality among the television people. Most of us brought our lunches in paper bags, and one or two days a week Eugene Hallman, the supervising producer of Television Public Affairs, would convene an informal lunch gathering in his big windowed office at the west end of the second floor, and we would sit around, some of us on the floor with our sandwiches and drinks in paper cups from the cafeteria, and talk about how to make better television and how to use it for the benefit of our audiences, to enlarge their world. When Hallman moved into the network programming office, Peers replaced him with Bernard Trotter, a soft-spoken, unpretentious redhead from Kingston who was a frequent encouraging presence throughout the department, dropping in on producers for a chat in their offices, and often quietly watching a production from an inconspicuous position in the back of the control room. Even the chairman, Davidson Dunton,[6] would turn up in a studio from time to time, in his low-key amiable way letting the troops know that he thought what they did was important.

There was adventuring going on in all the departments. Videotape had not yet arrived. Some programs were recorded for broadcast on kinescope, a modified 16mm film camera that recorded a slightly washed-out image directly from a black-and-white picture tube, but most went live, including big expensive dramas that filled the original drama studio, Studio One. Elaborate multi-level drama sets occasionally spilled over into a second studio, and later would fill the new Studio Seven, twice as big as Studio One, with what would now be thought of as movies of the week, sometimes a full-scale opera – *La Traviata* or *Carmen*, say, with the cast in Studio Seven and a live orchestra feeding the instrumental music from across the parking lot, from the storied old radio Studio G.

6. At the age of thirty-four, Dunton was appointed CBC's first permanent chairman (and CEO, though the expression was not then in use). He resigned in 1959 to become president of Carleton University, in Ottawa.

Once, gloriously, there was Franz Kramer's live production of Igor Stravinsky conducting the Toronto Symphony Orchestra. Up at Studio Four on Yonge Street, which had been a Pierce-Arrow car showroom, is now a Staples Business Depot, and was in the fifties and sixties CBC TV's home base for light entertainment and variety, Norman Jewison would be directing an elegant blend of comedy, dance, and big band variety. It was from Studio Four that the popular *Cross Canada Hit Parade* was produced live every week for years. Big cultural adventures like a major Shakespeare or an opera did not carry advertising; neither did any of the news, documentary, or discussion programs from the Public Affairs department. American imports, drama, and light entertainment were sponsored.

Right behind the elegant white-painted brick building, still there on Jarvis Street, which was the administration centre called the Kremlin, was the smallish Studio Six, a favourite of mine. There was something very friendly about that space despite the fact that the wooden floor vibrated when cameras were dollying. During the week it was the home base for afternoon programming for women, and on the weekend for the combination farm and garden series called *Country Calendar*. On the ground floor of the south side of the television building was Studio Two, the two-camera space where I had done *Junior Magazine*. Weekdays at one minute past seven it was home to Ross McLean's popular daily interview program, *Tabloid*, which was a frequent newsmaker. *Tabloid* introduced the extraordinary Joyce Davidson to Canadian viewers, with Percy Saltzman, a real meteorologist, not only doing the weather but developing an approach to interviewing from which I learned a lot.

A film unit operated out of a building on Front Street and developed a strong tradition of edgy documentary that was soon challenging the National Film Board.

One aspect of that collegiality was an openness and willingness to share and to teach. If I as the apprentice turned up in Norman Jewison's studio at the start of rehearsals, or in Ross McLean's *Tabloid* studio just before going to air, or David "Shit-Shit" Greene's drama studio, and asked if I could stand quietly in the background and watch and learn, the response was almost always generous: Here; sit over here, or There's a spare seat in the sound booth. And we, the apprentices, would be invited to ask questions during the breaks and to hang around for the post-mortem if there was one.

That spirit of sharing and fellowship began to erode in a few years, to be replaced by a more competitive, critical attitude, protective, defensive sometimes, or lofty and arrogant. But it was a warm and inviting collegium while it lasted, and that communitarian atmosphere contributed a lot to the energy and the loyalty that we brought to the new craft.

Management then seemed to share the spirit of risk-taking you expect from the front-line troops in a new enterprise. Ideas for new programs or formats or production styles were not, as they now are, submitted to committees for review. Single executives, sometimes at the fairly junior level of program organizer, made the decision and often made it virtually upon receiving the proposal. They either threw your idea out or approved it, or encouraged you to work it up a little more, and my recollection is that there was a great deal more approval and encouragement than the reverse.

Shooting the many discussion programs that I was handed in those early months (and I was given a lot of routine panels to produce, shows that my more experienced colleagues disdained), I began to experiment with lighting, eccentric sets, allowing cameras and crew to be seen in the shot, trying to naturalize the thing a bit and find a little relief from the inherent dullness of yet another discussion of some national policy issue.

There were programs called *This Week* and *Press Conference*, usually a matter of assembling two or three academics, journalists, or other professionals (again, almost always men), with a host/moderator, to discuss a prominent news story or public issue: Suez, capital punishment, women in the workplace.

Some were very popular. A bright and funny little guy, Cliff Solway, produced *Fighting Words* successfully for years and made its host, the crusty eccentric Nathan Cohen, drama critic for the *Toronto Star*, into a household name. You could find two or three major literary figures, both Canadian and international, gathered at Nathan's *Fighting Words* table first to play the game part – identifying a provocative and controversial literary quotation – and then to debate its merits.

At about the time I came on board, it was decided to try a television version of a long-time radio format called *Citizens' Forum.* For years CBC Radio had been inviting people in communities across the country to come to a local hall, hear two or three knowledgeable people discuss an issue of public policy, or the implications of recent events, and then join in the discussion, the whole being broadcast live to the country. Not something to corral a huge audience, but a steady and solid contribution to the national discussion, always attracting a good crowd to the hall and a modest but steady radio audience of listeners who cared about the country – citizens, in short.

Could it work on television?

We had studios big enough to pack a good size audience into, and the format had been used for a few months in that way. But a program organizer suggested that we deploy a remote production crew, who usually did sports events, and bring television out into the community instead of the community into the studio. Pierre Berton and Charles Templeton were suggested as moderators.

I remember thinking early on, as my concept of television as theatre began to take hold, that what we needed was not so much a moderator as the reverse: someone who would energize the place, raise the emotional and conflictual temperature. When I began to work with my francophone colleagues in Montreal, I was delighted to learn that their word for this function was *animateur.*

I gained confidence as a director from the challenge of surveying a site, like West Hall on the second floor of the U. of T.'s University College, my *alma mater*, and, with a remote broadcasts T.P. (technical producer: the person responsible for the crew and equipment), planning the disposition of cameras and lights, positioning of the truck, with its mobile control room, in a way that would allow me to conveniently go on set and return to the truck during setup and rehearsal. Before long I was really enjoying producing *Citizens' Forum*, and beginning to play around here too, with camera angles, lighting, and other aspects of the format.

I began to attract some small attention from the reviewers, who were amused by the playful camera work. When an early reviewer referred to this Pat Watson (the credit I took on screen) as a "she," I realized they were confusing me with the National Film Board screenwriter, Patricia Watson, who used the same credit. That is when I started to sign my programs Patrick Watson, and people began to address me as Patrick.[7]

It was during this period that I realized that television was not the medium I had expected it to be, was not primarily a vehicle for informing people (not, that is, in the somewhat academic and arrogantly teacherly way I had expected to use it), but was something closer to theatre. Eventually this perception would grow into a theory and a strategy.

One of the chores I was handed from time to time was the Sunday afternoon farm and garden show, *Country Calendar*, hosted by the gardening enthusiast Earl Cox. On my first assignment to that series, I was asked to produce and direct a documentary on harvesting for the frozen pea packagers, and got my introduction to 16mm film and the excitement of taking the camera out into the world. Of course, I hadn't the faintest idea how to direct the making of a film, and, as so often happened in those early months, it was the cameraman, Len MacDonald,[8] who showed me everything I had to know and let me take the credit for actually "directing" the thing.

I think the first regular series I was assigned to was the do-it-

7. Including my mother, who said she had always preferred it to Pat but had been afraid that some people would think it pretentious.

8. Len was a superb craftsman and a delightful colleague. Years later he and I began working together on an ambitious social documentary about the transformation of the community of Killarney, Ontario, that was about to take place when that isolated water-access-only fishing community was for the first time joined to the world by a road (to Sudbury). When Len was killed in a plane crash later that spring while filming in Alberta, I lost heart about the Killarney project and never finished it.

yourself program *Mr. Fixit.* The series had been developed by producer Desmond Smith and the program's star, Peter Whittall, as a straightforward set of demonstrations on how to cut dovetails for a kitchen drawer, use a fretsaw, or set mitre braces to make picture frames – basic carpentry and related skills for householders and hobbyists. Although the programs themselves were homey and unsophisticated, Des Smith had a habit of writing witty, Goon Show asides to himself on his scripts, perhaps to protect himself from the boredom of what this literate and experienced Englishman clearly did not find a challenging assignment. I was charmed by his witty marginalia, and I think it was in part those little verbal jokes that got me thinking about pumping a bit of laughing gas into the *Mr. Fixit* atmosphere. There I met a genuine television genius, Paddy Sampson, on his first assignment as studio director. He had most recently run the special effects department and still had access there, and between us we began both to expand the ambit of the series and to dream up visual jokes for it. Paddy was an Ulsterman who had worked as a lighting man in theatre, in the London West End. A few years older than I, he had been in submarines in the Pacific, and his anecdotes about the West End, and the British Navy, and his being British Ballroom Dancing Champion were so extravagant that for a while I thought him the most prodigious storyteller I had ever met, until bit by bit, through my encounters with his former mates and others, I found they all were true.

Paddy Sampson went on to produce pioneering symphony concerts for the Children's department, and then to become the dean of the CBC's Light Entertainment division. In the mid-sixties he began to work with American jazz artists and created a monumental two-hour special, *The Blues,* with a roster of the great names in that discipline. Over the years he became the favoured producer/director of Harry Belafonte, and did shows with Lena Horne and Duke Ellington, huge galas at the National Arts Centre in Ottawa, and a number of specials he brought me in to host.

But our humble start together was with a genial, somewhat

sloppy ("I'm an eighth-of-an-inch man") amateur carpenter, Peter Whittall, whose show had been intended to help people make kitchen cupboards and panel their rec rooms.

Largely provoked by Paddy, we soon moved far beyond the dovetails and the mitre boxes. In one (fifteen-minute live) program we constructed a hi-fi amplifier[9] and I found a way in our tiny studio[10] with only two cameras and no zoom lenses to shoot macro images of the soldering so that the tip of the soldering iron and the wires to be joined virtually filled the screen. In a subsequent show we built a complex exponential reflex bass speaker, a "folded horn," and offered plans to viewers who wrote in. In that tiny studio we actually assembled an outboard motor boat from a kit, over two weeks (two live fifteen-minute shows), having to cut the hull down from its intended fourteen feet l.o.a. to thirteen feet in order to fit it into Studio Five.

Paddy came up with a superb closing gag for a show that featured the Ramset, a big hammer for driving very hard nails into concrete (in order to put wood strapping, for example, on the concrete walls of a basement – we did two or three shows on building a rec room in your basement). The Ramset used a .22 rifle cartridge to fire its sharp case-hardened bullet-shaped nail through the wood and into the concrete. Peter spent most of one of these rec room shows demonstrating the thing with great gusto and a lot of noise (we filmed that part in my own basement). Then, live, in the studio, as he said good night to the viewers, he made a three-quarter turn away from the camera, picked up the still smoking Ramset as if it were a submachine gun, aimed it at a concrete block a few feet away, and appeared to be pumping bullets into it as the Ramset rocked and smoked. Recorded sound effects of a machine gun rattled out of the loudspeakers, and on the face of

9. A seven-amp four-tube affair made in Waterloo, Ontario, and offered to hobbyists in an accessible kit as the Wellington Seven.

10. Studio Five, in the basement of the old Television Building between Jarvis and Mutual streets. This studio had been the CBC's original *Howdy Doody* studio, Peanut Gallery and all. Later it was the *National News* studio for a while, then an announce and utility studio. One memorable day in 1964 Douglas Leiterman and I would use it to record auditions with Charles Van Doren, of *Quiz Show* fame, and later with Jimmy Sinclair, a former Minister of Agriculture (and father of Margaret Trudeau), both of whom we thought might be candidates for the host of *This Hour Has Seven Days*.

the concrete block, which Paddy had rigged in standard movie special effects technique, holes appeared in sequence, from left to right, spelling out MR FIXIT in block letters as smoke and tiny fragments of concrete were apparently pounded out of the block by the hail of bullets.

But the gag that changed my life was the water tap. It was based on the old magic principle of misdirection, which I realized could be produced by cutting between two cameras viewing the same scene from different angles.

At the end of our shows Rex Loring, the staff announcer and Peter Whittall's straight man, would often set up the following week by reporting that he had a problem he needed help with, and in this case it had been a dripping water tap. Rex appeared the following Saturday afternoon with a disconnected faucet in hand.

Peter, of course, made fun of him for the dumb idea of bringing the tap to the studio, but set about showing him what to do about the drips. I deployed my macro camera techniques to make the damaged old washer as big as a human head on the screen, and I think we spent the whole fifteen minutes on the niceties of this valuable little bit of domestic nuisance reduction. Then, at the end, Peter hands the tap to Rex, Rex looks admiringly at it, turns the handle, and water gushes out, and proceeds to fill the studio as the credits roll. This was sometime in the spring of 1957.

Ross McLean's office on the second floor of the radio building was next to mine. He was a bachelor then, and from his conversation one gathered that he read every magazine and newspaper, while watching television and listening to the radio. In the cafeteria he always had an observation to make to other producers about their work, as well as to performers, announcers, disk jockeys, newspapermen who had come by for an interview or a commentary program, and supervisors. He always did this very specifically and rather formally, and usually wittily, singling out some aspect of a recent program magazine piece that – at least in his formulation – merited comment. Monday morning after the water tap, he appeared suddenly full-frame in the doorway of my tiny office, his arms folded, his lips pursed in a slightly comic frown.

"All right!" he said. "How did you do it?"

We went downstairs for coffee. I do not now recall whether I stuck to Magicians' Secrecy, or told him how we did the trick, but most of the first part of what turned out to be a crucial conversation, perhaps for both of us, was his quietly probing my attitude toward the work and asking about my ideas and ambitions. At first I thought he was doing no more than cordially playing out his role as the dean of the Public Affairs producers, getting to know the new kid and giving him both advice and encouragement. I, of course, began to expound my notions about information vs. theatre and was gratified to sense that McLean was taking this embryonic analysis very seriously. After a while, he switched the conversation from my work to his own.

He said that he had been summoned to Ottawa the week before to meet with the chairman, Davidson Dunton, and that Dunton had given him a marvellous challenge. The chairman, who had been with the CBC for twelve years now and had enthusiastically helped usher in the television age, had been watching a lot and ruminating about how the service could be improved and had come up with an idea. Ross reported that Dunton had asked why couldn't we do a television equivalent of *LIFE* magazine? The idea had struck him as so perfect, so simple, Ross reported, that he had been uncharacteristically speechless; it was one of those "Of course" moments.

Dunton had told Ross that he would give all the support a chairman could give for the development of a television magazine, and that he would let the network program officials know that if they approved the project, they could count on the backing of head office. What would I call a show like that? Did I have any title ideas? A strong, popular title was essential, he thought. He wanted to do satire from time to time; had I seen some of the comic and satirical bits he was trying out on his daily interview series, *Tabloid*? He thought there wasn't nearly enough serious attention given to the human side of entertainers, including comics. What did I think about extreme close-ups in interview shooting? I must be tempted by them because he had noticed that in panel shows I tended to shoot more like a portrait than the accepted head-and-shoulders framing. Did my panellists ever complain that I was moving in too close on them? What did I think about the standard lighting arrangement where one side of the face was commonly lit at half the intensity of the other? Did I have any ideas about how we might link up several cities around the world and get discussions going with top experts, not by bringing them physically here, but electronically? It was an exhilarating, wide-ranging romp through a whole range of ideas that were always strongly linked to production issues, and to the way in which the program or the item was to affect the audience. This was very different from the brown paper bag lunch discussions on the floor of Gene Hallman's or Bernard Trotter's offices. They had focused on subject matter and social and political concerns; here was a guy who was thinking about cameras, lenses, sound, music, elegance of scripting, titles, framing, the physical stuff of which the program was ultimately made. And he was actually seeking opinions from me.

Then he asked a question I had not anticipated. He said that of course he would have to build a pretty substantial unit to produce this new program. Journalists would be attached to it full-time, experienced people who would produce items for the series either in the studio or in the field – he, Ross, couldn't do it all. He proposed to call these people story editors or item producers. (You had to be careful about throwing around the word "producer": the contracting people were scrupulous about the duties and rights attached to names.) There would also have to be a small corps of research assistants. Perhaps he would involve some freelance independent camera crews, especially for out-of-town documentary shooting. He would want a reasonable amount of original material from the United States and overseas. And he was going to need a number one, a first officer, someone to do a lot of the legwork, make contacts, write some scripts – come up with visual jokes – and, O wondrous, to direct for him from time to time, in the studio, so that he, Ross, could stand back and observe critically without being distracted by the athletics of waving your arms and calling, "Ready one. Take one. Two dolly in, pan slightly left. Good. Standby two," and being preoccupied with the moment to the point where you were distracted from the overall flow. He said he thought it was time the CBC reconsidered the idea of producers directing their own shows: it was asking too much. So he wondered if I would be interested in being that first officer, that number one? "I'd like you to think about coming on board as my co-producer."[11]

There was still a spring season to finish up, and I had already accepted a summer assignment, a travel show with a bit of dressy studio setting, perhaps a few feet of film, but mostly a vehicle for the authors of travel books to come in and do a lightly illustrated talk-to-camera version of their books. It was not onerous; I was one of three producers who would each take a couple of episodes.[12] A few editions of *Citizens' Forum* were still to be made, and probably some more joe jobs on *This Week* or *Country Calendar* for colleagues who called in sick or went on vacation. But by the time I came back from a brief holiday in the Lake District in the early summer, the magazine had its title, *Close-Up*;[13] the whole of the west end of the top floor had been dedicated to the new unit; Ron Krantz and George Ronald had been contracted as the story editors; there were two full-time research assistants,[14] two script assistants,[15] and a dedicated screening room. Nothing like that had happened before in CBC television: a whole *unit* dedicated to a single program series. We all thought we were pretty special.

11. We would say "line producer" now, perhaps. "Co-producer" now usually refers to a member of a partnership or consortium that is financially backing a production – usually a broadcaster. That is, if the CBC, BBC, and PBS all contribute money to a series that will run on all three networks, each of them will be referred to as a *co-producer* of that series.

12. My only really interesting one was based on the book *After You, Marco Polo* by Jean Bowie Shor and her husband, Franc, who had walked across Europe and the Middle East to the border of China to recreate the legendary travels of the famous Venetian.

13. Ross convened a discussion about whether to capitalize both words, and whether the hyphen looked okay. He scrutinized *everything*.

14. The late Lois Parkhill MacKenzie and Gail Hutchison.

15. Carol McIntyre and Patricia Clegg.

The next few years were an ongoing seminar with Ross as the prof, or perhaps it was a research establishment with a director and a team of juniors who moved from one lab to another, shared all kinds of work, and were called upon by the boss to be as inventive as possible and to take calculated risks. The management in those early years encouraged risk. New program ventures were not expected to be sure things; it was explicitly articulated by our supervisors that the only way to invent and discover was to take chances, and if things didn't work out and had to be cancelled, that was part of the cost of creating a new public service, opening up new territory, devising ways of bringing the world onto our viewers' screens in ways that had not yet been tried.

Ross McLean, however, had never failed at any of his television ventures. His casting choices – Elaine Grand on his early weekly series called *Living*, and the exceptional daily *Tabloid* group of Dick McDougall, Joyce Davidson, John O'Leary, and Percy Saltzman – set standards of hosting and interviewing. It was not just good luck and good judgment. Ross insisted that his performers regularly screen kines of their on-air work, in his presence, and be responsive to his brief and pointed notes. The *Tabloid* group, who went to air weekdays at 7:01 p.m., assembled every afternoon at 4:00 to screen the previous day's program. Often Ross would just say something like "See that? What you just did? That was great. See how well that worked?" Or "See what you're doing with your hands there? That's not very attractive, is it." I don't know of a producer at CBC or anywhere else today who so diligently guides and grooms the on-air people.[16]

For *Close-Up* Ross chose the veteran staff announcer J. Frank Willis (elder brother of the successful advertising personality and actor Austin Willis). In the spring of 1936 the neophyte Frank Willis had electrified Canada with his live reports from the Moose River Mine

16. In the early days of Toronto's CITY-TV, founder Moses Znaimer built his on-air group with a similar hands-on and detailed review of their work. He had a transforming effect on the style and tone of community-oriented commercial TV.

disaster, where his engineer used a wire fence for a transmitting antenna, and Willis sent out ninety-nine consecutive live reports, eventually picked up by nearly a thousand stations in Canada and the United States, as well as by the BBC.[17] Two and a half years later he broadcast live from the deck of the legendary schooner *Bluenose* during her last great race. He was a broadcasting legend, with a rich, slightly gravelly voice that was known across the country. But he had seldom been seen. Frank Willis, with his walrus moustache, deeply lined face, and intense eyes became another of Ross McLean's discoveries.

Close-Up was scheduled to make its debut on Sunday, October 6, 1957. I have no recollection of what we planned for the launch of what was about to be North America's first weekly television magazine program, because on the Friday of that week the Soviet Union launched the world's first orbiting satellite, *Sputnik I*, and it was clear that *Sputnik* would have to be the opener.

None of us got much sleep. We roused crews and journalists in London, Moscow, Washington, and New York, found someone with a telescope who could try for an image of the basketball-sized pioneer as it picked up the rays of the sun, and a radio operator who could tune into its beep (the news was away ahead of us with this, but we were trying everything we could think of). We found strategic experts to discuss the military and political implications and scientists to explain how the thing worked. When the weary team assembled in the control room of Studio One on Sunday night, to put the first episode of *Close-Up* to air, live to central Canada at 10 p.m.,[18] we had, in the space of less than three days, assembled what the press, audience mail, and CBC management all seemed to agree had been a breathtaking, globally comprehensive account of this extraordinary event.

There were no days off in those first few weeks. We would

17. A first for on-the-spot live reporting. The survivors were rescued on the eleventh day, and an exhausted Willis, who had slept at the site, reported live to the world as they emerged from the shaft. The broadcasting company was then known as the Canadian Radio Broadcasting Commission.

18. There was no videotape yet, so the network did not delay major programs. *Close-Up* for the first three years played at 11:30 p.m. in Newfoundland, 7 p.m. in B.C., and so on.

assemble for a story meeting on Monday morning at 10, Ross armed with any reviews from the morning papers. We planned interviews with major cultural figures, to be conducted by one of what Ross called his stable of interviewers: Pierre Berton, with whom I had worked on *Citizens' Forum* from time to time; Elaine Grand, who had moved to England and worked there with CBC news crews, and later with Allan King's film production unit. Charles Templeton, for years a prominent evangelist, had recently announced that he had lost his faith and become a critic of the evangelical movement (though still a friend of his mentor, Billy Graham). Ross McLean guessed that Templeton might prove a good interviewer, and indeed he did, contributing early on to a provocative investigative documentary on faith healing. Percy Saltzman would occasionally step across the hall, so to speak, from *Tabloid* to do an interview or a science feature. *Maclean's* magazine journalist Barbara Moon would contribute a number of pieces, and there were many more freelance journalists and entertainers.

Both Ross and I had been impressed with the work of a Southam Press correspondent in the Press Gallery in Ottawa, Douglas Leiterman, who appeared fairly often in the generally inoffensive regular appearances of politicians with a panel of reporters in the Ottawa series *Press Conference*. The majority of those reporters treated the senior politicians, especially cabinet ministers, with some deference. That was how you behaved with a minister of the Crown. Even the wise and knowledgeable *Maclean's* guru Blair Fraser, whose encyclopaedic memory and analytic mind made his questioning a delightful challenge to viewers and subjects both, would never come right out and label bullshit for what it was or squarely contradict a minister who lied or got it wrong. But Leiterman was different. In his quietly persistent way, he would seize on obfuscation or dishonesty like a ferret. "But minister," he would say, "last week you said the direct opposite; here is the quote. How do you account for the contradiction?" He was courteous but relentless. We had not seen that before. Ross had offered Blair Fraser a full-time story editor's position, and when

Fraser declined, Ross asked me what I thought of Leiterman. I was very positive. Ross said, "Let's get him." It turned out that Leiterman had just been told by Ross Munro, his editor at Southam, that they were pulling him out of the Press Gallery. He had been stringing for *TIME*, which offered to take him on as its Ottawa correspondent and offered him more money than the CBC could. But he had been doing some short parliamentary reports for CBC News as well as the *Press Conference* panels and was intrigued with the possibilities of the new medium. He joined the unit in November of that first year, and I took him to lunch the day he arrived. Here's his version of that lunch.

> *. . . you and I hunched over a tiny table in the crowded bistro at the Westbury – I had chicken soup – while you gave me a run-down on the mysteries of a tv studio and fired my imagination about how it could be used to engineer social change. After the lunch I thought, wow, if television is populated by people like this guy, smart, nuanced, intellectual, eclectic – heck, we can change the world. I'd earlier talked with Ross and was worried that he seemed more interested in celebrities than cerebral television. From you I got a different vector, and I was hooked.*

I recall that in one of our early conversations, when Ross was praising him for his doggedness in the *Press Conference* panels, Douglas told us that he had frequently been scolded by his Press Gallery colleagues, who warned him that if he kept on challenging ministers like that he would lose access.[19] He was undeterred, and a combination of determination, an uncanny sense for the visual drama in a story, and a fine eye at the viewfinder made him feel at home in television within weeks. We spent hours over lunches or sitting in the park talking about images, the virtues of lenses of different focal lengths, the possibilities of turning the massive, distracting cameras

19. Most of the senior Press Gallery journalists were associated with a party, even the best and most judicious of them. Arthur Blakely, who was with the *Toronto Telegram*, was of course a Tory. Even the luminous Blair Fraser was known to advise Louis St. Laurent and Lester Pearson privately, and so, as a Liberal, would have to be balanced, if cast in a panel, with a Blakely.

and sound recorders[20] into something discreet and genuinely portable. The first documentary film he made was called *The Road To Krestova*, an intimate, funny, and provocative look at the Doukhobor community in British Columbia. Douglas had been working in television some eight months when he directed *Krestova*, and it won the prestigious Ohio Award for television documentary.

Ross McLean was, as Leiterman had detected, interested in celebrities. He saw the Big Name both as a way of focusing audience attention on issues and as a source of strong biographical narrative. Sometime that season he began what became a staple of the series: a trip abroad for a crew and one or two interviewers to pick up several interviews in a day or two, with major international figures. Berton and Templeton helped line up that first basket of guests in New York, including the dying nuclear physicist Leo Szilard, who had worked on the bomb and was now an anti-nuclear activist. Also in that first group was the abrasive and popular CBS journalist Mike Wallace, whose aggressive style had set a standard for no-holds-barred television interviewing. The third interview would be with Vladimir Nabokov, whose novel *Lolita* was a new erotic sensation.

"You're going to New York with Pierre and Chuck," Ross said. "To direct." I became familiar with control rooms in New York and Washington, where we would lease facilities and crews from NBC or CBS. Once I engaged a small local station in North Carolina and did a live insert to the Sunday night broadcast with the ESP pioneer J.B. Rhine[21] out of his laboratories at Duke University.

Ross McLean had insisted from the start that building a big

20. The pioneering CBS journalist Edward R. Murrow called the TV documentary crews' equipment "the one-ton pencil." CBS and the other major American broadcasters were still shooting 35mm in those days, with something close to full movie crews. At least we were down to 16mm, although using bulky Auricon cameras and reel-to-reel 16mm magnetic tape sound recorders that were bigger than the cameras. All that would begin to change very soon, and Douglas Leiterman was one of the most diligent in pushing both the CBC film department and the much more responsive freelancers we worked with to find ways to bring down the bulk, the weight, the visibility, and the noise.

21. Professor Rhine invented the famous ESP cards, with their square, circle, triangle, star, and wavy lines, now used almost exclusively by magicians and other entertainers for tricks purporting to demonstrate mind reading or other forms of "extra sensory perception."

audience was not his primary concern, but rather to provide the biggest possible audience with television that would enrich their lives by lifting some meaning out of the chaos, take viewers beneath the gloss of celebrity to look for the human struggles and adventures within. Nonetheless, we were gratified when the early audience reports showed that we had substantial numbers, and the later ones showed those numbers growing. When we did an item on the dangers of smoking – a revelation, apparently, to a majority of our viewers – it was widely commented upon in the press, and – odd as it seems now – was a genuinely new use of the medium. When British Columbia's Minister of Highways, Phil Gagliardi, had his driving licence lifted for speeding, we sent Pierre Berton to do a playful interview at the edge of a highway near Salmon Arm. At the end of it, Berton presented the ex-minister with a bicycle, and Gagliardi accepted and rode off to a comical burst of music.

Newfoundlanders were canvassed on their feelings about being part of Canada, and most insisted that they were still Newfoundlanders ten years after joining the Confederation. Allan King sent us an absorbing documentary on the drunks and castaways of Vancouver's Skid Road. *Close-Up*'s broadcast of King's gritty, relentless portrait of a city's underbelly brought a whirlwind of letters and reviews and established King as one of Canada's finest directors. Satirical skits, sometimes performed by the versatile Frank Willis himself, poked fun at the CBC, among other subjects. There was a sensitive visual exploration of the portraits of Yousuf Karsh, an interview at the keyboard with an enthusiastic amateur pianist and rising film star named Christopher Plummer. McLean encouraged me to write and direct a complicated essay on the new discovery of DNA, for which I built in the studio a schematic model of a human cell that was big enough for Frank Willis to walk around in, pointing out the various elements, including the double helix.

The comic Shelley Berman, who invented the idea of extended sketches based on phone conversations with an unheard interlocutor, accepted Ross's brash invitation, came to Toronto, did one of his routines in the studio, and submitted to a live interview. Our interviews with entertainers were not puff pieces, but often probing inquiries into their lives and opinions.[22] Another celebrity initiative that did not work out was an attempt to get Oscar Peterson and Glenn Gould to play and be interviewed together. When Gould arrived in Ross's office to meet us and discuss the proposal, he held out his half-gloved hand aristocratically and as Ross reached to shake it said, with only a slight tone of mockery, "Careful!"

The poet Ezra Pound, who had been kept in a cage in public view in Pisa when American troops captured him there in 1945 (he had been making propaganda broadcasts for Mussolini), was by now incarcerated in St. Elizabeth's, an asylum in Washington. Ross suggested I try to arrange an interview. In the *Close-Up* section of the National Archives in Ottawa is Pound's genially terse reply to my letter: "Elementary my dear Watson: just get Grampa out of quad and we can talk turkey," and on the reverse a long tirade about the brilliance of Major Douglas, the nut who sold the theory of Social Credit to Bible Bill Aberhart, and the great benefits to the province of Alberta that flowed from its Social Credit Party.[23]

Elaine Grand sent a photographically brilliant if somewhat baffling filmed interview with the famously eccentric Dame Edith Sitwell, and a half-hour with Lord Bertrand Russell, which I still consider one of the finest television interviews ever and have often deployed as an artifact in lectures and workshops on the craft of the interview.

One day Pierre Berton, who was well-known for his love of the extravagant Yukon narrative verses of Robert W. Service, stuck his head in the door during a story meeting and said he'd just discovered that the legendary poet was alive and well and living in Monte Carlo; would Ross consider sending Pierre over? Ross said, Why not? And

22. It was Shelley Berman's first visit to Canada. Asked what he thought of a country that didn't even have its own flag he quipped, "Well, it's a start."

23. One of my few regrets in life is that I didn't think to keep that file when I left *Close-Up*. Roy Faibish used to scold me about that at least once every couple of years.

assigned me to talk to the travel department, engage a crew, and go to Europe with Pierre to produce and direct. Pierre arranged to meet me and my soundman at the Nice airport, where he had hired a tiny Citroen Deux-Chevaux for what proved a hilarious drive along the Haute Corniche to Monte Carlo, Pierre's long knees constantly interfering with the steering-column-mounted light switches, driving the oncoming motorists into horn-jamming rages as we careered along that dizzying road.

I brought a two-man crew from Canada and hired a second camera and a lighting electrician in Monte Carlo. We all turned up at the Service house, which clung to the side of a steep decline to the sea. Mme. Service graciously served coffee, and the old gentleman sparkled with delight at all this gear coming into his house and at the prospect of telling some stories on camera.

A few weeks later I remembered with poignancy the moment when Pierre reminded him of his age and asked if he felt any apprehension about dying. "Ach, no," Service said, his Scots origins still evident in the voice. "And by the way, wouldn't it be grand if I kicked off right here in front of the cameras during the interview? Wouldn't that make for good television?" We stayed with him for two or three hours a day for three days. When we wrapped, Mme. Service gave us champagne and petit-fours. I asked Service, as we sipped the champagne, if he had ever translated any of his works into French. Our faithful Monegasque crew had patiently worked for three days wondering what all the laughter was about, I said, and if he could do "The Cremation of Sam McGee" for them in French it would be a kindness. He said, Well, no, he hadn't translated anything, but maybe he could do it off the cuff. He went into a corner by himself and we could see him nodding and frowning, muttering away in French for a few minutes. Then he came back and sat down, and started in.

The Monegasque cameraman and electrician were wide-eyed as Service fluently spun out a French version of the grisly tale of the corpse on the sled and the hideous cold. And when the punch line came, one of them literally fell out of his chair laughing, as I ruefully looked at the cameras, all packed away in their cases, and said to myself, Why the hell wasn't I filming this?

Robert W. Service died only a few days before the interview was broadcast in September.

Our interview with Service made the Côte d'Azur seem an accessible and fertile fishing ground. That summer Ross dispatched Douglas Leiterman and Charles Templeton after the cultural greats of Europe and the U.K. on their Mediterranean vacation grounds. They came home with a full creel, including a spellbinding half-hour with the painfully stuttering W. Somerset Maugham, a wry and misanthropic Evelyn Waugh, and an almost incomprehensible but fascinating conversation[24] with Jean Cocteau. Allan King sent us a fine encounter with the then very frail Aldous Huxley.

I was able to persuade Ottawa to let me take a crew into Kingston Penitentiary and made what would be my first substantial documentary, and the first ever made inside a maximum security prison.

On October 23 of that year there was disastrous "bump" at Shaft No. 4 of the Springhill mines in Nova Scotia, and Ross dispatched me with a freelance cameraman, Robert Crone, to stay at the pithead until the survivors came up or were pronounced lost, and we came back with another strong documentary.

In an early and not very successful documentary project (on dialects in the Ottawa Valley), the Ottawa station's crews were all taken, so they sent me a young freelancer who had trained at Crawley Films and was a one-man operation. His name was Erik Durschmied, a brash Austrian with a rough sense of humour and enormous confidence behind the camera. We hit it off and agreed to work together again soon. It was an agreement that would lead to some groundbreaking adventures.

Within a few weeks of putting *Close-Up* on the air, other producers

24. Well, sort of a conversation; Douglas's French was not extensive and the eccentric author and filmmaker's English was pretty strange, but they patently were having a great time with each other, and of course we had the feeling of being in the presence of a legend.

had been stopping us in the corridors to say how much they loved it, and often to propose story ideas. But even in those early weeks, we were aware of some uneasiness on the part of the senior management, the first concrete indication that for some CBC officials the presence on the air of a popular and engaging controversial program was not entirely welcome. Charles Templeton had gone off to Sweden with a Toronto crew to look into the reputedly very tolerant attitudes toward sexual behaviour. The press discovered that the trip cost the CBC $12,000 (a vast, unheard of sum then) and scolded us for that, and management began to make some unpleasant noises. It soon got worse.

George Ronald reported in a story meeting that he had found a woman in Toronto who offered her services as a professional divorce co-respondent. In Canada at that time the only legal justification for divorce was adultery, and so consenting couples who wanted to dissolve a marriage occasionally faked an act of adultery – which had to be witnessed, of course, in order that disinterested testimony could be presented in court. The woman in question would, for a fee, agree to be in bed with the man in question when the private detectives allegedly working for the deceived wife would break into the hotel room or photograph the couple through the window, or otherwise produce evidence of the offence.

George Ronald filmed an interview with the woman, her face hidden in shadow. It made quite a sensation, and the *Toronto Telegram*, whose critic Bob Blackburn was generally admiring but whose editorial page often seemed out to discredit *Close-Up*, decided to prove the story was a fake. They found the woman, dubbed her The Shady Lady, identified her, and got her to say that she had lied to us. Then we discovered that they had paid her $2,000 to say so.

In the meantime, the then "field marshal" of the Ottawa vice-presidents, W.E.S. Briggs,[25] let it be known that he wanted Ross and me on the carpet in his office tomorrow morning to receive a personal dressing down. Our supervisor, Bernard Trotter, said tolerantly that

25. He had commanded the corvette *Orillia* in World War II, been awarded the D.S.C., and preferred being addressed as "Captain Briggs."

we had better go, not to be too upset, try to mollify the gruff old bureaucrat without acknowledging fault or committing to anything more than our already pretty high standards of authenticity and verification. We sat there for an hour while Briggs ranted and asked repeatedly, "Am I being understood?" We said that indeed he was, and, somewhat bruised, went back to work a little more cautiously.

I was fascinated with and almost close to Ross McLean, although few if any got really close. Jean Templeton, to whom he was briefly married, confessed to me shortly before her early death that she never had. Much later, Ross and I had a some very direct conversation, but for now it was the apprentice and the master, albeit a master who was very present, expansive, usually cordial, and generous with his time, and almost always either teaching or writing – even when he spoke. I mean that his speech was seldom spontaneous in the usual sense of that word; he thought before he spoke, almost always. Just as he dressed carefully, always shirt and tie and a suit or good-quality sports jacket, shoes polished, fingernails impeccable, so his utterances were not casual but dressed, planned, sometimes delayed for a few seconds as he visually shaped them. It was, he seemed to be declaring in his manner, better not to speak than to speak without any sign of wit, irony, or elegance. He usually cleared his throat before the first words. His left hand would sometimes restrainedly claw at the air as he sought a phrase, shaped a sentence, turned some words around so that something as simple as asking an assistant to bring coffee would become a linguistic event, a memorable utterance, if possible a joke. If he drank at all, it would be no more than half a glass of beer, or a few sips of wine, probably because he could not bear to be anything less than fully in control of his tongue. His insistence on careful structure had a strong influence on my writing, about which he was diligently and supportively critical, soon giving me the feeling that I was a real writer, a professional, capable of taking on any assignment he would throw at me, *capable of writing like Ross*, if I had to.

There was almost never anything about personal feelings in his discourse, although there was a constant flow of strongly felt evaluations of broadcasting, theatre, film, painting, that woman's clothes or this man's sense of humour, management's discourtesies and indifferences, a politician's rhetoric, a painter's brilliance or futility.

In those three *Close-Up* years when we at first shared an office and then, with our own offices side by side, were in and out of each other's space a dozen times a day, day after day, week after week, only once or twice did he say anything revealing of the person inside the armour and the mask. He was known to be dating the uncannily beautiful Joyce Davidson. When Joyce and I became close friends, she said of him, with an earthiness that was characteristic of her but would have much offended Ross, that he was "the only man in the world who never looks down when he pees." A fly on the wall at their dinner conversations would have been mesmerized by Joyce's flow of frank street talk and sharp social insights, set against Ross's measured, usually funny, and almost always ironic rejoinders and *pronunciamientos*, usually preceded by that careful clearing of the throat. One day after a discussion in my office about some issue or other related to the program, he seemed unusually hesitant about wrapping it up and getting back to his phone and his typewriter. He fidgeted in the corner for a while, tapped a pencil on the edge of the desk, looked at the ceiling, while I waited. Then he looked over, and away again as soon as he had spoken. He said, "Do you think I should ask Joyce to marry me?"

There was a second moment of vulnerability; I think it was over one of our frequent meals together. We had introduced a number of provocative American entertainers to our Canadian viewers. I had just had a call from a New York agent who said he was representing a brilliant comedian named Lenny Bruce, would we consider having him appear on *Close-Up*? We shouldn't pay any attention to what we might have heard about his dirty mouth and uncontrollability, he was a comic genius, far more interesting than that Shelley Berman guy – and it may have been at that same dinner that I reported all this to Ross and asked if he knew about Lenny Bruce and the reputation.

Then we got onto the subject of black entertainers. Would it be possible to get Duke Ellington for an interview? When would America grow up and give one of the great black musicians or actors a television show of his own? Or hers? Ross began to talk about Lena Horne, how she was so much more interesting than a dozen women who were prominent on television, what was the matter with them, the network bosses? He had produced a radio program with her in Vancouver, he said, seven years earlier, just before he came back to Toronto to work in television. After the program they had gone to a bar together, and sat side by side, and "There I was, sitting in a booth in a dark bar for two hours, with Lena Horne, holding hands."

My memory of the moment is clear; it was arresting. I remember the words, the unfamiliar wistfulness, the never-before-heard softness in the voice. Something close to tears in his eyes. After a pause I said, Well, hey! Why not phone her, invite her on the show, she'd come in a minute, that would be great.

And Ross McLean said, hesitantly, "I can't. She might not remember. I couldn't stand that."

There was one other moment of intimacy many years later. We had worked together for a few months on contract to Petro-Canada, preparing a sheaf of program proposals for them to consider sponsoring. They wanted Sunday night family entertainment that they could sell gasoline with. We hammered out proposals with ballpark budgets for at least twenty different kinds of series: dramas, hit parades, song and dance, an Ed Sullivan descendant. It was great fun sitting across the desk from each other banging away on a couple of Smith Corona Electric Portables (this is about 1983: pre-computer time). In the end the one they went for was *The Struggle for Democracy*, which did not answer their call at all but appealed to their bright, eccentric CEO, Bill Hopper. Ross and I read out the proposals, he first, then I, one after another, and were enthusiastically received, and that was our last practical collaboration.

Not long afterward he came to see me to say that he had been seriously out of work for a while. He had left the CBC after a wrenching alienation when management – who should have encouraged and rewarded his reaching out into wider fields as an executive producer – refused to let him continue the series of entertainment specials he had initiated and told him he would have to choose one series only and give up the rest. *Close-Up*, *Tabloid*, *Q for Quest*: which would it be; he could have one.

He had gone to the newly fledged CTV for a while, and then produced the successful, independent *Pierre Berton Interview*. Much later, when Douglas Leiterman and I wanted to bring him into the *Seven Days* unit to take charge of the comedy and entertainment features, we found that the CBC had blackballed him for his having left, and would not give him a contract. We wrote the contract in the name of his wife, Jean Templeton, and brought Ross in as a contraband producer. He re-established his credentials, took over that Sunday night slot after the death of *Seven Days* and Daryl Duke's one-year sequel called *Sunday*, and by the early seventies was program director of the Toronto station.

But now he was freelancing again and was worried about his finances. The Ryerson Institute of Technology had offered him a teaching job and he was deeply torn. He needed the money, but he always believed, he said, in the adage "Them what can does, and them what can't teaches." And he feared that if he accepted the job it meant he just couldn't cut it any more. "Patrick," he said, with evident grief, "I've lost my irony."

We talked for about an hour, and I told him how much I had enjoyed my teaching sessions at the CBC Training Centre in the years when a week or two's workshopping there was part of my contract for *The Watson Report*. I recounted the way in which I'd used Elaine Grand's Bertrand Russell interview from *Close-Up*. I remember thinking gratefully, that gloomy afternoon in our living room on Roxborough Street West, that now it was my turn to teach him something useful. I had the feeling that I turned him around, and, gratifyingly, about a year later he called to say he was having a fine time at Ryerson: would I come and speak to his second-year students, and I did that, and had a fine time myself.

And then he was dead. June 1, 1987. His heart just stopped. He was only sixty-two.

I was asked to speak about him at the ACTRA awards ceremony and to posthumously present to his brother Don an ACTRA Lifetime Achievement Award for Ross. I said that it felt very much like some of those early live broadcasts, when I would come down from the control room into the studio after we went off the air, to say thanks to the crew and the performers, and there was one guy who had really held the show together, and you wanted to get him in a corner and tell him that, but you were just too damn late because when you got there he had already left. My voice broke in the telling of it.

I quoted Ross again at the 2002 Gemini Awards ceremony when The Academy gave me (via the hands of Senator Laurier LaPierre) the Margaret Collyer Lifetime Award for writing for television. I said that I accepted the award in the name of my great mentor, Ross McLean, and that I thought in these days when the size of the audience and the economy of the budget were the only criteria most broadcasters seemed interested in, it might be useful each time we look at ourselves in the mirror and wonder if we really want to contribute to an industry dedicated to delivering to advertisers viewers whom we had stunned into passivity – useful to remember Ross's last question to a hopeful story editor (or co-producer) who was pitching an item in a story meeting. Because once you'd done the outline and guessed the budget and declared what and whom you'd need as crew and facilities, you had to answer that question satisfactorily or you didn't get to make the item. And that last question was "How will it *serve* the audience?"

Not "How will it *get* an audience?" but how will it *serve* them. That, my mentor taught us over and over again, by rhetoric and questioning and by example, was what a public broadcaster was meant to do. To serve. I will tell later how frustrating it was to try to get the management of the CBC to re-animate that motif during those dreadful years when I was chairman of the board.

All through the *Close-Up* years, Ross was still producing and directing *Tabloid*,[26] and pushing himself hard. He began to talk about looking for some more help at the producer/director level, and often asked me to take over *Tabloid* for a day or two, sometimes a whole week. Working with the *Tabloid* performers – Joyce Davidson, John O'Leary, and Percy Saltzman – was wonderfully convivial; they too took delight in trying things out. As I watched Davidson and Saltzman prepare and carry out their interview assignments, and then sit in the screening room with Ross (or with me, since Ross insisted that I do the follow-ups on the shows I produced), I learned the paramount lesson about interviewing: you must listen. Both those performers would study the notes and plan an interview carefully (although they seldom referred to their notes during the actual broadcast). But if they were assigned an interview at the last minute, with virtually nothing more than an introduction – "Sam Cranton is coming in at 7:15. He's running for Parliament in Digby West, and he has a new angle on the capital punishment issue" – they would dive right in with all the energy and engagement that accompanies genuine investigation and the asking of unrehearsed questions, especially questions that flow from what the guest has just said.

With five half-hours a week to fill, there was room to experiment quite a bit, and I began to slip out with a film cameraman and try some pure visual essays. When we learned that the last regularly scheduled steam locomotive would take its last run, I booked a cameraman and drove up to a locomotive graveyard near Barrie, Ontario, where we put together a wordless montage of the rusting, aging giants of the rails, with signs hanging on them saying BOILER EMPTY, birds nesting in the cabs, cinders still in the firebox. With the help of a talented cutter named Helga Faust, I edited it to a mournful music track – something like Samuel Barber's *Adagio for Strings* – ending with a pan from the decay of one of those colossal wrecks on to an adjacent active track, just as a brash young diesel loco came by, blasting its

26. The title was changed to 7:01, after a lawsuit in which a *tabloid* (!) newspaper charged the CBC with something like infringement of copyright. The CBC did not even fight this absurd suit.

electric horn. I was beginning to feel the joy and the beauty of the film image. By now the fact that I had been brought to the CBC to work in children's television was largely forgotten, although I still saw Fred Rainsberry from time, he very encouraging about what I was doing.

Daryl Duke, a former colleague from Ross's radio days in Vancouver, called from Los Angeles to say that topless dancing had become the new pop entertainment sensation and that he had persuaded a dancer named Carol Doda to film an interview in her dressing room; did we want it? It was a funny and innocent piece, but once more there was a rocket from Captain Briggs. Next, when Ross sent a film crew to the wedding of *Tabloid* announcer/interviewer Gil Christy, another vice-president, Bud Walker, declared incomprehensibly that this was the most tasteless thing that had ever been shown on television.

Those guys at head office. They did not consult; they pronounced. With the exception of the soft-spoken, always civil chairman, Davidson Dunton, they never came to see what we were doing, never sat down with producers for a chat about values and ambitions and what television was doing to the consciousness of the country (subjects that we were all speculating on). Our contacts in the Press Gallery told us that senior CBC officials were frequently seen drinking lunch with cabinet ministers and high-ranking bureaucrats at the Rideau Club, which was then just across from Parliament Hill. We felt, I think rightly, that a lot of the critical blasts we were getting from our leaders had their origins in those lunches, where an irritated call from a constituent would be relayed from MP to minister and thence to a friendly CBC vice-president.

In the spring of 1959 that Rideau Club connection led to the only serious incident of government interference with CBC programming that I am aware of in my sixty years of broadcasting and nearly fifty of TV. It was a radio program that did it.

The television producers formed a producers' association, I think in 1957 or '58. The founding president was Murray Chercover, a producer in the Light Entertainment department who soon became the founding president of CTV. I was made president of the association some time early in 1959. There was at that time a three-minute morning supplement to the morning radio news, a short daily talk called *Preview Commentary.* The prime minister hated *Preview Commentary.* The bloom had faded from Mr. Diefenbaker's rose as soon as he won his second election, a year after the first, and turned a minority government into one of the biggest and most unassailable majorities Ottawa had ever seen. Although the media exaggerate the importance of electoral politics, there are few more unhealthy developments in that small part of the Canadian democratic system than an unchallenged majority in the House of Commons. The journalists, having given the upstart his honeymoon (and a prolonged one at that), now began to play their part in telling truth to power, and challenging it, a role that becomes especially necessary when there is no effective opposition in the House.

Prime Minister Diefenbaker, something of a romantic to say the least, was at first shocked and soon resentful. They had all been so *nice* to him in that first heady year when the PCs had at last turfed out the Grits. Now the media were shooting at him from all sides, and what really rankled was that, adjacent to the CBC morning radio news – which absolutely everyone in Ottawa listened to, as well as a substantial audience of decision-makers across the country – was this three minutes in which a broad range of journalists, mostly from the Parliamentary Press Gallery, would come one at a time to give their take on the current state of the country.

Dief was outraged at the irreverence he was hearing on *Preview Commentary.* All those years when he'd been what journalist Patrick Nicholson called the lone wolf in the opposition, he had built a warm and trusting relationship with reporters; some said it was like nothing that had ever existed before. But when he began, as Nicholson said, "to walk on the water," the relationship changed. He would call reporters into his office and give them hell. The Gallery was accustomed to the long years of dignified silence from criticized Liberal ministers, and Dief's arrogance just made things worse.

The CBC was not popular in Parliament just then. The television producers at Radio-Canada, with the eloquent support of the tremendously popular on-camera essayist René Lévesque,[27] had gone on strike, and the strike had long outlasted Parliament's tolerance. Scarcely had that conflict been settled when a Radio-Canada drama marking the beatification of Marguerite d'Youville (the founder of the Grey Nuns) turned out to be a sexy drama with some wild scenes of the racy way the saint's husband had carried on in the early years of their marriage.

In that atmosphere any prime minister would have felt he was on safe ground to take a whack at the Corporation. While some of what follows is speculation, and the ministers and bureaucrats involved mostly denied that anyone had ever influenced anyone else, it is clear that Dief spoke to his Minister of National Revenue, George Nowlan, the minister through whom the CBC reported to Parliament. It was a bit like Thomas à Beckett and the "Who will rid me of this meddlesome priest!" story. Dief said something like "Don't they know who's paying their damn salaries? Get that abomination off the air!" George Nowlan's favourite contact at the CBC was not the impeccably correct chairman, Davidson Dunton, who in any case had left to become president of Carleton University a year earlier, but the acting chairman, Ernest Bushnell, a chubby, warm-hearted man who liked to lunch up the street at the Rideau Club, often with his pal George Nowlan. Nowlan called Bushnell, Bushnell said, Of course; nothing simpler, and decreed the cancellation of *Preview Commentary*, on June 22, 1959. There had been no consultation with the programmers.

We learned about it the next day from Frank Peers. On the twenty-

27. *Point de Mire* ("gunsight," or "aim" with a gun), Lévesque's weekly talk to camera, using a blackboard and chalk but mostly just talking, without script, was a model of natural television communication and played a role in generating what came to be known as the Quiet Revolution. A former war correspondent, Lévesque would nationalize Quebec Hydro when he was a minister in the provincial Liberal government. Then he became founding leader of the Parti Québécois, took it to victory in the provincial elections in 1976, had a great street named for him, and left a trail of puzzlement, admiration, and affection even among those who disliked his separatism. The Montreal producers, unlike the Toronto group, were a certified bargaining unit.

third of June he called the whole department together to tell us that he was going up to Ottawa to personally submit his resignation, carrying the signed resignations of his three top programming officers. He said that this was the only time that there had been any political interference with programming at the CBC, and that it had to be challenged. He acknowledged the loyalty of the producers and other program makers and urged us to keep the service going. He said he knew us well enough to expect that many of us would be inclined to resign as well, but that it was more important to keep the programs coming; his resignation would let head office and the cabinet know that a line had been crossed.

But Ernie Bushnell denied to the CBC board that there had been any directive from The Hill; the decision had been entirely his own, he told them, and the directors supported his cancellation of the program. Even without political interference, a president's cancellation of a program arbitrarily – no discussion with the responsible program people – would have been intolerable, but Frank Peers had told the troops that he was in no doubt about where the orders had come from. Within twenty-four hours I and about thirty others had submitted written resignations. They were not conditional, not a threat to resign, they were resignations, period. We were declaring that we would not work for a CBC that bowed to political pressure. I remember wondering how the hell I was going to earn a living.

Within a day or two the CBC board heard from another senior official that Bushnell had said in a conference call that he had indeed been talking to the minister, and had been told that "heads would roll" unless something was done about *Preview Commentary.* "Heads will roll" became a catch phrase in the press, and at this point the CBC board of directors regrouped, refused to accept any of our resignations, ordered the program reinstated, told Ernest Bushnell he no longer had their confidence, and instructed him to step down.

Nowlan and Diefenbaker lied and said there had been no interference, but Dief relieved Nowlan of his responsibilities as minister through whom, and before long changed the top management of the

CBC as well, appointing general manager Alphonse Ouimet as president and chairman. He also started work on the creation of an independent broadcast regulatory body, which would become the BBG: the Board of Broadcast Governors. (The CBC had been, till then, not only the national public broadcaster but also the licensing body[28] and the regulations policing agency.) (Which was, of course, outrageous and long overdue for a change.)

The work on *Close-Up* continued to be stimulating and rewarding, before and after the *Preview Commentary* affair. The series had become the premier television journal of current events. While the BBC's pioneering *Panorama* had established the magazine format, and very much influenced us, nothing like *Close-Up* had been seen in North America. Ross McLean's playful and critical mind was giving the series a distinctive edge and a yeasty sense of unpredictability. At the same time, we were often far ahead on major national and international issues, and so present on screens across the nation that access to major national figures was becoming easier all the time: *Close-Up* was a place to be seen, if you were in the public eye. When we proposed, in the fall of 1958, to originate the program live from the living room of the prime minister's residence at 24 Sussex Drive, the reply from the Diefenbaker office was rapid and positive. Events on an island a thousand miles away, as it turned out, impinged on that live broadcast in a logistical way.

In the early summer of 1958 I got a call from my cameraman friend in Ottawa, Erik Durschmied. Just on the chance that it might produce something, he had contacted an American photographer, Andrew St. George, because St. George had recently got himself into the camp of Fidel Castro, who was then waging his guerrilla war against the dictatorship of Fulgencio Batista in Cuba's Oriente Province.

28. Which meant that if you wanted to start a commercial radio or television station, you had to ask permission of the public broadcaster, who would also be your major competitor. No wonder the independents sometimes hated the CBC.

Erik's call was a lucky hit. St. George (who, years later, turned out to be working for the CIA – and probably used Durschmied for a cover) said he thought he could arrange a contact and that Castro might sufficiently trust a Canadian that he would allow a camera into the rebel camp in the Sierra Maestra. Would I, asked Durschmied, buy his footage for *Close-Up* if he pulled it off. I did not even consult my chief. I gave Erik my blessing, and off he went without even asking for an advance. He warned me that there would be little if any communication once he made it to Cuba. A few days later, he called from Florida. "I'm in," he said, not much more. And then for a couple of months there was silence.

Two months later he called again. He was safely back in Florida. He reported that he had been forced to leave in a hurry – Batista's secret police were on to him and he had barely made it safely out of Havana – but the film was being flown over in one of Castro's secret supply shuttles, and it was "sensational." He said he had welded a secret compartment into the back of his old Volkswagen to conceal his camera and had gone over to Cuba with the VW by boat. Against all advice, he had driven down the Carretara Central, past the sites of guerrilla engagements where there were still smoking wrecks of army trucks, to Santiago de Cuba in Oriente Province. He had met his contact after a few alarming delays and small misadventures, and then gone on foot up into the Sierra Maestra, where he had spent several weeks with Castro and his people, gone on a couple of raids and filmed them, and had interviews with Fidel, his brother Raul, and Fidel's lover and adviser, Celia Sanchez. Rather than risk Erik's taking the film back with him, which could have led to a firing squad had Batista's forces caught him, it was decided that Castro's people would airship the film to Florida, and Dursch headed back up the Carretera Central. On the way he was caught and, briefly, did face a Batista *soldateska* firing squad who (ironically) let him go because they thought he was an American and they had been instructed to do nothing to alienate Americans. Back in Havana in his hotel room, he'd received a warning phone call that the secret police were coming up the elevator. He had gone out the fire escape, had made it to the docks and onto a ferry that was just leaving, and had had to abandon the car and his camera. He would call as soon as he had the film in his hands and bring it to Toronto and we could get to work.

Weeks went by, and no film. Erik was still in Florida, and his phone calls sounded more and more despondent. He had tried every way he knew to find out where the film was, had met secretly several times with rebel representatives in Miami. I could tell from his voice that he thought he would never see that film. He was running out of money: could I send him a few bucks? I did. It was about the first of December when he called to say he had given up, there was no more intelligence coming out of Oriente Province, he guessed that either Batista's people had intercepted the shipment or it had been lost or forgotten about. After all, what was a few feet of film to a guerrilla force who felt they were on the verge of winning a revolutionary war? He couldn't blame them. He was coming home in defeat.

But only a few hours later, the phone rang again, and a jubilant Durschmied said that one of his guerrilla pals had just phoned from Mexico City, they had flown the film in there on a supply run only days after Erik had left Cuba, there had been a misunderstanding, it was still there, he, Erik, was on his way to pick it up.

As soon as we got it processed and screened it, I knew we had a superb documentary. In the meantime it was reported that Castro was fighting his way successfully up the spine of the island, the Batista forces were falling back, Castro could be in Havana by Christmas. We got to work in the cutting room. By Christmas day the film was just about finished, and the forecast now was that Havana would be in rebel hands before the New Year.

And we were originating from the prime minister's residence on New Year's Eve. The night Castro walked into Havana we dispatched Bob Crone and his wife, Vi, to film in the liberated city, hoping for a live feed out of the capital late on New Year's Day, when were scheduled to go to air with Erik's documentary. Ross chartered a Beech

Expediter to take him, me, and Charles Templeton to Ottawa for the New Year's Eve broadcast and back the same night.

The Sussex Drive program went off without a hitch. Dief was pompous, of course, but gracious and amiable. Templeton was in good form. It was the first time that the Canadian audience had seen live television from inside the residence. We were on the air at 10 p.m., off at 10:30 and airborne back to Toronto, where the final editing touches had been done on Erik's film. Bob Crone had managed to airship a few additional scenes of the rejoicing in Havana and the invasion of the presidential palace. We went on the air the following night, New Year's Day. A reporter was standing by in Havana to give us a few words live from the streets, which we used as part of the introduction to the broadcast and then cut to Erik's memorable footage, which is still being seen around the world in retrospectives of the Cuban revolution. The broadcast was a coup for *Close-Up*; it made Erik Durschmied's reputation and started him on what would be a spectacular career as a fearless and artistic shooter in the world's hot spots from Suez to Saigon. We became close friends, went to Havana together a year later to make a film on Castro's first year, and meet the man himself, and five years after that we were in China.

Late in 1959 the CBC acquired its first videotape machines. Now you could record a program whenever you wanted, and when you broadcast it later, unlike the faded and grainy kines, the taped broadcast was indistinguishable from the live. Videotaped interviews added a visual vigour and a new level of convenience when it came to grabbing, say, a visiting celebrity. You didn't have to book a film crew; there was always some spare studio time somewhere, so you could bring the guest in with relatively little notice, record the interview, and put it on the air looking as if the guest were there with you live in the studio.

However, there was no portable videotape. The recording machines were the size of a dining room buffet, the reels about fourteen inches in diameter and the tape itself two inches wide. So a one-hour reel of tape weighed about twenty pounds and took a great deal of shelf space. There was no way to edit the stuff, but that magical capacity to broadcast recorded programs that had all the sparkle of the live signal was a delight. Even without editing, videotape made possible the recording of dramas in segments of, say, twelve or fifteen minutes – acts – and then, for broadcast, played back from separate machines, or paused during a commercial and resumed afterwards, still looking like the real thing (I mean, live).

Then one weekend Douglas Leiterman and I went to the United Nations to do an interview with the Indian delegate to the United Nations, Krishna Menon, and discovered that the UN had its own videotape studio, which was available to broadcasters, and even better that CBS had opened a videotape editing facility that we could rent.

Douglas did the interview and I directed, in the UN studio, at around 8 p.m. Menon was icily cool and distressingly impressive as he argued that India ought to follow the Soviet model. We took the big reel down to the CBS facility deep in the bowels of Grand Central Station. The technician warned us that the editing process was still primitive and took a lot longer than editing film; he showed us the technique.

Mounted on the buffet-sized recorder was a flat panel about fouteen inches long, with a shallow trough along which the tape would slide after it passed by the recording heads. Four recording heads were set at 90 degree intervals on the edge of a disk that rotated at precisely 480 revolutions per minute, so that the heads passed *across* the surface of the tape, tracking it.

The slightly bowed lines running across the tape contained the raster, the picture information. The small tics at the bottom of the tape, positioned at every fourth raster line, were the synchronization pulses, keyed to the 60 cycle AC current, which kept the picture stable. On that flat panel were clamps to hold the tape firmly in place and a microscope focused on the surface of the tape. As you screened and identified a cutting point, the technician would stop the tape as close as possible to that point, refining his choice by listening to the slowed-down sound as he moved the tape back and forth by hand-cranking the reels, and then sprinkle on a little Freon[29] in which were suspended microscopic iron filings. The Freon evaporated almost instantly, leaving a faint pattern of iron filing dust that clung to the magnetically recorded tracks. The technician had to make his cut with a razor blade running through a slotted frame positioned over the clamped tape and note exactly where the sync pulse was in relation to the cut – one, two, or three transverse lines away from it. Then when he made the next cut, the sync pulse had to be in the corresponding position, so that after he had stuck the two ends of the cut tape together with a kind of super Scotch Tape, there would still be exactly four raster lines between sync pulses. If he was a fraction of a millimetre off, the picture would go out of sync at the splice, and roll distractingly in the frame until sync was restored, and so of course you had to try again.

But! When the splice worked, because the VTR image looked exactly like the real live thing, you had achieved the magical effect of an edit that did not look like an edit. That miracle was worth the labour. We stayed in that subterranean editing suite from ten at night till five o'clock in the morning. During that time we made the grand total of *five*, count 'em, *five* successful edits (and God knows how many that rolled and had to be discarded). But we thought we were right on the cutting edge of technology. What wonders! And the interview looked as though it were happening live.

Within a year we would be doing electronic editing, another apparent miracle, but delightful as that latter achievement was, there is nothing in my memory of technological advances that has quite the tingle of those five hours that night in the basement of Grand Central Station.

Ross McLean admired Edward R. Murrow's *Person to Person*,[30] where Murrow, from a CBS studio, interviewed celebrities and genuinely significant people who were captured by a remote unit in their

29. The volatile liquid used in refrigerators.

30. The program ran from 1953 to 1959. Among those interviewed were Marilyn Monroe on the back porch of the family home, John Steinbeck, and Harry Truman.

homes, the two locations networked together. The CBC did a similar series for a couple of years, hosted by the warden of the University of Toronto's Hart House, Joe McCully (I directed a couple of episodes). Now Ross wanted to try linking up a number of distinguished figures in different parts of the globe for a discussion of the state of the world's economy and offered me the challenge of figuring out how to do it. I huddled with a soft-spoken and courteous technical producer named Peter Taylor, and together we figured out a way to have Kenneth Galbraith in his study in Boston, Barbara Ward Jackson in her home in Sydney, Australia, and another person in London whom I have forgotten, in a discussion hosted by Percy Saltzman from our Studio One in Toronto.

Since videotape standards varied in different parts of the world, and a live hookup was not feasible in the pre-satellite era, we chose to go with film. It would be running at twenty-five frames a second in the U.K. and Australia, and twenty-four frames in Canada and the U.S., but that slight discrepancy we could handle; you can let film go a couple of frames out of sync before it's bothersome to watch, so we had about a four-frame cushion and could snip out the odd frame here and there and cut away to listening panellists from time to time. The locations were linked to the Toronto studio by a regular telephone line, so that everyone could hear everyone else, while the actual recording of the sound for broadcast was done on magnetic tape at each location.

When we were ready to start, I instructed the directors in each location to slate their films, one at a time, and then when the films were shipped to us in Toronto we could synchronize from those slate marks. It worked almost without a hitch, though Galbraith said to Jackson at one point, "I lost that, Barbara. I think you faded out somewhere over the Hawaiian islands." Whether or not the discussion was very interesting, there was great excitement about the technical achievement.

Travel to Cuba was still a casual matter. Ross suggested a follow-up to Erik Durschmied's Castro scoop of the year before, so in

December of 1959 Erik and I took interviewer Tom Hill with us to Havana and set out in search of the elusive Castro. He was known to have a number of favourite nightspots, some of them the kitchens of the city's major hotels, and we canvassed them regularly, while taking excursions to the sugar fields and putting together a modest portrait of the country under its revolutionary regime. At that time Castro was still trying to win the political and economic support of the West, and the Havana Hilton, when we arrived, plastered our bags with stickers declaring, "OUR REVOLUTION IS HUMANIST, NOT COMMUNIST." Two or three nights after we arrived, it was announced that Castro might show up at the annual general meeting of the Sugar Workers' Union. We just walked in with the hand-held Arriflex camera and a portable Nagra (then hand-wound like an old Victrola, and not exactly a sync sound recorder). Nobody asked for credentials –we went right up onto the wings of the stage, fairly close to the three armed guards who patrolled each side of the proscenium arch, and took a few shots of the crowd and the three rows of tables, on the stage, full of uniformed officials.

Castro arrived to sustained applause and took his seat at the centre table, where various bearded and uniformed men came to pay their respects. Erik said, "Roll sound when I get to the table," went into a crouch with the camera to his eye as if he were rolling, and duck-walked along the stage wing, almost brushing the guards aside as he came to them, and the guards demonstrating the power of the camera by letting him do so, out onto the stage, to the centre, still in the duck-walk crouch, until he was directly in front of Fidel, the lens at table-top level. Nobody paid much attention; they acted as if this were perfectly normal. At that point, Erik stood up suddenly, put the camera on the table, leaned across the table, stuck out his hand to the surprised dictator, who took and shook it, and then recognized Erik, stood up, grinned, leaned over, and embraced him.

When he sauntered back to the stage right wing where I was waiting, the armed guards were deferential.

"He says he'll be in the kitchen of the Hilton around 2 a.m.," Erik said. We filmed part of the interminable speech, went off to dinner and a nap, and then went looking for Fidel shortly after midnight.

I think it was not the Hilton where we found him, but another hotel. Erik introduced us, and Castro shook hands politely but declined to be interviewed. "Not now," he said. We kept on filming our portrait of the island under its new rulers. There were still many dissidents in Havana, who were uninhibited in expressing their distrust of the new regime, but hundreds of workers and street folks who were in favour. In a few days we felt we had something that would stand up well, the dictator's absence regrettable but not hugely so, and headed home to edit a documentary for *Close-Up*, "Castro's First Year," which Ross scheduled for early January. It had been a rewarding expedition; Erik and I worked well together and started to speculate about where next.

In the meantime, Douglas Leiterman and I spent a lot of time talking about lighting, lenses, the virtues of shooting hand-held or from the tripod. He now thought of himself as a documentary producer/director more than a journalist. We imagined what *we* would do if we had a magazine show all to ourselves. "We must find ways to make non-fiction more attractive to audiences," Douglas said. "After all, real life is more interesting in the end than fairy tales. *Bonanza* is a fairy tale. It's a very good fairy tale, but it doesn't touch real lives. We have to find a way to tell real stories as well as they tell the fairy tales."

I was still assigned to produce and direct other programs, and from time to time Ross, relentlessly on the lookout for ways to help people grow in the craft, would agree that *Close-Up* could do without me for a while, and that I might benefit from the challenge of something different. Arnold Edinborough, the editor of the Kingston *Whig-Standard*, wrote a dramatic script about military politicians, and asked for me to produce it. It was based on the recent history of de Gaulle and the Algerian crisis, and the stories of a couple of South American military regimes. I took over Studio Four, where I had occasionally gone to watch Norman Jewison directing the goofy and delightful *Alex Barris Show*, and spent probably two weeks away from the Public Affairs world, playing with sets and having a great time directing Edinborough and half a dozen gifted but unknown actors.

In retrospect it now seems improbable that Beverly's and my marriage would have survived those last years of our twenties had I stayed in the publishing business. Those first five years of trying to accommodate each other's very different personalities and needs had been hard work. We both were part of a culture in which divorce, while not forbidden, was seen as a failure of such magnitude that the old Methodist/Presbyterian matrix, even in our secular environment, made it hard to contemplate. But we had begun to talk about it: could we really keep going?

The arrival of our son Chris, in the spring of 1953, had at first given us a kind of reprieve, both of us dizzily in love with the energetic, lovely, imaginative little blond person. We took him off to Ann Arbor with us for the two summers of my doctoral studies, and his flowering personhood became a mediating force between us, the source of a great deal of agreement. But my frustration at the sense of confinement at W.J. Gage deepened my restlessness at home.

Like other couples in trouble, we told each other that a second child might help, and when I made the decision to leave W.J. Gage for the CBC, son number two, Gregory, was already on the way. And then the adventure of television was energizing; it kept bespeaking possibilities. That work and its rewards may have been a cushion. Gregory's arrival was, in fact, a strengthening of the partnership, and when daughter Andrea turned up less than a year later, we were soon spellbound by the overheard conversations between those two inventive storytellers, who shared a room for their first three years. We would keep on working at it, we said. When Andrea was ten months old, we spent much of that summer with Charles Templeton at his beach house on Georgian Bay, and it was there that Gregory gave Andrea the name that stuck: Boo.

Some time in that spring of 1960 Peter Meggs phoned from

Ottawa. Meggs and a senior radio producer named Doug Ward would later bring about the single most radical change in the CBC since the arrival of television. Assigned by senior management to study in depth the effects of television on the radio service and its audience, they had persuasively argued that the revenue produced from advertising on radio was now sufficiently small that it would be an appropriate move to eliminate advertising from the radio service, allow the commercial broadcasters to use that revenue, which they needed and the CBC really did not, and finally transform the radio service into a genuine public broadcaster.

But in the spring of 1960, Meggs was appointed regional director in Ottawa. His senior Public Affairs television producer, Michael Hind-Smith,[31] was leaving to go to CTV; would I be interested in taking over that chair? He said that both he and head office felt it was time to develop a reasonably well-budgeted national affairs series originating in the capital, and that would be my assignment if I wanted the job. I would also be in charge of the free-time political telecasts and the production of national affairs and political specials such as the forthcoming Liberal Party rally planned for the spring of 1961. Meggs promised that I would have a voice in planning both CBOT's local public affairs programming and its proposals to the network.

The salary would be $12,000 a year, and I would be expected to make the move at the end of the summer. It was attractive in every way. Even leaving *Close-Up* would be compensated for by having my own project to develop. I consulted Douglas Leiterman first. He was unequivocally encouraging. He was about to start a regular documentary series on his own, called *Document*, and he suggested that a few years on our own, keeping in close touch and unreservedly criticizing each other's work, would be a good preparation for the collaboration we'd been talking about. Ross McLean was characteristically encouraging about my Ottawa assignment. He seemed to take genuine satisfaction in his protégé's being offered a prestigious perch of his own.

31. Ross McLean called him "Michael Hyphen Smith."

Beverly agreed to undertake the arrangements for the move, and Meggs said that we could take a good long summer vacation and I could report on September 1, 1960.

I had a summer project. It would turn out to be one that delayed my move to Ottawa and transformed my life.

Chapter 8

INQUI'RY

FOR THE FIRST FEW MONTHS at CBC TV, I shared an office on the second floor with Gordon Babineau and Ted Pope. Babineau was an older man (all of thirty-nine), quiet and reserved. But Pope was a romantic, thoughtful, intense guy with whom I often went to lunch to throw around ideas about production and writing and television's potential as an instrument of social change. Ted had studied architecture at McGill. In the summer of 1951, Buckminster Fuller had been a guest lecturer there. Lecturer is probably not very accurate; what Fuller did was teach Pope and his fellow students the principles of geodesic construction by building a dome with them, a structure that stood for years near Morin Heights at the edge of the Ottawa-Montreal highway, serving as a hay barn.

Ted Pope had been enchanted by the brilliant, playful, and affectionate inventor and became converted to the geodesic faith. He had engaged Bucky to come to Toronto that summer of 1957 to make a substantial studio production about his work, *The Dymaxion World of Buckminster Fuller.* Ted had intrigued me with his stories about Fuller and invited me to come to the studio as much as I wanted to during production. It was to be recorded for later broadcast. The studio was full of Fuller inventions, including part of a good-size dome and a mock-up of the revolutionary 1933 Dymaxion Car, which was decades ahead of its time and had so terrified the big auto makers that they may have crushed it.[1]

The evening after the recording was finished, Ted Pope's studio director, Alwyn Scott, gave a party for Fuller and the crew in his apartment on the edge of what is now Lawren Harris Park on Rosedale Valley Road, and invited me. Fuller brought a couple of boxes of slides and a projector – this was not uncommon, I learned – and spent part of the evening giving the party guests an intriguing lecture on his career as an inventor. The lecture included a presentation of the geometry of the geodesic dome and a persuasive argument for the efficiency and economy of its construction. That same night I decided I must build one.

I fooled around with sketches and models for a while, trying to calculate the lengths of the different struts. The modest dome that I was planning would subdivide each triangle of the basic icosahedron[2] from which the geodesic is derived into sixteen smaller ones, and require five different lengths of strut (although so close in length that to the casual eye they appear equal). My younger brother, Roger, a geophysical engineer, came to my rescue with his spherical trigonometry and generated a table of the functions of the radius that would give me those five strut lengths. I built a balsa wood model almost a metre in diameter, and skinned part of it, leaving enough open triangles to allow me to reach inside and experiment with the placing of inner walls and furniture.

Beverly, the children, and I had moved into a compact two-storey, three-bedroom brick house at 217 Douglas Avenue, near Lawrence and Avenue Road. The mortgage was a challenge to my $7,500 annual salary, but there were no more long daily commutes from the suburbs: I could go to work on the then new subway. There

1. The car was involved in a fatal accident. When the Chicago press began to call it the Freak Car, Fuller's investors pulled back, but he told me that he was convinced Ford and GM had got to those investors.

2. The icosahedron is the most complex solid that can be enclosed by equilateral triangles, twenty of them. Each vertex is on the surface of a virtual sphere, and the more you subdivide those triangles, pushing each new vertex out to the surface of that virtual sphere, the closer you approach real (or apparent) sphericality: that is the principle of the geodesic structure.

was a workshop in the basement. The next step in the dome adventure would be to use that workshop to build a small two-frequency dome (the icosahedron's equilateral triangles broken down into four instead of sixteen smaller triangles). This would be a way to test some of the construction ideas by building what would become a miniature sleeping cabin for the kids and later a tool shed. It was eight feet in diameter, four feet high. Constructing the joints proved difficult; so did the waterproofing, but on the whole it worked out well.

Now we had to find a place to build. My mother and I explored some cottage country together in the fall of 1959, and on the road to Parry Sound, just under two hundred kilometres from Toronto, our eye was caught by the sign for Go Home Lake Road. A cruise around the shoreline in Reg Potter's eighteen-foot home-built pine square-bowed outboard sold us immediately. A week later Beverly and I went back with a rented outboard on a trailer and walked dozens of lots on the then newly opened lake, only a hundred or so already sold and developed. We chose two to bid on: sealed bids. My mother offered to help (we didn't have even a hundred dollars to risk), and we decided that while $1,000 was our reasonable limit, lots of others would bid exactly that; so we'd go in at $1,100. At the last minute we whimsically raised that to $1,111 and in February learned that we had beaten our nearest competitor by exactly that eleven dollars.

The lot is an acre and a half, with a small whaleback of red, rounded granite pushing out northwesterly toward the spreading waterfall half a mile away that feeds the lake from the Musquash[3] River. The rock on the lot climbs steeply thirty feet or so behind the one useful building site, and the water is deep enough all around the red granite point to dive safely into what was then the dark, perfectly clear, weedless water of a classic lake on the edge of the Precambrian Shield. Although there were adjacent cottages to the west and the south of our northeast "corner" of the island, they were hidden by rock and trees, and the closest visible neighbour would be

3. Or Muskoka.

on another island, half a mile north, where my mother was going to build.

I disassembled the Little Dome and put it in the back of a borrowed Chevrolet for our first trip into the lake in April. I bought some two-by-twelves and plywood flooring from Joe Bolyea, who had been on the lake long before it opened and was offering some goods and services to the invading cottagers. I drew up some plans, bought a tent to live in till the dome was up, and started to build, largely by myself.

My plans had intrigued both my brother Roger and Douglas Leiterman, who also successfully bid for lots on Go Home Lake. They both started to build domes based on the same math and the same general construction approach, which we were making up as we went along. We found a lumberyard that would precision-cut the struts, with angled rabbets along the two outer edges to receive the plywood skin, and another dealer who would precision-cut the required 150 plywood triangles[4] for the skin. In a garden show somewhere Douglas Leiterman found steel cups that would bolt together at the joints to hold the struts where they came together at each vertex. These cups had been designed for a garden shed not unlike my Little Dome, and we naively thought they would be strong enough for a full-size dome.

The three hundred struts (including some extras in case of breakage) all came up to the lake in the trunk of that same borrowed Chevy in one trip. The triangles for the skin were delivered by truck and were waiting for us one weekend, stacked in gleaming mahogany piles on the Government Dock. The total cost for materials, tools, fasteners, and glue, plus a tiny moulded plywood boat with a very old 10-horsepower Johnson outboard, was less than $2,000.

Many weekends during that spring I drove to the lake in our Volkswagen Beetle on my own or with a friend, staying in an old tent acquired at the Army Surplus store. The rain-sodden spring usually discouraged Beverly from bringing the kids. I worked away, rain or shine. Ted Pope came for an early session and gave the plan and the

4. Marine grade quarter-inch mahogany plywood, roughly four feet to the side.

site his blessing. Daryl Duke[5] came with me one Friday night on what turned into a drenching weekend, the two of us with water running down our backs as we slugged granite boulders into place and trowelled in mortar to build the stone pillars for the ten-sided floor, which at the lakeward edge was almost five feet off the ground. Beverly turned up that Saturday afternoon with my father, who had finally agreed to come and look at the property *his* frivolous wife had bought across the lake from the dome, against his advice. My wife glared balefully[6] at the two soaked men and said angrily, "Why don't you come home!" and left. We stayed on and finished the foundations that weekend.

Once the floor was laid, I moved the tent up onto it. Our digs were now sufficiently hospitable and approximately dry to make it attractive for the family as the weather warmed up. For extra rain protection, I stretched a big tarp above the tent, lashed to the skeleton of the dome, which had gone up very easily. Then I started laying in the dome's panels from the top, and soon we could dispense with the tarp (although the panels weren't sealed yet and leaked prophetically). By early August I was putting in the big windows, twelve huge triangles of double-diamond glass across the north face alone. The foot-high ventilator boxes around the rim, upon which the whole structure sat, were screened, and Bucky's surprising prediction that a hot day would draw air *down* from the vent at the peak and *out* through openings at the equator proved to be correct, so that it was sometimes cooler inside than out.[7]

Voices from outboard motorboats carry over water more than their owners realize, and we heard some entertaining comments from passers-by. "Hey, get a load of the crazy igloo!" was one. A local old-

5. It was Daryl who had sent *Close-Up* the slightly racy encounter with topless dancer Carol Doda, from LA. After the demise of *This Hour Has Seven Days,* he was given the Sunday night slot, and went on to a successful Hollywood career, most notably as the director of the hugely popular series *The Thorn Birds.*

6. Can you do anything else balefully besides glare?

7. The heat rising from the skin created a sufficient reduction in pressure at the rim or equator to draw air out at the floor level, and the reduction in air pressure thus produced within the dome drew cool air in through the rain-shielded (sort of) vent at the North Pole, or topmost vertex.

time carpenter dropped by for a skeptical look before the skin was on, hoisted himself up by his strong, gnarled hands so that his full weight hung from a pair of the seemingly frail little one-and-a-half-inch square struts, shook his head at the complete absence of give, and after a while, looking at the completely triangulated structure, said thoughtfully, "I get it: it's braced every way."

Which it was, although it was to turn out that the joints at the end of those "braces" were not as reliable as the geometry.

By July I was settling myself into a kind of bosun's chair, a plank in a rope stirrup hanging from a line secured at ground level and thrown up over the peak, so that I could work on the steep part above the Arctic Circle and below where the slope became gentle enough to hold a person without sliding off. I was now laying down fibreglass strips along the joints, buttering in a layer of the two-element resins that hardened into what looked like a hermetic seal. The air stank of chemicals that sometimes made me a bit giddy, but the place was gleaming and noble, the panels pre-stained a soft sage green, the north windows spectacular.

One day a message came by boat: "Call the office." Ted Pope, an amateur racer, was dead. His open car had flipped on a turn and shattered his skull. I headed gloomily for the city. One of the *Close-Up* staff met me tearfully and confessed that she had been "seeing" Ted (who was married) and that she was pregnant. There was no funeral, but there were solemn little gatherings of his pals, who, if few, were deeply fond of the wiry, ironic, hawk-faced guy, and all seemed stricken by his death. It put a dreadful stain on what had been shaping up as a triumphant summer in which Ted Pope had played a determining creative hand. I brooded about that death.

By mid-August the dome was sufficiently finished that I felt I could stop working on it – except for the occasional slinging of the bosun's chair to take a look at the leaks that materialized with every rain, even though it had seemed to be watertight the last time – and to do some swimming and canoeing and fishing with Chris, Greg, and Boo. We had a number of curious visitors. On the last weekend in August, Bob Smith, a friend from the Glebe days, came with his wife, Lorraine, and stayed overnight. It rained in the night. I woke up about six and saw a drip-drip-drip coming in not far from Bob and Lorraine's sleeping bag. Still in my pyjamas, I slipped quietly outside in my bare feet, managed to get our sixteen-foot aluminum ladder set in a fairly level spot on the wet rock, and leaned it noiselessly against the side of the dome. It was to be our last day there, and I knew it was a futile thing to do, but I wanted to be able to feel that I had at least closed off any leak I could see before we headed for Ottawa and left my noble hemispheric creation on its own for the winter. I would just find the source of the leak and slob on a patch of fibreglass with lots of goop. Take five minutes.

Those five minutes never happened. As I reached the top of the ladder, its feet slipped on the rock and it went out from under me. My left leg must have been hanging between two rungs, because as the ladder and I hit the rock, there was a loud snap from below, no pain, just a vast, stunning shock, and when I looked down at where my shin had been, arterial blood was spurting scarlet onto the rock. A foot that did not seem to belong to me was lying on its side, held on to the calf of my leg only by a small strip of pink, open muscle, beneath the jagged, dirt-encrusted edges of the broken tibia and fibula. As Beverly and Bob Smith bent ashen-faced over me, I remember saying, with some sort of mustered calm, "That's going to have to come off."

Beverly was heroic that day. We had not been comfortably close for a few years now, but she found a great deal of strength where it was embedded in her strong character, and marshalled all the available forces: a slab of plywood for a stretcher, a way to lay it across the gunwales of the little outboard to get me down to the dock, five miles away, and into the back of Bob's big station wagon, help from the neighbour to get word to my brother John, who was camping across the lake. She sat calmly beside me in the back of the wagon and told Bob to stop in at Coldwater, find a doctor, get me something for what by now had become a pain the size of the universe, a black hole that swallowed everything up. The doctor shook his head over the mess of my leg and gave me a large shot of, I think, morphine. It stopped the pain and made me giddy and flirtatious, and Beverly held on gamely.

At the Western Hospital on Bathurst Street, they were ready for our arrival, and before long I was on an operating table and mercifully out cold. When I came to, there was a huge cast down there, and somebody told me that the repair job had gone fairly well, although a number of nerves and blood vessels had been totally wrecked, I would walk with a limp for the rest of my life, one of the surgeons had wanted to amputate but the chief, Bill White, had said, No, we can save it, he'll be better with a partially functioning foot than with a piece of wood. The pain was ferocious, and I had developed a fever. I pleaded for someone to call my sister, Mary, who came over from Stoney Creek within hours. Something deep within had summoned up the times when I was a baby and she, assigned as my surrogate mother, had been all of my comfort.

The next day I was told that gas gangrene had set in. The only specific against gas gangrene in 1960 was the horse-derived serum used against tetanus ("lockjaw"). I had fortunately discovered on that sailing dock at Tamakwa that my one allergy is to that serum (and, as it turned out later, to any of its synthetic derivatives or substitutes). The amount required to stop the *Botulinus b.* bacterium that causes gas gangrene would have killed me in minutes. There was now no alternative but to remove the entire leg before the gangrene moved into my upper body. I remember feeling very calm and in charge when I signed the consent, even though my feverish hand rendered my already nearly illegible signature totally so.

When I awoke from the next bout of surgery, there was no more cast, no lump in the lower left side of the bed. For a day or two, I tried to make light of it and phoned friends to make jokes and comfort them. Mrs. Smith, a nurse whom I at first thought a bit dry and acerbic, warned me that I needed to let it out, to grieve. I told her, hey, I was going to be okay, this happened to lots of people.

Cards and gifts started to come in, a funny commercial card from Ross that had printed on the outside "All you ever think about is You

You You." And then inside, "Me Me Me." Under which he had signed, Ross Ross Ross. Pierre Berton sent me Leon Wolff's powerful *Flanders Fields: The 1917 Campaign*, which I dived into, learning dreadful things about the war my dad had gone through, things I had never appreciated from his stories in which it had always seemed inevitable that *he* would survive, whatever was happening to the others. Cataclysmic images from that book would swirl through the bouts of feverish delirium that the gangrene swept over me from time to time. This generated one prodigious nightmare.

The hospital bed had become a small boat that I was chained into, and the boat was stacked in a pile of similar small boats, each full of prisoners, on a sinister great ship at sea. I would fool them and escape. The next thing I knew I was standing in a vast corridor. The ship looked to be a mile long. It was throbbing dreadfully. Somehow I had, in my sleep, managed to slip out of bed without falling and to hop on one foot out into the corridor of the hospital in the middle of the night. As I stood there leaning up against the wall, an orderly found me, called for help, got me back into the bed. They put barred sides up on the bed and strapped me in; I raged against these echoes of the prison ship dream. As my mind cleared, I began to weep; I think I wept for five or six hours, appreciating, somewhere during that period, how right Mrs. Smith had been.

Visitors were discouraged because of the infection. My mother and father were allowed in once a day, and Beverly at will. The doctors were trying a variety of antibiotics for the gangrene, which was in the bloodstream even though they had cut away all the blistered muscles right up to and including part of the gluteals. A young Polish doctor, newly arrived in Canada and said to be very good about antibiotics, was trying massive doses of penicillin, unheard-of doses. The fever was blazing: my mind was seldom clear. I heard choruses chanting from the two electric fans in the room. I would wake up out of a delirious wander through the outer universe, to see that thoughtful young man sitting there, staring concernedly at me from only inches away. One day he said, "We think all that penicillin is working, finally. If it doesn't kill you, it may just kill the gangrene."

It was fearfully hot that September of 1960. The building was not yet air-conditioned, the slight breeze from the open window little or no relief. I fantasized cold beers. Once, half-asleep, I felt a cool hand on my brow and opened my eyes to Joyce Davidson's face bending close over my bed. She must have slipped in when no one was looking. Then I drifted off again, and she was gone. I woke again to see my brother John standing beside the bed with a funny smile, wearing a white lab coat, with a stethoscope around his neck. "Found 'em in somebody's office on the floor below," he grinned. "Didn't seem to be needed just now." He reached inside the lab coat and produced a glistening bottle of very cold beer looking like something in a television ad. He popped the lid. I guzzled. It tasted of anaesthetic and death, though the cold was lovely. I couldn't finish it, but I felt a wave of gratitude and was even able to laugh.

Paddy Sampson also sneaked by the security barriers, and grinned at me affectionately, telling me that – all on his own initiative – he had taken a team to the lake and closed up the dome for the winter, I didn't have anything to worry about there. He made me laugh with a couple of his elaborate jokes and cheered me up considerably.

When the heat began to build up in mid-morning, I would throw off the bedclothes and the hospital nightshirt and lie there naked. Mrs. Smith did not approve of this. She had been the one who confided to me that the night of the amputation the family was told that I was dying, would probably not last the night, and Father David Clarke had come in and given me the last rites. "We're not supposed to let ourselves get emotionally involved," she said. "But I went home and cried for you that night."

Much later it would appear that the surgeon who did the amputation didn't think I'd survive the night either; the incision looks as though it had been sewn by a second-year medical student hastily closing up a cadaver after an autopsy.

Mrs. Smith said one morning, when I grumpily threw off the sheet she had decorously laid across my naked midsection, "Well, but you'll have to cover up when the doctors come in this morning to examine the dressing." I frowned at her. I said, "Good God, Mrs. Smith, there's nothing here they haven't seen a thousand times, and the first thing they're going to do is take that sheet off." She said firmly that this may be so, but rules were rules. I glared. (Balefully?)

Mid-morning she came back and said the surgeon and the resident were on their way, and put the sheet back in place, and in they came. The usual "how are we doings?" and looking at the fever chart, the surgeon on one side of the bed, the resident on the other, Mrs. Smith standing by in case they needed her, at the foot of the bed, staring up the length of me, a bit crossly, I thought.

"Well! Let's have a look, shall we?" said Dr. White, the surgeon, and whipped away the sheet from my naked middle. I stared at Mrs. Smith (triumphantly, not balefully) and said, "Do you see my point, Mrs. Smith?" She stared directly at it and said with just the hint of a clever smile, "I certainly do, Mr. Watson." We became very good friends.

After about ten days the isolation sign came down from outside my door, and the visitors began. Joyce Davidson showed up again, this time with a beautiful classical guitar in a case, and a jazz guitarist whom she had commissioned to give me lessons. The kids were allowed in for one brief visit – only Christopher came, I think, and later said he had expected to see a lot of Band-Aids and was puzzled by the big round bandage where a leg used to be.

One morning I woke out of a deep sleep and looked up into the face of Erik Durschmied, who had been travelling, had arrived home in Paris where he now lived to find a telegram from Ross McLean, and jumped on the next plane. That cemented what had been growing into a solid friendship. Only eight months earlier, we had been tearing around revolutionary Havana together.

Erik is a complex, enormously cultivated artist who speaks German, French, and English with idiosyncratic gusto, and can get along in Spanish and Italian. He usually camouflages his extraordinary sensitivity with a rough, aggressive exterior that would conceal from a casual acquaintance the encyclopaedic knowledge of Western classical music, including opera and ballet, and a deep and visceral acquaintance with painting and theatre. He writes books of popular history on the theme of "the hinge factor" – those seemingly trivial matters like Napoleon's armourers forgetting the nails needed to spike their guns before the enemy captures them – the seemingly tiny hinges upon which the future of a battle, a country, or a culture may turn. He writes in English in a style that drives scholarly editors nuts, but sells worldwide in the millions. He is deeply loyal. I will write later about his breathtaking skill as a cinematographer, which turned our China film from what might have been a solid enough classic documentary into an impressionistic work of art. The rough-cast and sometimes brutal social insensitivity that is part of his camouflage disappears when the camera is on his shoulder, and he seems, through that lens, to sense the social dynamic of whatever situation he is in with such precision that the people being filmed seem to allow him invasions of their privacy and a spontaneity and naturalness of action and discourse that the camera, in most shooters' hands, characteristically turns off. To find him at my bedside that morning, despite the pain and the confusion, helped me feel that there was work to get back to, and that I was going to be able to do that before long.

The wound, however, was not healing. They had warned me that it might take months for the gangrene to leach slowly out of my system, and that until it did the wound would continue to drain. They did not warn me, however, about the single worst aspect of the thing: phantom limb pain.

I do not now remember exactly when it first expressed itself. The weeks in the hospital were pretty drug-soaked, and I have to suppose that quite a bit of that chemical intake was analgesic. I do vaguely recall that if I asked for painkillers they were ready at hand, and although there were some warnings about getting too accustomed to the narcotics, those warnings tended to abate whenever the resident took off the bandages and looked at the mess. But sometime soon after I moved in with my parents, back at 22 Bracondale Hill Road, to rest and try to build up some strength to complete the move to Ottawa and get to work on the new projects, weaning myself from the painkillers, I began to have overwhelming attacks of phantom pain, a burning sensation across the back of the non-existent toes and the ball of the foot, and up the instep, sometimes like a sudden electric shock that would cause my whole frame to shudder with wrenching spasms. Usually when I was vigorously active, learning to race up and down stairs on crutches, or driving a car, the pain would recede or vanish. It was at its worst when I got so tired that I had to lie down. The nights were torture. I was wan from sleeplessness. I remember meeting another amputee, an old man who had just lost a leg to diabetes, sitting on a bench in Hillcrest Park, and he telling me with profound grief that he did not think he could stand the phantom pain much longer.

In the evenings my father would mix perfect Manhattan cocktails. I never saw my father even the least bit tipsy, but he liked a glass of beer from time to time, had in later years begun to take a glass of wine with his dinner, and he loved a cocktail, just one, almost always a Manhattan, and very precisely made. When he saw how it helped me out of the phantom pain, he encouraged me to have a second, but no more. He warned me that I would have to watch it, using alcohol to deal with the phantom, but I blessed him for that little bit of relief. I tried Demerol at bedtime. It worked but it left me feeling groggy in the morning, mentally fogged, and seriously depressed. Joyce Davidson came by with her car, an automatic, and I was delighted to discover that I could drive it easily, but worried about how I would deal with a clutch – we still had the Volkswagen. Joyce introduced me to Wade Hampton, a sometime ski bum who had been crippled by polio, had founded a manufacturing firm employing only disabled people, and had brought in an industrial designer to make them an elegant forearm crutch, "The Canadian Crutch," and I was to be one of the few people to try them out, and to make recommendations for fine-tuning the design. After a few weeks on the conventional underarm crutch, I found the Canadian Crutches a bit unnerving at first, but it was such a relief not to have that terrible pressure in the armpit, and before long I could lope along as fast as any walking companion would want and go up and down stairs at a great rate without the always present risk, with the conventional crutch, of pole-vaulting to disaster. The pain was still terrible whenever I lay down.

Did Beverly come back and forth from Ottawa? That is not clear, but I think she had moved us into the house on Hillary Avenue, in Alta Vista, and came back from time to time. I asked her to come with me to visit Dr. White, the guy who had sewn me up as if it didn't really matter,[8] to see what he could tell me about dealing with this appalling phantom pain. He told me to act like a man, everybody got it, I would just have to learn to live with it. As we drove back to Bracondale that afternoon, I said to my poor wife, "I think I may have to kill myself." She knew I was serious.

By luck I ran into the son of a school friend of my mother's, a young surgeon who had lost a leg to bone cancer. I was lurching along Yonge Street on crutches, wouldn't have recognized him, but noticed this good-looking big guy walking toward me with a bit of a limp. He stopped me, introduced himself, and asked how it was going. I told him, bitterly. He said he'd had bad phantom too until he found a hypnotist and suggested I find a good doctor who used hypnotism or any hypnotist who was good at trance induction. He said that the hypnotist would use suggestion when the trance was established and the phantom would leave town. He was very persuasive.

Robert Anderson and I had worked together on his documentary about Nathan Schechter, an Ottawa internist who used hypnotism to cure all kinds of psychogenetic ailments and used it in the operating room. Anderson had filmed eye surgery with Schechter's hypnosis as the only anaesthetic. I made an appointment.

I did not like Schechter, but he was very good. I could not go into a trance, alas – never have been able to, though I have exposed myself to the droning persuasion of some of the best – but by giving

8. This interpretation of my ragged scar had not yet occurred to me.

myself over to his suggestion, I could lose the pain, totally. And it would stay lost for several hours. I was able to give up the Demerol. My morale and energy improved. I began to believe that this thing would be manageable. But it would not be until I was sixty-five that I would discover something that almost completely banished the phantom. For thirty-five years, I could count on a visitation eight or ten times a year of those wrenching electric shocks in the nonexistent foot, sometimes going on for thirty-six hours or more. Then suddenly an article in *Abilities Magazine* (I had become chairman of the foundation that publishes it) mentioned a food supplement, pycnogenol, an antioxidant made from pine bark. It worked. As long as I take some every day (now replaced by a less expensive antioxidant, grape seed extract), the phantom pain is never the totally disabling affair it was for so long.

The best therapy in those early days was getting back to work. CBOT's production needs had outgrown its tiny building, and staff members were being farmed out to rented quarters sometimes half a mile away. My first office was on the second floor over a bakery on Wellington Street. It was cramped, ill-ventilated, and hot. But I was working again. I had inherited Michael Hind-Smith's superb script assistant, Cecily Burwash, a lean, dry-witted, sometimes sardonic and vastly capable woman of about thirty-nine. She had a built-in roadmap of the politics of the station and shared my fondness for pushing the envelope here and there. We became a tight and trusting team within weeks.

I was going to work on crutches, my pant leg tucked into my belt or pinned up – sometimes with a slightly showy blanket pin, like the ones that private-school girls used on their tartan kilts. I had found a device that allowed me to drive the VW with one foot. That was another lift to my morale. I would sometimes totally forget about the absence of the leg while I was driving. Once when the left calf began to itch as I drove along, I leaned down absently to scratch it and burst into tears when my hand encountered air.

So this was the context in which I began to develop the program series *Inqui'ry*. I had inserted the diacritical mark in my early memos about the project, slightly mischievously, to indicate how I pronounced the word (I found *in'quurry* pretentious), and then later realized that it had some graphic potential and left it there on the screen and in publicity releases. Some critics, predictably, had fun with it, and Cecily and I would repeat the adage about "as long as they spell my name right."

For the thirty-nine editions per year that were the common allotment then, I had a budget that would allow me to do eight or ten substantial documentaries and some field inserts to studio-based reports; the rest was made up with interview or panel programs. Even with the panels and interviews, I wanted to give the program as much edge as possible, to break out and have a little fun from time to time, and to use my access to the nation's screens to bring citizens into a little closer contact with those aspects of our democracy that function and malfunction around the capital. Michael Hind-Smith had proposed that I ask Bernard Ostry to host the weekly half-hour. Ostry had been host of a weekly live phone-in and interview series called *Night Line*, and while his ironic and knowledgeable style was provocative, I wanted a host of my own choosing, and someone whose low-key and total credibility would carry a high level of controversy because of the host's solidity. I replied to Hind-Smith's memo about Ostry with one line: "Over my dead body," which was meant to be a joke but backfired because he showed it to Ostry. It is a credit to the latter's generous character that when he became Ottawa supervisor of Public Affairs TV, and thus my immediate superior, he humorously forgave me over our first lunch.

I had decided even before arriving in Ottawa that I would talk to Davidson Dunton about his hosting the new series. A university president who had been chairman of the CBC, Dunton had a low-key, quietly confident manner and absence of pretentiousness that made it impossible to think he would say anything he did not subscribe to. I went to see him in his office at Carleton, not very confidently. But Dunton remembered me from his visits to *Close-Up* and told me with quiet self-satisfaction about that early conversation in which he had suggested to Ross McLean that the CBC should create a television version of *LIFE* magazine. I had thought it a master stroke of programming inventiveness at the time, and was pleased to tell him so face to face. We had an excellent *tour d'horizon* about my intentions for the series, and a few days later he phoned to accept.

The next months continued to be therapeutic as I became more physically confident, certain that I was soon going to be ready for an artificial leg, get off those goddamned crutches, return to looking like a normal person, be rid of that sense, whenever I lurched into a room, of embarrassment as new acquaintances tried not to *look*, tried to think of something to say, or to determine if saying nothing were better. I wanted to be rid of the distracting empty pant leg. The rehabilitation was nourished by having this wonderful new investigative tool: a national program series of my own.

A CBC producer today would find it odd to be talking about "a program series of my own," the program decision-making process having become so hedged with the second-thinking of committees and checking up the line. But that management attitude of interest in and respect for the people who actually made the programs, despite its occasional lapses the closer one got to head office, was still intact in 1960. We were still being rewarded for initiative and risk. If you could make a reasonable case for a program proposal, orally or in a memo, the likelihood was that you'd get an okay the same day or the next day, and amiable inquiries from time to time: "How's that one coming along? Can I help? Did you think of contacting X or Y, I just remembered they know something about this issue . . ." – that kind of engaged and convivial support. The conviviality was important. You went out eating and drinking with your supervisors, or dropped into their offices with coffee and a bagel to throw around an outlandish idea. "Brainstorming" was still a young phrase. I sprang it on Ross McLean early in the *Close-Up* days, enthusing about the idea of the totally non-critical atmosphere of a session in which, for a while at least, you dismissed no idea, however outlandish. We did a lot of that, allowing outlandish notions to sit there on the table for a while to see if there just might be something . . . .

Management made the occasional arbitrary intervention, the funniest being the reaction to one of my studio sets. I designed and commissioned the building of a panel-discussion table that looked like a doughnut. It was more than six feet in diameter, and while that kept the participants a little farther away from each other than the ideal, it allowed me to put a camera on a "high hat" mount on the floor in the hole in the doughnut. The round table sat on an eighteen-inch-high platform, so that the camera was well below the surface, and out of sight, and I had a periscope made whose upper mirror came almost to the table top, but just out of sight of the other two cameras. This was to be used sparingly for low-angle extreme close-ups of the cabinet minister or other authority who was being grilled by my freelance journalist panellists, in what were becoming increasingly challenging encounters about policy and legislation. I called it The Hot Seat. I would hold back on the periscope shot until the journalists were really boring in and the guest was feeling the challenge, sometimes sweating it, sometimes glorying in his or her deftness in fielding every fast ball, and then, relishing the exact timing of the cut, I would go to that big, tight, low-angle, cinematic shot of the authority figure dancing his dance or polishing her phrases.

Audiences loved it; some of the guests did not. Their flacks would take me aside on the way to the green room after we went to black with something like "Did you really have to go *that* tight on the minister? It made her look very uncomfortable!"

I might say, "Well, I thought she *was* a bit uncomfortable for a minute; are you telling me you don't think she handled herself well?"

"No! No! She did a great job, she – uh – but you know, that shot, well it's a bit cruel, don't you think?"

It was talked about. Doug Leiterman, with whom I had a telephone post-mortem after almost every one of my programs and of his, loved it and began to talk of the Hot Seat as something we would want to use when we had our own program. He thought we wouldn't have to make a table like that; you could do an inverted periscope or have a camera on a crane swoop close to the floor, just out of line of the other cameras, and get the shot in what seemed to be an open and uncontrived set. But in the meantime he encouraged me to use the round table, though sparingly, and see which politicians would relish the challenge and which would duck it. I had to admit to Douglas – but I don't think to anyone else except Cecily Burwash – that the shot was, indisputably, very tough, and conceivably unfair. But my, wasn't it cinematic! I said, "If we warn the guest that we may use that shot, and they don't object . . ." That seemed fair.

Calls began to come in from head office, at first via the supervisors.

"Vice-President X or Y wants me to tell you to stop using that periscope camera."

"What did you tell him?"

"I said that we don't as a rule interfere with how our producers shoot their programs; that's a directorial skill we're not trained in."

I do not now remember precisely when we began to use the doughnut table and the periscope, but I guess that it lasted only one year. When I came back to Ottawa the next September after a month at Go Home Lake, my studio designer told me ruefully that the local management had ordered the table broken up while I was away. My instincts were to go to war; that kind of arbitrary messing in the producer's territory was really against the rules. But I kind of liked the guy who did it, Georges Huard, the local manager (whom we'll come to in a different context shortly), and decided in the end to say nothing at all, let them wonder what I was thinking, save it for an occasion when it might provide some leverage. In the meantime it was a good drinking story.

There were many occasions for drinking stories. Sammy Koffman's Belle Claire Hotel on Queen Street was a prime lunch spot for the Press Gallery, a few brave politicians from time to time, and some of the more interesting senior civil servants. You drank quite a bit at Sammy's along with your steamed pork hocks on rice or your thick rare steak. Martinis were very much in vogue and the precise proportions of gin to vermouth a matter of morally laden dispute.

At the end of the first season of *Inqui'ry* I commissioned a Montreal journalist named Jeanne Sauvé to do a series of in-depth interviews with some of the elder statesmen of the federal political scene, and in the summer, still slamming about on crutches, I was invited to stay with Jeanne and her husband, Maurice, at their summer home near St. Patrice on the south shore of the St. Lawrence. We spent three mornings filming an extended archives interview with the courtly former prime minister Louis St. Laurent, who lived nearby. Jeanne was later elected to Parliament, appointed Speaker of the House (the first woman) and Governor General (the first woman).

During the *Close-Up* days, Douglas Leiterman's interest in military and strategic issues had intrigued me, and I had caught the bug. As I began to strategize my long-term intentions for *Inqui'ry*, I was struck by the fact that while we were less than a decade and a half into the Cold War, the early fascination the media had shown for the international nuclear standoff had drifted onto the back pages, if anywhere. I thought that was wrong. I began then, and continued for the next twenty years, to insist on using my airtime to keep track of the global strategic situation, whether or not it was faddish in the press or other media, to keep myself up to date and to program fairly frequently about Canada's military and strategic policies and activities. I did many interviews and panels and at least two major documentaries on the state of our national defence system.

I had read a magazine article, perhaps in *Harper's* or *The Atlantic Monthly*, by a Harvard professor named Melvin Conant, the son of a famous president of that institution, James Bryan Conant. I phoned Mel Conant and offered him a contract as a consultant on strategic and other international issues. Although we met face to face only once, we became friends over the phone and he was extremely helpful. In today's technological environment it is amusing to recall a conversation in which he told me that there would soon be a network of stationary satellites orbiting the earth, and that they would transform both marine and aerial navigation, as well as weapons control. I thought he was drifting out of his usually rigorous intellectual world into something like science fiction when he told me that within a very short time it would be possible with a small receiver in a ship or a plane (I don't think he had foreseen the hand-held or private-car–based GPS receivers) to use common triangulation from three different satellites to pinpoint one's location on the earth's surface to within a few yards. "You're making this up," I probably said, and Mel said something like, No, he couldn't tell me who it was but he was talking to the guys who were working on it, and I should keep it quiet for the time being.

My conversations with Conant got me speculating about the value of our aerial anti-submarine patrols, and of submarines in our navy (tactically useless antiques, most of them, as now), and soon to feel very much engaged in and knowledgeable about the growing dispute over Canada's installation, at the behest of the United States, of nuclear-armed anti-aircraft missiles known as the Bomarcs.

I found a Canadian consultant too, an Ottawa University professor who was impressed by my knowing Conant and interested in what I relayed of his knowledge and strategic ideas. I shall call him Ian Gormley. He was delightfully paranoid, very clever, and claimed to be very much on the inside. There was not much he could tell me, he would say, but he could guide me on the principles and values of strategic issues I might be looking at, and could keep me from falling into embarrassing error. In fact, he was a mine of information about weapon strengths on both sides of the Cold War divide, quick to make it clear that President Kennedy was lying (he did not use the word) when he said that there was a missile gap in favour of the Soviets, and eager to help ensure that, as I went probing among the military and the senior defence officials and ministers, I would at least ask relevant questions; if they wanted to conceal or to be open, that was their concern.

After reading about the uses of sonar for detecting underwater objects, I began to speculate about using robotic sonar – seemed an obvious idea, unmentioned in the literature – so I phoned Ian Gormley. I asked him if anybody was planning to string a series of bottom-anchored remotely connected sonar robots offshore up the Atlantic coast, where we were now patrolling (expensively) by air and sea to detect intruding Soviet subs, whereas these things could just sit there, send anything they detected ashore for computer identification, and save us a whole lot of manpower and the wear and tear on our ancient patrol aircraft. As I finished the question there was a hiss of indrawn breath. "Who have you been talking to!" he whispered. I persuaded him that this was pure speculation, and then he was embarrassed at having given away a secret.

By the autumn of my second year at CBOT, I had spent the necessary fitting and training time at L'Institut de Réhabilitation de Montréal to be walking gingerly on my first prosthesis. Jeanne and Maurice Sauvé gave me a room in their comfortable house for the duration of my work at the Rehab, and were warm and humorously encouraging about my struggles with the wooden leg. These aids actually were carved from wood in those first few years, before the computer-generated molded plastic sockets with sophisticated hydraulic knee mechanisms we now use became commonplace. It was good to be back on two feet, now about fourteen months after the amputation. Before long I could drive a conventional car safely by just hoisting my wooden left foot up onto the clutch pedal by hand, and depressing it with what was left of my upper thigh. It sounds like a small thing but my morale soared. I no longer felt that people were looking at me pityingly when I walked into a hall. And people made jokes about the wooden leg, which we all enjoyed, perhaps I more than anyone. I made the kids laugh at a poker game at Go Home Lake once, playing with Arch McKenzie and his son, when after a failed bluff I picked up a small fishing knife from the table and jammed it into my wooden thigh with a curse – they still talk about that gag.

Inqui'ry had established itself as part of the Public Affairs television landscape. Provincial premiers answered my telephone calls, and it became easier and easier to arrange for the appearance of significant players. The CBC had moved Cecily and me out of the stuffy second floor over that bakery and rented us a delightful frame house just around the corner from the studios, the former headquarters of the Cummings Lumber Company. Cecily and I each had a presidential-style office with a green baize door, there was room for the new staff I needed to hire, my budget had been increased, we had a conference space in the outer office and ample room in my own spiffy quarters for a four- or five-person meeting. I flew to Winnipeg to meet Warner Troyer, whose work on a Winnipeg-based public affairs program I had admired, and discovered that he too was an amputee as well as a good interviewer and reporter. Over dinner I persuaded him to move to Ottawa and join the team.

As well as *Inqui'ry* I had other responsibilities as senior Public Affairs television producer, among them *The Nation's Business,* a fifteen-minute talk to camera that was broadcast at 7:30 p.m. every second week, the alternate weeks being similar programs on provincial affairs. These were free-time political broadcasts by ministers or opposition leaders or shadow ministers. This was still the Diefenbaker government, and Dief very much enjoyed his live talks to the nation. We developed an amiable if watchful relationship. He would walk in declaiming about the excesses and biases of the CBC, and then turn with a grin and say, "It's not you I'm complaining about, you understand; it's those awful vice-presidents in your head office." Once he came in looking particularly owlish, saying he had some serious criticisms of the CBC he wanted me to know about. As he settled into his chair in the tiny Studio Two, I warned him not to say anything really bad because I'd rigged his chair so that I could pull a cord and it would dump anybody sitting here into a pit full of alligators. The famous wagging old head nodded back and forth for a minute; then he grinned and said, "Can I think it?"

My son Chris was a Diefenbaker fan (something he recalls with a touch of pleased irony, having become national secretary of the New Democratic Party). I asked if he would like to come with me one day when The Chief was recording a *Nation's Business*, just to see him in person, maybe get to shake hands? Would he!

Chris would have been nine or ten years old then. I got him off school the next time Dief was booked, and as we were approaching the main doors after the recording I said to The Chief, "That boy waiting outside is my eldest son. He admires you a great deal and would be thrilled if you'd shake his hand."

Dief liked nothing better. While his aides fretted at the delay, he not only shook hands but took Chris aside for a private chat; they talked about a common interest, fishing. Chris was illuminated. Eleven years later I was making a call at Channel 13, CJOH, the Ottawa CTV station (where I had worked for a while), and as I arrived at the door Dief, now looking a bit frail, but still the Leader of the Opposition, was standing outside the main entrance with the group of journalists with whom he had just finished recording the CTV weekly parliamentary *Meet the Press.* Charles Lynch, Bruce Phillips, Tom Gould probably. They were blocking the way in, and I was manoeuvring to get by when The Chief noticed me. We had not seen each other for some years. I could tell that he had forgotten my name, but he nodded cordially, beckoned me to come over, and said, "How's that boy of yours, Chris, is it? He'd be twenty or so now, wouldn't he? Still interested in fishing?" He loved showing off like that.

Diefenbaker often sent one of his favourite ministers to *The Nation's Business*, a fellow Saskatchewanian, Alvin Hamilton, Minister of Agriculture. This minister's executive assistant was a skinny little guy with a big Adam's apple, Roy Faibish. Unlike many of the aides who came with their ministers, Faibish was relaxed and humorous, never complained about how the minister was lit or shot, chided his boss after the run-through with a charming mix of respect and insults, and filled the downtime with provocative conversation on subjects ranging from national policy to the poetry of Irving Layton or the latest discoveries in quantum physics. I thought I had never met anyone so widely informed and so wittily discursive. As the election campaign heated up and a Tory defeat began to look probable, knowing Faibish might be out of a job in the spring, I planned to go after him as soon as the news was out.

In the last few paragraphs I've referred casually to the recording of programs. By this time videotape (VTR) had transformed the production process. We were still using 16mm film in the field – there were as yet no field-portable VTR units. But the editing suite was already light years away from that primitive razor-blade-and-microscope arrangement Leiterman and I had thought so wondrous in the basement of Grand Central Station in the spring of 1960. Now we had electronic editing, in which you could preview a cut before it was made, the assembled edit taking place on one machine, with the original being fed from another. It was already much faster than film editing, which was still cut and glue (or Scotch tape). We had not yet got the idea of transferring our film to videotape for the edit, so the Steenbeck editing table, which had replaced the noisy old Moviola within my first year or so of being in the broadcasting business, was still the comfortable, preferred environment for thoughtful, creative cutting of film. The biggest impact of tape was the way it loosened up the scheduling of studios, allowing us to record programs that looked live, for later broadcast, making use of the overcharged studio facilities, in some cases close to twenty-four hours a day. But I think it also encouraged a sense of freedom and flexibility; I know that we began to be more playful as the VTR became a normal element in the production toolbox.

I made an elaborate documentary about Canada–U.S. relations, called *The Pull to the South*, and got far too clever with the shooting and editing, losing sight of the theme, and earning from Douglas Leiterman, in our regular debriefing, the devastating comment that documentaries were always better if the audience could tell what the subject was. A supervisor said something about the usefulness of "canons of relevance." It was a sobering lesson on being clever, an issue upon which I reflect further later in the book.

In December of that year, 1960, still groggy much of the time

Lucy Lovell Bate Watson, ca. 1926.

With Lucy and brother John, Woodside, 1930.

PW at eight months, in 1930.

With Stan and Lucy at the Woodside Avenue house, 1930.

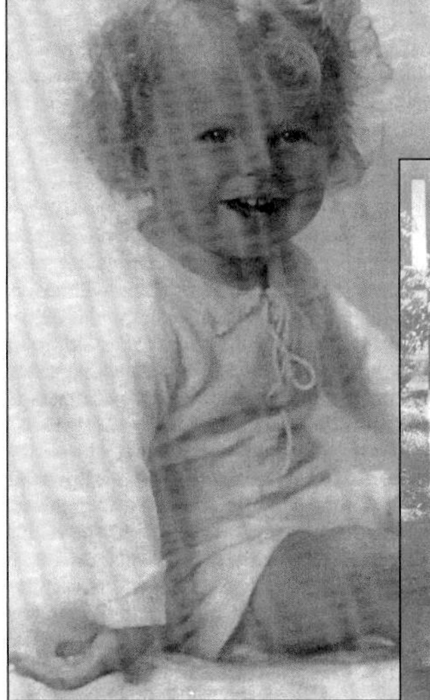

PW on the cover of *Saturday Night* magazine, 1931.

At the Woodside house, 1932.

John, Patrick, Mary, and Cliff, 1932.

PW, 1933.

At Camp Layolomi, 1936, PW nearest camera.

The Grade Five class at McMurrich Public School, PW centre front, Lawrence Harsar ("Hitler") 2nd from right, back.

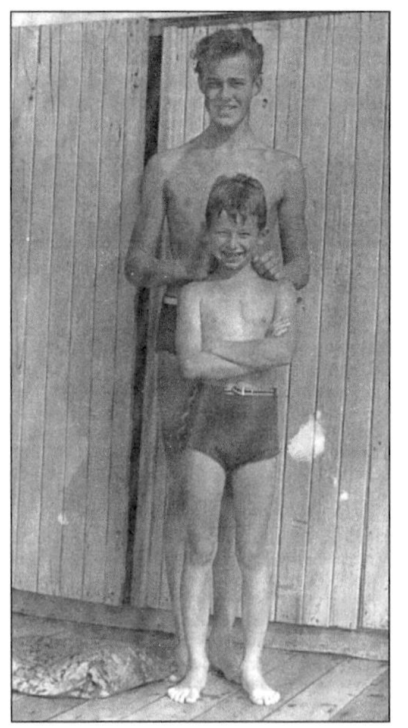

Cliff and PW after the day's sailing on Couchiching, 1940.

With Roger and Harry Bate, Port Burwell, 1938.

Stan and Lucy at Bracondale, 1941.

The manual training class at Hillcrest Public School, spring 1942. PW far right front row, next to him Bobby Green, who played The Kootenay Kid, and next to him Bobby Elton, whose older brother Chuck was the pilot who died with Cliff in the 1949 accident.

Lucy, Cliff, and PW at Bracondale, 1943.

The Ward McAdam quintet, Great Hall, Hart House, 1949. PW singing at far right.

PW as the King of the Sewers, in Giraudoux's *The Madwoman of Chaillot*, with Ann Murray, Hart House Theatre, 1949.

An Aykroyd Dinghy, Camp Tamakwa, 1951.

Erik Durschmied with Fidel Castro in the Sierra Maestra mountains, 1958.

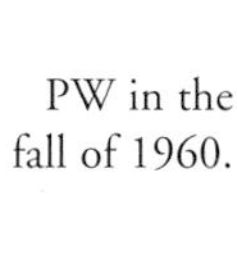

PW in the fall of 1960.

The frame of the original dome, June 1960.

The original dome, almost completed, 1960.

The original dome, with the experimental small dome, 1960.

Chris and Greg, the original dome, 1960.

Beverly (right) and Lorraine Smith, in the dome (with a single lamp) the night before the accident, 1960.

The Dome during reconstruction. 1963.

Left to right, Beverly, PW, Chris, Boo, Greg, with nephew Peter Green. 1964.

Greg, Go Home Lake, ca. 1964.

Boo, at the dome, ca. 1964.

Mark Lane (*Rush to Judgment*), on *Seven Days*, as framed by PW, 1964.

PW and the ambassador from Taiwan, Channel 13, New York, 1965, after the broadcast of *The Seven Hundred Million.*

Chris at the dome, ca. 1967.

Introducing my interview with Orson Welles, *This Hour Has Seven Days,* October 1965.

PW during the *Seven Days* period, 1966.

The dome in snow, ca. 1967.

On the beach at Europa, January 1968.

With Pierre Trudeau, Channel 13, Ottawa, 1968.

Lunch comes aboard the *Calypso,* January 1968.

With South Bronx street gangs, live, *The Fifty-First State*, New York, 1972. Photo by Charmian Reading.

WHEN WAS THE LAST TIME YOU SAW RAVE REVIEWS FOR A NEWS PROGRAM?

John O'Connor, New York Times:
"...refreshingly brash and impertinent. It affords a voice to groups and problems that tend to be slighted by television."
"...as unorthodox as turned-on viewers might expect from Channel 13."
"It will – it already has – upset influential powers..."

Val Adams, Daily News:
"...there is no question that the station can trigger a tumult."

Time Magazine:
Pat Watson is "one of the freshest faces to turn up on U.S. public affairs television in years."

Life Magazine:
"...like a muckraking magazine that gallops around your living room to a pop music soundtrack..."

Nat Hentoff, New York Times:
"This unpredictable news show is leaving the other local television news operations a light-year behind."
"The 51st State takes life as it comes, expletives and all."
"The very grit of the street is part of the texture of The 51st State."

Bob Williams, New York Post:
"...off and running in an inquiry into the ugly actuality of the breaking heart of Our Town."
"More than any other local TV channel, Channel 13 is getting into the ghettos – even those of the very rich..."

Marvin Kitman, Newsday:
"TV's first revolutionary, different, unpredictable news show."
"Rather than giving the news, they respond to it."

P.S.: It's membership week on Channel 13. We need your financial support to help keep THE 51ST STATE and all our programs going. Tune in any night this week. And call 581-6000 with your membership pledge.

"THE 51ST STATE" WITH PAT WATSON

10:00 TONIGHT AND EVERY WEEKNIGHT CHANNEL 13 WNET

Fifty-First State, New York poster and newspaper ad, 1973.

Robert Markle as Rembrandt, *Witness to Yesterday*, 1974.

PW as Leonardo da Vinci, Montreal, 1974.

At the controls of a Citabria aerobatic machine, Carleton Place airport, 1975.

PW bedding down the Twin Comanche, Sable Island, 1975.

Caroline outside the Café le Flore, Paris, 1978.

PW and producer Cameron Graham, Nightwood, ca. 1980.

Hosting a CBS Cable dance presentation,
New York, 1981.

Sarah with specs. Watercolour,
8 in. x 10 in. The author, 1982.

Caroline, Roy Faibish, PW Paris, 1981.

Sandra Kybartas, study. Pencil
10 in. x 14 in. The author, 1982.

Granddaughter Sarah Watson.
Pencil,9 in. x 6 in. The author, 1982.

Caroline driving. Pencil, 9 in. x 6 in. 1982.

Caroline reading. Charcoal, 10 in. x 12 in.

Robert Markle. Charcoal.
16 in. x 20 in. The author 1983.

Caroline, PW, and Peter Ustinov, Montreal, 1983.

Performing *The Book of Job.* National Arts Centre Studio Theatre, 1983.

Robert Duvall, Eric Fryer, PW, making *Terry Fox: The Movie* 1983.

with the after-effects of the surgery and the painkillers, and not yet on the air with *Inqui'ry* (which was first broadcast on Boxing Day), I got an unlikely phone call from a colleague in Montreal asking me to meet with a couple of McGill undergraduates, take a look at some of their comedy sketches and see if there wasn't a television venue for them. When I protested that I was in Public Affairs, not Light Entertainment, this regrettably forgotten person said, Yes, but these kids were doing very edgy satire on current events and in any case I would enjoy them a lot, they were prepared to come on their own to audition, what could I lose?

Christopher Dobson and Allan Shiach were performing as Bryant and Scott in one or two clubs in Montreal, Chris, twenty-three, being close to a law degree and Allan, twenty, in second-year English. Chris was a cherubic, curly blond upper-middle-class Londoner with a hint of the comic snob to him, and Allan a dark Mediterranean-looking Scot whose family owned the Macallan-Glenlivet distillery, he being the heir apparent and later chairman. Within minutes of the start of their audition, I knew that I really wanted to do something with these engaging young performers and their brilliantly written sketches. They were goofy in the *Goon Show* sense but also sufficiently pertinent and edgy to qualify as social or political satire. One of their best, which we later ran in an early edition of *This Hour Has Seven Days*, was a split-screen conversation between the British prime minister and the Soviet head of state, who announces jovially that the USSR has, heh-heh, just accidentally launched a ballistic nuclear missile and that London will be destroyed in, ahh, led uss zay, seven meenoots. When we did it on *Seven Days* the characters were Alec Douglas-Home and Nikita Khrushchev, with Allan playing the British P.M. ("Ah, now Nikita, it cawn't be as serrious as all thet; and how ah the wife and cheedren?")

I couldn't see how to fit them into my plans for *Inqui'ry* (I would now, easily), but the station manager, Georges Huard, was an open, affable man who shared that extraordinary taste for adventure so many managers seemed to have then, so I went to him brashly and liberated a few thousand dollars and a studio one night a week for a late-night ninety-minute comedy/jazz/interview program on the local transmitter, to go out at 11:30 Monday nights for a run of thirteen weeks. We called it *Nightcap.*

Noreen Young was a puppeteer who could sculpt recognizable caricature faces in soft rubber: heads inside which her fingers could open and close the mouths and manipulate the expressions. I had seen her interviewed on one of our local programs. I decided to use her skills to satirize politicians. We needed voices. A young Ottawa mimic was developing a reputation working service clubs and private parties, but had done no television. He could learn a voice with eerie verisimilitude after a few hours' practice from a recording of the original. We signed him on; his name was Rich Little. Bryant and Scott would interview presidents and prime ministers, animatedly caricatured by Noreen and voiced by Rich.

One of the switchboard operators, Carmen Browne, told me that her twenty-two-year-old son, Brian, had been studying with Oscar Peterson and now had his own jazz trio. I called Oscar; he gave Brian a warm commendation, and we made room in the tiny two-camera studio for a grand piano and a riser for the bass and drums. A few interviews with real people would round out the ninety minutes. We promised the audience that every show would contain one sketch based on a front-page article from that day's *Globe and Mail*, and we accomplished that by getting a friend in Toronto to phone us Sunday night at 9 or 9:30 when the bulldog edition of Monday's paper hit the stands. Chris and Allan and I would sit up until about two in the morning to write the sketch, and then reconvene at eight o'clock Monday night to block the show, rehearse the sketches, and get ready to go out live after the eleven o'clock news.

To open the first show, the two young comics arrived on camera in Chris's ancient blue MG, which they drove right into the studio through the loading bay and down the back service corridor. When I went into that studio a few months ago, I could not believe that its few square metres had ever accommodated all the goofy stuff we tried to do. We enlisted a tolerant staff announcer who was just the right shape to play a self-satisfied burlesque civil servant, "The Man in the Bowler Hat," and wrote short silent-film location skits for him that were quite frankly in the *Goon Show* mode, and which made our until then anonymous announcer into a minor celebrity.

Nightcap probably could not have played in Toronto and would have been precarious on the network, but Ottawa was a good town for a slightly precious mid-Atlantic goofiness. When the Russian ambassador agreed to be interviewed we were astonished, but nonetheless prepared a Khrushchev sketch for which Noreen made a puppet with two faces, one benign and one cruel, which she could instantly switch. When we afterward asked the ambassador what he had felt about being on the show, he said that he too "vas astonished." Well, it was astonishing that we ever got on the air in the first place, that we built a small but steady, almost cult-like following, who let the station know they loved us, and also astonishing that the station listened to that audience and renewed us for *A Late Evening with Bryant and Scott*, and then a third outing called, *Another Late Evening with Bryant and Scott.*

Alas, no recording of this work exists anywhere that I have been able to find. Queen's University's comprehensive listings (1952–1982) show no trace of it. It is gone.

Sometime during the second year of *Inqui'ry* I found a comfortable house for rent on a two-hundred-acre working farm on the Rideau River just north of Manotick, about a twenty-minute drive from downtown Ottawa. When we went to look it over, the kids were swept with excitement; we signed the lease and moved in in time for a summer on the river, the corn harvest, the fall start-up with a long walk to a two-room country school for Chris every morning, and some very nourishing family adventures in animal keeping and large-scale gardening.

I had been playing piano with the kids around me, inviting them to make up lyrics to the folk song melodies that were popular then, and that was the beginning, I think, of a practical interest in music that led all three of them to eventually give the professional music challenge a try. Boo, as I write, is still performing and recording her own songs – and singing and playing keyboard – with Boo Watson and Her Fabulous Band. Her first venture took place in that farmhouse when she was not more than six years old. I was fooling around on my own, vamping simply, with cords in A minor and E 7th, when she climbed up on the bench beside me and announced that she had just made up a song to my chords. She sang, to a simple melody of her own concoction:

When will my honey come back?
When will my honey come back?
I need my honey, 'cos I need his money,
Oh when will my honey come back!

By the time she was eleven or twelve the lyrics had become intricate and passionate, full of complex internal rhymes and ironies, and the melodies elaborate and intriguing. Her first CD, *Opening Moves,* made when she was just past forty, has a song she wrote for the person she was in love with when she was eighteen, one of the most moving on the CD. Greg would later move to Vancouver and play guitar professionally there off and on for more than twenty years, also writing and singing his own songs. And Chris, before becoming the national secretary of the New Democratic Party of Canada, would record, compose, play, and sing with Big Trouble, a Hamilton, Ontario-based country and blues group. That all began at the farmhouse on the Rideau River.

Two stately maple trees stood in front of the house, and in the early spring of 1963 we decided to try our hand at tapping and boiling the sap to make maple syrup. We got five or six gallons of sap, enough to boil down to almost two quarts of syrup, and spent much of a March weekend doing that, just adding more sap to the big kettle as the level went down, and watching the kitchen walls load up with water drops in the saturated room. As the process began to look as though it were going to have an ending, everyone took turns stirring. It was a tranquil family-centred afternoon, memorable because they were not common enough. A thoughtful, ruminative time as the liquid slowly boiled off the sap and the colour thickened. At one point a discussion began about what are you going to do when you grow up. Chris, who had begun to be seriously interested in hockey, thought that perhaps right wing on the Toronto Maple Leafs would be about as good as it could get (he was almost ten). Boo said decisively that medicine was the field for her. Greg was not much interested in the matter, but after a pause looked thoughtfully at me, a new puzzle having struck him, and said, "Dad? Why didn't you ever grow up to be anything?"

The year 1963 was a dramatic one. That noted apostle of peacekeeping, Lester B. Pearson, campaigned against Diefenbaker on, among other grounds, Canada's commitment to arm our obsolete Bomarc anti-aircraft missiles with nuclear warheads. Diefenbaker argued that this would bring us into the nuclear arms family and thus increase rather than decrease our vulnerability. Pearson's rationale was that we had made an agreement, we must honourably fulfil it, acquire the nuclear warheads and then negotiate their return to the United States.[9] Pearson won, in April of that year, and formed his first government. Diefenbaker was out of power and Alvin Hamilton was no longer a minister. I picked up the phone to call Roy Faibish.

Over lunch Roy was amiable and as conversationally engaging as always, but condescending about journalism generally and television in particular; he would rather talk about literature and did not seem the least bit anxious about his career. Something in that first conversation got us onto the aesthetics of film editing, and I quite spontaneously and innocently waxed poetic about the joys of the cutting room, in both film and videotape, about rhythm and pacing, lighting

9. Ask any national affairs journalist whether Canada ever became a nuclear power. Did the Bomarc nuclear warheads ever arrive? (Yes.) So what happened to them? Ask any peace campaigner. Chances are none can tell you. As early as 1968 I started asking reporters who had gleefully covered that part of the 1963 campaign; I never found one who had followed through and could tell me. That confirmed my desire to keep tabs on strategic issues, and when I came back to Canada to do the series that became *The Watson Report,* in 1973, I made sure that we regularly went to that file.

and lenses, all that craft texture that was and remains for me more intriguing than what is normally referred to as "content." It was the end of the lunch, and I guess I didn't notice a change in Roy's attitude, but he called me the next day and proposed a second lunch. "I'd like to hear you talk more about film editing," he said.

He said it was the aesthetics of film editing that hooked him, that when I was talking about the hands-on work of making a piece of film sing, it sounded like poetry to him, that, yes, he had made his career in politics (after a brief administrative role as a member of the Royal Canadian Air Force), but poetry was what really counted in life, poetry and love, and they seemed to come together when my eyes started to flash over the poetry of images, and, well, maybe he would give it a try, when could he start?

We agreed on September. His coming into my tent would have a powerful effect on the rest of my life.

Some time in, I think, the third year of the program, Frank Peers came to Ottawa as Vice-President, Programming, and the moguls at the Kremlin on Jarvis Street actually consulted program staff about his replacement as department head. Doug Nixon, then head of television, phoned me to say that they were thinking of making Peter Campbell the head of Public Affairs, did I think that would work? It was a generous, open conversation, in which I was able to say that while Campbell was a capable man, the troops did not really see him as a leader, and if they wanted strong leadership and a real sense of commitment in someone who would be liked, respected, and listened to, there were two choices. One was Helen James, who had been an important right hand to Frank Peers. Helen was wise, experienced, respected, and liked, but she was not young, and that might be an issue. The other choice, and I thought the best, was a portly Irishman named Reeves Haggan, who had started in Montreal when he immigrated, doing business programs in radio, then had become a program organizer in Public Affairs in Toronto, and was impressive in his judgments, his political astuteness, and his irresistible personality. They chose Haggan.

Born in Dublin, Reeves Haggan had served in the British Army Corps of Engineers as a Lieutenant in charge of stevedores loading and unloading on the docks of Singapore. When one of his men killed another in a brawl and was entitled to choose his defence counsel at the court martial, he chose Reeves, who had an arts degree from Trinity College Dublin but no experience that would qualify him to defend a man on a murder charge.

Reeves took the assignment, the man was acquitted, and Reeves became a very popular counsel to other court-martialled soldiers. After the war he was assigned counsel to a number of accused in the war crimes trials in Japan, where once more he achieved at least one unexpected acquittal. His commanding officer recommended that he study law, and back in England he did so, was called to the bar, and then decided to try his luck in the New World. I had been struck by him in the few encounters we had had over program development, and had simply no doubts that he was the best man for the job. Had he not been there, I doubt very much that *This Hour Has Seven Days* would have been accepted by management in the first place, and it certainly would not have survived without his prodigious tactical imagination and personal authority.

He had a huge memory, and often, in advising or making policy choices, he would cite precedents from the law, from the Bible, from fiction and poetry, and from his adventures in the British Army. He had that narrative skill that arrests attention and commends itself as truth, even though it may never have happened in fact. He liked risk takers but always took pains to advise us of the implications and extensions of the risks we might propose, usually leaving it to us to act or not. He was respected by everyone and loved by many. He assigned Bernard Ostry as my supervisor in the Ottawa region, and after some brief discomfort over my earlier rejection of him as a host, Bernard and I became and remain good friends. Scholarly, generous, with a penetrating intelligence and encyclopaedic memory, Bernard went on to have a distinguished career in both the federal and the Ontario public service, and as chair of TV Ontario; his life work is a paradigm of the best traditions of our public service, in which the public good is paramount.

In the meantime, the new Liberal government brought another challenge. I was going to lose Davey Dunton, my *Inqui'ry* host. One of the more significant creations of the new government was the Royal Commission on Bilingualism and Biculturalism, to be co-chaired by the Montreal journalist André Laurendeau and the Carleton University president, Davidson Dunton. I would need a new host when the series returned to the air in the autumn of 1963, and I began to entertain a mildly subversive thought.

I had been doing quite a bit of interviewing for my own series, but never on camera. There was an informal but well understood policy that producers do not appear in their own programs, but, curiously, nobody had raised any objections to my voice being heard as an off-camera interviewer; on the contrary, I had been encouraged to do more. It was hard to persuade experienced print reporters from the Press Gallery to do interviews the way I wanted them done for television. These journalists were knowledgeable and experienced craftsmen (no women in those days), and were skeptical of and resistant to my ideas about non-fiction theatre. It was easier to go and try out my theories on my own, and even though the sought-after objectives were vitiated by the invisibility of the interviewer, on the whole they were working well, my confidence was growing, and my supervisors were encouraging.

So I thought, what might happen if, when *Inqui'ry* went back on the air, *I* appeared at the home-base desk, announced Dunton's move to the Royal Commission, and without further ado got on with the presentation of the program? What happened was a cordial but firm telephone call from Doug Nixon, then head of the English television network, who began by saying that I had done an excellent job, very impressive, however he could not allow me to continue; it would concentrate too much responsibility (he did not say "power" but that is what he meant) in the hands of one person. "You can host the next two programs," he said, "but if you don't find an acceptable host in time for the next one after that, I am going to have to remove you from the series and probably cancel your contract." He was not unpleasant but the message was clear.

I decided to call Pierre Trudeau. I had felt from the moment I knew I was losing Dunton that if I could possibly find the right person (other than myself) the next host of *Inqui'ry* should be a French Canadian. I had been working in Montreal from time to time, occasionally volunteering to fill in for sick producers or to help out with projects that were short-handed. I had made friends with a number of my francophone colleagues, and hung around with them in bars and late-night restaurants like the San Tropez where the talk was nationalistic and heady, and I was feeling that the English television service was seriously delinquent about making French Canada better known to the anglophone audience. A French-Canadian host would help, especially an eminent one. Trudeau would be perfect. I phoned him and made an appointment to see him in his office at the University of Montreal, where he was teaching law.

In the meantime, Cameron Graham, a young producer assigned to a new national affairs series, had been auditioning for hosts. He knew of my predicament and suggested I look at his audition tapes of a young McGill professor of history. I screened the audition tape, which I liked very much, made a second appointment, and drove off to Montreal.

Pierre Trudeau and I had met during the Liberal Party's vast rally at the Ottawa Coliseum, during my first year in Ottawa when I was still going around on crutches, had hit it off well, and had kept in touch. Trudeau was familiar with *Inqui'ry*, to which he had contributed once as the subject of an interview on the growing nationalism in his province and twice as an interviewer. We chatted energetically in his office for about three hours. He was attracted by the prospect of access to a regular national audience, but the attraction supposed that he would be setting the agenda, not the CBC through me. "I have been thinking about getting back into the melee," he said. It was a time to move the country forward on a number of fronts – federal-provincial relations, social justice, international affairs – and a series like mine would be a great platform. But the more we talked the more it was clear to both of us that he would not be comfortable unless he had editorial control. Perhaps he had not considered this before my arrival, but as we talked he nodded acceptance of the principle that the Corporation must bear the responsibility for the content of the program, that I was effectively an officer of the CBC in that respect,[10] and that I would thus be the arbiter of the thrust of everything that went on the air. It was a cordial meeting, the longest talk we had ever had, and the basis for what became a lasting if not close friendship. We parted on the best of terms, and I headed for the bar in the old La Scala hotel, where I had a four o'clock appointment with this young professor[11] whom I had never met.

Laurier LaPierre and I hit it off immediately. We talked over drinks for no more than two hours and before we parted had reached an agreement. He too was looking for a greater involvement in the national scene, but had no illusions about using the screen as a platform: he just wanted to play a part in the unfolding national drama, become known, widen his horizons. He would start the next week.

The first long discursive *Inqui'ry* program planning meeting of the new season convened before my adventures in illegitimate hosting and my meetings that sunny October afternoon with Pierre Trudeau and Laurier LaPierre. Six or seven of us gathered in my green-baize-doored panelled office, Cecily Burwash and I side by side at the head of the circle, which included Warner Troyer, Jean Trébucher,[12] Wilson Southam, and Brian Nolan, freelancers who were sufficiently often involved in the program to make it convenient and productive for

10. Even though I was not an employee, but a contracting individual. Producers would later begin to press for staff positions, but during my ten years as a regular producer, I negotiated a contract for every assignment, renegotiated (usually yearly – I think there was one two-year contract during the *Inqui'ry* years) in order to press for pay increases on the ground of the quality of my work, and had no pension or health benefits.

11. Well, actually a month older than I.

12. A funny, brainy provocative man whom I would soon have to fire because he always needed "just a few more weeks of research" and seldom was able to complete any of the assignments I gave him: this is not his real name.

them to be in on the planning; Don Dixon, the production assistant and unit manager; the unit secretary; and finally the new boy, Roy Faibish.

It was at that first get-together that Roy announced, after we had surveyed the major themes and projects, that there was clearly something the matter with us, we had totally ignored the one matter that we should be giving priority to. What were we thinking of? We had gone around stories out of Quebec, international strategic and Cold War issues, the armed forces, major political figures, the Liberal first year, etc. But Faibish said he simply could not understand why we did not have China on the list, and in fact it was incomprehensible, given the range of international stories that the CBC was constantly covering, that the CBC had never made a documentary in China.

It was my turn to be condescending. I said, Look, he was new on board, if he had been around for a while he would know that we, like every serious journalistic organization in the West, for God's sake, had been trying to get into China for years, but there was simply no way, you couldn't even get them to talk to you, forget it, nobody could get in, nobody ever had.

Roy gave us what would become a familiar owlish look, followed by a small secretive smile. "I'll get you in," he said.

Two years ago he had been to Hong Kong with his minister, Alvin Hamilton, he told us, to help negotiate the sale of several million tons of Canadian wheat to China. The senior Chinese trade officials involved had come down from Beijing for the meeting. Roy had made friends with them, and maintained a correspondence with the senior trade official, General Ting. "Get me a ticket to Hong Kong," he said, "and I'll ask Ting to meet me there – he goes down regularly to meet foreign officials – and he'll get us in."

I phoned Reeves Haggan. I wonder what it would be like today, trying to get what I was asking for without documentation, simply on the bona fides of my own reputation and my vouching for a new associate. Reeves responded without hesitation. He said that because of the international implications of the thing he would have to get head office on side, but that he would do that, and that I could probably count on getting the necessary funds and permissions. It took him about three days. Faibish began to write letters to Beijing, and we all got on with putting together the program plans for the season and the familiarization of our new host with the staff and the routines.

It was the first time in the history of CBC television that a French Canadian was presenting a regular program to an English-Canadian audience. It seems remote and unlikely now, bizarre even, but in those first few months of Laurier LaPierre's tenancy of the *Inqui'ry* home-base desk, he generated some hate mail, most of it addressed to me or to the management: "Get that God Damn Frog off the air!" one memorably said.

Senator LaPierre (as he now is) has a mid-Atlantic accent with a strong British overlay, not at all French Canadian, although it is strongly coloured with something Frankish. He proved a quick study, a fine interviewer, a gracious and endearing on-camera presence, and – before long – a darling of the critical press. When President John F. Kennedy was killed in November Laurier rose beautifully to the occasion. Kennedy died on November 22; we had a program scheduled for the twenty-fifth. Our independence, as a CBC journalistic unit, was such that we did not have to consult with or defer to the interests and plans of the News department, and in those three days, with Laurier's help, we put together a response to that disaster, persuading the network to let us expand from our usual thirty minutes to a whole hour. Most of the journalistic response on television was event- and personality-oriented. Laurier argued strongly for a program that would investigate the significance for democratic citizenship and for the state of the American social fabric.

I had been reading for years the work of a Columbia University social philosopher, Sidney Hook, "an intellectual streetfighter," as one columnist called him, who by 1963 had become one of the most cited and most widely read social and political commentators in America. When I found him, with Mel Conant's help, he said that nobody else had called: I found that astonishing. We brought in the Dean of Law at Harvard, Mark DeWolfe Howe, and the dean of the Canadian historians, Arthur Lower. Laurier's deft and knowing guidance of the discussion gave us a totally absorbing hour, and even those network officials who had been a bit reluctant about giving us that extra time called within seconds of our going off the air, warm, sounding almost as if they were grateful

Laurier's confidence and grace were making themselves felt across the country. The hate mail stopped coming.

The *Inqui'ry* time was, in part, a time of healing for the loss of the leg: a very thorough healing too, partly because of the management attitude that still encouraged experimentation and respected the autonomy of producers. But it was also a kind of extended apprenticeship; I think I knew from the beginning it was a preparation for something more momentous.

Chapter 9

CHINA

IN DECEMBER OF 1963 Douglas Leiterman and I reopened a file that we had begun to work on the previous spring. In the years since we'd been together on *Close-Up*, we'd spent hours on the phone, and occasionally face to face, analyzing each other's broadcasts and speculating about what we might do if we ever had a decent budget and a time slot. Out of these conversations, we put together a proposal for an aggressive new weekly magazine and documentary hour, a proposal whose principal argument was that it would combine the by now demonstrated strengths of the two of us, in a collaboration aimed at conveying a running account of the way this country was functioning, politically, socially, sexually, culturally – to the widest possible audience. Reeves Haggan and his chiefs at the network called the proposal outstanding but said we were just too late (it was March) for the '63–'64 season – the budget allocations had all been made; why didn't we mull it over, refine the proposal, make it a bit more concrete, submit it again next year, not later than the end of January.

But by the late autumn of 1963 I was feeling tired and dispirited, despite the ongoing success of *Inqui'ry* and the delights and challenges of working with my new colleague Laurier LaPierre. I had been producing weekly television programs for six years. I felt stale, in need of a change of environment, something to stir up the old brain, a different context, maybe go back to school and start another Ph.D., go down to Harvard perhaps for one of its celebrated summer courses, but better to get off the continent altogether and into a different cultural and political atmosphere, France perhaps, even the U.K. Ken Black, a colleague who was then running the London office, told me of a Central Office of Information no-strings tour for offshore journalists, three weeks touring Britain, our choice of locations. I thought that would be a good opportunity to see some of my BBC counterparts, maybe take a look at Cambridge or the London School of Economics, or one of the northern universities, find a way to finance a year off, maybe get a bit of freelance television work while there to help pay the bills. And maybe it would refresh the decaying marriage and bring some perspective to it. Beverly had never been out of the country except for one brief flying visit to New York (she disliked flying), and she agreed that plunking ourselves down in a different world might be an instrument of renewal.

Cecily Burwash and I went up to Toronto one weekend in December to sit down with Douglas Leiterman and Beryl Fox and discuss ways in which their *Document* production unit might lend a hand with *Inqui'ry* while I was in Britain. Cecily could direct. She knew my visual style. Wilson and Roy could help her with the writing, but she would want some journalistic and planning support. We would try to thrash something out together.

That weekend turned into something very different from what we had planned. Over coffee before we had properly started, while gossiping about the past year – What was the matter with me, abandoning ship in mid-season? Did you see Mike Wallace's latest interview? Your broadcast on the death of J.F.K. was very moving, etc. – we got around to the subject of the previous year's proposal for a new jointly produced hour-long magazine. Doug found the file – it was just a one- or two-pager – and read it to the group. Someone said it was too bad that we'd been late for the budget deadline; we'd all be doing something different now. I said, Yeah, well, I didn't know whether it would have made any difference to my present state of restlessness, the sense of repeating myself. Doug said, But we'd moved on a good deal from then, what would the proposal look like if we were to redraft it?

We began to talk about that and soon got excited. Doug said, You know, one thing that is so wrong about most of CBC's public affairs programming is that it assumes a common interest among engaged citizens, it is preaching to the converted; it doesn't reach out for new viewers. And another thing: it still tends to be awfully considerate of the Establishment, of our various establishments, to take for granted that they are working pretty well. But a lot of people out there feel they are outside the system, that they're getting screwed by the system and by the establishments. They don't trust politicians, or police, or industry. They need something on television that gives them more of a voice.

The weekend went on a bit longer than planned. Douglas made a lot of notes. Every once in a while he would whip over to a typewriter and clatter away at a sheaf of yellows. After a couple of minutes he would rip them off the platen and say, "Let me try this on you."

By the time Cecily and I started back to Ottawa for the coming week's program, we had a draft proposal on those yellow second sheets that came in batches of seven with disposable carbon paper between them. Douglas and I refined it a bit over the phone during the next couple of days and then fired it off to our supervisor, Reeves Haggan. I think we ball-parked the budget at about $15,000 a week "above the line," meaning cash out for freelance personnel and travel. By far the bulk of the costs would be "below the line," meaning CBC facilities and services, office space and equipment, studios, staff film crews and services, and archives. Although Douglas and I were, technically, contract producers, not staff, our salaries would be below the line.

The core of that proposal was what we rather grandly referred to as The Manifesto. It did not suffer unduly from modesty or restraint:

> On Sundays at 10:00 p.m., a one-hour show of such vitality and urgency that it will recapture public excitement in public affairs television and become mandatory viewing for a large segment of the nation. . . .

> Items can qualify in terms of urgency, controversy, national interest, human condition, satire, beauty or art. [We] will range Canada and the world. Reporter-cameraman teams will pounce on significant events wherever they occur, looking not only at the news but at the reasons behind it. . . .
>
> Using special camera techniques we will probe dishonesty and hypocrisy. By encouraging leads from our viewers and inviting their alertness, we will provide a kind of TV ombudsman to draw attention to public wrongs and encourage remedial action.

The interventionist posture is clear, and in the light of the row the program eventually generated, it seems odd that management apparently accepted this declaration of intent without demur. But while Reeves Haggan, who would be the first to review The Manifesto, persuaded his superiors to fund and schedule the series, it is conceivable that in the interests of seemliness he kept the original Manifesto to himself and sold management by means of his own interpretive translation of our original proposal. This was the project that came to be known as *This Hour Has Seven Days.* At the time it was simply *The Mag.* We had no idea what to call it.

At about this time Roy Faibish and I met with the Leader of the Opposition, John Diefenbaker, to invite him for a full-length interview with Laurier LaPierre on *Inqui'ry.* He was coyly reluctant, but, as always, enjoyed telling stories, one of which I found very powerful. I asked him how he came to his view that capital punishment was wrong. He said that in his days as a lawyer in Saskatchewan he had defended an accused murderer. The only evidence against the man was the testimony of a person who claimed to have recognized him from his shadow on a window blind in the upstairs room where the victim was killed. The community was so aroused by the murder that this flimsy stuff was enough to convict Diefenbaker's client. He chillingly told how he had walked to the gallows with the condemned man, who was still shouting his innocence when the trap dropped and his neck snapped.

Then, said Diefenbaker, a few months later a priest came to him, saying that he felt he had to break his sacerdotal vow and tell the young lawyer that a man had just told him, in the confessional, that he was the real murderer.

I said with a great deal of feeling that if he stood up in Parliament and told that story he would have an abolition bill in a minute.

The Right Honourable John Diefenbaker wagged his head for a moment and then said, Yes, perhaps that was so, but what would people think of him for having lost the case? He was not joking.

When I went off to Britain for the tour in February, it was no longer in order to check out Britain as a place to take a sabbatical, but just a good break, in the company of some agreeable colleagues, a quick tour of a country it was time I got to know, a renewal of the friendship with Chris Dobson and Allan Shiach, almost a holiday before tackling the wind-down of *Inqui'ry*, the planning of *The Mag*, and – possibly, though it still seemed remote and unlikely – a filming expedition to the mysterious People's Republic of China.

Roy Faibish left for Hong Kong at about the same time that I left for London. He had a letter from General Ting, the Beijing foreign trade official. Ting would meet him in Hong Kong, with one or two other officials, to listen to a proposal. These things don't happen fast, Roy had warned; he might be there for some time.

In mid-February of 1964 I was asleep in my room in the Kensington Palace Hotel in London around two o'clock one morning when the phone rang. It was Roy Faibish in Hong Kong. "We're in," he said, and told me that I had better get cracking on the arrangements because our visas would be activated for the last week in April. The Chinese had agreed to give us two whole months. I would need to decide on a cameraman right away (I already had), and arrange for someone to keep *Inqui'ry* on the air until the end of the season in June, and be sure that Douglas Leiterman and I were in agreement about what had to be done to develop *The Mag* while I was away.

I hung up from Roy's call and despite the hour called Erik Durschmied in Paris. He crowed. His top cronies at the BBC had been trying to break through the Bamboo Curtain for years, he said, James Mossman and the BBC Current Affairs chief Paul Fox, the *Panorama* crew, wouldn't they all be jealous. He would be delighted to travel light, just the three of us. I had already been his soundman in Cuba; he would bring a hand-wound Bell & Howell for locations where we might need a second camera. He would train Roy to run sound too.

The rest of the London trip went by in a blur, my first visits to West End theatres (Joan Littlewood's *Oh What a Lovely War* was in its first incarnation), meetings with counterparts at the BBC, including Ned Sherrin, the executive producer of *That Was the Week That Was*, which Doug Leiterman and I were taking a lot of notes on for *The Mag*. We were wondering if it wouldn't be a good idea to import a third producer who had BBC and continental experience, maybe a strong *Panorama* man. I spent part of an afternoon on that with a young BBC producer named Jeremy Isaacs (now Sir Jeremy, later head of programming for Thames Television, founding chief of Channel Four, and producer of such mammoth series as *The World at War* and *The Cold War*). Isaacs said he was tempted. In the end he declined, but it was encouraging, even before we had worked out the design of *The Mag*, let alone produced anything, to find my counterparts at the Beeb giving me such positive notes on what we were planning.

Back in Ottawa I called Melvin Conant at Harvard about China. He sounded elated to learn that we were going and gave me a good oral sketch of the history of the Revolution. He said that for all the changes that Mao had wrought, the essentials of the culture were still intact. It was still a bureaucratic empire with Beijing at the centre, and the rulers, like the traditional emperors, still convinced that China was the centre of the universe and that not only the outlying regions but the rest of the world were inferior and owed them tribute. He got me to read John King Fairbanks's *The United States and China* as a guide to the Chinese state of mind.

Roy came back from Hong Kong, triumphant. We got immunization shots for every conceivable exotic disease, booked flights, made our wills, arranged powers-of-attorney. Cecily took command of *Inqui'ry*.

On April 22 Roy and I flew to Vancouver and the next day boarded a Canadian Pacific flight for Hong Kong via Anchorage and Tokyo.

Erik Durschmied met us at the Hong Kong airport. When Roy told him that we were booked into the staid old imperial-style Peninsula Hotel, he was a bit scornful. The Peninsula was dull and expensive, he said; we should book into the glitzy – but clean, modern, and inexpensive – high-rise where he always stayed, right in the middle of good cheap restaurants and shopping. Roy just looked owlish and suggested that Erik come with us, instead, to the Peninsula; he might learn something. That was the first of dozens of mutual attempts to put each other down; unlike some of the later ones, it did not escalate to the point where I had to mediate.

At the Peninsula the man behind the desk was deferential when Roy registered. He said that the Marco Polo Suite on the penthouse floor was all ready for us, and this young man, Benny by name, would be assigned to us twenty-four hours a day throughout our visit. Erik tried to conceal his bafflement.

Benny courteously led us to a special lift with a discreet plaque indicating that it went only to the Marco Polo Suite. As we walked from the lift toward huge double doors at the end of the hall, we passed two or three motionless men in pale green pyjama-style uniforms and round black caps, on watch, it seemed, in alcoves as we passed. Benny unlocked the doors to the suite.

The view over Hong Kong and the harbour was breathtaking. There was a central dining room with a polished walnut table, bowls of fruit, and vases of fresh flowers. To the left, down three carpeted steps, was a sunken sitting room with subtle floor lighting and a big round central table loaded with international periodicals and newspapers.

There were two complete two-bedroom suites, each bedroom with its own bathroom. The taps were gold-plated. Roy asked Dursch if he mightn't reconsider. Dursch reconsidered.

Benny said, "I take your dless fo' pless?"

Over the next few days we shopped for summer clothes and cameras, Erik having warned us not to waste our money on such things in Canada. I bought my first 35mm single lens reflex, a black-bodied Pentax, a couple of seersucker suits and a bright red lightweight nylon waterproof windbreaker. We lunched and dined with foreign correspondents. Most of them expressed unconcealed envy. *They* were stuck there in Hong Kong, watching from outside the border; *they* had decades of experience on the China file. Some of them were old China hands from pre-revolutionary days, unable to cross the border for the last fifteen years, and here were we, upstarts, naifs, it wasn't fair, but they wished us good luck all the same and said they hoped they would get to talk to us afterwards, and to see our film.

Three days later we took the train north through the Protectorate to Shen Cheng, walked across the bridge under guard, and were welcomed into the People's Republic by a severe-looking young woman who said that she would be our translator and guide as far as Canton.

Despite the familiarity of train tracks and British- or European-made locomotives (steam) and passenger cars, the sense of strangeness was powerful. More to do, probably, with anticipation and the feeling that we were breaking ground where nobody we knew had ever gone before, than with the level of the exotic in what we actually saw. There were water buffalo and rice paddies, peasants with wooden water buckets hanging from poles across their shoulders, ancient-looking men staring at us as we passed, with smoke curling up from thick cigarettes. Everyone smoked. Everywhere we went for the next two months we were offered cigarettes. Every meeting with officials (always more than one) began with cigarettes, which were always displayed in elegant china straight-sided cups or exquisitely delicate lacquered boxes.

We passed villages sporting big banners with slogans or exhortations, or quotations from Chairman Mao, which our keeper patiently translated. The smoke of a city appeared on the horizon: we were coming into Canton. Rickshaws and bicycles everywhere. Soldiers in light khaki uniforms, strolling the streets, often hand in hand. Pedicabs, some open, some with canopies, the passengers often formally clad in grey or grey-blue or black Chairman Mao suits. Pedicarts, two-wheeled wagons piled with goods, ridden by lean men in blue shirts, often barefoot as they strained to pump the pedals.

We were installed for the night in the Canton Hotel. The dining room was enormous, veiled in smoke, the smell of rich Chinese food overwhelming, a hundred or more big round tables seating eight or ten – you just grabbed empty seats where you could. Our interpreter/keeper bade us a courteous good night, saying she would pick us up in the morning for the train to Beijing, and we settled down to an immense dinner, rapidly served, surrounded by what seemed like every language in the world.

Most of the faces in that big room were not Asian. The Canton Hotel was where visiting businessmen stayed, and there were hundreds of them. At our table were a couple of Danes and a Belgian. Almost no women. After a while I realized that from a neighbouring table I was hearing the unmistakable accents of Quebec French. I accosted the man, a machinery salesman. It turned out we had several mutual acquaintances. He, like the journalists we had met in Hong Kong, expressed amazement that we were going to Beijing, that we had permission to film, that we were going to be there for two months. After dinner we went for a walk, unaccompanied, and watched street performers – jugglers and trick bicycle riders – and mixed with the crowd of mostly Cantonese people. It would be the last time we would walk in a Chinese city without attracting aggressive crowds who had never seen an Occidental, a white face. But Canton was a world crossroads. People were friendly, smiled, even tried a few words of English on us. We went off to bed saying, Well, it's not so strange after all: beneath the surface they're really just like us. It was a feeling that did not last.

After an all-day rail trip north, through plain and forest and across wide river valleys, we arrived in Beijing, where we were met by a new interpreter/keeper, a Party member named Lu Yi-ching, who would be with us for the entire shoot. "Mr. Lu" was how he expected to be addressed, and, for the first day or two, we were also Mistered. Lu was twenty-eight, lean, with an acne-scarred face and a habit of half-closing his eyes as he listened. He was severe but courteous and straightforward. He helped get us installed in our rooms at the Hsin Chiao Hotel, near the north wall of the old city and its beautiful high-arched fortress-gate that would be destroyed when the madness of the Cultural Revolution tried to destroy every vestige of the ancient emperors.

Lu then took us to meet Madame Chen, the foreign ministry official who would arrange our travel permissions and advise us as to what was allowed and what was not. After that first hour with Mme. Chen, Lu Yi-ching's attitude no longer seemed severe. Months later when we compared notes, neither Roy, Erik, nor I could recall her smiling. Her English was very pure, with a slight British cast to it. She had studied both in California and in England before the Revolution. She was about fifty-five. When we met with her, at least one other official was present, usually taking notes, seldom speaking. She carefully advised us about protocol. We would be expected to convey all our requests for filming to her, and also to a designated official in each place we visited. We were reminded that courtesy was de rigueur, and that people were not to be filmed without their agreement, even passers-by in the streets. When I roused over that one and was about to protest that this would paralyze our ability to make an honest portrait of life in China, Roy caught my eye with a minimally raised palm-down restraining gesture. In fact, Mme. Chen's advice and information turned out to be more helpful than restraining. As the weeks rolled on, we were seldom refused anything we asked for, and many of her suggestions proved worthwhile. The Hsin Chiao Hotel would be our base of operations for the next two months. When we travelled outside Beijing, we could leave our heavy baggage there and take only what we needed for each trip. We were required to return to the capital after each foray, to report to Mme. Chen and plan the next step.

For the first couple of weeks, we worked in the Beijing area, visiting factories and libraries and the legendary Forbidden City of the emperors. Along with a reported four million others, we went into Tian An Men Square for the May Day celebrations, and while our hosts wanted us to stay in the bleachers we successfully insisted that the people's view of the all-day extravaganza could be properly seen only from within the crowd. Once he accepted that this restraint would weaken the film, Lu Yi-ching actually seemed pleased to become part of the crew, carrying rolls of film and other gear, and helping us manfully whenever translation was needed. I carried Erik's little sand-coloured pebble-grain Bell & Howell Pro 600, hand-wound, with a tiny turret of lenses and 100-foot rolls of film, and worked the street thirty or forty feet away from Erik on the Arriflex, while Roy manned the Nagra. We used an old ivory-coloured Sennheiser, a highly directional nightclub microphone that gave excellent results in a situation like this, shutting out all the roar of the mob on its dead side, and focusing selectively on what it was aimed at. We kept shooting until the small hours of the morning, when the square, gleaming from the hoses of the street cleaners, finally deserted except for a few stragglers and the remnants of fireworks and a few torn banners and posters, gave us a perfect visual coda for the end of our montage of a long day of feverish, propaganda-laden slogans and marchers and acrobats, followed by the most spectacular display of fireworks any of us had ever seen. Much of that footage is built into the first five minutes of the finished film.

Sometime during those first few days of visiting local communes (one, to our surprise, a dairy farm with Holsteins and the claim of a world's record for milk production), we found two men who would be invaluable in guiding and interpreting the almost overwhelming sensory input of this extraordinarily expressive culture, where almost everything was new to us, and therefore noteworthy. Jacques Marcuse was a cynical and humorous Old China Hand from Agence France-Presse, who had only recently been readmitted to the country. George Hatem (Ma Haide) was a Buffalo, N.Y., physician and former juvenile delinquent who had come to Shanghai out of curiosity just as the Revolution was swinging into action, had survived the War of Liberation, offered his services as a public health specialist to Mao, become an insider, and among other successful campaigns virtually wiped out syphilis and leprosy from a culture in which they had been rampant. Roy Faibish did long discursive interviews with both, which served as invaluable narrative links in the assembled film.

Like every other visitor, we were taken to the Great Wall, a few hours' drive from Beijing. A first film about revolutionary China would have to visit the Great Wall, cliché or not. Some of our best shots were of soldiers squatting on the parapets with decks of cards, throwing down their trumps and laughing. The landscape was moody and impressive, though, and a soaring eagle, just north of the wall, saying something metaphorical about the threats from the north and the original purpose of the fortification, made its way into the finished film.

On the drive back to the capital, we passed thousands of cherry trees on a west slope, their blossoms spectacularly backlit in the late afternoon sun. A group of thirty or forty peasants with hand tools was climbing the path from the road into the orchard. Dursch called for a stop and unlimbered the Arriflex. I strolled up the hill with him, and smiled and nodded at the peasants as they went by staring at the white intruders with friendly curiosity. Toward the end of the line of workers was a thin young man a little better dressed than the others, not carrying a hoe, a severe-looking young man who addressed us very sharply. Lu explained who we were and showed him our Foreign Ministry passes. An exchange went on for some time, the young man increasingly sharp, Lu indefatigably patient.

When I asked what it was about, Lu held me off with a gesture at first, but then said with quiet exasperation that this man was angry because we had filmed his comrades without asking their permission.

I gently pointed out, through Lu, that in fact the peasants had pointed to the camera as they approached us and beckoned to us to take their pictures, it had not been our intention, we had stopped to film the beautiful blossoms, but the workers had invited us to include them.

The young man said this did not matter. We had insulted them by not asking. We would have to take the film out of the camera and hand it over to them. By now a crowd had gathered. Those faces that had moments before been grinning for the camera now echoed the young Party man's resentment. They were holding their hoes and sickles up like weapons. We were surrounded.

Erik said, Hey, why not give them the film, he could get some more cherry blossoms, no problem, but when Roy decided to stand on principle and try to talk our way out of it, I caught the spirit of it, and agreed. We would stand firm. Lu looked profoundly uncomfortable.

The young man conferred with some of the elders. He then made what sounded like a formal statement to Lu.

Lu blanched, but translated diligently. Whenever Lu began a line of interpretation with "You see," we knew there was trouble. "You see," he said, clearing his throat several times, "this man says that we are their prisoners now. He says that this is the People's Republic after all, and these are the people, and they don't, ah, they don't give a damn what the Foreign Ministry says, they are the authorities here. And they are going to, ah, keep us here until we hand over the film."

The young man added something.

"You see," Lu said, "he also says we must hand over the camera and all the other equipment. And then they will let us go."

The workers tightened the circle around us, unspeaking, holding their hoes and sickles with unmistakable menace. The sun was beginning to sink behind the western hills and the blossoms were no longer backlit. The road to Beijing was oddly empty. I looked querulously at Roy, who pursed his lips but indicated that we should wait.

Down the slightly sloping road from the north came a distant figure on a bicycle. The rider's attention was caught by the parked car and this knot of people surrounding a trio of Wai-jen. He stopped, dismounted, and came toward us. Our guards were sufficiently distracted that I was able to edge past them and approach the new arrival with my hand out. I bowed my head just the right amount and said, "Ni hao; wo-men shih Jia-na-da jen. Wo jiao Hua-hsiung. Dzhe-yi jen Lu Yi-ching deng-dze." Which I hoped meant "Hello, we are Canadian. My name is Wa-Shung, and this is Comrade Lu Yi-ching."

The man smiled broadly and said something welcoming. Lu seemed to be explaining to him that there had been a misunderstanding, and what it was about. The man asked a few questions, first of Lu, then of the severe young man and the elders.

With Lu translating he said, first to us, that he hoped we understood that in China one should never take photographs without people's permission. Of course we said that we understood that, and explained how we had interpreted the earlier smiles and beckonings to indicate that they wished to be photographed. Somehow this had not been checked out with the complete group, but this time the newcomer canvassed them all, and several honestly nodded agreement, yes, they had smiled and pointed at the camera.

But we still had not asked permission and had not had the courtesy to speak to the local representative of the party, had we? We had not.

Patiently, bit by bit, this man who turned out to be the Party secretary of a large neighbouring commune managed to get us all to agree that it might be very fine indeed for pictures of these excellent workers to be seen in Canada, along with the beautiful orchard, but that nonetheless we should apologize for our error, and give them a solemn undertaking that we would be more respectful of Chinese customs as long as we were guests in this country.

By the time it was over, we were all shaking hands all round, even with the prig, who actually smiled at the end. We left candies as gifts with the peasants, and I made a show of taking individual and small group photos of them with the Pentax. Roy made a speech about the mutual friendship of our two great countries. As the shadows began to deepen across the valley, and a long train with two steam locomotives came puffing up the distant pass on the east side, we got back into the car with much waving and expressions of goodwill on all sides, and headed back to the Hsin Chiao for a good big feed, and probably several bottles of an excellent beer called Three Goats.

Breakfasts in the Hsin Chiao were also very good. For about twenty-five cents Canadian we could have beautifully prepared scrambled eggs, generously garnished with two or three heaping tablespoons of exquisite salmon roe. With recommendations from every direction, we made an early visit to what was then called *The* Peking Duck Restaurant. It was an all-evening affair that began with the giblets, the feet and the heads, then moved on to slices from the rich, sweet barbecued meat, upon which there was always, it seemed, just the right amount of exquisitely crisp skin, all of this handled not with chopsticks, but with a thin pancake dipped in a special sauce, like a plum sauce. The feast finished with a huge bowl of soup, allegedly made from all the bones and other leftovers of that same duck. Or ducks. We went back frequently, always to the same place, no need of Lu after the first time; we made do with my fragments of street-and-kitchen Mandarin, and in any case there were no choices to be made except in the matter of drink, which was Three Goats, or a strong white wine – a little on the sweet side – and usually far too much of the favoured beverage for toasts, a fiery kerosene-like spirit called Mao-Tai.

Not all the proposals made to us were rewarding. In one northern city, Shenyang perhaps, our local contacts said they were taking us to something truly extraordinary, we would see when we got there, and took us off on an all-day drive through a barren semi-desert, to what turned out to be a deer farm whose most important product was ground antlers, a folk remedy for impotence. Lu Yi-ching was appropriately humiliated; he had not inquired enough into this "something truly extraordinary" and promised not to waste any more days like that.

Almost every day after lunch (and the lunches were commonly superb, as was the beer that washed them down, a different brew in every town and not a bad one in the lot), Lu would say that it was time for "a little nap." It usually was, but we supposed, with some evidence, that this was his opportunity to make his daily report to his superiors in the party. One day over lunch Dursch and I decided to slip off on our own, with the Nagra and the Arri, to see if we could pick up some casual shooting in the streets without the constant protocols and objections of insolent young party members, objections that Lu generally supported.

We had seen some new "workers' apartment buildings" on the road between the Hsin Chiao and the airport. It seemed unlikely that they were for ordinary workers; we guessed there might be something worth looking into there, and agreed that once Lu was out of the way during the "little nap" time, we'd come down from our rooms, grab a cab, and head toward the airport. This was perhaps three weeks into the trip, and I had picked up enough street language to order a meal, find a toilet, buy simple things, and tell a driver to head for the airport.

When we came abreast of those big red brick apartment buildings, I signalled the driver to stop and wait. Erik and I strolled along the walk between the buildings and into the central courtyard, well off the street, where a group of elderly women were gossiping off to one side, keeping an eye on a dozen preschoolers. Erik lofted the Arri, got in among the kids, down on his knees, and started to shoot. We had been offered kids before, including one chilling propaganda-heavy display at that Holstein commune where we were proudly treated to the fierce warlike anti-American chanting of a chorus of six-year-olds. But these were just easy-going kids, playing with sticks and little balls, a bit of human colour with no propaganda attached.

The old ladies, however, began to murmur among themselves, and almost before we knew it we were surrounded by a group of stern faces and a spokesperson apparently demanding to know what we were up to.

"Wo-men shih Jia-na-da jen," I said, "we're Canadians." I got out some version of the Chinese word for television and tried to smile reassuringly. They were not buying. We had produced our red cards from the Foreign Ministry that – according to Lu – effectively gave us permission to film all over China. The women couldn't read. The anger level was rising. I suggested to Erik that it might be time to make a tactical retreat. It was not clear that we would be allowed to do this. Then one of the women pointed behind us and said something emphatic. I looked around. An elderly man in a black pyjama suit was coming slowly up the walk from the street, blinking in the sunlight, smiling with cordial curiosity. We showed him our cards.

"Ah," he said. "You are Canadians." His accent had a British touch to it and his English, while slow, was fairly clear. We nodded. "Et parlez-vous français?" I said, "Oui, nous parlons français." He blinked at Erik's card. "Dies ist Deutscher nahme," he said. "Sprechen Sie Deutsch?" Erik said he did, and the old gentleman continued in English, evidently delighted with the encounter, calming down the women, who were deferential toward him. We explained that we had stopped by to film the buildings, which we had admired from the street, as we wanted to show our audiences in the West something of how modern Chinese people lived. Well that was just right, he agreed, a good thing to do. He lived on the second and third floors, two apartments for him and his children's families, wouldn't we like to come inside and film the apartments, some of the family were bound to be home. It would be conventional to say we couldn't believe our luck, but in fact something like this – maybe not quite this cordial – something like this had been the object of the exercise in the first place.

Upstairs in the old gentleman's apartments, we met one of his daughters and some grandchildren, and were given tea and invited to film around the apartment. After a few minutes, I said that we would like to interview him for the program, and he invited us to sit down in his study and do that. Nervous about the camera at first, he soon began to wax enthusiastic about the benefits the Revolution had brought to him and his family. Here they were, all together in the one building, plenty to eat and money left over for books and newspapers. "I marry my French wife, you know. I studied in Paris, in America. I speak French, English. I work a little every day, come home, to my family. You know, this a very good life!" He repeated, "A *very* good life."

Then he stopped and laughed a deep throaty chuckle, the camera still rolling. "But, but, but . . . you don't know who I am, do you!" He had apparently thought we had come to this place *in order* to see him, that we had known he was famous. "I was mayor of Peking [*sic*] at the time of the Revolution," he said. "My name Ho. Ho Sze-yuan. I was mayor of Peking in 1949!" And he laughed merrily at the joke, the joke on him, I suppose.

The mayor of Peking (the old Anglo form of Beijing) would have been, at the time of the onslaught by the People's Liberation Army in 1949, a very senior politician, almost the head of a nation-state. Over the next few days Roy Faibish was able to verify Ho's story, and even made contact with his daughter, with whom he kept up a correspondence for thirty years.

Ho Sze-yuan was known by Chiang Kai-shek's Kuomintang party to be sympathetic to the Communists. When the People's Liberation Army arrived at the gates of the city, Ho took his personal bodyguard with him and opened the gates to Mao's forces. The fleeing KMT left behind a unit with orders to assassinate Ho, but he went into hiding until the danger was past. It was not, after all, surprising that he was now, in his eighties, living a pretty comfortable life.

If Lu knew what we had done during that little nap he never said so.

Lu pleaded with us to tell him jokes. The one that made him laugh the loudest was the story of a man on a streetcar who asks a fellow passenger directions with a horrible, paralyzed stammer: "C-c-c-can yu yu yu you t-t-t-tell m-me when we g-g-g-get to K-k-k-ing Street?" The other passenger looks away and doesn't answer. Another passenger, offended at this rudeness, kindly tells the stammerer that

King Street is the next stop, and when he gets off there turns to the one who would not answer and scolds him. "Why in the world didn't you answer that poor fellow?"

To which the apparently rude passenger answers, "D-d-d-do yu-yu-yu-you th-th-th-think I want to get a p-p-p-punch in the n-n-n-nose?"

Lu collapsed into a chair over that one.

There were times when Dursch and I would see something we wanted to film, but did not want to alert Lu. We had already developed a game, which Lu found entertaining, of singing snatches of classical music to each other to see how long it would take the other to identify the composer and the work. Lu did not speak or understand French, so we began to use the singing, in French, to say something like, *Écoute, mon vieux, j'ai vu un char blindé derrière cette edifice-là. Arretons pour faire pipi, et peut-être il-y-aura quelque chose . . .*[1] All in vague operatic style. Erik would ask, Was that Puccini? And maybe we should stop just here, he had to stretch his legs . . . and sometimes manage to slip away with the camera for a few minutes while we sought out tea or a toilet or a discreet bush.

One day he concealed the camera and just said he was going for a ride in a pedicab, and got the pedicab man to take him up through some of the derelict old hutong neighbourhoods, narrow lanes of desperately poor shacks, right in the heart of the city, garbage and half-naked kids, Dursch shooting surreptitiously from within the privacy curtains on the pedicab.

This was not a planned or purposeful documentary. There had been little time to research from without, and virtually none within: we felt we had to shoot everything that moved. No Western camera had seen the face of China since the Revolution of '49, except for a couple of polemical films by one Brit and one Australian, both friends of the Party and both studiously overlooking poverty, violence, and issues of human rights.

We would get up in the morning and fire up the camera and try

1. "Hey, pal, I saw a tank behind that building. Let's stop for a pee, and maybe there'll be something."

to make some sense out of it later. Marcuse and Hatem provided a lot of running commentary that helped us do just that. We filmed a scene with an Italian journalist, Antonio Cifariello, who was trying to work alone as camera, sound, and reporter, and was going nuts at the restrictions and the lies. He had been almost paranoiac when he first met us outside the hotel and wasn't sure that we weren't some kind of plant. We recaptured the mood of that encounter, reconstructing it in a boat in the Bei Hai Park lake. (This is a considerable infraction of my own rules of documentary, but it is so powerful that I am inclined to forgive myself. Just this once.)

We had an exhilarating day with a group of ironworkers at a blast furnace just north of the North Korean border, and a moving, gentle encounter with an agricultural worker and new father on a rural commune in the same district. Bit by bit we were putting together a profile of ordinary life, occasionally touched by an official encounter, something that would have to be montaged together, to reproduce for our audience a model of the slightly surreal experience that we were having.

Erik Durschmied's camera was an extension of his person. He seldom looked at the light meter, unless the sky was particularly deceptive or the surroundings unusually bright or somber, and even then the meter would come out of its sack for a quick look at the start of the day's shoot, or the work in that location, and not be seen again. Shooting outdoors under broken cloud, with the sun going in and out unexpectedly, or shooting from a vehicle with the shadow changing at every turn or change in the height of surrounding buildings or foliage, his finger would ride the exposure tab on the lens, making adjustments up or down as the changing light demanded, seldom taking his eye from the eyepiece. When the footage came out of the lab, scarcely a frame was badly exposed.

He had proposed that we shoot almost everything with sync. And so even when we were going through a small boatyard up the river from Shanghai, shooting hundred-foot rolls on the Arri to keep everything small and unobtrusive, I would come along at his side with the Nagra and mark a card with the roll number, or even take a ballpoint to the palm of my hand, and clap my hands for the sync. We would do ten or fifteen feet, in close, the face of a worker bending over a wooden hull as his caulking hammer rose and fell. And when that footage came into the cutting room, there would be no need to dip into the sound effects library or send for the foley artist[1]: we had it all for real. It sounds cumbersome, but it became a comfortable habit, always having the Nagra on my shoulder, always ready for a makeshift clapper and I.D. There would be so many little bits of speech to pick up, or pebbles in a stream, or that caulking hammer, the whoosh of liquid iron pouring out of the blast furnace, the cacophony of a loom. There is no substitute for authentic sync sound.

A side trip to Nanjing (everyone was still saying "Nanking" then) produced some interesting footage at the university, and with the Anglican Bishop Ting and a couple of his clergy colleagues. We were surprised to find any religious activity still tolerated, and Ting and his fellow priests made it (obliquely) clear that silence on political matters was the price of survival. Later, in Shanghai (not yet a skyline criss-crossed by cranes as it is today, but already a city of nearly twelve million people), we dropped in at a Sunday morning service at a Presbyterian church, and filmed the sermon and some hymns, and talked with a member of the congregation afterward, who if he were a plant expressed convincing surprise at our presence and echoed the Anglicans' observations about political neutrality. Shanghai was a bit like Canton, buzzing with foreigners and enterprise, the great harbour full of international shipping.

Wherever we went there were bands of kids in white shirts with scarlet kerchiefs around their necks, "Young Pioneers." Two years later millions of them would become the cruel vanguard of Mao's insane Cultural Revolution, destroying so much of the country's architectural

1. Named for the Hollywood innovator Jack Foley, who with the advent of cinema sound began to figure out how to do appropriate footsteps, bird's wings, the creak and groan of rigging, as well as all those sound effects I learned in a radio studio, as recounted in Chapter 3, such as the cornstarch bags for walking on snow.

history, its scholarship, its nascent international goodwill, and how many millions of its educated, outward-looking citizens, the kind of people who are leading China into a major and constructive international role today.

Back in Beijing we found an old friend, Charles Taylor, now accredited in China for the *Globe and Mail.* He told us how, within days of his arrival at the Hsin Chiao Hotel, a local professor, with whom he had started an ongoing conversation, had the bad judgment to come to the hotel for lunch and was picked up by four agents on the street as he was bidding farewell to Charles after that lunch and hustled roughly into a car.

By the time Charles had turned up, we had been in China for weeks and had had no word from home. Mail was slow. Douglas Leiterman caught up to me in Shanghai somehow, telling me that he had secured offices for *The Mag* in a building at the corner of Maitland and Jarvis, a two-minute walk from the studios. We would have all the offices and cubicles we needed and our own film editing suites.

From time to time as we walked through a factory, say, or a commune, or down a street with our guides, Erik would sidle up to Roy and me and whisper, "Create a diversion." Roy was good at this. He would point to something, anything, kids dancing, or an architectural feature, and start an argument. "We would never allow anything like that in the West," he might say. Or "Those children look as if they are being held in a jail. Why can't they just play, like ordinary children?"

This would bring our hosts around us like a circle of mentors, to straighten us out. Lu would be translating as fast as he could go. Nobody would notice Dursch slipping away down a side alley to pick up a few shots of a family eating in a courtyard, or a couple hugging on a park bench, shots that Lu would have tried to stop his taking. Once in a rolling mill I indicated with a nod of my head that I wanted Erik to get some shots of a mass of idle machinery filling half the plant, machines that looked as though they must have been cannibalized to keep the rest of the mill working. He frowned and whispered,

"But they're not doing anything." "Precisely, my dear Watson," I answered in my best Sherlock Holmes voice, "the dog did *not* bark in the night." Dursch looked puzzled for a moment, then got it, laughed, and slipped away to shoot the derelicts while Roy and I distracted Lu and the local managers and party people. Erik still chuckles, when we meet, about the dog that did not bark in the night.

Despite my need to deceive him from time to time, Lu and I became very close. Often, when I had to keep Roy and Erik from leaping at each other's throats, he would watch from the sidelines and encourage me with minimal gestures and flicks of the eye. In China, as in much of Asia, men hold hands with male friends. I had found that striking in the first days, seeing a couple of army officers strolling hand in hand. One day in the north of China, as we were exploring a large rural commune, I suddenly realized that I had been walking hand in hand with Lu Yi-ching for more than an hour and had been unaware of its being in any way strange. I remember another sudden perception from that same afternoon. Although the artificial leg had given me some trouble with blisters and rashes in the first few days of the trip, by now it was working so well that I realized, during that same walk in the commune, that I had been on my feet for hours without the slightest discomfort. That is a phenomenon that comes and goes. The risk of being legless for a few days is always there, but when it is at its best I actually forget about it for a while.

We travelled nine thousand miles during those two months. I left a few days early, Roy and Dursch deciding to take a last fling in the deep west, to Sian, mostly landscape and rural stuff; but no Westerners had been to Sian; it sounded exotic. I had to get back to the office that Douglas Leiterman had opened on Maitland Street for *The Mag*. It was June. We were supposed to go on the air in October. We still did not have a title for the series, or a first show lined up, or a complete staff. I would have to sublet much of the editing of the China film and dive into the preparations for *The Mag*. And by then I was sick of China, the restrictions, the surveillance, the falsity. Tony Cifariello had encapsulated it, the hopeless bragging about the accomplishments of the Revolution, in his funny interview in the boat. "They brought me to a two-hundred-year-old forest. Vast, beautiful trees, thousands of acres of it. Do you know what it was before the Revolution? A desert."

There had been enough of those forests. I was sorry to part from Lu, though. We had been warned not to give gifts to any officials, but I knew how much he loved fountain pens. He obviously coveted mine. I bought him the most expensive one I could find at the Foreign Visitors' Shop in Beijing and coiled it up in a handwritten letter of farewell, which I told him was a scroll in his honour. He could find the pen in private after I was gone. He squeezed the scroll and smiled. We embraced at the foot of the stairs as I was about to board the plane for Moscow. We both had tears in our eyes. I never saw him again. We believe he was murdered during the Cultural Revolution, a man who had spent too much time with the Wai-jen.

Chapter 10

SEVEN DAYS

MY FLIGHT FROM BEIJING to Moscow headed northwest over the Gobi Desert, Mongolia, and Siberia. The aircraft was a big Tupolev with rear-mounted engines, not very full but very noisy. After an hour or so, I wandered about looking at the galley and the different passenger sections. What I supposed was first class was almost empty, with sprawling brown upholstered seats, very comfortable looking, so I tried one. A stern, matronly uniformed person addressed me very sharply in Russian. I replied, "*Ya ni panamaya pa Russki. Panamayityi pa Inglesi?*" hoping the words bore some resemblance to "Me got no Russian, you speak English?" She was not amused. I went grumbling back into the deafening steerage quarters.

Canada had no ambassador in Beijing in 1964; Trudeau would rectify that in a few years, but when I decided to return westward to Canada and spend some time in London on the way through, I sought advice before leaving from the British ambassador, who was Canada's diplomatic agent in Beijing. He was courteous and helpful, and warned me that there was some risk that the Russians might steal my film, probably from the hotel room, if I were stopping over in Moscow, which I very much wanted to do. He arranged for a junior from the Canadian embassy in Moscow to meet my plane and sent a coded telex recommending that they lock the film in the embassy safe as long as I was there.

The skies were clear for much of the flight over the Gobi wilderness. Through passengers were not allowed to leave the plane during the short fuel stop in Irkutsk, just inside the Siberian border with Mongolia, about as far east of Greenwich as Winnipeg is west and quite a bit farther north. A few hours later we were able to stretch our legs on the tarmac at Omsk, in western Siberia, and then it was only a few more hours to Moscow.

A tall young guy from the Canadian embassy was at the gate when I arrived, and took me straight through to the baggage pickup – I don't think I even saw a customs or immigration officer. There was nobody else in the baggage area when the conveyor started to roll, and happily my five big boxes of film (about eighty thousand feet, mostly in four-hundred-foot rolls) were among the first pieces to come through. I asked if he couldn't use his rank to get somebody to release them to us. I was exhausted and sweating with anxiety for the film. My companion said he did not think he would bother with that, leapt over the barrier, passed my three big pieces of personal baggage over to me, then the boxes of film all marked in Chinese characters, flung them onto a cart and went wheeling out of the building as if he owned the place. I was speechless, looking paranoiacally over my shoulder for the KGB. A car and driver were waiting, and the engine started up as we crossed the pavement toward it, the trunk lid open, my eyes still darting around fearfully.

As we settled down in the back seat, I let my breath whoosh out and turned to him with a big grin, saying, "Wha-a-a—?" But he cut me off, silently pointing at the driver. "Later," he mouthed.

Even in the dark days before Khrushchev's denunciation of Stalin, that first trip into Moscow was extraordinary. I had time for a few tourist sites, Lenin in his glass case, Nevsky Bridge, the underground, a couple of grand meals alone in the cavernous hotel. By grand I mean large with lots of vodka. I had phone numbers for a few correspondents from some major western agencies – Agence France-Press, where they would know Jacques Marcuse, and the guy from the *New York Times*. It was fun for a day or two bopping around the city, and spending good stories on the envious journalists. But soon I was lonesome and homesick and ready for my own bed. I called James Mossman in London, one of the top *Panorama* journalists, and a frequent Durschmied partner on difficult assignments around the world. I retrieved my film from the embassy and took a plane for London. Mossman and I had agreed to meet for lunch at the Ritz. Unthinking – after two months in a China where the suit and tie were not exactly part of the social scene – I gave all my clothes (except a summer shirt, tan cotton slacks, and my scarlet Hong Kong nylon windbreaker) to the bellman at the Kensington Palace just before sinking gratefully into a deep hot bath. I took my time over the London papers in the morning and met Mossman in front of the Ritz, he in an impeccable light tweed, a bit warm for June, I thought, but very smart.

He eyed my scruffy gear, sighed an "Ah well" kind of sigh, and nodded to me to come with him. The face of the maître d'hotel in the Ritz dining room was a study as it went from the cool outrage registered upon catching sight of me when we walked in, through a range of dramatic and finally accommodating expressions until he waved us to a table – a somewhat discreet table, but very nice all the same – and presently returned with the waiter, who brought champagne in an ice bucket, the maître d' nodding graciously to me, and Welcome back to The West, or something like that. I looked quizzically at Jim Mossman, but he just shrugged and tacitly suggested that I should not ask.

Mossman was off to Egypt the next day and gave me his elegant little apartment for the rest of my stay. I had four or five quite irresponsible and giddy days with the London friends, and then it was time to get back home and to work.

Beverly had stalwartly managed the move from Ottawa into a comfortable rental on Sheldrake Avenue in North Toronto by the time I was back. There was a mountain of demands from the CBC. I scarcely had time to hug the kids and tell a few extravagant tales before we gathered for the first staff meeting. Doug had brought together a lively and varied group and still had candidates for me to interview. We all were eager to get up to Go Home Lake, where the Leitermans also had a cottage, and much of the next bout of speculative planning would take place there. Doug remembers our sitting on a rock at the west end of the island with our feet in the water through a long afternoon, almost until sunset, talking about how we would do it, how to incorporate the Hot Seat format from *Inquir'y*. Who the best documentary camera people were, the strengths of the new staff and the familiar ones: Beryl Fox, now ready to make her own films after a few years at Doug's right hand; Warner Troyer, who had become a reliable interviewer on *Inquir'y*; Roy Faibish, who could be counted on to open some usually closed and unlikely doors.

We agreed that much of the strength of the program would come from recording hours and hours and hours of stuff. Both of us had found that extended discursive filmed interviews that went on long enough for the person interviewed to forget about being nervous almost always produced gems even if the first several rolls had to be scrapped. You had to keep listening for that little human opening that would suddenly illuminate the story with authentic feeling or insight. Budget officers scolded us about the hundreds of rolls of film not even sent for processing, because the only thing that mattered was in the last ten minutes. Videotape, still new, had begun to temper the old parsimony about shooting too much, film being costly and not reusable. Tape's shortcoming was that it confined us to the studio; there was still no portable VTR. The recorders were still the quads, those same machines the size of two coffins that we had spent the night with in Grand Central Station four years ago, with their two-inch-wide tapes and four-slot whirring recording heads that were so vulnerable to dust and smoke. Everyone still smoked in the control room (we had yet to make the connection between smoke and videotape problems, as the tape machines were always remote, never in the control room with us). But the editing process was now fully electronic, no more razor blades, and we were beginning to speculate about using the long studio interview to try for tiny moments of revelation that would enrich conventional documentaries whose location segments had been shot on film.

Douglas had introduced me to a comical and garrulously bright son of North Winnipeg named Larry Zolf, and a business reporter named Sandy Ross. He had already decided that CBC staff unit managers would not be able to move rapidly enough to meet our needs and had engaged a small freelance unit that would work out of our own office. He had canvassed designers and technical producers, secured the biggest of the Jarvis Street studios, Studio One, and had set an early October date for the opening program.

We still had no series title or third producer. We had screened hours and hours of the BBC's *That Was the Week That Was*, and while the rock and centre of what we intended was solid journalism, documentary, straight reporting, intense interviews, we also felt that cheeky outrageous satire would do a lot to win the affection and trust of our audiences. We said that newspaper editorial cartoons had established a tradition of journalistic satire: ours would be more effective. Neither of us was an experienced comedy producer. We went through the CBC's Light Entertainment roster. I had built myself a certain amount of confidence with Bryant and Scott and our *Nightcap* series, which was always topical as *The Mag* would always be, and often pretty outrageous, which we wanted to be too. But CBC television was rich in light entertainment programs then, goofy comedy inspired by Wayne and Shuster, who were still doing it, not often the edgy, pointed, politically cutting stuff we wanted to do, but well made, well acted, richly buttressed with music and costume and clever sets. We knew that a producer who had been able to crank out that kind of stuff every week would have a lot to offer.

So we invited Peter McFarlane to come to Go Home Lake and sit on the rocks with us. Peter had done a wide range of variety programs at the CBC and had been one of those producers at whose feet some of us asked to sit when we were new, to watch different kinds and categories of studio work. He was a quick, inventive director who had been invited to Australia to help get its television variety going, and after a couple of years in Sydney had come home to be head of variety programs at the new Canadian private network, CTV.

We described our ambitions for a program that would dig under the surface of each week's news, looking for the currents of social and economic and cultural energy that had kicked off events and coloured them, and into the minds and motives of the players and the victims, the ordinary citizens and the artists and the inventors, perhaps above all the ones who had power and who, we said (a bit earnestly, but we were right), ought to be systematically held accountable, in the public arena, for their stewardship of that power, and we would do that. We would keep the country up to date on why the rivers were flooding or receding, why the winds were blowing differently today from ten days ago, who the key people were who were acting out the theatre of our political life, our life in the courts of justice, on the great battle fronts of the Cold War and the little wars between little jurisdictions – all that stuff. I am sure we got quite carried away.

Peter McFarlane seemed to love it. But at the end of the day he said, Look, he couldn't give up what he had at CTV, where he had the chance to run several big programs. He was flattered by our invitation. He believed, he said, that we were on the threshold of something quite extraordinary, and he knew what we should call it. "There is only one title you can give this thing," he said. "You have to call it *This Hour Has Seven Days.*"

Doug Leiterman and I were polite about that. It was late in the day. Perhaps even a very bright guy would come out with a dumb idea at the end of a long day sitting in the sun by the side of the lake not far from a beautiful waterfall, listening to a couple of driven enthusiasts babble. And the dumb idea was just fun enough, and on target enough, that for the next few weeks we jokingly used it as the working title. Somebody put up a sign in the office, *This Hour Has Seven Days,* and fellow producers coming for a visit would say that for a moment they almost thought we were serious about calling it that.

We began to use the short form, *Seven Days,* in normal conversation, but after a while we realized that everyone was referring to the new project as *Seven Days*, even as *This Hour Has Seven Days*, and it wasn't a joke any more.

We knew from the start that Laurier LaPierre would be one of the hosts. While we wanted to do on-air tryouts with a number of interesting women – as third host – we also heard that Carole Simpson of *That Was the Week That Was* had moved to Canada, and we brought her in for some of the first few programs to sing some of the satirical stuff, play in the sketches, and handle some of the continuity and presentation. Douglas had campaigned hard to persuade the management that I should be the principal host. They agreed that I had done an impressive job during the two highly improper outings I had had on *Inquir'y*, but there was no way that I could produce and host the same series; they were adamant. We called Pierre Trudeau, who was vacationing in Spain. He said he would be delighted to appear on the program, perhaps do some interviews or some special reports, but he could not tie himself down.

We interviewed the man who became Trudeau's father-in-law, James Sinclair, who had been a minister in the St. Laurent government, a politician whom Douglas admired for his directness and integrity. Sinclair agreed to audition, and we booked the little *Howdy Doody* studio, Studio Five, where I had done *Mr. Fixit* in my apprentice days. Douglas directed while I interviewed Jimmy and then he interviewed me. At the end we all felt that it wasn't quite for him, and we went looking further.

I had long admired the dean of the broadcast acting community, John Drainie,[1] whose electrifying performance of Mr. Arcularis in the *CBC Stage* radio series remains in my memory the single most powerful radio drama ever. For no reason except that he was a giant of the craft, I thought Drainie might be a kind of aloof giant, but he answered the phone like a normal human being and impressed us with his solid credibility. He said that he would agree to read the scripts that were provided for him, and would accept our journalistic

1. Father of the editor of *The Literary Review of Canada*, columnist and broadcaster Bronwyn Drainie.

integrity on good faith, but would not read anything he felt he could not stand behind. We finally knew that we had our man.

And so *This Hour Has Seven Days* went to air, live from Newfoundland to the Manitoba border, delayed to the west, at 10 p.m. on Sunday October 4, 1964.

It is rough, that first program, but it still holds your attention. There is no opening title. The first shot is a close-up of a thick, elegantly bound and gold-embossed book, *The Warren Report* on the Kennedy assassination, which had happened eleven months earlier. The voice of Warren Davis, a staff announcer who would be with *Seven Days* throughout its run, tells us that the report was published seven days ago, affirming that Lee Harvey Oswald was the sole assassin. The book yields to a high-angle shot of an elderly woman being escorted through the studio (live, again), past the live audience, the hosts (whom we have not yet met), teleprompters, and other equipment, as Davis tells us that this woman is Lee Harvey Oswald's mother, and she believes the *Warren Report* to be ridiculous. As the logo (a bold 60/7) is superimposed, Laurier LaPierre's (unidentified) voice says, "Ladies and gentlemen: *This* hour . . . has seven days." And we cut to an (also unidentified) John Drainie.

The stories tumble out. The gangster union leader, Montrealer Hal Banks, his whereabouts declared unknown by the FBI and the RCMP, has been found only the day before, by a *Toronto Star* reporter, Robert Reguly, on a yacht moored in Brooklyn. Reguly is in the studio to tell us, live, how he found Banks and was threatened by his goons, and then we cut to film shot that Sunday morning, our air date, when Larry Zolf flew over the yacht in a helicopter and then, from dockside, tried to get Banks to talk to him.

This is immediately followed by a hot-seat interview with the Minister of Justice, Guy Favreau, in which LaPierre and Warner Troyer (unidentified) grill the politician relentlessly on the Canadian government's failure to control Banks and the contradictions in the official statements. Favreau is patient, almost deferential, accepting his responsibility to give an account of himself and his government, in this forum, to the Canadian people. The interview, edited from more than an hour of original material, is seamless, seems to be live, there is not a breath of waste. When the segment is finished it feels like an exhaustive report on the Banks case, and we are only ten minutes into the program.

Harpo Marx has just died, the day before our program launch. The next item is an affectionate obit, with a lovely, goofy encounter from five or six years earlier between Joyce Davidson and the comedian, followed by the film classic moment in which he plays a Rachmaninoff concerto while the piano progressively falls apart.

Then a bridge: a series of Ed Reid bird cartoons making fun of the pretentious language of the *Seven Days* Manifesto, "Drawing attention to public wrongs and proposing remedial action . . ." etc.

Footage of the arrest of a Mississippi sheriff, in the recent murder of civil rights workers James Chaney, Michael Schwerner, and Andy Goodman, along with gruesome shots of lynchings by hanging and burning, is followed by a moving interview with Schwerner's young widow, the whole segment foreshadowing Beryl Fox's powerful *Summer in Mississippi*, which will be shown in a forthcoming edition.

An impressionistic montage documentary on air travel safety looks forward to another upcoming major piece, my documentary *The Moment of Impact*, which I had commissioned Jim Carney to direct the previous February, the day after Air Canada Flight 831 went down in a snowstorm at St. Thérèse, Quebec, killing everyone aboard; the official report was about to be released and we had filmed extensively the investigation of the remains of the aircraft and the hearings that would eventually reveal a stabilizer fault in the DC-8.

A Second City satirical sketch on television advertising provided a transition into Robert Hoyt's live interview with Mrs. Oswald, which was followed by Warner Troyer and Laurier LaPierre again, this time vigorously quizzing Mark Lane (*Rush to Judgment*), who had documented all the evidence suppressed by the Warren Commission in which witnesses reported gunshots coming from a location on the opposite side of the murder site from Lee Harvey Oswald and the

Book Depository. I shot the Lane interview very tight, with what would become our dark signature lighting for the hot-seat interviews, framed hard left and very close, below the hairline and above the chin line much of the time.

Troyer and LaPierre were politely offensive, so to speak, challenging Lane to justify how he, one man, in a few weeks of investigation, could possibly claim to know better than the Warren Commission with its thirty thousand interviews, FBI investigators, and the full machinery of the American justice system. Lane held his own with dignity, and the effect was both riveting and distressing.

In a kind of palate-freshener, then, Lord Denning, the Master of the Rolls,[2] recounted in an ineffably aristocratic way a twisted, ironic, and funny legal anecdote about a suicide whose estate he had represented as a young lawyer when the man killed himself three minutes before his insurance ran out, in order to honourably acquit his obligations to his creditors.

And then we closed on what begins as a light piece, Larry Zolf's coverage of the Beatles' recent Toronto visit, funny streeters mixed with some footage from the concert itself, but then ends with wrenching scenes of hysterical girls in the medical emergency rooms under Maple Leaf Gardens, and others collapsing in screams of anguish and tears at the wire fence at Malton Airport as the Beatles' aircraft pulled away from the gate.

I said it was rough, that first edition. There was a full thirty seconds of black after the Davidson–Harpo Marx interview was introduced, an embarrassingly empty screen with some distant nondescript music: it was a clumsy late roll-in of the film, with no apology or explanation.

Today it is inconceivable to me that none of our on-camera people – interviewers or hosts – was introduced or identified. John Drainie at one point lost his teleprompter for an entire segment and had to work uncomfortably from the script on his desk. The Second

2. The third member of the Supreme Court of Judicature in England.

City script was weak, and those performers looked ill at ease.

But for all of these faults, the hour had vitality and authenticity. It was unmistakably live, there was nothing glib about it; that live walk-on by Mrs. Oswald at the top declared a lot about the attitude of the program, the reach, and the risk-taking.

Even in those first heady days we found ourselves in trouble with head office. We had announced on our first program, in a slightly spoofing tone, that the Queen would be visiting Quebec next week and that we would cover the visit. "No you won't!" management boomed. It was too provocative. There might be terrible separatist repercussions. A general directive had gone out that there was to be nothing more than minimal news coverage of her arrival at the airport. No film, no interviews.

We took the position that management was wrong to arbitrarily tell us we couldn't cover the thing. Erik Durschmied was in Canada at the time; with his mischievous eye he would be well paired with a brainy young director named Peter Pearson. They turned in a funny and journalistically authentic look at the pomposity of both HRM and fawning officialdom. Management was apoplectic, not at the piece itself but at our having disobeyed. That was the beginning of what would become almost two years of growing internal warfare.

The next few weeks would see Beryl Fox's unforgettable *Summer in Mississippi*, a rework of Bryant and Scott's sketch with Khrushchev and the British prime minister, David Susskind's gripping stand-up conversation with the real Nikita Khrushchev, and a roundup of reports and analysis responding to the news that China had just detonated its first nuclear weapon.

We broadcast Katie Johnson's funny and provocative encounter with Dr. John Rock, the Roman Catholic physician who developed the birth control pill. In the fourth episode Douglas Leiterman and Robert Hoyt interviewed the leader of the American Nazi Party, George Lincoln Rockwell, who, surrounded by goons in SS caps and swastika armbands, sucked a corncob pipe throughout the piece. "Send all the niggers back to Africa," he said, among other outrages.

That one got both Leiterman and me anonymous death threats and was condemned in the House of Commons. We read from an editorial saying that *This Hour Has Seven Days* was on every lip, and then took a dig at ourselves by taking cameras into the streets to ask people what *This Hour Has Seven Days* meant to them; none of them had heard of it.

There was a documentary profile of Muhammad Ali, another on a United Church minister charged with sexual misbehaviour with teenage members of his congregation, a JFK memorial feature by Daryl Duke, a number of ombudsman stories aimed at unjust laws or the tyranny of bureaucrats, and continuing bursts of satire, at first often borrowed from the zany London crowd who had made *That Was the Week That Was*, but increasingly of our own manufacture, and increasingly strong and socially trenchant.

By the time we closed down our fourth episode, we were able to report to our viewers that (despite our spoofing of our own success with the streeters who had never heard of us) we were now the number one Canadian program in the CBC's prime time schedule, even ahead of *Hockey Night in Canada*.[3]

The audience that traditionally turned out for public affairs programs was small. We knew we would do a great deal better. But when the numbers climbed to three million viewers we were agape. Decades later the CBC claimed that their multimillion-dollar, richly produced *Canada: A People's History* was the most watched documentary in the history of CBC television, with well over a million viewers for its opening programs. Apart from their calling those heavily dramatized programs "documentaries," even in their multiple releases (three broadcasts within the first few days), they came nowhere near the multiple million viewers that we were pulling in when we used the *Seven Days* hosts and studio look to attract our immense audience to the full-length documentaries that we scheduled almost every fourth week.

Our interventionist items were mostly well received by

3. The only Canadian series drawing a bigger audience was *Don Messer's Jubilee*, which aired at 7:30 Sunday evening. We rationalized by saying, Well, but that's not prime time.

audiences, though seldom by our masters at head office, and certainly not by the establishments that they challenged. Early in the second season, Jack Webster filed a film report from British Columbia about a mild-mannered official of the Indian Affairs department who, with the agreement of the band he was working with, had intercepted the family allowance payments that he and the band leaders knew would normally be wasted on drink. He soon accumulated enough money to build the first decent housing the sad little community had ever known, clean modest houses that the band members worked on themselves, with running water and central heating, the beginnings of a transformation from squalor to dignity. But the Feds said that he had misappropriated funds and fired him with no recourse. As we met him in Webster's report, he was earning his living pumping gas. By the end of that night's program viewers had phoned in – not at our instigation – to start a fund for the man, and by the end of the following week people from across the country had started a citizens' foundation in his name. Management said that was inappropriate; it was interfering with due process.

We learned that an Ontario farmer was languishing in the Penetanguishene institution for the criminally insane, for having allegedly shot at a tax collector. His psychiatric evaluation was ambivalent. A *Seven Days* researcher took a cameraman to the institution on a visiting day, their camera concealed under a napkin over a picnic basket, said they were cousins come for a visit, interviewed what turned out to be a perfectly sane if understandably angry Fred Fawcett, and broadcast it the next day. Within a week Mr. Fawcett was found officially sane and released. Management was furious with us for having obtained the interview under false pretences: we had compromised the dignity and reputation of a Crown corporation, the CBC.

Allan King turned in a poignant and humiliating intimate documentary on the life of an unemployed man in Hamilton, Ontario. Politicians and senior bureaucrats exploded, and once again management came down on our necks.

But the one episode that contributed more to the weeks of unprecedented open warfare that broke out in May of 1966 and led to the (probably timely) end of *This Hour Has Seven Days* was so trivial that many journalists hearing my account of it today wonder aloud if I might have got it wrong. I have not. In planning for the second season, we advised management that we were going to have an open telephone on the home-base desk and would, at the start of the first program, invite the five federal party leaders, Lester Pearson, John Diefenbaker, Tommy Douglas, Robert Thompson, and Réal Caouette, to phone in during the broadcast and accept our invitation to a hot-seat interview with Laurier and me. Head office, through the senior vice-president, Bud Walker, forbade us to do that, saying it would interfere with the political process. The decision was final. There would be no discussion.

We replied that extending the invitation during the broadcast was no more of an intervention than the telephone invitations we would normally make, and the rejoinder was We told you: no discussion. After consulting with our department chief, Reeves Haggan, Douglas and I officially advised the corporation, through Haggan, that if they insisted upon this we would simply fold the unit, cancel the series, and look for work elsewhere. It was a cliffhanger. We worked diligently toward the season's opener; Haggan fielded the brickbats and roars of outrage that Ottawa showered on him every day, and quietly let his masters at head office know that we were serious. We issued no publicity about the opening episode. September was drawing to an end. I don't believe any of us in the *Seven Days* unit thought we would have to cancel. With only a few days left, there were signs of mediation: head office wondered, through Haggan, if we would consider softening the challenge to the leaders in any way, perhaps drop the "hot-seat" designation, perhaps assign Warner Troyer and me, instead of Laurier and me? We hung in.

And then one day Reeves Haggan summoned us to the apartment of his deputy Peter Campbell, at four o'clock in the afternoon. Douglas and I and as many of the program staff as could safely leave their posts turned up to find a well-stocked bar, Reeves busily pouring drinks. He raised a glass to us. "You've won," he said. There was a flutter of applause and murmurs of satisfaction. Reeves held up his hand.

"But there is something I think you should be aware of," he said solemnly. "You never really win an ultimatum against the management. And you can be sure that they will have their pound of flesh."

But for the moment we were too close to opening night to think much about that.

There had been some major changes over the summer. In the late spring of the first season, John Drainie had been hospitalized for cancer surgery and said that his convalescence would not let him return to *Seven Days* before the summer break. Douglas, through Reeves, had asked management to allow me to sit in for Drainie on a temporary basis while we canvassed for a new host.

I had been struck by a *Maclean's* magazine profile of stunningly beautiful and electrically bright twenty-four-year-old Chinese-Canadian woman named Adrienne Poy and invited her to watch the program from the control room one Sunday night, to see whether she might like to join Laurier as co-host. At the end of the evening she said no, she had found it fascinating, but a little too rowdy for her taste; she would like to do something a bit more dignified. Before long she would be making her reputation through the women's afternoon series *Take Thirty*, and later as the first public affairs personality to have her name reflected in the program's title: *Adrienne at Large*, which went to air in 1974.

I did my best to fill John Drainie's shoes until the end of that first season, when Reeves Haggan proposed that we formally bypass the Corp's rule against a producer appearing in his own program by dividing the executive producership of *Seven Days* and the once-a-month documentary series *Document*. If I were to be the sole executive producer of *Document* and Leiterman the sole exec. on *Seven Days*, then – at least formally speaking – there would be no obstacle to my continuing to host the latter. Management, he told us, privately conceded that they very much liked my work as interim host and would now be prepared to let this nominal separation of powers legitimize my continuing. So we did that.

The season started strong and built well up until about Christmas. Management's tone was more conciliatory. President Alphonse Ouimet and Bud Walker met with Douglas and me in a room at the Westbury Hotel and said that they would reduce their demands on us if we would just give up the hot-seat designation and format and do the same kind of interviewing in a gentler environment, a round table, say. I regret that we agreed. It was one of the few concessions we made, and probably the wrong one. Some energy went out of the enterprise, certainly out of those encounters with cabinet ministers and other senior members of the Establishment. There was some restlessness among the troops, and Laurier, in an unguarded moment, was reported as having said the series had lost some of its pure journalistic energy.

In fact the series overall continued strong, and our audiences loyal, steady, seldom fewer than three million, including for the monthly full-length documentaries. Beryl Fox's *The Mills of the Gods*, her searing portrait of the horrors of the Vietnam war, won acclaim around the world. That film contains one of the finest documentary moments ever, when Erik Durschmied, who, with Beryl for the first time, after numerous previous shoots in that country, took his camera with him in the right seat beside the handsome and athletic young pilot of a Douglas Skyraider in a napalm raid on a suspected Vietcong village, the pilot rejoicing, "Look at them run! Look at them run!" as the villagers tried to flee the engulfing flames. As they returned from the raid ("Outstanding!" the young pilot exulted) Dursch asked if he ever had any regrets: after all they had just destroyed a few dozen women and children with flames from the sky.

"My only regret is that I never get to be down on the ground to see the results," the appealing young man told him. Whereupon Fox brilliantly cut to exactly that scene: a smouldering village, the blistered and blackened bodies of the children.

In that few moments of film, we had been taken convincingly into the experience of killing from the sky with impunity, of being with a boy, a really nice boy from next door, who knew, first-hand, what a kick it was. And, hating what he had done, we could not hate him. Jack Gould wrote in the *New York Times* that Fox's film was "a chilling poem of resignation to the inevitability of man's inhumanity to man," and Hugh MacLennan (*Two Solitudes*) called it "the most beautiful, disturbing work of art I have ever seen on television . . . . Its irony was subtler than Swift's . . . it was full of beauty . . . . It left one, curiously, with hope."

All in all, the second season was much stronger than the first, despite the softening of the hot seat. The interviewing was more knowing and sure and revealing. The editing was superb. The fine old print graduates, Ken Lefolii and Sandy Ross, had got over their need to fully contextualize, realizing that such work could be left to print: our job was to bring experience to the screen, and to engage our viewers. It became a commonplace throughout the land that Monday morning conversation around the water cooler would be about last night's *Seven Days*, "from one Atlantic to the other" as Créditiste leader Réal Caouette had once said in an interview. Some critics, like the *Toronto Star*'s Dennis Braithwaite, regularly scolded us, while others like the *Montreal Star*'s Pat Pearce and the *Toronto Telegram*'s Bob Blackburn were usually positive and always fair. It was a rare Monday when we did not get substantial press, and there was a gratifying number of questions on the floor of the House of Commons.

When Stan Daniels played an overzealous publicity agent trying to persuade Pope Paul VI to throw the first ball at Yankee Stadium during his forthcoming New York visit,[4] several citizens' groups (mostly Protestant) expressed outrage, as did some MPs on the floor of the House. I went openly to war with the president when CBC vice-president Ron Fraser issued a public apology without consulting the programmers. Things settled down quite a bit when the Roman

4. In the event the publicity extravagances of that visit were far more outrageous than anything in the Daniels skit.

Catholic Archbishop of Ottawa personally telephoned the prime minister to say what an excellent spoof it had been, that the CBC had finally succeeded in humanizing His Holiness.

The highest numbers any regular CBC public affairs broadcast had reached before *Seven Days* were *Horizon*'s, in the vicinity of six hundred thousand viewers. *Seven Days* opened to an audience of twice that, and the numbers climbed steadily, peaking at 3.3 million. In many different forms critics and citizens were telling the CBC that this was what it should have been doing all along. But inside the CBC, in the press, and on the floor of parliament a good deal of worrying was done about *Seven Days*' "lack of objectivity," and Douglas Leiterman would exacerbate that concern in a broadcast interview by saying that objectivity is a myth. Frank Peers wrote in *The Public Eye* that "the broadcast committee in 1966 [that same committee that convened to look into the *Seven Days* mess] agreed with Ouimet that CBC personnel should not promote their own views in CBC programs." It is important to note that they did *not* declare that journalists and hosts should *suppress or conceal* their own views. Indeed, they said explicitly that the CBC needs on-air people "with strong individuality and personal opinions, but who are aware of their biases, and are capable of keeping them in check." Management has tended to read "keep in check" as if it were "suppress and conceal." This is unhealthy. My argument has always been that concealing a journalist's own attitudes and biases keeps relevant information from the viewer, who needs to be able to take a journalist's bias into account. The tacit contract between journalist and audience is based on the supposition that the journalists will do their best to convey those aspects of the story that they deem most relevant. *And the journalist's training, experience, background, and prejudices are one of those aspects.* The challenge will then be to demonstrate that journalistic principles make possible a piece that is balanced and fair, even though the reporter holds strong views on the issues. The journalist should say, for example, "After studying and reporting on Kyoto for five years, I am not convinced of the value of the accord; but this week an impressive group of supporters from across the country . . . ." etc. This is much more honest and useful than the faking of "objectivity."

The objectivity question was an important part of the CBC management's growing uneasiness about our series. I believe that much of the talk about objectivity was really the rationalization of something else: their resentment at our slipping out of their clutches when they were trying to rein us in, of our cockiness, our unmanageability, our thinly disguised contempt for head office.

Reeves Haggan let us know that it had been a winter of discontent in Ottawa: we should be on guard. In the summer of 1965 Douglas Leiterman had his legs badly smashed in a car accident while directing a documentary, and nine months later, still weakened by that blow and by his determined presence in the offices and studios no matter how exhausted he might be,[5] opted for a couple of weeks on a Florida beach. Before he left, he came into my office, shut the door, and said that he and Reeves had been chatting, had agreed that management felt they could not deal with us as a team (we were always together when they came to complain in person) and that he, Douglas, was afraid that once he was out of the way they might come after me, might try to divide us.

He had not been away more than three days before Reeves stuck his head in the door to tell me that Bud Walker would be in the Kremlin the next day and wanted to see me at 11 a.m.

I still have the Day-Timer I took into that meeting, with my scribbled notes, notes that Walker would later say he had no idea I was writing, as he tried to bribe me to join with him and Alphonse Ouimet, CBC's president, in undoing *Seven Days.* He began by saying, "I am severing your relationship with *Seven Days.*" He said that they had no intention of losing the program. They would keep the title, get rid of the present hosts, invite Leiterman to continue as executive producer, keep the basic spirit of the series, just reduce the abrasion level.

5. Only days after they repaired his legs, he had himself carried into the control room of Studio One on a hospital litter so that he could supervise the next broadcast.

We chatted civilly; I said I would consider everything he proposed with the greatest care, and wrote down as much as I could.

The intention was to give me a series whose concept I had helped develop a month earlier, at a conference at the Mont Gabriel resort in Quebec, convened by Reeves Haggan and his Radio-Canada counterpart, Marc Thibault. Reeves and Marc had brought together their two departments of Public Affairs/Affaires Publiques for the first time ever, Reeves finding just enough bilingual anglophones in Toronto to give him a reasonable representation. Initially a bit nervous of each other, the two groups soon found that they shared virtually all the same problems and the same aspirations. The weekend turned into a kind of love-fest, with little pockets of radio and television people gathered around drinks far into the night, and four or five plenary sessions, some with well-prepared presentations and others more spontaneous. Jean Lebel and I had gone off to his room one afternoon, after a lunch conversation with two or three colleagues from both sides got us speculating about the possibility of a series that would be produced by a team made up of both CBC and Radio-Canada staff, and Lebel and I said – perhaps a bit frivolously at the time, and certainly cockily – that we would go upstairs and write a proposal.

We stayed in Lebel's room all afternoon and what we produced was one of the best proposals I ever worked on. The Corporation had tried a few times to get francophone and anglophone production teams to collaborate on a project, but it had never worked out, and our lunch group had concluded that it was because the orders had come down from on high rather than originating where program ideas best originate.

The one we came up with was to be called *Quarterly Report* in English, *Le Bilan*[6] in French. Four times a year we would report to the country on the condition of our democracy in its main categories of concern: health, education, the arts, trade, prosperity, justice, defence, politics. The productions would originate in Montreal, from two

6. "The balance sheet."

units each with its own executive producer, who, with his or her key staff, would decide on the content of the program: that is, the Radio-Canada exec and his senior program staff would commission the French-language program according to their best lights, their CBC counterparts would choose the topics for the English-language program; neither would be under any obligation to do the same stories.

But they would be obliged to share working space, facilities, research, and technical and office staff and make all their material available to each other.

This would mean that two experienced producers, each with strong track records in programming to their known audience, reporting through their own national supervisors (the Reeves Haggans and the Marc Thibaults) would still have that independence of decision for which we had fought so many hard battles from the beginnings of television. But they would do it within a context in which they had to negotiate with each other for access to the troops and the gear, and that would force them to be intimately aware of what stories each was covering, to look for ways of sharing in order to make the money go farther, and to really get to know each other's values and purposes.

That would inevitably lead to their doing joint work that they agreed upon only because it met their program and budget needs and ambitions and not because it was satisfying a management fiat about French and English collaboration. Lebel and I were crowing as we hammered out a couple of pages on his tiny travelling typewriter. By the time we brought the proposal into the plenary session those people had all fallen in love with each other. An air of euphoria was in the room. All these distant, probably hostile and politically troglodytic others had turned out to be people who shared your fears and hopes, distrusted head office as much as you did, and who had stuff to teach you and were interested in learning from you. The ground was already watered and fertilized when we walked in, and when we read out the proposal (I think Lebel did the English and I the French just for fun), the whole room got to its feet applauding.

"It's a sure thing" was effectively the message we got from both

Thibault and Haggan. It's just a matter of logistics, they said, and of when to start it and who would do it. (Both Lebel and I were up to our ears, he with his pioneer series *Le Sel de la Semaine*, and I with *Seven Days*.)

And so Bud Walker's offer to me in that cramped little office on the first floor of the Kremlin at 358 Jarvis Street on that April afternoon was that if I would go along with them on the reform of *Seven Days*, they would give me *Quarterly Report*.

As if, I thought to myself in my combined fit of resentment at this bullying and of delight that the war was coming out into the open. . . *as if they have the right to give me something I've made myself.* He even raised questions about my loyalty to the country: it would be unthinkable that I should be in charge of a program reporting regularly on the state of the nation unless I was a loyal Canadian. Walker said earnestly that some people, looking at the ways in which I had constantly challenged authority, had speculated that perhaps my loyalty was in question. That was the point at which I had the greatest difficulty keeping my cool, but I did so because by now I knew that he had exposed his intentions beyond recovery. Reeves Haggan agreed: Walker had done little but put obstacles in the way of our doing our best work – unlike the intelligent and generous-minded Al Ouimet, who had given Walker all this power.

It was that conversation in the Kremlin on April 6 that set off what would come to be known as the Seven Days War. Bud Walker had violated the Corporation's agreement with the producers that explicitly put into our hands the choice of performers, hosts, interviewers, and program content. I was aghast at the offer to do *Quarterly Report* in return for betraying my *Seven Days* colleagues. Douglas Leiterman and Bob Hoyt (who by now had become, in many ways, the First Lieutenant) decided to turn it into a public campaign and began to plan their strategy with the press. This made me uncomfortable, but what the hell, there was no way we were going to keep this quiet. I kept my sense of propriety to myself and went to war alongside my people, a war that we would win morally but lose technically.

This Hour Has Seven Days had its last broadcast on May 8, a month after that meeting with Walker in the Kremlin, a month that had seen us all summoned to testify before a parliamentary committee, the formation of a nation-wide Save Seven Days committee (masterminded by Hoyt), and an unheard-of intervention by Prime Minister Lester Pearson in the form of his own personally appointed mediator.[7] Douglas took the issue to the Toronto Television Producers' Association. Although deeply divided about *Seven Days,* of which many producers strongly disapproved, the association voted to withdraw services if management did not rescind its arbitrary firing of the hosts. Hoyt and his minions, directing the national Save Seven Days campaign, managed enough leaks and press releases and provocation of distinguished citizens into making outrageous statements to keep us on the front pages of the country's major newspapers every single publishing day for six weeks.

Reeves Haggan was refused his annual pay increase for the second year in a row and was told that it was highly unlikely he would be kept on as head of Public Affairs.

Bud Walker was humbled by Alphonse Ouimet after Walker had decided, quite arbitrarily, to move to Toronto and take over the network. Ouimet instructed him to return to Ottawa and relieved him of any serious responsibilities.

In the small hours of the morning on Friday, July 8, 1966, it was all over. Reeves Haggan and I resigned, Doug Leiterman was fired, Laurier LaPierre and the production staff were told that their contracts would be terminated forthwith.

The ultimate irony – no, *one* of the many ironies of that exhausting battle – was that Douglas Leiterman and I had said to each other, sometime before the simmering had reached the boiling point, probably early in the autumn of 1965, that we would bring it to a close at the end of that second season, with our last broadcast in May of 1966. By then it would have made its mark, established some directions, exhausted its freshness. We must not let it settle into routine, become

7. Stuart Keate, publisher of the *Vancouver Sun,* and a personal friend of the prime minister.

staid, too pleased with itself. After those two dazzlingly gratifying years, it would be time for us to step back, reflect upon what we had learned, devise something new, either together or separately. We would have done what we came together to do, it would be time to move on.

Perhaps the program would have had a longer life had we won the war against the management and become, as a result, morally obliged to keep going, despite what we had said to each other about closing it down after our two years of splendour. To be told over and over by your audience, by your ratings, by critics, even by some of your colleagues and chiefs, that you are doing something that has never been done before and doing it superbly is not likely to leave you in a state of humility.

We were already arrogant toward those head office troglodytes, who should have been long gone anyway, relics of the radio age who had never been able to come to terms with the volatility of television. We were high-handed with the News department and *its* arrogance toward us when we wanted library footage. But we did not think we were the be-all and end-all, and that we could go on forever. Ned Sherrin had told me in London in February of 1964 that he rang down the curtain on *That Was the Week That Was* because two years was the natural life of a program. And when Doug and I had that conversation in the fall of 1965, we were intuitively agreeing with Sherrin.[8]

A great deal has been written about all this. Eric Koch's book *Inside Seven Days* has a lot of the detail, is an absorbing read, and gets much of the tone and the purpose exactly right. Students of television wanting to study the program in depth will find most of what they need in that one engaging account.

But Koch missed something important. He saw *Seven Days* not just primarily but almost entirely as a social phenomenon, the device whereby a group of journalists and filmmakers deliberately tried to

8. Agreeing out loud, that is. Douglas Leiterman now says that he privately felt that *Seven Days* could have and should have gone on indefinitely, that it would have continued to evolve for years.

change the country, to confront our fellow citizens with our social failures and injustices and absurdities in the hope of moving the democracy forward. Eric did not really understand our stress on the cinematic, visual, pure journalistic, documentary, and dramatic intentions that gave the program both its distinctiveness and its power. Both Douglas Leiterman and I were close to obsessive about the image on the screen. That was the true *content* of the program, as we saw it: what the audience saw and heard. We *studied* movies. We saw that the stronger directors used enormous close-ups and lit them with little fill and strong backlight. We saw how smoke or haze in a scene gave it three dimensions, and not wanting to spend our always overstretched budget on smoke machines, we turned off the air-conditioning in the studio before a hot-seat interview and got all the smokers (a majority, in those days) to go into the studio and smoke it up for a few minutes before recording. This gave us that sense of depth, and a visible slash of hard backlight lancing down aggressively from the grid onto the guest, dramatically placing him or her on an exposed and menaced salient.

We looked on the interview as a form of theatre. For me, among the personal satisfactions was a growing sense that I *really knew how to do this interview thing*, an eagerness to find and reach another new level of bringing a person vividly to life on the screen. A remarkable number of those interviews grew into enduring friendships, among them an early one with the inventor Buckminster Fuller, and another with the painter Robert Markle, three of whose erotic drawings had been impounded by the police. Bucky Fuller became an important mentor, as did Robert Markle, who became my closest male friend until his early death. Both of these men will appear in later chapters.

Almost every interview was discussed at length before it happened and dissected scrupulously afterward. It was seldom that any interviewer would not be asked to screen the finished product and consider how it might have been better. Some of the editing sessions were extremely intense, and one was unforgettable.

Capital punishment was very much in discussion after fourteen-year-old Stephen Truscott's reprieve from being hanged for the murder he almost certainly did not commit. Someone said they thought Nathan Leopold was still alive, and wouldn't he be a great interview, a man who had narrowly been saved from being hanged for a murder he *did* commit, and had spent thirty-three years in prison. He and another Chicago teenager, Richard Loeb, had murdered an eleven-year-old boy on a whim, confident they had performed the perfect (motiveless) crime. They had been defended by the great Clarence Darrow Jr., who persuaded the court to sentence them to life plus ninety-nine years instead of hanging. Loeb had been murdered in prison, and Leopold was finally paroled in 1958.

I found him by telephone, working as a social worker in parasitic diseases with the Health Department in Puerto Rico, continuing the ornithological studies he had begun in prison in Chicago.[9] I asked him if he would agree that he was "Exhibit A," a prime example of a person whose life could make a case against capital punishment. He did, and got on a plane for Toronto.

I met him at the airport, and over tea in the old Four Seasons Hotel across the street from the CBC, I briefed him: we would record at least an hour and then edit it to its best running length. I reviewed the questions, and he warned me that he would not discuss the motivation for the murder of Bobby Franks. I said, "You know that I have to ask you, don't you?" He did; he just said he would not discuss it.

He then said that there was a condition. He wanted to sit in on the editing. I protested that we never allowed such a thing, but he made it clear that unless I agreed, he would not do the interview. He would not interfere, he said. He understood that the editing decisions were mine to make, but he was deeply curious about the process and would never have another chance. Briefly I considered consulting with Douglas, but I knew that this was a decision for me to make, that consulting would only muddy it, that Leopold meant exactly what he said, and I was not going to throw away the opportunity to interview him. We shook hands and he went to bed.

9. He published *Checklist of the Birds of Puerto Rico and the Virgin Islands.*

The whole interview was gripping. His soft-spoken courtesy and steady, emotionless blue eyes were riveting. I said, when he refused the question about what he was feeling at the time of the murder, that he had come here to present himself as an example of a man whose life had changed in prison, and who had become a valuable member of society, and that we could not understand that fully without knowing what his feelings had been then, and how they had changed. He said, "I understand that, Mr. Watson, but I am not going to discuss it." Calm. Not a flicker of those eyes. The studio was electrically silent.

Without telling the colleagues, I took Nathan Leopold with me to the VTR edit suite, and he sat there as promised, not saying a word for the three or four hours it took me to cut our seventy-odd minutes down to fifteen or so. When it was done, he shook my hand warmly, said he had found it most fascinating and thought my decisions fair and appropriate, and said goodbye.

I recently screened that interview for the first time since it went to air; it is still gripping.

In those cutting rooms we watched our colleagues' eyes as much as we watched the screen, and if anyone's attention wandered, we knew we had found something to cut, even when it was something of narrative or analytical significance to the story. If it was not strong enough to hold your attention, then it was wasting your time and that was irresponsible. Wasting the viewers' time was irresponsible. Broadcasting stuff that was not significant or compelling was an irresponsible use of the taxpayers' money. That was one of the principles that Douglas Leiterman had pronounced upon long before we came up with the Manifesto: in a universe of limited channels, where you were the one outlet that was meant to serve the country, not the advertiser, it was a misuse of your mandate and your funds to be anything less than compelling. To be boring or trivial was to be contemptuous of your audience. To make anything public that is of any value, a novel, a painting, a song, a movie, you have to respect your audience. That formulation was the underpinning of the program's morality. Our preoccupation with the image, with constantly making the picture on the screen so compelling that you could not turn away, was our way of saying to our audience, We know you're really smart, but we have seen some stuff you haven't seen, and we want to share it with you. *And we promise not to waste your time.*

Chapter 11

FLYING

While the end of *Seven Days* left me feeling morally secure (probably not a little self-righteous), it also left wounds that needed some healing time. I packed the family into the car, bought a twenty-five-pound bag of flour and half a case of gin, and headed to Go Home Lake to pound out my anger kneading loaves of fresh bread every day, and drinking sunset toasts to the memory of Bud Walker with martinis of exquisite precision, (5½ to 1: stir on ice with a cooking thermometer until it reads –1 Celsius). Larry Zolf came to visit and commented that the dough I was pounding so hard was symbolically Alphonse Ouimet's head. I liked that.

Donald R. Gordon, who had been CBC News's London correspondent during the early days of television, was now a professor of political science at the University of Waterloo. He got me an adjunct professorship in the department, beginning in October, and every week I drove over for a day or two, staying with Donald and his physician wife, Helen (an old friend from Glebe Collegiate days), and conducting a delightful, loose-format graduate seminar on media and politics. This gave me a good solid feeling of still being connected to the community, and briefly led me to wonder about picking up that long-abandoned Ph.D.

I also learned to fly, and that was very therapeutic. Partly, of course, I was bringing Cliff back to life. I worked at it diligently for the next couple of years and by late 1968 I had a multi-engine endorsement. I was checked out on a dozen different aircraft, and working on an instrument rating

Although as I write, I have not flown as pilot in command for fifteen years, the memories nudge me almost every time I see an airplane. The poetics and clarity of it are still fine. I can feel it in my hands. From my boyhood it had been something I would do one day, and in the spring of 1960 when I signed a contract to go to the CBC Ottawa station as senior Public Affairs television producer, I realized that at last, after those first years as a penurious family man – a family man too young, perhaps – I would at last have enough income to start those flying lessons. But that was the summer I lost my leg. As I was putting my life back together again, flying had been one of the many things I thought I would have to resign myself to giving up, but during the dispute over *This Hour Has Seven Days* I discovered I might be wrong. A very dear old friend from university days, Ben Marcus, by then a successful lawyer in Ottawa, had been flying for some years. Once or twice, sitting in the right seat of *Julie*, his ancient Cessna 182, I had taken the controls and gingerly put my prosthetic foot on the left rudder pedal. And Ben began to say, You could do it, you know. Al Goodman was giving me similar encouragement in rented airplanes out of the Buttonville airport.

One afternoon after I'd been on the stand at the *Seven Days* parliamentary hearings in Ottawa, Ben Marcus arranged for a friend who had an Aero Commander 500 to take me and a couple of the others back to Toronto, and they put me in the right seat. The pilot invited me to take the controls and showed me power management, synching the props, altitude holding – really quite a lot of stuff for a neophyte. I felt quite at home. Back in Toronto I begged Al Goodman for a few more flights.

Then, when the *Seven Days* battle was finally over in June of 1966, I phoned the flying school at Buttonville. I said I was interested in taking lessons, but that there might be a problem, I had a wooden leg.

The guy said, Hey, they were teaching a man who has two. If I can do it I can get a licence. I should come on out and give it a try.

The Ministry of Transport was perfectly straightforward: their attitude from the start was "Show us." They imposed a temporary restriction on my student permit and first private licence: I'd be allowed to fly only aircraft equipped with handbrakes; so I trained on a Cherokee 140. Then, once I had a licence, I took instruction on the Cessnas, 150s, 172s, and 182s, and worked out a tactic for applying the prosthetic toe to the upper part of the rudder pedal. I would lean back in the seat, lift my hip slightly and raise the knee of the prosthesis. This would cause the toe to depress enough that I could then press forward and put the necessary load on the braking tip of the rudder pedal. After a couple of weeks, I felt comfortable with it, went for a test ride to demonstrate that I was safe with toe brakes, and passed it easily.

Next was the multi-engine rating, taken on a wheezing old PA 23 Apache. And then I really began to want my own machine. Early in 1968 I bought into a partnership in a 1964 Twin Comanche, reputed to be challenging to fly, the smallest of all the current light twins, fast, easy on fuel, and this one, CF-UCH, fully equipped for instrument flying. The senior partner was Irving Shoichet, who ran a charter service at Toronto International Airport, Skycharter, and who offered to finish me up for an instrument rating as part of the deal. He was a low-key quiet, dry, ironic instructor. He called me "kid."

A few months after I finished the instrument rating there came the move to Ottawa and CJOH, and in Ottawa I took my commercial licence, then an instructor's licence with an aerobatics endorsement. The Twin Comanche proved to be, indeed, a challenge; it was several years before I found a technique for reliably landing it, in any configuration, without a bounce or two. But within months it was earning its way as clients learned that I could transport myself and a film crew to out-of-the-way destinations for thousands of dollars less than it would cost them to send us by commercial airlines. I paid down the initial loan and bought out the partners in less than two years.

Writing about flying – even for flyers – often seems self-indulgent, a bit like trying to be interesting while telling someone your dreams. Flying is a way of being in the world that demands poetry to be well communicated. There were some episodes of pure poetry, others of pure fear. Once, alone, landing on skis on the frozen surface of Lake Mazinaw to look for the petroglyphs that were allegedly inscribed in the cliff face, and not knowing enough about ski-flying to have tested the ice before coming to a stop on it, I broke through on takeoff, felt the borrowed Citabria stumble and slow, then, miraculously, pick up speed again and lift off. Once airborne, I banked steeply and turned back over the lake to look at the tracks of my takeoff run. There was a dark, spreading pool of water about a hundred feet before the tracks of the skis ended. By pure good luck, I had been far enough into the takeoff run that when I came to the thin ice and broke through, I was fast enough that the skis planed on the water: water-skiing, in effect. If I had landed on that patch of thin ice, only a couple of hundred feet beyond where I had come to a stop in the deep snow, the best possible scenario would have been that the fuselage would have stayed above water, and I could have radioed for help or climbed out onto the high wing and tried to wave to someone on shore. The worst possible scenario is one that I still wake up sweating about from time to time.

There were also some hilarious moments. Commuting to Teterboro, New Jersey, when I was anchoring *The Fifty-First State* for WNET Channel 13 in New York, I often flew down alone at night and back to Ottawa every other weekend or so to see the family and keep an eye on the few production projects I had been able to stay with through our Ottawa production house. It was quite magical to quit the buzz of Manhattan and walk from the bus down to the hangar at Atlantic Aviation, Teterboro, where both Lindbergh and Earhart had started their historic flights. Out at the threshold of the runway, usually nobody else flying that late, and the thrust of the throttles to the firewall, and the liftoff, and then the whole Manhattan scene glowing orange into view off the wingtip as you rose up above the low New Jersey coast; that was always a joy.

One night most of the trip north was in dry snow, on instruments, at eight thousand feet. Almost nobody on the radio. Too late for most airline service, just after midnight, as I recall. I had the Comanche on autopilot. I was scanning the panel routinely, when out of the corner of my eye I saw a blue flash that looked to be away off in the distance, dead ahead. *Lightning!* There is nothing as alarming to the pilot of a small aircraft as lightning, but it seemed awfully improbable to have lightning in steady snow at 20 below zero Fahrenheit.

I switched on the wingtip lights. The snow curled over the wings in a perfect demonstration of Bernoulli's theorem. Thin, dry snow. I switched off the lights and as I did so I caught another blue flash forward. I strained to see into the night. The airplane was sitting there perfectly steady, painted on the sky. I peered, another flash, but it seemed – out of focus. Which it was. Because when I refocused my eyes, closer, there it was, not miles ahead but right on the windscreen, a blush of blue flame running around the periphery of the Plexiglas where it met the metal of the frame.

A voice on the radio.

"Canadian civil Uniform Charley Hotel, go Binghamton approach control now, one-seventeen-point-niner."

I switched over. "Binghamton approach, Canadian Fox Uniform Charley Hotel, level 8,000."

"Squawk ident, UCH."

I pressed the Ident button on the transponder. "Check you level 8,000, UCH."

I said, "Binghamton approach, there's nobody else on the air, can I ask you a question?"

"Go ahead, UCH."

I described the blush of blue electric light. He said he'd never heard of anything like that and asked how bright it was. I said I would shut off the panel lights and hold a chart up to the windscreen to see if I could read it by the blue light. And he said something like, Yeah, stand by one, UCH, I have to work another flight.

I heard him clearing an Allegheny Airlines flight through the zone at 23,000 feet, probably deadheading back to base at that hour. I had the lights off. I held an approach plate (a small white landing chart, about four inches by six) up toward the windscreen, and moved it slowly closer to see if I could read it. There was a *SSSSSSSssssss!* (the acoustical part probably just in my imagination), as sparks arced from the windscreen to my hand. Just a slight tingle, but an impressive arc of more than an inch, must have been 30,000 volts, but with almost no amperage.

Binghamton was finished with the Allegheny flight. I called in and told him about the arcing.

Air regulations dictate that the radio be used only for necessary exchanges regarding traffic control, but late at night things are relaxed and pilots and controllers sometimes gossip a little. I heard the drawling voice of the Allegheny captain. It went something like this: "Binghamton approach, can I have a word with that Canadian pilot?"

"Go ahead, Allegheny 319."

"Canadian Civil Uniform Charley whatever you are, this here is Allegheny 319."

"Three-one-niner, UCH. Go ahead."

"Well now, I think I have a solution to your problem? You see, that arcing you-all reported? That indicates to me that . . . that you have either a very negative, or a very positive . . . *personality.*"

The business advantage of owning that airplane was manifest to my clients, and it paid for itself over and over again. But that was really just an excuse or a rationale for the profoundly satisfying experience of the thing. Hundreds of flights that each leave you with at least one ineradicable image. Coming back from Youngstown, Ohio, on my birthday in 1967, I was still a pretty new pilot, in a rented Cessna 210 with Robert Markle and my son Chris on board. Soon after dark and just crossing the Niagara peninsula, I call Toronto International for wind and runway information.

"We were right down to almost zero in heavy snow just a few minutes ago," says Toronto. During the pause that follows I feel the clear physical statements of fear beginning to enunciate in bowels and back and heartbeat and fingertips.

"Uhh . . ." says Toronto, agonizingly, ". . . but it looks like just a small local shower; you should be okay coming in."

And then we can see it. The whole spreading glittering mass of Toronto, thirty miles ahead of us, begins to be obliterated by the snowstorm that has just blown by the airport. The storm is haloed by the city lights, a rim glow on its top and bottom, and absolute black in its heart. It moves across the warmth of the city from left to right, eclipsing two million people. In a minute Toronto is gone: no statement of its life remains except the rim light on the rolling cloud. A few streamers of snow blow by below us. But after three or four minutes of what seem absolute silence, the three of us staring, speechless, into the black, the airport has come clear again, in the left of our vision, and tower directs us across its centre, out, and around, to line up on the diamond-flashing strobe lights that tell us which runway they want us on, and then, with a nervous bounce, we are down.

How lucky I was to have lived at that briefest moment in our history when almost anyone could learn to fly. Airplanes had become reliable enough to make it safe for everyone but the frivolous. Fuel was still cheap. Regulation and traffic had not driven the little guys away from the big airports. Insurance claims had not driven premiums through the roof along with the cost of mechanical inspections and parts. Dual instruction in 1966 cost me $16 an hour. Today it is ten times that, five times when adjusted for inflation. I paid $29,000 for a four-year-old Twin Comanche with only four hundred hours on engines and airframe. A comparable aircraft today would be five times as much, adjusted for inflation. Home-built ultralights are still an option, but they are noisy and dangerous – not intrinsically but because they fly outside the tradition of rigorous inspection and performance standards. Kids get killed partly because they don't inspect every cable and connection the way trained pilots are expected to do. Most of flying safely has nothing to do with coordination of hand and eye, but is embedded in the discipline of constantly checking everything, and that discipline is inconsistent with the atmosphere of the world of the ultralights.

When I got my commercial licence in 1971, I found myself in a dry period for television work, so having an unaccustomed amount of free time I took the training for an instructor's ticket and then got an aerobatics endorsement on that, and offered my services through the two flying schools at the Ottawa airport and also privately. I had expected that the most likely call on my time would be for instrument training, as not many flying school instructors are qualified for advanced instrument work. There was some of that, but unexpectedly I found that the most enjoyable teaching I did during those next few years was *ab initio*, the basic training of novice pilots. And, in that field, the most enjoyable sessions were with older student pilots, men and women in their fifties who weren't exactly sure that they should be doing this, but wanted to try it before it was too late. The interesting part was that their confidence was often precarious; they didn't have the cockiness of the teens and early twenties who made up the majority of the student pilot population. So I concentrated on those aspects of training that build confidence. One was stalls and spins, something that many instructors try to get out of the way fast because students find it alarming. Most of our training was in Cessna 150s or Cessna 172s, very stable and forgiving aircraft. In a stall the ailerons, which control bank, are awash in turbulent air and useless as control surfaces. If you don't put the nose down and gain airspeed, you will likely have one wing drop out from under you, and when it does so, then the other wing, reducing its angle of attack, begins to fly again while the downgoing wing goes deeper and deeper into stall. And that is a spin. Stalls can lead to spins, and spins kill. And that's why students are afraid of them. I think many instructors are too.

But I had discovered that you could hold the Cessnas in a full stall without recovering from it and not drop off into a spin as long as you kept the nose fairly straight ahead and the wings level using the rudder only, tap-tap with your toes. The airplane would nod gently left and right like a chicken pecking the ground, and drop at a modest rate of descent, with less than forty knots of forward airspeed. So that even if you never recovered and flew it, stalled, right into the ground, while you would certainly bend the airplane badly you would not likely damage yourself very much. I reasoned that should you have a forced landing over water or trees, you would be much safer touching down in this nose-up, low-speed attitude than you would if you went in at normal glide speed, so the controlled stall was an added safety manoeuvre to have up your sleeve. But I also discovered that once students had got the hang of putting the machine into this absurd and unorthodox attitude, and dancing on the rudder pedals to keep it from spinning, they loved it and asked to do it over and over. Best of all, they had lost their fear of stalls.

The other great confidence builder was forced approach and landing, or "short field approach." Here you practise how you would land in an unfamiliar field, say, overtaken by nightfall or bad weather or running out of fuel, but the engine still running and you fully in control. So you come in with a lot of flap on, very slow, just above stalling speed, using quite a lot of power, holding the nose as high as you can. Most of the work is done with power management; you need a lot of power when you are slow and "dirty" (flaps down full or two-thirds, landing gear down if you are retractable). But the lovely result is that your airspeed is only about forty knots when you touch down. So if you step on the brakes authoritatively, you'll be stopped in no time.

I remember one student, a fifty-five-year-old schoolteacher who was very diffident about his skills; in every session he wondered aloud if he should be doing this, if he *could* do it. It came time for the short-field forced approach. We were using a Cessna 172, a stable, reliable machine with good safety margins. My student was white-knuckled as we slowed close to the stall mark on the airspeed indicator, but, tense as he was, he was focused and responsive to my little nudges: "Touch more throttle now, hold it off, hold it off . . ." He came over the threshold of runway 21 not much more than fence-high. He flew it on and chopped the power when I called out to do so and stepped on the brakes. The little aircraft stooped forward on its nose wheel, and stopped.

"Whew!" he said. "I don't think I want to do that again."

I said, "Look out the rear window." He did. We had stopped so soon that we couldn't see the runway numbers behind us. Couldn't see pavement, even, only grass. In fact we had used about two hundred feet, the equivalent of the *width* of the runway.

There was a pause. My student said, "Did *I* do that!" And then he immediately wanted to do another.

My feelings about theatre helped too. One of the trials for any pilot in the early stages of advanced training is the first instrument ride, where you go up with a government inspector, put on the hood that masks the view outside, and submit to his trying to get you to make mistakes while you are flying by what you can see on the panel. I somehow conceived the notion that this was partly role-playing, and began to advise my students who were candidates for the instrument ride to rehearse the part of the cool, blasé old hand who, yes, has to go through this but it's really so, well, *ordinary*, you know. So you take it slow going around the plane to inspect it (mandatory), and you talk to the inspector as if *you*, not he, are the knowledgeable person, you do not defer, you act authoritative, cool, detached. All the things a good professional pilot is supposed to be. It works, and many of my instrument ride candidates reported back that they had done better than they had ever expected to do. So that was gratifying.

Being a minor celebrity had some perquisites. I was invited to try out airplanes that would never otherwise have come my way. In the mid-seventies the RCAF base at Cold Lake, Alberta, asked me to address an all-ranks full-dress dinner, and held out some pole time in a supersonic F-5 as an enticement. I was taken out on a standard search-and-destroy exercise, the pilot of my two-seat training version following another pilot at five hundred miles an hour about two hundred feet off the ground, on a simulated raid on an enemy gun position, which ended with the two fighters streaking almost straight up to about three thousand feet just before arriving at the target, then rolling inverted, diving to release their simulated ordnance, and then levelling off again just above the scrub and heading back toward base.

My guy said that now the formal exercise was finished, we could go and play, and invited me to take control and climb to thirty thousand feet. When we got there, he told me to set it in a 30-degree climb, hold it there, and firmly but not too quickly press the left rudder pedal to the floor. The airplane, on rudder only, flew an exquisite aileron roll to the left, levelling off again without hesitation as I released the pedal. "Can I try sump'n?" I said.

"Sure, go ahead."

We were firmly strapped in, of course, and the airplane would fly inverted as well as right way up. I remembered Cliff exulting about doing the split-S in a Vought Corsair, how he would almost black out when he pulled out of the almost red-line dive the manoeuvre ended in. I decided to try it – wouldn't go anywhere *near* red line, I said to myself – and rolled the machine over on its back, loving how easy it was with no propeller torque to mess up the roll, and how snug it was being so tightly embedded in the seat by all those straps and the G-suit. I pulled the power right back to zero and let the machine slowly fall out of the sky, inverted, until it was vertical and the speed was rising at an alarming rate.

"Uhmm . . ." said a voice from the back seat, "I would ease it out about now if I were you."

I could feel the G-suit pressure come on as we came back into level flight, and a sagging feeling in my cheeks considerably more severe than anything I had experienced in a light aircraft.

I don't recall what I spoke about at the mess dinner that night, but it evidently went very well, and the officers were generous with their thanks, even the pilot who had put up with my playful afternoon.

When de Havilland developed the Dash 7, a four-engined predecessor of the now worldwide commuter turboprop the Dash 8, I was invited to fly it while a film crew, directed by a one-time *Seven Days* colleague, Sam Levene, filmed a report on the newly developed sixty-seater. This was prototype number two. The test pilot put me in the front seat, gave me a basic tour of the panel, and then left it entirely up to me. I had a ball flying it on three engines, then two, then one, and then doing the same kind of short-field landing that I had loved to teach to those older students, the lovely big airliner with its reversible props coming to a stop in about the same distance you would do it with a Cessna 150, maybe less.

There have been helicopters and gliders and executive jets – something like thirty-five or forty different machines I've had the privilege of piloting for at least a few minutes. I won't fly again. I did that, and when the time came I gave it up. But my life was enriched by that incomparable experience of being alone in the sky with the droning engines and the moonlight and an expanse of open water ahead of you. Or by the exhilaration of dancing in three dimensions, of moving into zero gravity as you come over the top of a loop. Or by the unspeakable satisfaction of greasing it on so smooth that no one knows you're down yet – and when you look behind you, you can't even see the numbers.

Chapter 12

COUSTEAU

THE BIGGEST RESIDUE in my life from *This Hour Has Seven Days* was that I could no longer be a private person. For a time I was less than gracious about being accosted in public places, saying irritably that they must be mistaking me for my twin brother or other foolish discourtesies. One night Donald Sutherland and I were lining up outside Fran's Restaurant at College and Yonge for a midnight hamburger, and I was impressed with his generous response to the fans who, amazed to find him there, were pressing for autographs, gushing about him, and he acknowledging them as if they mattered. ("They do matter," he said quietly over our burgers. "They are the people we work for.") It was an important lesson: that courtesy is a prime value and costs virtually nothing.

Although after *Seven Days* the CBC had made it pretty clear that I was *persona non grata*, and I was feeling too bruised and tender to want to be anywhere near the place, there was some unfinished business. As executive producer of the series *Document*, I had accepted Allan King's proposal for a long-form cinéma-verité documentary about Warrendale, a radically permissive residential school for emotionally disturbed children. The film was in post-production at Allan's London production house when the *Seven Days* brouhaha ended, and Allan said he expected to have a fairly advanced cut early in the autumn. He had asked me to voice the narration as well, and because

I had been involved from the start and was convinced that it would be a very important film, I was reluctant to walk away from it. I saw Peter Campbell privately – he had been appointed head of Public Affairs when Reeves Haggan left – and we agreed that I would complete my duties as executive producer for this one project, quietly, without pay; he would smooth things over with the management. And so I was able to play my small role through to the end, formally accepting the finished film on behalf of the CBC: my absolutely final appearance as a CBC television producer. I went to London for a week or ten days in December to sit through the final stages of the fine-cut with Allan and his editor, Peter Moseley, and to polish the narration into its final form.

The film was pure experience, and we were doing everything we could to keep the narration to the minimum; as long as the viewer was not lost or confused, it would be better to let what happened on the screen tell the story. Almost every day Moseley would show us a bit of re-editing he had done that allowed a scene to work without the narration that had been drafted for it. And then there came a magical morning when Allan said he thought, now, that we could eliminate the narration altogether, would I mind that very much, and we were so pleased with ourselves that we knocked off early and went out for lunch, where we had a good bottle of wine.

Ironically, the CBC was so frightened of the film, particularly the repeated use of the word "fuck" (it was, after all, a house full of distressed kids, mostly adolescents), that they refused to broadcast it, even after it began to circle the world garnering international awards.

News of a fresh, independent-minded, Western-made documentary film on contemporary China also made its way around the broadcasting world. Felix Green, a British producer deeply committed to the Chinese Revolution, had been permitted to film there and his film had been broadcast and viewed with curiosity, but it was contaminated by his evident partiality. No Americans had been in since 1949, and no Canadians. The last Canadian film had been Grant McLean's

NFB production, *The People Between*, a strong, moving piece about the innocent victims of the War of Liberation. That had been fifteen years earlier.

So the interest in our film was high, and even before the CBC's foreign program sales operation had creaked into gear, NET, the National Educational Television network in the United States, expressed interest, and Paul Fox, the tough, inventive head of BBC Current Affairs – a friend and admirer of my cameraman, Erik Durschmied – had come over from London to have a look at some early sequences in the cutting room and committed the BBC there and then.

When it was broadcast in the United States, press reaction to *The Seven Hundred Million* predictably included some communophobic tirades for my having been too sympathetic to the PRC, while a number of viewers wrote to complain about my use of irony and my allegations of thought control. It is reassuring to be shot at from both sides about a controversial film. Makes you feel you probably got it right. In the meantime the film was being seen by millions of people.

Among them was David Wolper's production group in Los Angeles. Wolper's head of documentary production, Alan Landsburg, called to ask if he could send someone up to screen the out-takes. He was developing a production in which Theodore H. White, who had been in China for the Hearst papers before the Revolution, would do an extensive essay on the contemporary state of the country. The CBC sold them some of our footage, but the White film turned out to be more of an anti-Chinese tirade entitled *The Roots of Madness*, and as a result I had some bad feelings about both White and the Wolper group. Six years later, White returned to China, with President Nixon's party. Late one night after finishing a broadcast, at a friend's apartment in New York, I watched the press conferences upon their return. In response to the first question, Teddy White drew a deep breath and said, "For twenty-three years I have been wrong." I drank a bottle of Burgundy in his honour, fell in the street, and had to be helped on with my leg, which had come off in the fall.

Despite my disappointment in the Wolper film, Alan Landsburg and I became friends by telephone. We had never met. He had expressed warm admiration for *The Seven Hundred Million* and an eager interest in my doing a project for Wolper. The first one he suggested, assuming that I would leap at the chance, was a filmed walk across Africa with John Glenn, the astronaut, following the footsteps of Henry Morton Stanley in his famous search for the missing explorer-missionary David Livingstone in 1871.

I said, "Alan, I have a problem with walking any distance on smooth ground, never mind through the jungles of Africa." I told him about the leg. He laughed, and said never mind, he would find something else. The something else came late in 1967.

Wolper and Landsburg had begun what was intended to be a lengthy series called *The Undersea World of Jacques Cousteau.* Landsburg himself had written, produced, and directed the first episode, which he was then cutting in L.A. He had intended to do the second episode as well, due to begin shooting in the Indian Ocean on New Year's Eve, but he was reluctant to leave the editing of the first episode and was looking for another director. "Your French will help," he said. I said, hell, I would have learned French from a standing start for an opportunity like that. I had been entranced by Cousteau's first documentary feature, *The Silent World*, directed by Louis Malle in 1956. Cousteau had become an instant hero, and Malle's film I thought a work of genius. The notion that I would now be in Malle's shoes, directing this heroic figure, was irresistible.

Furthermore, while I had always preferred swimming underwater to swimming on the surface, and could still at thirty-seven stay submerged with mask and fins for close to three minutes, I had never dived with any kind of breathing apparatus, and the prospect of learning about that in the Cousteau team was impossible to resist. Landsburg brought me to L.A. to see some work-in-progress and sign a contract.

We hit it off even better face to face than we had by phone. We sat at an editing table with John Soh, the Okinawan-born editor assigned to the series. Soh is an artist at the editing bench, and a man with an encyclopaedic memory for filed outs and trims, a talent that demonstrated its value some weeks later when I returned with the negative to begin post-production. Alan Landsburg outlined the project I was to undertake. *Calypso*, the World War II wooden-hulled minesweeper,[1] had just picked up two "*soucoupes*" (saucers), one-man submarines designed to dive to a thousand feet. Landsburg showed me footage he had shot in the dockyards in Marseilles of the saucer-shaped yellow-hulled vessels being hoisted aboard by cranes. *Calypso* was proceeding now through the Red Sea. I was to meet Cousteau and his wife in Paris, fly with them to Tananarive[2] in Madagascar, and join the ship the next day off the northeast coast.

The diving cameramen were furnished by Cousteau, who of course controlled that aspect of the work. Landsburg had lost a good surface cameraman to another job and asked me to furnish a replacement. I called Douglas McKay in Vancouver, a good shooter, and a good companion who had done some poetic work for me on *Inquir'y*. McKay preferred prime lenses over the increasingly popular zoom. He especially liked wide-angle lenses. This was the kind of visual intent I wanted for outdoor adventure and nature footage. He agreed to come with me, but said, ironically, "I can't swim, you know, and I've never been to sea. But it sounds great. I'm on."

I raced back to Toronto for my birthday and Christmas, put together some kit, made sure the family's financial situation was under control, and wrote a new will. A couple of days later McKay and I were yawning and shivering in the early morning fog at Orly Airport, waiting to meet the Cousteaus.

Jacques-Yves Cousteau was not as tall as I had supposed. The drawn face and beak-like nose were strong, the eyes keen and appraising, the manner courteous. He wore his presence consciously, like a costume or a mask. He seldom even glanced toward the many people who recognized him as they passed in the crowded airport, but

1. Built at an Ohio boatworks on Lake Erie.

2. Now Antananarivo.

focused on the conversation at hand and the business of tickets and baggage. The thin mouth conveyed a hint of lofty amusement. He was less serious than I had expected; a strong sense of play was woven into an elusive, contained sadness.

Within the first few minutes of our meeting he was telling me, in English, a bizarre, graphic story of a painter named McEwen who "actually, you see, *fucked* a large fish he had just speared, you see, for contact with the vital forces of nature."

I would discover over the course of the next month at sea that he was vain, decisive, mercurial, impatient, inventive, careless, not humorous in matters pertaining to himself, quick to take offence, slow to forgive. He was contemptuous of politics and politicians, and of manners. "In a civilized world there would no need to say 'Please' and 'Thank you,'" he would say. At sea I would see the sadness surface in profound sighs, silent shaking of the head as if denying something, long silences. For now he was charming and helpful, putting his new producer/director at ease, courteously switching into elegantly accented English when he addressed Doug McKay, which he did with professional respect.

Simone Cousteau was small, tough, ironic, funny, a woman who clearly had always been very sexy. She, like her husband, was a mythic figure to me because of his book about the invention of what used to be called the Aqualung. I remembered the photographs of her swimming in the Mediterranean with him as he made the first trials of that equipment. He had found a cave twenty feet or so down, full of huge lobsters, and brought up several to just below the surface. Simone then reached down and apparently plucked them from the waves and held them up to the astonished gaze of nearby fishermen who were quite unaware of the submarine presence cruising around a few feet below her.

As he began to outline the objectives of the voyage, Cousteau took pains to put me at ease in The Presence – I would come to see how much he enjoyed the role – and during the flight we mapped out a rough plan for the shoot.

The film, intended to be the second in the series, would centre on the trials of the submarines, the *soucoupes.* The design of these vessels was new. Cousteau anticipated a good deal of technical revision. The chief diver and Cousteau's chief of staff, Albert Falco, was to pilot one of the *soucoupes,* something he had not done before, though he had been consulted on the design. I could see a coherent hour of dramatic documentary storytelling coming together around the early workouts, the obstacles overcome, the final successful dive to unprecedented depths, the suspense entailed in the attendant danger, the very different personalities of Cousteau and Falco. I was to share a cabin with Falco, a plump, cheerful, vastly competent Marseilles sailor. He had Cousteau's full confidence. When we got to know each other better, Falco would confide to me that the work went much better when "Jyc"[3] was not aboard.

Cousteau told me that he would develop the undersea scenarios with his crew of divers and diving cameramen, and would expect me to be at story conferences each day, which were also the tactical planning meetings. I would have to be ready to cover all the related surface activities, as well as any colour or side stories that caught my interest. He would provide a soundman who was an old hand with the crew.

With tantalizing stops in Cairo, Djibouti, and Dar-es-Salaam, and a fairly good sleep in the comfortable first-class seats of the Air France Boeing 707, we arrived in the early morning in Majunga airport, transferred to a six-seat Piper Aztec, and flew up the island of Madagascar at about seven hundred feet, over beaches, erosion fantasies, jungle, purple hills, toward Nosy Bé, about four hundred kilometres north of Tananarive.

I was exhausted, my stump blistered from more than twenty-four hours non-stop wearing the prosthesis. I felt old and stupid. (I have noted that this goes with fatigue and I give myself lectures about it.) A night in a resort hotel cured it. In the morning Cousteau was excit-

3. For Jacques-Yves Cousteau.

ed with news that the crew had captured a dugong[4] and were planning to film natives killing and eating it. "Of course, we will admit it is in captivity," he said, in response to a glance from me. Landsburg may have talked to him about my documentarist concerns for authenticity.

At Nosy Bé we boarded a launch, and by early afternoon, on December 31, 1967, we were being hoisted aboard *Calypso* in a considerable sea, 1,200 kilometres south of the equator. I was unsteady on my artificial leg, moving from the heaving launch toward *Calypso*'s rail. A wave lifted the launch and pulled it away from the side of the ship. I was left with my good foot hooked over the rail of the launch and the rest of me bridged across the gap, grasping at a line hanging from the ship, about to be dropped into the sea between them. I imagined myself crushed between the two vessels with the next wave. My foot was about to be wrenched from the launch's rail when I saw the boyish face of a compactly built shirtless sailor with an orange-blond Beatles haircut grinning cheerfully at my predicament. A single brawny, tanned arm came down and grabbed my hands. It was Maurice, the bo'sun. He lifted me aboard with that one arm as if I had been a suitcase. He grinned, nodded, bade me welcome, and got on with the business of offloading the launch.

Albert Falco, "Bébert," introduced himself and helped me take my stuff to the cabin I would share with him, insisting that I take the lower bunk. I asked if the crew were planning a New Year's Eve party. Falco rolled his eyes owlishly. We spoke only French together. "The Pasha [Cousteau] wants to film a dive tonight," he said. "With coloured lights. I don't know what it's for."

So that is how we spent New Year's Eve. Half a dozen divers and two cameramen went down the slide from the fantail, in full diving gear, and blundered around in the heaving moonless ocean for almost an hour with a meaningless cluster of illuminated coloured globes, to come to the surface all in a foul humour, with a few hundred feet of

4. Or "sea cow." A large, tusked, walrus-like tropical aquatic mammal.

film that would never be used, of a dive whose purpose no one could ever after explain. It was made clear that one did not challenge the Pasha about such whimsicalities; you just got on with it.

Wine was opened in the galley afterward, and everyone's good humour returned. There were about thirty of us. Cousteau graciously drank New Year's toasts to his men, and Simone served some candied delicacies. The sea was making up considerably, and I became aware of a growing sense of discomfort. I noticed the captain eyeing me. He had seen my green face, but for the moment did not let on. His name was Robert Maritano, a ruddy-faced, plump, cheery and aptly named professional from Marseilles, perhaps three or four years older than I. He accosted me suddenly.

"I've been watching you," he said. "I just realized, your French is – well, acceptable, but you're an English Canadian, aren't you? Not a Quebecer?"

"That's right," I said, a bit hotly, trying to keep my stomach settled, and deciding to match his tone, whether mock or serious, I added, "*Et alors?*"

"An English Canadian, anh? Ha. I was reading about the visit of our great General de Gaulle to your country, anh? 'Vive le Québec libre!' Anh? Ahh that was a great moment, ha! 'Vive le Québec libre!' Great, didn't you think?"

I was being tested. I took him on. In seconds we were locked into a hot political argument. The crew was all watching. So were the Pasha and Falco. And Doug McKay. The new film director was being worked over in public. I should have anticipated it. In fact I was relishing it, though I knew I was a bit hot under the collar.

Now the cook came and set pegs in the holes in the table to keep the glasses and dishes from sliding about as the ship heaved in the rising seas. The tone of the argument rose. I won a point, then Maritano won one. Nobody else spoke. Eyes flashed back and forth like a tennis match. I was on a roll. We were both flashing. I reached for another glass of wine. I was feeling great. I tossed back the wine. Captain Maritano grinned at me.

"Feeling better now, anh?" he said with a twinkle. "*Mal de mer* all gone, right?"

(Years later, sailing with Joe MacInnis and Caroline in the Gulf Stream, I would use the same technique to cure Michael Levine of pending seasickness by taunting him with anti-Semitic remarks until the adrenaline drove away the nausea, and then I told him how I had learned the technique from the captain of the *Calypso*.)

Calypso's planned route would take us north-northwest two hundred kilometres to the tiny island Les Glorieuses, then two hundred kilometres southwest to Mayotte in the Comoros Archipelago, then south through the Mozambique Channel, which separates Madagascar from the east coast of Africa, stopping at Bassas da India, a submerged atoll, and then, another hundred kilometres to Europa, a larger atoll with a tiny, three-man weather station. Then, if there were still time, to some submarine cliffs at the southern tip of Madagascar. The plan was to film the discovery of unknown underwater landscapes in each of these locations, if they were suitable. Bassas da India, for example, above water only at low tide, was said to have a virgin and inaccessible lagoon, and Cousteau had brought dynamite to try blasting a channel that would bring *Calypso* into the centre of this volcanic oddity, presumably a cauldron of ancient and wonderful marine life.

Les Glorieuses proved a classical Robinson Crusoe desert island. The sky was a brilliant blue, the sea moderate. The first dives revealed some interesting activity among egg-laying triggerfish, and Cousteau demonstrated his cleverness at scenarios, arranging for one diver to be filmed approaching dangerously close, until the triggerfish attacked him to defend their nests. The submarines were not ready. I put on mask, fin, and snorkel and went over the side to see if I could catch sight of the divers at work but they were too far away. I cruised around the ship, examined her barnacled bottom, and came back aboard. It was hot and sticky. My sheets were always damp and beginning to stink. My diary records that when I commented on this to my cabinmate, Falco, to explain why I always left the fan running, he said, "*Ah, oui; bientôt nous aurons des champignons!*" We had a couple of days of languorous weather and easy-going shoots on the bottom, but not much for me and my surface crew to do. Then the weather began to get rough and grey again; a hurricane was reported shaping up a few hundred kilometres to the north. We secured the vessel for a rough passage, and headed for Mayotte, in the Comoros Archipelago.

Mayotte was lovely, but the current was too strong for the divers, the weather was still rough, the skies grey, which always made Cousteau grumpy. Long silences and deep sighs. We headed south.

Between Mayotte and Bassas da India we sighted a sperm whale. The crew came on deck to watch, and we followed the whale for about an hour. The weather stayed rough. There was little filming. I was getting acclimatised, finding ways to don my artificial leg on the heaving deck and with the gluey moisture. I even made it up to the crow's nest to watch the whale. One morning the knee was seized up with salt corrosion, and I had to take it apart, clean it with emery paper, and thereafter keep it well lubricated.

Bassas da India, largely underwater except at low tide, proved uninteresting, a dying reef. We had hoped for excitement, for it had lain unexplored for a hundred years or more since its discovery. Cousteau grumbled over having to abandon his plan to dynamite an entrance through the reef to the lagoon. I talked him into filming his frank, spontaneous tactical discussions with Falco and the crew, and comments to the unseen director (me) about the troubles and frustrations, especially with the miniature submarines; he agreed but was uneasy. He preferred staging, rehearsing, and leaving nothing to chance. One evening we ended up in something close to a shouting match about the grammar of film, and conventions in the documentary.

"I don't want to listen to talk about *conventions and tradition!*" he snapped.

I said I didn't understand why he was so superstitious about the word "convention." Well, that triggered it! But later he became reflective, and surprisingly gentle, talking of the sadness he felt when he realized that his crew were afraid of him. Having a knack for accurately reconstructing conversations, I made diary notes, pretty well verbatim, of that conversation, and others.

Our next destination was the atoll Europa, about halfway between Madagascar and the coast of Mozambique. The clear waters outside Europa's reef would be ideal, Cousteau said, for the submarine trials. And as a bonus, the white beaches of the island are important nesting grounds for the great sea turtle. Cousteau had filmed the nesting turtles for *The Silent World.* Now he wanted a new sequence on the turtles for the television series. Europa would be our working base for a week or more.

When I came up on deck the next morning, the ship was hove to off Europa, anchored half a mile north of the reef, the atoll an appealing low shape beyond the slight surf seaward of the shallows. The inflatable Zodiacs and the launch were strung out on lines astern in the gentle current, their outboard motors in place. I was feeling especially pleased with myself: there were signs that the constipation that had troubled me for a couple of days was about to terminate. Perhaps the previous evening's *tripes à la mode de Caen* had had something to do with it. In any case, the signals were strong. I met Cousteau in the galley. We shared tea and toast. He had recovered his good humour. The weather was perfect, the sea almost calm. Maurice and his gang were busy about the *soucoupes*, preparing the cranes to hoist the mini-subs over the side. It would be our first day of serious filming. It was still just past 5 a.m. My insides now having progressed past a cheerful state of agitation to a rumble of urgency, I excused myself from the table and started off for the head.

This is what, in a screenplay, is called a Reversal of Fortune. The heads were out of order, blocked. The bo'sun's mate was on his knees with plumber's tools. "*Combien de temps!*" I pleaded, suddenly in pain, desperate. You know how it is when you are about to be relieved and relief is withdrawn. "How long!!?"

"Two hours, three, I don't know," the guy said. "It's a mess."

Cousteau found me on deck by the forward door into the cabin area, looking anguished. "What's the trouble?" he asked, kindly. I told him. He smiled.

"My boy," he said, "you are about to experience one of life's great gifts." Turning toward the work area abaft the main cabin, where Maurice and a mechanic were grumbling over the crane's motor, he called out, "Maurice, put the ladder over the stern."

"Patrick," he said grandly, as if about to award me the Légion d'honneur, "you will never have done this before, I am sure. And you will be grateful to me forever. Just go hand over hand along the lines joining the boats astern till you come to the launch. Hold on carefully, because the current is stronger than you can swim, although it doesn't look like much. Take off your bathing costume. Let the Great Sea receive from you what it is receiving from a million other maritime mammals every moment of every day. It will make you a part of nature."

He tended to speak that way sometimes. I did as he instructed. I am still grateful.

Europa had been home to a small garrison for a while during World War II, and there was said to be a cracked but serviceable paved airstrip in mid-island. A Piper Aztec from Madagascar would pick me up there at the end of the shoot. There was a weather station, a squat structure of thick coral walls with heavy corrugated iron roofing, manned by three Frenchmen from the island of Réunion. It was to prove a lifesaver before long. A forsaken graveyard of coral sand and eroded inscriptions was the only testament to a failed settlement around the turn of the century.

Maurice had got the crane working properly. I assembled my crew. Divers with cameras and safety equipment were lowered into the water, Falco got into the first of the *soucoupes*, it was hoisted overboard for a shallow test dive, and we settled in to work. Between takes I found time to go over the stern with a mask, fin, and snorkel, and free-dive the coral reef, my first. I was agog at the panorama of colourful life, the play of the light, the crackling of parrotfish eating the coral, the welcoming, healing feel of it, the clarity of the water. I seemed to be able to stay down on one breath longer than ever before, so entrancing was the spectacle.

I would in the end be thankful that Cousteau had decided to take another run at the story of the sea turtles. The submarines were endlessly troublesome. There were communications failures, electrical failures, and propulsion failures. The sea became rough again, and the *soucoupes* were breaking their lashings and shifting dangerously on the afterdeck. So was the heavy cylindrical emergency decompression chamber, a recently acquired device in which divers would leach out the overload of nitrogen after dangerously long deep dives.

Cousteau began to call the *soucoupes* "*Les Puces*" – "The Fleas." He became very ill-tempered. He and Falco snapped at each other, though Falco was by instinct a conciliator. In a journalistic environment this might have held some interest. But Cousteau was the proprietor of the project: there would be no ugly scenes. Well, not on film. Nor would we film in cloudy weather, if it could be avoided. "I do not like that," Cousteau would say, emphatically.

And, indeed, there was an uneasy feeling aboard. You could see it in the sailors' eyes. On January 10 at 2:45 a.m. the young Lieutenant Bernard woke us up. A radio signal advised that Hurricane Flossie, earlier reported to be safely distant to the north, had turned and was tracking toward us. The weather analysts at Réunion advised steaming to safe harbour on the west coast of Madagascar. In the meantime the sea was rising rapidly, and Cousteau had decided that Number One mini-sub would be lowered into the hold, while Number Two and the decompression chamber would both be loaded with pig lead and sent to the bottom of the ocean, out of reach of the wave motion and safely off the increasingly dangerous fantail. I roused Doug McKay. The fantail was brilliant with work lights, and we got some good footage. But after about two hours there was a further signal from Réunion: the hurricane would pass us by. Cousteau cancelled the emergency measures and we all went to bed.

By four in the afternoon the next day there was another hurricane warning. Much of the work preparing the decompression chamber and the second submarine had been undone. There was now a terrible sense of confusion and uncertainty. But in the end we stayed, Flossie kept her distance, and we got some good filming done. Cousteau had begun to approve of the way I was directing the surface material and his dramatic role in it as Guiding Genius. He now proposed that I extend my stay aboard for another month.

But by the twelfth of January the bread was stale, the water was short and beginning to taste, we were out of fresh meat and vegetables, and Cousteau decided to take a couple of days ashore. This would give the men some shore leave, and we could replenish supplies and take stock of where we were with the elusive scenario. The central role of the submarines was no longer possible, at least in the time I would have aboard if I were to return to Los Angeles as planned in the first week of February.

Tuléar,[5] about mid-island on the west side of Madagascar. A good safe harbour. We took on fresh water, fuel, and fresh meat, vegetables, wine, and best of all, fresh bread. Doug McKay and I went ashore in the blistering 44 degree (Centigrade) plangent sunlight, and found a Chinese grocery that sold cold Coca-Cola. Many of the crew were given the day off and roamed the region looking for girls. We all bought bolts of brightly coloured locally printed cotton. Sarongs would soon become the garment of choice aboard, when we were not working. I still have several yards of mine, unfaded and brilliant, and still sometimes wear it as a summer wraparound.

We went to the Oceanographic Institute, where they kept a lizard with three eyes, and a fish that walked on land. Then, warned that we would be watched all the time but would not see our watchers, we visited an eighteenth-century tribal chieftain's tomb a few kilometres north of the city. It was a two-chambered sloped-wall stone berm, about four metres high. We had been told that it was acceptable to the watchers that we climb and look over, as long as we disturbed

5. Now called Toliara.

nothing. The layout of the interior of the berm was two rectangles that seemed to be in the proportions of a classical Greek temple: the Golden Mean. On the ground in the centre of the smaller chamber were two rusted cutlasses, a Spanish helmet, an ancient ship's bell, and a Ming vase. When we clambered down again, panting and damp, there was a rustle in the jungle and suddenly two of the watchers were there in the clearing with us. Twelve or thirteen years old, half-naked, a slim boy and a girl with budding breasts. They stared at us calmly. The girl advanced, held out her left hand and opened it. There were four or five big locusts in it, alive. She pointed at them with her right hand, then to her mouth. She made signs and sounds of pleasurable eating, then offered the locusts to us. It is one of the serious regrets in my life that I did not accept that gift.

Madame Cousteau browsed the markets and came back aboard with baskets of steaks cut from the tender hump of the distinctive island cattle. That evening she took over the kitchen and served up salads with fresh tomatoes and radishes and peppers. She grilled the steaks and served them with a sauce made from green peppercorns that had steeped for weeks in a bottle of Johnny Walker Red, which she had brought along for the purpose. The crew banged their mugs on the galley table and cheered.

Mojé, a marine biologist stationed in Tuléar, had joined *Calypso* there for the operation at Europa. Mojé had been studying sea turtles for years. Several times he had tried in vain to send newly hatched turtles to his parent institution, the marine museum in Monte Carlo. They never survived the trip. The museum was an important sponsor of Cousteau's work, so there was common interest. Mojé enlisted my help, over a glass of wine in the galley. He said that the mortality rate among newly hatched turtles was prodigious: one hundred percent if they hatched in daytime. Frigate birds cruised the beaches and whenever a turtle nest erupted with its up to a hundred bite-sized morsels, soft-shelled and the size of a pocket watch, the birds screeched down and gobbled them up. Even if the turtles reached the sea, they were not safe. The young turtles can submerge for only a few seconds in their first hours of life, and the birds would swoop to the surface and pick them off. It was a major evolutionary puzzle, he said, that the hatching cycle and the reptiles' instincts still allowed daytime hatching, which was utterly anti-survival. Only if they hatched at night would they survive. Then the whole nest would make it to the ocean and be far away before the frigate birds awoke next morning. It would be fiendishly difficult to find a hatching nest in the dark, he said. The nests are buried, invisible, and the new turtles make no sound that could be heard above the surf. Nevertheless he was determined to stake out the beach at night and do his best. Now, if he were able to capture some living, newly hatched turtles, would I take a few back to France with me? Smuggle them out of Madagascar and into France? It was in the interests of science? "Of course," I said, negligently.

The first few days on the reef at Europa, in the Mozambique Channel just north of the Tropic of Capricorn, were idyllic. Although it was still hurricane season, the winds were light and the sea north of the island almost calm. Despite the vexing mechanical problems with the *soucoupes*, everyone except Cousteau was in a good humour. Diving cameramen not assigned to the submarine tests were getting good footage of the convocations of great turtles (up to 120 kilograms each) on the bottom, and even the actual mating procedure, never before filmed, Cousteau said, slapping his knee emphatically.

I went ashore for a couple of mornings with Doug McKay, the soundman, and Falco. We were able to approach and even touch the huge females as they lay, almost exhausted, with their tails over the holes they had dug for a nest to deposit up to a hundred soft spherical eggs before covering the hole again and then lumbering, painfully exhausted and dry in the baking sun, back to the safety of the sea. Sometimes, disoriented with fatigue, they headed inland, instead of back to the sea. The upper levels of the island, above the surf line, were littered with skulls and carapaces. Cousteau instructed us to take a couple of extra sailors ashore and film a capture of one of these lost ones, and their generously being turned and dragged back into the sea. Good for the image.

One day a deep dive yielded strange invertebrate, rose-coloured vulva-like shapes, with transparent bulbs and tentacles, which nobody had seen before and even Mojé could not identify.

The miniature submarines groaned and balked. Mechanics squatted in the shade of the after-deck awning, puzzling over engines and switches. Time stretched out.

Every morning at about 11 a couple of sailors crossed the reef in a Zodiac with heavy fishing line and big Williams Wobblers, trawled the shallows at top speed for a few minutes, and came back loaded with jackfish, grouper, edible barracuda, and other gleaming creatures. Sharp at 12, the young cook, "Couisteau," would serve mountains of raw fish, with fresh limes and bottles of soy sauce and nuoc mam, a Vietnamese sauce made from rotten fish that smells foul but goes wonderfully with raw fish. We gorged. Even the divers drank tumblers of chilled red wine with lunch and went back to the dive in the afternoon. At night the remains of the same fish would be served baked or fried or steamed, always with excellent sauces. Simone Cousteau, who seldom appeared above decks in the morning, would supervise the sauces and bask in the crew's applause.

The angular silhouettes of the frigate birds cruised the beach, silent, seldom moving their wings. We scanned the sky above the beach for the beginning of frigate activity that might betray a hatching. "It may be a bit early," Mojé said, "since they're still mating. But they have been here for a few weeks. I'll spend a few nights on the beach."

His second night ashore Mojé struck gold. I was having a smoke on deck about 10 p.m., when faintly from the shore, half a mile away, there came a series of shouts, fading and swelling with the soft currents of air. A flashlight was waving furiously. Cousteau had heard, through his open window, and came on deck. "What's he saying?" I asked.

"'*Les éclosions!*', I think," Cousteau said. "The turtles must be hatching."

It was too early in the trip to keep turtles aboard for the proposed trip to France, but now that the hatching had begun Cousteau said it would continue for at least two weeks. Falco took a Zodiac ashore and brought a delighted Mojé back with a bucket full of babies for us to admire before he released them over the fantail. "I just kept jogging up and down a kilometre of beach," Mojé said. "There was plenty of light from the stars. And suddenly I saw this swarm in front of me, making for the sea. There'll be more every few hours, now."

Cousteau, Falco, McKay, and I sat down in the galley and planned a shoot. McKay and I and the soundman and Falco would go ashore and film as many hatchings as we could. We would make a bath in a large plastic dome, under a tent, to keep a number of turtles for a night release – to be filmed in order to demonstrate the humanity of the Cousteau team. Most spectacularly we would film the desperate trek to the sea by the tiny doomed carapaces, the swooping, screeching frigates, the slaughter.

The sand was soft; walking on it with my prosthesis was very difficult, so the next day I left the leg on board and went ashore with crutches. We had two satisfactory days of this. On the morning of the third day, Falco dropped me on the beach with Doug and Marcellin, the soundman, for a last hour or two of the hatchlings, while he went back to *Calypso* to work on the submarines. He warned us to be ready for a quick pickup: a hurricane was reported to the north, and although it was hundreds of kilometres away, the sea might be making up within a couple of hours.

McKay mounted a wide-angle (9mm) lens on the Bolex. We stalked the beach for an hour or so, and suddenly the sand right in front of us began to heave and collapse, and a crowd of the babies emerged. Doug held the camera between finger and thumb and ran beside them in a half-crouch. With that lens he did not need the eyepiece; he just held the lens an inch or two above the scampering baby turtles. Sand flew from their little flippers. Frigates dived angrily and one even swooped under the camera for his hapless lunch. It was both tragic and exhilarating. All the hatchlings were eaten. Before this first nest had been destroyed, another hatched and the chase began again. When we saw them on the screen, these hand-held shots of the scurrying turtles, flinging sand as they desperately headed for water, would lure a number of Wolper's people into the screening room; they were brilliant. Cousteau waxed lyrical. Later, in the mix, Alan Landsburg set these shots of the march to the sea to fife and drum music from a Civil War film he had recently finished, and they would prove more compelling than anything else in the film, even the best undersea material.

So absorbed were we in the shoot that we did not notice the surf building impressively on the reef, nor hear the motor of the Zodiac until it was almost at the beach. Falco leapt out and ran up to us full tilt. "Hurricane coming!" he shouted. "We've only got a few minutes!"

We packed the gear, dumped a dozen baby turtles into a plastic bag with some seawater, and pushed the inflatable off into the agitated sea. The surf at the reef edge was spectacular, but I assumed that Falco could handle anything. I was wrong.

He made three tries to cross the reef. On the third we almost overturned. A Nagra and some tapes in a plastic parcel were flung into the sea and miraculously swept back into the boat. McKay, who does not swim, was very pale. Falco headed west for half a mile, then east. There was no way out.

He brought the motor back to idle and stared at me glumly. "That's it!" he said. "We're stuck. This is the advance sea from a hurricane that's done a lot of damage to the north. It will be here late tomorrow, maybe sooner."

Calypso had gone to the west of the island, the lee side, and was out of sight. Falco tried the walkie-talkie but got only noise. To McKay's relief and my dismay, we headed back to the beach. There we pulled the inflatable up to the tree line and started west. Falco said there might be a route through the reef at that end, in any case the surf would be less, he supposed. It was not.

Through the spray we could see *Calypso* lying half a mile away. We thought we could see figures scanning the shore with binoculars. Falco tried the walkie-talkie. Someone responded, but the interference made it incomprehensible. Presently an Aldis lamp began to blink in Morse.

"They've contacted the guys at the weather station here on the island," Falco interpreted. "They'll put us up. He says it looks as though the ship is safe there overnight, and in the morning he says they'll make a decision. There he goes again."

"Hmmph," he said after a few seconds. "*Garder la veille.*" (Keep watch.) "That's a lot of help."

The sunset was a huge red ball, shooting out flares as it hit the booming surf. I got McKay to lie on the sand and get a couple of minutes of it with the Bolex, with different lenses. Falco, anxious to get back to the Zodiac and secure it against the storm, was a filmmaker too and fretted patiently till we finished. Then he and Marcellin and McKay raced ahead. My arms were sore from that long march on the crutches; I lumbered along behind them as best I could.

Back at Turtle Beach I found them waiting at the trail that led to the weather station, half a mile inland. The Zodiac had been inverted, half a ton of flat stones piled on it, and the gear stowed in bags to be carried inland. One of the meteorologists had come down to meet us and was lending a hand. At the thick-walled coral stone four-room building they lived in another was making a spartan meal, mostly from tins. They had adequate water, they said, but supplies were low. They were due for a delivery in a week or so, but the storms might delay that, and there would be no fishing while the hurricane lasted, so it might be pretty slim rations. With their relatively sophisticated radio equipment, the meteorologists had good voice contact with *Calypso*. Falco picked up the headset.

After conferring with Cousteau he laid it out for us.

"*Calypso* will leave for safe harbour at Tulear not later than noon tomorrow," he said. "They can wait until then. In the morning they are going to fire a rocket line ashore, and we will pull a Bomba, one of the survival craft, ashore with the line. It will be full of supplies, enough for two weeks."

"Two weeks!" McKay said. "I've got a shoot in Vancouver five days from now. We were supposed to be back in Tulear on Thursday!"

Falco got back on the radio. "Tell them to send *whisky*, too," I said. He told them about McKay. He turned back to us.

"Well," he said, making his owl face again, "the Pasha wanted us to film as much of the storm as we can, but he knows he has to get Douglas away. So if you are willing to risk it," he said kindly to McKay, "you can try to make it back to the ship in the survival craft. And they'll put you on a plane to Paris tomorrow night. Goupil will come ashore on the Bomba, with the Arriflex so we can cover as much of the storm as is safe. And you will be on your way. If you are willing to risk it," he said again.

McKay was pale, but said, Well, he *had* to go, that was all there was to it. So Falco reported back once more.

"Don't forget the whisky," I said.

They didn't. We were back on the west side at dawn, the sea had built up overnight, and the wind was up to thirty knots. The rocket line made it to shore on the first shot, about two hundred metres from where we were gathered. All of us – my crew and the meteorologists – fell on it and began to haul the bright orange Bomba, an enclosed survival craft, toward us. As it came to the explosions of surf at the edge of the reef, it was suddenly launched into the air, twenty feet or more, tumbling over and over. "Pull!" Falco shouted. The tiny vessel sailed in the air like a kite for several seconds, all the pullers suddenly accelerated forward into the jungle, stumbling over each other as I fell and was left behind. Then the airborne shape inverted and plunged, miraculously righted itself again, smacked the water, was airborne once again for a second, and then was skimming toward us on the lighter sea inside the reef, bouncing like a skipping stone.

McKay, terrified at the prospect of making the return trip in that thing, stammered, "Too bad the Bolex is packed. "

The meteorologists cheered when Falco opened the cover of the beached boat. Inside were fresh meat and vegetables and bread, tins of coffee, dozens of bottles of red wine, and five gleaming bottles of Johnny Walker Red. And strapped in, crouching over the lot with his ironic eyes and his massive walrus moustache, was the undersea cinematographer Pierre Goupil, come to replace Doug.

We offloaded the Bomba as fast as we could. I hugged Doug. He ruefully climbed aboard and strapped in. Falco patted him on the shoulder before closing the waterproof curtains. I held onto his hand as long as I could. Falco said, and I translated, "Look, it could invert. Just hold on. It can't sink, and it will right itself again. And even if it doesn't it's waterproof upside down as well as right side up. You'll make it. Don't worry."

Doug gave a thumbs up and was sealed in. We waved to the binoculars aboard *Calypso*, the tension took up on the seaward line, and the orange capsule headed out to sea, stately at first, but bounding more and more as it approached the rocketing surf at the edge of the reef. Suddenly it vanished. It was gone. One second it had been leaping up and down at the edge of a kind of airborne Niagara, then it was gone. "*Putin!*" Falco said. There was a long ten seconds. Then the orange shape breached like a whale, only half-seen in a gap in the surf, and bobbed brightly toward *Calypso*. Two minutes later the crane was out, hoisting it over the fantail. They told me afterward that McKay knelt gravely and kissed the deck.

Calypso made a farewell signal on the Aldis lamp, and got underway.

There was far too much to carry in a single trip, and it took several hours to get all the supplies back to the weather station. The wind had risen to long rasping sighs that laid the palm trees on their sides. It carried a thin rain that tasted of salt and stung the skin. The meteorologists brought everything loose inside, bolted the two doors, armoured the windows with heavy teak shutters, and delightedly unpacked the generous crates of food as the sound of the storm outside grew steadily louder. I welcomed the presence of Goupil. Although he chewed his words through his thick moustache, so that his French was often hard to follow, we had vigorous conversations about film, social values, politics, and The Meaning of Life. As well as being a fine cameraman, he had a strong sense of irony and was the only one of the old guard aboard who said whatever he liked about the Pasha.

We had more Madagascar steaks, fresh salad, fresh-baked bread washed down with tumblers of red wine, and a gratifying double Scotch each to top it off. And then the power went off, as the storm hit the generator shed. We lit candles. The radios were dead.

A sudden staccato rumble made everyone start. The roof of the sturdy little building was made of heavy corrugated steel; it had been shaken by the wind like a thunder sheet in the theatre. That noise would recur, off and on, for nearly two days. And yet, comforted with our meal and laughing a bit nervously, we fell into our damp cots and slept fitfully until dawn.

The weather instruments were mechanical, so they continued to read the weather outside, even though we were virtually sealed in the building. By noon the winds were more than 120 miles an hour. Water was coursing down the inside of the thick door on the south side, although the door was solidly built, its boards smoothly joined with scarcely visible cracks between them. The barometer needle was still dropping. The roof roared its theatrical thunder. There were crashing noises all around, but shuttered in we could only speculate about trees uprooted and flying debris. There was no going outside to the toilet; the few pails we had inside were beginning to smell. The tension was considerable. We were snapping at each other.

I called a council of war. The three young men from Réunion (who, receiving most of their news of the outside world by daily doses of teletype seemed to me to speak French in staccato blocks, exactly like that machine) courteously accepted my authority without demur. I said that we needed some diversion if we wished to keep the peace, and that I proposed a program of puzzle-solving: brain-teasers. I thanked my stars I had a considerable supply stored away in that part of my brain that saves trivial curiosities. I proposed the Connecticut Commuter to one man, the Monk and The Mountain to another, and soon had them all worrying away over notepads in various corners of the little building, sworn to reveal their answers only to me, whereupon, if right, they would be assigned a new puzzle and I would keep score in a notebook the meteorologists gave me. I also used it for a diary. Peace was restored.

By nightfall the barometer needle was at less than twenty-seven inches of mercury. Falco said, "The eye of the storm will pass right over us." The wind velocity was dropping steadily.

Falco took charge of the cuisine. We had another feast and went to bed cheerful, Marcellin still muttering over his brain-teaser as he dozed off.

I woke in the night to silence. All the men were awake. Somebody lit a candle. We went into the instrument room. The quiet was eerie. The barometer needle was stuck against the bottom peg; the meteorologists all said they had never seen that before. Somebody gingerly undid bolts and opened a door. We went outside with candles. The flames scarcely wavered. In the distance, softened by the jungle growth between us and the beach, we could now hear the deep, echoing rumble of the surf. It was very dark outside. The air was fetid. We dumped the latrine buckets and pumped several *bidons* full of fresh water from the cistern. Falco shone an electric torch around in the crazed and broken trees. "Look." The body of a wild goat was impaled on a broken branch, twenty feet above the ground.

Now the low sky was beginning to pale. We went back inside. I felt nauseous and dizzy. "So do I," Falco said. "I have heard that low pressure can do that," he said. We went back to sleep.

By noon the wind was building again. Soon broken branches were banging against the shutters or caroming off the steel roof with a clang. The barometer needle came unstuck and began to rise slightly. The rain returned. We had a big breakfast of cheese and bread and coffee, and I got everyone back at the brain-teasers. Some solutions were very inventive. The roof began to thunder again.

"I think it is still building, this storm," Falco said, sometime in the afternoon. The roof was booming insanely. One of the meteorologists called us into the instrument room. Rain was driving horizontally through the fine cracks in the door; where the day before it had been pouring through, it was now like a pressure hose. He pointed at the anemometer dial: 145 miles per hour. It was no longer possible to keep our minds on puzzles and trivia, although the men afterward conceded that they had been a godsend. We sat huddled on the floor in the strong central part of the little building. After a while we were all shuddering at each explosion from the steel roof, our nerves very taut. This seemed to go on a very long time. Then someone said, "It is less now." We went back into the instrument room: 135 miles per hour. Then 130, then 120. We all stood and watched, as if the receding needle were a ship bringing rescue. It was getting dark. Falco proposed another feast.

By the next morning, although the winds still rose to a howl from time to time, we could go out again. One of the meteorologists got the dead goat down from the tree and proceeded to butcher it for dinner. Falco and I went down to the beach, although blowing sand still stung our cheeks.

Devastation. Waves had transformed the shape of the beach and heaped dunes against the tree line. The Zodiac, though half-buried, appeared to be intact. Surf was still rocketing into the air out at the reef line. Falco pointed down the beach. About half a mile away there was a turtle, apparently pausing before trying to get back into the sea. I went down to watch. I thought it raised its head at me as I came closer. Then I saw that this must have been an illusion; its skull had been sliced cleanly, a transverse cut, the anterior half of the head nowhere to be seen. We found several more corpses swept far inland. There were no birds. We heard the sputter of the generator coming to life. The radios were back in service. *Calypso* reported from its safe harbour in Tulear; she would be with us in two or three days. I was building shoulder and arm muscles from continuous crutch-walking. My hair was long and bleached, my skin the colour of mahogany: salt skin; it smelled good. I felt sexual and deprived. Falco and I explored the beach and the lagoon. As the tide swept up the narrow gut leading into it, Falco pointed out the food chain, sweeping in with the current as we watched. First the small herring, in schools, then jackfish and mid-size predators, followed by the sharks. At one point

Falco called out, "*Là! Là!*" and leapt suddenly into the current, disappearing for a second or two then coming to the surface with a four-foot ray grasped by its flailing wings. He brought it up onto the beach. "Perhaps you have never seen one of these before." We had not brought a camera with us.

Calypso reappeared grandly. She was standing just offshore as we came down to the beach one morning, as if nothing had happened at all. There was much backslapping and pouring of wine and telling of stories. The Piper Aztec from Air Madagascar would come in two days' time. On the day before I had to leave, I asked Cousteau for a lesson in scuba and he called a young diver, Siméan, to take me down for my first experience at what has since become a much-loved sport. With no lecture, no test, no more preparation than Siméan's injunction to not hold my breath, we went over the fantail. Nothing to it. Within seconds I was on the smooth white sandy bottom, watching turtles come and go, and the silhouette of the old *Calypso*, sixty feet above. A shark went by in the distance. I felt the delicious *frisson* of a first encounter.

A fifty-gallon drum of aviation fuel was manhandled ashore. The meteorologists repaired their two-wheel cart, which had been smashed in the storm, for the trek across the island to the airstrip. The night before we were to leave there was another hatching. Mojé kept half a dozen of the baby turtles in a discarded two-gallon plastic container that would do for the flight to Tananarive. We trekked across to the strip in the morning with the fuel drum strapped to the cart, the crew generously encouraging me to ride most of the way, and by ten o'clock we were airborne. The pilot (on loan from the French Air Force) turned the controls over to me when I told him I was familiar with the Aztec, and even let me fly the landing at our first stop at Tuléar.

Then it was up the spine of the island to Tananarive. The Air France representative put me up at his house overnight, where the bathtub, filled with sea water, was turned over to the turtles. In the morning my baggage had gone ahead. I waited in the car outside the terminal until they were calling for the stragglers, poured a little sea water into the bottom of a clear plastic bag, folded it into the glove pocket of my green wool Loden-Frey car coat, slung the coat casually over my shoulder, and then tried what I hoped was a nonchalant walk to the check-in. The Air France staff made a great fuss, thank God I had arrived, they had already loaded my baggage, *oh là là!*, and escorted me to Passport Control.

The bored officer had his stamp inked and suspended over the passport when he noticed a stamp with Chinese markings on it, on an inner page. "*De quoi il s'agit, ça?*" he said roughly. "*La Chine?*" I said, yes, I was a filmmaker, I had been filming in China four years earlier. "*Et Moscou? Là? Vous êtes communiste, vous?*" I kept as calm as I could, explained what I did for a living, played the Cousteau card (which helped a little, I thought). Then he noticed that my visa had expired the day before. I explained about the hurricane.

"You wait right here," he said peremptorily. Over at the gate I could see the Air France rep rolling her eyes and shaking her head. The man disappeared into an office a few metres away. Over the next few minutes a head would emerge, or two, frowning in my direction. I resignedly felt that the formerly colonized guys were getting some of their own back, using the power of their new independence to take it out on the white guy. Oh well. After three or four minutes the officer came back, gave me a stern lecture, and let me go aboard.

The attendants in first class were frostily polite until I showed them the turtles and explained that they were probably almost suffocated from my prolonged visit with Passport Control. "*O Marie-Celeste, O Virginie! Venez voir les jolies tortues!*" They sealed off one of the first-class washrooms with an Out of Order sign, made a bath in one of the wash basins with salt from the galley, and told me not to worry about a thing. If I dozed off they would come around solicitously whenever I woke to tell me that the babies were fine, swimming around vigorously, could they give them some shrimp? Some oyster? (It was too early: the third day only, Mojé had said.)

It was an all-day trip to Paris, via Dar es Salaam and Athens. I had sent a radiogram to Mme. Coenca at Cousteau's company, Les Requins Associés[6] and supposed she might meet me at Orly. I felt great going ashore there, swinging up the ramp with the turtles once again in a plastic bag in the Loden-Frey coat, horny and optimistic, my hair almost down to my shoulders, blond streaks from a month of tropic sun, and a tan worth a million bucks, and it was Paris!

The exquisite blond woman who approached me with a big smile as I reached the top of the ramp looked far too genial for the reputedly state-trooperish Mme. Coenca, but still: "Madame Coenca?" I asked, as she came up to me with an expectant look.

"*Mais non, Monsieur, je suis d'Air France*," she said, and explained she was doing a survey: how had the flight gone, could I just fill out a small questionnaire, they were trying to assess the first-class service or something like that. I brushed her off. I said I was just back from a month at sea with Cousteau and had important messages for his office, which I had mistakenly thought her attached to; I had to get through immigration and get to a phone.

She was *very* interested. Could she help? Was I going to stay in Paris? (We were now at the immigration desk lineup so I had time to stop and at least be polite to her.) Did I have a place to stay in Paris? (Yes, I had a cameraman friend.) Immigration was perfunctory. Nobody asked about the coat over my shoulder. I got to the head of the escalator and shook hands with the Air France woman. "Are you *sure* you have a place to stay in Paris?" she repeated. I was fretful as hell about the contents of my plastic bag. "Quite sure," I almost snapped.

I was half-way down the escalator to the baggage room when I realized what she was saying. Suddenly I thought, wait a minute, I mean this *is* Paris and . . . ! I scanned the upper level in vain. She was gone.

In my Paris hotel room I made a bath in the bidet for the turtles and went around the corner to the nearest Concaillerie for some fresh oysters. The babies went mad for their first meal, biting at each other's

6. "Associated Sharks."

fins in their rage to eat, and then went all tranquil and floated to the surface calmly. A man arrived by car two days later from the maritime museum in Monte Carlo, with a good-sized aquarium in the back. My turtles set off by road for the Mediterranean, and I got on my Air France flight for Montreal.

I spent most of March and a bit of April in Hollywood, living at the Roy Rogers Hotel on Sunset Strip not far from the Wolper cutting rooms, mostly walking to work, spending very long hours with the editor, John Soh. Cousteau came to Los Angeles for a few days and had a look when we were at an early rough-cut stage. He expressed almost ecstatic approval over what he saw, especially Doug McKay's 9mm lens running shots of the baby turtles heading desperately to the sea. Alan Landsburg was working on another script and preferred writing at home, so I had his very comfortable office as my writing room, and moved back and forth between it and the cutting room downstairs. One day Landsburg asked me to look after Marlon Brando, who was coming in to discuss a project, and Alan would be a bit late, so I had a chance to chat with the legendary actor, not yet fat, who was courteous and soft-spoken, expressing what I took for authentic interest in my account of the Cousteau adventure. Cousteau was in and out, back and forth to Europe, occasionally dropping in on *Calypso.* He was having an affair with a well-known middle-aged film star and asked me to drive them both to a television studio one night, where he was being interviewed. He was not very good on television, surprisingly; perhaps it was because she was there. He sent me a short filmed postcard from the museum in Monte Carlo, standing in front of the aquarium where my turtles were now nearly eight inches in diameter, and swimming strongly. "Ze turtles are doing well and miss zair master," he said, on the film. "See you soon in Hollywood."

That extravagant cordiality lasted until the day he saw the first fine cut and insisted I come back with him to Paris in a few days, rejoin the ship, leave Alan Landsburg and John Soh to finish the film, and get on with directing the next episode. I said, Well, I had to take a few weeks back in Canada, my friend Pierre Trudeau was running for the leadership of the Liberal Party and would likely be the next prime minister, and I had undertaken to cover the convention for the CBC, so I would be in Canada through most of April. He did that puffing noise that I had come to know as a sign of exasperation. "Then you are refusing my offer?" he said. "Just for a few weeks," I said. Then I would be delighted to get on with it. He puffed again, and left the screening room frowning. I do not think we ever spoke again. When I wrote him a few months later, Pierre Trudeau safely in the prime minister's chair and my *Undersea World* episode broadcast to favourable reviews, he never replied.

Chapter 13

BUSHNELL TV

ONE AFTERNOON I WAS SITTING in the control room of Studio Six, an old favourite of mine despite the shaky wooden floor. I had effectively won my directing spurs in that space, directing the *National News* when I was the new kid in the department, and had done my first fairly elaborate production there, with the legendary Nikolai Soloviov as my designer. On this afternoon I think I was being interviewed about some project or other on the afternoon program called *Take Thirty*, but I remember it not because of what I was there for, but because of the other guest, who was Zal Yanovsky of *The Lovin' Spoonful*. I was reminded of this recently when we stopped in at his restaurant in Kingston, Chez Piggy, a few months after his untimely death.

He and I were chatting in the control room that day in 1967 or '68, waiting for the producer/director to come and tell us what we were supposed to do on the show. The researcher was there, and the host or hosts, but no director, air time was fast approaching, and everyone was getting nervous.

Yanofsky said, Hey, that was cool, Watson was a director so Watson could direct the show until it's time for him to go on camera, and then, he, Yanofsky, would direct the Watson segment.

So everyone relaxed and that's what we did, as the regular director never showed up. After the show I asked Yanofsky where he learned to direct. "Well," he said, "actually this was the first time. But I've watched them do it a lot."

Late in 1966 Pierre Juneau at the Board of Broadcast Governors was commissioned by the government to design a new broadcast regulatory body, and he asked me to sit on a planning committee composed mostly of people from broadcasting, both anglophone and francophone, among them Professor Donald R. Gordon, the former CBC foreign correspondent who had brought me to the University of Waterloo as adjunct professor of political science in the wake of the *Seven Days* debacle. I would pick Don up at the Waterloo/Wellington airport in a rented Cessna – I had not yet acquired the Twin Comanche – and fly us to Ottawa, where the meetings were sufficiently frequent and extended to justify our sharing a furnished apartment. That work led to the creation of the CRTC (Canadian Radio-television Telecommunications Commission). There would soon develop a perception that Juneau was an adroit empire-builder, who deployed the classic techniques of encouraging division and dissent at the lower levels. When he became President of the CBC his network officials began to talk of his ambition to compete with the commercial television broadcasters on their own terms. Years later, at Peter Herrndorf's national conference on the financing of broadcasting, Juneau was there when I spoke of him in these terms. Afterwards he shook my hand sadly and said, "I made a lot of mistakes."

I was knocking about a lot from studio to studio and small job to small job in those years after the death of *Seven Days.* But the days when most television production was in the hands of independents like me had not arrived yet, and for a while things were bleak.

I got contracts for a couple of projects at Expo 67, narrations for pavilion films. The vigorous young Montreal International Film Festival asked me to join its board and help build the Expo film summer into what became a lavish success. We premiered *Bonnie and Clyde*, and spent much of the summer hosting and drinking with film people from all over the world. I proposed Moses Znaimer as a greeter and guide to all these celebrities. Moses spoke pretty good French and Russian then, and was a gracious host to the European and Soviet visitors. Most days the lounge at the festival's headquarters in the Windsor Hotel would find groups of producers, directors, actors, and journalists endlessly talking film or grabbing new partners for a quick trip up to a room and then back down to the bar or to that dizzying crowd in the lounge. Warren Beatty and Faye Dunaway hung around for a couple of days. Fritz Lang[1] came, the legendary Austrian director whom most of us probably thought long dead, and was gracious and funny and accessible.

One night Radio-Canada invited half a dozen people connected with the festival to discuss the City of Montreal's ban on Vancouver filmmaker Larry Kent's film *High*. Lang took part, and when the animateur came he introduced Lang as "*ce grande cinéaste, ce géant de l'art cinématique . . .*" and so on. Lang soon had the whole studio grinning as he responded insouciantly in several different languages, apparently not aware that he was shifting from one to the other, all of them accented except the German. It was something like this:

> *Eh bien, quand j'étais jeune réalisateur à Berlin – es war vielleicht in neunzehn hundert zehn, oder zwölf – je me suis dit, and I recall zis, you know, very clearly, das Ich müsste immer sehr – ahmm, vous savez, to be, you know, à prendre soin de ne pas épater les autorités, et les bureaux de censure, vile at ze same time to preserve ze integrity of ze films zat I was making . . .*

It was probably the only memorable thing about the panel.

The late Judy LaMarsh was the minister responsible for Expo and had an apartment in architect Moshe Safdie's intriguing jumbled pile of blocks called Habitat. At the height of the *Seven Days* wars she had proposed me to the prime minister as a candidate to replace Alphonse Ouimet as president of the CBC, and our discussions at that time had

1. *Metropolis, M, Dr. Mabuse, The Blue Gardenia, Beyond a Reasonable Doubt,* and about forty other movies in both Germany and America.

generated an agreeably complicitous friendship. She was travelling during most of the film festival period and gave me the Habitat apartment for two or three weeks, so I moved down there with the family, and Chris, Greg, and Boo had the run of the entire world's fair, day after day, without having to go through the gates.

One day at lunch in the Windsor Hotel I spotted Buckminster Fuller and went over to pay my respects. It had been about a year since the last time, and I was shocked to see him thin and drawn. He must be dying, I thought. The once stocky, plump, radiant little guy I had first met a decade ago and then become friends with after our luminous time on an interview set in 1965 looked as if he hadn't very long to live. But, no, he said exuberantly as he hugged me hello, no, he was fine, it was just that he had been having some pain in his knees and decided that he needed to get back to what he weighed when he was quarterbacking the Harvard football team, 125 pounds, so he ate only steak and orange juice, that was it, no carbohydrates, and the weight had just fallen off pound by pound, and he was within ten pounds of his goal and feeling great, the knees just fine, what did I think of the Skybreak Bubble, did I know his new book of poetry, *Intuition*, was out now, he had a copy for me, meet Iqbal here, Iqbal is from Iraq, he has an absolutely brilliant idea about quasars, old man, wait till you hear it, have you had lunch?

So those weeks on and around the fair grounds were lively enough, but apart from the small narration contracts it was shaping up as a dry time professionally. I began to fear that I was not going to have enough business to justify keeping my beloved Twin Comanche. The plane earned money as long as I was travelling frequently, especially if I were bringing film crews or other team members and thus saving my clients a good deal of travel expense. But if that business went away, the airplane might have to go away too. The prospect of losing it was very tough. For the next year and a half, I knocked on a lot of doors, made a great many proposals, and watched the bank account dwindle away.

In the fall of 1968, Ross McLean asked me to join his group at

The Way It Is as a freelance story producer. We assumed that the CBC management had got over the *Seven Days* thing – it was more than two years, after all. But when I went into the Kremlin to talk contract, the bureaucrat they sent in rather embarrassedly told me that the contract Ross had proposed would not be forthcoming. I could do a few interviews, perhaps a bit of co-hosting with John Saywell, but Ottawa had instructed him that under no circumstances was I to be given a contract with the word "Producer" in it.

Early in the season, I recorded a long interview with Pauline Julien, a fine singer and an apostle for the independence of Quebec. Somebody worried about it and sent a transcript to my former chief, Eugene Hallman, who had been promoted to vice-president of English Television. Hallman did not want the interview to be broadcast; it seemed to make the separatist cause too plausible, too sympathetic.

Ross and I called him on that, and I added that if he insisted I would resign from *The Way It Is* and let the world know why. There was a furious gathering at the Kremlin during which it seemed that Hallman sensed his fiat had been a mistake, and that he needed an out. I said it had suddenly occurred to me that he'd never seen the actual interview, only the transcript. Didn't he think it would be best if he screened the thing before making a final decision? He quickly agreed that judging a program by its transcript was impossible, and ended up reversing his decision, to our relief.

The interview was broadcast and well received. Of *course* it helped English-Canadian viewers understand why the idea of independence had seized so many outstanding talented people in Quebec: it was important to know about that.

John Lennon and Yoko Ono announced their intention to do a sleep-in in the Queen Elizabeth Hotel in Montreal, after they had been refused entry to the United States over a marijuana allegation. A story producer named Alison Gordon[2] proposed bringing a camera

2. The world's first regular female baseball reporter (for the *Toronto Star*), and author of *Striking Out*, and half a dozen other successful mystery novels whose heroine, Kate Henry, also happens to be a baseball writer.

crew to film their visits with the celebrities whom they had invited to come there and talk about war and peace issues, and that I get into bed with them and do an interview for *The Way It Is.* Their manager, Allan Klein, reported back that John and Yoko had agreed, so Alison and the crew and I flew down in the Twin Comanche, which Alison had dubbed Uncle Charley's Hotel, an affectionate play on the International Phonetic Alphabet convention for its call letters, UCH.

As we were taxiing in to the small private and business aircraft terminal, a Piper Aztec with U.S. registration was just shutting down across from our parking space, and I recognized the passenger who was awkwardly climbing out. It was Al Capp, the right-wing cartoonist who drew the popular *Li'l Abner* comic strip. I walked across the tarmac briskly to shake hands with him: I'd been reading *Li'l Abner* for as long as I could remember. I told him that we had something in common besides coming to the John and Yoko sleep-in: I too was an amputee. (Capp had lost his leg at the age of eleven when he fell under the wheels of a tramcar.) He looked at me grumpily and said something like "Well, you walk too damn well. You'll never get any sympathy if you walk like that." And went lurching into the terminal with a most pronounced limp. I thought it was a joke, but over the next two days, as we got to know what a dreadful person he was, I realized that he had been serious.

When it was his turn to come and talk to the couple in bed, Capp kept taunting Yoko, calling her Madame Nhu (after the Vietnamese politician). John Lennon got so angry that he abandoned his Peace To The World attitude, leapt out of bed with his fists up, and had to be restrained by Allan Klein. Tommy Smothers was there at the time – Alison and I had dinner with him later and found him to be a widely read and thoughtful guy – and so was Timothy Leary, high on something, gazing out the window of the suite at the statues on the roof of the immense church just west of the hotel, and dreamily murmuring about how lovely it all was. When Al Capp had finished his insulting visit he, oddly I thought, turned on a bit of charm for Leary and invited him to fly back to Boston with him, he had a couple of empty seats in the Aztec. Leary said, with a dreamy smile, "Why not, Al? It'll probably be the only time you and I will ever get high together."

My most unusual assignment for Ross, on *The Way It Is*, was the last program of the year in 1968. He suggested that I spend the full half-hour informally talking to the viewers, without a script, in response to their letters about the program. It was daunting until I got started, and then took on an energy and an intimacy that, looking back, still surprise me. I invited them to be tougher with us, and tougher with themselves in looking at challenging issues. I said I thought we all needed to be more open to the individuality of children, and more open about the challenges of human relations. I guess I was a bit preachy. I closed with the last stanza of Matthew Arnold's poem "Dover Beach": Ah love, let us be true to one another . . .

. . . [for] we are here as on a darkling plain
Swept with confused alarms of struggle and flight,
Where ignorant armies clash by night.

What was most memorable about that program was not the experience itself, although it had a nice clean, athletic feel to it, coming through smoothly with an unwritten half-hour talk to a national audience, and remembering the poetry without a flaw. What was amazing was the reaction: seven hundred letters within a few days. Audience Relations people told us that one letter represents two thousand viewers "who would have liked to write." Many of those seven hundred were deeply personal, some quite critical, but in a tone that felt like family. I replied to every one.

Those late sixties were a time of turbulence on the educational front, and Beverly and I found ourselves in considerable agreement about the need for some fresh air in the schools. While it seems odd as I look back on it, we did not much object when Chris decided, after finishing Grade Ten, that he would drop out for a while, and hitchhike across the country and take a look at life outside the institutional world. We also found ourselves working well together when Boo and Greg, with about twenty other adolescent kids and an astonishing amount of parental support, decided to start Superschool, a free school in a rented house on Beverley Street. For two years Superschool functioned, I think, quite effectively, the kids hiring their own teachers, handling a surprising amount of the house management on their own, staying up late, and probably smoking a variety of things, and even persuading University of Toronto administrators to sit down with them and seriously discuss ways for Superschool "graduates" to qualify for university entrance.

But apart from that collaboration, the marriage was not working for either of us. Beverly found some solace and meaningful work in the constant challenges of Superschool, and I stayed late at the office and tried to think of brilliant ways to earn money and make a mark in the world of independent television production.

Sometime in 1968, Allan King and I, feeling very complicit after our work on *Warrendale* together and the subsequent political wrangles over trying to get the CBC to actually broadcast a documentary that used the word "fuck" with such abandon, rented a three-storey brick house on Hazelton Avenue, in the Yorkville district, where I incorporated my small private production company, Patrick Watson Enterprises Limited. Allan and I had both somewhat alienated the CBC by then, and business was not brisk. When he began work on his landmark film *A Married Couple*, he at first wanted Beverly and me to be that couple, but the CBC was the only possible broadcaster and my presence in the film would not help it into the CBC schedule. Nor, upon reflection, would the rickety state of the marriage be much improved, we thought, by that kind of exposure, interesting as it might have been for viewers.[3]

We did work up a proposal for *Mondo Magico*, a global romp

3. The couple who did agree to live with the camera for a few weeks were divorced within a couple of years of the film's broadcast.

with Orson Welles visiting Indian rope tricksters and African buried-alive wizards, and Chinese necromancers – indeed magicians of all kinds – all over the world. Welles had told me, in the interview he'd given me in Paris in 1965, that he would go anywhere, do anything, to perform magic. We thought that in each location around the world – with a sleight-of-hand genius in Paris, say, or a big stage illusionist in Leningrad – we could finish the segment with Welles performing some intimate close-up magic for the local hero. His initial response was enthusiastic, but then the line to Spain (where he then lived, trying to get on with his elusive, obsessive *Don Quixote)* went mysteriously silent. One morning Allan handed me the latest edition of *Variety*, with a front-page four-inch column reporting that Orson Welles had announced the launch of a new project: a globe-girdling documentary search for the world's most amazing magicians, he to write, produce, direct, and of course star. He never did it, but the betrayal still rankles.

Allan and I also tried to find financing to buy that Hazleton building. It was going for just over a quarter of a million dollars. On Hazelton Avenue between Scollard and Yorkville! We asked Wilson Southam for advice (and perhaps hoped he would lend us part of the money or come in as an investor). Wilson, in a judgment he honourably deplores today, said we should not be foolish, we were filmmakers not real estate guys, we would only get into trouble, don't touch it with an *eleven*-foot pole. Within five years we would have been millionaires, but by then we were far away.

Roy Faibish and I had not seen much of each other since the *Seven Days* debacle. He had gone to work in private broadcasting and had become effectively the second-in-command at the Ottawa CTV station, CJOH Channel 13. Now he saw me floundering, and in the summer of 1969 he brought me up to Ottawa to work for him and Stuart Griffiths at CJOH. He had brought Laurier and me together there briefly in 1967 for a two-hour miniseries, a sort of *Laurier and Patrick's Canada*, in which we crossed the country talking to people we had always wanted to meet. The interviews I recall with pleasure were with the actor Chief Dan George (*Little Big Man*); Joey Smallwood, who had brought Newfoundland into Confederation; and the Abenaki activist/singer/filmmaker Alanis Obomsawin, with whom an instant spark of connection on first meeting grew into and remains one of the most important friendships of my life.

Stuart Griffiths, the man who had told me in 1953 that I had no future in television, now hired me as Programming vice-president for what he believed was going to be one of the country's major broadcasting initiatives. Griffiths was a brilliant organizer and an innovator. In the 1950s, as head of programming for the CBC's first English-language television station, CBLT Toronto, he scored a spectacular beat over all the American networks by putting a portable film lab and an editing suite in the plane that brought Queen Elizabeth's coronation footage back to Canada (there was no transatlantic satellite link then), so that it was ready to go to air when the plane landed, while the U.S. networks were still waiting for their wet negatives to come out of the lab. In 1957 he was scooped up by Granada TV in England, to be Program Controller, where he generated many of that new private service's outstanding initiatives, including the more or less eternal *Coronation Street.*

The Bushnell project was another ingenious Griffiths innovation: a conglomerate of TV stations and cable services linking Montreal, Cornwall, Kingston, and Ottawa. The revenue base would come from the subscribers to the dozens of St. Lawrence and Ottawa Valley cable systems he was going to buy, and that would allow him to finance a wide variety of original independent programming without totally depending on advertising revenue. It all depended on his getting CRTC permission to become a cable operator as well as a broadcaster, and Pierre Juneau, still chairman of the young CRTC, had told Griffiths that there was no obstacle: he could count on that approval.

So Griffiths had committed the parent company, Bushnell TV,[4] and had begun to build an empire. I agreed to move back to Ottawa.

4. Named for Ernest Bushnell, president, the same man who had been fired after the *Preview Commentary* episode.

Chris, Greg, and Boo, remembering those happy years on the farm at Manotick, pleaded for another farm, so Beverly and I decided to sell the house at 18 Glengrove West and buy a farm in the Ottawa Valley, near Carleton Place. We took temporary digs in the same apartment building where Donald Gordon and I had had our crash pad during the CRTC planning committee, and the night we moved in we left the television set on all night: it was the first moon landing.

Stu Griffiths started by hiring producers and executives, including – besides me – the gifted Nicole Sakellaropoula,[5] (who went on to give the country Peter Gzowski's *This Country in the Morning* – later *Morningside*), my old friend and colleague Laurier LaPierre, and an alumnus of *The Way It Is*, the producer and writer Alison Gordon. It only lasted nine months, but they were good months at first. Griffiths was so high on the prospect of becoming the first private television broadcaster to be at least in part free from the yoke of advertising that he encouraged me to turn my stable of unconventional and imaginative young producers loose on a whole lot of giddy projects

Sakellaropoula started a late-night live magazine show devoted to domestic and family issues, from a very non-consumerist perspective, and named it for the venerable off-beat Scottish weekly *The People's Friend.* Alison Gordon developed something called *Up Against the Wall* that was explicitly aimed at the hip sixties generation and raised a lot of eyebrows during its brief life.

One day she announced that she had talked her way backstage at the National Arts Centre where Frank Zappa and the original Mothers of Invention were about to give their last concert before breaking up. She had persuaded Zappa and the guys to come out to CJOH around midnight, after their show wrapped at the NAC, to improvise a couple of hours of television horseplay, their very last gig together. The only crew we could get that night was the mobile unit crew, who had to leave for Montreal and a football game by, at the latest, 4 a.m. So they would be going live to tape, probably starting

5. She later dropped the name of her first husband and reverted to her birth name of Belanger. She went on to become head of English language services at CBC Montreal.

around 1:30 a.m., maybe laying down ninety minutes of tape, they would see.

Imagine anything as shapeless and risky being undertaken today. Perhaps at Bravo!, but even there . . .

In any case, they pulled it off. I sat there at the back of the control room more often in a state of mystification than anything else, but Gordon and her director, Chris Braden, were cackling with delight, the whole control room had a marijuana perfume to it, the six or eight long-haired and T-shirted guests hanging around at the back were saying they had never seen anything so wonderful in their lives, and there was no doubt that Zappa and Motorhead and the rest of them were playing it right out at the end of the schtick.

The TP (Technical Producer) called a wrap at 3 a.m. He had to get the crew on the road with the mobile unit. They were taking some of the studio equipment with them, so they needed a little extra time. Zappa invented some kind of extravagant closing, Braden rolled the closing credits, and we retired to the empty lobby of the station to tell each other how wonderful we all were.

In the midst of the celebration, the TP came into that lobby with a long face to tell us that there was a problem with the tape, and it was mostly unusable.

Frank Zappa then gave one of the most generous performances I have ever seen. Alison Gordon had fallen back onto a couch in the lobby, pale, shaking her head blindly, unable to speak, the tears pouring down her cheeks. It would have been quite normal for a star of Zappa's stature to fly into a rage about the ineptitude of this bunch of amateurs and the waste of time: one would expect some kind of outburst. Instead, he did one of the most generous things I have ever seen in a showbiz environment (where generous deeds are, sometimes, quite spectacular).

Zappa sat down and put his arm around Alison, lightly patting her shoulder. After a while he said, "Listen. I've got an idea."

Gordon shook her head like a dog drying off, and gulped a few times, and became very alert.

Zappa said, Look, of course this was terrible, but he had another project he wanted her advice on, maybe they could work together on it, she should listen, it was really cool. And he then sketched the outline for, well, this great movie project – the onlookers could see that he was making it up as he went along, but I don't think Alison realized that until much later. It was a movie – perhaps she could come up with a title, they needed a title – it was a movie about how the Mothers of Invention had discovered that Colonel Sanders was really a profoundly evil would-be dictator who was trying to take over the world. Nobody in Washington would believe the Mothers, so single-handedly, so to speak, they had to plan and carry out a campaign to bring the KFC monster to his knees. It was like Howard Hawks' wonderful 1951 sci-fi flick *The Thing From Another World*, where you never saw The Thing (James Arness) except for a fleeting moment when it attacked, but you always knew when it was coming near because the Geiger counters in the Arctic research station would begin to click. In the Mothers against Colonel Sanders, whenever danger was near chicken feathers would drift in from the sky.

He kept this up for about twenty minutes, the whole room spellbound and laughing. Alison was laughing. There was lots to drink back at the hotel, Zappa said, why didn't they go back and celebrate, who needed to go to bed (well, I did) and off they all went.

In the new year the CRTC heard the Bushnell proposal and, despite Juneau's earlier assurances, turned it down. Stu Griffiths was stunned. Now, instead of the network he had felt so sure he was going to get, he was back to running a single station in a small city. He would bring in a good deal of CTV production, Graeme Kerr's cooking show, a few dramas and entertainment specials, but the empire was gone, the reason for hiring us all was gone. Griffiths said he would stick to his commitments to all of us, he wouldn't give up, there would be other ventures. But the atmosphere had gone black. In addition, I was not getting along with Roy Faibish, who seemed to be surreptitiously involved with someone or something not connected to the station and about which he was secretive even with his few close friends. The two of us were quite out of sync.

I left CJOH after six largely unhappy months. But during this time a new idea had begun to form, the first broadcasting idea that had struck me really hard since that winter in 1963 when Doug Leiterman and I and our band of kin-spirits had worked up the proposal for *This Hour Has Seven Days.* We called it *The Whole Earth Project* at first. Late in the autumn of 1969, before the CRTC pulled the rug out, I had brought Donald Gordon into CJOH to help develop a documentary series, and one day over lunch in the cafeteria he had said that television – especially news and current affairs – was so consumed by conflict and bad news that maybe what we should be doing was to invent a format that would make good news attractive and offer viewers some tools for living more creatively in their communities without having to numb their bruised sensibilities after a diet of TV crash and disaster by rushing out to buy the latest stuff. Which was, he said, the principal *raison d'être* for most television enterprises in North America anyway. This conversation led to others, Alison Gordon joining in with her limitless energy, and by the time the Bushnell empire came crashing down I knew exactly what I wanted to do next.

There is an important interlude in here. In October of 1970 James Cross, a British diplomat in Montreal, was kidnapped, and Pierre Laporte, a provincial cabinet minister, was murdered. The crimes were signed by a shadowy group of terrorists who called themselves the FLQ: Front de libération du Québec. In a famous few seconds of grainy black-and-white news film, Prime Minister Trudeau spoke to a CBC reporter with contempt about the "bleeding hearts" who were cautioning the government about not leaping into the fray with too many guns blazing. When the reporter asked him how far he was prepared to go, he replied curtly, with a hint of a sneer, "Just watch me."

We did not have to wait long. Within hours his government declared the War Measures Act (WMA) and began to round up hundreds of people connected to the Quebec independence movement, raiding homes in the night, taking people off in handcuffs, jailing them without charge.

I was friendly with a senior civil servant, Don Wall, who was one of the country's two top civilian security officials. We had met at a party at Arch McKenzie's house, the Canadian Press Bureau chief, and shared a fondness for singing rowdy folk songs to noisy unprofessional accompaniment. There was always lots of gin and lots of beer. Wine had not become the big thing it was soon to do, although I do remember its encroaching through those four years, and Don Wall's delight at discovering an Algerian red called Ben Afnam that came in imperial gallon jars with a ring handle on the neck, and cost just over $6 for the gallon. These are cultural notes, you understand.

Wall played the mandolin and I was getting to be fairly hot on the five-string banjo, thanks to Pete Seeger's instructional LP. We often lunched upstairs at Sammy Koffman's Belle Claire Hotel on Queen Street, well lubricated with martinis, ordered with meticulous precision even though the bar knew perfectly well, Gordon's Gin, 5½ to 1, straight up with an olive. It was not unusual for Wall and his partner, a more taciturn but also funny man named Don Beavis, to drink three of these very large inverted cone glasses at lunch, but neither of them ever slurred a word or boasted a secret or betrayed the tiniest indiscretion about the world of espionage and police and international intrigue within which they lived and breathed and had their being.

I knew that Wall, for whom I had conceived a great affection and respect, would be working around the clock on this WMA file, and I phoned his private number late one day, "Just to give you a hug," I said. He sounded grey and exhausted. It was the only time in our long acquaintance that he ever came close to giving anything away. He sighed and said, Did I know what the damnedest thing was about this whole affair? I didn't, of course.

"There is no FLQ, Patrick. There are a few little isolated gangs of two or three people, calling themselves a movement. It's not a movement. It doesn't mean anything, it . . ." And then he broke off. I told him, Well, I was thinking about him, we'd see each other when it was all over.

I don't think we talked about it again. I'm not sure. But I am sure that I was appalled at the way in which the majority of journalists fell into line, and the majority of MPs. The opposition did not oppose. The questions that Parliament and the Press Corps are designed to answer did not get asked. The War Measures Act can be declared only if local authorities declare there has been an "apprehended insurrection," and Quebec premier Robert Bourassa conveniently said that there was one. There was no evidence to support this declaration. But there had been a couple of mailbox bombings, one kidnapping, one brutal killing, and the country was enraged. Soon there were tanks and armoured personnel carriers in the streets, in both Montreal and Ottawa, and soldiers in full battle gear with weapons at the ready. It was more like a movie set than reality, but it was very real. The miserable kids who had taken Cross and killed Laporte were rounded up. A lot of people did time in jail and were eventually released. But the media were not screaming, as they should have, "What 'apprehended insurrection'? Show us some evidence." Neither was Parliament. The echoes of post-9/11 are striking. The only significant speech of opposition was from NDP leader Tommy Douglas. Douglas argued, correctly, that the authorities had all the power they needed under the Criminal Code, and that if the government wanted special powers it had an obligation to ask Parliament for them and make a convincing case, which it had not done. He accused the government of panicking, and said of his party that "we are not prepared to use the preservation of law and order as a smokescreen to destroy the liberties and the freedom of the people of Canada."

It was a powerful speech, listing the appalling lack of protection for civil rights in a nation that was still without a charter of rights. But it was only one voice, and the majority made fun of that voice, and for a while the police kept on breaking into homes and dragging "suspects" into jail without charging them.

Gordon Fairweather called, a thoughtful soft-spoken Tory MP (Fundy Royal). He and a couple of other Progressive Conservative MPs, David McDonald and Flora McDonald, were three of the few dissenting members, along with a young PC worker named Hugh Segal. The NDP had been steadfast in arguing for the preservation of civil rights, and Tommy Douglas's prescient speech was credited by a later leader of that party, Jack Layton, with turning him around on the issue – he had at first been in favour of the WMA. Among the governing Liberals, the only dissenting MP was Pierre de Bané, now a senator.

Gordon Fairweather told me that another young Tory volunteer, Bill Macadam, was organizing a book of essays questioning the imposition of the act, and asked if I would contribute a piece. I did, focusing on the delinquency of the media. Segal and Macadam were phoning around the country to round up the support of more writers. Much of it came from members of the Progressive Conservative Party: Eddie Goodman, the eminent Toronto lawyer; Dalton Camp; Norm Atkins; Dian Cohen, the economist. There were a few Liberals, too, including Lloyd Axworthy, and some eminent journalists including June Callwood, George Bain, Peter Desbarats, and Charles Gordon, Alison's brother and editor of the Brandon *Sun*. There were some academics, among them the historian Ramsay Cook and the principal of University College, Toronto, Claude Bissell. We considered ourselves, I think, a happy little band. The book was written, edited, and published by The New Press within a few weeks.[6] It was called *Strong and Free: A Response to the War Measures Act.*

I was on a panel in 1976 or '77 with Robert Bourassa – nothing to do with the subject – and I asked him afterwards about his support of the War Measures Act. Bourassa readily conceded that there had been no "apprehended insurrection," but said he felt that his government was not in control of the province and that the WMA was the only way he could think of to get federal help. Trudeau, upon Bourassa's retirement, called him "a wise and statesman-like leader."

6. ISBN 0-887770-086-1.

In the political world, the rhetoric of courtesy sometimes strains the truth, but this seemed unnecessary, and I regret that in our later frank and wide-ranging discussions about the challenges to the development of democracy in Canada it proved impossible for Trudeau and me to really explore the War Measures Act together.

But I am proud that my name is in that little book of dissent to something that is now, if remembered, largely remembered as a disgrace to our traditions of civil rights.

Alison Gordon and Donald Gordon and I initially called our how-to-have-a-life-without-shopping initiative *The Whole Earth Project*, after Stuart Brand's then popular *Whole Earth Catalogue.* That particular child of the sixties was a genuine catalogue of goods, publications, and services that people could use as a way to escape the consumerist tyranny: camping stuff; cunning and seductive tools for hundreds of dreamy enterprises in arts, crafts, and home industries from blacksmithing to gardening to wine-making; self-help books of every thinkable description.

It was probable, we thought, that the vast majority of *Catalogue*'s readers would never in fact *do* any of these things, or buy any of those lovely tools: they would mostly use the book as a kind of pornography of the creative life. But, we said, if television viewers could see vivid and dramatic short documentaries of other people actually building kites or weaving blankets or making goat cheese – or getting out in the community to animate a program for street kids or an environmental rescue – if the viewers could be taken into those experiences in the way that good, condensed, no-fat no-blab film can do so well, then maybe more people would actually start doing things themselves instead of intellectually masturbating.

We put together a fat book of photos, drawings, and sample scripts. It began with some tipped-in pages from the old *LIFE* magazine, a five- or six-page photo essay about a group of Girl Scouts in River Edge, a peaceable little New Jersey town. These kids had decided to clean up the riverbank, which was overgrown with scrubby trees and littered with junk, discarded tires and refrigerators, several generations of lazy discard both in and by the side of what had a century earlier been a clear-flowing pristine stream. The mess had been the focus of several municipal campaigns, none of which had amounted to anything: it was going to be just too damn expensive.

But the girls said, What if we all pitched in? And so they doggedly canvassed the churches, their families, their boyfriends, the Kiwanis and Rotary clubs, the local weekly newspaper – effectively the whole town, through that very catalogue of voluntary organizations that Alexis de Tocqueville had predicted a century earlier would be the spine and energizer of democracy in America. Of course the local Boy Scouts had to come on board; they couldn't be left behind by the girls. So did the YMCA and the one small synagogue. They decided on a forty-eight-hour weekend blitz, and they actually cleaned up that river. *LIFE* sent a small band of photographers. The result was an engaging, immediate photo essay that would cause anyone reading it to say, "My God! We could do that in *our* town."

And that is what we wanted our little films to do: lead people to say, "We could do that." We felt we could do a story like that in two minutes or less, taking account of the diminishing attention spans of television watchers. One of the beer companies had shown that a thirty-second commercial composed primarily of tightly shot and edited actuality films on unusual sports and recreations could very effectively give viewers a taste of and perhaps an appetite for actually trying something new, training bird dogs, for example, or tying flies. You said, "Gee, I could do that."

Struck by the power of colour photographs taken from the moon, we changed the name of the project to *Earthrise.*

It took us a few months to put together that fat book, at the same time beginning to canvass producers, potential sponsors, and broadcasters. Alison and I jumped in the Twin Comanche one day and took the plan to the Corporation for Public Broadcasting in Washington, where it was very well received. We dropped in on Nicholas Johnson, the radical young commissioner of America's broadcast regulator, the

Federal Communications Commission (FCC). He seemed enthralled by the project and assigned his senior assistant to try mapping out ways in which the Commission might lend a hand.

We also flew to a film location in Connecticut where we knew Donald Sutherland was working on *Klute*, and showed him the fat book. At that time he was very close to his co-star, Jane Fonda, and his dressing room was littered with books on political and social issues that she had pressed upon him. As our friendship grew over the years, I discovered that his reading was voracious and catholic, and that he shared my love of poetry and compulsion to show off by reciting at the drop of a hat. He took the time to go carefully through the *Earthrise* proposal and agreed to give us whatever support he usefully could.

It seemed about time to knock on the CBC's doors, but of course they were still closed to me . . . at least at the network level.

Coming downstairs from lunch at the Cercle Universitaire one day, I ran into a CBC vice-president who asked me, What was I up to these days? My obsession with *Earthrise* was in full sway, and I gave him the by now well-rehearsed spontaneous pitch, the ninety-second version that I deployed in order to bring conversations to a stop in parties and other gatherings. The man seemed impressed. He said he had never shared management's conventional view of my unreliability, and if I would give him my personal assurance that we were ready to work with the CBC in developing this project, he would get us in to see the new president, George Davidson, the elderly former secretary of the Treasury Board whom Lester Pearson had parachuted in for stability's sake after they had fired Al Ouimet. He said he was sure that Davidson would love our project; Davidson wasn't going to be there long; it would be great to leave a positive legacy. This VP said he would set something up and call me in a few days, and to my surprise, he did.

That meeting was one of the worst. Not overtly hostile, just blanketed by a ponderousness in stark contrast with the CBC I had grown up in a decade and a half earlier. The conveyor of the new attitude was the same Gene Hallman who had, in those early days, invited the gang of young producers to sit around on the floor of his office at lunch with our paper bags of sandwiches, to discuss how television might better serve the country, and with whom I had later gone to war over the Pauline Julien interview for *The Way It Is.* He was still head of CBC TV.

The president opened the meeting in a completely positive way: Watson had a project tailor-made for the CBC, he said, and he hoped we would come out of the meeting with a strategy for developing it.

I took them through the book and gave my five-minute pitch. Everybody in the room was nodding in excited agreement, except Hallman, who just pursed his lips and hung back. George Davidson canvassed the room. All positive. He then asked Gene, What do you think?

Gene Hallman said, Look, when they brought him a situation comedy or an outdoor adventure series, it was easy to evaluate because there were benchmarks, there were success or failure indicators for programs like that, it was easy to look at a proposal and just measure it against the criteria established by earlier successful programs. But this *Earthrise* thing – well, they had never seen anything like it. There was simply no way to evaluate it. Nobody had ever done anything like it. How could I expect the CBC to risk development money on something that had never been tried before?

He was serious. I guess he had forgotten *Close-Up*, *Seven Days*, *Citizens' Forum*, indeed that whole panoply of shooting from the hip and trying stuff that had never been tried before, because television was new, and he had been part of all that . . . .

But it was clear there was no point even arguing.

A Toronto advertising man, Jerry Goodis, saw me being interviewed on television about the difficulties of enlisting a broadcaster for *Earthrise*, and asked me to come and see him. He was in the news just then, having had a funny and noisy public dispute with Marshall McLuhan about the effects of advertising, and I was delighted to respond to his invitation: he had a reputation for getting things done.

He almost slavered over our book. He said, This was real television; this was what the medium was *meant to do*. Of course he could sell it. He would have a sponsor for us within weeks if not days. Don't worry. Leave it to Jerry.

The days became weeks. When he finally called, it was to say gloomily that every advertiser he had pitched on the project had said the same thing: it was anti-advertising. How could he expect anyone to sponsor a program whose message was that you don't have to buy stuff to be happy?

So it was over. We packed up the fat book and closed the little office. There had been virtually no income for almost a year. I was probably going to have to take out a second mortgage on the farm and sell the Twin Comanche. But the satisfaction of having devised a program series that I could *taste* . . . that someday, if we ever got back to the old spirit of public broadcasting, could provide an indisputably special level of that service to the viewer that Ross McLean had insisted on . . . I still feel that satisfaction, if a bit sadly, since the someday I refer to seems farther away than ever. In the meantime a temporary rescue appeared that was in some ways related to the spirit of *Earthrise*.

Within a few days a call came that put my feared austerity measures on hold, at least for a while. It was my old friend and former boss Bernard Ostry, Assistant Secretary of State, the title given to the deputy minister in that department. His minister, Secretary of State Gérard Pelletier, had asked him to commission a task force to look into citizen participation in the democratic decision-making process at the federal level, and Ostry wondered if I were free to head up the task force. The government had determined that there was a good deal of alienation from federal politics, that it wanted to know what people felt about their access to the processes of national government, and that it wanted to explore ways of more widely opening that access. Ostry proposed that I put together a small group of mixed backgrounds and travel across the country meeting with individuals and citizens' groups to see if we could come up with some answers.

The key group I assembled included a young Chinese-Canadian woman from Vancouver, a second-generation Ukrainian from St. Catharines, and an old-family francophone from Quebec. It would cost less for me to fly us around than to buy airline tickets, so there was at least a reprieve for CF-UCH. It was a lovely way to visit the country, fuelled by a modest sense of national purpose, in the good company of new friends, mostly young, all stimulating.

We soon began to feel that Canada's democracy was in pretty good shape, though, like de Tocqueville's findings in America just over a century earlier, it seemed more functional at the local level than on a national scale. We were struck by how little people knew about other parts of the sparsely populated country, and it was not surprising that they did not very much care about people they never saw. That seemed to be one area that the Feds could do some work on. It was striking how enthusiastic about distant parts people became once they had been there. Even die-hard Quebec nationalists who had set out on a business or professional trip to the West Coast – perhaps reluctantly or cynically at first – found that they could not suppress a leap of perception, a wild surmise, a gasp of recognition, when they looked down from 25,000 feet over the Rockies and realized that these majestic, brooding shapes also belonged to them. The few anglophone kids who had been lucky enough to be in a French immersion program that arranged for them to spend a summer or more with a family in Quebec inevitably came back to Regina or Lethbridge with a new sense of the breadth of the culture to which they belonged, of the legitimacy of regional feelings other than what they had grown up with, a love of that particular Quebec humour, and a greater understanding of what was driving the nationalist spirit in that province.

We thought perhaps there would be a way to make more of this happen, to move people around more. The vitality of local and regional pride and the involvement in local affairs that constitute the spine and muscle of effective democracy under the protections of rights of association and expression, and a fair shot, most of the time, at justice in the face of authority – these we found reasonably functional, more so than in most parts of the world, it seemed. So if we could just get Canadians to live the national experience more . . .

We inevitably ended up discussing the idea of national service, perhaps along the Swiss model, a year or two in which kids can serve either in the armed forces or in civilian social service that takes them to other parts of the country. By the time the young Swiss have finished their national service, they will have lived with families in every canton in the country and have been exposed to all the different languages and cultures, a powerful enrichment of the meaning of the words "I am Swiss." Could we do something like that in Canada, where the opposition to any form of national call-up is so powerful?

The final report we submitted was in two forms: the conventional sober cabinet document, in all its formality, and an artifact. This latter was in the shape of a good-sized pillowcase, made of strong, richly toothed drawing paper with the red and white flag printed on one side. It contained a number of objects, most of which were fictions suggesting that the proposals we were making already existed as programs. One of our favourites was *Take the Train for a Dollar a Day.* The flag/pillowcase had a poster in it rolled up in a cardboard mailing tube, a good-sized poster you could paste up on a wall, inviting you to travel across the country by train for a dollar a day.

Here is how we thought it could work. The government would demand of the railways, as part of the cost of doing business, that they attach a passenger car and a baggage car to every one of the hundreds of freight trains that criss-cross the country every day. Rudimentary passenger cars – even bring some of the old wooden-seat antiques out of retirement if they still exist, we said: the passengers will be on them for only a few hours a day, starting around 10 a.m. and ending at about 4 p.m. The baggage car would be equipped with bicycle racks. Priority access would be to families with kids able to ride bikes. We were big on bikes then. Everyone was reading Ivan Illich (*The Limits of Medicine,*[7] *Deschooling Society, Tools for Conviviality, Energy and*

Equity), and we admired the case he made for the bicycle as the central component of urban transportation. Our dollar-a-day families would get on the train in their hometown in mid-morning, get off at four and stay in a hostel wherever they found themselves, arrange through the system to stay with a family in the ultimate destination, move across the country by train and bike and get to know their fellow citizens. It was lovely to watch people going through the posters and other artifacts in the pillowcase, unrolling the train poster from its mailing tube, unaware that it was only a brainstorm, and exclaiming, "I didn't know about that! I'm gonna do that next summer with my kids!"

Our travels had also persuaded us that with the exception of CBC Radio, the media were not effective in giving Canadians a sense of the texture and spread of the country. Newspapers were especially regional, and we said, What about a national public newspaper more or less modelled on CBC Radio, funded initially with an endowment from the Feds but thereafter required to make its way through subscription income. Our other model was *I.F. Stone's Weekly*, which Izzy Stone and his wife, Esther, had produced in the basement of their small Washington, D.C., house, funded only by subscription, no ads, beholden to nobody, establishing it as essential reading for a sufficiently wide audience to keep it going for nearly twenty years (1953 to 1971).[8] *I.F. Stone's Weekly* was primarily a watch on Washington. Widen the scope, we thought, add in the kind of stories of communities functioning like communities across the country, follow no fads, hire a few diligent investigative journalists who were also very good writers – we were sure it was possible for a paper like that to be self-sufficient within a few years, and that it would pay off in the readers' knowledge of and engagement in national affairs that the

7. Also published as *Medical Nemesis.*

8. When Stone retired, still puzzled by the seeming absurdity of the Socrates story, a good man put to death by the State he had loved and served so well – and calmly accepting that death instead of escaping as he easily could have done – Stone learned ancient Greek in order to read the original documents and wrote a wonderfully provocative book, *The Trial of Socrates*, arguing that Socrates was indeed an enemy of the Athenian democracy.

government claimed it was concerned about. The best way to put such a proposal forward for discussion would be to publish an issue. Peter Gzowski agreed to be the editor and wrote much of it himself. When the idea surfaced thirty years later in front of a Senate committee looking into ownership concentration in the media, a search began for copies of the original paper.[9] My copy, along with the pillowcase and all its other artifacts, disappeared after I lent it to Fred Lebensold, the architect of the National Arts Centre. Nobody I know has a copy.

We delivered the pillowcase and the cabinet document, collected our final paycheques, were formally thanked and praised, "You'll be hearing from us," etc., and the task force stood down. Tom Spaulding, a CBC production designer from my early television days, now living in Ottawa, proposed getting together to look at some independent production prospects. I invited Bill Kurchak, a task force member who thought like an entrepreneur and independent producer, to sit in. Spaulding brought a literary agent friend from New York, Jay K. Hoffman. The meeting led to our incorporating Immedia Inc., with me, Spaulding, Laurier LaPierre, and Isabel Ripley as directors. We had no contracts and no immediate prospects, but there was a giddy optimism in the group. Gene Lawrence, a CBC producer and pal from the *Close-Up* days, came from Vancouver to sit in on some brainstorming sessions. Jay Hoffman represented Edward de Bono in the United States, and persuaded that author to come over at his own expense and work up a proposal for a television series on lateral thinking, which we would pitch first to the CBC and then to the world.

One day in the autumn of 1971 we all headed off to Sarnia (why Sarnia? I've no idea now) for a three-day think-in, to come up with as many Immedia projects as possible. Gene Lawrence and Alison Gordon came along. It was a kind of extended breakfast weekend, beginning over sausages and eggs at about 9 a.m. and going on well past midnight. We called Carbondale University in Illinois to ask

9. That Senate hearing was widely reported, and the public newspaper proposal brought a rush of reaction ranging from wild enthusiasm to nearly hysterical shrieks about mind control and state propaganda, the latter voices having totally missed the point.

Bucky Fuller to join us, but never succeeded in finding him. We designed any number of romantic and quite impractical initiatives and laughed a great deal. I suspect we all knew that it was unlikely to lead to anything, but there was something about that time, it didn't seem to matter.

I headed back to the farm, to tend the livestock and wonder about whether there were any cash crops we could raise that would help keep up the mortgage payments. A few CBC friends let me know that they had been trying to open a door here or there, but the bureaucratic shutout was still impenetrable, although I did get a few radio commentary gigs, fifty dollars here, fifty dollars there. Things did not look promising.

Beverly cast around to see what the chances were of a teaching job in the area. I tried to think of a clever book I could write in a hurry. Jay Hoffman said he could sell something, he was sure, another thriller maybe? Like *Zero to Airtime*? But it was hard to focus. I thought I would have to swallow my pride and call Roy Faibish, but then I learned he had left Channel 13 and was now a CRTC commissioner. As much as we could, we were eating what we grew. We had raised pigs that year, for the first time, and got a freezer full of pork. "Is this *Arnold* we're eating!" Boo demanded, when I cooked the first sausage breakfast. "Oh well, I guess it is. It's very good." When hens finished laying, we slaughtered and plucked and drew them and cut them up for stew.

Over drinks after an Immedia meeting, Laurier outlined a story he had sketched out for a movie about the War Measures Act. Tom Spaulding encouraged Laurier and me to collaborate on turning it into a screenplay, and within weeks we had one in pretty good shape: *Three Days in October*. It was a love story whose central figure was the daughter of a pundit known as the Voice of Quebec, also a major figure in the film. The rising Quebec star Geneviève Bujold, in a press conference for the launch of her film *Act of the Heart*, declared that our *Three Days* was going to be her next film. We began to get noticed by the press. The Immedia team said that I should direct – that would help bring financing – and that we should take it to the then fairly new Canadian Film Development Corporation. The CFDC's official mandate was to help fund movies made in Canada with Canadian subjects. Gratien Gélinas, dean of the Quebec theatrical community and much loved in the province for his comic folksy character, 'Tit-Coq, was the chairman of that funding agency, and we were surprised to get a letter asking us to meet with him, instead of the usual officials. That sounded like better news than it turned out to be. Gélinas scolded us for ten shrill minutes about the provocative nature of our screenplay, and the impossibility of any journalist's ever achieving the authority and status of our character the Voice of Quebec. "That could not happen in Quebec!" he said. "Quebec is not like that!" I asked him baldly if he were turning down our proposal on political grounds, and he replied equally baldly that this was exactly what he was doing. The CFDC was supposed to make its judgments on the dramatic and production merits of a script, and its potential for distribution and audience building, not on the values, political or otherwise, reflected in its story. In any case he was wrong about the pundit, who was modelled on the very real and much admired André Laurendeau. Gélinas did not even address the dramatic and production merits of the script. In retrospect it is astonishing to me that we didn't go to the press with the story and try to make a political issue out of it.

One afternoon Jack Willis telephoned me. He had been a stringer for *Seven Days*, bringing us a series of short documentaries, working from New York. I had not spoken to him since then, but I remembered him with affection, a lean, freckled baseball nut with a huge grin. He was now program director, he said, at WNET Channel 13, the National Educational Network flagship station in New York. Would I come down there, he wondered, on a six-week consulting contract? They could pay very well, and, understanding that I would have ongoing projects in Canada, they could cover my travel back and forth if I had to do some commuting. What was the project? Well, they were designing a news program for the station, aimed at the streets of New York, nothing like any news program the U.S. had ever seen before, and he wanted to put some of the *Seven Days* touch into it. Channel 13 had agreed that he could bring me in to help it get started. I changed the oil in Uncle Charley's Hotel and got out my U.S. charts.

Chapter 14

THE FIFTY-FIRST STATE

A WRITER WHO LEARNED his craft in Manhattan in the late sixties and early seventies wrote in the *New York Review of Books* that New York in those days was not really part of the United States at all: there were no shopping malls to be seen, no subdivisions or theme parks, "no born again Christians who had not been sent there on a mission."[1] It was more like an offshore cultural principality, he said. When I arrived there in the late autumn of 1971 its mythology – for me – was still one of lurking violence; I kept looking over my shoulder when I walked the streets, which at first I seldom did. But within weeks I forgot about being mugged, established my own paths around the central Manhattan watering holes and convivial eateries. Like millions of others I soon sensed the exhilaration of the city, at being in the Centre of the Universe, and at the myriad small characteristics that began to reveal themselves, such as the way in which one falls into conversation with total strangers in the supermarket checkout line, over a headline at the newsstand, at a table across the way in the coffee shop.

Jack Willis's call had come out of the blue. As I said, I hadn't seen him since he made the last of several fine documentaries for *Seven Days.* I had not heard about the surfing accident that had broken his spine and left him – according to the medical establishment – a

1. Luc Sante, in the November 6, 2003, fortieth anniversary edition.

permanent quadriplegic; so when I walked into his office on 59th Street West at Columbus Circle, I was shocked to see his emaciated frame, the canes, his twisted hands.

Jack did not make light of it; he just said we would talk about all that later, he wanted me to meet some people and get to work on what would become *The Fifty-First State.*

Both American critics and the press in Canada later wondered aloud if the program's title had something to do with my being Canadian, Canada often having been referred to as or speculated about becoming the fifty-first state of the union. But in fact the phrase had been Norman Mailer and Jimmy Breslin's slogan when they ran for mayor and city manager the year before, proposing that the greater New York area with its 30-million-plus inhabitants needed the advantages of statehood. Willis and his crew, with substantial funding from the Ford Foundation (then directed by the late Edward R. Murrow's producer, Fred W. Friendly), wanted a daily news program focused on greater New York, not on Wall Street or Broadway or any of the glitzy mythologies, but on the streets and the brownstones, the daily life, the subway, the crime, the economy, city hall, the bridges, the characters – the fabric of real life in the city. Jack contracted me for six weeks as a consultant on program development. I arranged parking for the Twin Comanche at Teterboro Airport, and a hotel room at 55th and 5th, expecting to be back on the streets in Ottawa looking for work in the new year.

But either late in December (1971) or early in January, a couple of weeks or so before the program was to go to air, the person slated to audition for the anchor position called in sick on the day of the dry run, and Jack asked me to sit in. It went well: a mix of film reports and debriefings with the reporter/producers who had made them, and a two-interviewer-one-guest rout with the irrepressible congresswoman Bella Abzug facing me and a smart young southerner named Robert Sam Anson as my partner. Anson and I managed to get Abzug refreshingly away from her usual bullshit-laden memorized lines and even she, after she recovered from the unusual experience of being contradicted and caught short, admitted that it had been a hell of an interview. In the debriefings with the people who had made short film segments, I upset a couple of reporters by asking questions they hadn't anticipated and did not have answers to. And then I went back to my office to screen some stuff and write up notes for Jack about the directions the program was taking.

Late in the afternoon, he limped to my office door with a big grin on his face and asked if I had any firm obligations in Canada for the rest of the year. Because he and the station manager wanted me to be the anchorman to launch the series and, they hoped, to stay with it.

The program made news in New York from its debut. Its success mirrored the success, eight years earlier, of *This Hour Has Seven Days*, and, not surprisingly (since Willis and I had met in the *Seven Days* camp), it was in some ways a New York–based daily version of the earlier magazine. Within a few weeks our audiences were large and loyal. I was recognized on the street, and in New York City that means they own you, and it was sometimes hard to get out of a cab or a restaurant without being cornered and lectured to. The press, from the beginning, was intrigued and before long our coverage was almost daily and almost always positive. There was no other news show like it. We paid no attention to the shibboleths. There was no such thing as a standard running length for a report. If an interview was going well, we let it run to its optimum length. If a film report merited three minutes, it got three minutes; if it merited nineteen minutes it got that. We went to air at 10 p.m. The station would not return to the network after we were off the air, so if we had a show that merited a full hour we did that. If we had only enough good material for, say, sixteen minutes, we did that. Occasionally we ran to midnight and beyond.

Jack Willis and I would sit there in his third-floor office at 8th and 58th screening with an item producer, and had the exhilarating experience over and over again of identifying exactly the same editorial and production issues.

It is standard practice in network television news for the anchor to question the reporter in the field. This is often a slightly fraudulent device intended to make the report look like a conversation, whereas the questions are really prepared either by the reporter himself or the editorial staff. But, as I had done in that dry run, I routinely debriefed the reporter/producers (live) on their filmed reports – a documentary on squatters in a tenement on the Lower East Side, an inside look at the New Jersey Mafia, a scientific breakthrough at Columbia University – by asking them to explain aspects of the story I hadn't understood, or spontaneous questions about what seemed to me to be pertinent stuff they had missed. The press and the audience mail and phone calls showed that our viewers became tremendously engaged in this process, the humanization of the journalists, their saying, Well, no, they did not know anything about that aspect of the story, but they would find out and report back tomorrow. After a while, the journalists not only got over their resentment at being asked unexpected questions, but began to pride themselves on being ready for anything I might come up with, and the debriefing process generated an in-house tradition of follow-up on stories that might otherwise have been forgotten.

Early in the series a producer named Tony Batten brought in a documentary about gang wars among young blacks in the Bronx. It was beautifully crafted, tremendously dramatic, a bit frightening. Jack Willis wondered aloud if there wasn't some way to get those kids sitting down together to see if there are peaceful ways of working things out? Or was the war motif more important than resolving conflicts?

"Why don't we ask them?" Batten said. He would try to persuade a bunch of their reps to come into the studio, watch the doc when it screened, and then it would be my job to put it to them: Do you all just want to make war all the time? What's going on?

Charmian Reading's great photograph (it made *TIME* magazine) shows the studio that night.

More than fifty young gang warriors were on the stage. They were eloquent and funny. At one point I said, "You guys claim that you're not militaristic, that you really want peace in the South Bronx, but all that gear you're wearing, all that insignia, that looks like uniforms to me."

A kid stretched out on the floor below my stool looked up solemnly at my impeccable dark green suit and turtleneck and said softly, "Man, you don't think *you* wearin' a uniform?"

The program went out every day into the streets of New York to observe its daily life and report on what was working well and what was working badly. We had several dedicated camera crews (16mm film was still the preferred medium for shooting "in the field"). While the identification of trouble and the search for remedy are always important functions of a committed journalistic enterprise and were central to this one, there was plenty of room for celebration, irony, and humour. We did not repeat the *Seven Days* use of the satirical sketch as a kind of dramatized televisual editorial cartoon, but we did broadcast excerpts from some comedy shows, the occasional profile of musicians and other entertainers, and street characters. There were some refreshing short wordless film essays that illuminated ordinary scenes. One jewel-like piece was simply farewells and welcomes at the airport balletically edited to Carole King's 1971 hit "So Far Away": "Doesn't anybody stay in one place any more? It would be so fine to see your face at my door."

Another was ducks marching portentously in Central Park to pompous military music, yet another the faces of poverty on the begging streets. There were similar filmic essays on architecture, the subways, newsstands, and cops.

The backbone of the daily broadcast consisted of solid and extended investigative studies of housing, municipal corruption, local and regional political issues, crime, prisons, nutrition and child care – the gamut of social and economic issues, almost always with a street edge. Not much on Wall Street or Broadway, unless we found something fresh and relevant to the life of the community. There was a good seasoning of literature and the arts. Early in the second season the controversial Scottish psychiatrist R.D. Laing[2] set out on a publicity trip across the United States to raise interest in a film about his new residential treatment centre. Network programmers asked him if he would like to have a television conversation with a well-known American – they could probably produce just about anybody he named. Laing asked for Norman Mailer. The network went a bit nervous about this: Laing himself was unpredictable enough, but the two of them together might be asking for trouble. They asked Channel 13 to lend me to the broadcast as a sort of moderator, in case things got out of hand.

We were on air for about two hours, all told, introducing the documentary on the treatment centre and then talking about it afterward. I did not really have to intervene at all, although I joined in restrainedly from time to time. The three of us got on harmoniously. There were some odd moments when Mailer's convictions about reincarnation made Laing look like a conservative, but the essence of the broadcast was a kind of eavesdropping on two huge intellects (and egos), fascinated with each other as much as with themselves, discovering each other and exploring the entire territory. We all went out for pub grub and beer afterward. It was an evening I was sorry to see the end of.

Reporters in the *Fifty-First State* unit who had at first bridled at my asking them questions they couldn't answer in the live debriefings on their filmed reports began to relish those sessions. One of them, Rafael Abramovitz, one day when I was pondering over a piece in which I thought we might not be giving adequate space to the wealthy "bad guys" (while the deprived "good guys" were well represented) said, memorably, "We're public broadcasters. *Our job is to give a voice to the voiceless.*"

While the streets of Greater New York were the *raison d'être* of *The Fifty-First State*, the war in Vietnam was preoccupying the whole country, and some of our more dramatic stories were about Vietnam veterans in New York. And when it was learned that President Nixon

2. *The Bird of Paradise and the Politics of Experience* and *The Politics of the Family* are his best-known books.

had ordered more bombing of Hanoi in December of 1972, some of the *Fifty-First State* journalists demanded a meeting with Willis and me to hear a proposal for a special program on the issue. They argued that the bombing was probably illegal, that it was a dangerous stunt that Nixon was using to try to make what must soon be a strategic retreat into something that looked like an American victory. They argued that the bombing so deeply imperilled the United States that it would be irresponsible of us not to give it major attention. They proposed to do this in our own special way, not following the conventional optic of the major broadcasters. They would involve a wide spectrum of prominent New Yorkers, in a live show that would effectively invite people to come to the studio if they could convince us they had something to offer. The live segments would be wrapped around filmed inserts, including material from Washington, where a team would head out that same afternoon to canvass opinion in the Senate and the House, *in extenso*, not the thirty-second sound bite[3] but serious interviews, with serious players being asked serious questions and given time for a serious response. We would go on the air the very next night at 7:30 and stay on as long as we were interesting. Because this was nominally an educational television service, we weren't constrained by advertising slots. We guessed that the program could go as long as three hours. Station management had to negotiate a release that night from NET network programming, but as Channel 13 was the flagship station of the system that was not difficult.

It was an extraordinary evening. Our own journalists would come to the anchor desk and brief me about the filmed report they were about to present (remember, this had all been set in motion over the previous thirty hours or so). There were live and filmed sessions with reporters, senators, and distinguished writers and scientists. Not many were in favour of the war; the tide of public sentiment had turned by then. Shirley MacLaine came in and read poetry by veterans of the war. As I introduced a film segment that would give me a bit of a break on

3. Not yet a commonplace, soon to become so, and then displaced by the increasingly useless shrunken bits, now often down to five meaningless seconds.

the set, I noticed standing just inside the studio door Hal Holbrook, the actor who had become suddenly famous with his stage presentation *Mark Twain Tonight!* As the film rolled, a PA came over and said that Holbrook wanted to say a few words to our audience, would that be all right? Holbrook came over to the anchor desk and shook hands gravely. I pointed to the stairs that led up to the makeup room and said we had two minutes. He was back at the anchor desk about five seconds before the floor manager threw me the cue.

I introduced Holbrook, assuming most of our viewers would know who he was, and then turned to him and said something like, "We haven't had time to discuss this; you just came in off the street. Why are you here?"

Holbrook said, Well, he was an actor, and had always believed that an actor should shut his mouth when he gets off the stage, and not exploit his fame trying to be clever in politics or in any other forum where he is not an expert. And he still believed that, but had been watching us tonight, and felt this was too important, he had to get involved. So he had come down to the studio, not to use his own words, but Mark Twain's: something called "The War Prayer."

Before our eyes he grew suddenly older. It was almost as if the famous moustache and sideburns were growing as we watched. He became smaller in his seat, frail, not the robust forty-five-year-old he really was, but seventy-something. His head went back, his eyes half closed. His voice was Mark Twain's voice. It said,

> O Lord our Father, our young patriots, idols of our hearts, go forth to battle – be Thou near them! With them – in spirit – we also go forth from the sweet peace of our beloved firesides to smite the foe.
>
> O Lord our God, help us to tear their soldiers to bloody shreds with our shells; help us to cover their smiling fields with the pale forms of their patriot dead; help us to drown the thunder of the guns with the shrieks of their wounded, writhing in pain; help us to lay waste their humble homes

> with a hurricane of fire; help us to wring the hearts of their unoffending widows with unavailing grief; help us to turn them out roofless with their little children to wander unfriended through wastes of their desolated land in rags & hunger & thirst, sport of the sun-flames of summer & the icy winds of winter, broken in spirit, worn with travail, imploring Thee for the refuge of the grave & denied it – for our sakes, who adore Thee, Lord, blast their hopes, blight their lives, protract their bitter pilgrimage, make heavy their steps, water their way with their tears, stain the white snow with the blood of their wounded feet! We ask of one who is the Spirit of love & who is the ever-faithful refuge & friend of all that are sore beset, & seek His aid with humble & contrite hearts.
>
> Grant our prayer, O Lord & Thine shall be the praise & honor & glory now & ever, Amen.[4]

It was a hideous declaration of the inhuman relish that takes over the soul of the aggressor. It was his way of saying to his country, This is what we have become.

Although it was hard to take my eyes away from Holbrook's anguished face, Mark Twain's face, I scanned the studio. It had gone totally silent. Not a rustle. Not a movement. Pete Hamill, the sportswriter, was standing at one side, wiping tears from his face. He was not the only one.

The prayer lasted about a minute and a half. It ended. Silence. I looked at Holbrook, and nodded, and looked at the camera. I said, "There is really only one thing to do for the next few moments. We will go to black, for thirty seconds." Our young director, a football director used to responding to the unexpected, took us to black for

4. Composed orally, dictated during the Philippines war, 1904–5, and published only in 1923. The full piece has a conventional church sending the young warriors off to battle in the traditional way, when a gaunt stranger enters, pushes the pastor aside, and tells the congregation that every prayer for war contains another unspoken prayer that they should listen to before their boys go forward. This is it. The "&" signs are in the original.

thirty seconds. The station just went dark and silent while we, and presumably the viewers, collected ourselves.

Thirty years later Alex Trebek, also a fine Mark Twain (he played the part in *Witness to Yesterday*), told me how in 1972 he had met Hal Holbrook during the Toronto run of *Mark Twain Tonight!* and asked him if he had ever thought of having Twain comment on current events, and Holbrook said, No, he did not think that would be appropriate. Well, this time he had found a way to do it.

We kept going that night until one o'clock in the morning. One of the interviews that I was handed unexpectedly was Robert Jay Lifton, a well-known author and professor of psychiatry, who specialized in the relationship between individual personality and historical change. Lifton saw connections between the national stance of the United States in Vietnam and the personality issues of frustrated individuals who turn to violence. He said that under Nixon it had become the Imperial Presidency. There was nobody to take him down, to tell him when he was making an egregious mistake. Lifton said that Julius Caesar, knowing the risks of that kind of power, appointed a man to walk at his side in procession, and when the crowd were bowing down and crying out "Caesar, thou art God," this man's job was to tug at Caesar's robe and whisper in his ear, "You're only human! You're only human." Nixon didn't have one of those, Lifton said.

As strenuous as that evening was, I had seldom if ever felt better in a live broadcast; the challenge of fielding all these surprises that came in, weaving them in and out of the planned material, staying on top of it all, working the studio like a musical instrument in a perfect logistical marriage of understanding with the director and the technical staff and the producers, was exhilarating. I don't think there was a single awkward moment, and I don't remember leaving the set even to pee, though I must have done. I had a lovely sense that it had been unique, one in a lifetime, and that I had done as good a job of work that night as I had ever done.

As we often did after a show, the staff and some outsiders headed up to Jimmy Armstrong's Saloon at the corner of 9th and 58th. Jimmy had been warned we'd be late. We were all regulars – Jimmy's was our local for lunch and dinner and beers and assignations and program planning.

I stayed behind for a while to talk to lighting and sound, and the technical producer, all the guys who had got the big studio ready for this marathon with almost no notice and kept it running like a broad, deep, smooth-flowing river throughout that unpredictable evening. It was a kind of post-show love-in of the craft, they telling me what a great job, etc., and me telling them I couldn't have done it without them, etc. And while this is all banal as well as true, it is just as vital a part of the humanity of the live television studio as it is of a warship at sea or a space crew in a shuttle.

I was about half an hour later than the rest of the program staff when I got to Jimmy Armstrong's Saloon. There were pitchers of beer all over the room and the hamburger chef was sweating over the charcoal grill. When I appeared through the door, they started to clap. They stood up. They cheered. The clapping went on for quite a while. Then, as it died down, Rafael Abramovitz's voice came softly from the back of the room: "He's only human; he's only human."

Once again as with *This Hour Has Seven Days*, an important broadcaster had demonstrated that in order to reach a substantial audience it is not necessary to treat viewers as meat to be sold to advertisers, that it is possible and rewarding to respect the viewers' intelligence. In the months after 9/11 when the major American television operators abandoned serious journalism to become uncritical channels for the prevailing views of the White House, it was provocative to recall those days when serious newspapers drew on *The Fifty-First State* for consequential stories, and everybody on the unit acquired a classified FBI file.[5]

5. When I used the Freedom of Information Act to file a request to see my own, the FBI wrote to acknowledge my request and inform me that they were not prepared to acknowledge that such a file existed, but neither was I to understand that it did not exist. I let it drop.

CHAPTER 15

BACK

IN THE LATE WINTER OF 1973, after that first dazzling year on the air, the management and board of Channel 13 were fretting about the audacity of *The Fifty-First State.* We were moved to an earlier time slot that deprived us of the luxury of running at whatever length we had good material for – a luxury that only a public television service could afford, by the way, and that other such services (there are few left in the world) might like to consider. Jack Willis tried to accommodate the management with a show of more upstairs consultation and downstairs restraint, but the great old journalistic soldiers like Selwyn Raab, a former *New York Times* man, and Al Levin ("Come on, Troop!") let us know that they were very dissatisfied. Some of the spirit began to go out of the enterprise. The atmosphere was reminiscent of that hateful *Seven Days* spring of '66.

In the midst of this descending gloom a couple of bright sails appeared on the horizon. Cameron Graham called from Ottawa to say that he had persuaded the network managers to sit still for some straight talk about the folly of the continuing blacklist of Watson. They had agreed that it was dumb to keep the walls up while I was earning kudos in New York and doing nothing in Canada except some relatively invisible production work through Immedia, and had accepted Graham's proposal for a new weekly parliamentary show that he wanted to call *Some Honourable Members,* a phrase used in

Hansard usually to identify the source of catcalls, choruses of "Oh! Oh!" or "Hear! Hear!" I would meet with two to four MPs every week – rarely a cabinet minister: they got regular news coverage, but the guys down in the trenches seldom did. We would try to give the country a more intimate sense of what was at stake for the people we voted into the Green Chamber, among other things preparing the ground for the televising of Parliament, which now seemed likely to happen within a few years.

It sounded good to me. A bit wistful about leaving Manhattan, I was nonetheless ready to come home and not inclined to continue anchoring a news operation while it was undergoing emasculation. I remembered the insistence of *TW3*'s Ned Sherrin that two years was the appropriate running time for any innovative television project.

The other bright sail came in the form of a visit from Laurier LaPierre and a Montreal producer named Arthur Voronka, who proposed over a splendid dinner at La Croisette on 1st Avenue that I host a series of two-person dramas, playing myself in a scripted encounter with figures out of the past. They already had agreement and funding for a pilot with Joan of Arc, to be played by the intriguing Sandy Dennis, who had starred on Broadway in *A Thousand Clowns,* beautifully played the ingénue in the Elizabeth Taylor–Richard Burton film version of *Who's Afraid of Virginia Woolf?* and the brave inner-city teacher in *Up the Down Staircase.* I told Laurier and Arthur that I doubted we had writers in Canada who could take the demanding format of a two-person drama disguised as an interview and make it sing. The proposed title was a winner, though: *Witness to Yesterday.* I said I would do the pilot for them and then decide about the series on the basis of how it went with Joan of Arc.

Before leaving New York I went to spend some informal time with Ralph Fasanella. Ralph was the son of immigrants from Bari in the south of Italy, who had discovered a talent for painting when he came out of the navy after World War II. A union organizer and passionate humanitarian, he was a powerful naïf painter with a strong narrative drive and a love of huge panoramas in which he depicted, in oils, hundreds of garment workers in a Brooklyn sweatshop, a massive union demonstration in the streets, lyrical family scenes from his childhood, and sprawling streetscapes of New York. It was Jay K. Hoffman, by then my literary agent in the U.S., who brought Fasanella and me together, proposing that I interview the painter for *The Fifty-First State*. Ralph was a great talker and the interview was a treat. Hoffman then sold Robert Gottlieb at Knopf on my doing a book on his life and art. *Fasanella's City* was a beautiful production with his huge *New York City* wrapped around the dust jacket. Gottlieb and my editor, Anne Close, declared themselves delighted with my writing, and a relationship was established. In those last weeks in New York Ralph took me around his haunts in the Village and showed me how to order pasta properly. We went to the movies together (he fell asleep in Fellini's *Roma*) and sometimes I sat with him late at night, watching him paint and mutter imprecations at the canvas, the union-busters, the politicians, or lyrical observations about women, the streets, colour, the smell of paint. He was a passionate little giant.

By early June I had wound down everything in New York, had some nostalgic lunches with the journalists, packed up my stuff, and moved back to the farm at Carleton Place. The domestic atmosphere was cool, sometimes frigid, but a good part of the summer was about getting my feet back on the soil, and my hands into it, reminding myself that part of my life was farming, that growing things and tending animals was enormously nourishing. In June my Vancouver friend Gene Lawrence brought me to the West Coast to record a marathon six hours of interview with Bucky Fuller, a life retrospective in which there were some moving moments of intimate personal revelation, and some of Bucky's most imaginative rangings through the universe in search of Great Truths. I don't think that material was ever broadcast, and since it was recorded on the short-lived one-inch videotape perhaps it never can be.

Paddy Sampson brought me to Toronto to do a similar piece, five hours of very personal interview with Harry Belafonte. The idea was to build a theatrical bio-epic on Belafonte, richly interwoven with performance material. The tapes were never broadcast, and as I write this I am fresh from a chat with Belafonte, at Jack Willis's seventieth birthday party in New York, about re-opening that file. That interview led to something that sharpened my need to deal with the marriage. A day or two after the recording session the phone rang at the farm, late in the evening. It was Belafonte, affectionately telling me that those hours we had done together had been, for him, a rare and wonderful event. "I really dig you, man," he concluded. I sleepily relayed all this to Beverly, feeling the glow of it. She said contemptuously, Yes, well, show-biz people were like that, weren't they? They would say anything.

Despite this, it was good to be back on the farm, a sense of homecoming, the same kind of thing I had felt after the Hollywood time with Cousteau, the comfort of feeling the roots thrusting back into the ground. There were trips into Ottawa to work with Cam Graham on plans for *Some Honourable Members*, or with Spaulding and Ripley on Immedia projects. There was time to play in the air. I took some aerobatics training and completed an instructor's licence. There was a Citabria at the Carleton Place airstrip that I could rent privately for the minuscule sum of $12 an hour, to practise aerobatics. But the central focus was the endless list of earth-bound projects and tasks on the Seventh Line of Beckwith Township.

From a journal entry:

1. *Examine hardwood bush with a view to cutting as much as possible for firewood, and replanting in oak, maple & poplar.*
2. *Collect stones at stone piles for barnyard and lane.*
3. *Enlarge garden. Onions as cash crop.*
4. *Set up tool area and work bench.*
5. *A sweet pea bed!*
6. *Calculate how much wheat flour & oats we use in a year and how much area we'd have to plant to produce that, & how to store and mill it?*

7. (See 2. above) use stones from stone piles to fill road down property.
8. Curtail late night talk & read sessions in good outdoor-work weather.
9. Build outdoor (shovel-out) outhouse.
10. Collect old fallen-down cedar fence rails and logs & store either under cover or well-stacked to prevent rot.
11. Change oil in tractor. grease tractor.
12. Clamps for sharpening axes & a good place to do that.
13. Repair cellar door.
14. Guest house. Dome?
12.[sic] deal with baler
13. Open south end of drive shed & clean up.
12 [sic] cattle pens for vet-work
13. SET UP ACCOUNTING SYSTEM!!!
14. Clear grass around Red Pine seedlings between new garden & barnyard
15. Weed new garden & mulch rest of corn.

It reads like a daunting list, but it was really a declaration of enthusiasm. Although the time in New York had effectively confirmed my relationship with Beverly as primarily a civilized convenience based on jointly owned property, and many of the daily journal entries record grievous tension and division, the farm gave us territory to share and action to agree upon. Chris and Boo had gone off on their own. Greg was still with us.

Perhaps it seems quaint that I actually considered growing onions as a cash crop, but they grew magnificently there, as did grain, and looking back I am puzzled and disappointed that I never did follow through on item 6: to grow our own grain and make our own flour. I was already making most of our own bread (and still do): what held me back then?

We bought cows and set up a modest breeding program. Soon the few chickens we had kept from the start became a few dozen and then over a hundred, and I sold free-range eggs to my CBC colleagues and the Domus Health Food store on Sussex Drive in Ottawa, even making a little money on these quaint transactions.

I was pleased to be back on the familiar studio floors of CBOT after nearly ten years, and less critical than I should have been about the initial design for *Some Honourable Members*, a rather cute miniaturized set of parliamentary benches, where I interviewed MPs about the salient parliamentary events of the week. Graham was a seemingly easy-going producer; it would take me a while to recognize the deep currents of commitment and inventiveness under that deceptive exterior. His script assistant, Nicole Rondeau, was the best in the business. Many of the old gang of technicians and other production staff who had worked on *Inqui'ry* were still there and contributed to my feeling of homecoming.

I began writing a novel, a thriller. It had been incubating on some of those flights to Teterboro and back, something about a flying journalist, no, a documentary cameraman, that would be it, a kind of Durschmied with a Twin Comanche, who uncovers some international conspiracy. Roy Faibish had for years predicted that the likeliest conflict between Canada and the United States would be over water, so I would devise a criminal plot to take control of the continent's water supplies, with corrupt officials and a movie-style archetypal villain. I told Laurier about it, and he came up with a great name for a sinister group masquerading as good guys: The Environmental Commando. Jay Hoffman sold the outline to Warner Paperbacks in New York and that brought in a Canadian hardcover publisher, Fitzhenry and Whiteside, where my editor, Ramsay Derry, helped me come up with what now seems a pretentious and too-clever title, *Zero to Airtime.*

It was great fun to write, a playful counterpoint to the somewhat boring and much too earnest *Some Honourable Members*, with its constraints of party balance and the absence of that lovely thing you can work up in a one-on-one. I asked for more one-on-ones (we did the odd cabinet minister solo), and Cameron Graham and the network people seemed to be listening.

I had the first draft of *Zero to Airtime* finished in January 1974.

The *Witness to Yesterday* pilot with Sandy Dennis turned out very well. She made the nervous, muddled style that had worked so well in *Up the Down Staircase* and *Virginia Woolf* seem to be exactly what the simple illiterate peasant girl from Lorraine must have been like, to the point where we could overlook the flat high-pitched Nebraska voice and be theatrically in the presence of the adolescent Strange One from the Loire Valley. Coleridge's "willing suspension of disbelief" may be an attractive metaphor, but it does not describe what happens emotionally and intellectually in the theatre. It is more useful to think that the task of the writer and director and actors is to *procure the assent* of the audience to a premise. This becomes a tacit contract with them, and then as long as the production is true to that premise, the audience delights in watching the challenge being met, allows their emotions to be engaged in caring about the fortunes of the depicted characters, and can, as Aristotle said, achieve a catharsis when that engagement is confronted with a consistent narrative and coherent characterization. *But we do not suspend disbelief.* We always know we are in the theatre. There is never any doubt about that. Let an actor fart audibly and accidentally, let one light crash down from the grid, even let something minuscule happen, a small error in timing, a line slightly fumbled, and it is clear that the critical attention has never been suspended, willingly or not. What we have done when it is well done is to fulfil the contract.

We were achieving that from time to time with *Witness to Yesterday*, and the subtly structured scripts that Patrick Withrow and Doug Scott were turning out not only persuaded me that I had been wrong about there not being enough good writers, they also encouraged me to write for the series myself. When it launched on Global in January 1974, it was well received, except by some of my Public Affairs colleagues, including Ross McLean, who worried that its fictions would erode the public's belief in the integrity of my real interviews. I don't think Ross was ever at ease with *Witness.*

Beverly and I were still heavily in debt from the lean years, so I decided I'd better turn more of that rewarding time on the fields and in the barns over to her, and try harder to sell television projects in the marketplace. My journals are a litany of financial worries. *Fasanella's City* had been well reviewed and had built me a warm relationship with Bob Gottlieb at Knopf, but it was never going to retire the debt. Tom Spaulding and I spent an evening with his clarinet and my piano, improvising around old swing standards and brainstorming projects for Immedia. Before long it looked like a very full season. We went to Alcan with a major series on the work of Buckminster Fuller, who had agreed to give us the rights in return for a share of the earnings. My New York agent, Jay Hoffman, a founding member of Immedia Inc., proposed a daily series on sex built around a psychologist and writer from Syracuse named Sol Gordon. Spaulding sold it to Global, and we hired Charlotte Gobeil to produce it under my executive producership. We called it *This Program Is about Sex.* We booked studio space at CJOH and contracted Chuck Weir and Jean Templeton to open each program with original comic sketches based on the theme of the day's show: Nudity in the home; language and sexuality; promiscuity and birth control. We did some location filming, but most of the series was live-to-tape in the studio, sometimes with dozens of participants. In one program we showed a film report on a group of rampantly promiscuous teenagers behaving outrageously and using very rough language to a studio audience of middle-aged middle-class women, whose discussion turned out to be remarkably humane and insightful.

Our host, Sol Gordon, did not turn out to be quite as humane and insightful as we might have hoped. Jean Templeton had to be replaced, and troublesome as she had been, the sketches were never as funny as they had been when she was at her best. Charlotte Gobeil turned out to be a superb wagon-master, marshalling all her resources, driving each demanding day in the studio (often two shows a day) with energy and confidence, and keeping everyone's spirits up with her outrageously visceral humour.

Global Television failed financially during the run of that on-the-whole enjoyable series (because of Gobeil's inspired production sense), but Tom Spaulding managed to get to the table early enough to get a sufficient percentage of what we were owed to pay our costs, while other independent producers were getting only about ten cents on the dollar.

The CBC invited me to host a whole evening devoted to the Arctic, with a live insert from the underwater explorer Dr. Joe MacInnis, whom I would be interviewing from a warm studio in Toronto while he was in a plastic igloo on the bottom of the Arctic sea. There would be several strong documentaries on Inuit arts and culture. For the first time, instead of just accepting their proposed fee, I got really aggressive financially, and proposed that they pay me the then very large fee of $5,000 for both hosting and helping to write and develop the three-hour special. As it turned out, most of my work was diplomatic, trying to keep the NFB and CBC people talking to each other. But in the end the broadcast went wonderfully well, and I fondly thought, for a while, that it might have established a new approach to the themed evening, something that looked seriously like public television.

With a group of concerned citizens, Abe Rotstein, Robert Fulford, Allan King, Kirwan Cox, and several others, I contributed to an ad-hoc group called the Committee On Television, whose objective was to try to persuade both Parliament and the CBC that the national public broadcaster's dependence upon advertising violated its mandate. CBC's commercialism was nothing like what it would soon become, but it was a trend, and we naively thought we could stop it. After all, Lister Sinclair, one of us, had just been named executive vice-president by the new president, Laurent Picard. But when we went to see him, he threw us out of the office, and allegedly told ACTRA officials that the committee was "Watson's personal vendetta against the CBC." That winter we took our arguments to the CRTC's hearing of the Corporation's licence-renewal application, but our presentation was far too earnest and moralizing. We were thanked politely and that was that. Laurent Picard invited me to go drinking with him after the hearing, and got angry, equating the committee with the character of the English Canadians, who were, he said, "defeatist, they don't know who they are, that's what your people sounded like." The tone improved a little after he scolded me for taking *Witness to Yesterday* to the enemy, Global TV, and I told him that the CBC had refused to consider the series because it wasn't sufficiently commercial.

Immedia began working with the Native Council of Canada, a group representing the Metis people, led by Tony Belcourt. One of the goofier but seductive proposals we made was to secretly film a "social research" project in which Metis pollsters would knock on doors in Ottawa's exclusive Rockcliffe district, home to senior bureaucrats and prosperous executives, and ask whoever answered the door how it felt to live in an area where you were not allowed to buy liquor (there was no commercial activity of any kind permitted in Rockcliffe), satirizing the do-good surveys that well-meaning anthropologists undertook in native communities. We also proposed installing a high-powered projector in a window opposite the white wall of the old Union Station building, and projecting a highly provocative documentary revealing the indignities suffered by Metis people across the country. One project that we actually carried out was *Moccasin Flats*, a documentary I wrote and directed about life in a native community in British Columbia, which won international awards.

Knopf president Robert Gottlieb sent me a *TIME* magazine piece by its former Moscow correspondent, Patricia Blake, who had interviewed an American citizen just repatriated after spending eighteen years as a prisoner in the Gulag. He asked me to meet with Blake, and then with her subject, Alexander Dolgun, to see if I thought there was a book in it. Around the first of February I flew the Twin Comanche to Washington and spent the first of what would become hundreds of hours with this man, delighted to find that his memory for detail, the texture of the walls of his cell in Lubyanka Prison, the smells in the room in which he first met Solzhenitsyn,[1] the plots of

1. Who writes about that meeting in *The Gulag Archipelago.*

the movies he recited to keep himself sane in solitary – all this was exactly what was needed to make a book sing. I flew on to New York, stayed overnight at Robert Gottlieb's Turtle Bay house with him ("That's Katherine Hepburn's back door, across the fence") and had a good talk about what kind of book it might turn out to be. "The thing you'll have to do," he said, "is find a voice. That's the key." He was affectionate and called me "boy." (I was forty-six). He assigned Anne Close, who had edited the Fasanella book. He agreed to pay the costs of my flying UCH to Baltimore once a week for as long as it took, and drew up a contract with an advance that suggested the debts might get paid off after all.

Alphonse Ouimet telephoned one day. Now several years into his retirement, as a former Crown corporation president he had an obligation to the national archives to do a memoir of his time of service, and he wanted to review the *Seven Days* story with me. Although he had been The Enemy during the battle for *Seven Days*, Doug Leiterman and I had never seen him as a Prince of Darkness. Unlike some of the immediate subordinates who surrounded him at head office, he was decent, intelligent, puzzled by the uproar his henchmen had got him into, and too weak to understand their role in it. I regretted that weakness, but had never felt the contempt for him that I had for his senior vice-presidents.

We met in his room in an Ottawa hotel, for what he had suggested might take two hours. I began by saying that I came expecting that he would be more likely to justify his role than to listen to me, and that I had always found him pretty authoritarian and very Jesuitical. "Well, what do you expect?" he said. "I was raised by the Jesuits."

In fact it went better than I had anticipated. Six hours later we were still at it and very hungry, and we adjourned to the hotel dining room for a steak and a bottle of good Bordeaux. Late in the meal, reflecting on the years of his presidency, I thought of something that I perhaps had not perceived before. I said, "Al, you never came to see us, the producers. Or if you did it was always to tell us to pull our horns in, to not spend too much. You never came to the studios, you never came to pat us on the back and tell us what a great job we were doing. You were the father figure, you know, and we needed that from you."

He said he found that an astonishing thing for me to say. We must have known we were doing a good job and that management thought so too, since we were given our budgets and our airtime, and we were all such confident and self-sufficient people; how could I say such nonsense about the father figure and needing to be patted on the back?

It was my turn to be astonished. He had been in broadcasting all his life and did not know that people who work in front of the public are profoundly insecure, in constant need of reassurance and affirmation that what they are doing is good. He looked at me with genuine puzzlement. "Are you telling me that all those brilliant announcers and interviewers and actors . . . are *insecure*? I can't do what you people do: get up in front of an audience and speak with assurance like that. No, no, I don't believe you. You've got that wrong."

In the meantime we were moving ahead with *Witness to Yesterday*. Zoe Caldwell played a seductive Catherine the Great, in which the principal dramatic line was her trying to seduce me, a witty and engaging script of Patrick Withrow's. Steve Allen came up from Hollywood and we sat at the piano together while he became an enchanting George Gershwin. Kate Reid was Queen Victoria and Chris Wiggins was Christopher Columbus. Richard Dreyfuss, in Montreal for the shooting of *The Apprenticeship of Duddy Kravitz*, agreed to do Billy The Kid, and persuaded me to let him ad lib, he knew the character, no need for a script. He gave us a chillingly monosyllabic psychopath, fingering a Colt revolver throughout and throwing me grunts and threatening looks.

Mavor Moore's Socrates was hilarious – "If you don't want to talk about philosophy, why did you invite a philosopher?" – and Barry Morse invented a nice piece of business, in mid-stream so to speak, when he played Shakespeare. I asked Shakespeare about the labour of writing with a quill pen, and illustrated the reason for my question by producing an elegant fountain pen to show him what modern writers write with (! – that was in 1974). This is what Morse came up with on the spot: Shakespeare takes the pen, intrigued. He tries it out, as anyone would, by writing his signature on a sheet of paper I produce, gazes at it for a moment, admires the pen, hands it back, and crumples up the paper to throw it away. I reach over and grab it before he can do so, and slip it into my pocket. Shakespeare looks surprised and asks, Why would I want to keep that worthless thing? I shrug, embarrassed, and mutter something about not wanting to make a mess.

Some of the best moments in the whole series were actorly insights. Donald Sutherland rejected the script for Bethune outright. "I *am* Bethune," he said. "Ask me what a good journalist would ask." I did, and there was so little to edit out, at the end of the day, that we made two shows out of it instead of one.

On the whole, though, the scripted shows with their plotted peaks and valleys and carefully devised narrative line of conflict between the two performers were stronger than the few improvisations we tried, and when we returned to the format twenty-five years later for History Television, we scripted everything.

In March I started spending my weekends in Alex Dolgun's house on the outskirts of Baltimore. I would clear Customs at Washington's Dulles International, and then hop over to the small airport at Gaithersburg, Maryland, where Alex would pick me up for what often became beer-soaked weekends, he seldom going to bed anywhere near sober. Nonetheless I came home on Sunday nights or Monday morning with cassettes loaded with vivid stories of his boyhood tearing around Moscow, where his Polish-born father was a Chrysler Corporation engineer on loan to the USSR. At the end of the war Alex got a clerical job at the U.S. Embassy.

He told me that he used to commandeer an embassy car in the evening, to look for girls and speed around Moscow with his boyhood friends, eluding the police when he had to by using his street kid's intimate knowledge of the city. The KGB finally decided that he might be spying and arrested him in the street. Whatever efforts his homeland made to rescue him were of no avail until, after eighteen years of prison camps and near starvation, and another ten of being confined to Moscow, he was repatriated by the personal intercession of Averell Harriman. By late spring I had about six hundred pages of cassette transcriptions.

That was a marvellous summer of writing. Beverly and I had a truce and met civilly about matters of beef breeding and slaughtering capons, but I spent much of my time alone at the Smith Corona electric portable. I set a quota of seven thousand words a week, allowed myself to go and play if I reached it, and *forced* myself to go and play if I did ten thousand. Play often began with an early drive over to the Carleton Place airstrip, three minutes away, to take the Citabria up for some snap rolls or hammerheads while the air was still calm in the cool of the morning. There was then a reserved space for aerobatics about fifteen miles south of the Ottawa airport. I could call the tower on my way over, and they would route any traffic around that space while I flipped the little blue cloth-covered machine around the sky, at first making myself sick until I realized you couldn't do that kind of thing on an empty stomach, and made myself eat a solid cooked breakfast before setting out. I was often airborne at dawn.

One amazing day I wrote nine thousand words between eight o'clock in the morning and ten o'clock at night. Alex's storytelling flowed out of the transcripts. Writing is such a lovely way to be in the world. Although I relished the solitary work, living in the same house as an attractive and active woman with whom I no longer had an intimate relationship induced a loneliness that metaphorically became almost visual as a kind of clock spring coiled up tightly inside my chest. A story began to form in my mind, a short story? Or a novel? I sketched out a few ideas about a solitary figure who meets himself, his . . . counterpart? His . . . I wasn't sure at first, but I wanted to examine the sense of self, of the isolate self, in the mirror of a living being who is both the other and the self at the same time.

I gave it a working title: *A Spring Coiled Tight.* The science-fiction device of having a man suddenly find himself face to face with his exact double, an electronically reproduced human being sharing all his physical attributes, memories, and skills to the point where neither could argue, even to himself, which was the original and which was the copy, had come to me from an early interview with Buckminster Fuller. Bucky had speculated, on camera, about a future teleportation booth, like a phone booth, into which you could step and dial yourself to Hong Kong, the booth scanning your atomic makeup much as a television camera scans an image. I remember thinking during the interview, Yeah, but the scanned original stays behind when the television camera transmits the image, what if that happened with Bucky's teleportation booth? The original person stays behind and his perfectly scanned reproduction turns up somewhere else. I got some encouragement for my fiction when news came that *Zero to Airtime* had been purchased for translation into Japanese.

At some point book reviewer Sandra Martin asked me to send her some thoughts for a piece she was doing for *Saturday Night* about the book or books that had most influenced writers when they were young. Selecting the book was easy: T.H. White's *The Sword in the Stone*, about the boyhood of King Arthur, which I had read when I was ten and have written about in Chapter Two. Now, in writing to Martin, I examined more carefully what White's legacy had been. I wrote, "The sacrament of objects and of craft was, I think, focused for me by White. . . . He allowed me to know before Blake about seeing the world in a grain of sand."

When I had finished the first draft of *Alexander Dolgun's Story: An American in the Gulag*, having done almost no revision, just writing straight ahead, looking for that *voice*, I sent the long manuscript off to New York with a letter to Bob Gottlieb asking him and Anne Close not to be too rough on it, it was just a first draft after all, but I felt I needed outside eyes on it before I even thought of revisions. And then went flying.

Quite a long time went by. Well, it may have been no more than a couple of weeks but it seemed agonizing and I did not have the nerve to phone and ask. I kept saying to myself, Look, they will both have to read it, it's a long book (almost two hundred thousand words), quit worrying.

But I worried. I came in from the barn one day and Greg was holding out the phone. "New York," he said. It was Gottlieb. He said, "Well, we've both read it, and we think it's perfect. Don't change a word. No, that's not quite right. The first chapter should really be the second chapter and the second chapter the first, I think you'll see that right away, and there will have to be some minor adjustments to make that work, but apart from that . . . the cheque on acceptance of manuscript is on its way. Here's Anne. She's ready to start copy-editing."

Just before the Dolgun book came out, in 1975, Bob Gottlieb handed me another assignment, my only real ghost-writing task. I was to go to London to sit with Linda McCartney for a few days, long enough to record enough interview material with her to write the personal essay in her collection of photographs, *Linda's Pictures*. I met her and Paul in the Apple offices, and then did most of the interview sitting on the front porch of their house in St. John's Wood, the musician being in one of his funky moods, Linda said apologetically, and wanting nobody in the house. The book came out a few months later, her first of what were generally well-received collections, mostly photographs of musicians.

Later that summer I met an old friend from camp days, Mario Bernardi, who had become conductor of the National Arts Centre Orchestra. I had been fooling around with the sheet music of Bach's two and three-part *Inventions*, very frustrated because they sounded so easy in the Glenn Gould recordings, whereas my fingers kept getting all tangled up as I laboriously slogged through the staves, my reading painfully slow. My thirty-some unbroken years of playing pops and jazz by ear had not provided me with a shred of understanding of how the fingers worked with even this simple contrapuntal stuff, and over lunch I asked Bernardi if he could recommend a teacher. The man he sent me to, Douglas Voice, was patient – intrigued, I guess, by the forty-five-year-old minor celebrity who was starting from scratch with this kind of music. Soon I was spending hours every day working through exercises, and, most rewardingly, disengaging my fingers from the paralysis of that matted tangle, muttering "Of course!" as the obviousness of what Douglas Voice was showing me made the music accessible. I stayed with the instruction for the next five or six years, and still happily play some of the *Inventions* from time to time.

In September the first payments from *Alexander Dolgun's Story* began to flow in. It was a main selection for the Book of the Month Club in both the United States and Canada. I decided to build a fantasy house, just as an investment, which I began to design in collaboration with a 1960s eccentric young log house builder named Glynn Shannan. We found a site on the Perth Road near Franktown and began scouring the county for derelict log buildings to cannibalize. With the Dolgun book now successfully in the marketplace, I resumed work on *A Spring Coiled Tight.* I was still feeling an overwhelming loneliness as the marriage steadily unravelled. Perhaps writing about it would help. Not an attractive theme, loneliness, but the science-fiction premise might draw the reader in.

When Peter Herrndorf became head of Current Affairs at the CBC about that time, he began to make waves. The CBC had traditionally been reluctant to use a performer's name in the title of a program. The fanatical fundamentalist William Aberhart, a radio evangelist who was premier of Alberta in the thirties and early forties, had given the Corporation an abiding sense of caution about broadcasting's potential for the abuse of power by a prominent individual. Entertainment programs had sometimes been named for their stars – Wayne and Shuster, Juliette, *Don Messer's Jubilee* – but never a public affairs program. In the fall of 1974 Herrndorf broke that tradition with a new series called *Adrienne at Large*, a Thursday-night half-hour of "personalized Public Affairs reporting" that ran for about four months. Now Herrndorf argued that my interviewing style had a lot to do with the unexpectedly respectable audience figures for *Some Honourable Members*, and that the best programs were the one-on-one interviews, so he now, in the fall of 1975, wanted to call the program *The Watson Report* and do primarily one-on-ones. Cameron Graham and I thought the title a bit odd for an interview program, but Herrndorf said it had a better ring to it than *The Patrick Watson Interview*, and so we agreed. I was glad I had turned down an earlier invitation to co-host the latest in the series of programs that had been tried in the wake of *Seven Days.* A Toronto producer named Glenn Sarty had called in the summer to discuss a new investigative program, *the fifth estate.*[2] The program had been designed by a fine, experienced investigative reporter, Ron Haggart. But there was something about Sarty's approach that had put me off. Maybe I had sensed an attitude that lay behind an astonishing statement Sarty would make at the end of that season. In the spring of 1976 the Public Affairs department convened the first national CBC public affairs conference that I had been invited to since my blacklisting. It was a collegial gathering. Here were friends from the earliest days whom I had not seen for years, and the discussion of the changing tenor of the country was intense and stimulating. I was asked to do a critique of *the fifth estate.* I gave it high marks, but suggested that it could lighten up a bit, do some playful and purely visual essays that would reflect more of the tone and texture of daily life in Canada, and try to remember that the arts were part of public life. Apart from that I was – sincerely – very positive about the series' investigative work. But when Glenn Sarty came to his summing-up, he shocked me by saying that while on the whole he was very pleased with the series, he seriously regretted not having advertising in it. "A good Cougar commercial would make it feel like *real television,*" he said. At the time I supposed it was idiosyncratic: that was just Sarty talking; he didn't really have a background in journalism. In fact, he was foreshadowing a profound change in the CBC Television's fundamental purposes and values.

2. Always in lower case. The title is a reference to the historian and democratic reformer Lord Macaulay, who, acknowledging the power and the democratic importance of the press, wrote that "the gallery in which the reporters sit has become a fourth estate of the realm" (The original Three Estates being the Lords Spiritual, the Lords Temporal, and the Commons). The latest Penguin dictionary wrongly identifies "the Fourth Estate" as being intended humorously.

Back in October of 1975 the first edition of *The Watson Report* marked another advance with the support of Peter Herrndorf. Capital punishment was coming back on the Order Paper, in what might turn out to be a definitive debate in Parliament. Firmly convinced that it not only does not deter murder but in fact generates violence and social anger, I had done many programs on the death penalty from the beginning of my work in television. One of *Seven Days'* more powerful segments had been an extensive report on the disgraceful Stephen Truscott case, and many of my colleagues agreed that the subject deserved special attention. Cam Graham and I had discussed the famous issue of journalistic impartiality, and I had been arguing for a while that for a journalist to pretend neutrality was a form of dishonesty, but that there were ways of being honest about one's partiality while still delivering a rigorously impartial program, in this case an interview. I had a clear view of how I wanted to do it, and we agreed that Herrndorf should be advised.

I had invited a homicide detective, Inspector Frank Barbetta of the Toronto Police, to be the first guest on the new series. I proposed to open the program with a concise outline of my opposition to the death penalty, and then introduce Inspector Barbetta as a cop who had been up against it in many a back alley, often with a gun in his hand, who had shot at least one criminal in the street, and who would argue compellingly for a return to the noose – which had been not abolished but suspended since the Turpin–Lucas back-to-back hangings in 1963. Herrndorf encouraged us, and said he would watch with care.

The result was excellent. Barbetta was a convincing cop and a genuine presence. The argument went on over drinks for some time after the close of the program. I had made it perfectly clear where I stood, and that exposition had provided a stronger context for and illumination of Frank Barbetta's argument than would have been possible had I adopted a masquerade of neutrality. Herrndorf sent bravos in the morning telex, and the press and audience response was uniformly positive.

Not long after that, Peter Gzowski needed two weeks away from his FM radio program *The Arts*, a two-hour live broadcast every afternoon, and his executive producer, Nancy Button, asked me to come to Toronto and sit in for him while he was in Halifax doing dry runs for a proposed late-night television show. The FM show was real public service radio, as his later classic, *Morningside*, would be for so many years. Each episode brought in a different musician or sculptor or curator. Every day, a group of writers and film directors met for a few minutes to brainstorm a screenplay, and by the end of the period we had it sufficiently completed to bring in some actors and perform a condensed version. On the last program of my tenure there, I introduced Walter Prystawski, the founding concertmaster of the National Arts Centre Orchestra, to a country and jazz fiddler named Ben Mink, and interviewed them together. When I realized during the live interview that Mink was an improviser who couldn't read music and Prystawski a classicist who couldn't improvise, I proposed a collaborative closing performance: Prystawski to play, from the score, a Haydn serenade, and Mink to improvise a contrapuntal or jazz accompaniment. They started it with about twelve minutes left in the program, and I thought, Fine, they'll play for five or six minutes and I'll have lots of time to wrap the show, thank everyone, tell the listeners that Gzowski will be back on Monday, say goodbye, and so on.

But the music was so enchanting I was unwilling to stop it. I slipped into the control room and asked Nancy Button to let them play us off the air, just fade under my voice for a minimal set of credits and thanks. I went back to the floor, grabbed a piece of staff paper, and wrote the thick bar and double dots that mean "go back to the beginning and start again," flashed it at the musicians, they nodded, I whispered my farewells from the other side of the room, and the classical pianist Monica Gaylord, who was also on that program, joined in, improvising brilliantly. When the red light went out to show we were off the air, everyone in sight was grinning maniacally, especially the musicians.

"I have never . . . ever . . ." Walter Prystawski tried to say, but broke up, and Ben Mink said he neither. It had been a glorious afternoon.

A few days later, back at the farm, Beverly said wistfully that she had found a side of me in those broadcasts that she knew existed but had not really experienced, and now knew that there were spaces in there where she could never go, and she had concluded that it really did not make any sense for us to go on together. I was grateful for her courage and her candour.

Jack Willis phoned at about that time to say that a new UHF television station was starting up in Santa Monica, they wanted him to program it, would I come out and help, host some shows, produce some. I discussed it with Beverly.

"You go," she said. "I'll stay here. It's time."

Chapter 16

A TRANSATLANTIC LOVE AFFAIR

THE SANTA MONICA PROJECT never did materialize, but it had provoked Beverly into articulating the separation that we had not been willing to face: it was, indeed, time. We agreed to share the house, she on the second floor and I on the first, until she had found digs of her own. She refused my proposal to move out and leave her with the farm. "Too many ghosts," she said flatly. We continued the somewhat bizarre arrangement (there was only one bathroom and only one kitchen) for a few months, and then she found a place a few miles north and I was alone, except when Greg sometimes stayed with me. I sold the cattle and the hens.

One of the first positive effects of the separation was the subsiding of a painful condition known as *proctalgia fugax*, a vicious cramp that had troubled me for about fifteen years. When I was recounting to Reeves Haggan the odd sensations of being alone, he said, "Watch out: you risk becoming very selfish." I think I did so. I entered into a series of relationships, most brief, some casual, some intense. Then, after a while, I decided it was time to cut myself off. "I'll become the bachelor recluse of Beckwith Township," I said to myself. Then I would lapse, resume, cut off again, lapse again . . .

Late in 1976 or early in '77 Terri McLuhan asked me to help with a project. We had collaborated during the *Fifty-First State* on her documentary, *The Shadow Catcher*, about the pioneer photographic work of Edward Curtis among the tribal peoples of the Northwest Coast. I had helped a little with the script, voiced the narration, and persuaded Donald Sutherland to do the voice of Curtis in the journal and correspondence excerpts that McLuhan had built into her excellent film. Now she had a feature, *The Third Walker*, that she wanted some script and directing help with. But the financing was very uncertain, so I agreed to work on the script and to be available for the shoot in Cape Breton in July provided she had her money in place by mid-June. I thought it unlikely, and that this might finally be the summer that Erik Durschmied and I would spend together.

Over the years Durschmied had repeatedly proposed that I come to Europe for a few weeks and just go driving with him, wherever we felt, spontaneously making up our itinerary day by day. "I know the continent like the layout of my house," he said, fairly accurately. "Wherever the car feels like going, we go." It was an attractive idea, but up to now I had never felt I could take that time. Now in the spring of 1977 as the likelihood of Terri McLuhan being financed in time for a summer production faded, I called Erik to see if the drive idea might still be on, and we agreed on a deadline. If there was no commitment to finance the film by mid-June, I'd fly to Paris.

So that is what I did. Dursch said he had all July free, come ahead. Maybe later in the month we could join his wife, Annelise, and the kids at her parents' cottage on the sea, at Falster Island in Denmark. I found a couple to house-sit the farm, and booked a flight.

I travelled light. Jeans and a denim vest with enough inside pockets for my passport, money, and tickets, and a tiny carry-on with a sweater, underwear, a couple of easy-wash shirts, not much more. Dursch had said he would meet me at the airport but when I got off the plane at Charles de Gaulle on the morning of July 4 there was a message that he had been obliged to go into TF 1, the main national television network, about a project: he would meet me at the downtown terminal.

Something had come up, he said. The BBC had commissioned him to produce a sequel to *A Short Street in Belfast*, a documentary on the Troubles, which he had written, produced, and photographed for them two years earlier. We would fly to Belfast together on Bastille Day, and shoot for a week or ten days, and I would run sound again, and right now he wanted me to meet his fixer and front-running researcher, the woman who had done that work on *A Short Street*, an Irish woman teaching at the Vincennes campus of the University of Paris and doing a Ph.D. on the role of the women's movement in the Irish Troubles, and knew everybody involved. "She's kind of eccentric," he said. "But very smart, and good at this stuff, and you'll get along just great."

We strolled across the Rond Point on the Champs Élysées, and a block or so farther north to a small café with little round tables on the street, where a lean somewhat cross-looking woman was toying with a cup of coffee. "Meet Caroline Bamford," Erik said, and left us to get acquainted while he loped off to TF 1. He would be back in an hour and then we would go to a screening room to review *A Short Street* and discuss what Caroline would do in Belfast by way of getting things ready for Erik to start shooting in ten days' time.

We were both a bit cross. Caroline had been having a very disagreeable spring and had agreed to the Belfast shoot with some reluctance, not very happy that her soundman friend Jim Morissey was being replaced by some unknown from Canada, of all places. I was jetlagged, needing a bed, pissed off to learn that our leisurely trip had turned into a gig, not very much mollified by being left with an irritable Irish stranger at a grubby little street café.

The first few minutes were pretty stiff, but then we got to exchanging some bits of autobiographical background. I learned that, born in Dublin, she had moved to London with her mother when she was nine, then at fourteen to New York, had done degree work at Boston University, lived briefly in Texas, taught high school in New Jersey, had a wide-ranging interest in and knowledge of literature, music, and art. It came out that we were both single, each recovering from a long connection that had left us a bit morally exhausted.

But we were soon laughing together, and ended up fairly cheerful as Dursch came to round us up for the screening. I was impressed with this researcher's comprehensive and generous-minded grasp of the Troubles, and with the fact that she was doing a doctorate on the story, especially that she was involved with the extraordinary women, on both sides, who were trying to bring the combatants to their senses.

The screening went well. By the time it was over I had to sleep, and Erik took me back to his flat in the XVIth. He was going to cook us an excellent dinner, he said, and in the morning we would jump in the car and head for Vienna via the Burgundy wine country and the Swiss Alps, how did that sound? It sounded great.

Just as we were finishing the guinea hen, Caroline Bamford turned up with some last-minute papers that Erik had to deal with. I invited her to stay for a glass of *framboise.* Soon we were in a mellow mood that rapidly became quite intimate. At one point, lapsing into the Dublin voice that I would come to learn as a signal she was moving up to another level of playfulness, she said, "Listen. I think you and I should fall in love."

I said, Well, no, I had fallen in love far too often in the last couple of years and had decided I was through with that kind of thing. "Ah sure now," she said, "we could fall in love for just a little while."

Erik and I bade her a warm farewell when we took off early the next morning, and began an easy-going drive through Burgundy. Dursch knew it all and loved to show off what he knew. In the town of Nuits-St.-Georges he bought bread and what he promised would be a memorable bottle of the eponymous wine. When we went into the *fromagerie* the woman looked at the bottle and said, "Monsieur, avec ce vin-là il faut un fromage *terrible*!"

We explored Geneva (a first for me), and then the astonishing Alps ("There's the Reichenbach Falls: remember Moriarty and Sherlock Holmes?") and on toward Vienna, another first for me. On the way we stopped overnight in Salzburg for a recital by the Janacek String Quartet, from Prague, in the hall where the young Mozart had first conducted an orchestra as a child. As the concert began, we could see his statue in the courtyard outside, and then as darkness fell and a thunderstorm came on, the staff brought out dozens of tall tapers and lit them. From time to time the music was punctuated by a rumble of thunder through the thick stone walls, and Mozart's profile was illuminated by the flash. This was a feel for the European heritage I had never experienced, and Erik, back on his home territory, was both generous and preening about being the one to bring me into it.

I decided to stay on in Vienna for a day while Erik drove back to Paris in time for his filming on the eve of Bastille Day. He had taken me to the Kunstmuseum to see that overwhelming roomful of Breughels ("Every known Breughel except one," Dursch said). Each one is worth at least an hour, and we had had only an hour for the whole room. I needed more. I booked a flight for late the next day that would actually get me to Paris before Erik would have completed the thousand-kilometre non-stop run in the car. But over dinner Erik said he'd just remembered, maybe the museum was closed on Mondays. He checked; it was. I would not get my day in that room until Caroline and I detoured via Vienna on our way home from Prague in 1992, and could do it leisurely together, taking breaks from time to time for coffee and Sachertorte in the museum's cafeteria, and leaving only when we had to race to the station for the night train to Paris. But that first hour, that introduction to the magic of the sixteenth-century Flemish genius, remains a landmark of memory for which I am as grateful to Erik Durschmied as I am for any of the other vistas he opened to me, not counting, of course, that it was he who introduced me to Caroline.

On the eve of Bastille Day I ran sound for Erik while he filmed a French Communist Party celebration on the Île Saint-Louis, where I was struck by the dancing of a large group of *sourds-muets* who, unable of course to hear the music, had delegated one or two members of the group to stand immobile, sense the rhythm from the band through their feet on the pavement, and transmit the beat visually to the group, who then danced ecstatically. I made a scene out of it in the final version of *A Spring Coiled Tight*, which I had brought on the trip for Dursch to read. His comments were encouraging.

The next day we shot some perfunctory stuff at the Bastille Day parade and then took an early afternoon flight for Belfast, where Caroline had found us a B&B and mapped out the entire week's shooting. It was a tough week, my first time in Ireland, my first confrontation with the sordid realities behind the news footage of livid anger and burned-out houses. The intractability of the thing. When we came to a day when none of the bookings had worked out, and Caroline proposed a trip to the Giant's Causeway, which even the all-knowing Dursch had never seen, I was too depressed by it all and chose to stay in bed.

The next day we were shooting a walking interview with a woman who had two sons in prison and was about to be tried for possession of an illegal weapon. She was credible and appealing, as we walked through a section of the Short Strand where every house but one had been burned and boarded up. As she finished her gloomy monologue with a forecast of unrelieved pessimism, we heard the crunch of tires whipping into the rubble-littered square behind us and turned around with camera and sound rolling to see what it was: a British Army jeep and a personnel carrier. Soldiers jumped down with submachine guns pointed at us. An officer approached. "Stop your filming," he commanded. I did not need to look at Erik to know that he would simulate shutting down the camera and lower it to his side with the wide-angle lens pointing at the army, as I did the analogous thing with the Nagra and the old Sennheiser microphone. They demanded our I.D. and ordered us out, and that scene became the final one in the film.

Caroline said over supper the last night that, look, here I was with the name of Patrick and an Irish grandmother and I'd never been in the country for God's sake and why didn't I stay on for a few days, Erik said we could keep the rental car and she could return it in Dublin when she went down to visit her father, and she would show me around at least part of the island. Dursch had a few days' business to do in Paris before he and I were due to drive to Denmark; so that suited him, and the next morning we drove him to the airport and set off for Donegal.

It was a superbly irresponsible and playful week, an amorous adventure with no strings because of course it would soon be all over and we would never meet again and so we could afford to fall in love for a little while with no consequences, and here was this amazing ocean coast, the breathtaking cliffs, the lyrical charm of the pubs and the B&B ladies, a Festival of the Maries in Dungloe where a comedian from Dublin made hilarious sectarian jokes.[3] Finally there was the long drive back east through the rain, through the armed checkpoints on the border, and to the Deer Park Hotel at Belfast International Airport. A depressing place in those days: we were taken up to our room under armed guard, locked in for the night, taken down to breakfast under armed guard and the same out to the car.

We parted very easily, it had been great *craic*, she said, we wished each other well, it was exactly what we had set out to make it: a travelogue, an adventure.

Denmark was sunny and relaxed. Long days on the beach and in the ocean, long seafood dinners with challenging explorations of myriad varieties of schnapps, warm hospitality from Erik's serenely beautiful lady Annelise[4] and her Danish parents.

I was about ready to head back to Canada. I came up from the beach one morning and found Erik on the phone. He looked up as I came in and said to the phone, "Yeah, he just came in. Want to say hello?" I took it and said, "Hello?" There was a pause. Then Caroline said hesitantly, softly, "Ah . . . I would really like to see you again." And suddenly I knew that it hadn't been for just a little while, that I had been, in fact, overwhelmed by this once irritable Irish person. I was on the next plane to Dublin.

We spent another week together, travelling in the west. One night when I was accosted by some Canadian fans in a great oysters-and-Guinness pub, Morans of the Weir, way out on the tide flats

3. Two nuns run out of petrol near a farm, and the farmer fills up a chamber pot for them from his tractor tank. They are gingerly pouring the fuel into their own car when Ian Paisley pulls up beside them, rolls down his car window, and says, "Ladies! I disagree with yer religion, but I admire yer fai-uth!"

4. Formerly married to Mark Lane, the author of *Rush to Judgment.*

south of Galway City, I saw that Caroline had no idea that I was a television celebrity, or anything but, well, some guy, a friend of Erik's who had offered to run sound for him in Belfast. She loved me for myself. After a few years of relationships that were inevitably affected by my being a national figure, this was powerful stuff. Even more powerful was her uncompromising honesty, about her own feelings and about my words and behaviour. She was like Robert Markle in this respect: always ready to take the risk of telling me exactly what she thought. More powerful stuff. I did not want this to end.

But word had come from Canada that Terri McLuhan had her money after all and was going to start shooting in Cape Breton in August, would I come. Caroline said, Well, she had a ticket to Boston anyway, for early August, she was going to visit some old college pals, why didn't she come up to Canada afterward and join me at the shoot, she'd never been to Canada. That eased the parting. So in August we had a week together on the McLuhan production, and then it was September and *The Watson Report* was starting up again. Caroline came for a visit at the farm in October, and I was able to plan a quick trip to Paris in November. We were constantly on the phone and writing letters. It was beginning to look like a very expensive and probably unsustainable relationship.

In the meantime, in addition to *The Watson Report*, there were a number of independent projects. Eric Till, my old colleague in the 1956 producers' training course, proposed casting me as the man who married Norman Bethune's wife, after the divorce, in a movie-of-the-week starring Donald Sutherland and Kate Nelligan, that he was shooting on videotape in CBC's big Studio 7. "Don't tell Donald; let's surprise him."

I went up to Toronto for the first day of rehearsal and bumped into Donald in the gents. "What are you doing here?" he said. I said I'd heard he was in for another run at Bethune, I hoped it would be almost as good as the *Witness to Yesterday* we had done together, would he mind if I sat in on rehearsals? The surprise came off very well, and for the next several days he and I and Nelligan became a familiar trio in the bars and restaurants, eating and drinking late after the rehearsals and shooting. I watched open-mouthed as those two traded dramatic recitations from the great poets, a kind of contest, who could out-recite the other, both of them deep into Shakespeare, Yeats, Auden, Dickinson, Millay. I recall Kate moving us both with Hardy's "Neutral Tones": *We stood by a pond that winter day / And the sun was white as though chidden of God . . .*" and Donald with Yeats's "An Irish Airman Foresees His Death."

In Studio 7, on the last day of shooting, there was an unforgettable actor's moment. Bethune is in the sanitarium recovering from TB, covering the walls with chalk murals on brown butcher's paper, when Frances (Nelligan) comes to discuss the final arrangements for their divorce. The scene is written to be played very cool, the two of them carefully suppressing any display, in the interests of an efficient, "adult" resolution of a marriage that has been riddled with conflict and rage. The dramatic intent was to arouse in the viewer a grief that the actors were not expressing. Both Kate and Donald played it impeccably. It was quietly moving, a transitional scene only, but a good one, with its own small but important enlargement of the characters. Eric Till called down that he was satisfied after the second take: would they agree to wrap the scene? Donald looked up for a moment, his eyes half-closed, and then made the hand sign for wanting to speak, and a mike was opened.

"I . . . I'd just like to try one more, Eric. May I?"

They went into it again, exactly as before. He is on his knees with his chalks and butcher's paper when she comes in, sits back up on the bed as they talk, she in a chair. The scene is about ninety seconds, maybe two minutes. It seems as though Donald is playing it exactly as before. Except that at the end, when she rises to leave, and he – up to then – had risen and coolly shaken her hand, this time, half a second into the handshake, he dropped to his knees. He threw his arms around her, his face in deep anguish. He moaned, three long words "I love you!" It was electrifying. Tears were flowing in the control room. Kate played it perfectly, just a tremor of emotion, then pulling back, gently disengaging, nodding, yes, she understood, but leaving him on his knees as she went quietly out of the room.

Later she told us about her triumphant debut in the West End when she was only twenty-one, I think it was in *Heartbreak House.* On opening night she had managed to cry real tears in a crucial scene, the whole performance had gone brilliantly, and she was given a standing ovation. Back in her dressing room she heard a soft tap on the door and a well-known voice saying "Gielgud here."

Thrilled and flustered, she threw on a gown and opened the door, would Sir John like to come in? No, he just wanted to say how splendid she had been, and could an old actor give her just a little bit of advice? "Of course, Sir John."

"Well," he said quietly, "it's just that . . . if *you* cry, the audience won't. Of course *I* always cry, but then I'm just an old softy."

I have found that story effective with actors when trying to get a scene under control, and even with documentary producers when they were trying too hard to, for example, force emotion into a segment with music instead of finding what was there in the documentary realities.

A strange thing began to happen to me over the next few years of *The Watson Report.* Perhaps it was because now it seemed to be all on my shoulders. I missed the camaraderie and teamwork of *Seven Days* and *The Fifty-First State.* In any case, even as I found the issues involved in each interview clearer and more graspable with every outing, I at the same time became more and more anxious about how each one would turn out, to the point where I sometimes found myself consciously hoping that there would be a breakdown of some kind, the guest would not show, the network would fail, anything that would allow me to avoid doing the interview. Sermons did not help; however firmly (and correctly) I told myself that the minute the tally light went on and I got out the first question I was going to be in charge, feeling buoyant, doing what I love to do – it did not dissipate that strange cloud of dread. "This is not you," I would say to myself. But it *was* me, it was becoming a characteristic, even though the interviews were getting better and better. There was, of course, the odd interview that frustrated me, and I dare say the audience too. I wrote in my journal about the impossibility of breaking through NDP leader David Lewis's "smiling mask of moral perfection" – a failure made especially frustrating because I liked and admired the man. But even as the interviews got better and better, that perverse fear insisted, that dread, that wishing the thing would go away.

But despite that odd quirk the work did keep growing more sure, more telling. Perhaps the dread helped. An encounter I had with Gingrich Trovimenko in December of 1980 remains, when I screen it even now, one of the best things I ever did. Trovimenko was head of the Canada-U.S. Institute in Moscow, a KGB cover. His English was flawless and he had a subtle sense of humour. I had been briefed by the Moscow desk at External, where the guys all liked and admired him, even though they knew – and the RCMP knew and everyone else knew but it was not said aloud – that the institute's professed mission to improve relations with North America was not without its less benign motives.

I knew that I could imply these things without actually saying them, and at the same time get in some hard questioning about the international stance of the Soviet Union, and indeed it went that way, a delightful encounter for me and the audience alike from the first seconds. And yet in the minutes before Trovimenko arrived at the station, I found myself hoping he would not come. Thank God he did. The conversation skirts misdirectionally around the implications of my knowing about the KGB connection, and his knowing I know, like a conjuring trick in which the audience knows what the actual technique really is, but enjoys the misdirection and the play all the same.

Others were less rewarding. When Israeli prime minister Menachem Begin announced a visit to Canada, I called Israel's embassy and arranged an interview with him. To fit his schedule, we agreed to record it a few hours ahead of broadcast. He was to be in

Montreal on a date in late October 1979 when we were supposed to be pre-empted for a sports event. Cam Graham persuaded the network to put us on an hour early, cancel the normal programming for that hour, and put on a special publicity effort. The major columnists gave us good advance notice.

All the Montreal facilities were taken for that night; so we had to book a sports crew and a mobile unit to drive from Ottawa to Montreal the night before and set up in a hotel.

I knew that Mike Wallace had interviewed Begin for *Sixty Minutes*. I phoned and luckily caught him between planes. He described Begin as terminally self-righteous. "If you ask him how the PLO terrorists are different from the Irgun [the anti-British terrorist group Begin was leading in 1948 when they bombed the King David Hotel] he'll blow up. He may walk out of the room."

"Any sense of humour?" I asked.

"None whatsoever," Mike said. "Good luck."

Late in the morning of the day of broadcast, and after the mobile unit had left for Montreal, a junior official at the embassy called to say that Begin's defence chief was arriving that same afternoon on a special mission from Tel Aviv and that unfortunately the prime minister would have to cancel his appointment with me in order to confer with this envoy and then later by telephone with General Dayan, who was in Washington. I said to the young official that he might want to convey to the ambassador that this could become an international incident: the interview had been confirmed from Tel Aviv a month earlier, it had been publicized nationally for a week, and a very large audience would be waiting for it. I told him how I had committed tens of thousands of dollars to transport a mobile unit and its crew to Montreal for the interview and that the network had taken a substantial loss in revenue by cancelling commercial programming to make room for it.

"Well, Mr. Watson," he said, "you must understand that these are very difficult times."

I asked to speak to the ambassador. It took about twenty minutes to get through. In a condescending and exaggeratedly confidential tone, he told me again about the man from Tel Aviv and the conference call with General Dayan, and regrettable as it all was, of course I would understand that affairs of state must have priority. I had a lucky hunch, and acted on it.

I had a list of Begin's Montreal engagements on my desk, and it was clear that he was heavily involved in fundraising. I told the ambassador that indeed I did understand about the primacy of affairs of state. But then I went on. "However," I said, very cool, "about one million Canadians, *very* interested in what is happening in your country, will be tuning in to see Mr. Begin's interview with me. And if it should turn out that the affairs of state to which you refer mean cocktails with the Montreal Jewish community, then I should have to report that fact to my audience. I hope you understand that."

There was a nice pause. Then the ambassador said, "Ah, Mr. Watson, what is the latest that you could record the program and still have it on the air at the advertised time?"

"Seven o'clock."

"I'll call you back."

He did so, within minutes, to report that, yes, they had been able to revise the schedule and Mr. Begin would meet me at seven o'clock.

When Begin walked in, he held his hand out disdainfully and informed me that I was a very lucky man. I said I thought perhaps he was lucky that I had not been obliged to publicly reveal that his staff had tried to get him out of a long-committed national television engagement in order to go to a fundraising meeting. The interview did not start well, nor cruise well, nor finish well. He never looked at me, only into the middle distance. I could not get him off his set pieces.

And the real reason that I failed to break through, and get at least a few minutes of genuine encounter, was that I broke one of my paramount interviewing rules and failed to ask a dumb question.

I had quoted the great Washington independent journalist I.F. Stone, who had written to the effect that he, Begin, had been brought, a reluctant third party, to the Israel-Egypt peace talks only by the intervention of Anwar Sadat and Jimmy Carter.

"Oh no," Begin said disdainfully. "After all, it was *I* who invited President Carter to Jerusalem. *I* brought President Carter to Jerusalem. How can you say *I* was reluctant! That was *my* initiative."

Now, despite my three or four days of intensive research, I could not recall Carter's having been invited to or going to Jerusalem. I felt dumb about that; I should know that stuff. How had I missed that? And I failed to do what you should always do in those circumstances: trust your intuition and ask the dumb question. Whatever happens will be better than if you do not. But I was reluctant to seem ill-informed in front of this arrogant guy, and so *I did not say what I should have said, namely, "I don't recall President Carter's going to Jerusalem."*

Because that would have made him vulnerable. He would have had to say something like "Not Carter: Sadat." And I would have said, "But you just said you brought President Carter to Jerusalem." And it might just have cut through the armour plate enough to give us even a few minutes of genuine exchange. An opportunity missed, and an interview bungled that might have gone somewhere had I only stuck to my own house rules and asked the dumb question.

But many of the interviews that season left me feeling euphoric and increasingly confident, and after a few months the curious and unfamiliar pre-broadcast dread evaporated.

I developed some other house rules during that season. I had learned from Douglas Leiterman the value of remaining silent after a dishonest or misleading answer to a difficult question, to let the weight of "dead air" do the work that conventionally one might try with an abrasive or contradictory question. Just let the dissembler sit there, knowing that the lie has been detected, and wait. I also discovered that leaning over and touching a guest's arm or shoulder, in the course of a tough question, can be both encouraging and disarming.

And that it was useful to label gobbledygook as such. Once Agriculture Minister Eugene Whelan, a circumlocution artist of no mean capacity, delivered, in response to a short sharp question, a very long answer almost certainly designed to either numb the interviewer's brain or to lead him away from whatever the difficult point was. Happily for me the answer was effectively indecipherable. I mentally counted off the seconds it had taken to deliver, and then rejoined with, "Mr. Minister, I have been listening to you talk now for approximately two and a half minutes, and I haven't understood a word of it: would you like to try it again? In English this time?"

It is remarkable how often it happens that a successful performer stops being diligently produced and directed. This is particularly true in news and current affairs, where, compared with drama, there is less of a tradition of the strong director constantly monitoring and refining the performer's work. In some cases eminent broadcasters become – to their loss – impatient with and intolerant of correction. In others the concern with journalistic issues may lead television news editors – and the journalists and presenters themselves – to forget that their first responsibility is to communicate clearly and without distracting tics. Female newsreaders on a Toronto radio station specializing in news went through a period when their voices developed a sarcastic nasal tone and a flip and overdramatized delivery. Nobody was producing them. BBC reporters all over the world, with few exceptions, indulge in a meaningless sing-song vocal delivery and wave their hands about distractingly when they should keep them still by their sides like a well-trained classical actor. (Watch Patrick Stewart as Captain Picard with this in mind.) Nobody is producing them.

It began to happen to me. Fortunately, Caroline won't be silent when I go sloppy. We were in London filming material for Cameron Graham's series *Lawyers* when she said one morning, "Does Cam like your hair like that?"

I said that Cam had not commented on my hair for a couple of years now. She said that she could believe that, it looked like it. Here, look in the mirror, do you really want to go on TV like that? And your pot belly? Has he asked you to do anything about that? He hadn't. And did you know that you've developed a distracting habit of rubbing your nose while you're talking to camera? Has he ever talked to you about that?

He hadn't. Since then, if I have to do on-camera work without Caroline's presence, I take the director aside, out of earshot of the crew, and say that I expect to be directed, and that if I'm distracting with my hands or postures or language or anything, I expect to hear about it. Of course my doing that generally pre-empts the director's having to say very much at all. But it's great insurance.

Chapter 17

CROSSINGS

THOSE EIGHT AND A HALF YEARS at CBC Ottawa ended with the last episode of *The Watson Report* on May 25, 1981. There was little time for regrets. The next few years leading up to *The Struggle for Democracy* and then the CBC chairmanship were packed with projects: the hosting of an entire arts cable service for CBS out of New York; co-hosting and writing for a series called *The World Challenge*, with Peter Ustinov out of Montreal; a starring role as an American news anchor in the Home Box Office MOW, *Countdown to Looking Glass*[1] (a prescient story of nuclear war breaking out in the Persian Gulf, which one Toronto reviewer called "superb"); my appointment to the board of trustees of the National Film Board of Canada and as a founding director of the Canadian Centre for Arms Control and Disarmament; Cameron Graham's series *Lawyers* (which would include the first television film of a real murder trial); a diving film with Joe MacInnis (and the renewal of my own scuba interest); an ongoing contract to host the PBS series *Live from Lincoln Center*, also out of New York; a one-man stage version of the Old Testament's Book of Job; the move back to Toronto; and a huge volume of family and personal transitions and changes.

1. September 1984. A number of people have reported seeing it in circumstances where, missing the opening and not quite getting the premise, they at first thought it was me as me, announcing the outbreak of a real nuclear war in the Gulf.

As well, *The Watson Report*, nourished by a healthy amount of press, brought me a flood of speaking engagements. Driven more than I should have been by the recent memory of months of no income whatsoever, I turned few down. That added a lot to the stress of those years, but it gave me a refreshed sense of the country. One week I would be speaking to teachers on Vancouver Island and the next to a conference of Anglican bishops in Ottawa. People began to ask me to solve extraordinary problems, as though my prominence in the media gave me some kind of encyclopaedic grasp on life. If I let that go to my head, Caroline was a healthy source of perspective.

Cameron Graham had established his reputation as the producer of solidly conceived and diligently produced documentaries. His *First Person Singular*, a biography of Lester B. Pearson in thirteen half-hours, broadcast shortly before Cam rehabilitated me with the CBC management and brought me back from New York, documented not just a man but a time. So did his eight one-hours on the 1957–1967 era, *The Tenth Decade*. He had made specials on Diefenbaker and on Trudeau as well, and went on to make series after series, and win an impressive string of well-deserved awards.

A pilot himself, and frequently a passenger in Uncle Charley's Hotel, he conceived of and commissioned a four-part history of aviation in Canada, entitled *Flight: The Passionate Affair*. He and Brian Nolan directed, and the production took us, often with me at the controls, to the site of the Wright brothers' first flight, and on to Gander for an essay on Transport Command during World War II and some time aboard a Concorde prototype that had come in for snow and slush trials. We went to Baddeck for a piece on Alexander Graham Bell's early aviation endeavours, and I flew the camera plane for Fred Gorman when we shot our World War I fighter sequence with a Nieuport replica from the National Aviation Collection. Fred shot from the front seat with the door off while I flew from the back seat of a Citabria. The Nieuport had been finished with the markings of the one Billy Bishop made his reputation in.

Graham commissioned the building of several exquisitely detailed radio-controlled models for the series: aircraft of which there was no longer any flying example, models so realistic in the air that experienced pilots and historians at the launch screening, warned to watch for "something extraordinary" in the second episode, failed to recognize they were not the real thing and were eloquent in their wonderment at our finding an extant and flying Fokker Trimotor or early Curtis open-cockpit flying boat. That series went to air in 1976.

In December 1975 or January 1976 Brian Nolan called asking if there was anything in my CBC contract that prevented my working for another network. He was with Bill Cunningham, a long-time CBC foreign correspondent who had worked from Saigon for years during the Vietnam war and was at this point head of news at the young Global network. They had been speculating about the remnants of the inner circle of Nazis, all dead now except for Albert Speer, who had served twenty years in Berlin's Spandau prison and was living quietly at the family home near Heidelberg. Speer's memoir, *Inside the Third Reich*, had just been published. On a whim Cunningham had picked up the phone, found the number in Heidelberg through the overseas information operator, and pitched Speer on the television rights to his book. Speer had agreed, without hesitation, and Cunningham, then running the news department at the fledgling Global Television Network, had committed a substantial budget to a biographical film. They wanted me to host and narrate the documentary, and to do a long biographical interview with Speer, which would serve as the spine of the film. "You'll love Berlin," Cunningham said. "It's a fun city."

Albert Speer was a young architect who had been introduced to Adolf Hitler in Munich not long after Hitler became chancellor of what was then the German Republic. There had been, Speer told me, an instant attraction between them, "not homosexual, but definitely homoerotic, that is the phrase that one psychiatrist suggested." Hitler, envious of Haussmann's magnificent nineteenth-century design for the centre of Paris, had decided to rebuild the centre of Berlin to surpass

Paris as the glory of Europe. In 1937 he named Speer *Generalbauinspektor*, the chief inspector for the reconstruction of Berlin. That put the thirty-two-year-old right at the centre of power, and Hitler cleared out an art museum next door to the Chancellery so that his young favourite was just the width of the State Gardens away from himself. Speer and Hitler's plan for the new Berlin was so grandiose that Speer's architect father said they were all insane. The centrepiece was to be a classical dome, soaring above the Brandenburg Gate to a height of almost a thousand feet, by far the world's largest, the avenues leading to it almost twice as wide as the extravagant Champs Élysées. Speer and Hitler travelled to Paris after the Nazis occupied it in 1940, and Hitler was filmed rubbing his hands with satisfaction: his Berlin would far surpass the City of Light.

The best known of Speer's architectural innovations is still his 1934 design for Hitler's vast rally in the stadium at Nuremburg, whose walls were composed not of stone or brick or wood, but of light, hundreds of powerful anti-aircraft searchlights on all sides of the rally site, so that at night it seemed to have walls soaring to infinity. Leni Riefenstahl's famous film *The Triumph of the Will*[2] is of interest mainly for the glamour of Speer's designs; without Speer there would have been no film and Riefenstahl would be unknown. When we filmed at the stadium it was deserted except for a group of American soldiers playing football. "Pass the fucking ball" was heard in the sound track when we were editing my stand-up in the marble seats of the stadium.

When Hitler's armaments minister, Fritz Todt, died in an air crash in 1942, Hitler replaced him with Speer, and that is where the greatest controversy of all begins. While Speer was the only top Nazi to plead guilty to war crimes at the post-war Nuremburg trials, he always claimed that he knew nothing of the Holocaust, and had no

2. Often carelessly cited as "the greatest propaganda film ever made," it is in fact a profoundly boring and repetitive series of march-pasts and crazed rhetoric that "leaves one only with an impression of insanity" (Lotte Eisner, 1952). It is painful to watch the whole thing. Goebbels hated it and would not use it. When it was released in the cinemas people walked out. There is a definitive study of this monstrosity by Brian Winston in *History Today*, January 1997.

responsibility for bringing in the slave labour that was extensively used in the armaments factories.

His book *Inside the Third Reich* is a spellbinder, and his well-verified account of how he drove around Germany countermanding Hitler's mad order to destroy the country by wrecking the water and power supplies, the "Scorched Earth" policy, gives him an appeal despite his disturbing affection for The Fuehrer. He was, indisputably, an extraordinary architect. Later scholarship shows that he did know more about the Final Solution to the Jewish Problem than he admitted to, and that he was in fact complicit in the slave labour imports. He remains a complex, difficult, yet strangely appealing figure.

When Moses Znaimer heard about my Speer project, he phoned me in a state of consternation. He said that Speer was evil, that I should have nothing to do with the man who had masterminded Hitler's rise to glory, that Speer would bamboozle me as he had others, and that if I was perverse enough to go ahead with this project would I promise him, please, to consult Simon Wiesenthal, the famed Nazi hunter at the Dokumentation Zentrum in Vienna, before I met with Speer.

I said that I thought my journalistic principles and experience would guide me through whatever mystifications Speer might put in my way, but I promised to speak with Wiesenthal.

Brian Nolan and I flew to Frankfurt in March, and I called Wiesenthal. He astonished me by saying at the outset, "I hope you will do nothing to harm this man. He is a good man. I have spent many hours questioning him, and I believe him."

To his credit, Brian Nolan was more skeptical than I was. We met Speer first at his home on the Wolfsbrennenweg in the outskirts of the beautiful old city of Heidelberg. He was as urbane, charming, and witty as he had been described. Through several hours of interview, both in his house and in the hotel in Berlin where he had spent his first night of liberty after twenty years in Spandau prison, he insisted that while he had heard rumours of atrocities, he had been warned by senior officials not to enquire into them. He admitted to naiveté in not doing so. He continued to maintain that he knew nothing of the slave labour, and when I said that I found that impossible to believe, he just shrugged and said he could understand my skepticism, but that he had kept himself deliberately away from the dark side of things.

Gitta Sereny's 1995 biography *Albert Speer's Struggle with Truth* convincingly reveals that he was lying about both the Holocaust and the slave labour: that he was at the famous Wandsee meeting and had not, as he claimed, left that meeting before the Final Solution discussion. And yet Sereny found the man who came out of Spandau apparently reflective and penitent, a sympathetic figure: "In this Speer I found much to like . . . ." she wrote. She saw him as a man who was, in fact, able to avoid seeing things that he felt he should not see. She found acquaintances going back to his adolescence who identified that as a central characteristic.

Our seventy-two-minute film reveals, I think, his complexity and his contradictions, as well as his charm. It remains an important document of the man's life. It earned me the 1977 ACTRA award for best television journalist in Canada.

I am still a bit troubled about not having found a way to press Speer more effectively, nor to have found the evidence Sereny was later able to confront him with that proved his complicity to be greater than he had admitted. But it remains a landmark film, and for me and Brian Nolan a landmark experience in the making of documentary.

Overlapping *The Last Nazi*, Cameron Graham secured the rights to Peter C. Newman's book *The Canadian Establishment*, and we began to work on what became a seven-part series, which I hosted and for which I did the major interviews, working with a number of directors. The series was broadcast in 1980, rebroadcast extensively during CBC TV's fiftieth anniversary year in 2001, and still shows up on the Documentary Channel. Then in 1985 we worked together in a similarly designed eight-part series based on Jack Batten's book *Lawyers*, also with a number of writer/producer/directors.

One of the filmmakers whom Cameron Graham had brought in

on *The Canadian Establishment* was a quiet, slightly diffident, wise-looking writer/producer/director named Ted Remerowski. I remember deciding early on that he was someone I would like to work with again. I think it may have been while we were in mid-stream with that series that Anthony Westell[3] said lightly one day, commenting on the range of material in the Cameron Graham canon of documentary series, "When you two finish this one, you should think about doing a series called *The Struggle for Democracy*." At the time Cam Graham was too preoccupied to pay attention. *The Canadian Establishment* was more than a full-time job. But a journal note has me talking about the democracy idea over dinner with Moses Znaimer and Peter Watkins of *Culloden* fame, some time in 1979. I remember sounding out first Peter Herrndorf, when he was head of Current Affairs, and later Bill Morgan when he took over that chair, and both of them telling me that, yes, it was a great idea but the age of the CBC's ability to fund major documentary series was pretty well over, and likely the only way I could get support for a project that would entail filming all over the world would be to find a sponsor. CBC would match what the sponsor put up, not necessarily all in money; some would be in services, staff, office space, crews, etc. But the bottom line was to find that sponsor. It seemed an unlikely prospect.

In the meantime, Graham came up with another proposal, this one much grander and of much more extensive implications than anything either of us had ever considered. As early as January 1974 he had been talking about a nightly interview program.

The use of stationary satellites had already transformed the long-distance transmission of telephone and television signals. But while television news was making extensive use of this new facility to move news clips around the world, Cam Graham worked intensely for a couple of years to develop a project that would, he said, transform television itself. In February when he asked me to meet with him and John Kerr from the network office in Toronto, he described it simply

3. Then dean of the School of Journalism at Carleton University, where Cameron Graham was a visiting associate professor.

The dome.
Acrylic 24 in. x 18 in.
The author, 1983.

Photo: Leonard De Silva

With Caroline at her cottage on Go Home Lake, ca. 1984.

The wedding day, Dublin, 1985.

Markelangelo, by Robert Markle (PW as Adam, Markle as God). Acrylic, 34 in. x 20 in., 1985.

The continuing beers: Robert Markle and PW, 1987.

PW and Caroline, Go Home Lake, 1986.

At Go Home Lake, 1988.

Marlene and Robert Markle.
Oil on canvas, 24 in. x 30 in.
Caroline Bamford, 1996.
From a photograph by
Stephen Williams.

Roy Faibish. Oil on canvas, 30 in. x 24 in.
Caroline Bamford, 1996.

Erik Durschmied, ca. 1995.

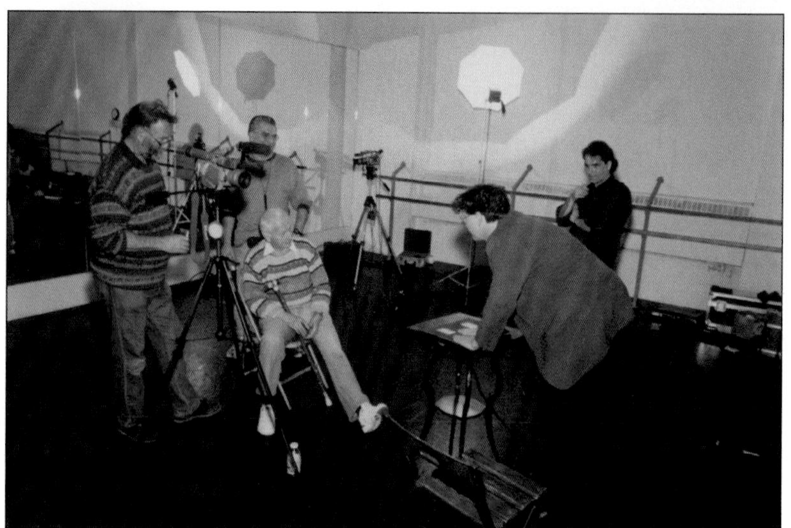

Directing David Ben during the filming of *The Making of The Conjuror*, 1996.

At the Shaw Festival, with Daniel Zuckerbrot and David Ben, 1996.

Performing magic on Members' Day, Shaw Festival, 1996.

as a nightly interview program, based in Ottawa, connecting me to guests all across the country. Kerr's first reaction was so positive that Graham had alerted me to the possibility of launching the project sometime in 1975, but in the event he kept on elaborating it until its final thickly documented form in 1979 or 1980.

He began to refer to it as *The Satellite Program.* He did most of the development work himself, with the knowledgeable collaboration of some of the technical staff at CBC Ottawa.

The Satellite Program envisaged a nightly magazine, hosted out of Ottawa and transmitted across the country by satellite, with inserts originating from locations to wherever we could fly or truck a satellite dish. Not stations on the already familiar network, but an Inuit village, say, where a new artist had been discovered or a dreadful crime committed, a south Saskatchewan county devastated by storms, a laboratory in Prince Edward Island, a town hall where a crucial civic decision was being debated. The project would own a couple of aircraft – not fast or sophisticated, but big enough to carry a two-man camera crew and a small satellite dish. Mobility would be the project's watchword, mobility and the tying together of the whole country through this new technology – and the technology was changing rapidly.

Finally, when all the technical, financial, and logistical issues had been described to the last detail, in a binder that was some two inches thick, Graham sent it off to Don McPherson, then the programming network in Toronto. The response was immediate and enthusiastic: financial and schedule planning would begin immediately. This was exactly where the future of the CBC belonged. Graham was a genius. Revolutionary idea. Of course Watson would be the host. Give them a couple of months to do the necessary internal selling to management, work out the finances, deal with the politics; they would be back to us.

The silence that followed was not, at first, alarming. This was a huge project and would take a long time to set in place. But that silence went on for what became a ponderous wait. When Graham phoned Toronto for a progress report, he was asked to be patient, things were moving ahead, and then the silence continued.

When it was finally broken, in the summer of 1980, Cam told me that Peter Herrndorf had called, a bit sheepishly, to announce that in fact the new newsmagazine would be produced from Toronto, which had the facilities to coordinate all these out-of-the-centre inputs, and it would be, uhmm, under the executive producership of Mark Starowicz, who, while he had not exactly worked in television, had a national reputation for his groundbreaking radio series *As It Happens.* Starowicz could not, of course, be expected to engage a host (Watson) with whom he had not worked, but he would certainly find a role for Watson, perhaps as a roving journalist/interviewer. As host of the new program, to be called *The Journal,* he would bring Barbara Frum over from *As It Happens.* Herrndorf said they should be ready to go to air as early as January (1981). Cameron Graham would be offered some form of contributing producership, which would require his moving to Toronto. *The Watson Report* would be terminated in the spring of 1981. There would be no more network money for documentaries out of Ottawa, although if Watson were able to find some outside money for *The Struggle for Democracy,* it would still be considered. Cameron Graham was understandably wounded. He was in a rage at first. Then the rage transposed into a kind of grief, bitterly tinged with a sense that he had been abandoned by the employer whom he had so diligently and productively served for so long, abandoned, betrayed, and perhaps cheated. Although they said in Toronto that *The Journal,* while it bore many resemblances to *The Satellite Program,* could not, after all, really be said to be the same project, could it?

That final year of *The Watson Report* went well. Curiously, I still sometimes felt that weird anxiety, that perverse hope that a program would be cancelled. By the final year of the series it was beginning to fade, and, mercifully, never returned.

Caroline and I continued our extended courtship in Ireland and France and Canada. The following summer I planned to spend a lot of time in Paris. Robert Markle, whom I had interviewed for *Seven Days* when some of his drawings were impounded by the police in 1964, had by now become a mentor, drawing teacher, and close friend.[4] He had stayed with me in New York during *The Fifty-First State*, and I was often at the farmhouse that he and his wife Marlene had found near Holstein, two hours from Toronto, or at his rangy sixth-floor loft/studio in a former casket factory in the city. In that summer of 1978 he had finally agreed to his first (and, sadly last) transatlantic trip, when the Artists' Jazz Band, in which he played tenor sax, was invited to play at the Canadian Cultural Centre in Paris where the members' paintings were on display. Caroline invited him to stay with us at her little flat in Menilmontant, and for a few lyrical days we cruised Paris together, including a six-hour visit to the Louvre, which Robert quite transformed for us with his passionate response to the treasures there and his teacherly discourse.

Later that summer Caroline revealed, in a somewhat off-hand, almost diffident way, that she had a black belt in karate and invited me to visit her class with Sensei Richard Lee. If I'd had any doubts before that evening at the Dojo, watching her move along the spectrum from quiet authority through fierce aggressiveness to the slow contemplative grace of the Tai Chi with which Sensei Lee began his evenings would have banished them. But there were no doubts by then, except about how long we could maintain this transatlantic relationship. One of us had to move. One afternoon at Roissy Airport we literally flipped a one-franc coin, and on that basis, in late 1978 Caroline agreed to give Canada a try. With Ben Marcus's help we secured her landed immigrant status. She arrived in February of 1979. I picked her up at Montreal with the Twin Comanche and flew to Carleton Place, and dipped a wing as we circled the snow-covered airstrip so that she could see the large WELCOME CAROLINE that I had stamped out in my snow boots. After a few months at the farm,

4. See my biography of Robert Markle in *The Canadians: Biographies of a Nation, Vol. III* (McArthur, 2002) or in *The Omnibus Edition* of the same titles (2003), and the History Television documentary from the series of the same title, available on cassette from the History Television Online Boutique.

we left it to Beverly, and moved into Nightwood, Caroline's name for the log house I had built near Franktown.

Caroline was upset at the move. It was not I who had drawn her to Canada, she teased me later; it was the farm. Its tranquil isolation and endless walks had seduced her, and now she had to go through the dusty business of moving, albeit only a few miles away, to a place she had no investment in whatsoever. She was finding the Ottawa Valley bleak after ten years in Paris, a lot of cultural adjustment to make and a radical change in her daily life; she was uneasy about how my friends and colleagues were going to react to her sudden appearance as the most important person in my life. As it turned out she was welcomed with enormous warmth. Reeves Haggan made her feel she'd found a piece of Ireland in Canada, especially when he told her about hearing her uncle Tom Martin preach in Dublin. My mother fell in love with her. Ben and Angela Marcus made her welcome in their home. Laurier LaPierre treated us to an enormous dinner at Les Halles, in Montreal, and made her feel like royalty. Roy Faibish, Robert Markle, and Sandra Kybartas seemed almost as smitten with her as I was, and so the stress of this drastic change in her life was cushioned by affection and admiration.

Sandra Kybartas is a production designer in movies and television with a string of impressive titles in her resumé. When Caroline met Sandy in the Windsor Arms' famous bar, the 22, on her first visit to Toronto, they were sisters within the first ten minutes. Sandy flew back to the farm with us then in the Twin Comanche, and the three of us stayed up long past midnight, night after night, exploring quantum physics, poetry, existentialism, jazz, Bach, the politics of oppression, the nature of play, Caroline and I discovering that this Kybartas person knew something about everything and was one of the best conversation partners ever invented. I had to go off for a day or two with Cameron Graham on the *Canadian Establishment* project, and the two of them stayed on at the farm gardening, doing target practice with an old .22, drawing and painting, and talking talking talking. When we moved to Nightwood, Sandy turned up there with gratifying frequency, and the talk went on, seasoned with wry comments on the goofy design of the place, since Sandra Kybartas also has a degree in architecture.

Nightwood is the two-and-a-half-storey log building I had conceived with a couple of young local builders, Glynn Shannan and Jim Connell. We used 150-year-old ash logs from a former smithy in Ferguson Falls and designed and constructed a tall granite fireplace and chimney, high ceilings, an open-plan ground floor, galleries and surprises on the second, and an improbable roof line. Jim carved a great pine tree in bas-relief on the thick pine front door, and Jacob Lischer, a local blacksmith, made the lock and latches and wrought iron hinges, the bottom set of which represented the twisted roots of the pine tree. You can see the building still a couple of kilometres west of Franktown at a bend in the Perth Road.

The logs took some time to settle into their new configuration, and some nights, especially when the temperature dropped suddenly, they talked, protesting audibly and at length. One night we heard soft, slipper-shod footsteps coming hesitantly up the wide plank stairs from the living room to the oddly shaped hallway outside our bedroom door. There was no one else in the house, or *had been* no one else in the house. It was about 2 a.m. There was finally nothing to do but get up and turn on some lights and confront this hesitant stranger, who turned out to be a bat, possibly rabid, insanely flopping up those stairs one at a time and sufficiently confused by the sudden light to be taken up and thrown out. Bats filled the spaces between the vaulted ceiling and the roof; clouds of them emerged at dusk. We rationalized this nuisance by saying they were keeping down the mosquitoes. The mosquitoes did not seem to understand this.

Living in that talkative, improbable house, with not a great deal going on at first except the weekly *Watson Report*, Caroline and I got to know each other well. We went through a lot of the testing that is part of early days. We started flying together. I had an instructor's ticket endorsed for aerobatics, which she at least tolerated in the back seat of Marvin McPherson's Citabria.[5] We found a Cessna 140 we could rent for a song, and I began to give Caroline her *ab initio* training as a pilot. She was a natural hand on the controls, completely at ease in the air.

One day, teaching stalls and stall recovery at about five thousand feet, I noticed that the air was so clear we could see the Arnprior airport's triangular layout about twenty miles north. The air was lovely and still, a hint of fall in the colours. I said, "Let's try something a bit different," took control for a moment, shut off the engine, pulled the nose up into a stall, held it on the edge just long enough for the propeller to stop turning, and then handed her back control of the now silent airplane, only the soft rush of air over the skin and struts announcing that we were in motion, the sound increasing and decreasing with the angle of descent and its accompanying speed.

"You're a glider pilot now," I said. "See if you can make it to Arnprior. Just keep it on its best glide speed (around 70 mph) and we should make it." It was as if she'd done it a hundred times, one hand relaxed in her lap, the other gently easing the nose up or down whenever a small bump in the air had to be accommodated, the wings steadily level, the nose pointed at the old World War II training strip. It was perfect. We didn't power up again until we were within less than a mile, and that was just for safety as she could have greased it on, right in the middle of the strip, with no need for power at all.

From time to time on a whim we would put the nosewheel bar on the Twin Comanche, tug it out of the old corrugated hangar at Marvin McPherson's strip, and head off to Montreal or Toronto or New York for a weekend. It was an idyllic time, even though we knew that my major source of revenue was about to dry up, although for the time being Knopf was still sending me royalties from *Alexander Dolgun's Story: An American in the Gulag.*

5. Which he still has, at his own private Carleton Place Strip: I flew it again twenty years later (with Marvin in the front seat), when I stopped in at the strip on a Sunday afternoon during a promotion tour for Volume II of *The Canadians: Biographies of a Nation.*

Maybe something would come out of the Starowicz project. He and I did have some early, wide-ranging conversations which, for a while, had suggested that he was thinking globally and adventurously, so the fact that he had been quiet for a few months was not really disquieting. But he had been very quiet. We read a great deal. The house was full of music and company, a great fire roaring on the big granite hearth. Sandra Kybartas would turn up after a design assignment in Ottawa and stay for a few days of non-stop talk, very literary and philosophical and cinematic. Roy Faibish would come for dinner, sometimes with a new companion, sometimes with his big cast-iron Creuset full of Irish stew and once, memorably, mussels in cream with Pernod. There was much reading aloud. One weekend Faibish, discovering to his alleged dismay and shock that most of us had never read Herman Melville's *Bartleby the Scrivener*, drove all the way back into Ottawa to get his own copy so that he could read it aloud, eight or ten of us gathered spellbound in the firelight around that soft, almost hypnotic voice.

I bought an ancient and not very good grand piano, and took some more lessons, and a harpsichord, which I learned to tune by ear according to some of the ancient pre-tempered-scale tuning regimes: pure fifths all through the scale and then slightly flattened thirds, was that it? Counting the beats on the thirds.

We put in a good-sized vegetable garden, foraged for lamb's quarters and wild asparagus, and for wild mushrooms in the eight or ten acres of old pine woods on the property. Caroline was widely knowledgeable about funghi and was diligent with microscope and textbook when there was a find that was hard to identify. I can still see one feast we served in a bowl almost as big as a wok, heaped with eleven different species and sauced with a secret ingredient. One weekend of wet snow and freezing rain, Caroline's suitcase of Gauloise cigarettes that she had brought from Paris a year earlier was finally exhausted and neither of us wanted to venture out in that awful weather. So we just stopped smoking. For good. Without trying.

Night after night, at ten o'clock, we listened to Gilles

Archambault's seminal *Jazz Soliloque* on Radio-Canada's FM service. I nominated him for the CBC's annual President's Award, and to our delight he was chosen.[6]

One evening I reached down from its almost five-foot shelf one volume at random from my father's *Interpreters' Bible.* I had never understood why he'd bought the enormous set, but when Lucy had invited me to go through his shelves after he died, *The Interpreters' Bible* had seemed something that for its sheer mass and dignity should be kept in the family. I had never opened it. How could a Bible take up those many thousands of pages? The volume I chose turned out to contain the Book of Job. Interesting. I knew nothing about Job except that his name is part of a cliché about patience. I remember from that same night, as I sank deeper and deeper into fascination with this ancient, powerfully poetic encounter between a deeply good man and an egotistical, self-righteous, irresponsible, and perversely nasty God, that I looked up at some point and said to Caroline, "This is a movie." I began to think about making something out of it. That thought would eventually take me onto the stage of the National Arts Centre in Ottawa.

It was during that period that Moses Znaimer and I tried to interest the CBC in making some more episodes of *Witness to Yesterday.* When the Corporation turned us down, Moses decided to go ahead with the resources of his young, street-smart television station CITY-TV. There was some fuss over the title, as the original productions from Look Hear Productions in Montreal had been sold to Doug McDonald at Film House in Toronto, and the original producer, Arthur Voronka, was threatening legal action if we made more programs without involving him. We flirted with *The Immortality File.* Finally Moses proposed producing thirteen programs under the

6. Years later, when I went down to an audio booth in the basement of La Maison Radio-Canada to record French narration tracks for the Radio-Canada version of *The Struggle for Democracy*, I heard the familiar, soothing Archambault voice coming from a control room as I passed. When he looked up from his notes at the end of the introduction to the next record, he saw me watching him. He clicked in after a second (we had never met), rushed out, and without a word we embraced warmly, his producer waving at him frantically to get back to the microphone.

rubric of *Titans*. We rented an elegant private house in Rosedale, to represent my house in which the guests would be invited to step out of the shades of the past for half an hour and visit me in my own living room. It was a very different style from the original cinematic and formal approach of the 1973–1975 *Witness to Yesterday*. It seemed to fit the texture and feel of videotape (the originals had been set in a stylized manner and shot on film), although in the end I thought the videotape realism and immediacy of the set and the image worked against the fantasy of the concept: the slight remove of the film image had worked better.

But we made thirteen lovely programs. Marilyn Lightstone and I collaborated on a script for Nefertiti, which she also played brilliantly. Andrea Martin was a hilarious and convincing George Sand. David Calderisi's Napoleon was excellent. John Marley (the movie producer in *The Godfather* who wakes up in bed with a severed horse's head) was an appealing Albert Einstein, and even played the violin. When the actor scheduled to play Alexander Graham Bell fell ill, Moses suggested I play the part, so I worked up a Scots voice, climbed into some elaborate makeup, and interviewed myself.

As we prepared for this production in the spring and summer of 1981, my mother was stricken with cancer and went into palliative care at the Salvation Army's Grace Hospital in Toronto. Lucy presided over her last months in a magisterial way, calling in members of the family and doing her best to mend a rift here and encourage a new venture there. Caroline had come to love her very deeply, and it seems in retrospect that until she had to go back to Paris, we were almost continually back and forth between Nightwood and Toronto, the old Twin Comanche running up a lot of hours.

With a steady and growing stream of invitations to speak all across Canada, I soon found that I had no appetite for or skill in managing the business side of public speaking. Moses Znaimer said one day that his lawyer operated as an agent for some of his clients, a man who, while he was only in his mid-thirties, was already being described as the top entertainment and media lawyer in Canada. His name was Michael Levine. Moses told me that as well as Moses himself, Michael Levine's clients included Peter Newman, Robert Bateman, Karen Kain, Timothy Findley – it sounded as though he touched every conceivable field of the arts, as indeed he does. I told Moses it sounded a bit daunting and perhaps my needs would not be very interesting to such a big player. Moses said simply that if we got on well together, and Michael Levine decided he admired my work and liked me personally, he would be very generous, often putting in hours (for which his normal billing rate was . . . impressive) on his own hook for a client whose career he wanted to advance. We had our first meeting, hit it off exceptionally well, and thus began a friendship that has continually deepened, enriched by collaborations in some of the best projects of my life.

Caroline's mother, Casey,[7] had come to stay at Nightwood during the idyllic Indian summer of 1980. It had been a lively, funny visit. Casey read aloud to us from *Finnegans Wake* all through one evening by the fire. Despite the busy commuting to see my mother and get the *Titans* project up and running, and despite the uncertainties about the CBC, there was a calm, pervasive sense of rightness about the world. *The Watson Report* was to be over in May, but there was another ending, closer to home, before that.

Casey died in April. She had opened a bar on the Rue St. Denis, just opposite Le Square des Innocents. It is a part of Paris whose pavements, before the gentrification of the area, were well supplied with ladies of the night, with whom Casey had made friends, allowing them to use her patio area to cruise after she locked up around 2 a.m. (good security for the bar) and then sometimes inviting them in for a morning coffee-and-Armagnac. Casey was an enthusiastic painter, and used Casey's Irish Bar ("The Best Irish Whisky in Paris," the sandwich board said) as a gallery where she could display and sell her landscapes and still lifes. She died in London during emergency heart surgery. Roy Faibish was living there by then, lobbying for Ted Rogers who was hoping to develop cable TV in Britain. Roy, with the help of

7. Muriel Philamena Crossgray Furey.

his secretary and future wife Barbara Calvert, had the funeral arrangements all in place by the time we got there with Caroline's brother, Russell, and sister, Gabrielle, and generously found places for most of us to sleep in his Hampstead flat.

Then we had to go to Paris to deal with Casey's Irish Bar. Erik Durschmied was about to take off to his summer house in Denmark, and invited us to stay in his big apartment in Le Marais, within walking distance of the bar. Caroline, Gabrielle, and Russell decided to keep it open for the summer, the best earning time, and then to sell it. For several weeks I helped out in the bar, then went back to Toronto to spend time with my mother and also to try building a relationship with Mark Starowicz and his yet-to-be-broadcast *The Journal*. Mark had given me a desk in the new *Journal* offices on Carlton Street; so I had a place to leave my stuff.

When he learned that I was staying with Durschmied, and that Erik was just back from North Vietnam with a lot of raw film that he intended – after his holiday – to build into a documentary for the BBC, Mark suggested that perhaps Erik and I should form a two-man documentary team specializing in trouble spots. He proposed that we should, as an experiment, see if we could within a week or ten days edit the North Vietnam footage into five ten-minute episodes, as might be used five nights in a row on *The Journal* (which was not intended to go to air until the New Year). If we set ourselves the goal of doing the edit that rapidly, the experiment would demonstrate whether Starowicz's concerns for timeliness could be handled by the Durschmied–Watson team. Erik and I agreed to try it, and I raced back to Paris.

In just over a week, working about eighteen hours a day in the comfortable cutting room in Erik's big flat on the Rue Rambuteau, we succeeded in cutting thousands of feet of film into five short episodes, with music and narration (mine), and, feeling very pleased with ourselves, reported triumphantly to Mark Starowicz in Toronto. He said that his first lieutenant, Richard Bronstein, was in London, why didn't I give Bronstein a call and have him step across the channel to look at the stuff, he was practically in the neighbourhood. We seemed to have the basis of an agreement for what would be a dream assignment. Caroline and I would find a place to live in Paris, which she had been missing a lot despite the delights of Nightwood. She would keep the bar going after all, while Erik and I charged off around the world on hit-and-run assignments to challenging places, coming back to edit them overnight in his flat, and perhaps establish a new form: the five-part series of short docs. I phoned Bronstein in London.

Unfortunately, Bronstein was yawningly uninterested. Why should he take the trouble to fly to Paris just to see a few films?

Responding to the proposal that we get ourselves into difficult parts of the world, Erik and I had opened discussions with the First Secretary of the Chinese embassy in Paris, a Mr. Pi. Mr. Pi was fascinated with our accounts of filming in China in 1964, and soon said he would arrange for us to make a return trip, all he needed to show his superiors was our official accreditation. *The Journal* never did provide that accreditation.

It was soon clear that we would not be working with *The Journal.*

Lucy died in July. The last time I saw her she was apparently in a coma. The medical staff told me that she would not likely regain consciousness, but might live for a considerable time. I went in to see her and sat quietly by the bed for about an hour, she breathing peacefully and looking remarkably content for a dying eighty-two-year-old woman. After a while I stood up and reached out my hand, remembering all those comforting times in childhood and adolescence, she by *my* bedside, when she would reach out her hand and rub my head and tell me it was going to be all right. I put my hand on her forehead.

She pursed her lips and said, distinctly, "Patrick?" And opened her eyes. I threw my arms around her and burst into tears. "Now now now," she said, "what in the world are you crying about?"

Casey's Irish Bar was lively and profitable, although I found it a bit tough some nights when Caroline would stumble into bed at 3 a.m., her hair reeking of tobacco smoke. By mid-August she was exhausted and decided to leave the bar in Gabrielle's capable hands for a few days and accept Erik's invitation to spend some time on the ocean beach at Falster Island. We had not been there many days before a call came from New York. Jack Willis had a new project. CBS was starting a new arts channel, available exclusively on cable. Jack had agreed to program it; would I consider joining him as host? Host of what, I asked. Of the whole service, he said, every program. Come on over and meet the troops and we'll talk about it.

Caroline got an offer on the bar and decided to keep it going until the closing day in October. I moved to New York in early September. CBS had found us a fine apartment high up above 57th Street, just west of 8th Avenue, from which we could watch the blue jays sweeping in by the hundreds from Central Park, just north of us, to perch on the sills of our building. CBS Cable had taken a big studio on 48th Street, laid out a false hardwood floor over the entire space, and brought in different sets, mostly composed of works of art, as the environment in which I would introduce every single program to go out on their cable service. Sandra Kybartas came for a visit, chatted up the series chief designer, David Mitchell, and ended up with a contract as his hands-on assistant designer for our presentations of *La Cage aux Folles*, *Private Lives* (Liz Taylor and Richard Burton's last), *Dance a Little Closer (*Alan Jay Lerner's musical, which closed the night after it opened when the critics called it "Close a Little Faster"), Balanchine's last two Stravinsky dances and Peter Martins' first (*Magic Flute*) when he took over the ballet from Balanchine. There was a nine-foot Steinway grand that I could use to demonstrate ideas about some of the musical programs. When we did a documentary on abstract expressionism, they brought in about a dozen big Rothkos and hung them from the grid for me to walk among as I introduced the film.

About twenty percent of the programming was original, including some dance and drama productions, and a very strong daily interview program, *Signature*, whose host/interviewer Greg Jackson was never seen, and whose voice was close enough to mine to earn me some credit I did not deserve.

It was a breakthrough service. William S. Paley, the man who invented broadcast networks and founded CBS, had proposed it as a way of putting back into the world of broadcasting some of the immense wealth that he and CBS had made there. It was budgeted to lose $40 million in the first year, that loss shrinking to zero only in the sixth, and then turning into steady and irreversible positive revenue after that, as the cable (and later satellite) subscription base went into its inevitable high-growth curve. The programming was on what Jack Willis called "a wheel": a block of three hours of original programming would be repeated seven times, and then changed for a brand-new block. Jack wisely knew that in the expanding universe of dozens of channels, many of them appealing to the same audience (PBS, for example, and the new New York–based BRAVO), viewers would not be staying with one channel, but if they knew that they could always count on three hours of fresh stuff from CBS Cable, at a certain block of time when they wanted to watch TV, there was no need for us to give them new programming all through the day.

The launch party was at the storied New York Public Library's lion-guarded central building on 5th Avenue. Bill Payley came over and grasped my hand when I walked in, and said, "Patrick, it's got the *feel.*"

Which it had.

But feel was not enough. The money men at Black Rock, the soaring black-glassed CBS head office on 5th Avenue, were not happy about the financial haemorrhage of those first few years. If Bill Paley wanted to "put something back," why didn't he use his own millions, not the company's? And when he stepped down from the chair of CBS when the arts service was less than a year old, it did not take them long to move in and close down what had been a noble experiment. But we did have a second season, since the programming was committed for it before Black Rock began its move. Caroline and I were put into a fifth-floor apartment at 40 Central Park South and were revelling in the joys of living in Manhattan. I could walk to work at the studio, which was now in the main CBS production centre on 57th Street west of 9th Avenue. Once again, as in the *Fifty-First State* days, I experienced that New York thing, the feeling audiences have that they *own you.* Very different from Canada, where I can often see people across the aisle in a supermarket whispering behind their hands as they recognize me, but more often than not never saying anything. In Manhattan, cab drivers and people in the streets would take me aside and tell me how to properly run CBS Cable. One man in a shop on 57th Street said, "You're the guy with white hair on that arts channel. There are no guys with white hair on TV. How come they let you on?"

I had two weeks on and two weeks off. We rented Nightwood and took a flat on St. George Street in Toronto, where I had contracted with the CBC to help Ted Remerowski finish a six-part series on China. That relationship bloomed, and as the idea of a series on democracy took further shape, I came to feel that Remerowski would have to be part of it.

The Journal went on the air. It was wide-ranging, politically smart, and visually ugly. The joke on the street was that while television had long been called "Radio with Pictures," *The Journal* was television without pictures. There was seldom anything on the arts. Offended by the constant panning over banks of monitors and other equipment that linked segments, designed I guess to show how technically swift these guys were, I called Starowicz and suggested that he think about featuring a Canadian visual artist every week, painter or sculptor, fill a studio with works of art, with teasing identification that would set up an appetite for a major piece on the said artist to be featured on the final program of the week, on Friday evening. Mark said he couldn't imagine that anybody would be the least bit interested.

The street was buzzing with stories about the money that was being spent, the chartered jets kept waiting at a thousand dollars an hour until a crew was ready to fly off to a distant location for a breaking story, the luxury suites in foreign hotels for reporters and producers long accustomed to CBC's less than lavish travel guidelines, the stories thrown away, unfinished.

By late spring of 1982 after less than six months on the air, *The Journal* announced that despite its promise to be the ongoing ever-present magazine of current affairs for the whole of Canada, it was closing down for the summer. It had been such a demanding first season, they said, that the staff was exhausted and needed the summer to rest.

Cameron Graham and I conferred by phone and agreed that it was a disgrace to take the program off the air for the summer: *we* were not exhausted; we would put together a skeleton staff with Brian Nolan and Ted Remerowski and a few freelancers, I would host it for the minimal scale fee, we would keep *The Journal* on the air.

We took the proposal to Don McDonald, the acting head of News and Current Affairs. "You guys are heroes," he said. "That's so generous. That's brilliant. I'll take it to the network."

When he called back it was to sheepishly admit that he did not know how he could have been so naive. The summer cancellation had nothing to do with the press release. It was not the staff that was exhausted, it was the budget. The network had been forced to dip into reserves to keep the thing going, even into the spring, and would now have to give the summer evenings over to American movies, which could be had cheap and would sell advertising to help make up the shortfall.[8]

By late in 1982 it became public knowledge that CBS Cable was being shut down by the money men at Black Rock. I got a call from John Goberman, a former symphony cellist equipped with bad puns and a fine production sense, who was executive producer for the PBS series *Live From Lincoln Center*: could he come to Toronto to chat? He had been watching me on CBS Cable and now that it was winding down he wanted to discuss my hosting the Lincoln Centre series.

8. A tradition nobly continued by our former public television network, which now fills its prime-time Sunday night slot with American movies that you would have to pay a couple of bucks to rent at the corner store. That is about what the CBC pays for them, and as of early 2004 a few advertisers were still willing to buy space in them even though viewers were becoming less and less willing to put up with the interruptions.

We hit it off well, and within weeks Goberman had arranged for the extension of my H-1 visa. There began what would turn out to be a delightful assignment, seven years of it. It took me to New York for two or three days every six weeks or so, to walk out on the stage of Avery Fisher Hall, with Zubin Mehta, Kathleen Battle, Marilyn Horne, Schlomo Mintz, Luciano Pavarotti, Christoph von Dohnányi, Pinchas Zuckerman, the musicians of the New York Philharmonic – dozens of superb guest performers. Watching the NYPO's principal flautist Paula Robison was like watching a ballet dancer, as her tall body and humorously arched eyebrows echoed the intricacies of the music. Backed up by the extraordinary Lincoln Center and Metropolitan Opera stage crews, and technical and production people from my old *Fifty-First State* home, Channel 13, I was getting a regular hit of one of the things I love best in television, something now very rare, a genuinely live broadcast with all its risks and rewards.

Some of the artists were impossible. The soprano Beverly Sills had become head of the New York Opera Theater, and when John Goberman proposed I interview her during a production of the Corsaro production of *Carmen*, my journal quotes her as responding that "I will not be *interviewed* in a program from my own theatre. This is *my* theatre." But her behaviour was unusual. Most of the celebrated artists were gracious and focused, and some, like Luciano Pavarotti and Marilyn Horne, were simply great company and great partners in a conversation, on or off camera.

The budget included travel and accommodation for Caroline, nominally as my keeper and wardrobe supervisor. Caroline had lived in Manhattan in the '60s, and we had developed our familiar paths and watering holes, I showing off to her those I had discovered during *The Fifty-First State*, and she to me from her teenage days there (which had included a year taking the bus over to New Jersey five days a week to teach English in a private Catholic school when she was eighteen). What amounted to a couple of days a month did not justify an apartment, so we arranged to leave some basic gear with the concierge at the Mayflower Hotel on Central Park West near Lincoln Center.

Once, early on, Caroline was in Paris when a Lincoln Center date came up, and was unable to come with me. It was a relatively undemanding show – a symphony concert with no special guest stars. So off I went, alone into Manhattan in time for an afternoon of rehearsal and blocking, and back to the hotel for a rest and a snack around five in the afternoon.

I had a quick nap at the Mayflower and started to dress around seven. Then I discovered that I had not brought my dress shoes; all I had were the white sneakers that had become my habit for the preceding few years. It was too late to go out shopping for shoes – I had no idea where to look, Goberman and Kirk Browning, the director, would be out to supper so I couldn't consult. I thought, Well, they never shoot me below the waist anyway: it'll look odd but what the hell.

And so in an elegant tux (left over from the CBS Cable days) and bright white sneakers – new, fortunately – I walked along 62nd Street, crossed Broadway at the islands and by the wide staircase and the fountain outside the entrance to the Met, and around and into the back door near where the Channel 13 mobile unit was parked.

The stage manager frowned at the sneakers, but then shrugged and said he guessed that the cameras wouldn't see them. I walked through my positions with the cameras, and then stood by the head of the stairs waiting for the conductor, Zubin Mehta, to come down for the last few pointers (I would be interviewing him at the interval), and then curtain time.

At about six minutes to eight, the elevator door opened and Zubin Mehta came out, sweeping his eyes around the backstage area as he habitually did, and characteristically grinning with anticipation. He nodded genially at me and started across for our pre-show quick exchange. The bright white evidently caught his eyes; I saw his glance drop to the floor. Then back up to me, the grin broadening. A moment's pause, and then he said, "Patrick, that is class." That was the beginning of my affecting white sneakers with evening dress, an affectation I still enjoy.

New York felt more and more homey, with Lincoln Center and the Mayflower as the home bases. We had acquired a pair of Wang computers. John Goberman had Wang computers in his office, too; if I felt like writing I could borrow one and take my work home on a diskette (five and a quarter inches). The old acquaintances from the *Fifty-First State* days were often around for a drink after work, or a dinner. One day I got a call from Russ Thomas, who had given me jazz guitar lessons in Ottawa in the early sixties when I found the classical guitar a beautifully distracting therapy for the dolorous after-effects of the amputation. He was now playing in the Dizzy Gillespie band, had become a Black Muslim, and changed his name to Sayyd Abdul al Khabyyr. We had an affectionate reunion. Evenings in the bar at the Mayflower would bring ad lib encounters with film actors and television folk, and the talk often went on most of the night. One morning at breakfast there I saw Leonard Cohen at a table across the room. He waved, came over to my table, and proposed lunch. "Very important lunch," he said mysteriously.

When I got back to the hotel around 1 p.m. with Caroline, he was there with a lovely blond woman in her early thirties, and a bottle of Dom Perignon was cooling in a bucket by the table. "This is my agent," he told us. "She has just achieved something extraordinary. Fourteen years ago my rights to 'Suzanne' were cheated out of me by a brilliant scoundrel here in New York. Today we got them back. Cheers."

But delightful as the Lincoln Center assignment was, it did not *engage* me as much as a good documentary, or acting in *The Book of Job* was about to do. The interviews at Lincoln Center, rewarding as they were in many ways, had to serve two or perhaps three "clients": the audience, the interviewee, and Lincoln Center. If Beverly Sills behaved in a self-important manner, I couldn't call her on it. I couldn't really challenge people. Instead of serving the audience as the prime and perhaps the only constituency, I had to be careful about the artists, careful about the enterprise, careful to protect Lincoln Center. That divided my attention, and I think attenuated the results. The associations with the artists and exploring the life of the Center and of Manhattan and the arts community – all those were charming; but the intrinsic values were thin compared to journalistic or documentary interviews.

Back in Toronto, we moved first into a third-floor apartment right in the centre of town, not far from Bloor and Yonge, and then to a house almost directly opposite, on the same street.

Caroline, a Dubliner who had lived in London, New York, Boston, Houston, and Paris, and had at first been somewhat condescending about my native city, now began to say nice things about Toronto, that perhaps it was a real city after all. I accepted an appointment to the board of trustees of the National Film Board.

There was a lot going on at the Board in those years. The recent Applebaum–Hébert report on the cultural agencies had recommended turning it into a non-producing academy, the old production staff were close to paranoia, and the Board was fighting back effectively. A bill had been drafted to change it from a sub-department of government into a Crown corporation with the same kind of independence as the CBC. The women's studio, Studio D, declared that it wanted to separate from the rest of the institution. Commissioner François Macerola told them, "Go ahead, fine. And as soon as you do I'll create another Studio D."

Macerola was working against a lot of resistance. He was presumed to have been appointed as a hatchet man, he was Italian, he was tough, he had done the unheard of and fired people for incompetence.

There was a lot of controversy – and I was very much in the middle of it – about films by Paul Cowan, Donald Brittain, and others in which dramatic simulation and other devices were used in a way that led the audience to believe they were seeing a documentary film of real events. It was a lively time.

In March or April of '83 Michael Levine proposed me for a

cameo appearance in *Terry Fox: The Movie.* I played a feather-encrusted eccentric old chicken farmer with a peg leg, who cheers Terry on in his run. The production had the peg leg custom-made for me, a real Long John Silver kind of peg with no knee, just a short hardwood stick with a rubber tip. It was surprisingly easy to walk on, although just putting on the leg was a bit tetchy since the day of the shoot was less than a week after I had come out of surgery to repair two inguinal hernias. Robert Duvall, the one major star in the production, was a courteous and good-humoured fellow actor.

Caroline and I re-opened the geodesic dome at Go Home Lake that spring. We had scarcely seen the place over the previous few years. I took the peg leg there thinking – wrongly, as it turned out – that it might be easier than my regular prosthesis for walking over the uneven rocky land around the dome. Caroline's M.D. brother, Russell, came for a visit and brought a rented windsurfing rig. He suggested I try it. I said I had enough difficulty standing up on solid ground and that the movement of the board would inevitably cause the knee of my prosthesis to buckle. "Try the peg leg," Russell said. I did. It worked. We became almost compulsive about board sailing, graduating to a pair of fairly sophisticated boards and cruising together all over the upper part of the lake. When I finally managed to get the sailboard up on the plane, the peg leg planted firmly against the mast step and the right leg bent deeply, hanging away out on the boom and flying down the spume of the singing waves, it felt like being at one with the universe. Once in November as we were sailing in tandem toward the falls, not a soul on the lake but us, a bald eagle hove into sight and flew over our heads at less than a hundred feet. There were days of pure enchantment on those boards.

I began painting, watercolours and acrylics, and drawing, portraits mostly, in pencil and charcoal.

Joe MacInnis asked me to work on his film about the discovery of a ship that was wrecked while searching for the remains of the Franklin expedition. I agreed to write the film for him, working with the brilliant editor Bill Mason. Mason and I came up with the title *The Land That Devours Ships.* Joe MacInnis is not only an underwater explorer but also an M.D. who specializes in underwater medicine. He got Caroline and me interested in diving, and before long we were heading off whenever we could to Dick Birch's homey Small Hope Bay Lodge on Andros Island in the Bahamas, where we progressed from neophytes to certified divers and then into some extraordinary cave diving, in one case to three hundred feet, along the then unspoiled reef that made Small Hope Bay a mecca for divers.

Something started me thinking about *The Book of Job* again. I chatted about it over drinks with Nicole Belanger, Peter Gzowski's producer, and she suggested that to try out its viability with a popular audience I should work up five ten-minute segments and read them on *Morningside* during Holy Week. That went quite well. Producer John McGreevy phoned and invited me to lunch. "Let's do it on the stage," he said. "As a one-man show."

He introduced me to John Wyre, the percussionist founder of the group Nexus, suggesting that Wyre could provide a musical and sometimes almost sound-effects-like and contrapuntal accompaniment that would enrich the acoustical texture of the one-man show. Wyre worked inside an eight-foot-square cage hung with gourds, cymbals, bottles, and other unconventional percussive instruments. We set him stage left. I worked largely from a throne-sized chair upstage. Stage right on a lectern there was an enormous family Bible with gilt-edged pages – a sometime birthday gift from my daughter, Boo. We decided to tease the audience at the opening by letting them think for a minute or two that I was going to read the whole thing, rather than perform.

The text of my play was taken verbatim from the King James Version, edited down to eighty-five minutes from the approximately four hours it would have taken to do the whole book. I devised individual voices for Job and his wife, for Satan and God, indeed for all the characters (nine in all, plus the narrator). But I opened downstage in my own persona, laying in the background of the story. Job, if he existed, is said by some scholars to have been a substantial Jordanian sheikh in the second millennium BCE. I suggested that it might have been a story told in a big striped tent, cushions down front for the children, rush lights in sconces around the edge, the women veiled, that the audience should imagine themselves in that tent, the major-domo calling for the children to be seated and the rush lights to be lit, and then calling out, "Let the storyteller begin."

Then I would move stage right, to the Bible, and read the first five verses, establishing Job's substance and character, "perfect and upright, and one that feared god and eschewed evil." Now having found God at his throne with his sons around him, as I came to the line "And Satan came also among them" (with a soft, sinister rattlesnake sound from John Wyre's cage), I moved rapidly downstage and began to play with my characters.

McGreevy had put us into the Nathan Cohen Studio Theatre, part of the Young People's Theatre complex on Front Street, and before that run was out in December, we had an invitation to bring the production to the Studio Theatre in the National Arts Centre in Ottawa, where we played ten performances, most of them sold out.

I had done much of my line-learning deep in the woods at Go Home Lake, well away from the neighbours, finding that shouting the lines helped me to remember them, and in the process discovering that there is an astonishing amount of dramatic humour in the Book of Job. The three dreadful comforters, I realized, could be played at a level of absurdity that would leaven with laughter the tough moral and spiritual investigation that is the core of Job's dramatic odyssey. But when we opened in the Nathan Cohen Theatre, nobody laughed. I was playing broadly, but not extravagantly so. I said to McGreevy after the second performance, a matinee, "Why aren't they laughing? I can feel them on the edge of laughter, but they're holding back."

McGreevy pondered and came back to my dressing room when I was changing for the evening performance, with a triumphant gleam in his eye and a characteristically wicked grin.

"I know why they aren't laughing," he said. "They think they're in church. One doesn't laugh in church. You have to give them permission to laugh."

What a penetrating directorial insight, I thought. And when I went downstage that night in my own persona to tell them about the historical background, I ended the backgrounder by saying that C.G. Jung's *An Answer to Job,* his last book and his favourite, had been an important guide in my development of the play. I said that the most extraordinary thing that Jung said about Job was this: The reason for the Crucifixion was not that God had decided to come down to earth and suffer for the sins of man, as is commonly said. The truth, Jung said, was that it was God's way of saying to mankind, "I'm really sorry for what I did to Job."

After a beat they got it; the laughter was released at last. So that when I brought on the comforters (I had a different voice and body language for each), they could laugh at those absurd figures too.

McGreevy had warned me that I might dry, and we had marked key points in the big Bible, to which I could stride dramatically if I had to, as if planned. I never had to. But after four or five performances at the Nathan Cohen, with no hint of even hesitation, McGreevy came in and played a director's game with me by suggesting something about how it's always on the fifth performance that the actor dries. It has to happen once. It's inevitable . . . etc.

Sure enough, that night there came a point where I had Job sink into his seat in despair, his head hanging down for a few seconds as he tried to summon strength to go on. I realized, as my head slumped, that I had no idea what the next line was. I would have to cross stage right to the damn Bible. I took a few breaths, then looked up at the audience, about to make both facial and hand signals that would seem to meaningfully propel me toward the big gold-edged pages. The moment I met the eyes of a woman in the front row, frowning at me in perplexity, as I had been silent a touch too long, that very moment the line came to me: it was "I know your thoughts," spoken in the tone in which we would accusingly say in ordinary conversation today, "I know what you're thinking."

It was a frightening experience every night, but nourishing as well. After every performance, people found their way to the dressing room to talk about that great issue that has been written about in Melvin Tinker's book *Why Bad Things Happen to Good People.* I discovered that Job's repentance in the end is less a matter of his submission to this cruel, self-centred and irrational Jehovah, than of his realization – before the mighty poetry of God's last great rhapsody about creation – that the beauty of the created world is so unfathomably mysterious that it is beyond the capacity of mortals to question or challenge the Creator. I don't think you can make that discovery by scholarly study of the Book of Job: you have to speak it, or hear it spoken, dramatically and loud. It is one of the most powerful poems in any language. But when it was all over, I said to myself that I thought I would never again have the resources to do anything that demanded so much daily courage.[9]

We talked about taking it on the road, to play it in churches and town halls all across the country and invite audiences to engage with the Bad-Things-to-Good-People issues after the performance. But a number of other projects materialized, projects that were too compelling to turn down. In fact *The Book of Job* was over. Neither Caroline nor I had the faintest premonition of how overwhelming the next few years would be.

9. There comes the odd day when I feel differently, that it would be very fine to go on stage with a fine director like our friend Diana Leblanc, and work it up again, and for God's sake at least make a video this time, our failure to do so twenty years ago being one of those great puzzles.

Chapter 18

THE CHALLENGE

SOMETIME EARLY IN 1985, Daniel Bertolino came up from Montreal and outlined a substantial bilingual television project on the rich and the poor around the planet, which he called *Le Défi Mondial: The World Challenge.* It was based on a book by Jean-Jacques Servan-Schreiber, and was to be produced in both French and English. Servan-Schreiber would appear in it and would be present as a consultant in the studio. Peter Ustinov had agreed to host it and had accepted the producers' proposal for a co-host for the English-language version, a way of securing funding from Telefilm Canada. Would I be that person? And would Caroline act as a kind of performance critic in the studio, to assure the francophone producers that the hosts' English-language delivery was satisfactory? We were both to be involved in the scripts, Caroline doing much of the translation from the original French drafts, and I writing most of my own copy. Although we were troubled by the polemical quality of the Servan-Schreiber argument, we managed to inject some historical and journalistic balance, and went cheerfully off to Montreal.

Ustinov was slightly hostile to Caroline in this role until the first day's recording when she asked him to look at the playback of a section that she was, she told him, pretty sure he would want to re-do. He was a bit huffy until he screened it. Then when he realized that she had saved him from looking very bad, his characteristic generous good humour returned and they became friends. We all did. It was enchanting to sit there with him at the cast table between takes and watch him drawing caricatures of the technicians, captioned cartoon jokes on events in the news, landscapes, imagined faces, intriguing abstracts. The captions were almost always puns, often multilingual, usually playing on the French title of the series, *Le Défi Mondial.* One depicted him, me, and producer Daniel Bertolino as a trio of plump, aging, Lautreckian whores. The caption: *Défi de Joie.* Another showed him and me, aged, trembling, cobwebbed, under a clapper board that announced "Program No. 3,567."

He was legendary for his storytelling. Many were about other actors and movie adventures around the world, but the best were just ordinary things that had happened to him in the previous few days or hours. Every day brought jokes, each one a polished miniature, often of the kind that take a second or two to connect: "When I was in Moscow last month a senior bureaucrat said, 'We don't like to boast, but here in the Soviet Union we have built the biggest microchip in the world.'"

That studio on Crescent Street was illuminated with laughter. Bertolino and his partner, Catherine Viau, treated us royally. The place was supplied with superb coffee and the best croissants ever.

The series also drew on some of our journalistic and other contacts. I telephoned Washington and renewed my acquaintance with President Kennedy's Defence Secretary Robert McNamara – who had played himself in *Countdown to Looking Glass* – and got to him to agree to an interview for *The World Challenge.*[1] I invited Pierre Trudeau to have lunch with Ustinov and me, and asked him if he could eat in a Montreal restaurant without being harassed. He said, "I imagine you and Ustinov get hassled more than I do, but if you go to a high-class joint like the Ritz they leave you pretty well alone." We went to the Ritz, and Ustinov kept Trudeau laughing through much

1. He was very frank, pronounced America's rejection of Cuba a mistake, the nuclear arms policy "insane," the U.S. popular reluctance to share the wealth "a disgrace." He had already, in *Looking Glass*, been equally frank in admitting how wrong his policy had been on Vietnam. In the wake of 9/11 he published a book attacking the Bush policy in Iraq and the growing U.S. imperialism.

of the meal. He also told us about how as he sat waiting to interview Indira Gandhi he heard the fusillade that killed her, and on the spot dictated a short essay into his tape recorder. Later a security officer who had overheard Ustinov announced that he must confiscate the tape, and said roughly, "Is it necessary to say that six minutes elapsed between the first burst of gunfire and the second?"

"I said it is, because it is the truth. A lot of people will forget exactly what happened. In any case even if you take my tape, if I am called on the stand I would have to tell the truth, and I will be talking to many people in the meantime. You cannot control what I will say to them, so why bother to censor my little tape?" He was allowed to keep the tape.

The nicest moment in the lunch came when he told Trudeau about the world's biggest microchip. Pierre looked baffled for a couple of seconds, and then his face was transfigured from the usual watchful, almost sinister mask into a helplessly laughing adolescent. As we drove away from the Ritz in a taxi, Pierre having chosen to walk back to his office, our young Lebanese cabbie said, "That was Mr. Trudeau, no?"

I said, "Or perhaps someone who looks very much like him."

The driver squinted through the side window and said, "Ye-e-e-ss. Looks *very* much like him. But of course Mr. Trudeau is much taller."

Back in Toronto between *Défi Mondial* sessions, Caroline and I were learning our way into those new Wang computers, chosen because Wang's word processing system was then the only one that offered a bilingual capacity. It cost us more than $10,000 to get set up with two computers and two dot matrix printers. The computers had no hard drive but had to be fired up with a succession of five-and-a-half-inch floppies, which you had to change each time you got into an advanced aspect of word processing. The onboard RAM was 128k. I learned to program, rudimentarily, in BASIC, and went online with THE SOURCE, a primitive e-mail online database and chat service, fairly expensive, based in Virginia, played games, chatted online with strangers on the other side of the world, and thought myself a very advanced technocrat indeed. I was soon spending an absurd amount of time learning how to do what was rudimentary and not very useful programming:

```
10 FOR X – 1 TO 1/25.6E + 32
20 PRINT X, X+1, X+2, X+3, X+4
30 NEXT X
etcetera.
```

For a while that sort of stuff became something of an obsession, and I took extraordinary satisfaction in being able to write a BASIC program that would calculate the cumulative value of a savings program over *n* years at so much deposited per year and a stated rate of interest. Another program that I crowed over like an adolescent was a game that calculated how thick a pile of paper would become after any number of folds the player chose to (theoretically) make. After something like twenty folds the program tells you that your pile of paper now reaches out to the orbit of Saturn. I still have it written out proudly in a diary, even though none of my present-day computers has BASIC installed in it any more. Probably just as well. As much fun as that primitive programming was, it seriously invaded my sleep; all night long I would be writing in my head,

```
9 INPUT "HOW MANY FOLDS WOULD YOU LIKE?"
10 FOR F = 1 TO N
20 T = 2^ F
30 PRINT "NO. OF FOLDS"; F, "NO. OF THICKNESSES"; T
```

It just wouldn't let me alone. This went on for months.

I excused myself to my journals saying that this training was helping me debug the Wangs when they crashed. Twenty years have not completely cured me of this malady and the misapprehensions that generate it.

Cultural notes:

We had bought our first VCRs early in 1983, one Betamax and

one VHS, but were still using a big three-quarter-inch Sony Umatic deck to play work in progress. The Betamax home system became obsolete within the year, but Sony's Beta cameras were moving in on film as the preferred professional production tool. VHS home video was burgeoning. By the summer of 1985, even the tiny community of about two hundred cottages served by the Minor's Bay Marina at Go Home Lake was keeping the marina's new video rental shop hopping. Another cultural note: the original Rubik's cube that had mesmerized me four years earlier had been superceded by the four-frequency cube (sixteen squares to a face instead of the original nine), and during a Christmas visit to the Markles I found myself unable to wholeheartedly join the party until I had solved it too.[2]

University of Toronto professor Franklin Griffiths came over one afternoon with a young friend named John Lamb, who had developed a proposal for what would become the Canadian Centre for Arms Control and Disarmament. They were assembling a board of directors and asked me to join. Conrad Black would be on the advisory council, Edmonton oilman Bob Blair would be on the board, they felt it possible to have an effect on Canadian policy, and thus hopefully on what then seemed to be the very gloomy global scene, President Ronald Reagan having announced that he would put billions into his absurd and unworkable missile defence system nicknamed "Star Wars." I remember my disbelief when one of the Arms Control Centre directors, Gary Smith, predicted that Reagan might go down in history as having signed the arms control agreement of the century.

We were soon going to have to get serious with our documentary project about democracy, or else find another project substantial enough to pay the rent. *Le Défi Mondial* had been an enchanting interlude.

But there would be one more interesting project before *Democracy* took over our lives. During the CBS Cable time, the newly

2. About two years later these enchanting puzzles, which had been on every street vendor's cart, in every convenience store, were forgotten, gone, invisible, and I had forgotten the solutions.

appointed CBC president, Pierre Juneau, had come to New York to consult with me about personnel choices and policy issues. Now he called to know if I would be interested in putting together a new proposal for a second CBC television channel, two earlier proposals having been turned down by the CRTC. My old pal John Kennedy was assistant program director for the network by then, and over a few beers we plotted out what kind of a second service might be practicable, of service to the country, and achievable with the $5 million that Pierre Juneau had said was all he could muster at the start. Juneau agreed to have Kennedy seconded to work on the project.

CBC owned the licence for the parliamentary channel. The parliamentary channel went dark on Friday night when the House rose, and stayed dark until Monday. We designed and wrote the first year's schedule for a service called CBC Weekend, a mixture of arts and programming, no news, perhaps a small documentary component, mostly repeats but a modest amount of original arts programming. The CBS Cable experience was an influence, of course. I told Pierre Juneau that I would not ask to be paid, but only the assurance that if the proposal were approved then I would be given first refusal as operating head. We finished the plan two days short of our three-month commitment, and John Kennedy and I made an oral presentation in the War Room at head office. Juneau made a gesture with his hands, rubbing his fingers together. "It is so clear!" he said. "So palpable! I can feel it." He asked me to come to the next board meeting to pitch it. I did. My presentation, purely oral (no insulting PowerPoint,[3] no documents, just a talk), won me a standing ovation.

Juneau said, "I'll call you in a week. I think you may be right that we don't even have to go to the CRTC. We'll just do it."

The call never came.

Well, a call did come, but not from Juneau himself, and not for weeks. Whoever it was said, Look, there was going to be an election in the fall (1984); there might be a new party in power. It would not

3. For more on PowerPoint as a communications obscenity, see Edward Tufte's book, *The Cognitive Style of PowerPoint* (it's only about 40 pages).

be prudent to launch such a radical new project before the election. In vain I protested that the opposite was true.

September 1984 brought Brian Mulroney to power with the biggest electoral majority Canada has ever seen. There was no way that Mulroney was going to agree to *any* expansion of the CBC's ambit, however modest, CRTC or no CRTC. CBC Weekend was dead.

However, even before we knew it was dead, I got a call from Bob Foulkes at Petro-Canada in Edmonton. They wanted to start a new series of commercials, long on useful information and short on the Big Sell, and would I consider being their on-camera guy, and become a national spokesman for the corporation. Foulkes, who was V.P. communications at the time, is a thoughtful and strategically minded guy, and when I explained that as a journalist I could not compromise my visible independence by selling gasoline, he was not offended but invited me to lunch to discuss "a whole bunch of ideas."

Foulkes and I and two of his creative staff met in the old dining room at the King Edward Hotel and kicked ideas around, and out of that discussion there bloomed the idea of Petro-Canada's sponsoring a Sunday night series of family entertainments, and would I write up some proposals for such a series? I have written in Chapter 6 how Ross McLean and I worked together hammering out proposals for everything from sophisticated dramas to a Canadian version of the Ed Sullivan show. Just before the oral presentation in Ottawa, I decided to fold into the presentation a one-pager on what Caroline and I were now calling *The Democracy Project.*

Michael Levine came to that meeting in Ottawa, in case it might lead to anything practical. The proposal I thought they would like was the elaborate, hosted variety show modelled on Ed Sullivan, and Ross thought they'd like the Canadian theatre-based drama series. As Ross and I took turns reading, we were gratified by the beaming smiles from the advertising and PR staff members. Petro-Can Chairman Bill Hopper was attentive and asked the occasional pointed question, but did not seem much engaged.

Somewhere around proposal number 17 or 18, I brought out the page on *Democracy*. I could see the advertising staff's genial expressions darken and a few heads begin to shake. When I finished, Foulkes said, Well, that was very interesting but it did not exactly meet the call, of course, could we move on please? But Bill Hopper rapped on the table where he sat on the other side of the boardroom. He said, "Hold on a minute. How much would that democracy thing cost?"

I said I thought it could be done elegantly for about $5 million. "Hell," Bill Hopper said. "I can get that without even going to my board. I like that idea. Let's hear the rest of them, but so far that is the one that I like."

The ad men were suddenly smiling again. Within a few days, back in Toronto, Michael Levine was organizing the tactical talks to set the project in motion. It happened that fast.

At the first of those meetings, the senior person there – not Bob Foulkes – said that of course all the outlines, treatments, preliminary scripts, and shooting scripts, as well as the early edits and fine cuts, would be sent to his office for approval. As I was glowering and gathering myself for what would possibly have been a response sufficiently shirty to scupper the whole enterprise, I fortunately glanced in the direction of Michael Levine. With what I have come to recognize as a characteristically tiny ironic smile, he signalled me to cool it, and said, with great dignity and firmness, that they had better reconsider this, ahmm, request, because they would have to understand that a documentary series conceived and signed by Patrick Watson, one of the country's most distinguished and etceteras, would not have credibility with an audience who knew that it had been submitted for approval to an advertiser, that the CBC would never broadcast it under those circumstances, that the whole concept depended on the absolute independence and integrity of both the producer and the broadcaster, and that he was sure that when they spoke to Mr. Foulkes they would find him in agreement.

That meeting broke up on a sour note, but within two days a twinkling Michael Levine was on the other end of the telephone saying that, yes, he had spoken both with Mr. Foulkes and with Mr. Hopper, and that we were going ahead, and wasn't it a good thing that I hadn't blown my top in the meeting with the ad men?

One day in the spring of 1984 when I picked up my mail and opened the *Atlantic Monthly*, an article leapt out like a starter's pistol. It was a condensation of *Strong Democracy*, a new book by Rutgers University political philosopher Benjamin Barber. His message was that you can't really *define* democracy, you have to live it. Yes, it is about the governed choosing who is to govern them, and about power above all, but it is not just about elections and politicians and congresses and parliaments. Just read de Tocqueville: he found the real power of democracy not in the Congress or the Executive or the judiciary, crucial as those devices were, but in the way in which local citizens, free under the constitution to assemble as they wish and to speak and to publish, could get together in their own small communities to determine how they were going to live their lives.

Barber wrote intriguingly about the vital nature of public space – what an idea, *public space*! No real democracy without it, he declared. I had to know more about this. Freedom, he said, consists first of an inner spirit capable of a range of investigation from passionate flight to profound calm, *whose instrument is a vigorous imagination.*

I raced out and bought the book.

It is a difficult book, *Strong Democracy*. The *Atlantic Monthly* condensation had been a colloquial, breezy read, but the book was intended to make academics take its author seriously, and Ben Barber would later confess that he probably should have forgotten the academics he was trying to impress, and gone for the same broad international popular readership that propelled his later *Jihad vs. McWorld* into twenty-two translations and world sales of a million copies.[4]

But for all its academic jargon, it was worth the slogging, full of ideas, an almost spiritually driven celebration of this brilliant writer's

4. His newest book, *Fear's Empire*, has been printed in eight foreign editions, and *Strong Democracy* re-issued in a "Twentieth Anniversary" edition.

conviction (one he shared with Benjamin Franklin and de Tocqueville, among others) that in the long run the mass of citizens will make better decisions than will any rulers set over them without the sanctions and accountability that democracy entails. But this would work only when that public space is protected, and will work better when public space is increased.

I had to talk to this guy. Maybe he would agree to join the team as our academic adviser. I called him and set out for New York on September 10, 1984. On the plane I read the comic strip *Shoe* in that day's *Toronto Star*. Shoe said, "It's hard to be an individual all by yourself." That's a democratic insight, I thought. Without community, there is no language. Without language, the imagination cannot flourish. Without imagination, there is no liberty. Without liberty, there is no democracy. Nearly every idea I came across now had to be wrestled into some kind of relationship to democracy.

Ben Barber and I met at the Mayflower and walked across Columbus Circle for lunch at Alfredo's. A bigger man than I had guessed, stocky, forty-five, big sleepy eyes but nothing sleepy in the brain. Garrulous, expansive, humorous, a great talker, and an attentive listener. I went back to the hotel after lunch and wrote extensively in my diary, quoting him at length. We had dived right into issues. I assumed that he would be a great enthusiast for the role of citizens' groups. "Well," he said, "yes, I mean partly. You see, the trouble is that once they've been heard they are likely to return to not caring, and I fear they contribute to the separation of private and public."

On the popular appetite for capital punishment: "I'd rather have a functioning participatory democracy in which the citizens are sometimes wrong than a rule by elites who are sometimes in advance of the public. Elites are sometimes wrong too, you know. In this case I believe that people will declare a prejudice more vehemently than they will approach the formulation of public policy in which they have a stake and over which they have real control. That may be idealistic, of course. But if I didn't believe in the general tendency of an informed and deliberating public to arrive at better decisions in the long run than elites would, then I wouldn't believe in democracy. If democracy means the enactment of popular prejudice then I don't want it. I'd prefer representative elites."

The long run was important, he said. You can scold democracies for their short-term failures, but the only valid criticism is that which looks at decades or half-centuries or more, and compares that history with totalitarian states over the same time.

He said, "The best democratic leadership leads and then disappears, having . . . *facilitated* . . . you know, that's the word I prefer. Having helped the people in the task of governing themselves. The great charismatic leaders are dangerous because their charisma covers their dirty tricks. Or allows the people to forgive them. Like JFK.

"And then when he is taken from them, the people feel impaired. In fact they are impaired while he is there because they trust him too much. They let him take too much from them. The best democratic leaders are going to lead the people to need him less, not more."

Heady stuff. I said, "Isn't it asking a lot of citizens to give up the symbolic power of a leader they love?"

He said, "I say democracy is asking a lot of citizens."

I knew we were started. Three weeks later I was back in New York, huddled with Ben in his apartment on West 96th Street, drafting the first outlines.

Cultural note. In October 1984, Ben Barber told me that the CIA had started this great thing in the universities called the Internet. I'd never heard of it. Way better than your commercial e-mail services, he said. Worldwide. Great mail tool. Great research tool. It was available only to university faculty, but he would try to get me on it. He did not succeed. But the engine was running.

In the meantime the CBC had approached Michael Levine about something else. They were about to launch a new weekly half-hour television series devoted to business, primarily small business. It would be called *Venture*, and it was considered a difficult challenge to engage an audience with this kind of programming. Would he approach me about hosting it, at least for the first year, to help get it started? *The Watson Report* was recent enough to be well remembered by CBC viewers, and there had been enough press on my New York adventures to keep my name in the public eye. The new Current Affairs chief, Bill Morgan, said my helping to launch *Venture* would get it off to a good start. Michael Levine told Morgan, Fine, Watson does that for a year, and you commit to partnering on *The Struggle for Democracy*. Morgan has agreed to this, Michael told me; I'd better go and see him.

Well, he had a gift for the blandishments, Bill Morgan did, and a sly irony and humour. And he said, "Nobody else in Canada has your storytelling skills, both writing and on camera. If you launch *Venture* it will be on the road map within a month. Without you it'll take us a year."

I'm not good at standing up to this kind of stuff. But at least I had the sense to tell him I'd think about it. I had to consult Caroline. I still didn't want the distraction. But Caroline saw the tactical advantage. She said, Look, I had said I could stay on the Film Board, it would mean contacts and maybe some production help. Maybe I could fit *Venture* into the plan, and if it would firmly bring the CBC in on *Democracy* . . . ?

We set up another meeting, with Bill Morgan and Denis Harvey, the head of English Television. Michael said he was now confident that the *Democracy* budget would come in at half a million an episode, we needed only a third of that from the CBC, and a good part of their investment could be in staff and services. So they would get a five-million-dollar series for less than a million and make good use of staff they would have to pay anyway. Denny Harvey nodded for a minute and then said, unequivocally, "If Watson does *Venture*, we're in."

On November 20, my journal notes, Levine and I had "dinner at Panache, plotted Britain, signed the *Venture* contract."

Under the leadership of an enthusiast named Duncan McEwan, the *Venture* staff started assembling material in the fall of 1984, and on the eleventh of December I went in to meet them and get started. That same day Pierre Juneau announced the early retirement or layoffs of nearly 1,700 people.[5] There were rumours that he would be visiting Toronto soon to explain to staff just how dire the CBC's position was, and invite people to join forces with what he believed was a broad public base for a Save the CBC movement. I doubt very much that there was such a public base, even that long ago, Juneau already having increased the amount of advertising on television to the point where viewers were having a hard time knowing they were watching a public broadcaster. But even if there were, I noted in my journal, the corporation itself was so rancorously divided within that it would have proven impossible to work with such a movement in a united way.

The *Venture* people were experiencing the mixed feelings of survivors. One of the two senior story editors was a bright and funny journalist named Margaret Wente, for whom I did interviews on a number of very satisfying assignments. "She of the secret smile," I wrote in my journal, "the best story sense of anyone on the show." Stories were already in development, a dry run was planned for the following week, and I was soon writing copy, recording narrations, and sitting in on editing sessions. "McEwan's editorial judgment is not bad," I told my journal, adding "No. Very good."

By the first of December Michael Levine had recast the *Democracy* budget at $700,000 an episode, which is close to what the actuals were when it was all over. Roy Faibish announced that he and his executive assistant, Barbara Calvert, would marry in London on December 8, so we went over via Dublin for a few days' family visits, and took the opportunity to chat up the management of Radio Telefis Eirann. They were enthusiastic but not rich, offered some crew and facilities for any shooting we might do in Ireland, but no money. Their head of programming asked why we were going to the private sector for a British partner, instead of the BBC. I said that it was because of a long experience of not being able to sell the BBC anything, and of their lofty condescension. He smiled a slow smile and

5. In my diary for that day I noted, "I believe it is the best disaster the CBC ever had," having been struck over the previous year or two by the numbers of people sitting around doing nothing, but "It will be a killer," my diary note adds, "for some of the management people who have to carry it out."

said, "We've been there." In London we opened talks with Central Independentl Television and tried to set up a meeting with their top man, Richard Creasey, whose decision would be crucial.

Back in Canada Cameron Graham's series *Lawyers* was still in production. Ted Remerowski had proposed covering a murder trial, and Cam and I had gone to see the Chief Justice of Ontario, the Hon. William Howland, to see if he would recognize a provision in the law that allows cameras into a trial for educational purposes. Mr. Justice Howland not only agreed to permit our filming, but helped us select the murder trial of Linda Clow, where he found a combination of legal niceties, a small city setting (Kingston), and a presiding judge who could be counted on to collaborate. The documentary finished up strong enough to persuade Current Affairs head Bill Morgan to give it two hours of broadcast time.

Clow was convicted of second-degree murder. There were a few months of anxiety when the Chief Justice told us that he might have to forbid the broadcast because of complications arising from Clow's appeal. But in the end he telephoned to tell me that he was "very pleased" with the way it turned out.

Ted Remerowski said he felt that a key witness who was manifestly psychotic and paranoid should not have been admitted, and that Clow herself and the interests of justice would have been better served had she taken a plea for manslaughter, and served six or seven years in a medium-security institution, instead of the ten years minimum she would do in maximum security, likely to come out sexually abused, addicted, and well equipped to pick up a life of crime. Our discussions over this project cemented my conviction that Ted would bring a great deal of insight and production elegance to *The Struggle for Democracy.*

Cameron Graham, however, despite his having made yet another breakthrough for the CBC with the first-ever filming of a murder trial, was dispirited, anxious, and alienated. There was nothing for him downstream once he was finished with *Lawyers.* He felt that management had abandoned him. I was sure we could work something out with him for *Democracy.*

A few months earlier I had approached former prime minister Pierre Trudeau about the *Democracy* project. I wanted an extended interview about what this intellectual had learned about democracy once he had launched into politics, and also continuing access to him for advice on the complex issues that I knew the series would confront me with. He had agreed to the latter, but was holding me at bay about the interview, saying that he had made up his mind, once out of office, that he would stay away from the media, give himself to his family and his memoirs, and not risk opening the door to an avalanche of badgering producers and journalists by appearing on a major series like ours. "It's the most interesting of all the projects I've been offered," he said, "but . . . I feel I have to keep a low profile now."

One evening Caroline and I were waiting to cross Yonge Street for dinner at the storied (and much missed) Cibo Ristorante, when Senator Keith Davey came up to shake hands. He said he had dined with Trudeau the previous week and had "urged him to do the project with Patrick Watson."

"He gets thousands of invitations, you know. But he goes into his office every day and reads the mail and tells his secretary to turn everything down.

"I told him he should go down to New York and do the UN thing they're after him for. He could go down in the morning once a week and be back by 11 p.m. But he said, 'Yes, but then who would teach the boys Latin?'"

In fact Davey was thinking about a biographical proposal from Cameron Graham, but it later turned out that Trudeau thought he meant our *Democracy* project, and had evidently not completely closed his mind to it. The development of the series was being noticed in Ottawa. When I consulted Geoffrey Pearson about working conditions in the Soviet Union – he had been ambassador to Moscow – he urged me to make use of External Affairs staff, saying he thought they would go out of their way to be helpful. Not long afterward, I called Ron Halpin on the Moscow desk in Ottawa, who said, "We've been told about your series. We'll do anything we can to help."

Robert and Marlene Markle came down from their farm at Holstein to stay with us over Christmas, when we had Caroline's friends Leonard da Silva and Claire Rado from Paris also visiting. Ever since I had met Robert, my love and admiration for him had grown to the point where he was in my mind every day. He had become my closest male friend.

A fine artist, an extraordinary wit, a great drinking partner, and a natural philosopher, had he been formally trained, he would have been a spectacular teacher. Well, he *was* a spectacular teacher. Fat, often unshaven, his shoes and trousers spattered with paint, an old green peak cap advertising Red Man chewing tobacco, seldom without an open bottle of beer after eleven o'clock in the morning, he was also graceful, meticulous, fastidious, and systematic. Watching him dance with a woman, lightly, circling as if up on the points, you would have thought him trained in ballet or at least in ballroom dancing. If you made the mistake of using your jam knife on the butter at the breakfast table, you heard about it with genuine indignation. In his studio upstairs in the old farmhouse in Egremont township, everything was in place and the sense of order far overcame the paint-spattered randomness.

He said once, "The deepest underlying impulse, human impulse, is toward orderliness."

"So that is an aesthetic judgment about human nature," I said.

"I think it is maybe even more than that."

"Prior to that?" I said. "So it becomes a position from which to make aesthetic judgments, to do criticism?"

"I think so."

I said, "I'd be interested to see if you could develop that into a theory of justice."

He said, very slowly, "That would be very difficult."

I said, "But it would be interesting to study a number of classical cases, criminal cases, litigations, etc., to see how they reflect not the cultural sense of good and bad but of order."

He said, "Only order is prior to good and bad."

I have said before that he was one of the people who made Caroline feel welcome when she moved to Canada. He did not go out of his way to do this; he was ready to love her because I did, but when he began to know her the friendship became deep and comfortable. Once I came into the living room when he was staying with us, Caroline having got up early to do her exercises there. She does her morning routines nude. And there was Robert Markle, the painter who painted nude women more than any other subject, sitting on the sofa pronouncing about some musical subtlety, the two of them chatting away as casually as if they had bumped into each other at the corner coffee shop.

Although he looked unmistakably like the pure-blood Mohawk he was, it was about two years before it struck me that he was an Indian. He did not downplay it; he said once he just wanted to be known as an artist, not as an Indian artist, and there was some risk that if he reminded people of his heritage they would be unable to see around it. It was not until he was forty that he began to explore that heritage, and went back to the reserve, and found new streams of spiritual and cultural strength there.

Visiting him and Marlene in the winter of 1985, Caroline and I took a couple of strenuous hours to shovel a walkway for Marlene all down their long driveway one morning when we awoke to waist-deep snow. It was like a corridor with lovely vertical walls.

We had no sooner finished than the local snowblower guy came by unexpectedly and cleared out the whole drive in ten minutes. "Our path!" Caroline said in dismay. It had vanished. Robert looked at our glum faces and said, "Never mind. The path's still there. He just took the walls away." For years after we would ask, and he would reply, "Yep; your path's still there."

He made me think about the partnership of folly and wisdom, of play and work. He was equally pleased with himself in both modes, and would probably have characterized his folly as a form of wisdom. It was from his example that I learned the necessity of respecting both aspects of my own imagination.

There were many times of wonder with Robert. I had sat at his kitchen table, the centre of gravity of the house, doing watercolours under his instruction, thinking that there was probably nowhere in the universe a happier man than I was for those few hours.

When Robert asked me once, with his characteristic mock grump, what I would like for Christmas, I reminded him of a pencilled cartoon he had whipped off once, showing me in shorts with a leafy branch growing out of my wooden leg. I had lost it and suggested that he do another like it, in ink, something I could frame. He and Marlene turned up on my birthday, December 23, with a parcel, a framed picture I guessed, and when we opened it on Christmas morning it was a richly textured comedic version of Michelangelo's Sistine Chapel God and Adam, with Robert as God floating on a cloud composed not of angels but of strippers in G-strings and pasties, the Markle/God's hand languorously reaching out to a naked me with my left leg transmogrifying into a thick, twisted, and leafy vine. Years later Caroline met me at the airport after a New York shoot, to drive to Go Home Lake for the weekend, and said that she had on a whim, just that morning, decided to move Robert's painting from where it hung in our downstairs screening room up to the sun-splashed kitchen that Sandy Kybartas had recently designed and built for us on the second floor. That very night the house caught fire. Our tenant on the third floor called the firemen in time to save the house, but the fire destroyed the screening equipment, monitors, the Umatic deck, hundreds of cassettes, and over a thousand books in the room where that painting had, until the day before, always hung. It is still upstairs in that sunny kitchen.

Robert Markle said to Caroline and me once, over breakfast at the Roxborough house, "I love you two so much, it's silly." We would have only six more years of that love.

Over that same Christmas break I read Barbara Tuchman's *A Distant Mirror*, and began to wonder whether a documentary series could be built with that combination of narrative immediacy and solid historical reference, and at the same time *engage* an audience, as Tuchman's book does, with a deep sense of meaning for their own lives. Early in the year, as if there was not enough to do, director Robin Spry called to say he liked my screenplay for *Alter Ego*, and would I do a rewrite for him, just a few revisions?

Another diary entry soon after shows that with the Arms Control Centre, the film board, the *Democracy* project, and *Venture* all going at the same time, I was on airplanes as many as six times a week. I began to collect airline liquor miniatures as a kind of, what, *trophy* of all this mad activity? This collection kept growing for the next ten years. I wrote of myself in the third person that

> *"PW sometimes has difficulty distinguishing between what he wants to do, & what he wants to see done. Sitting on boards represents the latter and yet leads to his doing things he does not really want to do (attend board meetings.)"*

Roy Faibish called from London to say that Prime Minister Brian Mulroney had asked him if I would be a good person to head up the Canada Council, and that Roy had told him, No, Watson is not an administrator, he's an executive and a creative person. Find something else. A few weeks later Mulroney told Roy he wanted me as president of the CBC. This was another point at which Roy Faibish had a transforming effect on my life, and I step out of the narrative line briefly here to sketch a portrait of this extraordinary man.

CHAPTER 19

ROY FAIBISH

THE FIGURE OF ROY FAIBISH has flashed through these pages from time to time. Now, because of the magnitude of his influence on my life and on the late-twentieth-century history of Canada, I have to take a few pages to place him, to try to say who he was, to leave some record here of that enigmatic, sometimes magical, and always powerful presence.

When he died at the age of seventy-two, in March 2001, his widow, Barbara, asked me to come to London and conduct the funeral; he had considered me his best friend, she said, despite the difficulties. It was impossible not to agree, although to convey to the mourners both the love and admiration that I had for Roy and at the same time to convey to those who knew him well that we shared some of the mystery about him – that would be a challenge.

There were about forty people at the ceremony. Some had come from Los Angeles, one from Paris, several from Ireland and Canada. It was not to be a religious ceremony, but Roy had spoken a lot about his Jewish heritage in the last years, and it was comforting and right that his Kaddish be said.

The Canadian senator Jerry Grafstein asked to speak. Senator Grafstein seldom speaks for less than half an hour, but this time he disciplined himself to a crisp, moving six minutes.

I spoke, I think, not much more than that. I told of our meeting in a television studio, of the China adventure, of his immense knowledge of and love for poetry and the incomprehensible range of his reading, his generosity and his adventurousness. I said of the darker side only that there were several different people living within that one compact body, probably more people than I had got to know, although I had seen many of them, and that the challenge to Roy himself of keeping all those different persons straight was perhaps one of the sources of the overwhelming pain he seemed to have lived with in his last years. There in that chapel in London, from the faces of those who knew him best, I could see what I needed to see. When the time came to press the button on the lectern that would send the casket back through those doors behind me, I felt that I had paid him a farewell he would have approved of . . . after we had argued about it for a while.

Coming into an argument with Leroy Abraham Faibish you had to be very well prepared. He could talk knowledgeably about quantum mechanics, international strategic issues, the agriculture of northeast China, the real reasons for the breakdown of the peace talks in Saigon, the poetic influences most affecting Ezra Pound, the chemistry of psychedelic drugs, the history of the State of Nebraska, the eating and sexual habits of Al Capone or James Joyce or Pablo Neruda or W.B. Yeats.

He could quote Yeats, at length, and did so, frequently. In the midst of a heated discussion or an exchange of e-mails, Yeats's words often seemed to be, for Roy, a more appropriate response than a declaration of his own. Here is an e-mail, in response to something from me about trouble in the *Democracy* production unit:

```
Date: Wed Nov 25, 1987 2:37 pm EST   **RECEIPT
From: Roy Faibish / MCI ID: 254-9554

TO: * Patrick Watson / MCI ID: 270-9941
Subject: YOUR DEMOC. PRODUCER.
Pass this to your floundering Democ. Producer:
```

"These masterful images became complete
Grew in pure mind, but out of what began?
A mound of refuse or the sweepings of a street,
Old kettles, old bottles, and a broken can,
Old iron, old bones, old rags, that raving slut
Who keeps the till. Now that my ladder's gone,
I must lie down where all the ladders start,
In the foul rag and bone shop of the heart".

Chao
RF

Many of those quotations from Yeats were uttered in ways and on occasions that wrenched in your heart. Or he might shock you with a deft and unnerving placement of "But love has pitched his mansion in / The place of excrement."

With a voice that could drop into a soothing softness that the world's great actors should have paid money to learn, he could produce a feeling of tenderness and wonderment from Christopher Smart, with "For in my nature I quested for beauty: But God, God hath sent me to sea for pearls." Or, as he regarded his cat, another Smart that he loved, also from *Jubilate Agno*,

For I will consider my Cat Jeoffry
For he is the servant of the Living God duly and daily serving him.

He had a knack for retailing a line that would stick with you for life. He was the only person I ever knew who loved and read and reread Ezra Pound for pleasure, not out of scholarly duty, and would nail into your consciousness Pound's astonishing verbless two-line masterpiece about a Paris metro station . . .

The apparition of those faces in the crowd:
Petals on a wet, black bough.

. . . and then go on with the eagerness and wisdom of a great professor of poetry to tell you exactly *why* this was so good, the explanation often varying, freshening, as he made new discoveries somewhere in the profound pools of insight in his own magnificent brain, a brain some of us thought must have a couple of extra layers in it, extra folds, extra convolutions.

He would say that he knew something about what might have led to the death of Marilyn Monroe, something that he could not share, because she had confided it to him with an absolute restriction, which he must respect always.

He had come to be a major adviser to Prime Minister Mulroney through the same lovable, rough-hewn Tory politician with whom I had first met Roy: Alvin Hamilton. Roy had come to work for Hamilton after a few years in the RCAF, where he had been assigned to Air Vice Marshall Fred Carpenter. When Diefenbaker made Hamilton his Minister of Agriculture, the unilingual Saskatchewan man realized he needed some francophone competence in his office and brought in the young Mulroney, a Quebecer with an Irish heritage and a perfect fluency in French. Only nineteen, twelve years younger than Roy, Mulroney struck up a close friendship with the executive assistant, took many of his assignments directly from Roy, and the two agreed that should either of them ever run for office the other would be on call.

During Roy's time in Hamilton's office, he was also an informal policy adviser to Prime Minister Diefenbaker, who had given his family some legal help in Saskatchewan when Roy was a boy, and to whose ear he apparently had instant access at almost any time, advising on everything from nuclear war to the price of eggs. He almost certainly made a major contribution to Diefenbaker's northern policy, "Roads to Resources," and to the crusty old Tory's insistence on the virtues of cultural multiplicity and the equal value and status of all citizens, whatever their race or origin. After he left politics to come and work with me, Roy maintained his gossipy connections with politicians, not just Tories; hobnobbed with Pierre Trudeau; helped shape the policies of the CRTC; and would never, for the rest of his life, stop doing his best to get people of influence to consider major issues of water conservation, world peace, the importance of China, and a whole spectrum of other issues that he was constantly investigating.

Roy liked and trusted Mulroney, but by the time Mulroney became leader of the party, Roy was solidly ensconced in his new life in Britain as a broadband expert at British Telecom. He had no desire to come back to Canada, which he now felt to be something of a cultural backwater. But he came over a couple of times to see Mulroney and advise him informally, especially about key appointments, and planted the idea that I should be asked to take over the CBC. When Mulroney became prime minister, he offered Roy Faibish anything he wanted; he could be chief of staff, or even Clerk of the Privy Council, the highest public servant in the land; Roy turned Mulroney down, but said it hurt him grievously to do so. He just couldn't come back to Canada. He had married Barbara Calvert, a freelance computer programmer from Northern Ireland, who had come to work for him as a secretary/assistant when he arrived in London. They had a lovely cottage on Strangford Lough in Co. Down, Northern Ireland, and an airy top-floor flat in Chelsea. He said he had his seat on the board of the London Library, the Tate within walking distance till his back went bad, and the Victoria and Albert, and the National Gallery and the theatres and concerts and a substantial income from the shares he bought after he helped privatize British Telecom, and a seat at Margaret Thatcher's dinner table from time to time, and the ear of a few wealthy and influential Europeans, and a seat on the board of an international consortium of investors led by Simon Murray (who was at the funeral), including Henry Kissinger, and meetings three times a year in Bangkok and Singapore and Paris and Rio de Janeiro . . . why in the world would he ever want to come back to Canada, a country that had, after all, "rejected him in the first place"? (What he meant by that I never understood.)

Having in the early 1960s established friendships in Beijing that he maintained through correspondence, he continued to find ways to return after our filming expedition, even before the end of the Cultural Revolution, and in the last decade or so was going out to China almost every year, sometimes armed with investment commissions of some kind from Simon Murray and the consortium. Once, shortly after I had become chairman of the CBC, he called from London to say that he had decided on the eve of leaving Beijing that, by God, he had never been to Vietnam, wouldn't it be great to see what was happening to Saigon since it became Ho Chi Minh City? And whaddya know! It's become a bustling centre of commerce, and you guys at the CBC ought to get out there and sell them French-language television programming, French is still the second language, they have an enormous need for low-cost programming and would far rather get it from Canada than from France. What a great idea, I thought, and rushed off to put it on the president's plate and get staff working on it. I later had reason to think that he had never in fact gone to Vietnam, but the idea was a great one all the same.

Back in the *Seven Days* period, we were following up Isabel LeBourdais's book arguing that Stephen Truscott was not guilty of the murder for which he had been sentenced to hang at the age of fourteen (and reprieved by Prime Minister John Diefenbaker). We wanted to talk to Truscott's mother but nobody knew where she was, or how to get to her, but it was Roy Faibish who found his way into her home and her confidence and sent back a brief, unconventional interview so powerful that it made Laurier LaPierre wipe away a tear on camera (we had not seen the interview before we went to air), a tear that would haunt the senator for the rest of his life.

Not only had Roy done the journalistically impossible and got us permission to film in China – *and* with a degree of freedom that astonished the journalistic community – but out of the China adventure we had become close, loving friends, exchanging intimate details of our lives to each other, things we would share with nobody else. Roy had been a presence and a strength when my first marriage began to come undone, a comfort not only to me but to my first wife.

When Caroline arrived uncertainly in Canada, he made her feel as though she were bringing rays of illumination and wisdom into the deprived backwoods, and brought her champagne and impossible clarets, and once came and sat for three days outside the drive shed splitting wood for our fireplace. He said he needed the exercise for his upper body, his ten-mile walks weren't doing it, he would just sit there, he said, and split maple and elm for a few days (elm is almost impossible to split by hand) and he did, and the pile grew around him as he tossed the split pieces this way and that way until he disappeared inside a growing volcanic cone of firewood from the interior of which you could hear the thump and whack of the axe and every few seconds see another split bit arc up through the air and land on the rim of that growing ring of bright wood.

He told stories of his adventures with a kind of brio that made those adventures into scenes from a screenplay. In the days leading up to the launch of *Seven Days* we were deploying a lot of resources to find the Mafia-bound leader of the Teamsters' Union, the Canadian Hal Banks. Roy reported to a program meeting one day that he had been down to the mansion in rural Quebec, with its barbed wire and electric fence and high stone pillars and locked iron gates, had hidden in the tall grass by the stone pillars until a laundry truck came with a delivery, had sprinted out and jumped onto the back bumper of the truck as it went through the electronic gates, found his way into the house, and got away with it by some fiction when he was discovered prowling inside. He reported back to us that Hal Banks was, in fact, not there.

Our time together at Bushnell Television was rough on the friendship. When the enterprise that had led his chief, Stuart Griffiths, to bring me there with such promise foundered, perhaps Roy felt uncomfortably responsible for having led me into something that evaporated, or perhaps he imagined that I was resentful. Whatever the cause, I saw in him for the first time a great store of anger, and we fell out severely. We did not see each other for about two years, but I missed him a great deal.

We finally regrouped, under some pretext or other, agreeing to meet for dinner at the Hungarian Palace on Albert Street. He was predictably late. I wrote in my journal, as I waited over a glass of Sancerre, that while I would never be completely at ease with him again, and was anxious about the reunion, there was no doubt that "when we are on together, *we are really on.*" And that "being on together" meant, more often than not, an elevated language and deep, intuitive communication about Bach, or Mozart, or a painting, or a poem.

He wept, openly, over Rosalyn Turek's recording of Prelude No. 8, in six flats, from the *Well-Tempered Clavier*, and insisted that I learn to play it with the same almost impossibly soulful languor as Turek's. He would rage scornfully at Glenn Gould's "total misunderstanding" of Bach, just as a Chomsky might rage at the global corporate conspiracy or a Wiesenthal at the Holocaust. He would bring wide-eyed young women to the farm or to Nightwood and whisper that he had at last found the answer to the eternal puzzle of life, and he was going to forsake all else.

There were some mysteries that never got resolved, and about which he was reluctant to talk. His mother was the source of one. While he had often talked of his childhood in Saskatchewan, his parents, and other relatives, it was always in the past tense. There was never any indication of a living relative except for a sister in Los Angeles. Then one day as I was about to leave for a trip to Alberta, he asked me to visit his mother in an Edmonton hospital; she had just had her leg amputated for cancer, he said, and I could probably be of some comfort. I made the visit and discovered yet another sister, as well. Roy was mildly indignant when I suggested that he should have told me about these people. Of course he had told me: I had just forgotten. Only after his death did I learn that there was a brother in British Columbia.

He told me a few months before he and Barbara married that the doctors had advised him that he might have to have a colostomy, and that he would commit suicide rather than "impose that on anyone." I said this was nonsense, it was no worse than my lost leg (I did not believe what I was saying), and that it would be criminal to deprive the world of a brain like his because of something that thousands of people were living with and discovering to be something in the order of a substantial nuisance but not a disaster. "Well, the old brain's not too good either," he said. He meant memory problems. Well, hell, we all have memory problems after sixty or so, and he was still quoting Yeats and Pound and disputing arcane details of quantum theory; the brain looked pretty good to me, I said.

In any case, in 1984 the wedding went ahead in the Chelsea Registry Office, "same room Ringo got married in," Roy said. And soon he and Barbara were flinging off on extravagant junkets on the Orient Express, and exhibiting the signs of a marriage that was deeply founded and permanent. Roy had Barbara's head sculpted in bronze. He detected a strong artistic gift in Barbara and helped her build a studio inside the same ancient County Down stone walls the other part of which had become a superbly stocked wine cellar with what appeared to be a fortune's worth of exquisite wines in it, mostly French, although he had been forced to stop drinking wine for medical reasons. Barbara turned out to have, indeed, an exceptional talent as a textiles artist, which got her exhibitions and sales in Dublin, London, Frankfurt, and Paris.

The colostomy did not prove necessary, but Roy was in a lot of pain from about 1980 onwards. He had to have surgery for nerve pressure on the lower spine, and began to walk with great difficulty, and was growing deaf, which he hated, and angrier and angrier. The great Irish dinner parties he had presided over at Tully Hill Cottage, the Strangford place, had been, in those first years in Northern Ireland, the best parties in the world. There would be scholars and poets and musicians, and elderly farm wives and artisans, and he would introduce this poet, who would read or recite, or me doing a bit of magic, or Barbara's latest wall hanging, with a graciousness and poetic generosity that won him the hearts of people all across the county. Then as the pain grew worse, those parties began to reflect the anger; he would shout at people and drive them away.

The crustiness would come and go. Perhaps it had always been there, only to be exacerbated by the later physical pain and sense of frustration over the walking difficulty, the deafness, the insomnia. When we had the press launch for *The Struggle for Democracy* at Canada House in London, when it came time for questions I noticed Roy getting to his feet at the back of the hall, whence he called out to me, very aggressively, "Just what makes *you* think you have anything significant to say to the world about democracy?" I was tongue-tied for a moment. When we met for a drink later, he said that he was just trying to set me up in an interesting way, but it had not sounded very much like that at all.

I have something of the order of ten thousand pages of correspondence from Roy Faibish, several thousand of them on paper, two or three feet of folders in a file case, and innumerable diskettes of e-mail. Thousands of those pages are fascinating, detailed, concrete, and complex accounts of meetings and readings and opinions arrived at and discoveries made and theories developed. A late e-mail told me how he had been walking in Central London and suddenly some sentences from Lionel Trilling's critical writings had come into his head with such clarity that he was startled. Being close to the British Museum, he had dashed in to find a copy of the book from which he thought they might have come. Wasn't it amazing? There they were, word for word, just as they had come into his head. And he put them into the e-mail, three or four pithy, wonderful, critical sentences.

They looked familiar. I felt I had read them, those same pellucid observations, within the last few days. I looked in the latest issue of the *New York Review of Books.* There were the lines, in a review of the great fat anthology of Trilling's essays that had just been published, exactly as Roy had sent them, "from memory," the same beginning, the same ending, the same ellipses . . . .

I should have left it alone. Regrettably I confronted him with it. He raged back. He accused me of the worst kind of bad faith. He said in any case his copy of the NYROB hadn't arrived yet, so he *couldn't* have read it there. And I fear that we never recovered from the damage, we two. Barbara told me soon afterward that many of those great friends around Strangford and Portaferry were deeply puzzled and distressed by the way he was, and some of them just found it too difficult to be with him after a while. Among those friends was the gentle and generous Billy Brown, the mathematician who had helped found Britain's Open University and had pronounced himself pretty damn impressed with Roy's ability to talk about mathematics when he clearly didn't know any, and the lady who ran the pub, and the neighbours. Simon Murray, at the consortium, was loyal and attentive to the end. Now Roy and Barbara began to pass in the night, she often going to London when he was at Tully Hill, and he to the Chelsea flat (where he died) when she was in Ireland. Few friends came to drink the wine with him and he spent a great deal of time alone.

I was at the Edinburgh Festival in the late summer of 1998, and knowing that Roy was at the cottage and never went anywhere, I caught a cheap flight to Belfast City Airport and rented a car. I would just drop in on him, so that he couldn't make excuses. I *needed* to see him. I pulled into the little courtyard behind Tully Hill Cottage, parking outside the stone wall of the legendary wine cellar, and watched him emerge blinking from the chair in the sunroom, off the kitchen, where he spent most of his time. He was bent and frowning as if he didn't know who it was, but after a moment he said, gruffly, "It's you, eh! I just got a case of an incredible 1983 St. Émilion, six hundred pounds a bottle. I'll get a couple; you can try them out. I can have a taste but that's all. Wait right here."

He came back out into the sunlight, still bent and frowning, with three seductive-looking bottles, and in we went to the sunroom where he pointed me at the corkscrew and some glasses. He was breathing a bit noisily, not wheezing, but puffing a bit as though the walk to the wine cellar and back had been too much. I sipped the wine and he sniffed at it and shook his head with admiring approval. We talked in short bits, and then he would muse, away off somewhere, and then come back and ask about Caroline, or the magic interests that had taken me to Edinburgh, or some other relatively trivial matter, puffing and grunting and frowning, apparently very uncomfortable.

The phone rang. He frowned, looked at me glumly, said he'd better take it, grunted, picked it up.

Instantly his face, posture, and demeanour changed completely. "Simon?" he said briskly. "Now listen. I've been talking to San Francisco and I think they were right after all, and you should buy." He was crisp, chuckling into the mouthpiece, totally cogent, his eyes sparkling. "Sure! Sure! I'll see you in Paris in two weeks. Great! Goodbye, Simon." Then he hung up and slumped back into the chair, puffing, grunting, frowning, as miserable as before. I saw him once more, in London. We were together for three or four hours. He did all the talking. Most of it was angry, much of the anger aimed at me.

A few months later he was gone, really gone. And now I am sorry that I was ever angry at him about anything at all. Barbara wrote to me,

> *Yes, he was a grumpy, aggressive old man before he died, but grumpy aggressive old men are ten a penny. . . .*
>
> *His appetite for life was as large as his appetite for good food and wine. He loved entertaining and was a lavish and generous host. He loved cashmere sweaters, Brooks Brothers' shirts and hand made Italian boots. He was great fun. He also had an amazing ability for walking into a room at a party, picking out the dullest looking person, asking them one question, like "Where were you born?", or "Where did you study?", and extracting from them some gem of information that suddenly made them the most interesting people in the room. He welcomed strangers into his home and treated them as warmly as his closest friends.*
>
> *Many friends were helped through relationship breakdowns. He would talk to them for hours, calmly going over the same thing again and again, making them think rationally when they were in emotional turmoil, and he would never seem exhausted or irritated no matter how long this went on. He got his niece Holly through a marriage breakdown, giving her a*

home and emotional support for six months in London. She called her second son after him.

He helped people who had lost jobs, emailing and telephoning contacts, forwarding CV's.

Everyone remembers the first time they met him. The most common thing people say about him is that he was the most extraordinary person they ever knew.

Amen.

Chapter 20

VENTURE

In the last months of 1984 there was so much going on that I noted in the journal that I literally did not know what day it was without consulting my Day-Timer.

Perhaps because of all that stress, phantom limb pain, which had been infrequent for a few years, began to hit me hard every few days, sometimes insisting for up to thirty-six hours with high-voltage jolts that made my whole frame shudder. I would wake up at 4 a.m. soaked in sweat. My blood pressure was up. Both Caroline and I seemed to carry those excesses into recreation, and by midsummer of 1985 I had wrecked my right knee and shoulder by too much strain on the sail-boards.

We listened to a lot of Mozart, moved the television set into the bedroom, and watched trash. Drinking prodigiously. Frequently hung over. My dreams were full of journeys begun but frustrated. In one I find they have cancelled the railway, but I must get to Ottawa. A big steam locomotive comes into the station and stops. Its last stop. Sad and famous people get down from the silent train, along with a big black bear, its paws outstretched in supplication. I find a shallow trough the width of the former track, stretching along the old rail bed; it will take me to Ottawa. It is brilliantly painted. I am running along it as fast as I can go, with a sense of joy and nostalgia. "I helped paint this thing!" I shout to everyone I pass.

Sometimes Caroline and I speculated about dropping all this deadline-driven stuff in favour of projects that were purely ours, and purely playful. She proposed a couple of screenplay ideas: a Don Quixote written expressly for Donald Sutherland, a drama based on Germaine Greer's account of the sixteenth-century female painter Artemisia Gentileschi.

I was having a lot of head colds and insomnia. I joined the YMCA and forced myself to brave the hideously slippery (to crutch tips) floor of the showers to get myself into the pool sometimes five times a week for a half-mile swim. That seemed to help with the phantom limb, and with those appalling sleepless nights.[1] Soon the Y became an essential agent for cleansing away these continued accumulations of pressure and obligation. I remember one afternoon late in the winter, or early spring, as the sun began to climb in the sky again, and as I ploughed up and down with a fin on my good foot and a diving mask to keep the chlorine out of my eyes, how the rippled webs of sunlight on the bottom of the pool turned the afternoon into a Caribbean holiday.

It was on one of those days at the Y that John Kennedy told me grimly he might be one of the 1,700 people that Juneau was about to let go from the CBC; they were pressing him about early retirement.

Venture went to air for the first time on January 7, 1985. The opening program was a magazine with four crisp segments: "Radio Wars," a feature story about competition between radio programmers and the prize they are after, market share, the greatest number of human ears they can deliver; "Mortage Wars," on the battleground of the home loan business; "Bryston Amplifiers," the success strategy of a company in an industry whose failure rate is 99 percent; and finally a profile of Canada's richest banker, Edgar Kaiser, which Margaret Wente and I had to fly out to B.C. to rescue from its initial not very

1. Sometimes there was fun in them. One night at Go Home Lake, thinking about the dome, I came up with a formula for calculating the sum of the internal angles of a polygon S=([n-2] x 180), a simple enough and probably ancient and common formula, but I didn't know it before. Later I started silently reciting poems in my head, and began to learn new ones, and now (the insomnia still a common visitor) have dozens of poems I can draw on, and learn more almost every month.

successful production by our Vancouver stringer. There was no advantage to going live and no need for the cumbersomeness of a studio, so I did the introductions and links in the office with a single camera, and the program was assembled in the office. Reaction to the opening program was universally good.

One day during that first month, Conrad Black called to ask if I knew Lister Sinclair well enough to invite him to lunch in the Argus Corporation boardroom. "He's always been an intellectual hero of mine," Black said. Lister was puzzled but flattered, and off we went for what turned out to be a bizarre hour and a half over a flat dry pizza and an inferior bottle of red wine. The bizarre part was the Sinclair–Black contest, each of them trying to outdo the other in their knowledge of European history, mostly military. Black did most of the talking, and at the end took Lister's hand graciously, thanked him profusely, said it was one of the most stimulating conversations he had had in years, and showed us to the door amiably. Lister muttered in his beard as he limped along, wondering what *that* had all been about.

Late in January Cam Graham and Brian Nolan brought me to Ottawa to record the last bits of narration for *Lawyers* and asked if I could come up with a philosophical piece as an ending to the final program: they had not yet found a shapely way to end both the hour and the series. That last hour was about three lawyers in three quite different circumstances, one of them the British barrister and writer John Mortimer (*Rumpole of the Bailey*). At the end we see one of them, a thoughtful and able Quebec barrister, paddling his canoe out into a dark lake as he reflects on the day in court. He had just got a couple of clients out of what would probably have been a modest and even deserved jail sentence. I found myself pondering it during the recording of the narration bits, and in a five-minute break wrote this:

> *Neither the instruments of the law nor the materials it has to work with are perfect. The law is not about perfection. Neither is it about the truth. Despite the oath we swear in*

court, none of us can tell the whole truth: we can only tell what we know.

And when Maître Jolin paddles out to contemplate the reflection of his day in court, it is not the image of some ideal of justice that he seeks, but only to know if he has done the best he could with what he had.

Then Jolin's voice is heard, reflecting that "the priest asks 'How many times?' But we have to ask, 'With whom?' It's in the details." And my final comment as the canoe paddles off:

Details? It is details amassed over a thousand years that make up the work of Louis Jolin, John Mortimer, Nancy Murray . . . . Lawyers.

—- 30 —-

It felt good to be able so easily to find a line that had a delicate sense of coda to it. All this accumulation of documentary work was bringing me a sense of confidence about the writing. I wrote in my journal that evening:

These are the satisfactions of the day these days, good existential satisfactions too, even though they do not endure. But when C. gets out the old tapes as she puts together the raw materials for our Demo tape [for *The Struggle for Democracy*], *and I stick my head into the screening room to catch the odd one going by, I can relive some of those satisfactions in a way that is available to very few in the ordinary course of life, & to very few broadcasters in the days before videotape. . . . Perhaps before the magnetic pulses have all decayed I can get some of the work onto laser disc & leave a mark that will last a little while.*

For the first few months *Venture* was exhilarating. The best stories were about start-ups by small entrepreneurs: a couple in Moose Jaw opening a computer consulting business in a town where there were as yet only a handful of people with computers. A co-op in the Maritimes, with a strong sense of social involvement. A First Nations trapper on the West Coast with an inventive approach to marketing. I was writing a lot of copy for short reports and rewriting a good deal for the story editors, and told my journal that there was "actually a good deal of pleasure to be had from hack writing" (which is true). I knew a good many of the camera and sound people we worked with, and while I was technically not supposed to be directing, I usually got involved in lighting, trying to get some modelling and shadow into the kind of images that normally, because it's easier, are shot with boring, flat overall lighting. If you are going to deploy all these sophisticated technical resources to send images through the ether to millions of people, I would argue, why not make the images interesting? I pressed for visually intriguing pictures both in the studio and on location. That was sometimes contentious but usually fun. I was moving back and forth between the old familiar top documentary crews on Cam Graham's *Lawyers* series and the younger technicians at *Venture*, and feeling increasingly confident – cocky is probably an appropriate word – about my ability to do a stand-up to camera in one take without a script: usually an exhilarating stunt, especially if the piece is fairly complicated and even more especially when I find, as I'm delivering it, a felicitous rewrite that I can build in without hesitating. Now as I moved through airports, people were coming up to comment on *Venture*, almost always favourably, and often with good suggestions for out-of-the way stories about entrepreneurs – about *ventures*, in fact.

I worked up some notes for a *Venture* board game. I imagined a strategy and tactics game that would interlock production, labour relations, management, sales and marketing, capital, price-equity, options, automation, foreign exchange, taxes, regulation, taking illegal risks, and the stock market. There would be a set of mailboxes where you could register a number of initiatives *(Ventures*, of course): start or buy a business, develop a takeover proposal. As in Monopoly, any player could take a randomized proposal from the computer or a pile of cards (Buy 10,000 shares of X; Hire Industrial Spy to Steal Design Secrets; Double Your Marketing Staff), act on it, sell it, or reject it. There was a lot more detail. The game would be elegantly made with a padded dark green or burgundy leather board and case, gold-tooled leather, a built-in microcomputer and random-number generator, and sculpted pieces in polished metal. The broad objective is to make a profit while benefiting the economy, on the theory that if everyone wins, the total winnings are higher for everyone and the society at large is more prosperous. A political observation, of course, with implications for the relationship of the co-op movement to corporate globalization. I'm sorry the game never got made.

There were some irritatingly wasteful times, four of us flying to Ottawa once and spending an entire day to get an interview with a cabinet minister that would give us only ninety seconds of air time. But many of the stories were first-rate. In February, working with Margaret Wente, Nick Hirst, and Peter Raymont, I put together a full half-hour on Union Gas's attempt to block a takeover by Unicorp. Raymont and Hirst had lucked into a shareholders' meeting where it first surfaced, and we built it into a strong, integrated story that was revealing of the corporate world, and best of all held audiences with a strong narrative grip.

But then management began to agitate for more attention to investing and the stock market. Unwilling to acknowledge that a lousy time slot (10 p.m. Monday) and almost zero publicity might have something to do with the unimpressive audience figures, they deluded themselves into thinking the problem was with Duncan McEwan's determinedly populist approach, and wanted it to go more downtown. The weekly listings said simply, "Venture: Business." The publicity people had placed no human interest stories out there and had made no use of my fronting the show as a publicity tool. For eight years *The Watson Report* had built a name; now they were abandoning it.

Feeling insufficiently engaged – not only because of these absurdities but more importantly because things were beginning to buzz on the *Democracy* front – I just could not muster the energy to fight that folly. Commercial broadcasting was saturated with investment stories and stock market reports; *Venture's* gift to viewers was embedded in its storytelling about entrepreneurs, managers, innovators, and people who took risks. There was simply no need for the kind of stuff they were agitating for.

The program began to lose interest for me, the more it moved into Bay Street and the closer we got to believing that we would soon be making *The Struggle for Democracy.* One day in early March, Bill Hopper phoned from Ottawa to say, "We're in, firmly, for a million plus. I just want to make sure that you're not so lean that you may be forced to give up some control to an investor who saves your bacon with the ten percent you need and demands a lot of control. We want to know how much equity we're buying. So Michael Levine and Claude Morin [from the Petro-Can office] can start negotiating."

I said, "Negotiate: that means there's an envelope."

He said, "That's right. We're putting all our chips on you. Claude knows my bottom line."

It was time to shed *Venture.* I had received a visit from a Quebec program host named Robert-Guy Scully, a compulsive flatterer so good at his game that he got to me, saying he wanted to become a really good interviewer and wanted to work in English as well as his native French. He is fluently multilingual, speaking Italian, German, and Spanish as well as the Canadian languages. Would I advise him on his interviewing technique? Were there any opportunities I could think of that he might exploit in English television? I called Michael Levine. I said I was getting ready to leave *Venture* and would he like to meet a candidate to take it over. Scully flattered the hell out of Levine as well. Later on that year, he did take over from me on *Venture.*

In the spring of 1985 you could still get a champagne supper for two at The Courtyard for under a hundred bucks. The Cold War was beginning to seem less intractable. The boy Gorbachev had replaced the invisible Chernenko. The Great Powers were about to meet in Geneva. Robins were singing in Ramsden Park in the first week of

March. We booked a couple of weeks of underwater time at Small Hope Bay. There was a good smell in the air.

Chapter 21

DEMOCRACY

THAT MARCH '85 visit to Small Hope Bay was rich in many ways. Although I had a bit of a cold, and some trouble with my ears as a result, doped up with Actifed I made my first night dive and noted that while I was delighted to find how much could actually be seen, the dive made me aware of how much I needed to learn. The next day we had our first visit to the legendary Blue Hole, which would become a favourite over the next few years, with its endless intricacy of cavern and tunnel. I got to two hundred feet for the first time.

An encounter with another diver reminded me how little one can anticipate the results of one's work. On the dive boat during the first two or three days, I had noticed a woman in her late twenties who walked with some difficulty, with a cane. Polio, I thought. Peter Douglas, the big black affable adopted son of the lodge owner, had spoken of her as "a Canadian artist." She handled herself well underwater. On the boat I was puzzled by the way in which she was quite obviously avoiding me. Once she even had to step over my peg leg to get to a seat, and it was clear that she was deliberately looking away.

The next day I was dozing in an outdoor hammock at the edge of the water when I heard a voice say, "Patrick?" It was the artist, Lynda Lapeer.

"Listen," she said, "I've been avoiding you, because the emotion was too much. It's okay now. But you changed my life, and when I saw you I didn't know what to do."

When she was hospitalized, she had read my book *Fasanella's City*. It had, she said, spoken to her so strongly that she knew she must paint. The hospitalization had been for a viral infection that left her totally paralyzed at first. Her husband, Michael Benan, encouraged her to start painting and brought her materials in the hospital. Shortly after she'd begun to walk again, he had died. The whole thing was overwhelming her. She left me slides of her work, which was a kind of affectionate approach to landscape, populated landscapes, not a little affected, I thought, by Fasanella.

The night before we left, I read aloud my satirical poem about the origins of the name "Small Hope Bay," poking fun at some of the family and staff,[1] and then we talked late into the evening with Lynda Lapeer and a Texan couple about will, intelligence, and computers. Much of the joy of that lodge in the eighties was the talk in the evenings. Next morning, the lodge's pilot let me fly his Aztec most of the way back to Fort Lauderdale, and then it was back to Toronto and some serious work on the *Democracy* project.

I had commissioned Paddy Sampson to make a promotional reel of excerpts from my on-camera work over the previous ten years. It's always an anxious moment to look at programs you made years ago and supposed were good. But this turned out to be heartening: it would be good stuff as we took the *Democracy* project into the marketplace. I remembered author Morley Callaghan (then eighty-three) at Paddy's CBC farewell party, saying affectionately that Paddy was, above all, "a reassuring man."

I bought my first Tandy Model 100 laptop computer, the most finger-friendly keyboard I've ever used, despite its tiny (128K) onboard memory, and set up the Wang to automatically receive files from it over the phone. During the production of *The Struggle for Democracy*, that little Tandy travelled around the world with

1. See "The Ballad of Small Hope Bay," in the Appendix.

me, at least three times, and recorded tens of thousands of words – correspondence, narrations, "pastoral letters" to the crew.

In late April I was flown to Ottawa to testify in defence of the CBC, the Corporation having been charged for allowing a journalist to film in the corridors of a courthouse (not in the courtroom). It seemed absurd, given the breakthrough we had made with the Linda Clow murder trial. It was not politically acceptable to complain that the bright and aggressive prosecutor of this case – a case that revolved around the use of the camera – was David Lepofsky, who is blind. Films and videotapes were being screened as formal exhibits for the court to consider, including our *Lawyers* episode on the trial of Linda Clow. Lepofsky asked the court to refuse to qualify me as a television expert, on the grounds that I did not have a university degree in social sciences and had not made "scientifically valid experiments" to support my conclusions about the social dynamics of television. He was doing his job, but his attitude made this very bright man appear to be pretty disconnected from the real world. Judge Vanik thanked me warmly for my testimony, and defence counsel David Scott said, "If that doesn't do it, nothing will."

But nothing did; Lepofsky won the case for the Crown.

On the last day of April, Caroline said she had been thinking about my saying for the last couple of years that I thought we should get married, should make that public and formal commitment that marriage represents. Well, she said, now she agreed; let's do it. I was euphoric. We went to Go Home Lake to celebrate. Duncan McEwan was so pleased about the (as yet not public) marriage news that when he needed me back in town for an interview with the chairman of Sony Corporation, he sent a seaplane, and I got to fly it to Toronto Island and back, and a whole lot of things began to feel pretty good.

On August 3 Alanis Obomsawin and I were having tea in the second-floor kitchen at Roxborough Street when the phone rang. When I came back from the call she said, "Who was that?"

"Mulroney," I said. "He asked me if I would agree to be president of the CBC."

He had said there were indications that Pierre Juneau was considering early retirement, and that he understood and respected my concerns in that regard. He non-committedly acknowledged my proposal to move head office to Toronto. (The film board's head office was in Montreal, I said: why shouldn't CBC be in Toronto? In any case, it would be need to be reduced to about a tenth of its present size. Under successive presidents it had become vastly bigger than the small coordinating body it should be. He said nothing about timing. Roy Faibish had assured me that Mulroney knew I would not drop the *Democracy* project before it was finished. I tried to put the question of running the CBC aside, to get on with assembling the team and the tools I needed to run *Democracy*, as we had come to call it.

Petro-Canada came through with some cash in mid-year. Michael Levine now felt legitimately ready to conclude an agreement with a couple of offshore partners. He set up a meeting in London with Richard Creasey, the head of special projects at Central Independent Television of Birmingham. Michael's earlier discussions with more junior people at Central had gone as far as drawing up some rough budgets, and having preliminary discussions regarding what kind of services they might put in beyond their cash contribution. In fact, they had agreed in principle to advance £400,000 against their revenue from all foreign distribution, with our commitment to buy back all our U.K. crewing from them at favoured-nation rates. But by November they were getting nervous and said they wanted out of the deal. The only way to rescue it was to get to Creasey.

Caroline, Michael, and I met with him over breakfast at the Royal Thames Yacht Club in the fall of 1985. He was courteous and friendly, and spoke warmly of what he had heard of the project. But he warned us over the orange juice that Central would not be able to contribute in the way that some of his juniors had been considering, and said that he was meeting with us because there had been some level of commitment and he felt he had to do what he could to steer us to more promising partners. We had already met with Montrealer Jake Eberts's company Goldcrest, the unconventional people who made *Gandhi* and *The Killing Fields*. Like almost everyone to whom we pitched the project, they were full of praise for it and made predictions of its success. Now here was another Love-Your-Project; Not-for-Us.

But Creasey had not met Caroline and me before, and by now our grasp of the project had become hard-edged and specific. During that breakfast, Creasey confessed later, something caught him strongly enough to contest with his better judgment, and by the second pot of coffee he was rubbing his hands, saying that maybe, *just maybe*, he could do whatever was necessary to bring in Central Independent Television PLC, after all.

Next we went to Pittsburgh to meet with the people at WQED, who had surprised us (after the initial good reactions from New York and Los Angeles) by being the one PBS station that wanted to talk concrete details. WQED did a lot of work with National Geographic, one of the few major organizations still insisting that the documentaries they commissioned be done on film instead of video, so they understood my insistence on film. They had a film unit; they were comfortable with film, shared my preference for the film look, and said they would draw up an agreement.

The agreement with the CBC was by now firm enough to start putting together a unit. We quickly lined up Ted Remerowski as senior producer, and, as line producer and production manager, Nancy Button, whom I had met subbing for Peter Gzowski on his FM arts show and who was now working in television.

We were getting CVs from dozens of people looking for research jobs, people who spoke four or five languages, Ph.D.s, one young woman who sent along a brilliant paper on Ronald Reagan's crazed "Star Wars" proposal, The Strategic Defence Initiative.

A good part of the CBC's contribution was to be office space, clerical help, editing suites and editors, and most importantly producer/directors. Although many CBC people were anxious about the future of the institution, some of the candidates we interviewed displayed a condescending attitude toward our project. At least two of the people we decided to hire were among the condescending ones, but in the end, ironically, they turned out to be invaluable.

And so by the time we were ready to go to Ireland for our wedding, even though none of the offshore co-production agreements was yet nailed down, we felt it made sense to combine the wedding trip with a first shoot, which was somewhat audacious as we still had no solid commitments from partners other than Petro-Can.

We are not religious people in the conventional sense. Formally speaking we are both Christians, Caroline having been more or less raised Church of Ireland, a sister church to my Anglican affiliation. Never quite as emotionally and intellectually involved as I was in that brief period in my twenties, she had found a similar joy in ritual and ceremony when she was confirmed in the magnificent and storied St. Patrick's Cathedral, in Dublin. I had been in St. Patrick's only months before and had sat at Jonathan Swift's desk with the man who was then the latest inheritor of Swift's mantle as dean of St. Patrick's, Victor Griffin, who was well-known to Caroline's family.

I had gone there to interview Dean Griffin for CBC Radio about his stand on a proposal to entrench in the constitution Ireland's opposition to abortion. A referendum was about to be held, and I had learned that Griffin was fighting it not on religious but on political grounds. He argued that embedding a sectarian element in the constitution was a violation of Ireland's advanced tradition of authentic republicanism. While he was theologically and personally offended by abortion, as a republican he considered it a matter of personal conscience. The republic would injure itself, he said, by yielding to the Catholic majority on this issue.

When I had finished the radio interview, I asked for a minute of his time on a personal matter, and told him that while the lady in question had not yet completely come around to my way of thinking, I was hoping to marry a woman who had been confirmed here in St. Patrick's, and as a divorced person would I have a problem if we wanted to be married here in the cathedral, Caroline's pastor at the local church in Malahide having refused?[2]

Victor Griffin glanced at the arched ceiling and pursed his lips for half a second, in a glance-and-purse I would come to know as characteristic, and gave a little sideways dip of his head in the Dublin way, and said, "Ah well, yeah, there'd be a couple of t'ings to be dealt with. Y' know? But *I'd* marry ye."

So as we were trying to decide between Toronto and Dublin, Roy Faibish found out about it, and was categorical: there was no other place in the world for that wedding. Once he had articulated it, it became an imperative.

There was, in fact, only one t'ing to be dealt with: Dean Griffin had explained that we had to have a civil marriage first. This was not Church of Ireland law, but Irish civil law – another instance of a clerical intrusion into a republican body of civil law.

"Some of me fella clergy say that the ceremony we perform after the civil ceremony is simply the Church's way of blessin' a marriage that's already taken place. But I'm goin' to tell you, Patrick Watson: when I marry you and Caroline Bamford in St. Patrick's Cathedral, *I'm goin' ta* marry *ye.*"

Paddy Sampson and his wife, Bette Laderoute, came over to the Roxborough house to be witnesses as a rent-a-rev from Markham performed the ceremony. We agreed over dinner that we would do the real thing in Dublin. Paddy and Bette would come. Dean Griffin suggested November 30, Swift's birthday. Perfect.

The outlines that Ben Barber and I had begun to assemble a year earlier were for a series organized around nations: the French experience of democracy, the United States, Canada, the fragile South American countries that had cruised back and forth between democracy and

2. It is not widely understood outside Ireland that Dublin's two cathedrals, Christ Church and St. Patrick's, are both Protestant. The Protestant dean Jonathan Swift had endeared himself to the Catholic poor by standing up for their rights against the murderous and economically vicious policies of the ruling British, in the 1700s. Now his late-twentieth-century successor was outraging the Irish Catholics with his stand on the abortion issue, but he never lost their respect.

dictatorship, Israel, Japan. Of course we had to begin with the first historical democracy, in Athens in the third century BCE. The modern writer who had most crisply recounted that experiment was Sir Moses Finley, a kid from Brooklyn who had caught the ancient Greek bug young and gone on to do his doctorate at Rutgers University, just before the U.S. went crazy with its post–World War II anti-commnist hysteria. Refusing to testify before a congressional committee about a colleague allegedly sympathetic to communism, he had been denied tenure, had gone off to England to take his chances, ended up as the senior ancient historian at Cambridge, knighted for his services as a scholar, and recognized worldwide as one of the best. His book *The Ancient Greeks* gives a compact, lucid, and engaging account of the Athenian democracy. I wanted that on film. He was said to be frail and fading. Remerowski began to make arrangements for us to meet him in his home in Cambridge in December, a few days after the wedding. We still had no budget, no crew, and no firm commitment from our British partner to supply a crew. We might have to borrow Ed Long, a CBC cameraman then based in London.

In October I had the first of a series of meetings with Pierre O'Neill, then head of French Television Current Affairs at *La Maison Radio-Canada* in Montreal. I wanted to do the *Democracy* series simultaneously in English and in French, and to host both versions. I expected much more resistance than I found. O'Neill is a courteous, open, adventurous man, and while he was cautious about the unheard-of proposal for an anglophone to front a major series on Radio-Canada, he remembered that *Seven Days* had built an astonishing following in French Canada (twenty years later I was still getting street recognition in Montreal and Quebec City), so there would be something of an audience base. He did not need to warn me that there might be resistance and resentment among the more nationalistic production people at *La Maison*. It turned out that we were wrong about that, however; most of the resistance came from management.

We were still patching up *The World Challenge*, and almost every trip to Montreal entailed at least a few hours of voice-over recording, or rewrites, or editorial consultation with Bertolino. We were beginning to screen completed episodes in early November. They were promising, but I was not confident about the producers' approach to the final versions – graphics, titles, music, and so on. A prophetic anxiety, as it turned out. At the same time, *Venture* was wearing me down, and Duncan McEwan and I were beginning to have some sharp encounters when he wanted me to do interviews or agree to items that I thought bad for the show or bad for me. In addition, Bill Morgan, the CBC head of Current Affairs, wanted to turn *Venture* into a business section of *The Journal* and assign McEwan to the *Democracy* project as the CBC's liaison. Rumours were flying around 790 Bay Street. Morgan had allegedly offered *Venture* to Mike Harris from CBC News without saying anything to McEwan or me. McEwan was in fact going to be fired, let down easy with the *Democracy* assignment (that was reassuring!). The atmosphere was CBC gutter gossip at its worst. I stayed with the board of trustees of the NFB, which took up relatively little time. There might be a collaboration there, I hoped(!), when we finally got underway with the actual production of *The Struggle for Democracy.*

Live from Lincoln Center was still enjoyable because Manhattan always is. In November 1985 I met Aaron Copland during an eighty-fifth birthday concert dedicated to his music. I felt I was doing good on-camera work. But I was getting more and more anxious to shed everything except *Democracy*, and we were moving in that direction.

By mid-November we had confirmed the interview with Sir Moses Finley for early December in Cambridge, and meetings with the Central Independent Television producers and money people to get that partnership up and running.

Caroline was in Malahide preparing the wedding. On the day I left to join her, there was a last flurry of *Venture* stuff and commissions to Remerowski about staff. Peter Ustinov phoned from Hamburg and said grandly, "What I do will pass, but what you and Caroline are about to do will last. Lots of love." Robert Markle grumpily refused to come to Ireland for the wedding ("If I get more than a hundred miles from home I get a nosebleed"). Our office manager, Debbie Wood, gave me an extraordinary yellow boutonniere to wear on the flight, with a sprig of ivy grown "from my own wedding bouquet." I was quite high on all that by the time I got to the airport. The British Airways agent sensed something, asked about the flower, and bumped me into first class.

Caroline's aunt Mai and uncle John Kirker had offered us their thatched seventeenth-century stone house, Casino, for the reception. It is just across the road from Malahide Castle, where Boswell's diaries were discovered in 1946. The wedding guests virtually took over the Grand Hotel in Malahide,[3] although there were only about ten of us staying there. For two or three days, we gathered around a coal fire in the lounge, drinking Guinness and feeling Irish. The first afternoon my sister's husband, Lloyd Green, got into a baseball argument with Roy Faibish. They were like a couple of kids with their card collections. The whole room watched spellbound as these two dignified Gents of a Certain Age tried to outdo each other with obscure trivia: "I bet you don't know who caught the foul ball that won the 1942 World Series for the Cardinals over the Yankees?"

"Sure I do, Walker Cooper, the catcher. But *you* don't know who the shortstop was who caught the grounder just before that and threw the runner out at first."

"Well, I know who the runner was . . ." It was mesmerizing. Until then I had always thought Faibish's boasting about baseball was fraudulent. Quite properly, before the wedding Caroline stayed at her father's house and I at the hotel. We walked every afternoon at Black Rock, the waves crashing in and sending up cascades.

I wrote in my journal, "I cannot remember being so full of a sense of the holiness of acts & of things & places & of human speech."

The wedding, in the Mary Chapel just east of the reredos, was like a polished stone. A small children's choir in blue and white surplices sang "Sheep May Safely Graze" in the gallery above. Soft light flooded

3. The town where Caroline's father also lived, about half an hour from central Dublin.

through the stained glass.[4] The organ announced the bride with a Bach trumpet voluntary.

When Dean Griffin pronounced us man and wife, he made a flourish with his gold and ivory brocaded stole that left it draped perfectly over his hand, as it enclosed our own clasped hands, the stole's crimson oval and cross perfectly centred. I had never seen that before. He kissed Caroline warmly as we came out of the cathedral, "Right on the smacker," she said afterwards.

Caroline's brother, Russell, drove us back to Casino in the rain, made a wrong turn in the Liberties in central Dublin, and got lost. We were twenty minutes late. Everyone else was still outside in the pouring rain. Mai and John had not arrived yet. The house was locked and the catering staff inside couldn't figure out the code. The burglar alarm went off and the police arrived. Russell raced around to the back and found the hidden emergency key. Typical Irish, we all said.

The party, when we finally got in, was warm and funny and soaked in affection. Best man Roy Faibish was characteristically ironic, and chose a poem by Robert Graves for Kate Nelligan to read, beginning

Why do fine women
Marry such terrible men?

Caroline's sister, Gabrielle, made a speech saying that Caroline and I were two orbiting bodies whose rotational velocities occasionally matched, thus giving us the opportunity to join, and that we had met in strife-riven Belfast and found peace in the midst of war. Roy quoted Christopher Smart:

For in my nature, I quested for beauty.
But God, God hath sent me to sea for pearls.

The dean stayed to the end, and kissed me when he left. Right on the smacker.

4. Including the one that shows Jesus going among the people, with the inscription "I was thirsty and ye gave me drink," and a brass plaque beneath it: "This window is a gift of the Guinness family."

We spent our wedding night in the Grand Hotel as if it were the first time ever, had breakfast with my sister, lunch at Casino with the guests, and headed off to London and back to work.

London was great. Reflecting on both the wedding and the work session, I wrote in my journal on the way home that it had been the best trip ever "to these here parts." Kathy and Allan Scott (he was the *Nightcap* comic in 1961) gave us a lavish second wedding party, where director Nicholas Roeg shot an elaborate "home video" of the rowdy evening. We went up to Cambridge on my mother's birthday and filmed with Sir Moses Finley in his study. He spoke about the rise of the Athenian democracy as if he had been there, about Pericles as though they had just parted in the Agora a couple of hours earlier. He was tired, his eyes gleaming out of dark circles, but the mind and the poetry were vigorously alive. We recorded more than an hour with him, only a few minutes of which ended up in the finished film, but a transfiguring few minutes.[5]

In London, Richard Creasey came through and decisively commissioned the Central production group. Ted Remerowski made an elaborate presentation to them of the concept and initial structure of the series. Ted tends to say "I dunno" a lot, as a kind of pause-word. It was entertaining to watch the Central producers' initial doubts about this mumbling, diffident guy ("Are we going to have to work for *this* dummy?") transform in the course of his hour-long presentation, as Ted gathered steam and the intricately coherent tapestry of his mind unfolded in front of them. He had transformed the earlier nation-based concept into a thematic structure: The Rule of Law; The Military and Democracy; The Last Citizens (Women); Money and Democracy; The Tyranny of the Majority. There would be one hour primarily about the dramatic, revolutionary experiment that produced the United States, but the rest of the programs would explore

5. The rest is still among the 400,000 feet of footage from that project, which we have archived in climate-controlled storage ever since. Finley died six months after we filmed with him, and cameraman Ed Long died a week after Finley, of meningitis, having been sent home from a Toronto hospital with some Tylenol for his "headache."

our themes in several different cultures. More and more, guided by Ben Barber, we were coming to understand that, in a sense, there is no such thing as democracy pure and simple: it is a word applied to a crazily differentiated patchwork of systems and structures derived from the cultures in which they grew, ranging from the direct democracy of Athens through the Iroquois Confederacy and the ancient consensual tribal *Khotla* in Botswana, to the rigid formalism of Japan, all sharing a relocation of power from elites to citizens.

The word "citizen" was taking on increasing power in my mind, in my vocabulary.

Except for those initial dollars from Petro-Canada, there was still no real money. Caroline and I took a look at the staff and facilities budget, and the blanks beginning to fill in on the shooting schedule, and realized we would have to dip into our own personal resources by February 1986 if the partners had not yet opened their purses. I had better keep on with *Venture* as long as I could, and accept anything else that came along with a reasonable fee attached. Aida Moreno called from WGBH Boston and pitched me on hosting their *Masterpiece Theater* 15th Anniversary Special. Alistair Cooke would introduce me, and I would interview him as well as cast members from *Upstairs Downstairs* and other luminous programs from that series. That worked out well, in February, and then we were off to Monte Carlo for the launch of *The World Challenge* (it was snowing in Nice when we arrived). Eight people were in the group: Bertolino had even brought his mother over from Carcassonne. After my presentation to the marketing crowd, I finally saw, for the first time, the finished programs and was appalled at the relentless music, my own wooden performance, and the cumulative moralistic effect of the scripts, which I had somehow missed when we were in production. A critic from *Le Monde* challenged me about it afterward, but far less critically than I had expected (or deserved).

I called the Musée Océanographique to inquire after the health of the sea turtles I had brought from Europa in 1968, and was saddened to learn that they had not done well in the aquarium, and had all been released into the Mediterranean two years after my adventure of smuggling them into France.

Remerowski and I began to spend a lot of time together. When my spirits sagged, contemplating the prodigious size of the challenge, he would invite me to screen other people's work on the subject and would point out how far beyond anything we saw we were now beginning to reach. I would realize how clear we were becoming about what the issues were, filmically and intellectually, and cheer up again.

There was still a deliciously distracting whir around the CBC presidency. At an NFB board meeting in Rouyn-Noranda, Alain Gourd, the deputy minister of communications, treated me with a mixture of deference and amiability that left me feeling he must know something. I had no idea how I would handle the ongoing production of the *Democracy* project should Mulroney confirm his offer. It seemed only prudent to make some plans, but apart from Caroline and Michael Levine, I thought I could not confide in anyone. Roy Faibish called from Ireland to say that the prime minister now expected Pierre Juneau to step down on his approaching sixty-fifth birthday, so it would be a retirement, not a resignation. That seemed probable enough to set me listing people I would want to bring in – I knew that the place could not be radically reformed with the existing senior officials still in place.

I persuaded Jack Willis to come to Toronto and screen a few days' worth of programs. I wanted him to take over the English television service. Michael Levine was hostile at first, but I said we could import American stars to play hockey and baseball and head the cast in a Canadian movie: why not bring in a brilliant programmer? They would not have objected to a Brit (and never had – the CBC had put a great many in senior positions). Jack was a production star in PBS. He had been an important contributor to *This Hour Has Seven Days.* Michael came around to my thinking. Jack and I had three or four giddy days of screening and brainstorming. He said that his wife, Mary, would be reticent about moving here, but that they were willing to give it the five years I felt it would take to rebuild the CBC into a genuine public television service, one that would win back its popular constituency and Parliament too. I would just have to sublet a great deal more of the management, editorial, and production work on *Democracy* to Ted, Caroline, and Nancy Button, and delegate tactically whenever I had to leave the president's office to go on location.

By the late spring of 1986 we had most of our team together. We settled into CBC office space at 415 Yonge Street and started planning for the early shoots. The CBC has always been a rumour mill, but that spring was especially rife with fearful speculations about the destruction that Juneau's next budget cuts would bring. One day George James and Michael Gerard, the two CBC documentary producers we had chosen, came anxiously into the Yonge Street office to say that management had just told them officially that they were assigned to the *Democracy* project, but that the uncertainty level was so high they weren't ready to believe it until they heard it from me.

Now the whole team was meeting for long sessions over the philosophy and attitude of the series, as well as the specifics of each program. It was beginning to feel like a unit. We screened dozens of films together, looking for new techniques and ideas, and noting excesses and errors to be avoided. We invited producers of unusual works to come and talk to us about making their films. Marian Marzynski was a favourite. His mischievously personal PBS documentary, *Russia: Love It or Leave It*, was screened over and over again. It had a combination of topicality and timeless relevance that was something we wanted to achieve.

Almost every member of the group had a film they wanted to dissect with the rest of us, and the discussions were long and vigorous.

Ted Remerowski came to me with a long face one day to say he was afraid we were going to have a lot of trouble with Michael Gerard, who had brought in ten complete outlines of his own and pronounced our own outlines to be inadequate. I said as long as we have really good people the chances are they'll be difficult; let me know if I have to intervene but in the meantime just let him get to know us better. I was remembering the Central Television producers' initial reaction to Ted, and how they had come around, and was confident that Gerard would too, which he did, though as Ted had predicted he was often very prickly. Many of us were prickly much of the time. In one meeting, after thrashing through some depressing budget problems, I raised the issue of Caroline's accompanying me on all the trips. Ted had reported some cynical whispering around the unit about doxy time for the boss. So I knew I had to deal with it straight out, remind them that it was our series, Caroline's and mine, we had intended from the start to work together, there was no way we would agree to be separated for months at a time, and that we would get more done if I had her help and support in the field. I wrote in my journal,

> *Nobody takes account of the fact that moving around is hard for me, and that I am too proud to yield to pain and its resultants until too late, and that she anticipates the problems and keeps me out of trouble. I cannot seem to manage that on my own. In the meeting I unfairly accused Nancy Button of icing C from the Iceland trip without consultation, and she rightly got a bit shirty about that and there was certainly a good deal of tension in the room. Michael was good, describing it as a situation not of our making but with contending legitimacies, and we established the rule that C. will normally travel except on the most rudimentary trips, and that we both will do our damnedest to conserve when and where we can.*

There were frequent blowouts – with Michael Gerard, with Nancy Button, with Michael Levine, and between Caroline and me. We were all feeling driven to do something extraordinary and the edge was pretty sharp much of the time.

But in fact they all delivered, often brilliantly and often with surprises. One evening in April, Michael Gerard invited us to dinner at his home with Mujbir Saad, an official from Tripoli whose sons were at Canadian universities, and an elderly blind Libyan scholar from the

University of Toronto. By the end of the evening, largely due to Gerard's adroit steering of the discussion, we had agreement in principle for a couple of weeks' shooting in Libya and an interview with Colonel Qaddafi. "He is not the head of our government," Saad told us. "We have no government, you see." His colleague the scholar demurred quietly, but said very seriously, "Colonel Qaddafi will be the last dictator in Libya. After him we will be ready for pure democracy. I think you will find it already growing."

We set dates for the first round of official filming, in June, in Iceland, Ireland, and Belgium. I felt a growing sensation of being on the threshold of consequence. Michael Levine, officially our executive producer, pulled off a series of prodigious deals, handling the legal and financial intricacies in such detail that they produced a set of big books, which he would later use as the basis of law lectures at Osgoode Hall. All this was accompanied by an acute sense of risk, of the possibility that all this effort and money might not, in the end, produce the major opus Caroline and I had dreamed of. How could it? It was just another round of documentaries, after all. My dreams began to reflect the magnitude of the thing. Journal, April 30, 1986.

> *At 4 am I awoke in tears having dreamed that pine trees could no longer grow. It was devastating. I wept for a good half hour, and felt restored by the weeping. Cosmic. The most powerful images were tiny black seeds, which seemed so perfect and so vital, and yet all the experiments that had been done failed to make them germinate, and while the existing trees would continue to live out their normal life span, there would be no new ones. This was utterly certain. It was like saying there would be no more children. An end-of-everything dream.*

We now had an agreement with Lester and Orpen Dennys for a book to accompany the series. Louise Dennys would edit it and was talking about a first-class production, richly illustrated and marketed internationally. She knew Ramsay Derry, who had edited my first novel, *Zero to Airtime*, when he was with Fitzhenry and Whiteside.

Derry was now a freelance editor, and Louise proposed that he begin drafting and organizing chapters and illustrations, to give an armature to work from when I could get away from the project long enough to do some finished writing. After a few weeks, he and I agreed that it wasn't working out. Ben Barber agreed to come in as my co-writer, and that proved another productive and amiable collaboration. Caroline had added location photographer to her portfolio of duties on the project. One vivid, sunny memory we share with equal delight is of Louise, Caroline, and me, in our stocking feet, with hundreds of pages and photographs laid out on the floor of Louise's Spadina Road apartment and the three of us roaming among them giggling and moving them about as we worked through the layout of the book.

After six months of shooting and assembling some preliminary edited segments, we booked the Prince of Wales Hotel in Niagara-on-the-Lake and convened an international colloquium of historians and documentary makers to look at what we were doing and guide the next steps. A year before going into production, we had held the first such gathering, mainly to talk about the nature of democracy, and to identify some of its crucial turning points across the span of history from Athens to the present. Jack and Mary Willis had come from New York, Cam Graham and Anthony Westell from Ottawa, and the philosopher T.M. Robinson from the University of Toronto. Now that we had more money to work with, we were able to bring people from around the world. Anthony Sampson (*The Anatomy of Britain, The Arms Bazaar, Mandela*) flew in from London. When snow closed the Boston airport and Henry Steele Commager, at eighty-four the dean of the American historians, could not get a flight, Bill Hopper sent the Petro-Canada jet to pick him up at another small airport near Harvard. We had a sociologist from Malaysia and our resident political philosopher from Rutgers. It was a daunting group and my producers were very nervous, dragged unwillingly to the table, so to speak. But when they showed some excerpts and outlined the plans, the colloquium's response was unequivocally excited and positive; the ideas that flowed were concrete and helpful, and the informal convivial evening sessions over food and drink convinced the whole team that we were doing something very special indeed, that the historians and other outsiders really admired what they were doing.

But the next two years would be mostly running hard and not resting or playing nearly enough. The panorama that presents itself when I look back casually is all airplanes and crossing oceans. We circled the globe three times. In one forty-day period we flew to Australia, filmed in Sydney, then up to Alice where I did stand-ups in a hot air balloon to set up our investigation of aboriginal culture and politics, much of which we shot at the magical Uluru,[6] which of course we had to climb. Well, I couldn't, but the others did. From Sydney we flew north across the Pearl Sea to Port Moresby in Papua New Guinea, where we were refused entry over a minor visa problem, and put right back on the same plane for its return to Sydney, whence we flew to New Zealand for a week, largely working with a group of Maori, then to California by way of Hawaii, New York for a couple of pickups, back to Toronto for a couple of days of rest, screening rushes, meeting with the unit, getting field reports, then off to the airport again for London, Nigeria, Rome, Tripoli, London again, then Jerusalem.

To extend the discussions that had begun at home base and been amplified in the colloquium, and to keep them going during the shoot when we sometimes had four crews on the road at once, all over the world, I began to write a series of letters to staff, some of which I jokingly called "Pastoral Letters." Some were sent directly to Louise Dennys and meant primarily for the book, but most went to everyone in the group. Month by month my sense of what we were after and of what the subject entailed was becoming more assured.

In May of '86 I wrote,

> *It has been conventionally said that government is an instrument for keeping human beings from their natural inclination to wipe each other out, and that in the state of*

6. "Ayers Rock" on the older maps.

> *nature, as Hobbes said, life would be nasty, brutish and short. I have come to the conclusion that this . . . fails to take into account the natural appetite for society, for talk, for social intercourse, that characterizes the human experience. Human animals become human only with the arrival of language; language is the distinguishing mark, and language is by nature social, gregarious, collaborative.*
>
> *It seems to me a more interesting and resonant view of the human experience to include – in the mix of motives that lead to government and civilizing institutions – this aspect of the human experience which is not violent but affectionate.*

Between trips I was often in Montreal negotiating the details of our French version with Radio-Canada. Among his management colleagues, Pierre O'Neill had found both encouragement and resistance to the idea of my hosting the series on the French network. A few years earlier, when the CBC announced it was opening a bureau in Beijing, I had applied for the post as both bureau chief and correspondent. That was at about the time of the decision to terminate *The Watson Report*, when there did not seem to be much television opportunity for me in Canada – before that summer of our mothers' deaths and Casey's Irish Bar, and the Jack Willis rescue call from CBS Cable. I thought I had more experience in China than any other CBC regular, and I was very excited about being both camera operator and correspondent, and reporting to both the French and the English networks. I auditioned confidently, but they turned me down because my French was not sufficiently elegant.

That would not be a problem with *Démocraties*. The lines would be largely scripted, and the improvised or on-the-spot stand-ups would be supervised by a francophone producer. One of those producers was a humorous energetic little guy named Pierre Castonguay, who had been the Radio-Canada rep in London when we were in the early phases of development and enjoyed making jokes at his own expense about how he had originally told me – in London – that Radio-Canada would *never* agree to have a series like that hosted by an anglophone. The other, Max Cacopardo, was a younger man, unknown to me, but endlessly enthusiastic and wisely helpful.

But the senior Montreal network people said that if the network were to get its money's worth they should give me an on-air sidekick who was well-known to the Radio-Canada audience. Would I be prepared to work with Robert-Guy Scully, they asked. I agreed, and, on the whole, it worked out quite well. We shared some stand-ups. It was clear that I was the principal figure, and he a kind of interlocutor. Pierre O'Neill would afterwards say that it had been an unnecessary encumbrance, two hosts in the same program, and the audience numbers were probably not at all helped by his presence. But it had been such an extraordinary advance to have come this far in getting the two networks to collaborate – nothing anywhere near as substantial would happen again until Mark Starowicz's *Canada: A People's History* – that I was never seriously inclined to argue against the pairing of Scully and me.

Radio-Canada had come in later than we had hoped. We had to shoot twice in some locations – Athens was one – to redo key scenes in French, and we added some subjects – the French Revolution, for example – that we had not explored in depth in the English version. Cacopardo and Castonguay were fine teachers, and sound man Robert Reed, under the pretext of adjusting my microphone, would often whisper in my ear some suggestions about my idiom or pronunciation, which gave my French stand-ups a colloquialism they would otherwise have lacked. (He whispered because that was the producers' job, and they were perhaps a bit reticent.)

However, in the recording studio, doing the voice-over narrations in French, Cacopardo and Castonguay were diligent and unrestrained, and refined my speaking of the language more in those few weeks, I suspect, than had all my years of conversation and reading.

There are many swish pans and blurred images in my memory of this period, but tons of details in the journals I was compulsively keeping, mostly on the primitive Tandy Model 100 with its tiny memory now enlarged by means of a plug-in bar of additional chips, to 768kb (yes, kilobytes), in six banks that each had to be accessed separately. Sometime along the way the first outboard three-and-a-half-inch floppy disk drive arrived, so I could make security backups. Remarkably little was lost, although I left the computer in airplane seat-back pockets in Harare and Buenos Aires, among other destinations, usually rescued by the irreplaceable and irrepressible sound man, Ian Challis.

The displacement of time zones and cultural frameworks was dizzying. In March and April 1987, we were in Nigeria, Zimbabwe, Australia, New Zealand, Switzerland, and Liechtenstein. But among the confusion of blurred images and sleepless nights are also dozens of etched and unforgettable scenes.

An Israeli soldier from two hundred feet above the desert in a sky almost blackened by parachutes yelling down, "Will you get that fucking camera out of the way! I have to land right there."

Standing at the edge of the Libyan desert, a deep wadi to the north of us, a helicopter pad close by, Mujbir, Caroline, and I, and the crew. A clutch of small buildings in a copse of stunted trees. An open ceremonial tent, where Colonel Qaddafi holds official meetings. A few armed men in uniform, one of whom has told us to wait by the tent. Our driver has taken the car away somewhere out of sight. Ian Challis says, "Shall we take bets where he'll come from?" He is looking at the helicopter pad. Caroline says, "Down there," pointing at a path that leads over the edge of the wadi and disappears.

Twenty minutes later, Qaddafi arrives up that path with a single armed soldier at his side, a woman. He shakes hands. The interview goes well, Mujbir translating fluidly. Qaddafi laughs a good deal. His confidence is radiant. He fields the hardest questions with dignity. He tells us, Yes, it is regrettable that some enemies of the revolution have been killed, and that he finds the public spectacle (they are hanged in the football stadium) disgusting. But if they had not been killed, there would have been many uprisings, maybe civil war, soon he will abolish capital punishment, the country will move unhesitatingly toward true democracy. Abruptly it is over. He rises, shakes hands, strides away. I signal to Francis Granger, who whips the camera off the sticks and onto his shoulder, and trots after the tall retreating robed figure. Soldiers appear out of nowhere, holding out their submachine guns to block the cameraman. Qaddafi looks back, grins, says something gently to a soldier. The weapons are lowered. Qaddafi nods to Granger, and they continue along the path over the edge of the wadi and disappear. Granger tells us later that he stumbled and fell while circling for a better sight line when Qaddafi stopped to stroke a baby camel on the steep slope, and that the dictator courteously bent over and helped him up. Ian Challis asks Caroline, "How did you know where he would come from?" Caroline says, "Just as we were getting out of the car, I saw a man going down that path carrying a silver tea service on a tray."

Images on the screen in the cutting room. A bound man being led to and then tied to a thick post set in the sand on a Nigerian beach. As he protests his innocence of the theft for which he has been convicted, the firing squad lets loose and his body is riddled, slumps, and is still. The Nigerian newspapers carry letters of complaint later that day: the television transmitter had failed that afternoon and people had been deprived of watching the executions.

Television executives sitting around a boardroom table in Moscow as I pitch them about collaborating on the project. They have been screening scenes from film already shot. They express amazement at the range of the series, at the quality of the storytelling. "We would really like to get involved, but . . ." It is Perestroika time, and the atmosphere in the city is much gentler than it was even a few years ago, but we're still a long way from the end of the USSR, and it looks like a no-go on bringing in the Russians.

Japan. A public meeting on a hillside above the nuclear reactor at Kashawazaki, where the citizens are courteously but firmly questioning power executives about the cooling system and its effect on the fishermen. The executives are replying courteously and in detail. Some kind of accommodation seems to be in the making. This is how authority deals with the citizens in Japan, we are told. It is called "Nemawashi," which means "Going around the roots" to build consent.

Sitting in a classroom at the National Military College in Argentina, not long after the end of the Dirty War, listening as officer trainees are taught about their role in society; they are the guardians; they must believe this; if all else fails, it will be up to them to preserve Argentina; it is a sacred duty. I reflect that the generals who held the country hostage all those years had all sat in these same desks and learned this same mission. By contrast, walking with the Mothers of the Plaza da Mayo, in their continuing protest against the Dirty War that had killed so many of their children, and filming with the residents of the shanty towns, in the earth-floored shacks of cardboard and empty oil drums whose desperate inhabitants still somehow were finding the spirit to hold on. Or in India, the earth sheds that quarry workers and their families lived in, workers who were effectively slaves to the quarry owners, in the midst of the "world's largest democracy."

Filming an all-day *Khotla*, the centuries-old tribal democratic meeting in a village in Botswana, where every adult, man and woman, has a say, and decisions are not made until the entire assembly agrees. They handle municipal matters here. For a while the discussion is about an as yet little known issue, which we hear as the only English word they use. It is AIDS. The principal speaker says that there is far too much talk about this AIDS thing, they should get on with more important matters. Nobody in their village has the disease, after all.

(Less than two decades later, almost half the adults in Botswana had AIDS.) The currency unit in Botswana is the Pula. This is the Setswana word for rain. It is also used as a salutation. When it is time for us to leave, the (elected) chief makes a little speech about us, and the entire village rises to its feet, the warriors waving their ceremonial weapons, and the whole village chanting, Pula! Pula! at the top of their lungs. I still have a crisp one-Pula note in my wallet.

Shooting a stand-up in sunlight at 11 p.m. at the site of the Althinge, the democratic Icelandic parliament that first assembled here in the tenth century, where the tectonic plates separate and the valley is more than a mile wider today than it was for the first Althingers. They wrote laws that Iceland's schoolkids can still read, so little has the language changed.

Standing on the sidewalk in Londonderry on July 12, as the boy in a stocking mask beside me throws a flaming Molotov cocktail at a British Army armoured car.

Looking into a pit full of flaked marble, near the Agora in Athens. The archaeologists on the dig tell us they have just concluded, on the basis of one small inscription on a fragment of pottery, that this is probably where Socrates lived. And two days later, crawling on my hands and knees into the depths of a tunnel less than four feet high which, in Socrates' time, was a silver mine, and shooting a "stand-up" there to remind us, in the midst of all this excitement about that brief ancient experiment with democracy, that the miners here, who dug out the silver by hand, were from that 30 percent of the population who were slaves, and, like women, were not citizens.

Here is a journal entry about a strange mishap on the day we filmed in the Swiss canton called The Appenzel, where they still made legislation in a *Landsgemeinde*, an outdoor assembly of the entire citizen body (which did not, ironically, include women at that point). This was written on the Tandy 100 in the spring of 1987.

> *First thing was a trip up the Cable Car to Hoherkast, shooting my piece to camera on the way up and some scenics on the way down. Piece to camera went fine. Breakfast was waiting at the restau at the top. At the end of the breakfast I pushed my chair back too fast from the table; the legs caught on a lip of lino or something on the floor. Whatever it was I went over backwards and cracked my head fairly hard on the floor. Didn't hurt that much and I did not feel stunned or anything, just a bit shocked and surprised.*
>
> [On the next shoot, at the Landsgemeinde] *David* [Gerrard, the British director] *says that he came into the room a few minutes later and asked me if the take was all*

> *right, and that I said, "I'm waiting to hear a playback." I remember that at that point I was looking at the script and feeling very puzzled about it somehow. Dennis Fitch said, also puzzled, "He just heard the playback."*
>
> *I suddenly knew that he was right, but at the same time that I could not remember doing it. I was shocked and frightened at the sense of confusion. David said, "Perhaps we'd better get you to a doctor – it's that bang on the head you had this morning."*
>
> *I looked baffled. "This Morning!" (I thought, But that was days ago.) I could not remember much of the sequence of the morning. I thought, They would do a gross neurological first. I checked the vision in each eye. Then I brought my fingertips together. They were shaking. Fear. I asked Elaine to go over the details of the morning. She did, quickly, solicitous in a low-key, careful way. As she described things we had done I could remember most. But there was still a huge confusion about time, especially the previous few minutes in which I had done an almost faultless standup from memory, spoiled only by this genius from Swiss Radio hissing and waving at me. That part I could remember.*
>
> *I memorized the next piece to camera and moved down to the street again to do it. Everything else seems to be all right, no headache, no confusion, I can remember poems I know, postal codes, what we have to do tomorrow. Of course the dreaded word Alzheimer drifts momentarily by . . . .*

And more memories: India this time.

Climbing out of a boat on the shore below Varanasi, after a trip along the Ganges to see the Ghats. The boatman pokes with his oar at a round pink object half-submerged among the garbage and debris along the edge. It is the head of a child, most of the skin already gone. The boatman shrugs. I compulsively reach for my Nikon, but in the end do not even take the lens cap off.

Riding down a river in Eastern Nigeria in a boat loaded to the gunwales with villagers going shopping in a downstream town, doing a stand-up to camera about village democracy in that country, and having a man across the boat call out, asking where we came from. I tell him Canada. "And the cameraman? Where does he come from?" Jamaica, I answer. "Ah," called out my interlocutor. "I thought he was not from Canada . . . because of his CULL-OR!"

Driving across that country with a Canadian flag hopefully mounted on the windscreen, we are warned that there are bandits on the roads, that we must never get out of the car. Offer them money but never roll the window down more than an inch or two. Watch out for tires left in the road as obstacles to make you stop. Just bulldoze through. Foreigners who do stop and get out of their cars to move the tires out of the way are generally not seen again.

My regret that I listened to Michael Gerard's thoughtful insistence that Caroline not come on the Nigeria trip, because of the danger. She is one of the world's more accomplished survivors, to begin with, and what good would it do either of us for me to die alone in Nigeria?

The constant, intent concern to not waste time, to make the best use of every resource. Here is another journal entry.

> *Tuesday 6 Sep. (1988) Spent the morning at CBC Paris office. Had to walk there and back. Taxis hard to find. After lunch to the Sorbonne, and prepared prof Michel Vovelle, the "Bonze" of the bicentennaire, for what I hoped would be a planned, concise interview, with segments not more than 1min 30. He was superb, to everyone's amazement. With passion and a twinkle, came in at 1min pile* [precisely] *on the subject of The Declaration of the Rights of Man, equally concise on La Terreur, a little less good on the heritage of the revo, because I did not prepare him that well. I told him he deserved a medal for being so generous in COMPRESSING his speaking time. Christiane Rondeau* [the production assistant] *said I deserved a medal for producing such compression out of*

a scholar, and I thought so too. Shot the whole interview on less than 300 feet!

More scenes:

The small screening room at 790 Bay Street, where we have assembled perhaps thirty people to screen what we at last think is a pretty good cut of "The Last Citizens," a difficult program that Ted Remerowski chose to do himself, one that has been in the cutting room for a very long time. As is our custom, we have invited a few people who don't even know about the project – a mail boy, some secretaries, a stranger we met in the coffee shop – so that the majority in the room, who work on the series, can hear what some virgin viewers think. A substantial part of the hour is about the long struggle of several Canadian women's groups to entrench gender equality in the Charter of Rights and Freedoms. At the end of the screening, people get to their feet and applaud the shyly beaming Remerowski. As the applause dies away, a deep voice from the back, Ben Barber's, says sourly, "I didn't understand it at all." All the references to pressure groups and institutions, in the news for the last few years and totally familiar to all of us, had been incomprehensible code to the one non-Canadian in the room. Our offshore audience will be at least ten times the size of our Canadian audience. Back to the cutting room.

Fine-tuning the narration in the cutting room with Ted and the senior editor, John Gareau. I write by hand, in pencil, on legal-size foolscap. We try a line. It doesn't work. I crumple it up and throw it across the room to the wastebasket. I always miss the basket. Ted always scores with his tossed crumples. We each do several dozen crumples a day. I keep missing; Ted keeps hitting. It becomes a thing.

Screening a rough cut in the CBC's VIP screening room at Film House, on Front Street, for Bill Hopper, our principal sponsor. It is really too soon to show him anything. You never show rough cuts to lay people. But Hopper is paying a lot of our bills and he wants to see a selection of work in progress, wants to see bits of Athens, bits of Zimbabwe, bits of Argentina. I'm seeing some cuts for the first time.

I think it looks pretty good. The lights go up. Hopper turns around and grins at us. "I guess you guys know what you're doing," he says dryly, "but that's about the most boring confused hour and a half of television I've ever seen in my life."

Crushed. (But we say to ourselves, Of course, you never, *never*, screen rough cuts for a lay person.)

The day the call comes from Ottawa, many months later. We had sent Hopper a finished copy of the opening program, "Genesis." There has been an anxious week of silence. The call is from an assistant. Mr. Hopper wants to see Remerowski and me in his Ottawa office tomorrow. Stomach cramps.

We are shown into an empty boardroom and sit there without speaking for what is probably five minutes but seems an hour. The door opens. Hopper comes in with the cassette in his hand. He looks at us slyly for a moment, and then says, as he sweeps his hand toward the champagne bucket and glasses we had not noticed in the corner of the room, "This is the best damn documentary film I have ever seen in my life."

I had still not given up on Pierre Trudeau. With only a few weeks of shooting left I tried again, telling him about the range of material we now had, the perplexities and challenges, our distribution commitments in Britain, the U.S., and internationally. I said it would be an opportunity for him to tell the whole world about his experience with the Canadian democracy, and that it seemed to me a kind of obligation.

This time he did not say no straight out. "When do you have to know?" he asked. I said that in just under two months I would have to lock up the final shape of the program, so, let's say six weeks. "I'll call you within six weeks and give you a definite answer," he said. He was travelling, would think about it while he was abroad, would be back in a month and would call soon afterward.

At around the five-week mark I woke up one morning at seven o'clock and told Caroline that I had just had a vivid dream in which Pierre had phoned and accepted. She scratched my head affectionately and chuckled something about wishful thinking. At ten o'clock that morning the phone on my desk rang. "Mr. Trudeau is calling," a secretary said, and on he came to say that, yes, I was right, he had an obligation to do this, he was reluctant but he knew he must, would I call in two weeks after he'd settled down from his trip, and we would set a time.

And then when I made that call, two weeks later, he had changed his mind again, he was very sorry, it was the floodgates thing again, he couldn't bear having to tell all the other journalists with whom he had long-standing cordial relationships that he would not do something with them when he had done so with me, and, please, I must not ask him again.

So I buried it.

In December of 1988, about three weeks before the first broadcast of the *Democracy* series, Tom Axworthy gave his wife an elaborate party at the Mount Royal Club in Montreal and invited me because I worked on the *Heritage Minutes* with him at the CRB Foundation. I was standing in that crowd with a drink, about twenty feet from the door, when Pierre Trudeau came bouncing through it, all eyes turning in that direction. He paused at the threshold and surveyed the crowded room. His eyes lit on me. He called across in a loud voice, "Well! Patrick Watson! I hear that you are about to launch a big international television series on democracy. Why the hell didn't you ask me to take part in it?"

Every eye in the place turned on the idiot producer who had made such an egregious omission, such a goof, such an idiotic goof. Trudeau glided by me on his way to shake hands with Tom Axworthy, and winked conspiratorially as he went by. I admired that joke; I remember it with affection.

The Struggle for Democracy/Démocraties went to air simultaneously on the CBC's two networks, in French and English, in January 1989. It was the first program ever to be hosted by the same person in both languages. Bill Hopper gave us a spectacular launch party at the National Gallery. I bought a radio-controlled toy car, a jumbo-wheel pickup truck called *The Hopper*, and sent it whizzing across the hall to the Petro-Can chairman during my thank-you speech.

In the United States, PBS launched the series in July. Central Independent Television, who had the international distribution rights, reported within months that they were getting orders from the major English-speaking countries, from Hong Kong, and ultimately from some forty countries around the world, including the emerging new democracies in Eastern Europe. In the spring of 1990, Caroline and I and Remerowski shot a follow-up episode, "The Wall Goes Down," in Romania, Czechoslovakia, Poland, and Russia. When we were flying from Prague to Bratislava, I was approached by several people who that week had been watching the series on Czech television. The whole series is available to students free in a number of libraries across Canada. History Television has rebroadcast it several times, as has iChannel and Access, and the number of times I am still approached about it on the street or in public places is extraordinary, almost fifteen years after its first broadcast.

I believe that *The Struggle for Democracy* was the last major Canadian television documentary to be shot on film. Video was on its rampant way, and none of the film cameramen who worked with me in those years is still shooting film, though some still have their old cameras and many are wistful about the old medium. Some say it will soon be only a memory. I have been predicting it will have a revival, but then, nostalgia, as the joke goes, isn't what it used to be. In the making of the *Heritage Minutes*, I have insisted on using film for the original shoots, because the cinema look needs the grain and latitude of film, which even digital video has not yet achieved. Audiences know intuitively that if those elements are absent, then it is not a real movie, but some producers are ignoring that, and putting up on the big screen images that look like high-definition television – which they are. Some critics comment on this when dismissing a film. I am told that video will soon be able to imitate the grain and other traditional cinematic qualities of celluloid and emulsion, and if that happens it will be interesting to see for how long audience taste will continue to favour them.

I had launched into making *The Struggle for Democracy* from what soon began to seem a naive state of ignorance. We had assumed that while the world was full of peril and disaster, nonetheless the spread of reason and the retreat of superstition, although slow, were steady; that there was an irreversible momentum toward the universal recognition of the value of the human person and of that person's rights to liberty and growth; that there was wide and growing agreement about war and genocide, and increasingly effective international covenants and institutions and mechanisms committed to building toward a peaceful world. Much of what I discovered travelling through the thirty-odd countries we filmed in, some of them just emerging from nearly a century of dictatorship, reinforced that optimism. Even in the foulest grip of the corruption and cruelty and civic paralysis of a Nigeria, say, I thought I discerned a core of dedication to the long task of cleansing, of taking the lumps and the indignities that came with insisting on social justice and on tolerance and liberty and shared values. Here was an Anthony Ukpo, Colonel in the Nigerian Army, provincial governor with effectively dictatorial powers, using those powers to bring the tribal peoples together in a sort of proto-parliament, to give them the experience of the give and take of debate in an environment that supposes that all sides have rights and have dignity, and are to be met with as something like equals. Here was a brave and outspoken lawyer, Gani Fawehimni, in and out of jail for his irrepressible insistence on calling corrupt authority to account, but not destroyed, not discouraged, still turning up in the news twenty years later, still doing it: that had to mean that thick as the corruption was, cruel as courts were, some seeds had been sown and there were men and women guarding them, watering them, nourishing them, risking their lives to get them into the sunlight.

But in the years since, there has often appeared, on the surface of the daily news and out of the great currents of disaster in the Kosovos, Malawis, and Rwandas of the world, clouds of inhumanity and violence that sometimes seem as if they will billow and rise and overwhelm the courage of the Fawehimnis and the Ukpos, or the goodwill of Les Médecins sans Frontières, or the determination of the European Court of Human Rights or the muddle-headed impotence of the agencies of the United Nations in the face of determined militaristic imperial powers. The apparent willingness of the great pioneer democracies to allow civil rights to decay, and power to flow into the hands of the wealthy elites, while the working people who produce that wealth are kept hypnotized by the dominant consumerist morality, is perhaps the dreariest of the signs of change in those later years.

Nancy Button organized a tremendous wrap party shortly after the launch. She had enough left in the budget to invite everybody and give them a very good time. I was able to say things about Canada, in my speech to the troops that night, that I am not sure I could say today. I said:

> *I have been reinforced in my conclusion that Canada is in fact the most vigorous, fresh, effervescent and profitable of all the nations that I have met. And this is not just the fond fancy of a patriot. It is a conclusion that I came to young and keep on finding confirmation for. That this Canada of ours has an opportunity, especially now that we have reached real maturity and independence, constitutionalized and agreed upon, to prepare for the world's contemplation such a model of civility and social justice and human fulfilment for all our citizens, that everyone the world over will say of us, as many already do, "There now! That's how it should be done."*
>
> *Not to be the world's smartest trader or most steadfast soldier or brilliant inventor or dazzling entertainer, though we excel in all of these more than many of our people know – being a bit reticent when it comes to advertising our accomplishments – but to draw the world's eyes and the flattery of its imitation because we are wise, imaginative, generous, just and civil – to our own and to all.*
>
> *As you saw in the sales reel, one day, filming in a pub in Australia, we decided to put the camera on the legs and ask a*

few drinkers, as we had been asking around the world: "What is democracy?"

And there was one guy in a beard and a pony-tail . . . NOT one of our producers, by the way, who said, "The trouble is that Democracy basically says that ninety nine half wits will make a better decision than the one person who knows the facts."

Well, after filming the struggle for democracy all over the world, you know what? I think I've ended up . . . on the side of the half-wits.

Here at home, and across much of the global territory where democracy established itself over the past couple of centuries with the shedding of much blood and the painstaking humanity of courageous men and women relentlessly putting themselves on the line for personal liberty, for the end of slavery and the defanging of racism, for literacy as the essential tool of the modern democratic citizen, the equality of the sexes, the rights of children – after all that work and sacrifice, much of it focused and energized and brought to an accelerated fruition by a world war and the unleashing of the nuclear weapon – after all that work, over a few short years the idea of the citizen seems to have gone into eclipse.

The concept of the public good and the assumption that people who share the benefits of membership in a nation have things to do together, have a continuing common enterprise in the endless business of making the land they stand on more and more nourishing of the fabric of democracy, of the great bake ovens of community, of all the great singing and striving and building and rejoicing that flow from making real the great – and it always seemed to me inevitable – entrenchment of human capacity that happens to a country when the dream of democratic citizenship becomes a universal reality – these, however, appear to be withering. The idea of civic virtue has been replaced by the seemingly irreversible myth of the consumer as the ultimate state of grace. *To shop is to be fulfilled*: that is the new civic religion.

The media, especially television, are almost completely in thrall to that religion. In 2002 I signed on with a new international group committed to finding a way for television to achieve some of its potential as an instrument of awareness and of social and democratic and civic growth through something called IWT, International World Television. It was conceived and developed by a former CBC journalist/producer named Paul Jay, who has tirelessly beaten a track around the continent to persuade hundreds of journalists[7] to help him build this service, which would be paid for entirely by its viewers around the world, and would be dedicated to solid journalism unbeholden to any interest except the needs of its members to be honestly informed, and the high professional commitments of its editorial staff.

As he was developing the website, I wrote to Paul Jay that I had an overriding concern:

> *I am more and more struck by the preoccupation, in existing television journalism, with disaster, crime, violence and dysfunction, and the almost complete invisibility of the myriad success stories from around the world. The global rise in literacy and fall in infant mortality are invisible to television. The tremendous spread of alternate energy would be a huge source of hope for the world were it known about. Even in Canada, where we used to have a national public broadcaster and still do have at least one regional public broadcaster, how many Canadians know about the huge wind power development in Alberta? We all know it's the oil capital of the country; but oil is going to run out and wind is not. How many Americans, numbed into despair by images of erosion, forest fire, earthquake, pollution and disappearing species, know that 50 million acres of the North East US have been successfully reforested, that the Red Wolf has been rescued from extinction and now roams wild, that wild turkeys, declared extinct in Wisconsin in*

7. Among the forty-five members of the founding committee by the beginning of 2004 were Gore Vidal, Jonathan Schell, Lewis Lapham, Francine Pelletier, Charles Benton, Bob Blair, Naomi Klein, Odelia Bay, Amy Goodman, Tariq Ali, and Afsan Chowdhury.

the late 1800's, have become so plentiful we're soon going to have to encourage hunters again because these birds have become a menace to grain farmers (I know this from personal experience right here in Mono Twp [where we were living at the time]). *Nobody is reporting these things on TV, and we need not only a systematic major documentary thrust about success stories, but also to seek them out for the daily newscast as well. We must not fall into the Bad News Sells syndrome that has infected everyone else.*

I am becoming convinced that it is very much in the interest of Global Corporatism to keep bad news on the screen. The viewer is so powerfully persuaded by the night's review of death and disaster that the opportunity for personal salvation represented by buying happiness off the shelf or at the car dealership becomes insanely seductive. The notion that one might become involved in any kind of personal, community or international action aimed at bettering the world is rendered inconceivable by the relentless display of a world that is only getting worse, a world in which comfort and assurance can be found only in a shop. How the hell can anyone begin to imagine there's any hope for democracy if they take their information about the world only from TV news?

When IWT becomes a reality, if I am allowed anywhere near the policy engine I am going to press very hard on this button. This is not polyannaville or comfort blanket stuff: this is saying that unless people know that we have in fact made real progress in critical areas, then despair will become universal and buying stuff will be the drug that everyone turns to when they could be turning to their neighbours and saying, let's get together and put up a turbine, clean up the stream, plant a community garden, teach kids how not to get AIDS, start an adult literacy centre, force our government to give us a top-quality public education system . . . .

It has become quite impossible for citizens to judge from the generally available sources whether the world is getting better or worse, whether we are killing more kids with weapons and pollution than we used to, or whether the information buried in United Nations reports or books of modest circulation – reports, for example, on the global reduction of infant mortality and the global increase in literacy, or the amazing overnight appearance of thousands of women elected to public office in Pakistan – whether such things offer any hope against the massacres and disasters so beloved of television news editors.

Had I the energy and suppositions of success that drove me into *The Struggle for Democracy* the next major enterprise I would undertake would be a world health report, an assessment of that kind of balance I wondered about in my letter to Paul Jay. We are appalled by the accounts of 800,000 people hacked to death in Rwanda. *But it did get reported, in the end!* A hundred years ago it would not have. Journalists were not routinely swarming all over the world (and often getting killed for their efforts). The European powers that controlled so much of subequatorial Africa could massacre whom they wanted and conceal all the evidence. If a million kids died of smallpox in China, who would ever hear of it? So what the world needs now is an ongoing synoptic account of how we are doing. Beating away inside this writer's aging ribcage there is an irrepressible conviction that as human knowledge increases so does the recognition that we *do* have common enterprise, we citizens of the world, that we *do* have stuff to do *together*, that we have the tools and the instruments to clean up our air and water and make sure there is enough for everyone, to change human behaviour on a global scale.

A few years ago *Le Monde* reported part of a conversation between the then French Minister of the Interior, Jean-Pierre Chevènement, and a group of journalists who were pressing him on the long vexed issue of foreign workers in France, especially Algerians, and the widespread hostility of the native French to granting French citizenship to these immigrants.

Chevènement came up with a phrase so banal in its language that it almost slips by you the first time. He said that perhaps it was time to redefine the criteria for citizenship in France. Popular sentiment seemed to hold that you could be a *real* French citizen only if your *arrière, arrière, arrière grand-père* had been born in France, only if you were a member of *la vieille souche*, the old ethnic stock. Perhaps, he proposed, perhaps a more useful criterion would be your commitment to the values of the nation. M. Chevènement then suggested that from now on the one criterion for citizenship of France would be "*le partage d'un projet commun*," sharing in a common project. *Sharing in a common project!* The simplicity of the words and the grandeur of the idea! It seems to me to describe the approach we have taken in Canada, where you get to be a citizen by demonstrating that you mean to live here, you have studied the laws and institutions sufficiently to know what it is we intend in matters of civil relations and are willing to sign on, to share the common project of making that civil society function.

I admire that formulation; it holds the seeds of the dream of world citizenship. I used to trot it out in conversation with committed Quebec nationalists, asking them to make lists of the things of consequence about which they could agree with Canadians across the country, and the things about which they could not make common cause. Interesting how long the list of agreed items was, the components of the common project: the sacredness of children and the environment, the importance of education, health care, peace and stability, the tolerance of racial difference, freedom of movement and of expression . . . and the brevity of the list of differences: a few things about language and borders and names.

And I thought, Expand that to the world. Systematically work up lists, around the world, of those things we can all agree on, and those things we disagree on, and find ways for us to live with our differences (as we often do by creating borders and naming nations) and might that not move us toward a definition of citizens of the world, citizens who share convictions about the sacredness of children and of the environment, the importance of education, peace and stability . . .

Of course there would be huge differences with regard to religion and superstition, tribal differences, differences about who belongs and who does not. But it would be a start.

In any case: there is a project for you, reader, if one reason for your having opened this account of a life largely spent in television is that you too would like to make something of value in the medium: How about an ongoing global assessment of how we are doing?

You could call it *Quarterly Report.*

Oh, by the way: both the English and the French versions of the *Democracy* series won the country's highest awards for documentary that year.

Chapter 22

MACHINATIONS

A DIARY ENTRY ON October 2, 1984, casually recounting a lunch with Caroline in the midst of a day happily working away at outlines for *Democracy*, contains an indicator that was not taken seriously at the time.

> *Pam Wallin was at the next table in Cibo. . . . Rumours that* [the only recently elected] *Prime Minister Mulroney will try to squeeze out Juneau + replace him with Peter Herrndorf, David MacDonald,*[1] *or me. I doubt very much the premise. Larry Zolf's very funny guest column in* Maclean's *last week contradicts rumours of Tory War against the CBC & I incline more to Zolf's view than to the conventional rumours.*

The prime minister's first phone call in 1985 was mellifluous and seductive in intent. Faibish had apparently persuaded him that I was the one to take charge of the CBC. That theme resurfaced when later that year he invited Caroline and me to dinner at 24 Sussex, with Roy and Barbara Faibish, to explore where the CBC might go under a new president. Mulroney did not hide his distrust and dislike of Juneau, and I was sure that Faibish was nourishing those attitudes. During Roy's tenure as a commissioner on the CRTC, he had characterised

1. The United Church clergyman who had been the minister responsible for the CBC in Joe Clark's short-lived government.

Juneau's chairmanship as divisive and damaging. Then when Trudeau named Juneau to the presidency of the CBC, Roy was outraged. "He's a former cabinet minister, for Christ's sake! The journalists will never trust him. They'll see him interfering in political coverage even if he doesn't do a thing. And if there's ever a Conservative government they'll kill him."

Now there was a Conservative government, and they were trying to kill him. Apparently I was a candidate to replace him, and I was torn.

It had seemed so clear and simple when Roy Faibish first asked me to consider the presidency in the fall of 1984. I had refused instantly and my refusal had been untroubled by second thoughts. Now my perception of it all was a dark mirror image of what I had seen earlier. I agreed hesitantly to be available should Juneau decide to leave early, as the prime minister had suggested he might. I had no idea what a prodigiously inert and resistant mass the CBC senior management was. I was eager to get my hands on the place and start putting some of my ideas into effect. I still felt it was possible to restore a national constituency for the CBC by reversing Juneau's drift into commercialism and rebuilding the television service as a genuinely engaged and totally service-oriented public broadcaster. I had put together a notebook of ideas about dealing with the unions,[2] revising the schedule to meet the challenge of the multi-channel universe, tidying up the administrative mess, and radically reducing the stifling burden of useless bureaucrats.

The biggest obstacle was the damage such an all-consuming job might wreak on our relationship. Caroline was cautiously encouraging, but I knew she was anxious. Furthermore, the idea of a government firing a CBC president for political reasons was anathema, a crude and dangerous violation of the arm's-length relationship. Roy was doing his best to persuade me that it was in the interests of the survival of the Corporation, since as long as Juneau was there a Tory government would consider the CBC to be the enemy. But it was still

2. To two of which I belonged and still do: ACTRA (the performers' union) and The Writers' Union of Canada.

a political move; it was against all the best traditions of public broadcasting in Canada, including the express intent of the Broadcasting Act, which firmly protects the CBC president from government interference. Now my being even in part the government's instrument in this outrage was an appalling prospect. Although Roy was also doing everything he could to persuade me of Mulroney's strengths and virtues, I was uneasy. I also believed that a majority of his cabinet disliked the CBC; I expected that they would see the successful removal of its president as a beachhead from which to launch further attacks.

But at the same time I thought Juneau was making CBC Television look more and more like an American commercial broadcaster. Denny Harvey, the vice-president of English Television, had almost whimpered to me once as we walked together down Bay Street toward his office building. "Every time there's a financial problem," Denny said, "Juneau calls me and says, 'Sell more advertising.'"

When Juneau was first named president, he had come to New York, where I was hosting the CBS Cable network, and consulted me about personnel and about the possibility of my joining his team. I declined, but later, when CBS Cable closed down, he engaged me as a part-time policy consultant and I had spent a good deal of time in the war room at head office through a number of strategy planning sessions. I had seen him being influenced by the smooth-talking John Shewbridge, and watched with astonishment the way Juneau was charmed by former TVO chairman Ranald Ide, his principal outside policy adviser.

This was distressing. We had had a long relationship. When he was vice-chairman of the Board of Broadcast Governors, he had brought me in along with Donald Gordon, Harry Boyle, and others to devise a way of requiring the commercial broadcasters, especially the new licensees in television, to provide Canadian programming. That had been an intellectual and political adventure, with a group of stimulating colleagues. While the industrial and bleakly quantitative Canadian content rules that emerged from the process were unsatisfying to me because they did not insist on content of social, cultural, or historical value, nonetheless they were an advance over what existed and quickly had a significant positive effect on radio and on the production of music in Canada. It was exhilarating to have been a part of that process, and the process itself had led to the replacement of Diefenbaker's Board of Broadcast Governors by the new Pearson-mandated CRTC with Juneau as its first chairman. I felt I had helped put him there and I had been hopeful that what I thought to be his exuberant Canadian nationalism would lead the commission to effectively demand of Canada's commercial television system the kind of quality programming that Britain's Independent Television Authority was exacting from their commercial broadcasters.

This did not happen. For a while it looked promising, especially in the light of the boom in Canadian popular music, which was a direct result of Juneau's insistence that Canadian radio stations play Canadian songs. But it never really worked in television, and soon the CRTC was seen as an instrument of insuring that new TV licensees were sound business propositions, whatever programming they might bring forward. When promises of performance were violated by new licensees, the CRTC did little about it.

But I still felt affection and a lingering admiration for Juneau, and a distaste for the politics of it all, so I was relieved when Roy called to say that the tactic now was to lay off and assume that Juneau would step down when he reached the age of sixty-five, in 1988, and that the question of my participation might be raised again closer to that date. I breathed easier and focused on the *Democracy* project, now, in mid-1986, in full swing.

At this time I was still on the Board of Trustees of the National Film Board of Canada, and an April 1986 journal entry after a meeting of that body in Edmonton notes that part of my enjoyment came from my seeing it as a training ground.

> *Note that I am enjoying nfb board experience to some extent because I am practising for corprez, among other things working a lot in french, and importantly seeing the country.*

In fact, the PMO had not yet given up on moving against Juneau, and a few little ripples from that wave would reach me from time to time.

When we started principal photography for the *Democracy* project in Iceland in June 1986, and then went on to Ireland and Belgium, I had still not said anything to Michael Levine about Mulroney's overtures regarding the CBC. A journal entry from that same summer, just back from that first shoot, shows that the idea was still nagging.

> *Sunday, 13 July 86. At Roxborough. Peter Newman came over yesterday to look at the computer, and Michael Levine came to watch.*
>
> *Peter, who is working on Mulroney's biography, said, "The staff have been told to prepare suggestions for changing DM's and for replacing Juneau . . . Mulroney feels he has dealt with the Ministers* [there was a cabinet shuffle in July] *and now it is time to make more changes. Your name is on the list for CBC along with Adrienne Clarkson and Peter Herrndorf. They don't think Herrndorf is a serious candidate. They told me I could probably have it if I wanted it but I said I was definitely not interested."*
>
> *I thought about it a lot over night. I decided it is getting close to time to talk to Michael. In the morning, Caroline said: You have to start getting Machiavellian about this. No. She said that last night. I was thinking the same thing. In the morning she said, "Maybe IT IS time to talk to Michael." . . . .*
>
> *It was manifest that he was more than very pleased and offered all help and undertook secrecy.*

The prime minister later that month told Peter Newman that he still wanted to offer me the job, and asked Peter to seek a view from Michael Levine on his behalf. Levine told him to remind the PM that first I would have to finish *The Struggle for Democracy.* Michael also told Newman to advise the PM that I would not cease to be a presence on air, and that Mulroney should ask himself if that were acceptable. If I had hoped the issue would shut up and leave me alone for a while, to let me give the *Democracy* project the attention and energy it needed, I was to be disappointed; the CBC presidency issue kept rattling my cage. Filming the story of the democratic experiment in ancient Athens, in August of '86, I was relayed an "urgent" message to contact the PMO. I called the contact I had been given in the PMO, Ginette Pilotte; she was on vacation and no one else knew anything about it. Fret.

"I find it onerous," I said to my journal early in September 1986, "not to be able to share my bursts of excitement and enthusiasm and perplexity about the CBC presidency with any of my working colleagues except C." By the end of September it was back on the surface. Roy Faibish was in Canada briefly and he, Michael Levine, Caroline, and I had a serious discussion in our kitchen about how to dispose of my financial interest in the *Democracy* project "upon my becoming President," the journal says. Roy was conveying that much of a sense of imminence. I had talked to Jack Willis about the possibility of his coming to program the English Network, and was working on a political strategy and language that would make it acceptable to import an American for that job.

> *In the meantime,* I wrote on October 7, 1986, *the CBC is struggling on with an invisible president, a demoralized staff, and no clear indication of what it should now be doing. Monday night's schedule, which I recorded for Jack Willis, consisted of a Canadian made cartoon (series), The Raccoons, which has nothing to do with Canada in any discernible way except industrially, followed by American Sitcoms right up to the National at 10PM. No indication all evening, until the News, that the CBC is meant to be an expression of the Canadian experience.*[3]

3. Not much better eighteen years later, when the Saturday night major offering is almost always an American movie you could rent at a video shop, the schedule is so cluttered with advertising it is usually difficult to tell that you are not watching a commercial channel, and the program heads are planning "great things" with so-called reality television, a further abdication of their responsibility to broadcast the best of what Canadian writers, artists, and citizens have to offer.

Speculation was on the street about the presidency. Ivan Fecan (who later became vice-president of English Television during my chairmanship) confronted Michael Levine about it, saying "It's either Patrick or Moses Znaimer, isn't it!" Michael was noncommittal. A week later there was an e-mail from Roy Faibish in London. My journal:

> *Message from Roy . . . PM phoned the other night to say "Juneau is being difficult" but the PM hopes to find the Auditor General's report helpful. Juneau has a contract . . . that makes it difficult to move him.*

Well, the contract referred to was the Broadcasting Act, in whose protection of the CBC president I deeply believed. None of this was helping me sleep at night. But by God, I wanted to get the CBC moving out of its inertia, and I still was naively unaware that the senior management had the power and the skills to render such movement nearly impossible.

I arranged for Jack Willis to come to town. Together we went deeply into program issues. He proposed a new approach to daily news on TV that would get rid of the "knee jerk" stuff he found wearisome on *The National*, and turn it into pure mandate programming, which would deal only in matters of significance to Canadians, including of course a strong international section. He said, "I can't find much to distinguish it from any good U.S. network news show."

Now Peter Newman entered the picture again. My journal for October 27, 1996:

> *Peter Newman came in at 4:05. He had made an appointment some time ago, through his secretary, "just for a talk." He brought a tape recording of his conversation with CBC Executive Vice President Bill Armstrong in which Armstrong says that [Juneau] is ready to go if he can go with honour and with assurance that his successor is not a patronage appointment . . . Peter correctly rejoined that he did not think a Government could commit in that way before the incumbent was gone. Armstrong said that of course they had*

> *heard my name and that I was "a great friend of Juneau's" . . . Newman, I, and Ian Anderson in the PMO think it might be a trap. Newman's group, The Friends of Public Broadcasting, are drafting a letter asking J to resign . . . Peter stayed twenty minutes and then went off to meet the Friends. He cannot be the spokesman because he is too closely associated with the Prime Minister. Peter said, "How was Mulroney when you saw him? Does he know how much trouble he's in?" I said I thought not, but asked if the Liberals are poised to get rid of Turner. Newman said they were not. I said, "Then Mulroney will win the next election."*
>
> *I find this whole business, waiting to know if I am going to have to deal with the CBC and at the same time trying to stay bright and strong on the Democracy Project, just exhausting.*
>
> *And it leads me to drink too much at night, to seek some oblivion. Old story, n'estce pas?*

My journal shows that in April of 1988, shortly after our *Democracy* shoot in Switzerland, Caroline said kindly, over breakfast one morning, "The CBC presidency is over. You should forget about it now."

Early in the winter of 1989 I was approached by Gordon Fairweather asking if I would consider chairing an institution the government wished to found, an initiative of Joe Clark, then Secretary of State for External Affairs, to be known as the International Institute on Human Rights and Democratic Development. They sent an official to sound me out and brief me; it sounded real, not unattractive, but totally in conflict with the CBC possibility. Clearly the PM and his foreign secretary were not in cahoots on this one. I sent a handwritten note to the PM telling him about it, and saying clearly that I was committed to standing by for his CBC proposal if it was still real, would he let me know? I never received an answer, but I think that my instincts had already turned down the Fairweather proposal. I agreed with Roy Faibish's arguments against such an institution, when he wrote in April:

> *It is presumptuous and duplicative and Canada has far too much to be defensive and apologetic about to start a high profile organization. There are civil rights, economic rights, legal rights, cultural rights, that need addressing in Canada. What the 3rd world needs most, whoever they are these days, is to learn something from Pacific Rim Countries. One of the least democratic countries in the world is South Korea. What will an Institute like this be able to do? Zero. Yet there is a lot the 3rd world can learn from S. Korea.*
>
> *Take the money they might spend on the Institute. Double it. Then establish 15,000 Bursaries for students from undemocratic /undeveloped /suppressed countries so that they can spend 3 or 4 years each at a Canadian University. If there is anything of value to absorb they might absorb it and then go home and help build their countries at least having experienced the quiddity of Canada. And keep doing it till year 2000.*

I had been maintaining for years in public fora that, for all our faults, Canada's most useful gift to the world was the example of a civil society. Roy's thinking paralleled my own, and helped me see that I was not the appropriate person for Joe Clark's new institute, flattered though I had been at being courted by the admirable Gordon Fairweather. Helping straighten out CBC would contribute more, I thought, to making the country's civil society better known.

That same winter of 1989 raised the prospect of a promising television project. Roy Faibish had been travelling to China regularly since the end of the Cultural Revolution in 1976, scouting business opportunities in China for the financial interests to whom he was a contract consultant. Sometimes he took a copy of *The Seven Hundred Million* with him, arranging screenings in a friendly embassy and inviting old Chinese contacts, who in turn brought new ones to the screenings.

He reported that the younger officials were especially fascinated to see the portrait of pre-1966 China that the film conveyed, as most of China's recent historical memory had been eradicated during the Cultural Revolution, along with a good deal of the architecture and other aspects of the face of Old China. Roy had reported a growing interest among the young officials at the China International Film Co-Production office in our making a second film comparing the China of the eighties with what we had filmed in 1964. Sometime early in 1989 I began a series of conversations with a young enthusiast in that office named Ma Qiang, who proposed an idea that seemed interesting and perhaps even marketable: a film retracing the 1964 film's itinerary, comparing what we had filmed then to the China of a quarter-century later. I added an angle that I thought would convince investors.

It had to do with our interpreter, Lu Yi-ching. I had had no word from Lu since we wistfully parted at the Beijing airport twenty-five years earlier. Roy had tried to find him on several of his visits, but without success. Roy concluded that Lu had been in serious trouble during the Cultural Revolution. It was easy for a zealot to attack a rival for political sins then. The monstrous kids loosed by Mao as "Red Guards" had ostracized, sent to prison, and even killed thousands of innocent intellectuals for supposed crimes against Communism. Lu was an easy target; he had spent a lot of time with foreigners. His membership in the party would not protect him.

Reflecting on Lu's fate one day, it occurred to me that a film could be made called *The Search for Lu*. We would shoot hand-held video with one of the new generation of high-quality home video cameras, making ourselves look as much as possible like tourists. We would just show up in places where Lu had lived or worked: the Institute for Foreign Languages, the Foreign Ministry office that assigned interpreters, his home village if we could track it down. We would go into police stations and offices and show people Lu's photo, or, even better, footage of him speaking, played back on a portable miniature VCR. And we would say, "Did you ever know this man? Can you tell us where he is?" In this way we could visit many of the sites featured in the original 1964 film, keep a running line of inquiry, and at the same time reflect the changes that the quarter-century had wrought – including the predictably fascinated reactions of contemporary Chinese viewing, in our film, aspects of their country that were forgotten and had vanished. In 1964 official China would never have permitted such an informal, improvised approach: everything had to be planned in advance, with permissions secured. But Ma Qiang was able to persuade his seniors to approve the approach. It was now June 1989. A couple of days later Ma called me back to tell me about a gathering of students in Tienanmen Square, where there was a growing demonstration calling for increased democracy. "I've just come back from a meeting with Zhao Ziyang!" he said, and told me about this amazing scene in which hundreds of students sat around one of the senior statesmen in the country, and exchanged ideas about democratic reform, and Zhao told them that this mattered very much to him.

Ma asked me to fax him newspaper accounts from the Canadian papers, so he could photocopy them and post them on walls and electricity poles, as the Chinese media were suppressing the story.

And then on June 10, 1989, in a flurry of gunfire and mangled bodies and bicycles, with that dramatic picture of a brave lone student confronting a tank in the square, it was over.

I tried for three days to call Ma, but got no answer. It was about three weeks later that he managed to call me. He sounded close to tears. He said that official hostility toward foreign media was so intense that he was convinced it would be at least a year before we could even re-open the negotiations. So our project was dead.

A few days later I was in New York on my own when Caroline called to say that the prime minister's office was urgently trying to find me; she had not given them my New York number. I called. They wanted me to be chairman, not president. The new broadcasting act, not yet passed, would divide the functions. I would preside over the policy-making deliberations of the board; the president and CEO would put the policy into action. They had to have a rapid answer. They understood that everything would depend on the relationship between the president and the chairman, could I fly to Ottawa the next day to meet the new president? As I took off from LaGuardia, there was a half-drowned American Airlines DC 9 in the water off the end of one of the runways; the accident had happened the night before. I looked down on it as we banked to the north. "The decay of that colossal wreck," I thought. It felt ominous, somehow.

I had been asked to keep the visit a secret. I would be met at the airport and taken discreetly to a hotel where Paul Tellier, the Clerk of the Privy Council, would introduce me to his colleague and friend, Gérard Veilleux, Secretary of the Treasury Board, who was the presidential nominee. But nobody showed up at the Ottawa airport, and I had to get on the phone to the PMO and try to keep up this ridiculous secrecy thing while finding someone who could tell me where to go. I was told that a room had been rented in a grubby little hotel. It would be in Paul Tellier's name and the desk would give me a key. Tellier and Veilleux might be a little late. Unfortunately there would not be any room service available, it was not that kind of hotel, if I needed anything could I pick it up on the way in? Terribly sorry.

The hotel was terribly sorry too, there was no room booked, they knew nothing about it at all. I was sitting there fuming in the lobby, pretty well decided to head home and forget it, when Paul Tellier came in the door with Veilleux in tow. Tellier stayed only long enough to get us started, and then left us alone. We got along famously. Veilleux had an appealing eagerness about him, a sharp, ironic sense of humour, and a twinkle. He said he knew a lot about management but nothing about broadcasting, and that he would look to me for guidance. We agreed to meet again in Toronto in a day or two.

In the meantime I asked Pierre Trudeau whether he thought I should accept the chairmanship. "No, I don't," he said. "If you have no executive power, they'll eat you alive. Whenever there is a major issue, the government will do everything it can to set you and the president against each other, and so will your own staff. Don't touch it. It'll kill you." When Veilleux turned up a few days later, as promised, he and Caroline and I sat in the kitchen at Roxborough

Street for a couple of hours, going over the proposal and getting to know each other a little. I told him about Trudeau's warning. He agreed that the risk was there, but said he thought that we could handle it if we worked closely together. The conversation was cordial and concrete. I thought I could make it work. And I was increasingly aware that if I refused it, my colleagues and friends in the profession would be baffled and resentful.

After Veilleux left Caroline said, "Do you really think you can work in a couple relationship with him?" It would be easy to say I wish I had listened to her, but I think we both knew that it was too late. And in fact, I think she was wrong: Gérard Veilleux and I could have helped transform the place, together, had we been among friends.

CHAPTER 23

THE CBC AGAIN

ONE AFTERNOON LATE IN 1989 I came out of my sixth-floor office to head for the boardroom. Ahead of me I saw John Shewbridge walking down the hall with Gérard Veilleux, touching the president lightly on the elbow as if guiding him along the corridor, bending in his courtly way to whisper his courtly British syllables into the president's willing ear. I said to myself, "The seduction has begun."

I had been explicitly warned about it by Al Johnson, who had preceded Pierre Juneau as president. I had called Johnson in Africa soon after the first Mulroney probe about my accepting the presidency. He had been encouraging, but had one overriding caution. "You'll risk being taken over by head office." The majority of the senior vice-presidents in head office, he said, were very adept at taking control of these fly-by-night prime ministerial appointees who were nominally president and CEO of the Corporation, but seen by the entrenched bureaucrats as a bit of a nuisance, slightly politically tainted, outsiders who could, during their fixed term, be managed in such a way that the relatively tranquil long term tenure of those VPs on the sixth floor at 1500 Bronson Avenue would be undisturbed. They, the VPs, would be there long after the presidents went on to other things; they had the *real* mandate for the running of the Corporation.

Their technique, he said, was to seek an early private interview with the new boy, and then tell him earnestly that they had been waiting for someone just like him, what a relief to at last have someone in the president's office who would *understand*, who was a real manager: now they could really go to work at last and realize the great potential of the grand old institution, and revitalize it, and re-win popular support and parliamentary support. "They'll never pull that kind of wool over *my* eyes," Gérard Veilleux had said, when I passed on Al Johnson's warning to him. "I'm amazed anybody would fall for that kind of stuff." But here he was, nodding in earnest agreement to whatever Shewbridge was telling him. I felt a combination of superior sophistication (*I*, in any case, would never be taken in by these guys) and anxiety about the extent to which the seduction might already have made it difficult to get Veilleux to listen to the real broadcasting concerns I believed the Corporation had to address.

My diaries show that during our period of getting acquainted, Veilleux devoured whatever information and ideas I could bring. I had first worked at the CBC forty-six years earlier and had been deeply involved with it, except for a few intervals offshore or in private broadcasting, for thirty-three of those forty-six years. Veilleux spent hours quizzing me on corporate structure, broadcasting values, ideas, techniques and traditions, and personnel. He was an astute questioner, a careful listener, and a quick study.

Until then I had been inclined to dismiss Pierre Trudeau's warning, but his "they" had been the wrong "they." He meant the politicians. The real "they" were among those entrenched senior executives at head office.

When I had learned that John Shewbridge was now Vice-President, Planning, and that he had still not succeeded in putting together the Canadian Programming Cable Service in the United States that Juneau had assigned him to develop seven years earlier, I had spoken to the president about him.

At first Veilleux seemed to hear me when I pointed out that Shewbridge had no executive experience and that his brief stint as Program Director in Edmonton had not gone well. I said I thought the U.S. cable channel initiative was a strong idea, if fairly obvious, and that Shewbridge deserved credit for proposing it seven years ago. But I said that what was needed now was somebody with entrepreneurial skills and contacts, an outsider with a good head for business, somebody used to making deals in the United States. Someone to press the matter, bring it to a head, discard potential American partners who were clearly not going to produce, and take a mandate from the CBC to bring it off.

Veilleux at first agreed. He arranged for Shewbridge to meet with Michael Levine, whom I had suggested as the make-happen person above described. But now a few weeks had gone by, and one day Veilleux said, "You know, you may have underestimated John Shewbridge. He knows this Corporation from top to bottom. He's a tremendously hard worker. So, I'll watch him on the executive skills side, and backstop him, and we'll see how he and Michael Levine get along."

Veilleux later reported to me that there were obstacles more serious than I might have realized in getting the proposed U.S. cable service underway. In that phrase I could hear another warning I'd been given early on. Harold Redekopp had said in Edmonton, when I first toured the regions as chairman designate, that whenever I asked for real change at head office I would be told that there were obstacles more serious than I might have realized. My journal notes (October 1989) report his saying,

> *"Here is how head office will react . . . . They will say, 'Of course what you want to do is desirable. But unfortunately there are certain intractabilities here that are not of our making: they are demanded by the auditor general, for example. . .'"*
> *(&c, &c.)*

Well, the intractabilities would persist, on this and other files. Ironically, it turns out that I was not immune to the seductive skills of those senior VPs. They managed in at least one key issue to persuade me, falsely, that some of the major changes I had dreamed of were going to become corporate policy and were being built into a long-term and radical renewal of the mandate and direction of the whole institution.

After a series of long private talks with the president, and at his suggestion, I drafted a seven-thousand-word paper in November 1991, entitled "Distinction or Extinction": it was a detailed strategy for returning the CBC to its intended status as a genuine public broadcaster. I argued that the public's willingness to keep paying the almost billion-dollar annual parliamentary allocation was eroding, because most of the time CBC Television, both in its choice of programs (like that famous Monday night schedule I note above) and its overburden of commercials, looked too much like just another commercial channel. I showed how, within the existing financial structure (always declared by management to be *the* obstacle to serious change), we could *overnight* transform the place, bringing to Canadians only programs that reflected the country, its needs, its laughter and its tears, its aspirations, its realities. It would be done with programs that were broadcast only to leave their audiences richer than before, never just to hold them anaesthetized and ready for the advertisers' messages. The new CBC would strive for a wide audience while making sure that special constituencies (the community of ideas, the arts, the policy elites) who now felt themselves abandoned were also well served, and served by programs that were designed to open those worlds to wider audiences.

It would not be necessarily devoid of advertising: I have never been doctrinaire in that regard. While advertising has little legitimate place in a public service, there may be imaginative ways to include a modest amount once you've established guarantees that program decisions are not to be altered by advertising concerns. Hockey broadcasts, given the nature of most sports commentary, are probably better with a few commercials than without. But a new relationship would have to be established with advertisers in which it would be understood that honesty and good taste in advertising were a *sine qua non* requirement, that the CBC would display advertising only between programs (I had at one point suggested an evening half-hour composed entirely of the most elegant commercials available, for which advertisers would, of course, pay a premium).

And I said we must get our people out into the community, find a way to get schools involved and get programs into schools, and in other ways make it clear that the CBC, unlike other broadcasters, was not there just to *get* an audience for revenue purposes, but always and only, as my mentor Ross McLean had insisted, to *serve* an audience with valuable programming that respected their intelligence, and that they could get nowhere else.

The president strode into my office within hours of receiving the document. He said something like "Tremendous! Tremendous! This is exactly where we should be going. I'll put it into the works right now. It may take a little longer than you hope, and it's going to have to be done right. So I'm going to give it to our best people to get working on."

Nearly two years went by. We found ourselves in some major problems between the French and English services, problems that required delicate diplomatic work both at the board and with the managements concerned. There was a fight at the boardroom table over moving *The National* to 9 p.m., and another over news policy, which consumed a huge amount of time as we wrestled with the development of a policy book that would satisfy the board and our critics but be manifestly the work of the journalists themselves. The most corrosive of these was over the regions, when I was in radical disagreement with Denny Harvey and the president over the decision to cut regional program budgets with proportionally equal severity. I argued that some regions – St. John's, Newfoundland, or Windsor, Ontario – had very special needs and could not be treated as if they were the same as Winnipeg or Vancouver.

With this sort of thing demanding prodigious attention and energy, I allowed my prime concerns to slip into the background. And then one day I woke up and said to myself that it was time to find out what was happening to "Distinction or Extinction." The answer was that they were planning a "complete repositioning" of the corporation's whole role, image, and function, that the thrust of my paper was central to it, and we'd be seeing the presentation of the strategy in a few months. When the repositioning was at last unveiled, it was all cosmetic and no trace of my initiatives was to be found in it. I have included the full text of "Distinction or Extinction" as an appendix. When Gérard Veilleux and I met again eleven years later for what turned out to be a frank and affectionate review of our time together, and I asked him about it, he said, "Patrick, we were sandbagged."

In the spring of 1993 I had to take some time off for surgery: a hip replacement. The president was talking about leaving before his term was up. I realized that the forces of inertia and the skills of The Manipulators were such that if I were to achieve anything of the strategic thrust I had hoped for I was going to have to start a more Machiavellian process of building alliances and destroying enemies. I had trusted too many. I was not sure I had the stomach for any more of it.

Gérard Veilleux did resign about a year before his mandate was up and went off to take a crash senior executive MBA before moving to Power Broadcasting. While we had been at loggerheads on many issues, his going left me wondering why I should stay on. Although there had occasionally been some fierce disagreements, we had been straightforward with each other and had agreed on enough issues to accomplish a few quite difficult changes. Among those changes was the radical shrinkage of head office, which had become a multimillion-dollar cathedral of redundancy, and which we left behind sufficiently reduced and rationalized that it would soon become possible for a new president to close it down altogether.

Another accomplishment seems not to have survived subsequent president-chairman teams. Many presidents and chairmen had seen the board of directors as a nuisance to be manipulated. I believed it ought to be an effective expression of the needs and wishes of the shareholders, who for me were always the citizens, not the government. Not all my fellow directors agreed on that. And even though I did not succeed in persuading the government to discard the patronage principle, and instead to appoint board members for their abilities and their credibility as representatives of citizens, I did succeed, partly by summoning my best rhetorical skills in front of that board, in developing a strong sense of national accountability.

Veilleux said that he too believed in a genuine role for the board. A new bylaw that required the president/CEO to have the approval of the board for any appointments at the vice-presidential level or above was his initiative. Previous boards had regularly been fed expensive lunches with good French wines, with important decisions saved for the afternoons when everyone was sleepy or anxious to get away. Veilleux knew about that and expressed contempt for it. We shared the view that directors who felt they were taken seriously were a resource not only in strategic planning but also in "representation" (read lobbying), as many of them were politically well-connected. A few of the directors were astute managers and policy people who had become disaffected over the years.

Veilleux and I had gone into our mandate with a cynical board, many of whom were only putting in time and enjoying a few perks; we came out with a largely loyal and committed group of public-spirited citizens. I retained a particular affection for Gilles Boulet, a professor of history at the University of Quebec, and for Glen Wright, who had his own insurance company in Waterloo, Ontario. Both had a genuine commitment to public service and a magisterial view of the responsibilities and opportunities of the board itself. With both, but especially with Glen Wright, with whom I often flew back to Toronto after board meetings, I was able to have long, searching (and often playful) conversations that soon settled into genuine and open friendships.

We had found a corporate bureaucracy that was grievously obese. During my initial walk-around of the head office at 1500 Bronson in the fall of 1989, I went into one department of fifty people, not one of whom could give me a clear description of what role he or she or the department played in the Corporation. I reported this to Gérard

Veilleux; he repeated the experiment and within weeks shut the department down. We had a big budget cut to administer. It should almost all have come out of the bureaucracy, and while we were not as ruthless there as we should have been, we made a start. I regretted some of the program cuts, and some could have been avoided. I am told that hundreds of program people are still angry at me over that, and I can't blame them. But they did not see the depth of the bureaucratic cuts that saved many of their jobs. And for the first time we began seriously to trim the fat, in a coherent way, so that all those people I used to see sitting around in offices reading paperback books, and all those who were available for lots of extra work when I devised *CBC Weekend* or needed more hands for *The Struggle for Democracy*, were, by the end of our mandate, either doing genuine work or were gone. And it was not done chaotically.

We also made some modest headway toward partnerships with private broadcasters and cable services. More importantly, we established policy in that regard: it was to be a strategic objective to expand those relationships. After decades of a lofty arrogance toward the private broadcasters, the institution now declared officially that working closely with the private sector was a necessity. The arrogance remains to this day, and the general discourtesy of CBC managers, especially toward the independent producers who supply most of the programming now, is legendary. But the relationships are building and without them the cost of doing business would be far greater than it is, and audiences for CBC programs, which belong to the citizens of Canada, much smaller.

We instituted a policy of journalistic accountability, in an era of shrinking public confidence in journalism. That policy resulted from the board's initiative and was devised by the journalists. We declared as policy that too many programming decisions were driven by ratings and the hunger for advertising revenue. Nothing was done about that, but at least it was declared, and that helped prepare the ground for the modest advances in that direction that the management attempted for a while in the first year or two of the new millennium.

But there remained a number of directors who could not abandon their private-sector principles and who continued to think that the CBC should be a money-making device, not a unique service to the people of Canada. The next independent chair after me made no secret of her wish that she could take over as CEO and use the place to make money. At the top programming levels of the English Television services, the prime value still appears to be audience ratings and advertising revenue. The rhetoric has changed, but the programming profile still reflects those values.

That was our biggest failure, Veilleux's and mine. We did not get the board's commitment on the authentic public broadcasting morality, on the necessity of building constituencies, of being memorably distinct. And at a level of lesser but still great importance, we did not succeed in the perennially elusive task of bringing the French Language and English Language services into a fruitful (and financially effective) collaborative relationship.

Casting over the pattern of accomplishment and failure, I felt that staying on after Gérard left would depend a good deal on who the new president would be. There had been rumours about Bob Rabinovitch, but I knew them to be unlikely as he had recently taken over the presidency of Charles Bronfman's company Claridge, Inc. But when the minister invited me to his office to tell me whom he had chosen as the new president, I hadn't the faintest idea whom he would name; I was confident only that it would not be the man who had been acting president since Gérard Veilleux's early retirement, Tony Manera.

In fact, I had been surprised by how well Manera had functioned as an interim CEO. He briefed and consulted with me regularly and cordially, and handled himself at board meetings more adroitly than he ever had as senior vice-president, when the directors had often felt he was less than ingenuous. Years earlier, he'd had a distracting habit during meetings of sucking a mint and moving it around with his tongue, from time to time pushing it into view under his moustache. I was afraid it made him look unsure of himself in front of the board, and had once asked Veilleux to speak to him about it. For a while the mints were absent; then they returned.

But now he seemed more graceful in his new captaincy than he had as a First Officer. He was courteous to the directors, firm when he had to disagree but never sharp. He explained his decisions carefully and generally quite well. He still hobnobbed with Shewbridge. But when there were difficult matters to deal with, such as the PMO's opposition to Michèle Fortin's being Vice-President, French Television (her husband was alleged to be an *indépendentiste*), Manera went through all his options very carefully with me before tackling the politicians, and persuaded the government to drop its inappropriate campaign against the capable Mme. Fortin.

When it became urgent that something be done about the Vice-President, English Television, Ivan Fecan having left and Jim Byrd having taken on his duties till someone could be found, Tony decided to promote Byrd to acting vice-president and made a good case for this against the opposition of some directors, and myself, that this would unfairly raise Jim's expectations of being confirmed in the job, which Tony said he had no intention of doing. He said, Look, Byrd was a good man, he was doing the work, he deserved the pay and the status and the authority, and had been quite straightforward in accepting that it was temporary and that he was not a candidate for confirmation. Manera's manner at the *in camera* board meeting in which this was discussed was also straightforward and quietly confident, as he most often was during this period, both with me and with the board.

He talked wistfully of his gardens and his greenhouse. Although he was diligent in his duties, he seemed to be thinking a lot of retirement. Now that he had occupied the CEO's chair, if only as acting president, he'd come a long way from the shy little Italian immigrant kid, as he described himself, and spoke proudly of that and warmly of the country that had made it possible.

So I was quite unprepared for the minister's announcement that he had appointed Manera president, not acting, the real thing. I told him frankly that I thought it a strange choice. I said I would see what I could do to help make it work out. I went back to head office, sent around a note of congratulations, and suggested that the new president and I meet for a strategy session the next day.

That session did not happen for two months. From an open, courteous, and congenial executive, Manera had reverted to the silence that I had come to know in the early months.

Finally he asked for an hour of my time late one afternoon. He began with routine matters, the date of the next board meeting, some discussions with the minister about financing, and some minor staffing issues. He then said that he had decided on a replacement for Ivan Fecan: it would be John Shewbridge. Jim Byrd would revert to his old position and program the network under Shewbridge's direction.

For a moment I was uncharacteristically speechless. And then characteristically too outspoken. I recounted some of the extraordinary encounters I had had with Shewbridge. I reviewed the now eleven-year-old story of his being assigned by Pierre Juneau to develop a partnership with an American cable operator to provide CBC programming to U.S. viewers, and how after endless trips to Florida and California, there was still no deal in place seven years later when Veilleux and I arrived. How Michael Levine, the country's best-known entertainment lawyer and negotiator, whose vast catalogue of foreign sales of Canadian artists of all kinds is unmatched, had offered to help, and when he asked Shewbridge what the business plan was, was told there was none, and was shown the door.

I remember saying, "Tony, I hope you have not said anything to Shewbridge about this, or to anyone else, because I don't think the board will approve it, and I have to tell you frankly that I will do my best to make sure of that." And then my shock when he said he had not only informed Shewbridge that the job was his, but had discussed it with another board member, Bob Kozminski (an able Winnipeg businessman, straight as an arrow and very diligent) before he had raised it with me, the chairman. Did he not think that was a bit irregular, I inquired. He admitted it was, perhaps, but that it didn't matter, his mind was made up. There was no point bogging down in minor courtesies.

But this was not a minor courtesy. The board had voted unanimously, three years earlier, that appointments at the vice-presidential level could be made only with their agreement; did he not remember that? Manera shrugged. I closed the meeting abruptly saying that I was going to canvass the directors, and that if he succeeded in making what I thought was a very damaging appointment, I would have to resign and to say publicly why.

Somehow, before I had even completed my calls to the directors over the next days, the news leaked out. I got an incredulous call from John H. Kennedy, former head of Television Drama (English TV) and now regional director for British Columbia. He had hosted a gathering of regional directors and their senior staff at which the rumour of Shewbridge's appointment had been bruited. When it became clear that this was not the trial balloon they had supposed, the mood turned very black. Someone had asked Kennedy to call me, to verify or deny the rumour, and to plead for my help in reversing it if it were true. Kennedy said that every person at that meeting – he had polled them – disapproved of the appointment and that several had said flatly that they would leave the CBC should it happen.

A special meeting of the board was convened *in camera.* Some directors were angry with me for being obstructive and were sympathetic to the president when he said my intervention and threat of resignation were an abuse of the chairman's power. I said, Hell, the chairman has no power in this institution; the Broadcasting Act says that I am to preside over meetings of the board; that's all. I said that my commitment to the health of the institution was stronger than my personal situation anyway, and I would do whatever I had to do to stop this appointment. I then proposed that we adjourn, let things cool down for a few days, and reconvene by telephone in the coming week.

That conference call was the turning point. The wise, patrician, scholarly Gilles Boulet, of the University of Quebec, proposed that since the board had indeed agreed that process must be followed for senior appointments like this, we simply have the candidate assessed professionally as we had done with others. The head-hunter Manon Vennat had won our confidence over two or three earlier appointments. Boulet said he hoped that both the president and the chairman would agree to engage her to review Shewbridge's credentials and particularly his reputation with and acceptability to the men and women in English and French television with whom he would have to work.

I was confident about what Mme. Vennat would discover, and readily agreed. Manera gruffly agreed as well; it was clear that the board was in no mood to reject a reasonable solution to a nasty impasse.

Glen Wright, whose careful and humane analysis of management problems had been very helpful to the board from the start, offered to chair an *ad hoc* committee to manage the Shewbridge affair. The next board meeting was to be in Fredericton, late in February. It was agreed that we would settle the Shewbridge question at that meeting.

The Fredericton meeting began well. Early on in my chairmanship, I had established the tradition of an informal Chairman's Dinner, no staff, on the first evening (of what was usually a two-day meeting). And so, there in the Sheraton Inn Monday night, after a day of committee meetings in which Manera behaved calmly and genially, we went through the first layers of a five-year financial plan, and the mood was quite positive. There was no mention of the Shewbridge issue.

I stayed on with a few of the directors who liked a late-night drink and some banter. They asked for some magic, and I did a couple of new, intimate close-up tricks I was working on. Then Brian Peckford proposed poetry, so we exchanged recitations, he with Tennyson, I with Yeats. Gilles Boulet joined in. We had enjoyed an evening like this in Quebec City a few months before, and while this one was not quite as wide-ranging as the one in the Château Frontenac, it closed off the evening in a way that made the following day's potential for conflict seem remote. We rose from table late, mellow, convivial.

Next morning I woke up early with a sudden brainstorm about producing a monthly or quarterly cassette to be distributed to all MPs and all CBC employees, a digest of our best programs. I lay there in bed getting very excited about it. CBC's image was by then deeply confused among the public because of that desperate obsession with ratings and advertising revenue from which I had failed to convert either management or the board. I thought, At least if the MPs and employees could see the best of the brilliant programs that some of our people are turning out, and see them uncontaminated by interruption and the hucksters, that might help us toward the kind of drastic reforms I had proposed in "Distinction or Extinction."

At 7 a.m. I called Robert Pattillo, VP Communications, and pitched the monthly cassette idea over breakfast. He responded very positively; we got quite worked up over our coffee and croissants, and Pattillo agreed to cost the idea as soon as we got back to Ottawa.

I was in a sunny mood. I thought I knew where the Shewbridge thing would go, and now here was a fresh idea that should get our people thinking again about the issue of defining Canada's public broadcaster in the age of a thousand channels.

The full-board formal meeting was scheduled for 9 a.m. Glen Wright's *ad hoc* committee had been meeting since early that morning and still hadn't appeared. As chair I was, of course, delaying the meeting until they were ready. We waited in a room across the hall, the staff, the other directors, the president and I. I expected Manera to be pacing a bit; it was his normal style in anticipation of an important decision. Suspecting what was going on, and supposing he did too, I was impressed with Manera's air of detached calm.

Glen came in looking as if someone had been shot. He said *sotto voce*, "We have a problem." Manon Vennat's report had been extremely negative. She had not been able to find anyone inside the Corporation who had anything good to say about Shewbridge, and several executives had convinced her they meant it when they said they would leave if he were appointed. The resistance was particularly angry within the French service, where recent attempts to procure more collaboration between French and English television had been looking fruitful. Now they were saying that the appointment of this man would be a sundering. Glen Wright said that he had briefed the president, who had said that if the board supported Vennat's recommendation, despite his earlier agreement to abide by it, then *he* would resign. Glen proposed that he, Glen, take the chair for the next phase of the meeting, once I had taken us through the preliminaries. It would be better, he suggested, if the directors heard and discussed his committee's report without our being there, the president and I. Manera and I would retire to the coffee room with the staff, while Glen and his committee reported to the full board.

I convened the meeting. We dealt with the agenda and a few other pro forma items, and then Manera, the staff, and I left. In that adjacent anteroom, in sight of the closed boardroom door across the hall, we all chatted and joked, a bit stiffly. And waited.

It dragged on. At about the twenty-minute mark, I phoned Caroline and told her what I was speculating. Showdown time. At about the eighty-minute mark, Glen came out and beckoned Tony into the hall. Then he came back to the anteroom and took me aside to say that Manera would now tell the meeting that he was about to submit his resignation to the PM, as he would not accept that the board could overturn his choice. He and I returned to the meeting, Glen Wright still in the chair.

Several members, most eloquently a Calgary broadcaster named Thompson McDonald, pleaded with Manera to reconsider. McDonald was magisterial and lucid about the governance issue at stake, and the potential damage to the CBC. The wisest and most persuasive of them all was Gilles Boulet. He said this was not a vote of non-confidence: it was a difference of opinion over a candidate. "No one is forcing anything on you, we are just asking you to come back with another candidate."

Manera was adamant, and sat with his arms folded. He was trying to appear dispassionate and dignified, but he was losing ground fast with the board. One member told me afterward, "That is when it *became* a vote of non-confidence; it had not been so before." Glen Wright looked troubled throughout. Dramatically he called three times for any member who wished to reconsider the Shewbridge appointment. None did.

We agreed that the committee that had sought the compromise would be the committee to work with Manera on the transition. Tom Wilson and Nancy Juneau both approached me privately: would I consider being the interim president? I said, Yes, but there would be strong opposition.

We had lost two hours of a planned five-hour meeting. We bulldozed through the whole agenda in the time remaining. I called Bill Neville in Florida. Neville was the longest-serving member of the board, a staunch Tory who always checked his partisan guns at the door and was intensely diligent about his administrative responsibilities and deeply loyal to the institution. He was flabbergasted and angry at the news.

We packed for home. Manera in the hotel lobby wished us a good flight as if nothing had happened.

Walking out to the plane I said to Thompson McDonald that while I of course had not heard the committee's report on the headhunter's findings, I gathered that they confirmed the assessment of the candidate that I had given to the board from the start. "In spades!" he said. "Much worse than what you said. Irrefutable."

On the plane I sat beside Pattillo but did not tell him anything except that it was going to be all right, we could talk later (board members John Crispo, Brian Peckford, Glen Wright, and Tom Wilson were on the plane). But at the Toronto airport Glen took Pattillo aside, asked him to stand by for forty-eight hours and told him why. He phoned me at home shortly after I got there – to tumultuous applause and hugs from Caroline, by the way, and a bottle of champagne – and Pattillo said, "Well, you didn't tell me the important part!" I said, "Better you got it from Glen. Glen should be canonized," I said.

As we sipped our champagne, Caroline's face darkened. She had met Manera a few times, and her characteristically draconian character assessment was working in its prophetic mode. She said, "He'll back down, you'll see."

"Who? What do you mean?"

"Manera. He'll find an excuse to withdraw the resignation. You'll see."

She was right. The next morning (the morning I wrote the last of the ongoing Shewbridge Affair diary notes on which these paragraphs are based) brought the news that the PM had asked Tony to reconsider, and that Tony was trying to get Glen Wright and corporate counsel Gerry Flaherty to agree on a statement that would find fault with the board process, and was still pushing Shewbridge, but said he would not resign if the board would agree that the process was flawed because he and I had not been in the meeting where it was all decided.

I said I couldn't remember bullshit having ever accumulated quite that deep. There was a whole series of conference calls and side calls and lobbying and fretting. It was pointed out to Manera, apropos this nonsense about flawed process, that he had declared his resignation *before* the meeting started, so that clearly the flaw had not affected his behaviour or thinking then. And that he had been offered every opportunity to reconsider and had refused.

Through the day – with some canvassed directors saying with asperity that there was no way they would agree that the *board* was at fault – language was hammered out that Tony said he would buy. A bit reluctantly, I was persuaded by Glen Wright that I had established a new power position, got what I wanted, saved the Corporation from a disaster, and should accept this too, as the language was really anodyne ("it might have been more appropriate had the President and Chairman attended the *in camera* meeting" . . . or something like that). Manera's published account of his time at the CBC slides over the whole episode. He makes no mention of Manon Vennat's report, saying that "some respondents expressed reservations about [Shewbridge's] management style . . . if you dig deeply enough you can find some reason not to hire anyone."

Much of the negotiating had been done on the car phone, as we drove to Larch Hill, our rented country refuge north of Toronto, with Caroline driving and me making detailed entries on my Poqet computer. One of them said, "I am really fed up talking, thinking, writing about this shit."

It had been a battering four and a half years at head office, nourished and made tolerable – often even pleasurable – by the deft and loyal support of Nicole Latreille, my executive assistant, and by Laurier LaPierre's hospitality and constant wise counsel. Eighteen months into it, when the government still gave no sign of enacting the changes to the Broadcasting Act that would make my independent chairmanship official (I was, until then, "Acting Chairman"), I had proposed stepping down but had been talked out of it by Veilleux and by my personal advisers. There had been the problems with "Distinction or Extinction." Now I had at least the satisfaction of having helped spare the troops Shewbridge's being put in charge of CBC Television, but I was exhausted. Two weeks later, I told them I was leaving. Suddenly I could see the sun again.

Chapter 24

THE NINETIES

LARCH HILL WAS A FRIENDLY, decrepit house on 150 acres in Mulmur Township in the Dufferin Highlands an hour and three-quarters' drive north of Toronto, looking down on a hill of silver birch rising above a five-acre pond and a paradise of long walks, secret places, even a section of the unique Bruce Trail. We rented it from 1992 to 1996 and it was a godsend during the years at head office. I would take off my shoes and stand barefoot (it works with one foot as well as two) on the land, smelling the clean air, chanting an old Ojibway song to the four winds, meditating to shed the confusions and hypocrisies of the CBC and become healthy again. After the final episode with Manera and Shewbridge, I was far enough gone to need more than a year of Larch Hill's healing, deferring a lot of work, mowing the rolling meadows with the landlord's cranky old Massey-Ferguson tractor, swimming and canoeing in the pond, and visiting the beaver.

For all its creakiness, the house welcomed visitors. Weekends were often full of conversation and feasting. I made a long home video on New Year's Eve 1994, with our guests Laurier LaPierre, Sandra Kybartas and Harvey Crossland, Marilou McPhedran and Alanis Obomsawin. Laurier cooked. We all danced in the snow at midnight. Alanis sculpted an eccentric snow owl and Kybartas a seven-foot-high head with Easter Island eyes, an ice glaze, and huge silver earrings.

The next New Year's Eve we had a bigger party. At about 1 a.m. we had a magic visit from a flying squirrel who came to the birdfeeder and seemed perfectly happy with my bringing out the video camera. Robert Pattillo held forth magisterially. Sherri Kajiwara read people's palms. Bill Reid phoned from Vancouver to wish Alanis Obomsawin a happy New Year, and he and I had a brief funny chat about the time I asked him to join the board of the CBC and he said he couldn't because he was not a Canadian, he was a Haida. The convivial magnetism of Larch Hill was a bath in which all that dreck of the CBC head office years at last dissolved and flowed away downstream. It was an environment in which I could get back to writing imaginatively instead of tactically. I wrote a lot of the *Heritage Minutes* at Larch Hill.

There were just enough projects to keep up a running contact with the real world, but much of that first post-CBC year was given to our getting back in touch with each other, Caroline and I, and with the land and a measure of coherence and authenticity. Caroline discovered, with the help of an extraordinary teacher named Kate Kabacynska, that she had a gift for portraits in oils. The high-ceilinged, beautifully windowed Larch Hill living room was soon a studio redolent with turps and oil, and festooned with paintings and charcoal sketches. The intellectual and social life was being fed with a lot of play, and earth, and physical stuff that it had been deprived of for too long.

We went diving at Small Hope Bay, and read indiscriminately. Working with my hands in wood or iron or stone was therapeutic. I fussed away at things on the little garage workbench, and enjoyed driving the car or the old Massey-Ferguson tractor up onto a home-made ramp and getting underneath with tools and a work light to wrestle with a recalcitrant shaft or a bearing. Shifting like this into manual labour that makes demands on your improvisational skills has always been an activity that sends packing the clouds of strategic anxiety and has – for me – strong intrinsic rewards. I still remember with pleasure the day in 1941 when the wringer stopped working on the washing machine, and my mother threw up her hands in dismay, it was wartime, you couldn't get parts and you couldn't find a repairman. I was eleven. I took the thing apart. The drive shaft going from the electric motor at the bottom to the wringer's transmission perched above the tub was a half-inch-square rod made of a relatively soft steel, and the harder steel of the socket at the upper end, fitting less snugly than it should, had worn the shaft, rounding off the square corners so that the shaft turned freely in the square socket. I lifted the shaft out of its base to look at the other end. You could see that it sat in a square socket down there too, but a better-fitting one and in any case one that was not the same distance from the end of the shaft. If I just turned the shaft end for end, the upper socket would have square corners again. It worked. My mother said she was grateful but not amazed. That was better than if she had said she *was* amazed. I still feel proud of that, as I did of ramping up the old Morris Minor outside our rented digs in Ann Arbor, during the first Ph.D. summer there, and replacing the big end bearings in the four connecting rods. These days at The Ridge, our little retreat an hour north of Toronto, I still head for the workshop when the clutter from writing gets too clotted, or the politics of foundations and broadcast establishments and production houses gets too much. With the turn of the millennium I found some ancient apple trees sprawling decadently at the edge of our pine woods, and have been turning their deliciously dark-grained wood – this is very simple stuff – into shoe horns and salad servers, the process always taking me out of the perplexities of production work, and incidentally delivering up objects that are a pleasure to the hand and the eye.

In 1993 the sculptor Kirk Mechar brought us *The Artist's Way* by Julia Cameron, and we both read it and took up the author's suggestion about writing spontaneously and thoughtlessly every morning first thing before breakfast, everything that came into your head for half an hour or forty minutes, before Good Morning Darling, before coffee, just write, by hand, don't re-read, don't plan, don't think Journal, or Great Thoughts, or Get That Dream Down: just write. This was a device for banishing the left side of the brain, for letting the unfettered imagination do whatever seemingly purposeless things it wanted to do.

Not really purposeless, of course: expression is seldom purposeless. Julia Cameron promised that the Morning Pages would enlarge one's access to the imagination, and free up the creative impulses – as long as one did it uncritically and never looked back. They became part of the start of almost every day.

During the chairmanship, poetry had resumed a prime position in my mind, not only reading more widely, but also finding that I needed to memorize and speak poems of consequence. Yeats's "The Second Coming" was a port of entry, both rich and elusive; it can bring a room to a long and pondering silence. So can Auden's "On the Death of William Butler Yeats," and some of his songs from the 1933–34 cycle, which includes the so-called Funeral Blues made famous by the movie *Four Weddings and a Funeral*, especially one that I found went well in the mouth, that begins

At last the secret is out, as it always must come in the end
The delicious story is ripe to tell to the intimate friend.

I have found that I share with other performers and poets who like to speak poems aloud a feeling that it is difficult sometimes not to edit a little bit, for one's own voice, hoping that if the authors heard me speaking their work they'd recognize the justice of my small revisions.[1] I began to explore translation, intrigued by the challenge of rendering into French some poems that seemed, on the surface, to be untranslatable, including ee cummings's "anyone lived in a pretty how town." Occasional verses celebrating birthdays and other occasions began to flow from the pen, poetry sometimes being more satisfying by hand than by machine.

And there was some serious purposeful reading, as well. Having been humiliated in the Croft Chapter House by Northrop Frye in my first undergraduate year, I had never read his books. I at last felt it was time to make up that deficiency. I went through his *Anatomy of*

1. For example, "for the ears of," instead of "to tell to," in the lines from Auden here given.

Criticism three or four times, to make sure I was getting it, shaking my head with amazement as page after page had me muttering, "Of course! Of course! Why didn't I see that before?" I chuckled with delight at his Shakespeare lectures, ploughed full speed through his two books on the Bible, *Words with Power* and *The Great Code*, slowing down again for *Fearful Symmetry*, which seems to be a life-long study that one picks up and reflects on at length, perhaps one chapter, maybe two, and returns to again and again.

Anatomy of Criticism offered a number of tools for my work as a writer and producer, and I began to use Frye's observation about Milton's *Lycidas*, poets of that time knowing what their responsibilities were and Milton's response to the death of a dear friend not some desperate "O God how can I deal with this!", but rather a measured *What does poetry expect of me, in dealing with the death of Edward King?* When a director working on a *Heritage Minute*, say, wanted to show the world how clever he was, do something never seen before, really break new ground, I would quote that passage and say, You know, we are making movies here, popular movies, not a new art form: What do movies expect of us? In dealing with the story of . . . ? I found that helpful. The imperatives of form.

At least two beaver families were living in the Larch Hill pond, knocking down some of those silver birch for which they had no real use, and messing around the swimming area. But while they were troublesome, they were also entertaining. We found we could call them with a kind of schlooping sound in the mouth, and that they would learn after only one or two repetitions that this might mean an apple or pear was forthcoming, and put on hilarious shows as they rolled around the floating fruit trying to get it into their mouths all at once, or to take it under for a more leisurely meal. We came upon one lodge we could walk right up to, very quietly, and listen to the mewing and muttering and chuckling that filtered up through the blow holes, and speculate about what conversation was taking place in there.

For more than forty years I have been aware of some curious visual aspects of my imagination. Often, waking up in a dark room, I will discern the distinct shape of a dark creature, or creatures, in a corner of the ceiling or clustered around a fan or a picture frame, often ape-like, but sometimes a face, sometimes a cluster of small objects, disappearing after a few moments. When I close my eyes I often see a face behind my eyelids, sometimes recognizable, sometimes my own face, often incomplete, sometimes the face of a complete stranger, in great detail, a bearded young man, an ironic woman, those faces often turning or changing expression in the few seconds of their presence. Sometimes when writing a scene in a novel or a dramatic script, if I close my eyes as I ponder the development of a scene, there will be an image, like a moment in a film, in which the camera will move, or someone will come into the shot, presenting me with a new bit of action or character, something totally unexpected. This can be a bit eerie at times. Often a whole line of dialogue, or a story outline, and occasionally a bit of verse, will just be there, in my imagination, on waking up or on turning from one form of activity to another.

One morning I woke up at Larch Hill vividly recalling a book I had read when I was six or seven years old – maybe younger; it was published in 1934 – *Flat Tail* by Alice Crew Gall and Fleming Crew, and said to myself that it was time to write *my* book about a beaver. I dived into the published research and thought about beavers every day. Soon visitors were made to sit still for at least part of a dinner party as I tested chapters on them. They were encouraging, and the manuscript of the novella, *Ahmek*, was finished in a few months. It took a few years to find the right publisher, but when it came out finally I was repeatedly asked to read from it to school groups and answer questions about it from Grade Three and Four and Five kids who were endlessly gratifying in their excitement about the characters and about the natural history.[2]

The *Heritage Minutes* began like this. It was in February of 1988 when we were spending long days in the cutting room with *The*

2. In 2003 the television rights were acquired by a major animation house, and as of this writing that project is in script development, and the novella has just been re-issued in paperback by McArthur & Company.

Struggle for Democracy, working like hell to get it ready for its air date then only eleven months away. There were still a few pickup shoots to do but most of the work was post-production, recording and re-recording narration segments, and working with Micky Erbe and Maribeth Solomon on the original score, which they were writing for a symphonic orchestra.

One day Michael Levine said he wanted me to go to Montreal for a brainstorming session at Charles and Andrea Bronfman's CRB Foundation. The foundation had a double mandate: the promotion of peace in the Middle East, and, at home, the promotion of Canadians' interest in and understanding of our national heritage, our history.

Charles Bronfman had an idea about making some short historical films, Michael said, and had invited a couple of dozen media people and historians to sit around the boardroom table for a day, prospecting for an original and convincingly practical response to what seemed on the surface a simple call, but turned out, upon reflection, to be brilliantly challenging.

That call, which sounds so simple as to be almost banal, was just this: Charles said, If we can use sixty seconds of television to persuade Canadians that cornflakes are interesting – or Cadillacs or tampons – couldn't we use the same amount of time to persuade our fellow citizens that this country is interesting? That we have a meaningful past, we didn't just get here by accident? That we have triumphs to celebrate and tragedies to mourn and learn from? I want this to be especially appealing to young people, Charles was saying. They're not getting their history in school any more. Not enough, anyway. You tell me convincingly how to do it and the foundation will fund it – at least through the pilot stage and then we can see if anyone is interested.

I did not want to go to that session. I had three editing crews going full-time, there were problems to solve every day, rewrites and test screenings, and I had only so much energy. I told Michael Levine, Look: I can't afford the time to go to Montreal, it will be a day and a half with the travel and the mandatory socializing, I'm working on something important, we've been at this for years, millions of dollars are in play, you are the executive producer for God's sake, you have as much at stake as I have, we only have a few months left.

As has mercifully been the case on a number of occasions when I have told him grumpily that I am not interested in some cockamamie new initiative, it's not in my line of work, find somebody else, Michael Levine patiently but determinedly insisted. In fact he became imperative. He has a technique. He says, interrupting my rant, "Patrick!" I stop. He waits. He lets the silence sit there for a moment. Then, again, "Patrick! . . ." And then a deep breath, and then, "Listen to me. Trust me on this. You have to do this."

I went off to Montreal, grumbling, and sat through the first hour or two in that boardroom listening to people talk about NFB animations, or sitting Pierre Berton down on a log in the forest to tell one-minute anecdotes. I fidgeted and fretted.

But then somebody said, Young people are interested in movies; why don't we make movies? And somebody else said, Hey, we were talking about sixty-second pieces, not two hours, and somebody else said, Well, hey, what about sixty-second movies!

I would like to be able to say that it was I who proposed this idea. I cannot do so with confidence. But I do know that I stopped thinking this was a trivial meeting. It might after all be possible to respond to Charles Bronfman's inspired call with something fresh and powerful, something that was, at the same time, a familiar form. Movies only one minute long. Astonishingly, before that day was finished, it was agreed that we try one, and that it should be about the Underground Railroad of the mid-nineteenth century when thousands of American slaves made their way secretly into Canada and freedom.

I undertook to commission a script from Patrick Withrow, who had written so many strong episodes of *Witness to Yesterday*. The CRB Foundation's media consultant, Patricia Lavoie, brought us a director/cinematographer, Richard Ciupka, who had also worked on *Witness to Yesterday*. Ciupka was the artist who set the style for the *Minutes*, both dramatically and cinematographically. When the executive committee of the CRB Foundation saw Ciupka's finished minute on the Underground Railroad, and loved it, and learned that to make the *Heritage Minutes* at this level of cinematic excellence was going to cost a lot more than the fifteen or twenty thousand dollars per episode they had hoped for, they decided that the foundation needed a sponsoring partner. To find that sponsor we had better go into the marketplace with more than one pilot: one might be just good luck, an accident: Let's make two more, they said, and if they're all as good as this one, we'll have a persuasive case. The executive committee asked me to assume the role of creative director on the project.

Charles Bronfman, throughout the ten years that his CRB Foundation funded the *Heritage Minutes*, made almost no interventions regarding content or style, but the three he did make were memorable. The first was his insistence that I make a *Minute* about the origins of a street name in Winnipeg: Valour Road. It used to be called Pine Street, and three boys from that street, living within a couple of hundred yards of each other, had gone off to fight in the 1914–18 war, and had all been awarded the Victoria Cross, "For Valour." When I argued that telling three stories in sixty seconds was going to be nearly impossible, Charles just said he was glad I said "nearly" and would I please do my best. He wanted it to be the third pilot.

I drafted a first script. It came in at about four minutes. I tried another, and then another. After three or four versions I reported exasperatedly to Charles Bronfman that I'd got the thing down to just under two minutes but couldn't see how to get it any tighter. "Good progress," he said. "Keep trying."

At that time Caroline and I had been developing a television series starring Robert Markle. Robert had introduced us to the small independent brewery at Creemore, in the Dufferin Highlands, and as a beer enthusiast he was watching with great interest as more and more microbreweries sprang up all around us. One morning over breakfast in bed at the Enniskeen hotel in Newcastle, County Down, where we were visiting Caroline's father, we saw a charming BBC program, one of a series whose host/presenter walked around Scotland visiting small distilleries, interviewing the distillers, sampling the whisky, and on the way giving us an unusual and congenial tour of the Highlands.

Caroline said, We should do a series with Robert, just like that, on the microbreweries in Ontario. Trina McQueen, who was then head of information programming at CBC television, agreed to invest a crew and an editing room in a pilot, Harley-Davidson provided a gorgeous touring machine for Robert to ride from town to town, we all agreed that Robert should sketch and paint in the places he visited, bits of architecture, perhaps local eccentrics, and visit the local newspaper editor and other interesting citizens as well as watching how the beer was made (and sampling it), so that the microbrewery would become the focal point and energizing principle for what was really this articulate artist/philosopher's essay on the community that housed the said enterprise. Caroline would produce; I would direct; we would call it *Something Brewing*.

A few days after that conversation with Charles Bronfman, I was driving to Creemore to meet Robert and Caroline when the solution to the Valour Road problem just dropped down out of the sky, a sudden perfectly clear device for dealing with the time issue: tell only two of the stories but make it seem as though you were telling three. I fired off a note to Richard Ciupka asking him to come up with a couple of two- or three-second purely visual transitions in which we would see three soldiers, and I would do a line or two about the three of them, but we would actually dramatize only two of the stories. It worked. Suddenly I felt I could tell any story in sixty seconds and was hungry for the challenge.

It was several months after that first brainstorming meeting before we had the three pilots complete and convened with the board again to screen them. By now we knew that, whereas producers, crews, editors, and even processing labs had charged us far less than the normal fees for the work they put in on the pilots, the actual production costs would be comparable to the production costs of a quality feature film, on a minute-by-minute basis. It was a heavy load, even if we did find a partnering sponsor.

We screened in the boardroom, and when Charles looked around the room for reaction there was some hesitation; it was his money after all, and the directors all knew how much this was going to cost, that it would eat a substantial part of the annual budget just to make half a dozen or so more.

Leo Kolber, now Senator Kolber,[3] has been a major adviser to Charles Bronfman for decades. He has a severe exterior that conceals a sensitive and humorous mind. I did not yet know what that exterior concealed and was somewhat intimidated by Mr. Kolber, who reminded me of Mr. Wemmick in *Great Expectations.* When Charles detected that he was not going to get a quick response from around the table, he said, "Leo, what do you think?"

Leo Kolber rose sternly to his feet. I felt sure that heavy weather was coming. His first words were "Well, I don't know what we're wasting our time for . . ." and my heavy weather now looked like a cyclone or at least a major thunder strike. "These things . . . " he went on, scowling fiercely, ". . . these are the best damn things I've ever seen in my life. I think we should just get on with it."

We produced about thirteen in the first year, almost all directed and photographed by Richard Ciupka, who wrote some of the scripts. I largely took over the writing, and over the years we have had some magnificent submissions from citizens, some professional and some just enthusiasts.

When my role as an independent producer was constrained for a while by the demands of the CBC chairman's office, we brought Robert Scully in as my francophone counterpart, to take some of the creative director's load off my shoulders. For a couple of years, he took charge of the development of about a dozen of those *Minutes* that were to be originally shot in French.

Of the sixty-five *Heritage Minutes* we have produced so far, about

3. See his recent autobiography, *Leo: A Life.*

fifty of them are as satisfying to my standards as anything I have ever worked on. They are based on trusting the viewer's capacity to intelligently interpret tiny clues, fragments of language, shots lasting less than half a second. We found that we could dispense almost entirely with expository material, let background information be inferred from the dramatic action. We said we would prefer viewers to be forced to infer rather than waste time on exposition at the expense of drama, and we deliberately left much of the referential information fragmentary or even left it out altogether because we wanted the viewer to ask questions afterwards, to want to know more, to turn to a companion and ask, "Did you get that? Do you think they really mean that the guy who invented Superman was a Canadian?" Much better that than a totally satisfied response, than turning away from one of our little dramas thinking they now had it all.

I have included in the Appendix the script for the *Minute* on Emily Murphy, which I wrote expressly for and in collaboration with Kate Nelligan, our first foray into pure monologue. I was going to direct Kate myself, but had to leave the country on CBC business when it was due to go in front of the cameras, so I contracted Holly Dale, the writer/director of *P4W*, who had done a fine job for us on the Agnes McPhail *Minute*. When she saw the half-page script for the Murphy story, Dale protested that it was far too short, it could be done easily in thirty seconds, I should write more, flesh it out. I said, Well, she didn't know Nelligan. Nelligan would use every second. But I also felt that it was stronger to leave it a bit cryptic. You will see from the script that it begins in the middle of a sentence, a little speech almost an aside to an unseen listener as if we had come in *in medias res*, and that there are few complete sentences.

We had early on agreed that we should shoot the *Minutes* in a 35mm wide-screen format so that they could be shown in cinemas if they were good enough. It was a year or so after they were launched that Michael Levine completed an agreement with the Cineplex chain, and we launched the cinema versions with "The Naming of

Canada"[4] in one of their big houses at Yonge and Eglinton, with an audience of high school students. Even I, having written the script and supervised its completion, was surprised at the immense amount of additional detail that shows up on the big screen, and at how much more powerful this version is than what appears on television. I began slipping quietly into movie houses whenever a new cinema version was released and found that people were applauding them. Each cinema release runs for the life of a print, which is six to eight weeks. After a few years, I asked the Cineplex people if it wasn't time that we started reruns, but they rather stiffly rejoined that it was company policy never to run anything twice (not even *Apocalypse Now*? I should have said). Now that the ownership and management have changed, we are going to re-open the subject, as there are several generations of new moviegoers who have never seen the *Minutes* on a big screen.

Within five years the *Minutes* had become a part of the national cultural life. I guess the first proof of this was the spoofs that began to turn up as elaborately produced sketches on the CBC's *This Hour Has Twenty-Two Minutes* and as inserts on the Comedy Channel. Nothing says quite so eloquently as parody that you have become an institution. In 1998 a new independent history foundation, Historica, took over the CRB Foundation's heritage work (with a generous financial assist from Charles Bronfman).

When I visit schools on Historica business I often ask a classroom how many know what a *Heritage Minute* is. Usually about half the hands in the room go up. I then point to one of the students who has not raised a hand and ask if they can tell me anything about, say, a terrible disaster that took place in Halifax harbour during World War I, and the kid will get up and give me back my script, sometimes in considerable detail. At their maximum popularity, according to an informal but thorough audit, the *Minutes* were being shown more than 3,600 times a month, across the whole television, cable, and satellite system.

4. Our dramatization of First Contact: Jacques Cartier's coming ashore in Iroquois territory, and mistaking the phrase "kanata-kon," which means "to the village," for the name of the Iroquois nation.

In 1997, with the help of Allan and Gary Slaight and the staff at Standard Broadcasting and their networking and production company, The Sound Source, I wrote and produced five pilots of radio versions of the *Heritage Minutes*, and over the next few years pestered the Historica board of directors for funds to produce a full cycle. In 2003 they agreed, having been promised generous donations both from Standard and from Rogers Communications, and we are, as I write, more than halfway through the production of two hundred of these little radio dramas, ninety seconds instead of sixty. In April 2004, when I played a couple of them for an audience of about five hundred at the Canadian Association of Broadcasters in Quebec City, I saw people wiping tears from their eyes during the episode about the Irish orphans in Quebec in the 1850s, and later I was stopped in the corridor by people who said they found the radio versions more powerful than the films.

When the *Heritage Minutes* were still in their infancy, the CRB Foundation experimented with another initiative. When teachers started phoning to request videocassettes of the *Minutes*, the projects manager, Deborah Morrison, was asked to think about ways of getting school kids more actively involved. She put me on the road for a while, visiting schools to help kids write scripts and produce home video versions of the *Minutes*, and I reported back that their instincts for dramatic structure were so well instructed by the thousands of hours of television they had watched that it took very little Socratic method time – half an hour, say – for a Grade Five class to come up with a *Heritage Minute* script that was worth producing.

Morrison, speculating about further devices for involving the young people, arranged a meeting with the Manitoba Historical Society, in the fall of 1992, where the idea emerged for history fairs modelled on the by then well-established science fairs. The Winnipeg group thought perhaps they could enlist four or five hundred kids for a trial run the following spring.

While the proposal at first suggested conventional topics – prime ministers, the birth of new provinces, war heroes, and inventions –

there were much more original initiatives from the kids: How did Portage Avenue get its name? Was Louis Riel's mother a witness to her son's execution? Who invented the famous Lake Winnipeg barges and why? By the time the fair was assembled in May they had to book the Winnipeg Convention Centre, because those four or five hundred kids had blossomed into a crowd of five thousand. They set up a display in an arena, with little booths and artwork and artifacts and sculptures. The foundation decided to keep developing it, expanded it to four locations in '95, and in '96 added a national fair, in the summer, and funded the travel and accommodation for kids from across the country.

While the foundation put in enough money to send staff out to the participating communities to help with the organization, and then to transport selected students to bring some of the best exhibits to an annual national fair, by far the greatest resource applied to this project came from volunteers in the communities: service clubs, individual teachers and librarians and others, local newspapers and radio stations.

When Deborah Morrison asked me to visit that first national fair in Prince Edward Island, I was not very enthusiastic. I had not paid attention to the fairs project. I thought of it as a distraction from the "real work" of the foundation (the *Minutes*) and a draw on financial resources that should have gone into my productions. But that weekend in Summerside turned me around completely. The young people chosen from local fairs were assembled on the May 24 weekend in an unused hangar at the old RCAF base, which had been set up with dozens of small booths that the kids had fitted out with drawings, paintings, maps, models, costumes, photographs, and other archival material, each booth manned by one or two young people who were eagerly telling their stories to the three thousand visitors who came through the building that weekend. The ones that struck me the most were two that had originally been shown at the regional fair, in May, in Charlottetown. One boy had studied in detail the engineering plans for the fixed link, the not-yet-completed PEI causeway, and had built a large-scale model. There were a number of good agricultural and political stories, and the booth that best illustrates the value of these Heritage Fairs was fronted by two eleven-year-old boys. It contained some mysterious and very big chunks of broken, rusted farm machinery, a number of drawings the boys had made, and several ancient catalogues. Their story was that driving in the countryside with the father of one of the two friends, they had asked what that weird-looking rusted old machine was, lying by a farm gate. The father didn't know, but imaginatively suggested they drive in to the farmhouse and ask. They found an elderly retired farmer, who explained the machine, and dug up an old Massey-Harris catalogue showing what it looked like when it was new. Over the next weeks the boys found more relics and a neighbour with a front-end loader and a truck who helped them collect some of the artifacts, and put together their display, in which they were able to tell their fellow Islanders something that nobody else knew. They had done this work themselves; nobody else had ever done it before. They *owned* it.

Those two eleven-year-olds stood there with such proprietary pride that they brightened up the place. I forgot my resentment over having to "waste my time" at a Heritage Fair and became a booster. The next year in British Columbia, two boys at one fair had done a history of money for which they had converted a discarded doll's house into a miniature museum with tiny glass display cases of ancient coins and banknotes, had written and recorded a humorous story of a penny and its journeys from pocket to pocket and all the strange other coins it had met over the years, and had developed a board game that taught you about pounds, shillings, and pence, dinars, rupees, yen, and yuan.

At one fair I met a twelve-year-old British Columbian girl with a French last name who had set out to track down the family legend of an ancestor who was famous in Quebec, and found him, the first-ever francophone judge of the superior court of Quebec. She had discovered the parchment with the Royal Seal and signature naming him to that court, which she had on display in her booth along with published letters the judge had written to newspapers, and photos of the line of succession right down to herself.

When Historica took over the CRB Foundation's heritage, the Heritage Fairs came with it. Last year more than two hundred thousand Canadian children took part in fairs from coast to coast.

While my personal satisfaction in the production of the *Minutes*, both radio and film, is as high as anything I have had in my sixty-plus years in the media, I now feel that the Heritage Fairs are the single most important program that Historica operates. The children who do this work learn existentially that history begins with the question "Mummy, where did I come from?" and moves out into the community in expanding circles that take the investigator through the family, the neighbourhood, the regional community, the nation, and finally the world, in search of the meaning to be found in the quest for our sources. They learn that history does not have to do with the memorization of the dates of battles and legislation or the names of kings and premiers, useful though these may occasionally be, but in enriching our understanding of what it is we are doing here where we live, and why, and how both absurdities and accomplishments came into existence – and perhaps discovering some directions for the future that the past intrinsically suggests.

During the nineties the performance of magic tricks captured my attention again. Something about that period in the 1940s, after the end of *The Kootenay Kid*, something about Glebe, the choir and the jazz quartet and the string ensemble, and song and dance on stage, and perhaps the model airplanes and the kites . . . anyway, something happened that relegated magic to a secondary position for almost fifty years.

But over that half-century I had kept alive a small repertoire of impromptu tricks with coins and string and paper napkins, which I would trot out for kids from time to time. And when I became a professional television director and producer in my mid-twenties, what I had learned in magic about directing and misdirecting attention and creating illusions of continuity of action where none existed proved useful.

I have written above about the Peter Whittall television series *Mister Fixit*, and how Paddy Sampson and I devised some magic-based program endings for that series. And every once in a while, through the television years, I would learn a new trick. In one episode of my comedy series, *Nightcap*, in Ottawa in the early sixties, I engaged an old schoolmate from Glebe Collegiate, Roy Cottee.[5] We had performed variety acts on the stage together at Glebe, comedy song and patter numbers. Now Roy was a part-time professional magician. That night, forty-odd years ago, Roy performed the wonderful rope trick, "The Professor's Nightmare," and taught it to me in the studio after we wrapped. I still enjoy performing it.

But from the Glebe Collegiate days on, there had been a swirling cloud of opportunities and demands that somehow put my magic into a side pocket: personal upheavals and family moves; the distress of the war; the career; obsessive sex. It apparently never occurred to me (as it has occurred to many who practise sleight of hand and the making of illusions) that magic might be a capital instrument for getting girls into bed.

While I was chairman of the CBC, I had a couple of rooms in Laurier LaPierre's house on Fairmont Avenue, and Laurier being an irrepressible host insisted that I entertain regularly – buffet dinner parties for thirty or so senior bureaucrats, other broadcasters, people from the arts community, and head office staff and officials. At one of the first of those evenings, our friend Emmanuelle Gattuso turned up with her new companion, Allan Slaight, the president and owner of Standard Broadcasting. (They would marry soon after.) I had met Allan Slaight in his days at Global Television, but we had not gotten to know each other. That evening Emmanuelle told me that Allan was feeling particularly good as his new book on Stewart James had just

5. Roy Cottee, seventy-five years old as I write, is still performing, busking and clowning in the streets of Ottawa's Bytown Market, and still using magic in his act. The Ottawa branch of the International Brotherhood of Magicians is named after him.

been published. James was an elderly, prodigiously gifted and productive but little-known Canadian magician. Emmanuelle said the book really was a magnum opus. So when I got around to renewing our acquaintance a few minutes later, I congratulated Allan and said that I would love to see the book.

"Well, it's really just for magicians," he said.

I told him that I had performed a lot of magic when I was younger, and named some of the tricks that were still in my repertory. Allan said, "Who turned you on to magic?" I said it was a little Maltese magician in Toronto and got no further because Allan interrupted with a delighted "Johnny Giordmaine? Me too!" And next morning a copy of this hefty (almost a thousand pages), richly produced book was sitting on my desk at head office. I took it home for the weekend and it seems in memory that I didn't get out of bed all day Saturday except to scrounge around to see if there were a deck of cards in the house. There was not. This seems odd today, since you now can't walk through more than a couple of rooms without seeing at least one deck of Bicycles or Bees or Tally Ho's. But in my young magic days I had never seen a good card trick, had formed the notion that all card tricks were as dumb as the crudely obvious one about the four burglars that some of my public school friends had failed to fool me with, and if there were any cards in the house they would be left over from the bridge and poker days, by then in the distant past.

I worked up trick after trick out of *Stewart James in Print: The First Fifty Years*, over which Allan and his late writing and magic collaborator, Howard Lyons, had laboured for fifteen years, from Stewart James's original documents and hundreds of hours of conversations and demonstrations. I learned card tricks and coin tricks, rope tricks and tricks with newspapers and paper money. I proposed lunch with Allan, and we showed each other tricks, and I learned to my delight that he had been performing professionally in Saskatchewan, as a teenager, when he had a day job in his father's radio station in Moose Jaw. He said that he was still inventing and publishing tricks and was deeply involved with the magic community.

I dropped in at the Browser's Den of Magic in the plaza at Bathurst and Eglinton, and discovered that the proprietor, Len Cooper, offered lessons. So I took him up on it, $25 an hour, in the evenings after the store closed, sitting at an ancient card table learning sleight of hand. One Monday morning at the Browser's Den, Thomas Baxter was looking after the shop so Len could have a day of golf. We became friends. Tom, like many mature and thoughtful magicians, is a careful and enthusiastic teacher, and soon he was taking me through a litany of the classics: the cups and balls, the linking rings, a number of the classic card tricks. We later collaborated on a screenplay about a young magician, a girl with a physical disability who discovers she has a prodigious talent for sleight of hand, becomes corrupted by her celebrity, and has to find her way back to her decency.

With Tom Baxter's guidance, I began to add a little round of magic to those chairman's parties at Laurier LaPierre's. I reported on my progress to Allan Slaight from time to time, and soon he invited me to come to one of his legendary evenings in the coolly elegant Romanesque house that was once a dry-cleaning factory at the end of an obscure lane in North Toronto. Soon I was performing bits of magic for strangers and new friends, and sensing myself falling into a new obsession, a welcome obsession with its capacity to cause the dismalness of the CBC head office to fade into the background.

Caroline was at first disdainful, and once threatened to divorce me if I ever performed in public as embarrassingly as I had at a charity at the Smile Theatre Company, where both Slaight and I had been invited to do some stage magic – and were both less than brilliant. After a while she came around, seeing both the nourishment that magic was giving me, and, later, especially after I began to work with David Ben, seeing how lovely really good magic can be.

One of the evenings in the Slaight–Gattuso house was a turning point. Allan had proposed by phone that we do a duelling magicians routine for the next party, I to open, he to close with a mind-reading routine, and the meat in the sandwich to be provided by a professional magician named David Ben. I had heard of this young man, that he was an all-round performer with a strong sleight of hand repertory. A former tax lawyer with a graduate degree from the London School of Economics, he was said to be severe in his judgments of other people's performance, intolerant of anything but good, clean, elegant work. I was working on a sleight of hand piece, a modern classic with a banknote, to which I had added some presentational angles of my own, and had practised to the point where I was pretty confident. I decided to risk the disapproval of D. Ben, and do my version of the Mismade Bill, a trick created by Allan Slaight's late collaborator, Howard Lyons.

It was, in the event, slightly unnerving. Allan Slaight's living room entrance is framed by a pair of soaring black marble columns as you come in from the hallway, and they served us that evening as a proscenium for the performance. As I came between them for my opening number, David Ben, whom I had only just met and perfunctorily shaken hands with (he had arrived late), stood just out of sight of the audience of about thirty people in the living room proper, and looked over my shoulder as I undertook this sleight of hand piece in which a bill "turns inside out." My presentation suggested that the real reason for the government's proposal to replace the bill with a coin was that magicians had discovered it was possible to fold the two-dollar bill in such a way that it would be permanently transformed when unfolded. "Mismade" was Lyons's term: the corners would migrate to the centre of the bill and the centre to the corners.

It went very well. There were gasps. I gave the transformed bill as a gift to a lady in the crowd, who behaved in a suitably stupefied way, and I took my applause. Allan then introduced David Ben, who produced a deck of cards and proceeded to do about fifteen minutes of graceful, funny, apparently improvised and totally baffling card magic. Allan finished with something called a Book Test, also totally baffling, to enthusiastic applause.

Over drinks a few minutes later, I found the tall form of David Ben bending owlishly over me, with what I at first interpreted as a wicked expression, playfully wicked as it turned out, for he said, "You know that, ah, that trick of yours . . . that was very well done. We should talk."

We began to have lunches together. David told me that he was earning a good living at magic, working corporate gigs mostly, some small parties, travelling a lot, doing a fair amount of public speaking using magic to illustrate some ideas about creative problem solving. He felt it was time to do a classical stage magic show. "I can make up magic tricks the way Cole Porter wrote songs," he said, "but I need someone to . . . ."

"Write the book?" I said.

"That's it: write the book."

We began to spend a lot of time together, and by the time I stepped down from the chair at CBC head office, we were close friends and had begun to shape a show that was based on the stage spectacles that the great British and continental magicians used to present a century ago at London's Egyptian Hall and St. George's Hall. Allan Slaight had been chairman of the Shaw Festival at Niagara-on-the-Lake. The Shaw Festival's mandate is theatre that was on the boards in Shaw's lifetime – Shaw himself, of course, Pirandello, the early Kaufman and Hart, Chekhov, Ibsen, Pinero. When David opened discussions with the Shaw, Slaight put in a good word for us with Christopher Newton, Shaw's artistic director. David was proposing that we do a late nineteenth- or early twentieth-century-style show composed entirely of magic that Shaw himself – who was an enthusiast – might have seen at one of those legendary halls. In the late winter of 1995 we made a dinner date with Denis Johnston, who called himself "Literary Dogsbody to Christopher Newton," and the festival's managing director, Colleen Blake, to tell them what we had in mind.

At a table near the back of the Indian Rice Factory on Dupont Street, with waiters coming by from the kitchen with steaming bowls, David and I pitched the show. David did a lot of magic and I did a little. He loves to improvise and to take advantage of whatever circumstance he finds himself in. The passing waiters with their savory freight just added to the fun and the mystery. Denis Johnston has said publicly[6] that he had come to the dinner with no intention regarding the magic show, no interest whatsoever, it was just that he had always wanted to meet me and here was an excuse to do that. But the evening caught both their imaginations, and they said we had a good chance for the summer of 1996. We booked the library at the Prince of Wales Hotel in Niagara-on-the-Lake (where Caroline and I had convened the *Democracy* symposium a decade earlier) and set up a lunch meeting with Chris Newton, who brought along his deputy artistic director, Neil Munro. Our original proposal had been for a modest show, largely sleight of hand, which might be presented in the Shaw's Courthouse Theatre. But when Chris Newton asked us to check out the Royal George Theatre on the way in, we instantly saw the possibilities of a complete period show: not just period magic, but a period character; not just tricks that Shaw might have seen, but a whole show.

Before the others arrived, we worked out the basic idea for a show that would almost be a drama: David Ben would play the part of a cocky young Canadian conjuror, sometime early in the twentieth century, who has come to London, booked St. George's Hall, and set out to show that London crowd some really spectacular magic. Then after lunch David did a few tricks. Newton and Munro had rehearsals to go to and seemed a bit distracted, but to our astonishment, as they got up from the table, Chris Newton turned to Colleen Blake and said, "Pencil it in for next season."

We called the show *The Conjuror*. He would be a brash young guy who boasted about his international performing successes and acted as though he had a lot more to show London than London had to show him. The Royal George's classic nineteenth-century stage, with all the gilt and red plush, and a first-rate backstage setup would allow a good range of illusions. Much of the real work on the concept, script, and shaping of *The Conjuror* took place over five intense months of rehearsal and writing in a big ballet studio in the Canadian

6. In the CBC Television film *The Making of The Conjuror*, by Daniel Zuckerbrot, also broadcast on the A&E channel in the United States.

Children's Dance Theatre on Parliament Street. We had the mirrors and plenty of space to work with. David began to rehearse there five days a week, often accompanied by his long-time roadie, Suleiman Fattah, who would be both the backstage operator and an onstage assistant. Before long the rehearsal and writing – seldom really separate activities – began to take over our lives.

We would start into a trick with only the elements, and see what happened as we tried to fit the trick to the character. The character began to take on texture, and one element of his personality that played nicely into both the writing and the structuring of the trick was our decision that he was a guy who shamelessly dropped the names of his "good friends" around the world who had helped him with the development and understanding of his art. But while this might be offensive in a serious character, we would make it into a self-deprecating joke. He would say, "While performing in Vienna last month, I spent some time with my good friend Sigmund Freud, a physician of the mind who . . ." etc. Or (in the second season) "Over lunch in Calcutta last year, with a young journalist from Lahore named Rudyard Kipling, I listened with delight as he told me tale after tale about children and animals in that magic land. 'Kipling,' I said, 'you must put these in a book. You must call it . . . The Jungle Book.' And so delighted was he with my suggestion that he took me through certain half-deserted streets, where white men never go, to meet The Fakir of the Roses." This led into the presentation of that great classic of stage magic where a seed planted in a flower pot sprouts before our eyes, grows into a bush, pushes out buds that open into roses; the magician then plucks and tosses real fresh roses to members of the audience.

David had been the only young magician to whom the legendary Toronto master Ross Bertram showed the secret of a card trick he called "Five-Zero-Five." The performer takes five cards out of the deck, shows them to the audience, and one by one, taking his time, throws them into the air, where they vanish and then one by one return to his fingertips. In its original form, it can be done elegantly in about ninety seconds. We built a story called "The Vanishing Points," which stretched the trick to five minutes and made it work on a big stage in a large theatre, which is not easy with card tricks, and when we played a later version of *The Conjuror*, with no card tricks in it at all, to try out a more large-scale illusion feel of the show, the one piece missed by people who had seen the original incarnation was "The Vanishing Points."

We agreed that the purpose of the show was not to send audiences out into the street muttering resentfully something like "How the hell did he do that!" We wanted them to feel illuminated, not impaired or stupid because they couldn't figure it out. "These aren't puzzles for the audience to solve," David would say. "They're mysteries for them to wonder at."

It was watching David Ben refine another classic, the Egg Bag – it was first described in print in 1584 and is certainly much older than that – that led me to a new concept of what magic is for. The climax of David's version transfers most of the magic into the hands of a child invited from the audience, who, by waving his or her hand over the manifestly empty bag, causes the egg to appear. I saw that magic is about *giving* to an audience more than about showing them something or impressing them with brilliance

Some fellow magicians expressed disapproval of our closing with David's eerily lovely version of Okito's famous Floating Ball, which he had spent years researching, through Okito's letters and newspaper reviews,until he felt he had discovered the exact choreography and some details of the method that the world-famous nineteenth-century Dutch master had never revealed. David choreographed it precisely to the Adagietto from Mahler's Fifth Symphony, the same yearning music that haunts us in *Death in Venice.* Magicians would say, "That'll never get you a standing ovation. You want to end with a standing ovation." And for a standing ovation you need something big and brassy with a boffo surprise at the climax, whereas this version of the Floating Ball is haunting, lyrical, memorable, almost sad at the end.

When I did my lobby-rat duties after our performances at the

Royal George, my eavesdropping exit polls, I would hear people say "Wasn't that lovely!" with a touch of awe in their voices. That was what we had hoped for, had designed the piece for. Teenagers coming out of the theatre shaking their heads with dreamy smiles and saying softly, "That was so *cool!*"

Who needs a standing ovation?

Ticket sales for *The Conjuror* were strong and reviews were all positive (except for the *Globe and Mail*'s). That summer of 1996 in Niagara-on-the-Lake entrenched David Ben internationally as a magician of distinction, and gave me an itch to do more directing. The Shaw Festival brought us back for a second season, with a largely different fifty-minute show in the Royal George, and David agreed to give them a ninety-minute combination of parts one and two at the end of that second season, as a gala fundraiser for the festival.

We got to know Lindsay Sharp, the executive director of the Royal Ontario Museum, who showed up at the Slaight dinner table from time to time and demonstrated a childlike delight in the magic that Allan and David and I would trot out over the demitasses. I love the theatre in the basement of the ROM, not so much for its intrinsic qualities, which are uneven to say the least, but because I saw my first *King Lear* performed there, and, through the offices of the University of Toronto Film Society, made the acquaintance of the great cinematic classics in that same hall. Lindsay Sharp made the theatre available to *The Conjuror*. Over the next two years, we did two successful runs, continually polishing and rewriting, and I loved being part of that great old beloved institution, the ROM. I discovered that directing a dedicated professional on stage was more rewarding than actually performing magic. Although I have not given up performing, working with this guy has taught me my place.

Our friendship has deepened and solidified. I have watched not just David's growth as an artist, but also his bottomless love for and commitment to his family. He is a hockey dad who might well create a new category in the Hockey Hall of Fame. He has invited his sons into the magic arena, without pressing them, to the point where they know and parody some of his routines. Harrison Ben's hands are seen handling cards in our Dai Vernon biographical film. In the last incarnation of *The Conjuror* the elder of the two, Courtney Ben, was the costumed star of one of the most memorable of the big illusions, and earlier had helped his father develop what one New York magician and critic of magic deemed the finest piece of magic he had ever seen.

In 1998, when David proposed a smaller stage show, almost pure sleight of hand, Lindsay Sharp offered us the gallery just off the ROM's rotunda, to the left, where I had spent hundreds of happy boyhood hours prowling the geological display. That's where the huge lodestone used to be, floating in some kind of dense oil in a round brass tank, with a rotating three- or four-inch cylinder of iron on a crank that you could reposition to cause the big natural magnet to rotate toward the metal. The gallery was temporarily empty pending the development of a new exhibition, and we built our own 175-seat theatre in it, in the round, with a small stage only four inches above the floor, the seats well-raked, so that nobody would be farther than about eight metres from David's hands when he was downstage. We called the show *The Conjuror's Suite*. The premise was that when magicians came in from out of town to see *The Conjuror*, they would often come home with David afterward and pass the night away showing each other the latest adventures in sleight of hand. Tonight would be that kind of magic.

Again there were classics such as the Ring Off Stick, and again David choreographed them to classical music, contriving night after night to come to the climax of the trick – even when working with up to four volunteers from the audience – exactly in sync with the final coda of the music. The Ring Off Stick he turned into an elaborate drama in which, after the standard mysteries of a borrowed wedding band mysteriously and repeatedly penetrating a wand held by volunteers from the audience, he invited the wife of the owner of the ring to come to the stage for a special magical ceremony over the ring – which then mysteriously vanishes as he is about to hand it to her.

At that point begins the overture to *The Barber of Seville*, accompanying David in what seems like a completely goofy search for the ring. Wordlessly he points the woman toward a ribboned Birks Blue Box that has been sitting in full view on a chair, stage left, throughout the show. He indicates that she should bring the box centre stage, untie the ribbon, and remove the contents. Inside the box is a smaller box completely wrapped in ribbon. It takes the guest some time to unwind the several yards of it. Finally, there in her hand is a small jewel box. She opens it. Inside is a rose. On the stem of the rose is her husband's wedding ring. She finds this on the last note of the overture, and magicians in the audience gasp at the audacity of it.

But my favourite piece in *The Conjuror's Suite* was David's reworking of another classic, The Torn and Restored Cigarette Paper. It's an elegant and simple piece (uncomplicated, that is – not easy to do). You take out a packet of cigarette papers, remove one, show it, tear it in half, put the halves together and tear them in half, showing the four bits stuck to the ends of your fingers. You roll the bits into a ball, which never leaves the audience's sight, and even in a fairly big theatre, if well backlit, can be seen clearly at the fingertips of the upheld hands. The ball is then unrolled, slowly, and the paper is seen to have been magically restored to its original size. Bonnie Beecher's lighting turned it into a breathtaking drama, with large shadows of hands on the drop as the magic unfolded, "a Caligari atmosphere," David said.

David was rehearsing it one day. In the theatre, besides me and the stage manager and Suley, were Courtney and Harrison Howlett-Ben, David's sons. He suddenly stopped and said, "Patrick! I've just had an idea. I want to try something. Cue the music again when I signal you." And he invited Courtney, then ten years old, to come and kneel on a chair with its back against the rear edge of the small green-baize-topped performance table, centre stage. He whispered to Courtney, just loudly enough so that the audience could hear every word and yet it would seem intimate and private, "Do as I do." He gave Courtney one cigarette paper, while he took another, and in a measured way led his son through the first tearing, then the second, and the display on the fingertips, the rolling into a ball and the presentation of that ball between the outstretched index fingers.

"Now," he whispered, "I'll go first." He snapped his fingers magically, unrolled his ball, and the paper was restored. He nodded to Courtney. Courtney unrolled his paper ball. Four torn pieces tumbled to the tabletop.

"Oh-oh!" David said apologetically. "We forgot to snap our fingers over yours." He rerolled the fragments, put them on the boy's palm, snapped his fingers, Courtney unrolled the ball, the paper was restored.

We have on film the look of transfiguration of kids invited from the audience to share this moment. The faces of their parents were often the best thing to see in the whole evening, though. As the young volunteer went back to his or her seat, David would call out, in his stage whisper, "Wait! Wait!" The child would turn back toward him. "*Don't tell anyone how you did it!*" David said, with a grin.

This was for me a kind of summit of the giving we had agreed we wanted to build into our magic shows. A tough-minded long-time New York–based professional and critic of the craft, Jamy Ian Swiss, came to Toronto for the opening night (as did magicians from Chicago and Hollywood). Jamy sat with me near the back of the little theatre. At the conclusion of the Torn and Restored Cigarette Paper, a trick he has often used to close his own elegant act, Jamy turned to me and said quietly, "That is the best magic trick I have ever seen."

He was not talking about the sleight of hand.

If my rediscovery of the pleasures of performance magic began as an escape from the dreariness of the CBC head office, it soon became a somewhat regressive obsession, much as magic does for kids who find out at the age of eight or ten just what a delight it is to do something that amazes an audience. And there is, indisputably, a great pleasure to be taken from that amazement. I suspect that the reason more boys than girls take up magic, by a ratio of maybe a thousand to one, is that boys need power and attention. Our culture demands performance from males in ways that it does not from females. Boys are deprived of the natural and essential mystery of the woman's body. Making things disappear, or levitate, or multiply or be created from nothing is a natural function of woman-ness: boys are unconsciously reaching for something female when they pick up the wand.

And then, when life becomes more intricate, and rewards for the work of investigation and labour and the building of something of social value that did not exist before become manifest, the majority of those boys leave their cards and thumbtips in a drawer somewhere and get on with life.

But some never stop needing to amaze, and while many reach a point where there isn't much else they can do, and their performances seem tired and routine (magic has a bad name as a result), there are still a few who move up to a new level of reverence for the craft, who constantly explore and grow. The best are those who recognize that they have a tacit contract with their audience, and that this contract includes respect for the audience's intelligence and personhood. Good magic uses the props and the sleights and the lighting and the music, not for its own sake, but for the building of a relationship with a community. David Ben has founded a not-for-profit organization, Magicana, dedicated to teaching and archiving magic, particularly that of great Canadian magicians, and organizing programs in which professional magicians teach sleight of hand as an instrument of building self-confidence in children who are mentally or physically challenged. He is a man who constantly has to be involved with his community, and that is reflected in his performance. Through his good offices, and Allan Slaight's, I have been able to meet some of the princes of contemporary magic. The best of them are teachers at heart.

The columns of the magic publications are weighted with reports of performers who seem to delight in humiliating their audiences. The magicians to whose work audiences return again and again are the ones who give, who make us feel clever for anticipating them, or blessed for having witnessed the extraordinary. It looks as though my having chanced upon some of these generous people in the latter years of my life is going to keep my hand in the craft for the foreseeable future. Forgive the pun.

My parents encouraged my early ventures into performance – the magic, the radio drama, speaking in public. It seems to have become a need. Caroline will say, if I am going through a grumpy period, that it's been too long since I've done a television program. I miss the challenge of the regular broadcast interview assignment.

I have written about the strange experience, in the mid-seventies, during *The Watson Report*, of the anxiety crisis in the hour or so before a live program began. I suspect that, among people who perform professionally, something like this may be more widely shared than is commonly acknowledged. I was sitting beside Luciano Pavarotti in the sixth or seventh row at Avery Fisher Hall one afternoon while Zubin Mehta was rehearsing an orchestral piece and the great tenor was waiting for his rehearsal time. I asked him how he felt at times like this, a couple of hours before a major concert that was built around and depended entirely on him. He looked at me thoughtfully for a moment and then said, "We always feel sad."

As my hands begin to lose the precision and sensitivity that the best sleight of hand requires, I am performing tricks less often. In reality, I don't have the patience and the discipline for the literally hundreds of practice hours needed to bring a fine sleight to the point where you can perform it with assurance and grace. The professional magicians with whom I've become close, David Ben and Jamy Ian Swiss and others, are always practising. There are no idle moments for a serious magician. I seem unable to give that much time to magic. Yet in a sense for me as a public speaker or a television host, it is also true that there are no idle moments. When I am not physically active, or reading or writing or playing music, my mind is often busy with some kind of performance scenario: how I might present a complex idea to a lay audience; how I would approach the teaching of a graduate seminar on the uses of the imagination. Even giving a reading from one of my works of fiction will be a performance that I plan with care, and then approach the moment always ready to change that plan, to improvise, to read the audience's eyes as Bucky Fuller advised me to do forty years go, to respond to and try to learn from the occasion.

There are, however, long and nourishing idle periods when all of this conscious tactical activity goes to sleep, and I gaze dozily for an hour or more at the lake or the valley, or swim lazily, or wander around the piano keyboard with no particular intention. Like sleep itself these interludes of contentedly doing nothing at all seem to be not just physically and emotionally nourishing, but also to allow the inventive parts of the unconscious mind to roam unencumbered for a while and find their way into new perceptions. It frequently happens that after a day or two's purposeless musing by the lakeshore, or mindlessly working with my hands in my little workshop, or just sitting and staring, a story idea will appear or a problem be solved. It happens in dreams too. *Ahmek* came out of a period of idleness and plenty of time in bed. I woke up one morning remembering that it would be Mary's birthday tomorrow, I should call her, and in the act of sleepily reaching for the phone a poem came into my head, pretty well fully-formed. Although I have massaged it since, to tidy up the meter and sharpen an image here or there, the following is close to exactly what appeared, unbidden, that recent November morning:

SEVENTY-FIVE
My hands are the hands of seventy-five
And my feet much older than that
And my forehead feels more like a century
Of going without a hat

But my dreams still scare me with phantoms and monsters
Or tempt me with breast or brawn
Or hand me the keys to the universe . . .
(Which I then can't find in the dawn.)

Or the missing clue for the crossword
Or a birthday verse for my wife
Or the place where I left my wallet last night
Or the ultimate secrets of life

Dreams give you a lot to hang on to
When the engine begins to run rough

And as long as they're playing me movies like this
I'll always have more than enough.

Michael Levine is always identifying fresh talent and going leagues out of his way to help young people make a start. He became interested in a young actor, David Hirsh, and asked me to do some work with him on voice and body language. Hirsh told me he was fascinated with Oscar Wilde's *The Picture of Dorian Gray*, and together we worked up a proposal for a television program with a director and a group of actors rehearsing a dramatic version of *Dorian Gray* for the stage – a way of taking a television audience into that backstage process. I brought in a director friend, Diana Leblanc. I played the artist who paints the original portrait. The program is a montage of director and actors reading around an onstage table, in preparation, backstage gossip and interplay in the dressing room, portions of scenes with the director working over the actors on set, and segments of finished scenes. It is a workshop, and Leblanc and I thought it might be the pilot for a whole series. It did not become so, but Bravo! broadcast it, and it played very well.

In the mid- and late nineties as History Television got underway in Canada, the Historica Foundation decided to help fund a series of one-hour biographical documentaries, to be called *The Canadians: Biographies of a Nation*. I was asked to advise on the development of the series at the pilot stage, and later I was offered the position of commissioning editor, narrator, and program host. This came close to being everything one could want in a broadcast contract. Although I was not actually producing and directing, with the support and encouragement of the executive producer, Patricia Phillips, and her business partner/husband, Andy Thomson,[7] I worked closely with the filmmakers, undertook hands-on guidance in the rewrites and edits, spent lots of time in screening rooms and cutting rooms,

7. In 1987 Thomson and Phillips had gone from Montreal to Edmonton to produce a television project about dinosaurs in China, had started a small company for that production, Great North Productions, which grew into a major Alberta film and television production centre, since absorbed into Alliance Atlantis, where Phillips and Thomson were vice-presidents in the short-lived AAC FACT division.

and did the satisfying work of voicing the narrations.

But I think the best part of my work on *The Canadians* was the opportunity to share with other filmmakers a lifetime of tracing my way through the paths of the documentary. Whatever the seductive power of performing, I think teaching is a deeper part of the legacy I have from Stan and Lucy, my mother and father, teachers both. To go on location with a director, to sit in the cutting room over an intractable editing puzzle, or to find the articulation of a solution that has just been eluding all of us as we frown through a screening in which something is almost perfect – these are the kinds of things that lead to a sunset's feeling as though the day up to now has been pretty damn good.

Daniel Zuckerbrot is a producer/director whom I had met over *The Making of The Conjuror* back in those months of rehearsal in the Canadian Children's Dance Theatre studios. David Ben and I agreed that he could bring a crew in for a few hours of speculative shooting during our rehearsals, and he turned up a few days later with Neville Ottey and Ian Challis, the A Team from *The Struggle for Democracy*. Those few hours stretched into days, generated an engaging documentary on the development of a stage magic presentation, and gave me the experience of watching a quiet, modest, low-key, and confident documentary director at work. Daniel Zuckerbrot and I became good friends. I brought him in on several episodes of *The Canadians*. He made *A Love Story*, the biography of Northrop Frye, a project that History Television declared to be pretty improbable for their audience until they saw the passionate and compelling film that ensued. I felt that I had found someone who could help me deal, through the making of a film about it, with the death of Robert Markle, a loss that had left a very large space.

It happened not long after we had completed the pilot of *Something Brewing*. Driving home to his old farmhouse one evening after visiting friends in Mount Forest, Robert's pickup slammed into the back of an unlighted tractor and he died instantly. Caroline and I were diving at Small Hope Bay when it happened, and flew back the next day to be with Marlene and the gathering mourners at the farm. Daniel Zuckerbrot's film, *The Life of Robert Markle: An Investigation*,[8] orbits his beautiful and gracious widow. The film has helped me – and many of Robert's friends report the same phenomenon – to deal with the vacuum his death left in its wake. I would have written more extensively about Robert in this book, but my biography of him in the Omnibus Edition of the books based on the television series is my farewell. The okay term today would be "closure." Robert Markle would have turned up his nose at that word.

In the second or third year of *The Canadians: Biographies of a Nation*, Michael Levine asked me to meet with publisher Kim McArthur, about their idea for a series of books based on these biographical documentaries. Kim McArthur had already done a successful translation of the *Heritage Minutes* idea into book form, *Just a Minute*, written by Marsha Boulton. But Kim and Michael had been stymied in trying to find a writer, or writers – or indeed someone who would bring the writers together – to make books based on *The Canadians.* She asked me if I would consider stepping in as general editor. I spent an evening in front of the fire doing one of my imagined scenarios: conversations with writers whom I'm trying to enlist for these books. Who will they be? What will I ask them to do?

A great deal of my own professional writing during these last fifteen years has been book reviews and comment pieces for the periodical press, *TIME*, *Maclean's* magazine, *Books in Canada* latterly, and more than anywhere else for the *Globe and Mail.* In one of those imagined conversations I telephoned television and film critics – John Doyle, the late Bob Blackburn, and Brian D. Johnson – to ask them if they would be interested in doing a kind of extended review of an episode of *The Canadians* – the kind of long review that the *New York Review of Books* often carries, which allows you to think you know the book without having actually read it. I proposed that we engage a stable of critics, pay them a fee comparable to what they would get if

8. "Investigation" was Robert's favourite word.

they were doing freelance reviews of television programs, and send each of them four or five cassettes with an understanding that in this environment they were not going to be encouraged to dump on the films they were reviewing, but do what they would do for a newspaper or a magazine where they wanted to interest their readers in the program under consideration.

Now I began to feel that I knew exactly what these "reviews" would look like, and to feel some enthusiasm at the prospect of working as an editor with some of these interesting writers. So I said I would bang off a sample for Kim McArthur to consider. I dug out the cassette of Bob Duncan's episode on the life of Percy Williams, the Olympic runner.

It was an extraordinary day, the day I wrote that sample chapter. By the time I was three pages into it, I knew exactly what the "voice" should be, as Robert Gottlieb had so helpfully said when I was starting into Alexander Dolgun's story two decades before. And then, by the time I was halfway through, I knew who was going to write these things: me.

The writing poured out. In three days I had a chapter off to Kim, with a note proposing I write the whole book myself. She phoned back ecstatically. Go ahead, she said. Over the next three years we did four books, three volumes of sixteen short biographies each, followed by an Omnibus Edition that compiled them all. Hugh Graham helped me with volume three. The writing was enormously satisfying, and the books did very well.

There appeared sometime in the seventh decade of my life an awareness that all those years of writing to deadline, writing words for people to speak in broadcasts, writing to the demands of a specialized form like the documentary, writing to a particular and fairly narrow audience, as in the dozens of book reviews and current affairs essays for newspapers and magazines, all this discipline salted with excursions into playful or adventurous fiction, or focused by the intractable need for compression in writing the *Heritage Minutes* – these had generated a confidence in the process, a confidence that had grown imperceptibly until one morning I woke up and was aware of it. I would feel it in the screening room with a director from whom I had commissioned a documentary for History Television, or in the cutting room with the editor of a *Heritage Minute.* If something was wrong I knew why it was wrong and how to fix it. What to colleagues and cutters and commissioned producers might have seemed impatience and irritability felt to me like an almost complacent sense that everything was going okay, let's get on with it.

At the same time the elusiveness of the truly fine, the yearning, like Yeats, for the possibility that one day

> . . . before I am old
> I will have written him one
> Poem maybe as cold
> And passionate as the dawn . . .

. . . that hunger would still wake me up in the night with the seed of a story to be told, or a form to be tried, or a line of verse . . . things that then seemed even more elusive at sunrise but still demanding attention and speaking of work yet undone. The desire to write something that, as Sir Philip Sidney said, might keep old men from the chimney corner or children from play. Sometimes something light, almost trivial, a joke or a bit of classy doggerel, sometimes vast, sprawling works of huge intent, that I knew I would never do, don't know how to do . . . and yet . . .

One night there was the glimmering of a story about a falcon. Was it Yeats's falcon, turning and turning in the widening gyre? No, this was a cheerful story, a playful story, not a falcon, an accipiter, a goshawk, that was it, a playful goshawk.

But as I began to get her on paper, she wasn't playful at all, she was a ferociously snobbish old dame, raised in an aristocratic household in the Old Russia, somehow having found herself brought across the ocean to North America, loosed in the north woods of Ontario. And over the next months, retreated to for relief from tasks and deadlines, for play, yes, but something more than play as a humanity and a moral intent began to invade the story, the book evolved into a fable for adults, a small thing but my own and now my favourite, which McArthur has just published as *Wittgenstein and the Goshawk.*

Looking back. I think you're supposed to look back, at the end of a memoir. In the following chapter, reflecting on the craft of television, I write about some of the things I learned at that level, and I think that throughout this book I've been able to draw some threads together. I also want to make a couple of observations about Canada, my country, the great cradle whose rocks and lakes and pines nourished me, and whose teachers and strivers and risk-takers and reformers helped me to see how a society might move steadily toward the authentic, institutionalized recognition of the value of the person, of the imagination, and of liberty.

For most of my career, broadcasting was a significant arena in which to contribute to those advances, but that field is now shrinking toward the vanishing point. Public broadcasting in Canada was meant as a buffer against invasion by the commercially driven American broadcasting system. The early days of television were a time of experimentation and risk-taking, when producers and managers alike were searching for ways to employ the medium to make the best of Canada known to more Canadians, to reveal the problems and challenges for the betterment of the whole society, to enlarge the meaning of the word "citizen," through the sharing of experience. Bit by bit that motif has been submerged by the competition for viewers and for revenue, a rage for numbers that is steadily eroding the proud commitment to artistic and social adventure that was once widely shared.

Along with the clutter of the airwaves by too many channels and too much hucksterism is the cluttering of the screen in "information programming" by short summary banners in bottom screen and side panels or even mid-screen inserts of headlines and promotions, so that it becomes impossible to pay concentrated attention to the reporter or the scene that is ostensibly the report of the moment. This represents the same kind of contempt for the viewer *and also for the on-screen reporter and image* that has been inflicted on us since broadcasters began to make screen credits impossible to read. Screen credits to directors, writers, performers, and designers were meant to acknowledge creative contributions. Audiences wanted to know who the artists were, whose work they might want to look for in the future. When you take an old program out of the archives, in the few frames containing one or two names – which are, by the way, left on the screen long enough to read them – you can read and absorb the identities of people whose work you would look out for in the future.

Bit by bit, pressure from funders, unions, and managers began to force onto the screen more and more names of people who had simply made routine contributions, doing their jobs, names of no interest to viewers. Producers responded by rolling the credits quickly, rendering them illegible. Then they began to squeeze them into a narrowed panel beside which was added a new panel, also almost impossible to read, promoting an upcoming program. The viewer, the people "credited," and the makers of the upcoming program are all insulted by this practice, and it is difficult to understand why the perpetrators imagine that any good is being served.

Audiences, not surprisingly, are falling away.

In the 1960s regulators decided that commercial broadcasters should be required to do more for the privilege of their licence than just rebroadcast American shows they could buy cheaply. The CRTC developed elaborate regulations to put "Canadian content" on the screens of broadcasters. But the shareholders of those companies had not signed up for that reason: they quite properly wanted a maximum return on their investment. Nonetheless, the regulators were encouraged by the early and unexpected success of their radio regulations demanding that music stations carry a substantial percentage of Canadian music. Some grumpy broadcasters complained that there wasn't any decent Canadian music, and even if there was, Canadians wouldn't listen to it. They were spectacularly wrong. Canadian singers, songs, and artists began to take off not only at home but abroad, as the result of – of all things – a *regulation!* Maybe something like that could work in television.

The trouble was that instead of demanding quality and relevance to the Canadian experience, the new regulations were (and remain) primarily industrial: if the key players – producer, director, writer, principal performers, key technicians – hold Canadian citizenship, no matter what the subject matter might be, the program can qualify for funding. Since the late sixties the funding agencies have multiplied to the point where I have listed more than twenty in the Appendix. This means that much of the money intended for the production of Canadian programs actually goes to pay the salaries of the people who run these agencies. The cost of the application and hearing processes also generates an increased burden on independent producers who have to devote a prodigious amount of time to learning the elaborate rules and scheduling protocols, and filling out forms, instead of making programs. In this way millions of Canadian tax and obligatory "philanthropic" dollars are wasted every year.

The result is that there is seldom enough money for quality production that reflects Canadian concerns and realities. Dramas are commonly preferred if they are so location non-specific that they can be sold abroad, and that really means sold in the United States. Other kinds of programs – documentaries, house and garden, home crafts, health, and getting-on-with-life programs – are sought by broadcasters at the lowest possible price. Few get made that are of specific interest to Canadians. For the most part, neither broadcasters nor producers can put together enough money to produce anything airable unless it can be sold in more than one market. That often means that program judgments are being made by offshore "co-producers" who have zero interest in our content concerns, and independent producers here report increasingly on their being bullied by British and American co-producers whose youthful officials are interested only in the bottom line, have no experience in the making of programs, no concern for the welfare of audiences, and an arrogant attitude toward program judgments that are made for any other concern than profitability. The new fad of so-called "reality" programming is driven entirely by this kind of greed.

I keep thinking that it would be so easy to fix, were the political will available. Here's how. Relieve the commercial broadcasters of all regulation concerning Canadian content. Let them do what they do best: local news and current affairs, and prime-time replay of low-cost American entertainment. Canadian audiences love the stuff, and that is a cheap way for them to get it while also serving the advertising business in Canada.

Take all that funding from the twenty or so agencies, put it into the CBC's budget, tell the CBC to get out of American movies and out of the advertising business, *and then make uncompromising demands on the country's genuinely public broadcaster, that it produce a wide range of the best possible Canadian programs.* These would include high-risk experiments. It would include the transformation into television drama of some of the highly successful and original theatre that is being produced in regional theatres from St. John's to Victoria – some of it, by the way, from non-Canadian playwrights – Shakespeare, say, or Michael Frayn.[9] The programming would have to reflect the regional and provincial origins of a great deal of that funding, but not just for industrial reasons as is the case now, where you can do a murder mystery set in an unnamed Midwestern city (a city that just might be Chicago, say) and get Alberta government funding for it as long as the people who make it live and work in Alberta.

CBC could lead the way in this by a radical remake of its programming, right now. I've demonstrated how to do that in "Distinction or Extinction" in the Appendix to this book. The Corporation would then be in an admirable position to go to governments and say, See what we're doing? We could expand that threefold if you gave the public broadcaster the unique mandate for Canadian programming and let the private broadcasters get on with what they

9. The author of *Copenhagen,* a brilliant, profound, morally, and spiritually challenging drama that represents for me programming of foreign origin that should be considered Canadian content because it is profoundly meaningful to Canadian audiences. Ditto, say, Ibsen, Molière, Shaw – all offshore playwrights being welcomed by theatre goers across the country, but not on CBC TV. (Any more.)

were designed for: to give shareholders a return on their investment. CBC has repeatedly demonstrated that it is not interested in such a glorious opportunity, but would rather show the private broadcasters that it can compete effectively with them. As who couldn't with a subsidy of several hundred millions per annum?[10]

But that is an aside: I meant to look back on some broader aspects of cultural and social change, some of them quite dramatic. For example, in the unembarrassed expression of affection, coloured or not with an acknowledgment of the omnipresence of the sexual sensibility, we have moved a considerable distance in my lifetime. I think this has contributed to freedom. If a man ever kissed another man during the first thirty years of my life, there was no question that Something Was Going On. (Unless it were Russians or Frenchmen, in which case it was understandable, it was ceremonial, it was convention, and in any case it was only on the cheeks.) The first time I was kissed on the mouth by a man was after five days in Vancouver when I had been assigned to Buckminster Fuller, as his "keeper" during a series of speeches and seminars, getting him to the hall on time, and seeing he was fed and watered. It was one of the longest times we had had together and was full of affectionate and intimate conversation. And when I said goodbye to him at the gate to his flight, he grabbed me by the ears, smacked me on the mouth, and said how much he loved me.

That was surprising. In latter years I observe lots of men besides myself, grown men whose heterosexuality is in no question, kissing each other affectionately on the mouth. Friends gathering at private cottages go swimming naked together, in mixed groups, and while they seldom talk about it,[11] their pleasure in the expressive sexuality and attributes of each other is obviously a component of this still somewhat daring activity. I think that is a part of the growth of liberty that our traditions and institutions have fertilized.

10. The total allocation of public money in 2003–2004 was just over a billion dollars. Of course, there are no perfect solutions, the big problem with this one being the dangerous concentration of power in the hands of an already arrogant organization. I persist in believing this is not unsolvable.

11. Even this is beginning to change.

I have written about the scabrous racism and exclusiveness in Toronto when I was a boy. Racism and tribalism are so deep-rooted in most people as to seem ineradicable. But the institutionalizing of racial equality and the dignity of the individual, while perhaps never able to eliminate feelings of racial and family and tribal difference and superiority, can, in fact, change behaviour and thus change attitudes. It used to be a truism to say that you cannot legislate morality, but history demonstrates that in fact you can. When the United States legislated the end of the segregation of the races in schools and on buses and at drinking fountains and in public places, it was at first necessary to bring out the army. But now if you are in a gathering around a television set, and on the screen a black man kisses a white woman, the chances are if you ask around nobody will have noticed that what just happened in that program was something that forty years ago would have been unthinkable and twenty-five years ago would still have occasioned public comment.

Here in Canada the steady enlargement of the part of the population deemed to be citizens is encouraging, and is also an important demonstration that morality not only can be legislated, but must be. It takes time for attitudes to change. People in our culture whose prejudices are deeply set against other races, cultures, or social "classes," members of the opposite sex, or of a different age group, usually consider themselves to be civilized, reasonable, tolerant democrats. We are often unaware of how strongly our behavior is influenced by attitudes of which we are unaware, and during the making of *The Struggle for Democracy* this was brought home to us dramatically in at least two instances, one of them excruciatingly embarrassing to me – and very, very instructive.

Among the precious and enduring friends we have found during the making of television programs is the activist lawyer Marilou McPhedran. Marilou has selflessly given most of her adult life to the cause of justice between the sexes. She is a founding member of LEAF, the Women's Legal Education and Action Fund, and a tireless traveller to whatever part of the world summons her to work with women in campaigns for justice and equality. In 2004 alone she was in Malaysia, Pakistan, India, and South Africa, as well as writing the dissertation for her LL.M. (Master of Laws) degree in comparative constitutional law. We had met socially in the seventies, but where I first came to understand the strength, character, and stature of this woman was during the shooting of "The Last Citizen," a program about women's slow rise toward equality in the western democracies. Marilou McPhedran was a key member of a band of warriors who recognized that Pierre Trudeau's proposed Charter of Rights and Freedoms did not, in fact, guarantee anything of consequence to women. When she discovered that her male political friends and contacts all said that it did indeed specify the sexual equality that she and her colleagues were demanding, she realized that a campaign would have to be fought, and with considerable ingenuity. She led a group of women who invaded Parliament Hill, knocking on MPs' doors, diligently and insistently corralling every possible ally, infiltrating so successfully that security staff apparently thought they were parliamentary employees. In the end they brought it off and secured Clause 28, without which – as the one-time sanguine apologists of the earlier draft of the Charter finally agreed – women would have been left out in the cold. And while the drama that propelled this very strong segment in the documentary came out of the character and determination of Marilou McPhedran and her sister campaigners, their strategic and tactical genius, and the conflict with the men who tried to dismiss them, the strongest lesson for me was that those men were not wicked, they were complacently at rest in the comfort of their power and unable to see that what they were offering was not justice but patronizing condescension. It was necessary to fight that through to its legislative conclusion in order to cause the courts of law to begin to make the judgments that would make the news that would bit by bit begin to change attitudes within the culture at large. A process that is, I think, underway but only just.

That was not the embarrassing episode, though. Early in the filming of *The Struggle for Democracy* Ted Remerowski built a sample reel for sponsors and partners and invited the key members of the production group, Caroline and me and Nancy Button, to take a look at it and give him his comments before he locked it up. It was, to say the least, thrilling. Even though we were only a few months into the shooting, the geographical and thematic scope of what we looked at that day was enough to make us feel that we had the wind in our sails in a great way. Except.

Ted asked each of us in turn what we thought. Caroline said she would like to wait until Nancy and I had said our pieces, which were very positive indeed. And then Caroline asked quietly if any of us had noticed that there was something missing from the undoubtedly very impressive twenty-minute reel? We shook our heads, puzzled. Caroline said, "There is not a single woman in the whole piece."

We had not noticed, neither Ted, Nancy, nor I – people who quite honestly and diligently were building a major international film project about justice and equality. Had we been questioned in any forum about the importance of the equality of women in the growth of the democracies, there is no doubt that we would have been unequivocal about it. But we had not noticed that there were no women in the demo reel. Our ideas were reasonably advanced, I think, but our attitudes were still shaped by centuries of male complacency.

The great waves of immigrants after World War II seem to have been one of the most important instruments that allowed Canadian institutions for civility and our declarations of fairness and equality to finally find a footing – to *set* – or almost so. There is still a long way to go in recognizing the strengths and rights of our First Nations (and of women), but compared with the racism and male complacency characteristic of the thirties I grew up in, the progress has been monumental.

Yet in the last twenty-five years, our leaders have stopped talking about the main currents of this growth toward civility. Parliament itself has become a catcalling arena. Politicians and pundits wring their hands about low voter turnout and political indifference, but why the hell should citizens take seriously a costly chamber whose main activity appears to be the hurling of insults? The media contribute to the trivialization of electoral politics by the ten-second sound bite lifted out of the scrum. They encourage the catcalling and the smart-alecking in those panel shows that are offered as a forum for exploring public policy but usually turn into a contest to see which participant can come up with the cleverest defamatory lines. A similar egoism seems to be widespread in the community. Drivers on the streets of our bigger cities have forgotten how well common courtesy smoothes the flow of traffic, and anger at the wheel is increasingly a part of the urban driving experience. Social anger, I call it, and speculate that it follows inevitably when the teaching of the social values of respect for fellow citizens is abandoned in the classroom and in the public discourse of political leaders, and the prime value is the self-gratification that drives the consumerist culture we have become.

Hypnotized by the mythologies of the bottom line and fiscal prudence, and the (usually dishonest)[12] shibboleth of small government and the sacredness of private enterprise, governments have put health care into jeopardy and education into the sink. All across the country, governments have quite knowingly and deliberately encouraged the scourge of the gambling casino to blight the land because it is a source of revenue that allows them to pretend that the cost of public programs has been reduced, when in fact commercial gambling contributes to the poverty and mental anguish while providing employment and rehabilitation for a few. The irony of this moral and spiritual sickness being promoted by governments,[13] whose mandate is supposed to be the well-being of the governed, is surpassed only by the irony that gambling has become the economic mainstay of many First Nations. This is painfully poignant, but it is inappropriate to

12. I say "dishonest" because in so many instances the great recipients of public resource have been the huge industrial complexes (defence industries, aviation, resource industries, etc.) and it is somewhat less than ingenuous for the leaders of such beneficiaries to say that public enterprise has no place in a progressive modern state. I would be delighted to debate this with anyone in any forum: David Frum at a meeting of the Fraser Institute, say.

13. Note: *Promoted,* not just tolerated – I am in favour of citizens having the liberty to do stupid and hurtful things as long as they don't hurt others – but what governments are doing in this field is deliberately seducing citizens into wasteful and hurtful activity in order to appear to be fiscally prudent.

blame the chiefs of those communities: they have been abandoned to poverty and despair by white governments for so long that providing prosperity for the members of their Nation is not something they can reasonably be expected to turn down on the grounds that it is spiritually, physically, emotionally, and economically damaging to white people and morally corrupting to their own.

The physical health and imaginative and intellectual strength of the people who make up a democracy are its greatest source of wealth. Poor, sick, alienated people cannot produce and cannot consume, so even if your values are so cynical and primitive as to think that shopping is a social value and consumption is the purpose of life, you are screwing yourself if you contribute to a society in which poverty and ignorance are growing.

Is that happening in Canada? I am heartened somewhat by the evidence that so many young people across the country are vigorously eloquent about their love of their communities, their commitment to the democratic ideals, kids who are engaged, are giving, are involved. But I fear that they are all, in a sense, the rich kids. The kids who have enough to eat and get driven to school every morning, and that we are turning away from the challenge and the opportunity to secure a future for all our kids, to make sure that the potential Einsteins and Graham Bells and P.K. Pages and Beethovens don't fall through the cracks and vanish because they are too hungry to think or study or invent or compose or take chances or grow. A friend wrote, "We are become too brusque a nation." I worry that I may have contributed to that, by pushing so hard for aggressiveness in journalism. I look at the vacant superficiality of television and I worry that I may have contributed to *that* by insisting that television must not be boring, preachy, and condescending.

As I have said at the end of the chapter on *The Struggle for Democracy*, contemporary journalism is not serving us with the ongoing review of the balance sheet, the annual (or quarterly) reports on the gains and losses of civilization versus barbarism. All the same, on the whole I incline to the considered and rational view that, slow as it seems, and largely because we are crying out against our barbarities instead of concealing them – that on the whole we are moving slowly toward civilization.

But every so often, in the middle of the night, my heart keeps sneaking up on me and whispering that I might be wrong.

Chapter 26

ASPECTS OF STYLE AND METHOD

THE FIRST, GREAT, OVERRIDING LESSON that I learned early in my long career as a television interviewer is that more than anything else you must *listen.* Listen to and intently watch your subject. Follow the leads offered you. Be prepared to abandon your plan whenever you detect an unexpected opportunity for a spontaneous and thus likely honest exchange or response. And the second great lesson in a sense subtends the first. It is that the subject or subjects being discussed in the interview, what I call the "referential content," is of only secondary interest. The prime interest is the person being interviewed and the dynamics of the relationship with the interviewer. The television interview, unlike an interview for the written press, is a piece of theatre. It is not an essay or a lecture or an article, and definitely not a documentary. (Of course, good television documentaries usually make use of interviews, and in that context the rules may be different.)

Listening and spontaneity are connected. In the late 1960s Buckminster Fuller persuaded me to stop writing the talks I was increasingly being invited to give all across the country (as a result of the popularity of *Seven Days*). "What you want to say is already in your head," he would say, arguing that if you *speak* to the hall instead of reading to it, and respond to what you see in people's faces – a form of listening – you will make a much stronger connection with them, and will actually learn valuable lessons about the strengths and weaknesses of your own ideas. "Trust your intuitions," Bucky always said. And for nearly forty years that is what I have done when speaking in public.[1] I know I've mentioned this before, but it is important enough to bear repetition.

Parenthetically, one of the most ruinous technical innovations in the field of public speaking is PowerPoint. Used mostly to project on a screen the printed text that the speaker is reading to the audience, it reinforces four destructive elements: it underlines – were that necessary – the sad fact that we are being read to, not spoken to, it renders even more impossible the speaker's capacity to sense and respond to his audience, it makes it very difficult to comprehend the text, and perhaps worst of all it is deeply insulting to that audience. To demonstrate with costly technology your assumption that they will not be able to understand what you are saying without being able to read it at the same time is an act of both self-contempt and contempt for your listeners.

I have seen one use of PowerPoint that was appropriate and genuinely effective. My magician colleague David Ben uses it to spring visual surprises on his audience, to challenge them with puzzles that could not be conveyed any way but visually, and to do inventive conjuring tricks. But he is a rarity. Most users of this lamentable crutch, apparently unaware how blatantly they are advertising their lack of confidence in the value of their message, use it as a kind of stun gun whose principal effect is to render the whole experience a waste of time or worse.

The foundation for these ideas was laid at the dinner table when I was a boy. Conversation at that table shaped a great deal of my view of life and of what was expected of me as I grew up. My parents and siblings were good storytellers, my father, Stanley, and eldest brother,

1. With a few exceptions. In the spring of 2004, when my own university, Toronto, awarded me an honorary degree, the occasion felt like the kind of homecoming that demanded something special. So for my convocation address I wrote a poem. It was very, very well received, and helped confirm my sense that in the world of "reality" television and schlock there is a growing appetite for the hearing of carefully wrought language. I have included that address in the Appendix.

Cliff, superb. So I caught the idea early in life that when you gave an account of the events of the day, you looked for a beginning and a middle and an end and tried to give your gossip some narrative shape. Even put it into rhyme and meter if you felt up to that, the Dad being particularly deft at taking some fragment of your story and capping it with a bit of doggerel. He also loved retailing bits of light verse, and would do Lewis Carroll's "Jabberwocky," or one of A.A. Milne's little masterpieces from *When We Were Very Young* or *Now We Are Six.* I wrote in Chapter Two about his reciting Milne's "The King's Breakfast" whenever we ran short of butter at the table. At some point I realized that without consciously trying I too had learned that little comic poem, just from hearing my father say it.

So whether it was shunning the frumious bandersnatch, or going back to bed in disgust because the Alderney said that marmalade was nicer than butter for the Royal Slice of Bread, or just trying to outdo your siblings with the narrative effects of your account of a ruckus in class or a stolen kiss on the playground . . . at that big walnut table at 22 Bracondale Hill Road you knew that *structure mattered.* Because while all this exchange – which often included the Dad's sometimes horrifying accounts of trench warfare at Ypres and Vimy and Mons – was usually based on real events (except perhaps for my brother John, whose talent for invention and embellishment was exemplary) I think we all tacitly recognized that emotional and social authenticity was conveyed better by a well-shaped tale than by a simple cataloguing of events.

It would be decades before I began to think analytically about that aspect of narrative, in both fiction and non-fiction. It is an area of speculation that continues to fascinate me now in my eighth decade. How the sensitive ear of novelists, playwrights, and actors can capture and convey the tone and texture of our social life in a way that allows us to recognize when the story and characters portrayed are us, or somebody else, and cast a glow of illumination, bring what Edmund Wilson called "the shock of recognition."

Within a few months of my apprenticeship as a CBC Television producer/director, I became aware that the new visual medium was not quite the instrument of public instruction and information that my superiors seemed to believe it to be, and that in this respect it was different from both print and radio.

As the new boy in the department, I was given a great variety of talk show and documentary assignments, mostly the former, often filling in for the regular producer when he was absent or overloaded, and sometimes just attached to another producer's program as part of the training process. CBC television producers were then in most cases their own directors, imitating the norms of BBC television. The divisions of labour now common in the industry had not yet been worked out in anything like the fragmented and specialized way they are now. I never heard the phrase executive producer until the 1960s, and while we producers were all directing our own programs, most of them live, we seldom referred to each other as directors, and the first time it ever occurred to me that my programs would look better if I sublet the directing to someone who thought *only* about that aspect of the production was some months into the making of the series *This Hour Has Seven Days.* Douglas Leiterman and I were jointly functioning as both executive producers, producers, and, on alternate weeks, directors. Directing was like finally getting your hands on the controls of the airplane and taking it into the air after months of raising the money and building the machine and planning the round-the-world flight. Directing was Making Images. It was the key part of shaping the program. It was working with the lights and the lenses and the technicians and all that lovely equipment. And it was taking command, the front lines. Like taking the regiment over the top after weeks of strategy and charts. It was the real thing.

But we had to face it, Douglas and I: with the weekly challenge of finding the stories, commissioning their production, and shaping an hour of compelling television every week, and spending whole nights in a videotape editing suite or hunched over a 16mm film editing table with a bleary-eyed editor, we were not doing a very effective job in the control room. And so we hired a director, David Ruskin, a bright, feisty little guy with a fine eye for lighting and design who lived, breathed, slept, and dreamed directing. It was Ruskin who refined the distinctive *Seven Days* studio look and style. A large part of directing is macho stuff, and in retrospect it is regrettable that Douglas and I stuck to our macho guns as long as we did.

But back in the fifties, in those first months of producing and directing, when I would be doing a *Citizens' Forum* panel discussion one night, a *This Week* political interview or discussion another, occasionally sitting in, at their request, as guest director for one of Ross McLean's daily *Tabloid* magazines or even the venerable *Country Calendar*, I began to realize that careful, thoughtful, reasonable discussion was not what held viewers to the screen. It was vigorous dispute and strong images that did the trick. I would ask friends and family for their evaluations of my shows and regularly hear that they had thought so-and-so very wise and intelligent, but had found other things to do, whereas those rascals shouting at each other – was it about Suez? or about capital punishment, they couldn't remember, but boy it was a great show, the way they got at each other.

And a kind of formulation or principle began to emerge. I said to myself, This is not an information medium. It is . . . *theatre.* It may be dealing with factual information and opinion about current events, but when it works it works because it engages the viewer emotionally the way a play does, and I have to decide whether this is worth all the effort when it seems that audiences cannot tell you the next day what anybody said on a program that they all agree was enthralling, spellbinding, absorbing, and all those other words they used after you'd presented something in which the participants came close to shedding blood.

Bit by bit I began to fit it all together into something resembling a theory. *This Hour Has Seven Days* was where all those theoretical speculations and mumblings first came together in a single incarnation – not of my own devising by any means. Leiterman and I had spent three years trying things out, arguing, writing policy papers, testing our ideas on often unsympathetic fellow broadcasters and journalists. But the product as it evolved and kept on evolving was unequivocally *theatre.*

In the mid-seventies my contract for *The Watson Report* included a few days every year conducting workshops on interviewing at the CBC's training centre in Toronto. I often began with my declaration that virtually nothing that is said in the course of a television interview will be remembered by the audience, unless they have a prior and special interest in the subject being discussed, the "referential content." "The words spoken are never remembered," I would say, and was usually met with some angry responses. Many of the trainees were moving into television from print or radio, and a few were fresh out of university. I would a bit mischievously keep at them on this issue, while they were protesting that, What the hell, you, Watson, you've made your reputation as an interviewer, getting people to tell you stuff; are you saying it was all a waste of time?

As soon as I had them properly worked up, I would bring out an artifact, usually Elaine Grand's *Close-Up* interview with Lord Bertrand Russell. Grand was still a gamine-looking radiant beauty, and Russell had a reputation as a ladies' man. She seemed to be literally sitting at his feet, in a room in his house, with cushions on the floor. She led him through an account of his life, his early education and the dawning realization that he had a special mind, his delighted discovery of mathematics, especially Euclid. She asked about his young encounters with famous people in his father's house, his philosophical explorations, and, in the latter part of the conversation, his political experience as an anti-nuclear activist, for which he had gone to jail.

At the end, when she asked him (after this full and richly recounted biography), "Lord Russell, what has given you the greatest pleasure in life?" we expected an intellectual answer. Russell's eyes twinkled mischievously. He put his fingertips together and squeaked, "The greatest *pleasure?* Oh, I should have to say, passionate private relationships."

I knew the students would remember that line, and perhaps his joke about tame scientists who worked for governments and produced results their employers wanted, and thus were "like a parson, telling lies for money." But I was equally sure they would remember almost nothing else. I would swear them to fair play, take no notes, just watch it as if they were sitting at home. In one memorable session, when the lights went up after the screening and I asked what they thought, it was clear that they had been so absorbed that they had forgotten what the issue was.

One young man said, "We have been in the presence of greatness." Another said, "This has been a real privilege; thank you." Another said, "The steel-trap mind! I have never seen such a demonstration of logical argument!"

"Well, that's great," I said. "Give me an example of this logic that struck you so."

The student said, Well, it had been all the way through, all Russell's arguments had been brilliantly logical. I asked for an example. He looked flustered. Then he brightened. He said, "Well, his argument about banning nuclear power. I mean that was brilliant."

I asked what the argument was. He didn't know. He looked around, floundering. Nobody could help him. One reason nobody could help him is that there had been no discussion of nuclear power. Russell had said that a nuclear *weapons* test-ban treaty would be more useful than trying to ban all nuclear weapons, because the former was achievable, and the latter was not; he had not mentioned nuclear power. But that week was the week of the meltdown of the reactor at Three Mile Island, and the media were full of the nuclear power issue. My student's recall of the Grand–Russell conversation had been contaminated by the plethora of talk and image all that week about nuclear power.

After that demonstration of the difficulty of remembering what is said on the screen, we could really get down to business in that workshop. They all agreed that the experience of the interview had been very valuable, even if they couldn't remember the content (the "referential content"). And so bit by bit they came around to language of their own that connected to my theory about theatre, the experience of the person, and the importance of conflict and other dramatic principles.

In those early years, learning to write and direct documentary films as well as to produce and direct live studio programs, I experimented for a while with comedy and dramatic re-creations in my documentaries. Mercifully I soon realized that while some of these quite *undocumentary* elements were very amusing for me to produce, the most satisfied viewer was me, the director; they weren't doing much for the audience, and in some cases were seriously irritating and distracting. The word "distraction" was added to my lexicon of terms that helped me to think about what I was doing. I saw that in every form of communication anything that stood out, that was not completely integrated into the communication, would weaken the transaction. It could be something as apparently trivial as the inappropriate use of quotation marks, or the unconventional use of capital letters or other devices like the asterisks in *The Education of H*Y*M*A*N K*A*P*L*A*N.* It could be a wrongly used word, whose accepted meaning the writer did not understand. It could be an overwrought metaphor or other image, an overstated emotion, even something as simple as an unnecessary adjective or adverb. Young directors are particularly susceptible to the temptation to use camera and editing devices not designed to enhance the communication but rather to show how clever they are.

This is not a hermetic rule: there are times when a short flash of exuberant, celebratory, or athletic language (or camera or editing) will transmit more about the author's passion than would the most painstaking analytical description. I made a cautionary note to myself once: "We must watch against the wintering of our words in an excess of linguistic prudence" (itself a distractingly self-conscious line, which I have to admit pleased me at the time). But for the most part in film, fiction, the essay, even on the platform, if the reader or audience is made aware of your cleverness, they will become conscious of the environment, will be nudged awake, so to speak, notice what is going on in the room, be taken away from the spell of transmitted experience you have been so diligently trying to create for them.

As I thought about these concepts and kept using them to identify moments that didn't work, or that somehow injured a work, whether a movie or a novel or a poem,[2] the things that *stick out* (like those italics just now?), that word, distraction, became an indispensable aid to my seeing and hearing how to improve the integrity of any communication.

Well, I was learning, in the context (then) of non-fiction and journalism and especially the documentary, something that experienced cinema and stage people understand profoundly. Your task is to create an experience. In a movie or a play or indeed a documentary, it may be a *world* you're creating. You must make that world perfectly and constantly consistent within its frame. You must do everything you can to make it impossible for your reader or your audience to withdraw, to step out of that world, until the work is complete. Sometimes you can see a cinema director lose his nerve and introduce an expository device or a bit of irrelevant sideplay, or an overload of emotionally manipulative music: something that may be entertaining in itself, but does not belong in the same movie as everything else, and so constitutes a distraction. It takes the viewers out of the world the director has worked so hard to bring them into. The best movie and theatre people know that very well (although vanity or polemic can sometimes skew their judgment). It is what they are about, creating worlds. I began to learn it doing documentary films.

That is why, as a commissioning editor for documentaries, I took as one of my first tasks to persuade the producers and directors that they should not use dramatic re-creations. There are many reasons why dramatization harms a documentary. An important one is that documentary budgets do not permit the sets, locations, props, costumes, and other production values, or the fees to skilled writers and

2. My mother had good instincts here. She showed me a charming poem in the *New Yorker* once, an evocation of the courage and risk of a small airplane in a thunderstorm. She knew I would be interested because of my own flying, but she said, "What's wrong with this poem?" It was perfectly clear. There was a *distraction.* The poet had used the word "trudging" to describe the little craft's difficult passage through the storm. "Airplanes don't *trudge*!" my mother said, right both about the poem and about planes.

actors, which will produce an effective and satisfying dramatic moment. Most documentary makers are not trained in theatre and cinema and don't know how to direct actors effectively. Audiences are conditioned by movies to tacitly demand refined skills and quality resources on the screen if they're to take drama seriously. Those skills and resources are seldom available to a documentary producer. It is a tribute to the quality of our best movies that they look so easy; novice doc makers think, "I could do that; let me show my stuff." But in fact they seldom have that kind of stuff to show. By the time we reached our fourth season with *The Canadians*, I had not only succeeded in almost totally eliminating re-creations, but had, for the most part, won over the directors who used to turn to dramatized bits almost routinely as a solution to parts of the story for which they could not find authentic documentary material either spoken or visual. Many of them came to appreciate the satisfactions of working out an inventive solution using only documentary material.

But even if a dramatized insert is really well done or is very simple it will still usually be a distraction. The viewer has suddenly been asked to step out of the world of authentic experience and into a fictitious world. The viewer is momentarily distracted by this dissonance. The whole communication has been weakened. And the strengthening of the communication must be the ever-present imperative, for all of us in the craft.

I recognize that it may seem trivial to conclude a memoir of three-quarters of a century with some observations about the principle of distraction. It would have been more conventional to attempt something grander about Truth and Beauty, or The Good Society. When I was about twenty, I found a metaphor for the purpose of life, a metaphor which, at the time, I labelled as useful only until something larger and wiser presented itself. However, this metaphor, a raw and uncomplicated existentialist image, has not yet yielded to something larger and wiser. It is this:

Place your hands with the palms toward you, the fingertips

spread just a finger's width and touching. Then move them so that the tips of the fingers of each hand are just inside the space between the tips of the opposite two fingers. Let the left hand represent the self, and the right hand the world that the self will encounter. Move the hands slowly together so that the fingers interpenetrate, very slowly, the self moving deeper and deeper into the world of experience. That world contains all the people whom you will love or hate or pass by, the sands and the oceans, the ideas, the images of the galaxy, the mysterious exploration of your own imagination, the inexplicable gift of invention, the pain of loss, the joys of the body.

Any life, however long and adventurous, will penetrate only a small part of the way; there will always be space between the fingertips and the opposite web. But the aim is to go as deeply as you can. And if you choose as the main enterprise of this interpenetration the sharing with others of what you discover as you press the tips farther and farther toward the web, sharing through poetry or narrative or image or music (the sides of the left fingers touching more and more skin on those of the right), and if you take seriously the value of that sharing, then you will do well what you have set out to do only if you try to understand those with whom you are sharing, and to understand them with respect. A juvenile mind may think that using those others as objects from which to profit will be a rewarding experience, but it will not: in the end it will be empty. Only by understanding your reader, your audience, your viewer, your listener, as a part of that deepening of the fingers that is the reason for your life, and you as a part of theirs, only then can you begin to come close to the experience of fulfilment.

It is elusive. You will seldom feel that you've achieved it. But every once in a while you will *know* . . . .

You will know that you've found your way into some measure of that exhilarating state that language and image and music are so essential to, of being an individual who is part of a community. Shoe said, in that comic strip I read on the plane to New York, "It is hard to be an individual all by yourself." In fact it is impossible. Scientists know they have made a discovery only when the community has tested it and given a measure of assent. Artists, leaders, parents, explorers, poets, none of them can do what their discipline exacts of them unless they do it out of a deep understanding of the community, both intuitive and studied. We approximate truth and assurance only when we find that the language or the symbol or the equation or the image we have produced procures a measure of assent, and even then we know we have not achieved an absolute. But we are on the path. And that is a lovely place to be.

APPENDICES

APPENDIX I

CONVOCATION ADDRESS, THE UNIVERSITY OF TORONTO, 2004.

Community depends upon two words
To keep it strong: the words are "We" and "Us."
Unless those simple monosyllables
Pump through the blood with vivid images
Of all the towers we might build together
Fields that we could cultivate
And seas to dive and navigate, and roads
To map, and courts that we convene to call
Ourselves to be accountable for all
The treasures we've been handed from the past . . .
Unless those two short words, the "we" and "us"
Unless they both contain a resonant
Cathedral full of things we have to do –
To do together . . . then the people sharing
This great stretch of land – (and land is our
Religion, in this Canada) – those folk
Will simply be
A vast conglomerate
Of things called
Me.

Me's are okay: I'm glad that I have one.
Keeping them nourished, loved and entertained
Drives science, keeps us at the wheel, the bench,
The keyboard and the plough, is, in the end,
What poetry and art most celebrate.

But there's a dreadful spectre looming close,
Sliding its cunning tentacles deep inside
The ancient miracle that is the self,
That conscious, yearning, loving bundle of
Inquisitiveness that we each are given:
The starting point from which to find our way.
Towards the stars.

The spectre? It's a self *without* community,
Me's with no us, I's without a we.
A mass of appetites for gain and junk
Corralled into a great consumers' mob
And driven by the new morality
That's preached with all the media's costly power
Day after day, night after night, to tell
Us that if we don't buy . . .
We'll go to hell.

Unless we troop out daily to the mall,
Acquire the latest SUV, the best
In laptops, real sweet gear, and all the rest . . .
We'll be depressed.
Headwaiters will ignore us, friends desert,
We'll be nobodies nobody respects
And what is worse, we never will have sex.

That is the media's message now, McLuhan,
It started off that way when you were doin
What you did – a half a century
Ago – right here – and; now it's really all
We ever hear about what life is for.
Back then, in 1950, we were just
Emerging from the shroud of war that clung
And choked the furthest reaches of the globe
Six years, almost, of burning flesh, the sky
Scarred with the incandescence that means not –
– Not dawn, or hope, or blossoms opening
But carnage, ruin, and the end of days.

Yet out of those six years there grew
Amongst us, here, an irrefusable
And urgent chorus about *us* and *we.*
How *we* could do it, *we* could fight and win.
And at the end, late but mercifully
At last we opened up our doors to those
Whose lands had been destroyed in those burned years
And made ourselves a coat of many colours.
A Just Society, we said we'd build.
We talked like that. A while, at least, we told
Each other that was what we had to do.

Will we ever talk like that again?
The truth is that we do. Our *governments*
May be preoccupied with bottom lines
And fiscal probity – but all across
The land, women and men, especially
Young folk, have reached across the ancient lines
As if they never had been drawn, the lines
Of gender, wealth, inherited excess
Of every kind, insisting that each one
Of us be given to and called upon
With equal measure for what we can bring
– As me's and I's – to the community.

And here's the essential centre of it all:
The wealth and strength of all community
Is vested in that one distinguishing
Miracle of this unlikely thing
We call the mind:
                    Imagination.
Imagination. That capacity
To see a thing that does not yet exist,
And make it. Fashion it from what we have
At hand. Machines and goods, and poetry
And strokes of colour on a canvas, which,
Improbably, become a human face
Vivid with rage or radiating joy.
Song, we make; and different ways to be
Together in the world. That many-coloured coat.
Which formed itself before it was described,
And took us ages to imagine that
There might be something greater than . . . the Tribe.

Imagination is the only tool
We have, the only source of wealth, of growth,
Of cutting those old bonds:
                    Imagination.
And so, to those of us who teach, who preach,
Manage, inquire, investigate, bring kids
Into the world and try to guide their hands
Towards those strokes of colour that become
The marks of meaning and of love: for us

Who work at making universities,
Or books, or moving pictures on a screen
There is one eminent imperative:
To nurture the imaginative act.
To say, each time the child picks up the pen
And makes outrageous lines upon the page,
To all inquiring persons, large or small
Who doubt, and ask, and test unquestioned truths –
To say to them, "Now that was int'resting.
Did that feel good? You like to try some more?"

Now let me close with words not of my own
But of another and much older world.
It is fit and seemly when we gather here
For ceremony, on the land, above
The now deep-buried streams that once ran free
And clear, right here beneath our feet: the land
And streams where our First Nations had *their* hunt
Their dwelling and *their* ceremonials –
To leave you with the words a member of
Perhaps the world's first constitutional
Proto-democracy – the great Six Nations –
Might well have said:
Their words for Gratitude
And Peace.
Nya; wen.
Nya:wen koa.
Skenen.[1]

1. Say (approximately) "NyAH-weh. NyAH-weh GO-ah. SKAH-no."

The Ballad of Small Hope Bay (1984)

A diver arrived up in heaven one time –
An awful old sinner – and that long climb
From earth's restraints to the Heavenly Gate
Took him so long he was almost late.

But he put down his fins and his reg and his mask
And he said, "Now I know it's a lot to ask,
And I don't deserve it, but do you think
When you've checked me in, I could get a drink?
And after that, like when I was alive,
From time to time you could let me dive ?"

Well! Saint Peter smiled a cryptic smile
And he said, "We've had a good look at your file
Why you've broken hearts and everything
From unpaid debts and rendezvous
That you failed to keep, to nights full of booze
The virtuous life was beyond your reach
You might say you're a genuine Son of The Beach."

Now the diver's heart was beginning to sink
But Saint Peter said with a nod and a wink
"Now buck up son, don't faint and turn pale,
There's another part of your earthly tale
And the Lord is fond of his sons and daughters
Who've come to terms with his Great Green Waters

"And it says in here that you've given thanks
by feeding the fish and filling the tanks
that you stuck with your buddies and shared your air,
and, hung over or not, you were always there
when they needed a hand to go for the boats
or coach the newcomers or swim for the floats
It seems – in the water – you're one of the best
So the rest is forgiven; we'll grant your request."

And he lifted him up and he waved his hand
And there was green water and palm trees and sand
A rickety jetty, compressor and shacks,
With wet suits and BC's all hanging on racks
And a bar like a boat with tall bottles, quite phallic
Being poured by a beard who said, "Hi there, I'm Alec."
(And he thought that he *knew* him; recalling a storm
and a pilot who flew like his hands held a charm)
and there, standing square, in the door of the kitchen
Half jokin', half scowlin', half laughin', half bitchin'
Festooned with fish basket, stew pot and egg beater
Roasts of beef, loaves of bread, bags of beans –
That was Peter.

And to give *him* a hand with that savoury cargo
All smilin' and huggin' her baby was Margo.
(Who sneaked up and turned off our poor hero's air
"Just to see if you're still on the ball," she declared.)

Just then it was time for them all to go divin'
On a boat half submerged because Ivan was drivin',
While all the time hurling rude insults at Mike
About how to get docked without busting a spike
From the ladder to make us all worry and tremble
While up on the dock all the people assemble
To bid a farewell to these divers so goofy
And waving her powerful hands there was Newfy
And clutching a tall double scotch, cool and frothy
And decked out in whites was the matriarch, Dorothy.

(I *know* that Frothy and Dorothy don't rhyme
But I'm tryin' to please; don't give me a hard time!)

And waving a six-metre flag, quite unique
Was a man in a tan that's applied by batik
Cos' he hasn't been out in the sun for a week,
That was Jeff, buzzing in on his bike from Fresh Creek.

And beside him, in warm but intense dialogue
With a hairy young man who resembled a dog
Was Patti, who seemed to be just about swooning
As she philosophised with young Willem de Kooning.

Oh the names of the place was confusin' and loose
With this dog they called Bill and a boy they called Moose
And Darnelles and Danielles in various sizes
And a Gabrielle too whose accent would win prizes.

But the *Crowning Event* – with a tidal commotion
A huge scallop shell rose up out of the ocean
And standing within it all rosy and bare
Although modestly holding her long golden hair
In the way that you're sposed to when painted by Titian
Was a radiant, leonine, full-bosomed vision
An angel, a goddess, a queen or a Rosi, a
Tattoo on her left breast said Shop at Androsia
Beside her in trident and beard Dick NEPTUNE
Who turned and bent over and showed us a moon.

And when our poor diver saw all this display
He looked at Saint Peter, and started to say,
"When I arrived up here all sinful and grey,
I had little hope I'd be treated okay . . ."

But the Saint put him off, and said, "'Small Hope,' you say?
From now we'll call this part of heaven Small Hope Bay."
And ever since then, up to this very day
We're still calling this part of heaven Small Hope Bay.

EMILY MURPHY[1]

A *Heritage Minute* by Patrick Watson

ONE SINGLE CLOSE SHOT, SPOKEN TO CAMERA, AS THOUGH THE CAMERA WERE A PERSON IN THE ROOM.

But the Supreme Court of Canada agreed, you see.

I could not become a senator because, as a woman, under the British North America Act, I was not a person.

I, Emily Gowan Murphy, author of the *Janey Canuck* books, pioneer in the war against narcotics, first woman police magistrate in the British Empire.

But not a person.

So we took it to London. A group of Canadian women, labouring ten long years, against ridicule. Husbands saying, "There, there, dear."

Until those noble lords of the Privy Council agreed.

(Very distant, light musical chord, for punctuation)

Nineteen hundred and twenty-nine.

I, Emily Murphy of Alberta. And all Canadian women after me.

Persons, under the law.

(*Pause, mischievous smile)*

(Laughs) And so we could sit in the Senate, after all.

1 This was played by the exquisitely beautiful Kate Nelligan. The real Murphy was fat and dour, fanatic to the point of fascism on drugs, and a eugenicist who advocated the sterilization of the "unfit." While the *Minutes* are, after all, fictions, not documentary, there is some discussion as to whether this one should be withdrawn or remade.

The following is my 1991 summary paper to the CBC board of directors, about returning the CBC to the role of a genuine public broadcaster. Apart from a few edits for clarity, and to shorten it slightly, it is in the form in which it was finally circulated to the board a few months before our summer retreat, in the summer of 1994, effectively my last official function as chair. It begins with the covering letter to the members of the board.

(Cover letter)

I am circulating all directors with the enclosed memo from Bill Neville which is self-explanatory. Bill suggested that I append the paper I prepared for Gérard Veilleux in November of 1991, to aid in the development of what became the Repositioning Strategy. Although it sounds, in its details, much more like an Action Plan than anything the Board should be actively involved with, it does contain a good deal of thinking that is pertinent to Bill's concerns and I am sure you will understand the spirit in which I am distributing it. I have made some editorial modifications for clarity. Some references, e.g. to *The Journal*, are of course anachronistic; I leave them in, in the interests of History.

Having just helped host a reception for the amazing team of Brits, Russians, one French, one Israeli and one Canadian who drove *on land!* from London, through the Chunnel, to Moscow, through Siberia and out onto the Bering Straits ice (in Canadian tracked vehicles) . . . where they sadly met open water and had to take an airlift to Alaska, thence to New York via Toronto, and seen that their 8 hours of documentary were all shot on "home video" Hi band eight Sony consumer cameras, I would just add one note to my paper, that in the interests of democratizing our television we absolutely have to look at ways of encouraging citizen contributions, in home video formats. This should be a strategic objective for both media and democratic and financial reasons.

I too, like Bill Neville, will welcome your thoughts, and we should be well prepared by the time we get to our Summer Retreat, which I hope will include some key staff for at least part of the brainstorming.

I wrote this paper at the request of then President Gérard Veilleux in November 1991, and delivered it to him to aid in the development of what became the Repositioning Strategy. I would like now to share it with the Board, as I believe there are some components of my strategy, not yet incorporated, that might merit reconsideration, and I would be grateful for the views of the Directors.

Patrick Watson
January 12, 1994

DISTINCTION OR EXTINCTION

A STRATEGY FOR THE SURVIVAL OF CBC TELEVISION

" . . . so that every time you select a CBC channel you know where you are . . . and you're glad to be there."
(The Chairman's Speech Book, 1989/1991)

"Cherchez le créneau. . . . You have to have a ***position*** *. . . You can't win by not making enemies, by being everything to everybody."*
(Ries and Trout: *POSITIONING,* 1981)

A SUMMARY OF THE STRATEGY

(I) TOTAL DISTINCTIVENESS. The decline of a political will to support CBC Television is due to confusion about its role. The only way CBC TV can survive is to become *ruthlessly and unremittingly distinctive.*

(II) FEASIBILITY. The objective is achievable within present levels of funding and without sacrificing CBC TV's reach to a substantial majority of Canadians.

(III) RAPID AND SOON. The transformation should take place suddenly and soon, not step by step.

(IV) THE PROFILE. The basic principles are these: (1) *DISTINCTIVENESS:* All programming carried on both English or French Television shall be of a kind, character or quality not available from other sources. (2) *SERVICE*: Programming will be designed always to serve and never to exploit or simply to win our audiences. Note: not 'some programming' or 'most programming,' but *all.*

(V) THE PROFILE (2). Distinctiveness in style, comprehensiveness and authority must be palpably present in News and Current Affairs programming; distinctiveness in quality and dramatic power in drama; distinctiveness in style and boldness in variety, entertainment, comedy and satire . . . and in Talk Shows.

(VI) SENSE OF PLACE. Responsive to new technologies and to a need for a greater sense of Presence in the country, programs will strive for a vivid sense of place. The CBC distinctive look will get us out of the studio and into the streets, the landscape, the towns, the architecture of the country. Information Programs will be anchored from real places instead of studios, and as many network programs as possible will originate regionally, visually acknowledging where they come from.

(VII) CROSS-CULTURAL. For reasons of distinctiveness, financial advantage and responsibility to mandate, cross-cultural (CBC/SRC) initiatives will be privileged.

(VIII) REACH. Programmers will be charged to achieve these objectives in a way that retains a **large reach and popular appeal,** while at the same time rewarding those members of the Community of ideas, the Policy elites, and the Arts Community, who now feel neglected by Public Television in Canada.

(IX) CHARACTER. An important proportion of programming will be designed to be outspoken, provocative, groundbreaking, so that in an era of blandness and the studious avoidance of controversy, audiences will rely on the Public Broadcaster to cut through the flab.

(X) SCHEDULE. Recognising the new environment, *all major programming* will be frequently replayed within days if not hours in different time slots in order to accommodate the majority of viewers who seek to satisfy their special interests on special channels, and who cannot always watch first releases. This will include major news and current affairs programs. At least one prime time evening will be devoted to The Best of the (Previous) Week.

Archives and inventory will be combed for creative possibilities of rescheduling, including fresh ideas for their presentation and surroundings. **And an aggressive publicity will promote these programs as the treasures they are.**

(XI) ADVERTISING. Will be clearly seen to be serving programs, not the other way round. Independence from the influence of advertising (while not abandoning advertising) will be energetically pursued, as will collaboration with advertisers, industry, to upgrade quality, taste, honesty in advertising.

(XII) OUTREACH. Publicity will be overhauled to become focussed, specific, aggressive, and fresh. There will be increased presence of CBC employees and on-air people out in the community. Special efforts will be made to interest young people in the CBC, through internships, other direct-involvement initiatives, as well as programming. Cross-promotion between radio and television services will be aggressively developed.

(XIII) POSITIONING. A major task will be the development of a slogan or declaration that is simple, obvious, niche-pre-emptive, memorable. *CBC and YOU,* is not quite it (for reasons developed below). Neither is *Pour Vous Avant Tout.* Neither is *Public Broadcasting in Canada.* But the need is imperative.

(XIV) CORPORATE WILL. Some ideas in this paper have been presented to Network officials in the past. The reply: "It won't work." Now we have to recognize the critical position that public television is in, and to require of programmers and planners that they tell us *How To Make It Work.*

The Strategy Developed

(I) TOTAL DISTINCTIVENESS. *The only way CBC television can survive is to become ruthlessly and unremittingly distinctive.* This message has been flowing into the Corporation from across the country for some years now. It has been expressed with particular trenchancy by those Citizens who trust and use CBC radio and cannot understand why CBC television cannot or will not give them the same satisfactory sense of being especially for Canadians.

Policy elites have been among the more vocal, speaking with some contempt of our television service by comparison with the American PBS. Too many of these people seek out about PBS chiefly for its elegant British Drama, its ballet, symphony and opera – programming that is fairly elitist, earning PBS an audience too small to really justify its being considered a Public Broadcasting System. But tactically speaking they constitute an audience that is of special importance to the survival of the CBC. It is not appropriate for CBC to neglect them. The Policy Elites are *influentially* dissatisfied clients. This is a concern that democrats sometimes overlook.

So are members of the Arts and Intellectual community. They are also joined, ironically, by a general public who, while finding satisfaction and authority in the CBC's mainstream information programs, to a disturbingly large extent do not see the CBC as doing a job that is substantially different from the private broadcasters. It is English TV that is seen as the unsatisfactory component. Based on the performance of English TV, many Canadians are not clear why CBC deserves its $1bn of public moneys. Especially poignant is *Corporate Strategy Inc's* finding that amongst Francophone Quebeckers the distinctiveness of Radio-Canada TV is even lower than is CBC's among English Canadians. However, the affection that French Canadians retain for Radio-Canada is reassuring.

Many of the Corporation's own planners and programmers are now convinced that distinctiveness is the only route to survival. The Board of Directors inclines in the same direction. The provocative question is How? and Is it achievable? The main thrust of this paper responds to these questions.

(II) FEASIBILITY. The strategy is achievable if the program schedule aims at being both **popular and financially realistic.**

(1) Financial Realism. If the strategy is developed in the hope of and dependent upon increased funding it will remain a dream. Instead, the Corporation must now face radical changes in the way in which programs are produced, delivered, and scheduled. New technologies and collective agreements, when realised, will contribute important efficiencies. A new approach to repeat scheduling of major programming will bring greater value for money, as well as greater reach (see section X).

Once the strategy is achieved the Corporation will be better positioned to argue the case for financial security. Then enhancements of the new strategy will become possible. But the changes will have to come first.

(2) POPULARITY. For a few years the conventional wisdom held that zapping with the remote channel switcher had brought an end to channel loyalty. In fact this was never the case for specialty services, such as PBS, CNN, and Newsworld. Viewers sought them out. However, some of those specialty services do not have the reach needed by a genuine public television service; CBC's strategy must avoid the trap of narrowcasting too tightly.

The popularity of our best programs is demonstrable. *Les Filles de Caleb* is a stunning example. Making our best available to a demographically wider audience through repeats will only increase their reach. Adding a component of arts and classical programming, if done with a mandate to make those programs as popular as possible, will not only satisfy constituencies in the community of ideas (including the Policy Elites) but also – if deliberately targeted in this regard – make such forms as opera and other serious music, accessible to audiences who now avoid them. More on how to achieve that below.

The policy directive must be unequivocal about being both distinctive, of service, and popular.

(III) RAPID AND SOON. The winning back of the Political Will cannot be achieved piecemeal. It requires boldness and decisiveness. Just as the Corporation rejected piecemeal solutions to the 1991–1992 funding shortfall, the repositioning must be radical and sudden. It should be announced as soon as agreed upon, and launched when ready, all at once not bit by bit, not waiting for the illusory advantage of a Fall Launch (though not avoiding it either), but on the air as soon as possible, avoiding only the low-viewing season from May 15 to Labour Day.

The Corporation is haunted by a reputation for indecisiveness and lack of clarity. A major concern in the pursuit of this strategy is to extinguish that reputation. A programming *Revolution* will generate curiosity and excitement among the general public, and – where it counts (with the Policy Elites, the business community, the Community of Ideas, the Arts community, the Capital-C Citizens, and Parliament) – an important measure of approval for decisiveness, independent of the content of the changes. Whereas a layered, staged, little-by-little evolutionary approach to the New Positioning would be fatiguing, encourage backsliding and self-doubt, and leave the Public relatively indifferent. Independent of the content of the changes.

(V) & (V) THE PROGRAMMING PROFILES. The content, however, is crucial. The basic principles are these:

(1) *DISTINCTIVENESS:* All programming carried on both English or French Television shall be of a kind, character or quality not available from other sources. While this implies a predominantly Canadian schedule it also includes quality foreign programming, including American, that is not otherwise readily available to our audiences.

Achieving distinctiveness will, among many other tasks, entail a rigorous re-examination of News and Sports policies. And even Weather Reports should be distinctive, reflecting primarily the need to be useful and meaningful.

In News (more of this below) there should be a tough-minded reassessment of our present pre-occupation with electoral politics. We now neglect other areas of leadership and change, (such as science, commerce, the Community of Ideas, and the Self-Management of communities) to which Electoral Politics are often only a response. We have a responsibility to better investigate and report such matters, independently of the field of electoral politics.

In Sports, we must undertake a review of the appropriateness of our commitment to big-ticket spectator sports at the expense of community, participatory and youth sports (CPY Sports).

These latter are seldom celebrated with the same panache we accord to what is essentially a profitable form of show business. Community, participatory and youth sports are of much greater significance to the health, survival, entertainment and informational needs of our audiences and of our Country than are the big-ticket Sports. And big-ticket Sports are widely available elsewhere. It is argued that "Hockey is part of our culture." That is correct: hockey *is* part of our culture, and *television now neglects most of the hockey that is played in this country!*

The revenue implications of abandoning big-ticket sports will have to be faced squarely. This issue contains one of the starkest confrontations between revenue and the need to be distinctive and to appropriately serve as only the Public Broadcaster can. At the same time, our approach to CPY Sports must crackle, excite, compete for the big-ticket audience and create its own stars. The stardom of big-ticket heroes is, after all, no accident: they are the product of a Celebrity Machine. CBC must consider both the values and risks of applying such a machine to CPY sports.

The concept of distinctiveness is intimately connected with the essential Public Broadcasting idea of Service. We now proceed to deal with the idea of Service, and it will quickly be seen how the Service focus brings with it an inevitable distinctiveness.

(2) SERVICE: *Programming will be designed always to* **serve** *and never to exploit or simply to win our audiences.*

"Exploit" means using programs or programmatic devices to keep audiences in place to be advertised at or measured for ratings purposes. Now, large audiences are important to a genuine Public Broadcaster, and this proposal, while arguing for a unique and distinctive service (and for a service that will build loyalty and commitment) does not propose *pandering* to elite tastes but rather building a service so meaningful, civilized, significantly entertaining, concerned for "little people" (as well as for big curiosities), that it continues to reach a substantial percentage of Canadians each week.

"Serve" is not confined to serious information; it also means to entertain with quality material: graceful or outrageous, intelligent or zany, reassuring or provocative: but never simply exploitive. The pushing of well-worn Stimulus/Response emotional buttons, as in the Greed Game Shows or the sitcoms based upon cliché and stereotype, and requiring laugh tracks to induce the illusion that something amusing has taken place, are examples of the exploitive.

"Serve" also means to inform *relevantly.* In the present media universe of information saturation it also means to inform both broadly and intensively, avoiding cliche and ritual coverage. An example of ritual coverage is the exaggerated attention conventional media pay to electoral politics, particularly at the Federal level, and the exaggerated indifference shown to the Community of Ideas, to the business community, to the Citizens (those men and women and youth who undertake some responsibility for making their communities more prosperous and civilized) where there is at least as much leadership to be found as on the hustings and in the legislatures.

"Serve" also entails the exploration of our times and of our past through drama, in a way that allows us to find meaning (including laughter, irony, grief, inspiration, anger, direction, absurdity) in our ongoing existence as a community. This does not exclude situation comedy or situation drama such as MOM P.I. or STREET LEGAL. But it does call for the advancement of kinds of drama now rarely seen, except for a small number of specials:

dramas that come out of the passion of Canadian Writers for the characters, stories and issues that move them, dramatic recreations of our past (not necessarily different from the passions just referred to) . . . *and the great classics.*

WRITERS: We shall deal with the special problem of the *Classics* shortly, but first there is an important observation to be made apropos the passion of writers:

There is a large number of writers working in English and French, in poetry, fiction, non-fiction, and theatre, whose work is not much tapped for television because it is not meant for television. But some of these writers are strongly in touch with the Canadian spirit and the Canadian character, and to develop the drama that tells Canadian stories compellingly to Canadians will mean tapping into this well of writers to seek out those among them who can adapt to the medium, and give them the technical help they need to do so.

It may also mean seeking out those televisually hip, very experienced makers of television who have never been invited to work from the heart but who already know television skills to their fingertips: the commercial producers, writers and directors. Much of their work is brilliant, but it is by definition exploitive. Many of these exquisitely skilled craftspeople are an untapped resource for powerful television drama.

So, seeking heart and soul among the Televisually Hip, or seeking to develop Television Hip among the relevantly passionate: both directions need even more cultivation than we have yet undertaken.

THE SPECIAL PROBLEM OF THE CLASSICS

Both our French and English television have largely retreated from major productions of the "difficult arts", opera, classical theatre, ballet, serious music. Although such programs have (especially in French TV) been an important component of our distinctiveness in the past, they have not won large audiences. World class curtain-to-curtain performances are already available to a large number of Canadian viewers via PBS, and we will rarely need to reach for this relatively small and specialised audience. There has been pressure on us to broadcast NAC performances. Our producers and programmers have correctly resisted this pressure.

But, as with most vacuums, there is an opportunity here. Our television could accomplish an important public service, re-establish a large amount of lost good will in the Arts Community (and to some extent with the Policy Elites), and enlarge our CROSS CULTURAL activities, by taking a distinctively television approach to this kind of performance. This could entail making the Classics and other "serious" forms more accessible and interesting to those who now find them obscure and inaccessible. I would also argue that similar opportunities and obligations exist to help those whose education and tastes isolate them from important popular forms like Rock Music: to help such viewers become more aware of and understanding of the powerful messages these forms contain about What Is Going On.

One demonstrably effective technique for doing this is to build substantial non-fiction stories (i.e. journalistic reports or documentaries) about the making of such performances: documentaries that include substantial and intriguing elements of performance (from rehearsals, for example). Storytelling appeals to everyone; if these programs are made with a strong storytelling thrust they will draw audiences who might never before have considered going to an opera, for example. Our programmers, given this general objective, will be inventive. Milos Forman's teen-oriented, anachronistic and outrageous AMADEUS introduced a lot of surprised people to the wonders of Mozart. Mandating our programmers with the strategic objective of provoking the interest of those now outside the sphere of these artistic experiences will produce other forms *which have not yet been tried yet because this objective has not been mandated in the past.*

TALK: English TV has untapped opportunities for provocative, daring, low-cost talk shows. One area that cries out for attention in both English and French is media review. Richly salted with excerpts (especially from television) and driven by tough, funny, outspoken criticism.

With producers, writers and others there to reply, a series of real donnybrooks can be created around all kinds of media production including journalism. There is an opportunity here. It could be a major weekly event, giving unrestrained opportunities to Citizens as well as professionals to tackle issues of taste, relevance, Hip &c., and at the same time give audiences a wide sampling of current media fare. *La Bande des Six* is exemplary in this regard, deserves some enriching (in terms of performance segments and perhaps the participation of a larger number of distinguished producers and others whose work is being criticized) . . . and more publicity and a better time slot.

(VI) A SENSE OF PLACE: Consistent with our commitment to be a reflection of the country to the country our television should exploit every conceivable opportunity to originate in a real place, buildings, public spaces, art galleries, malls, landscapes, streets, abandoning the sterile, mechanistic environment of the studio.

Major current affairs magazines such as *Le Point*, *Midday*, and *The Journal* should be encouraged to move around the country and assemble themselves in front of people where possible, and in front of identifiable backgrounds. Some producers may argue that their technical requirements make this impossible; it would then be time to paraphrase De Gaulle's "Alors, c'est simple, changez vos amis" and say to them, "Fine, change your technical requirements."

Venture has demonstrated the ease with which a magazine program can be assembled with one camera in an office. Now is the time to move it and other programs outside, to sites that contribute to a constant sense of a presence in the country. This one move alone would have a profound effect on our distinctiveness and on giving Canadians a sense that we are *of* them and not just *for* them.

In this connection, all network programs that can be produced in the regions instead of from Network headquarters should move, and perhaps move again periodically. *And they should be produced in an environment that speaks of place!*

The studio should be reserved for those aspects of drama and some variety production that cannot be produced elsewhere. Management must be prepared to expect resistance to this initiative, and to be vigilant in distinguishing excuses from real reasons.

(VII) CROSS CULTURAL PROGRAMMING. Not only should cross cultural initiatives be privileged, but there must be an incentive program to engage and develop bilingual producers, who can work with their other-language colleagues on an equal footing. The budgetary advantages of collaborative production should be made more apparent to producers: that is, they are helped to see how their productions can be enriched by spreading, say, a budget and a half over two programs. Consideration might be given to a bonus system, or at the very least to a preferential hiring posture for producers able and eager to work cross-culturally.

But there is an important warning to be attached to this part of the strategy. At no time should programs be preferred *only* because they meet cross-cultural objectives. They must first and foremost be programs that work well for their target audiences, otherwise the initiative will attract contempt and will fail.

(VIII) REACH: Programmers will be charged to achieve these objectives in a way that retains a **large reach and popular appeal,** while at the same time rewarding those members of the Community of ideas, the Policy elites, and the Arts who now feel neglected by Public Television in Canada.

Some may argue that there is a contradiction embedded in such a mandate. But our best programming, as noted before, is already so demonstrably popular that *a priori* we are justified in making the demand, and committing to the effort. The Corporation has not always asked of programmers that their first concern be large audiences, particularly when undertaking new initiatives to fill a programming lacuna. In the area of arts programming producers have often been allowed to accept the idea that they are programming to a minority. This idea should be discouraged. (See above on *The Classics.*)

(IX) CHARACTER. (An extension of distinctiveness.) It includes such obvious and relatively trivial devices as the omnipresence of a corporate logo in the corner of a screen.[1] But it also means seeking ways to avoid the blandness of much television. In an era saturated with selling, nice-guyism, false charm and bland vapidity, CBC audiences will be grateful for television, especially but not only information television, that is direct, outspoken, irreverent, innovative, witty, and above all meaningful and not wasteful of our attention.

We should eschew the appearance of wheedling that comes from our thanking viewers for watching our news programs (they should feel like thanking us!). Our news should make its way on its comprehensiveness, authority, accuracy, fairness and balance, and meaningfulness.[2]

VIOLENCE AND NEGATIVISM: We should make a public commitment to attack the twin diseases of gratuitous violence and negativism. The former is easier: we now deal with it very well. The latter is much harder.

The issue is fraught with danger. In drama, violence can be an exploitive device, a substitute for the subtler kinds of human conflict that make drama meaningful. We do not much dabble in this kind of violence, but it rears its head occasionally, in a minor way, when *Street Legal* lawyers engage in fisticuffs in the office, not very likely behaviour for Canadian lawyers and certainly an admission of dramatic poverty on the part of the screenwriters.

It is far more common, in all kinds of dramatic production, when actors are directed to shout at each other in order to simulate conflict. This is a television disease and our producers have fallen into it. It is a prime indicator of dramaturgical poverty, and somebody should be saying this to our programmers.

However, the wholesale bloodshed characteristic of US TV, and for the most part deeply and cynically exploitive, a kind of pornography designed

1. One element of this paper that actually was adopted.

2. Newsreaders should *never* say "Thank you for watching." They should stop wasting precious airtime by greeting and thanking reporters. "Hi, Edward, how are you?" and "Thanks for that, Edward." "You're welcome, Peter." How can that possibly be said to be of service to the audience, when there is not enough time to allow us to hear interview inserts for more than a few seconds?

to keep viewers hanging in, numbed and ready for the advertising message, has not become a major component of our TV culture. We should, however, openly note our concern and state our commitment, *but without yielding to a dreary puritanism* or, more importantly, *without falling into the trap of censoring the murder of Julius Caesar, the Crime of Ovide Plouffe, or the Carnage of the Killing Fields.*

But negativism in journalism and commentary: now *there* is a challenge! And a danger. CBC journalists and Current Affairs people are already subjected to so much scrutiny that to demand more compliance of them would begin to smell of and maybe approach censorship. And it would throw into doubt our already suspect (in some quarters) commitment to journalistic independence.

So, while vigorously defending, publicly and within the Corporation, the independence of our journalists, this paper proposes institutionalizing an ongoing Journalists' Forum, a continuation of the O'Neill/McQueen 1990 initiatives, into which critics, articulate citizens, Board Members, international thinkers, would be invited to question our practices, traditions and habits, forcing our people to articulate the attitudes and principles (cultural underpinnings not always explicit) that guide their work.

The culture of negativism is deeply set in journalism as a craft or profession. The reflexive search for contradiction is a function of the inquiring mind. It has a very important function in journalism as in science and scholarship. But we, seeking always to take the leadership position in everything we do, must be vigilant in avoiding unthinking, irrelevant, and ill-placed negativism, and diligent in seeking out significant and relevant news of positive, creative, constructive events.

Bad News is arresting. It is easy to communicate. It is often significant and important. But accomplishment, constructive achievement, and socially and politically positive events (except in naturally dramatic circumstances such as the arena of competitive sport) require more effort to be communicated with excitement and with that quality of theatre that the small screen particularly favours and needs.

Further, journalists are appropriately anxious not to be caught in naivety, not to be "taken in" by the skill of Public Relations specialists, not to be seen as unskeptical, unquestioning. In an era of massive, brilliant, expensive PR, much of it conducted by governments, in the era of Spin Doctors, journalists are right to be on guard.

But they are not right to habitually and by convention favour negative stories. And they are wrong to habitually insert a "but" or a "however" into every report as a convention to demonstrate impartiality, balance and their fairness. Analysis of reportorial sentence structure reveals that the **"but** syndrome" is so ingrained, so endemic, that the B-Word is sometimes used as a connective to a clause that in fact contains no negation of the preceding declaratory sentence. Here is an example: "*A new process for safely incinerating radioactive waste underground by nuclear explosions has been announced in the Soviet Union.* ***But*** *environmentalists here say that the idea is being taken very seriously in the West as well.*" "And" would have been the appropriate connector, but syntactic habit and the psychology of contradiction will often induce the inappropriate use of the B-Word. Watch for it. The B-Word and its variants have assumed the imperative and sanctity of litany. This kind of automaton, reflexive search for "the other side" is probably a substitute for the more careful, difficult research that is required to reveal genuine significance and genuine context. It gives the *illusion* of the questioning approach, while in reality often achieving nothing more that the satisfying of a grammatical or semantic formula. The remedy will be for editors, especially assignment editors, to stress the importance of significance and context, to give journalists the time to pursue the same, and to be on guard for negative code words as a substitute for intellectual rigour.

FRAMING: Screen time is so limited and so precious that producers should be asked to consider whether they need some of the window-dressing, music &c., that conventionally introduces programs. Such devices can be important. But attention should be given to the ways in which drama, particularly cinema, has largely abandoned such conventions, getting us quickly into the meat of the matter, sometimes spreading out opening credits, for example, over the first several minutes of dramatic development. This paper argues that particularly in the case of News, our viewers, wanting authoritative and meaningful reportage, might be grateful to bypass the antique introductory conventions and rituals of music and graphics and get quickly into substance.[3] Other programs should be scrutinized according to the same principles. Avoiding wasteful conventions could become a distinctive part of our character.

(X) SCHEDULE. The idea of replaying all major programming within days if not hours may be the single most contentious element in the strategy. In order to achieve an all-mandate, all-service schedule instantly within existing resources it will be necessary to substantially reduce the number of original hours. In the past, reducing original hours has usually meant reducing the number of episodes in series. This paper proposes instead that we

3. Musical transitions, now beloved of the otherwise fairly crisp BBC News World Service on television, provide absolutely no service to viewers and waste our time.

recognize the significance of the 50+ channel environment and respond by making it possible for people to seek out what they want on the specialty channels, the sports specials, the movies &c. and still be able to find our outstanding programs as well as our regular flagship information programming in alternative time slots.[4]

Over and over again we hear people complain that while they heard Episode 4 of *Les Filles de Caleb* was marvellous, they missed it: when can they see it again? Or that *Love and Hate* was great and they missed it. And so on. This concern can be met, and Canadian content enhanced, by offering a replay the next day in daytime, one late night per week (or more) for quality repeats, and one prime time evening a week consecrated to the Best of Last Week, including Current Affairs.

Such an evening would be spiced with a panel of Appreciators and Critics, saying why they chose these as the Best of Last Week. Comments would be brief, trenchant, provocative, demanding more and better, in the same mood as the Media Review suggested above in (V) under TALK. There might be an audience-voting component, with some weekly acknowledgement for the viewer of the week whose Program of the Week was picked, perhaps in the form of a free Cassette of that program and a pin or medallion for the Viewers Choice Club.

By establishing a firm and predictable pattern of repeats, publicised energetically both in print and at the time of original broadcast and surrounded by enhancements such as the panel attached to The Best of Last Week, we will build expectations and audiences, rationalise the fragmented-audience, multi-channel environment, and entrench our distinctiveness.

When such a pattern of repeats has been proposed in the past network managers have tended to say, "We can't do that; it won't work; we don't want this to be a network of repeats."

But that was then; this is now. Now is the time for them to be required to *make* it work. It is unrealistic in the new environment to accept the old answers and refuse to venture into new modalities.

It should be remembered that when it was proposed to move The National from 11PM to 10PM, the CBC's competitors happily predicted

4. In 2002 I extended this theme in an article in the *Globe and Mail*, proposing that the CBC devote an evening a month to repeats from the specialty channels, "A Festival of the Specialties," commissioning a panel of viewers across the country to nominate favourites and selecting two or three hours of the best Canadian programming to be found on Discovery, History Television, Discovery Health, etc. I argued that the CBC has always had an obligation to reflect the best of the Canadian cultural scene, that television is now our principal cultural activity, and that this would be an excellent way of broadening the specialty audiences, at low cost to the Corporation; a win-win situation for both sides. There was no comment from anyone at CBC TV.

disaster for the CBC. The conventional wisdom was that competing entertainment programming would kill News and Current Affairs at that hour. But CBC stuck to its guns and the success of that bold move is history. It is time to be bold again.

In this regard it is also time to consider once more the potential value of moving the National/Journal package to 9PM, cf the British experience. Such a move would be appropriate in the new environment. Audiences would be pleased to settle in for an hour or more of quality entertainment *after* the news. Market testing would be helpful here.

(XI) ADVERTISING. There is a growing conviction among some of our programmers that we should be out of advertising altogether; a segment of the Public Broadcasting constituency agrees.

This paper proposes that the essential principle should be this: that *advertising must serve programs and not the other way around.* It is widely agreed that we must should try to end the interruption of long-form drama by advertising, and seek other ways to avoid the total subjection of craft and art to the advertising imperative. Clustering has been proposed and should be pursued.

THE COMMERCIAL CORNER. A weekly or even daily half hour of Best Advertising, in which, among other enhancements, advertisers, agencies and commercial producers would compete for awards, and in which-long form advertising would be encouraged.

This paper also recommends that the benefits and costs of ceasing to solicit advertising should be studied as an alternative to a limit on minutes-per-hour. The advertising community would be advised that we will welcome their coming to us to seek space adjacent to programs or in the Advertising Half Hour. Contract officers would of course be retained. There would be a substantial reduction in sales overheads.

In addition we would establish a council on honesty and taste in advertising, perhaps connected to the COMMERCIAL CORNER, so that the Corporation might become proactive in the pursuit of higher standards. Industry contacts report that many advertisers are ready to discuss socially beneficial advertising. This paper proposes opening this dialogue with a small number of demonstrably likely players, such as Petro-Canada, and seeking to build a community of responsible advertisers, layer by layer, perhaps honouring them in the COMMERCIAL CORNER.

In the same spirit, and perhaps out of the same office, the development of special relationships with major advertisers willing to undertake responsibility for the development and broadcast of quality programs should be pursued. These initiatives might be a function of the CBC Chairman or his office, with initial discussion to be held at the level of chair or CEO with likely corporations.

The CBC could become a World Leader in the pursuit of responsible, honest, tasteful television advertising. This would be an appropriate role for the Public Broadcaster.

(XII) OUTREACH. Publicity will be overhauled to become focussed, specific, aggressive, fresh. In this regard we need new people and probably outside help. Much of our self-promotion seems cute, unsystematic, themeless, ill-thought-out, relying more on slogans than on substance, ignoring the special character of Public Television (perhaps because it has not had a sufficiently special character?).

There will be increased presence of CBC employees and on-air people out in the community. Some of our people have been exemplary in this regard, especially among radio staff and performers. But the attitude that supports and rejoices in this personal involvement with the community, perhaps normal in small communities, does not seem part of the Network TV Culture; perhaps it should become so.

Special efforts will be made to interest young people in the CBC, through internships, other direct-involvement initiatives, as well as programming. Accommodation should be sought where necessary with the appropriate unions, and collaboration with departments of education, school boards and local school officials, to make possible an ongoing program of attaching young people to aspects of program production in a regular way, with quick turnover and high volume. This should be done in radio and in television. Radio appears to have been leading the way. The strategy should aim at so interesting young people in the making and broadcasting of programs that they will not only become members of our constituency but also attract other members of their family and peer groups because of their pride in their participation in significant broadcasting.

We should also be more present in the schools as a source of useful teaching tools.

Cross-promotion between radio and television services will be aggressively developed. This is a curiously neglected area. Perhaps a certain journalistic puritanism in some areas leads producers to be contemptuous of the activities of their fellow-broadcasters in the same or the other medium. But those broadcasting activities are a significant part of the national life, often more meaningful and useful and entertaining and helpful than the endless display of political activity, rhetoric and posturing that seems to need no justification.

The challenge here is to demonstrate to programmers and journalists that a curiosity about what is going on on ***our*** airwaves is of significant interest to ***our*** audiences and remind them that *significant interest to the community you serve* is a fundamental criterion for journalistic choice of subject matter.

(XIII) **POSITIONING.** A major task will be the development of a slogan or declaration that is simple, obvious, niche-pre-emptive, memorable. "CBC and YOU," is not quite it; neither (despite the brilliant balletic commercial that vehicles it) is "Pour Vous Avant Tout": both are echoes of McDonald's Hamburgers' "We Do it All For You," and sound equally insincere and hucksterish.

"Public Broadcasting in Canada" doesn't do it: it is not only dry and institutional, but places us second to and inferior to PBS, which has, in marketing terms, pre-empted the phrase Public Broadcasting *as a marketing slogan.* It does, however, contain a key word that may serve us: that word is *Canada.* In view of the powerful response to the President's moving and repeated declaration in front of the CRTC, "I chose Canada," it seems there is a clue here to be pursued.

The 1981 marketing classic *Positioning,* by advertisers Al Ries and Jack Trout, declares this:

> Positioning theory says you must start with what the prospect (*i.e.* Audience, or Public) is already willing to give you.
>
> We need to study what that is for CBC, and then build upon it.
>
> *I think what our publics are ready to give us is* ***Canada.***

Slogans like "CBC: Excellence in Canada," and "CBC: Putting Canada First," or "CBC: Canada's Longest Defended Border," are approaches worth analysing. They are perhaps not quite there. But in several decades of the CBC publicly declaring what it stands for, that ringing presidential declaration to the CRTC is (apart from a number of splendid program screenings) the most spine-tingling moment we have ever had; perhaps we should look for a way to rekindle the tingle, through our slogan, by calling on our Citizens to *Acknowledge their Country.*

(XIV) CORPORATE WILL. While this paper has identified some predictable centres of resistance to a program revolution, several factors contribute to its acceptance:

• First an unequivocal and felt need both within and without that the time is past when we can or should compete with commercial broadcasters on their own terms.

• Second, a strong feeling on the part of programmers that they can, if supported, effect substantial change.

• Third, a fear of further diminution in national support.

• Fourth, a new sense of respect for Corporate Management and for the value of collaboration and teamwork.

• Fifth, a new recognition of the value of interregional collaboration and of the threats to regional programming.

• Sixth, a growing appreciation by all that the old environment for broadcasting is gone for good.

In face of these factors a resolute Board and Management should be able to bring these changes about with the necessary despatch and clarity. But a solid front will be necessary, therefore the development of consensus among the Board, key managers, planners and senior program people is vital. Now is the time to do this, and half-measures are not appropriate.

Broadcast Funding Agencies

Alberta Film Development Program (Alberta Foundation for the Arts) – **www.affta.ab.ca**

British Columbia Film – **www.bcfilm.bc.ca**

Canada Council for the Arts – **www.canadacouncil.ca**

Canadian International Development Agency – **www.acdi-cida.gc.ca/dip**

Canadian Television Fund – **www.canadiantelevisionfund.ca**

Enterprise Prince Edward Island – **www.techpei.com/**

Film New Brunswick – **www.gov.nb.ca/filmnb**

Manitoba Film and Sound Development Corporation – **www.mbfilmsound.mb.ca**

Newfoundland & Labrador Film Development Corporation – **www.newfilm.nf.net**

Nova Scotia Film Development Corporation (NSFDC) – **www.film.ns.ca/**

Ontario Arts Council – **www.arts.on.ca/**

Ontario Media Development Corporation (OMDC) – **www.ofdc.on.ca**

SaskFILM – **www.saskfilm.com/**

Société de développement des entreprises culturelles – **www.sodec.gouv.qc.ca**

Telefilm Canada – **www.telefilm.gc.ca**

Private Sector Funding Organizations: Film and Video

Canwest Western Independent Producers Fund – **www.cwipfund.ca**

Harold Greenberg Fund *(click on Corporate Info)* – **www.tmn.ca/**

Independent Production Fund – **www.tmn.ca**

New Voices Fund – **www.toronto1.ca/programming.php**

Shaw Television Broadcast Fund – **www.shaw.ca/scpi**

New Media Funding Agencies

Bell Broadcast and New Media Fund – **www.bell.ca/**

Interactive Multimedia Arts & Technologies of Canada – **www.imat.ca**

MultiMediator Strategy Group Inc. – **www.multimediator.com/sg/**

Ontario Media Development Corporation (OMDC) – **www.ofdc.on.ca**

Telefilm Canada – **www.telefilm.gc.ca**

INDEX

N

O

NOTE: *Page references containing* n *refer to footnotes on those pages.*